183

# Ships of North Cornwall

### JOHN BARTLETT

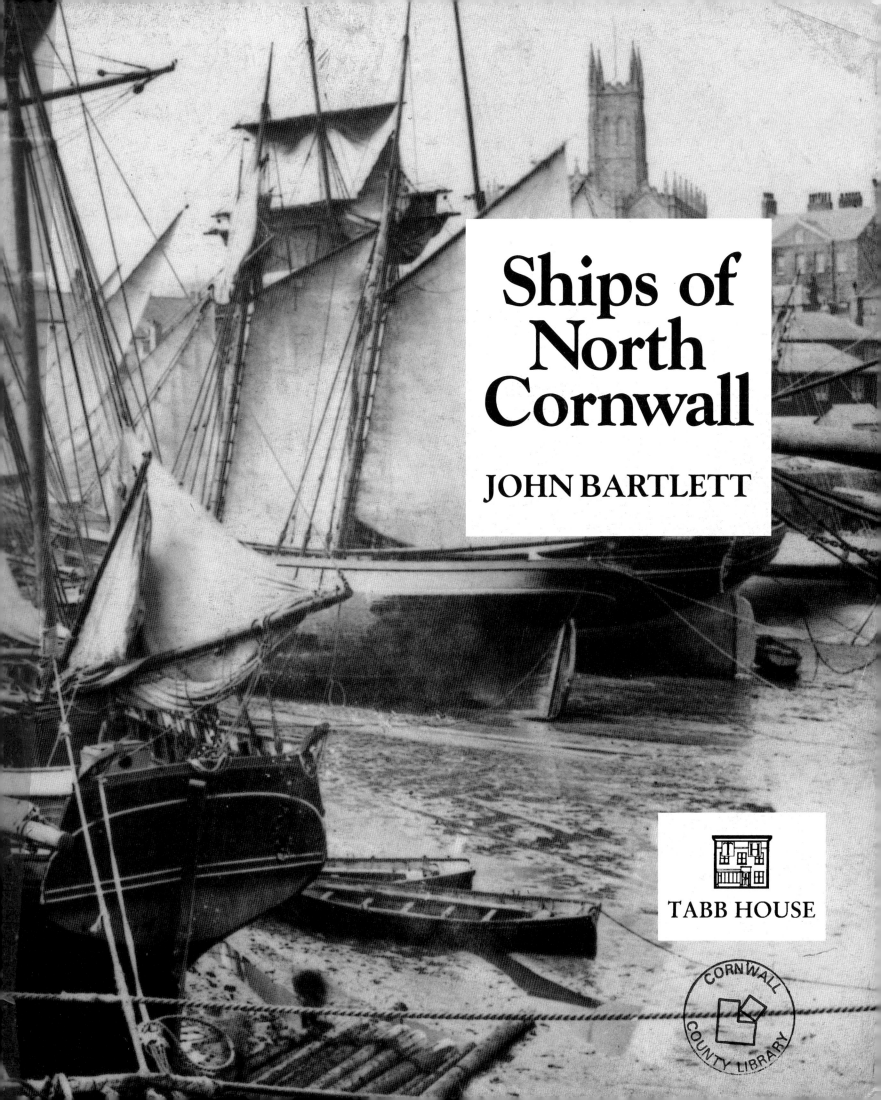

# Ships of
# North
# Cornwall

## JOHN BARTLETT

### TABB HOUSE

First published 1996
Tabb House, 7 Church Street, Padstow, Cornwall

ISBN 1 873951 03 5

British Library Cataloguing-in-Publication Data:
A catalogue record off this title is available from the British Library

Monochrome and Colour Reproduction by Lithocraft, Coventry
Printed and bound by Clifford Press Ltd, Coventry

# CONTENTS

# FOREWORD

FOR many centuries men have been earning a living out of the sea which bounds the North Cornish Coast. They have fished and traded from all the creeks and beaches from St Agnes to Hartland: granite to London, coal from Wales, slate from Delabole, timber from Quebec, china clay from Newquay and even emigrants from Padstow to Canada. For most of this time the life at sea was very much taken for granted, tragedy being all too common, and even today losses at sea still happen.

The centre of this activity was the port of Padstow, but it is not easy for today's visitors to recognise the former site of a thriving shipyard or to visualise the seasick emigrants setting out for a new life in Canada and catching their last glimpse of Trevose Head. Yet many Padstow traditions live on: May Day is still celebrated with the 'Obby 'Oss, men still earn their living fishing and the sound of the maroons calls out the lifeboat crew.

We are fortunate that John Bartlett is here to tell the whole story. John has been a regular visitor to the area since he was a child and has had a lifelong interest in ships and the sea. A successful Civil Engineer, his work has taken him to many parts of the world, and he has applied the logical skills of an engineer to his research for *The Ships of North Cornwall*. His great interest and enthusiasm have led him to produce an exceptionally well researched book which covers the history of the North Cornwall ships in all their forms. The book covers the period from Padstow's first recorded named vessel The MARY of 1377 to the new Rock Ferry delivered this year.

The main strength of this book is the way that every chapter is backed up with detailed research from contemporary sources. In the case of the early ships the information comes from Port Books dating from 1565; later chapters are supported by extracts from local newspapers and official reports. The appendix and tables are well organised and allow the work to be used as a clear and concise source of information on particular ships and their owners.

I am most grateful to John Bartlett for producing this fine book, which will become a classic of its type. Everyone who reads it will enjoy it and will learn a very great deal about the vessels of North Cornwall.

Captain G A Hogg, RN
Hon. Curator, Cornwall Maritime Museum

# ACKNOWLEDGEMENTS

THIS book has taken several years to write: happy years because of friendships made, and because of the generous help of many people.

I was fortunate to be invited to join the South West Maritime History Society, and to attend the maritime conferences organised annually at Dartington by Dr Stephen Fisher of Exeter University. Membership of the Society for Nautical Research, the World Ship Society and the Devon & Cornwall Record Society has provided much useful information.

I have haunted the Public Record Offices at Chancery Lane and Kew, the Guildhall Library, the National Maritime Museum, the offices of *Lloyd's Register* and the Royal Institution of Cornwall. The search for North Cornish ships has taken me to numerous museums, libraries and archives in England, Wales and overseas, the most distant being in Hobart, Tasmania. The people at all these establishments have been unfailingly kind and helpful.

The Records Branch of Customs & Excise allowed me the run of their archives, and E.T.W. Dennis & Sons Ltd., who publish *Olsen's Fisherman's Nautical Almanack*, let me work through their unique collection of early editions.

The names of some of the following people will be found in the picture credits, but they have contributed far more than photographs. Jim Nurse, Charles Waine, David Clement, Peter Ferguson, Barry Kinsman, Barbara Jones, B. Dudleigh Stamp, Alison Grant, Joyce Youings, Jolyon Sloggett, Malcolm McCarthy, Roger Penhallurick, Terry Belt, Martin Benn, Paul Parry, Tony Pawlyn, Ralph Bird, Malcolm Darch, Todd Gray, Peter Stuckey, Kemal Ahamed and the late Christopher May have all generously contributed time, advice and invaluable information.

Joyce Greenham introduced me to the collection to the Newquay Old Cornwall Society, including W. H. Verran's notes. C. J. Davies, who has made the most thorough search of newspaper reports and other sources, was kind enough to make available his list of ships built in North Cornwall, so as to confirm and correct my own work.

Thanks are due to Peggy and Douglas Shepperd and Bob Acton for allowing me to reproduce Captain Sydney Bate's narrative in Chapter 13 as it appeared in their book *The Story of Port Navas*. I am grateful for all the other permissions from sources named in the text.

This book was inspired largely by the works of Basil Greenhill and of the late Grahame Farr, both of whom have helped me wittingly and even more, unwittingly: but the two people who have been most actively involved in making the book a reality are George Hogg and Barbara Atterton. George, who amongst other things is Curator of the Cornwall Maritime Museum at Falmouth, has smoothed the path to publication, whilst Barbara, who had no special interest in Cornwall or ships four years ago, has done so much more than feed it all into my word processor that she should perhaps be cited as co-author, save that might make her responsible for my errors.

Errors aplenty there must be in a book of this nature. The date of a newspaper may be given in place of the date of the event it recorded: a statement may refer to another ship of the same name. Ships sometimes stay in the registers long after they have ceased to exist. Accounts of a given shipwreck vary so widely that it is difficult to believe that they describe the same occurrence.

Files giving references to the sources of information used have been placed in the Cornwall Maritime Museum at Falmouth. I would be most grateful for any corrections and additions.

J. V. Bartlett, 1996

# LIST OF ILLUSTRATIONS

## Colour Photographs

## Drawings by the Author

## List of Maps, Plans etc.

To the Seafarers of North Cornwall
Past and Present

# 1 THE SETTING

*On either side the river lie*
*Broad fields of barley and of rye*
*That clothe the earth and meet the sky . . .*

A. Tennyson

---

THE River Camel rises on Bodmin Moor, and flows south through Slaughterbridge and Camelford past St Breward and Merry Meeting. The tiny River Allen rises just west of Camelford and also flows south to join the Camel above Wadebridge.

These upper reaches were the scene of two important battles. In 542 AD King Arthur finally caught his treacherous nephew, Moldred, on the banks of the Allen. The bloody battle lasted two days with 'an uncommon slaughter of the best troops of the Britons who were no longer able to stand against the Saxons. Moldred was killed on the spot and Arthur, being mortally wounded, was carried to Glassenbury where he died aged ninety years, seventy-five of which he had spent in the continual exercise of arms'.[1] The Cornish Britons gradually allied themselves with the ever-encroaching Danes against the up-country Saxons, and in 824 AD they assembled again on the banks of the Allen and fought 'a most sanguinary battle' against Egbert's Saxon forces near Camelford. 'Many thousands fell on either side and victory remained undecided.' The presence of the Danes probably meant Viking longships in the Camel. The name Slaughterbridge appeared on the map.

Later, Athelstan subdued Cornwall, so when the Danes came back to Cornwall in great strength in the tenth century, they came not as allies but as invaders and 'foraged the country, burnt the towns and destroyed the people'. The Anglo-Saxon Chronicles tell how, in 981, St Petrocs (Padstow), was ravaged and in the same year much harm was done everywhere along the sea coasts in Devon and Cornwall.

Close to Bodmin the Camel is still a rocky stream, but there it turns northwest and flows for five miles to Wadebridge in a sheltered wooded valley which provided sufficiently level going for the second steam railway in the world, the Bodmin-Wadebridge mineral railway, opened in stages in 1833 and 1834.

Wadebridge is the lowest crossing point on the Camel. The original bridge was started about 1485, and the seventeen-arch structure has often rivalled that of Bideford for beauty, longevity and, in recent decades, traffic jams. The tide reaches Wadebridge and a mile further upstream at spring tides. Like some other early structures in Britain, parts of the bridge are said to be founded on bales of wool as a means of avoiding subsidence on soft ground.

It is the remaining five miles of the River Camel's course to the open sea which has moulded the character of Padstow over the centuries, for until the coming of railway and motor road, it left Padstow an isolated community which could only be reached through long, steep, narrow lanes, or by boat or ship.

Although the various accounts differ considerably, St Petroc, (and should his name be likened to St Patrick or should it not?), spread Christianity in North Cornwall. He then visited Rome and returned to live with his followers at Petroc's Stow (or Place) which was later shortened to Padstow. He died there in 564AD. His remains were removed later to Bodmin which became an important ecclesiastical and administrative centre. It seems that the cathedral church at Bodmin was also known as Petrocstow, and historians differ as to whether certain references are to Bodmin or Padstow.

The natives of Cornwall, once they joined Christendom, played their part. In 1147 under Don Alonzo, they distinguished themselves in the liberation of Lisbon from the Moors. They sailed on many of the crusades: when Henry III's son, Prince Edward, fought his way to the Holy Land, he was accompanied by a Cheyne, a forebear of the Cheineys of St Teath, (past which the Allen flows). Edward I, as he became, relied then on Cornishmen, as did Edward II when he subdued Wales and Scotland in the 1290s; his senior lieutenants included de Prideaux and Sir Walter Molesworth, two family names which will recur in this book.

At the time of the Domesday Book, Padstow was one of the few settlements on the north coast of Cornwall. In that part of the country one can picture the settlements or manors, about five miles distant from each other, many of them little more than large farm buildings. Padstow would have been rather more substantial, with its monastery, but still just a small hamlet with a place to beach boats, and a rough track to Bodmin. And thus it remained for several hundred years.

> From Padstow Bay to Hartland Light
> Is a watery grave by day or by night.

That is one of several versions of a jingle which was drummed into the mariners of the Bristol Channel. In the days before the lighthouse was built, it was doubtless:

> From Hartland Point to Padstow Bay
> Is a watery grave by night or by day.

The navigational dangers of this coast are dealt with in more detail in later chapters, and they were sufficient to ensure that any ship which did not need to close the land tried to keep well clear. Thus, as long as England's maritime affairs were principally concerned with warring against France and Spain, North Cornwall had little to contribute. There was little danger of the area being invaded: there were virtually no facilities for ships, not even a safe anchorage, and the few small locally based vessels were too far away to take part in any assembly of a fleet, say at Plymouth, to meet any challenge from the enemy. As Oppenheim says[2] it is not surprising that we do not hear of the appearance of an enemy on this coast except in the shape of an occasional privateer.

In the history of the wars against France and Scotland in the first half of the fourteenth century, we find the first mention of Padstow ships. To raise fleets, the king ordered 'arrests' and 'embargoes' of shipping, and his ports were assessed to provide so many ships and men. None of the original lists survive, but instead conflicting copies were made in the sixteenth century and later.

On 12th August, 1326, an order was made on nine Cornish ports, including Oldestowe (one of the many names of Padstow: there are still numerous Olds in the local telephone directory.*

In 1336 Padstow was one of the many ports which sent representation to London to discuss shipping matters, and in January 1337 there was a 'general arrest of shipping' in which Fowey, Polruan, Truro, Looe, Lostwithiel and Bodmin took part. Anyone familiar with Bodmin will know that it has never been a port, whereas the monks and laity of Padstow were administered through and by Bodmin. It seems certain that instructions to Bodmin were meant to apply to Padstow.

In 1342 there were major expeditions to Brittany. An undated list[3] shows a total of 119 vessels, including two barges from Saltash, one from Looe, two ships and a barge from Falmouth, six ships and a barge from Fowey, Polruan and Lostwithiel combined, and one barge from Padstow. This gives some indication of the standing of Padstow in Cornwall, and of Cornwall in England. According to the 'Roll of Calais', (the Crecy campaign and the siege of Calais), in which between 1,000 and 1,600 vessels took part, Padstow sent two ships and twenty-seven men in 1346, but the figures are very doubtful and some historians believe they represent assessments before the event instead of actual performance. Nevertheless Padstow had become a recognised port capable of supplying a minimal number of small ships.

The first Padstow ship of which we know the name is the MARY.

In September 1377 the MARY of Padstow owned by one Hamely (later the Hambly family?) of 60 tons burden, was in Plymouth waiting to sail to Bordeaux 'for the autumn vintage'. The only reason we know about her is because she and her owner were involved in an acrimonious lawsuit which ended up being recorded in London. But she was, for that time, a goodly sized trading vessel, and it is clear that the trade with France was already well established.

In 1400, Henry IV supplemented his fleet by ordering ports to build and equip ships at their own cost, and Padstow and Lavantstye were jointly to provide one balinger, that is to say one small clinker-built coaster with oars and square sail. In the king's service a balinger was supposed to be able to carry forty soldiers. It is interesting to note that in the Second World War a ninety-foot steam drifter was considered capable of carrying sixty troops.

A. L. Rowse's book *Tudor Cornwall* was the splendid result of extensive research which, read carefully (and there are 450 pages) gives us the most comprehensive picture available of life in those times. In investigating the decline of the monasteries he came upon the case of Prior Vyvyan of Bodmin who on his deathbed desired Nicholas Prideaux of Padstow to arrange the election of Thomas Mundy from Merton Abbey to succeed him. But he and another incumbent fell out about the tithes upon fish landed at Padstow:

It appears that the fish tithes of Padstow had been leased by the convent to Christopher Tredennick for forty years at £4 per annum (Star Chamber Proc. Henry VIII, ii. 18/25). Some time before his death he made over his lease to his young children.

On 4th November, 1533, the prior had caused Thomas Coles, one of his monks, Nicholas Prideaux, William Vyvyan, Richard Sawle and a body of yeomen and labourers, some sixteen in all, to pounce upon the young Tredennicks, seize their father's lease of the tithes and a quantity

of fish, six barrels of white herring worth £4, and 20 couples of hake, mullet, etc. worth £4. On 24th November, the prior in person, with the same following of servants, made a more interesting catch (Star Chamber Proc. Henry VIII, vol ix, no.44). It had been the custom at Padstow 'time out of mind' for some of the inhabitants to make joint-stock voyages to Ireland for fish, dividing the proceeds among those who had set out the ships on their return. In September 1533 John Carmynow set forth the tenth part of three ships the JOAN, the ANTHONY, the NICHOLAS, with 28 bushels Cornish of salt, 7 bushels of flour, 3 hogsheads and 3 barrels of beer, and 33s. sterling in ready money. On their return the prior's band entered the ships and took 6 barrels of white herring, 400 hake, etc., to the value of £7. John Carmynow was determined to get something of his own back; and on 3rd December he took his opportunity, attacking Richard Sawle, the prior's servant, with a band of seven, and wresting from him £2 worth of fish (Star Chamber Proc. Henry VIII ii; bundle 29, no.55). Sawle claimed that Carmynow was 'a man of great possessions and kindred' within the county and that he himself was but a poor man unable to sue him at common law. The case came before Star Chamber. The prior was determined to assert his rights; it meant that there was no love lost between the priory and people like Carmynow, who belonged to the class which was to prove most dangerous and most hostile to the monasteries.

Thus JOAN, ANTHONY and NICHOLAS join the MARY amongst the names of early Padstow ships, and like the MARY we only know their names because of a court case being carried on in London and duly recorded. Padstow continued to play a lowly role in the context of trade and war with the Continent, but her connections with Ireland became more important. With the prevailing south-westerly winds her ships could fetch Cork and Baltimore and reach home again comfortably, and the alternative routes, entailing land travel up-country and out to Wales, were abominable. It was reported in 1579 that Padstow had been declared a Post Town for Ireland. Leland wrote *c* 1533:

Padestow, a good quick fischar toun, but onclenly kept. This toun is auncient, bearing the name Lodenek in Cornische, and ye Englisch after the trew and old writings Adelstow [c.f. Oldestow], Latine Athelstani locus. There use many Britons [i.e. from Brittany] with small shippes to resorte to Padstow with commodities of their countery and to by fische. The toun of Padstow is full of Irish men.[4]

Carew, writing towards the end of the sixteenth century, wrote that Padstow 'hath lately purchased a corporation and reapeth great thrift by trafficking with Ireland for which it commodiously lieth'.[5]

The existence of a packet service from Padstow to Ireland seems to be absent from the available records, but perhaps the following episode, quoted by Hippisley Coxe[6] tends to confirm that at least some such service existed. There was a ship called NEWKEY, 13 guns, with a crew of twelve under Captain Ley:

seventy-one Irish passengers, and fifteen French prisoners. In November 1744 she was attacked by a French privateer called PIERRE & MARIE, manned by Captain Jean Lacost of Morlaix and a crew of forty-seven. The Irish refused to fight, but two attempts to swarm aboard by the French were beaten back by the English, who were outnumbered by almost four to one. At the third attempt Captain Ley, who had a broken shoulder blade, surrendered. The casualties aboard NEWKEY were one of the crew and thirty-one of the Irish passengers dead and

---

* A few years ago an American, seeking to establish contacts with his ancestors, advertised in the Cornish papers and gave a party in St Minver parish for all those with the family name Old. Luckily he had prospered in the New World because several hundred people turned up, despite it being harvest time.

another thirty wounded. Captain Lacost treated the English well, putting Captain Ley to bed in his own bunk, because he said they were brave fellows. The Irish he set adrift in the NEWKEY's long boat to row to Ireland which lay about thirty-six miles away. One can only imagine that the success — or perhaps the celebration of this success — went to the French captain's head, because he became convinced that Hartland Point and Lundy were the French coast. When he realised his mistake, he promptly surrendered to Captain Ley, who brought the ship and both crews into Barnstaple.

Although all this was a century before the major construction of Newquay Harbour by Squire Treffry, there had been a quay at Newquay for many years and it is possible that the NEWKEY packet boat was named after it, and made use of it when wind and tide served.

The absence of records in the sixteenth, seventeenth, and eighteenth centuries makes it particularly difficult to set down a comprehensive history of Padstow ships. These years are rich with history for British shipping, both naval and commercial, but Padstow was literally a backwater. The little ships which brought supplies and took away the products of farm, mine and quarry, were of critical importance to the local communities, but they were so trivial as to be scarcely mentioned in the history of the great ports (and Bristol was pre-eminent) whence they came. There was no Lloyds to record their comings and goings. If one comes across a sloop named, say, MARY, or a brig named DISPATCH, the problem is to discover which of several hundred MARYs is the vessel in question, and one finds fourteen brigs named DISPATCH in *Lloyd's Register* of 1790.

Nevertheless, it has been possible to form a picture of the sixteenth and seventeenth century shipping at Padstow, principally by examining some old port books which have survived, and the story is told in Chapter 4, 'Early Ships'.

I have somehow written a chapter about Padstow's setting without mentioning the beauty of North Cornwall. The scenic beauty of the Camel estuary in all its moods and seasons is breathtaking. The sight of the great seas breaking on the rocks is majestic and terrifying. If you walk around Pentire Point and on towards Port Quin in the spring time, with the sea pinks in full bloom, you will be entranced by the wild flowers and the wild life. If you are lucky, you will see a seal near the Rumps or a basking shark in Lundy Bay. The Cornish chough is no longer to be found and puffins are rarer than they used to be, but guillemots, razorbills, fulmar petrels, oyster catchers, cormorants, gannets and other sea birds abound. Within the estuary and higher up the river all manner of wading birds are to be found. Sailing offshore, with the wind off the land, you can smell the flowers, the farms, the hay harvest, even the dew.

But we take all these blessings for granted and in this book the only use of the smell of the land is as an aid to navigation.

Padstow, June 1906. A famous photograph with the Scots built GUIDING STAR on the left, and Barry pilot cutter No 5 on the right. Between them the eye runs down to the Lower Yard, previously Mr Carter's, and Brea Hill in the distance.
*Photo by J C Burrow*

# 2 PADSTOW AND THE DOOM BAR

*Sunset and evening star,*
*And one clear call for me*
*And may there be no moaning of the bar*
*When I put out to sea.*

A. Tennyson

---

## The Harbour

IF the origins of Padstow as touched on in the previous chapter are partly hidden in the mists of time, it is possible to be more certain about the construction of the port itself.

Until the sixteenth century, the site of Padstow could be described as a muddy bay surrounded on the landward sides by low cliffs. Boats and small ships were doubtless built on the beach above the high water mark, and launched at high water spring tides. Other vessels would be beached to be unloaded or repaired. If there were stagings or walls against which to unload, no records remain. Then, in the early years of the sixteenth century a jetty or quay was built on the north side of the bay, roughly where the large red brick building stands, which has recently been rebuilt. This jetty created calmer conditions in the bay, encouraging the construction of the inner harbour walls, and the reclamation of the beach area behind them on which to construct roads and the waterfront buildings. Gradually over the seventeenth and eighteenth centuries, the inner harbour of Padstow emerged with the shape and character much as we know it today.

The start of serious shipbuilding at Padstow towards the end of the eighteenth century led to further harbour construction, and by 1830 Mr Carter's dock and slip had been built north of the inner harbour, and a seawall had been built south from the Custom House with building slips close to the harbour, and a 'mast pond' behind the wall over 1,000 feet further south.

The Prideaux-Brune family retained the freehold of great tracts including along the shore from St Saviour's Point to Dennis Cove, so apart from an area around the Custom House owned by the Avery family, and another immediately to the south of that owned by John Tredwen, all the harbour expansion was over their lands, but they appear to have made leaseholds available to the advantage of the port and the community.

A crisis arose in 1835, as described in the shipbuilders' chapter, when the Admiralty objected to Tredwen's ambitious plans south of the harbour, but once that had been settled in his favour, there was nothing to prevent the construction of docks, slipways, seawalls and other facilities all shown on the 1839 plan, although at that time there were yet more plans to reconstruct the mast pond at the south end of Tredwen's works which were duly carried out.

The next and most dramatic reconstruction took place in the 1890s. On 31st October, 1881, the *West Briton* carried the following news:

It has finally been decided that the railway built from Wadebridge to Padstow would take the 'water line of route' on the St Issey side, rather than a route through Little Petherick which would have entailed expensive tunnelling at Tregirls' farm and, on its final extension to Harbour Cove, more tunnelling near Prideaux Place. The engineers, Messrs Galbraith & Church were requested to commence their survey at once.

It is perhaps comforting that, even in Victorian times, public works took a few years to come to fruition, and it was not until 27th March, 1899 that the line from Wadebridge to Padstow was finally opened.

As the railway construction approached Padstow from the new bridge over Little Petherick Creek, first of all it cut off Dennis Cove and its former shipyard from the estuary, then the construction broadened out to include the locomotive turntable and the goods yard. John Tredwen's seawall, which impounded the mast pond was invaluable as a retaining wall for all the infilling materials. And his 'wet dock' into which most of his ships had been launched became the new railway dock for fishing vessels. The railway ran on northwards all the way past the Custom House and onto the south pier of the inner harbour which had been there for some time but which was widened and extended.

Wooden shipbuilding had come to an end in the Westcountry yards in the 1880s, making it possible for the railway construction to proceed to the port area along the waterfront through the abandoned shipyards. The railway company achieved its ambition of a holiday route to the north coast, but in the process made it virtually impossible to build or repair ships at Padstow except at the lower yard (originally Carters).

The port (as opposed to the shipbuilders and the sailing ships) undoubtedly benefitted from the railway. Coasters which had previously gone to Wadebridge mostly came to Padstow instead. One of the principal changes was that fishing vessels could land their catches at Padstow, and the fish would be on fast trains to the upcountry markets within hours. By 1904 it was clear that the port facilities were totally inadequate to deal with the hundreds of fishing vessels from Brixham, East Coast ports and even from Scotland, which swarmed to Padstow in the early months of each year, so in 1910 Parliament passed a Bill under the powers of which the Harbour Commissioners and the Railway built the present large 'railway' dock, removing all but the last vestiges of Tredwen's earlier walls. The work was completed by 1916, and remains in service today, apart from the railway itself. The present North outer jetty (from which the ferry to Rock departs except at low water) was completed between the wars.

During and after the Great War, the fishing never reached its previous intensity and people speak of Padstow being in the doldrums between the wars. But the annual visitation of the fishing

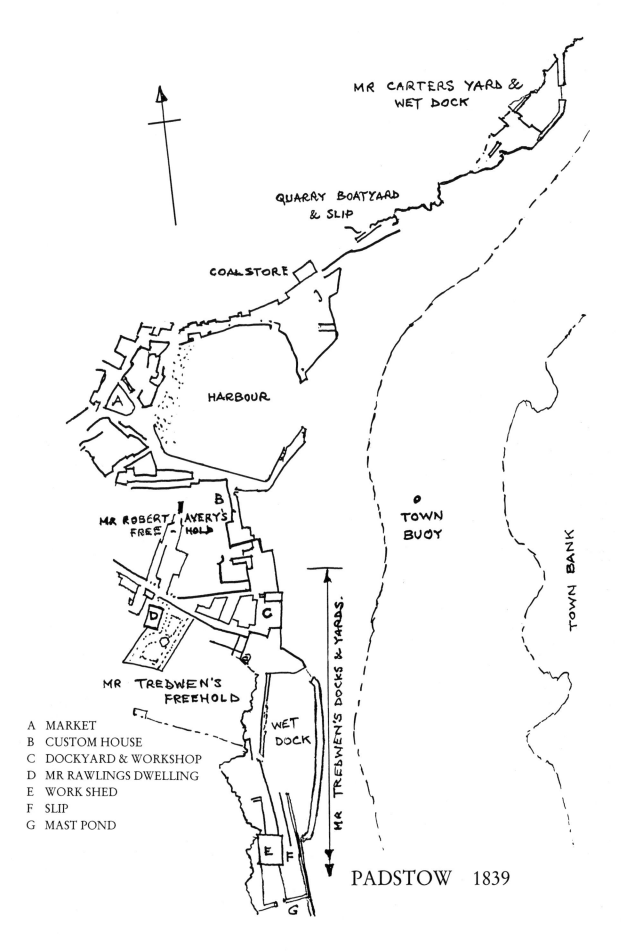

MR CARTERS YARD &
WET DOCK

QUARRY BOATYARD
& SLIP

COALSTORE

HARBOUR

TOWN
BUOY

TOWN BANK

B

MR ROBERTS AVERY'S
FREE - HOLD

D

C

MR TREDWEN'S
FREEHOLD

MR TREDWEN'S DOCKS & YARDS.

WET
DOCK

A   MARKET
B   CUSTOM HOUSE
C   DOCKYARD & WORKSHOP
D   MR RAWLINGS DWELLING
E   WORK SHED
F   SLIP
G   MAST POND

E   F

G

PADSTOW   1839

fleets did continue, and also the harbour carried quite a substantial trade of timber ships from the Baltic and steam colliers from Wales with coal, and coasters came and went with building materials and other goods to be trans-shipped to and from the railway.

Looking at Coastal Movements in *Lloyd's List* for August 1933, chosen at random:

**TANNY** (a small Bristol steam coaster) arrived on 5th August from Bristol, and sailed for Cardiff on the 8th.

**M.A. JAMES** (a famous old schooner with an engine) arrived 5th August from Runcorn.

**PENRYN** (a ketch owned in Appledore, too small to be in *Lloyd's Register*, arrived 5th August from Barry.

**LADY THOMAS** (A Liverpool steam coaster) arrived 6th August from Ayr.

**WELCOME** (A Gloucester auxiliary schooner) arrived 6th August.

**MARENA** (a small steamship owned by County of Cornwall Shipping Co. Ltd) arrived 9th August from Hayle.

**TORPOINT** (Cardiff coastal collier) arrived 19th August from Ayr.

**FLORENCE** (a small steam coaster) arrived 19th August from Barry.

**ZILLAH** (a Liverpool steam coaster) arrived 21st August from Runcorn and sailed 24th August for Jersey.

But despite the activity, the times were hard. The average age of these nine ships was over thirty-four years, and what is even more remarkable, they all survived to face the U-boats and Stukas of World War II at an average age of over forty. But they were none of them Padstow ships, and in that respect Padstow was definitely in the doldrums between the two world wars.

The Southern Railway, as it became, can justly claim that this activity was sufficient to justify such a large dock in such a small port, at least up to 1939. After the second war, however, Padstow really was in the doldrums as far as shipping was concerned; the annual migration of trawlers and drifters to Padstow fell away completely and only inshore fishing remained. Since 1967, when the railway was closed, cargo vessels have only visited Padstow sporadically, bringing in coal, cement or timber, and in the last two decades Padstow has ceased altogether to appear in the reporting of shipping movements in *Lloyd's List*.

Fishermen, like farmers, are seldom happy with the weather or the government, but in the last ten or fifteen years trade with Europe has greatly benefitted Padstow, and Padstow has bent every effort to benefit. Crabs and lobsters have become crucial to the local economy, and the port has been increasingly busy. The capital invested in Padstow fishing vessels, if not their number and size, has soared, and it is not unusual to see enormous refrigerated container lorries loading shellfish for Paris on the quayside.

In the period 1988-1990 another stage in the construction of the port was achieved when the inner harbour was converted into an enclosed dock. The gap between the old inner North and South piers was reduced, and a gate placed between them. The gate is kept open an hour or two each side of high tide and closed for the rest of the time to retain water in the inner harbour. Thus a yacht entering the Camel estuary on the flood tide can sail into the inner harbour, moor alongside, and stay afloat in comfort and safety. That may be compared with some earlier episodes described in the chapter on yachts. The arrangement has also proved popular with some of the fishing vessels.

This civil engineering work enclosing the inner harbour has already greatly increased the traffic and the revenue, but it was also needed as a means of protecting the lowest areas of Padstow from flooding. In times of flood warning, when a tidal surge is expected, the gate can be kept closed (as on the River Thames at Woolwich), and the walls and gate now constructed will keep the waters of the estuary out of the town.

## The Doom Bar

The last few pages have described man's contribution to the shaping of the estuary. Nature has played a more dominant role.

The Admiralty charts of the north Cornish coast show the bottom of the sea for miles offshore to consist of sand and seashells. There are, of course, some exposed rocks, and some gravel, but sand and shell are the predominant features. In recent millennia the sea has driven countless millions of tons of sand, with a high content of crushed shells, into the bays and harbours of north Cornwall. The beaches in effect stretch for miles out to sea. The sand driven into the Camel Estuary has formed the Doom Bar and the Town Bank. When it dries out at low tide there is a secondary effect; the prevalent west wind blows the sand particles eastwards in the estuary, forming the great sand hills stretching from Trebetherick to Rock opposite Padstow, and more sand moves in from the sea to take its place.

Gilbert's *Historical Survey, 1817-1820*, contains the following passage:

This part of St Minver, according to common tradition, has undergone a change of an extraordinary nature, solely occasioned by the great increase of sea sand which has blown over the country for the space of several miles. Under the principal sand hills, they inform you, a town formerly stood, which reached from Porthilly Church to that of St Enodoc, a distance of rather more than a mile: and the benefits of the harbour which now belong to Padstow on the opposite side of the water were then solely confined to that of St Minver.

This belief was doubtless nourished by the fossilised remains of a forest which were sometimes exposed at low tide in Daymer Bay, and by the fact that access to St Enodoc's was only possible through a hole in the roof since the rest of the church was buried in sand at the time. But if there was ever a town, it was well before Domesday; and it was Padstow not St Minver which suffered destruction by the Vikings even earlier.

The shifting sandbanks in the estuary have always been a menace to navigation. Throughout the nineteenth century and well into the twentieth century there was relatively deep water close to the rocks on the west side of the entrance from Stepper Point to Hawkers Cove, and the navigation channel went from there up to Padstow.

The *Admiralty Pilot* of 1872 describes the situation:

Stepper point, the northwest boundary of the entrance to Padstow harbour, is high, bold-to, and free from danger . . . Within Stepper point are three capstans and several bollards just above the high-water mark, and warps are kept in the capstan houses.

The navigable channel is closely confined to the bold shore within Stepper point by an extensive tract of sand named Doom bar which stretches out from Trebetherick point and Brae hill on the eastern shore, and occupies four-fifths of the mouth of the estuary; it is the northwestern extremity of this sand or the 'Ketch' which is only a cable's length from the shore, and a little within the point, that constitutes the special danger of Padstow harbour . . . Above Hawker's cove the channel is winding, shallow and irregular up to abreast Padstow.

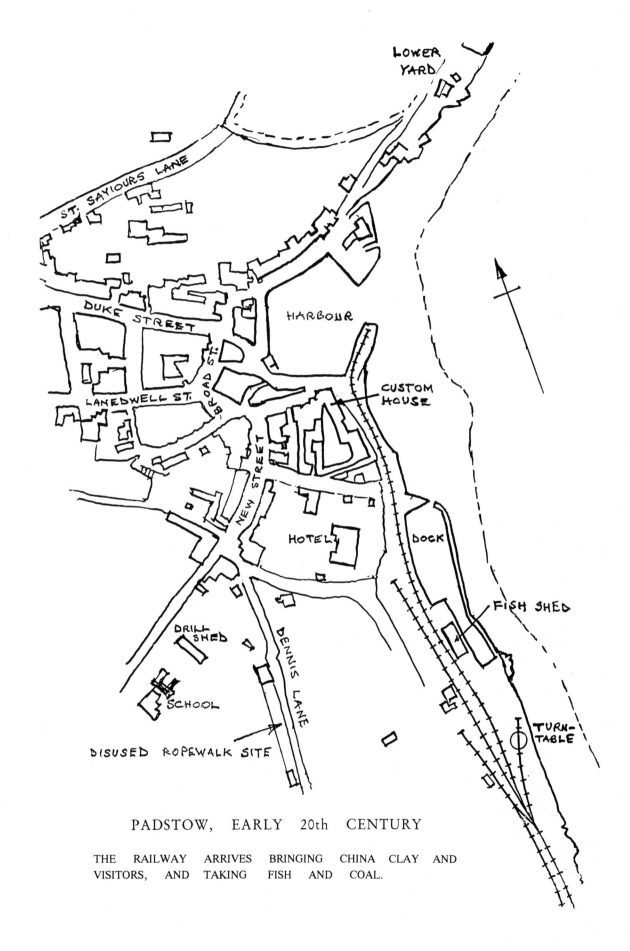

LOWER YARD

ST. SAVIOURS LANE

DUKE STREET

HARBOUR

BROAD ST.

LANEDWELL ST.

CUSTOM HOUSE

NEW STREET

HOTEL

DOCK

FISH SHED

DRILL SHED

DENNIS LANE

SCHOOL

TURN-TABLE

DISUSED ROPEWALK SITE

PADSTOW, EARLY 20th CENTURY

THE RAILWAY ARRIVES BRINGING CHINA CLAY AND
VISITORS, AND TAKING FISH AND COAL.

There are six licensed pilots at Padstow, who are always on the look-out at tide-time by day and night. They cannot board vessels outside Stepper point in heavy weather . . . but they may be obtained immediately the vessel has rounded the point. The charge is 10d per foot inwards and 4d per foot outwards.

*Directions*: The best time for entering Padstow harbour is from half flood to high water and it should not be attempted from half ebb to quarter flood, except in a case of absolute necessity.

Round the sloping extremity of Stepper point closely and keep within one-third of a cable along the straight shore of steep cliffs . . . and if a pilot cannot be obtained, run in as far as Hawker's cove and anchor close in abreast it. Should the vessel have lost her anchors, proceed a third of a mile farther and lay her upon the soft ground of Harbour cove where she will be secure in nearly all winds.

To proceed up to Padstow, the assistance of a pilot is necessary, for both the height and shape of the sands occasionally change.

*Caution*: The ebb stream during springs runs strongly out of Padstow harbour, and several wrecks have occurred from vessels attempting to enter on a falling tide, and with the wind scant.

Another point requiring careful attention is, that with winds from the westward, when the port is more generally required for shelter, baffling winds will be found within Stepper Point, and if unprepared, drive a vessel to leeward onto the Doom bar. Standing in therefore in such circumstances, have an anchor and warp ready, and with a press of sail round the point closer, and either shoot into the leading wind, or as far as possible towards the rocks and let go, when the ship will be in comparatively smooth water and assistance from the shore will be promptly rendered.

The *Pilot* also states: 'The channel [up to Padstow] may be sailed with winds between N. by W. (north about) to ESE as they will be found steady.' In other words, with the prevalent winds from the southwest and west it was difficult or impossible to fetch the channel up to Padstow, and it was necessary to proceed with great caution and the assistance of the local pilots and hufflers, drifting up with the tide, taking advantage of every favourable slant of wind, tacking in the narrow channel, and at times 'dredging' or dragging

an anchor along the bottom to keep the vessel in the fairway. The smaller vessels had sweeps (long oars) to give them steerage way.

Even in moderate weather, lack of local knowledge often caused stranding and wreck. The most common occurrence was a ship sailing in round Stepper Point with the tide at half flood, following the advice of the Admiralty pilot. Behind Stepper, she loses the wind completely, but the flood stream carries her on up the river. Thus her sails are caught aback, and instead of driving her forwards, they take all way off her and she can no longer be steered. Quite a number of vessels drifted onto the Doom bar in those circumstances, and although some got off on the rising tide, many were carried further onto the sands in the breaking seas. The timely assistance of the pilots, the gigs and the hufflers was essential. The following three newspaper reports from the *West Briton* will describe the danger:

*9th December, 1864.* On Monday, a dead body was picked up at Polzeath, supposed to be one of the crew of the LADY ELIOT, which was lately lost at the entrance of Padstow harbour . . . It will be remembered that the LADY ELIOT was lost not by coming into contact with Stepper Point or stranding on the Dumbar, but was literally overwhelmed by the roaring surge. Fast ebb 2 hrs. before low water springs. Wind against tide. It cannot be too generally known that at such a time of tide, with a gale from the NW or WNW, there is scarcely a chance for the ship which attempts to enter Padstow. The 'flaws' come down over the hill [Stepper Point] and take the vessels aback: they strike on the Dumbar and destruction is inevitable. If vessels are so frail as to be unable to keep to sea and wait the flowing of the tide, it would be far better for masters to run them on some sandy beach. Had the LADY ELIOT been steered into Polzeath Bay, every soul would probably have been saved.

*5th January, 1866.* On Saturday forenoon, during a heavy gale from the SW, a barque was seen making for Padstow harbour, and about noon she brought up about a mile within Pentire Point. The barque proved to be the JULIET of Greenoch from Demerara for London, laden with rum and sugar. About 10 o'clock pm she went to pieces and a considerable portion of her cargo has washed ashore and been picked up

In westerly gales seas break across the whole mouth of the estuary.

A Lowestoft sailing trawler running for Padstow under reduced canvas past Stepper Point, with Pentire in the background. She's already out of the worst of the sea, but how will she fare when she turns to starboard into the river and loses her wind? She'll need more canvas in double quick time to keep off the Doom Bar, and her crew may have had no sleep for several days.
*Royal Institution of Cornwall*

at Polseath Bay. About 280 casks of rum, out of over 400, have been recovered, but none of the sugar has been saved. A man called Wm. Ham of Carveth, St Austell, who has been working at Wadebridge for some time, went to the wreck and drank so much rum that he died from the effects. A medical man attended to the patient with a stomach pump, but it was to no avail. At least 100 casks of overproof rum were stove against the rocks, and the spirits mingled with the salt water in the hollows have been scooped out, and a great deal of drunkenness has been the result.

*25th March, 1869. Shipping Casualties, Padstow*
Friday night — The Schooner PEARCE on Doom Bar, but got off. The brigantine SARAH WILLIAMS of Portmadoc ran into Hell Bay [Polzeath].
The schooner MORECAMBE BELLE of Barrow from Pomaron with sulphur ore, put in in distress.
The HELIGAN of Falmouth lost sails and jib boom.
The brig ST PATRICK of Youghal lost sails and bulwarks.
The brigantine CONSTANT of Penzance lost jib boom and sails split.
The Prussian barque DEVITZ was wrecked near Gull Rock.
The Austrian brig SLAVEN, Falmouth for Gloucester with grain, after

scraping the coast near Hartland, finally brought up near the Moles riding the gale but quite seriously damaged. She had Capt. Volk of Falmouth in charge as pilot.

In 1872 Padstow's first tug, Captain Hutching's paddle steamer AMAZON arrived, but although she doubtless offered some assistance downstream, she had to earn her living towing ships and barges up to Wadebridge, and could not spend her time day and night in the Narrows waiting for ships to round Stepper. In any case, 10d per foot for pilotage was all that could be afforded and did not include towage.

Throughout the nineteenth century proposals were made to remove the Doom Bar. Training walls or breakwaters were to be built out from the Trebetherick shore to speed up the ebb stream and scour it away. Anyone who has seen the seas breaking on the bar in a northwesterly gale would realise what a massive construction would be required. On more than one occasion an even more ambitious scheme was proposed; in 1881, Silas Nicholls, Civil Engineer, proposed clearing the bar of sand 'by making a tunnel

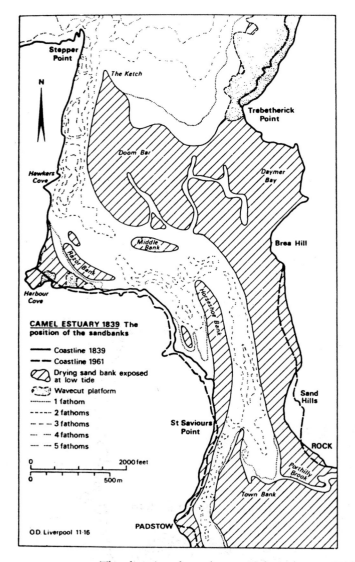

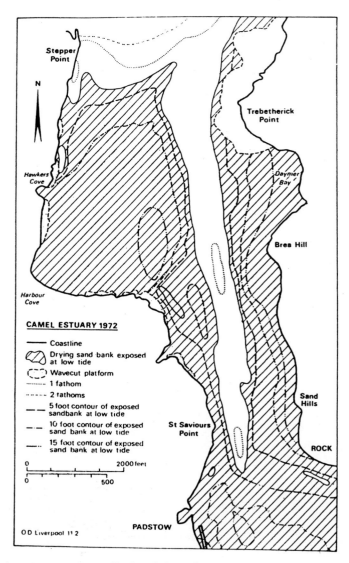

The changing channel up to Padstow.     *With acknowledgements to Sue Handford and the Padstow Echo*

from Butterhole through Trethelick farm somewhere to Hawkers cove.' Presumably the tunnel was to have been just above sea level and the sand transported through by a mineral railway and dumped in the sea.

Very substantial quantities of sand have been removed and spread over the fields inland, but the quantity of sand in the estuary continues to increase to this day, both on the Doom bar and on the Town bank higher up the river.

The 1872 *Admiralty Pilot*, as always, has other interesting information:

Padstow is a place of call to the steamer trading from Hayle and Bristol for both passengers and goods; it is also a coastguard station.

The chief imports are coals, timber, and manure, and the exports are copper and other ores and grain.

In 1867 the number of vessels belonging to the port were 133, tonnage 12,005; of sailing vessels which entered there were 704, tonnage 35,111, steamers 26, tonnage 2,476 whilst the number which sought shelter only were 1,000.

There was a depth of 9 ft at Wadebridge at springs (as opposed to 16 ft in Padstow) but Wadebridge accounted for more than half the trade of the port. 'Rock with its small quay, is on the opposite side

of the estuary from Padstow, and divides with it the remainder.'

The 133 vessels include all those registered at Padstow, and therefore all the ships of Newquay and the other outports. The number of ships entering were, however, only those entering the river, not including Newquay, Port Isaac, etc.

Clearly the Hayle steamer only called twice a month (presumably at springs), and throughout 1867 she must have been the smallest of Mr Pockett's screw steamers, the HENRY SOUTHAN, which measured just under 96 net tons at that time, otherwise the recorded tonnage would have been greater.

The figure of 1,000 ships seeking refuge in Padstow in 1867 is most revealing. Here is real confirmation that, despite its dangerous approaches, Padstow was the only real port of refuge between Land's End and Barnstaple Bay (which had its own considerable problems). One might suppose that most of these 1,000 ships would have sought shelter in times of westerly or northerly gales, of which there may have been as many as thirty per annum: on that basis, a typical gale would have brought twenty ships round Stepper Point, and occasionally twice that number, all seeking the services of the six watchful pilots, some of them happy to run themselves ashore on 'the soft ground of Harbour cove', but the rest desperately seeking room to anchor in the Narrows close to the rocks, with the breakers

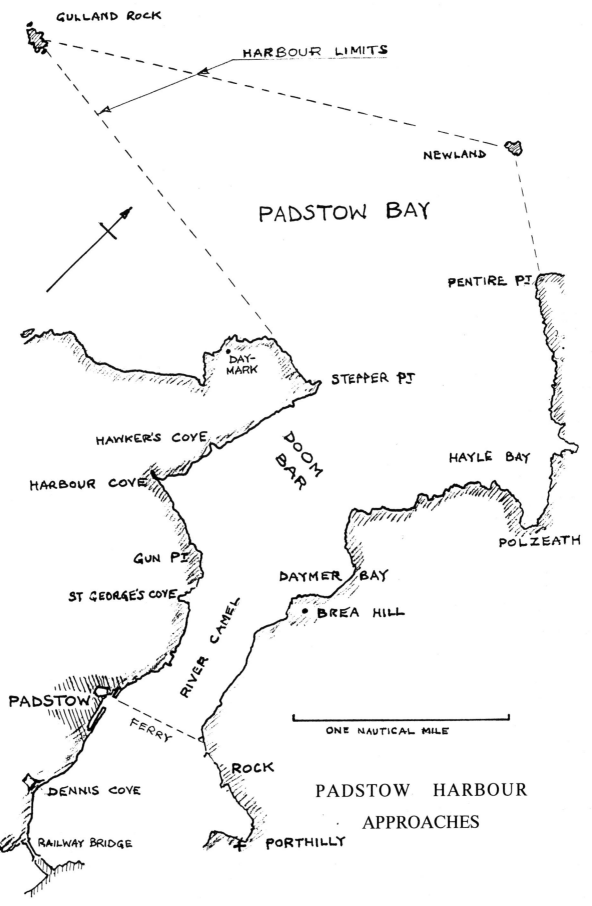

In spring in the early 1930s the trawlers of Yarmouth (YH) and Lowestoft (LT) filled Padstow harbour. Shown are TRITONIA, HILDA COPPER, LORD KEITH and JACKLYN with at least fourteen others visible astern of them.    *Royal Institution of Cornwall*

on the Doom bar to leeward ready to penalise any error of seamanship.

But not all the ships seeking shelter were in such desperate straits. It is surprising how often, for instance, Padstow schooners sailing from Runcorn, with coal for Falmouth or Fowey, had to take shelter in Padstow in December, and found themselves forced to be home for Christmas. And who shall blame them: they had to pay for the privilege, some with their lives.

In the present century, the configuration of the Doom bar has altered drastically. To put it at its simplest, the gradual silting up of the Narrows on the west side adjacent to Stepper has increased the speed of the ebb tide on the Trebetherick side, and scoured the present entrance channel.

The increased amount of sand in the estuary has resulted in there being virtually nowhere to anchor and remain afloat at low water, except of course, that one can now proceed to the inner harbour and remain afloat in peace and comfort at all states of the tides.

## The Organisation of the Port

As far as the administration of the port is concerned, the Church, the Duchy and the Lord of the Manor wielded the power in the early years. It says much for the people of Padstow that the first modern departure from the normal administration of ports in Cornwall was the formation in 1829 of The Padstow Harbour Association for the Preservation of Life and Property from Shipwreck, the activities of which are described in the chapter on lifeboats.

In 1844 the Padstow Harbour Commission was set up by Act of Parliament, with twenty-six commissioners, two of whom were appointed by the Duchy of Cornwall and the Lord of the Manor, (the Prideaux-Brune estate), and the remainder were elected by the ratepayers of all the parishes surrounding the estuary.

For Treasury and Customs purposes the Port of Padstow extends for miles along the coast in both directions, as described elsewhere in the book and includes all the outports. The powers of the Padstow Harbour Commission apply to a more limited area but it includes all the waters of the estuary and the navigable river, and extends seawards to waters within lines joining Stepper Point to Gulland Rock, Gulland Rock to Newlands, and Newlands to Pentire Point.

Even a small port requires a panoply of official and semi-official services, such as harbourmasters, pilots, receivers of wreck, coastguards, controllers of customs, and tidewaiters.*

The surveying of ships is an important function. There is the need for the vessel to be measured and registered, the legal requirements for her to be seaworthy, and finally, if she is to be acceptable to charterers, insurers and the owners of cargo, the desirability of her to be acceptable to a classification society, which in the case of British ships (and many others) almost always means being surveyed and classed by Lloyd's Register of Shipping, which has been carrying out this work for well over 200 years.

Padstow ships were predominantly surveyed at Falmouth, and the Falmouth surveyors visited Padstow to inspect ships under construction. For the period 1830-1840, Padstow was temporarily considered important enough to become a 'Survey Port' in its own right. John Tredwen was a subscriber to *Lloyd's Register* (one of about 600, the vast majority being Londoners), and John Parnall was appointed surveyor for Padstow and Boscastle though 'not an exclusive servant of the Society' which he would have been at most of the major ports; the nearest surveyors competent to deal with steamships were at Falmouth, Bristol and Swansea.

The independence of Padstow was illustrated by the early formation of the Padstow Shipping Assurance Association. On the walls of the London Inn, Padstow, is still preserved a list of the ships insured by the Association in 1856, and one evening I believe I established that there were sixty-five or more named ships from the 26 ton smack JAMES & ANN to the 700 ton barque INTREPID. Judging by the number of hostelries in Padstow, there must be other historical documents yet to be examined. A parallel Newquay Mutual Marine Insurance Association Ltd was established in 1869 and lasted until the Great War.

The Padstow Harbour Commissioners found their role was somewhat circumscribed by the activities of the railway company in the period 1899-1967, but since the closure of the railway they are back in full control, although recently reduced to ten in number to ease the administrative burden.

What does the future hold for Padstow? One of the possibilities is 'tidal energy'. In the 1980s studies were made[1] of river estuaries around Britain which could most successfully provide power by building barrages and generating electricity by passing the tidal flows through turbines. The schemes to harness the River Severn and the River Mersey are well known, but of the smaller estuaries, that of the River Camel was considered to be one of the most promising.

Much would depend where exactly the barrage might be built across the estuary. The further downstream the barrage, the greater the volume of water trapped above it and therefore the greater potential to generate power. There would be a lock for shipping, and conditions for water sports might actually be improved. The effects upon the natural environment would need careful assessment.

But what of the Doom bar and the Town bank? It was Rennie, the famous civil engineer, who proposed the breakwater built out from Trebetherick to increase the scour and sweep away the Doom bar in 1836 soon after he had completed London Bridge. It may well be that a tidal barrage scheme would have the same ends in mind, as the presence of vast volumes of sand above the barrage would reduce

Padstow, the North Quay, May 1933. The East Coast men have gone and Padstow's only steam trawler ADELE PW3 is laid up before being sold back to Lowestoft. Outside her is berthed the Gloucester ketch ISABELLA, herself to be hulked at Rock in 1936.
*Royal Institution of Cornwall*

Padstow, the South Basin (the Railway Dock) *c.* 1934. The famous Irish schooner MARY B MITCHELL is on the left: the coaster ELSIE ANNIE of the Wexford Steamships Co. Ltd is waiting for a cargo.
*Royal Institution of Cornwall*

the quantity of impounded water, and the efficiency of the whole project.

* Just as ratcatchers have become rodent operatives, so tidewaiters have become customs officers.

UNTIL the eighteenth century Padstow was designated a 'creek of the harbour of Plymouth and Fowey'. By a return to an Exchequer Commission in the Trinity term of the 29th year of Charles II, the port of Padstow was appointed from Perran Sands (where it joined with St Ives & Hayle) to the county boundary with Devon near Morwenstow, to which point Bideford had already been appointed.

Padstow therefore included about sixty miles of wild, rocky coastline with occasional beaches, as well as the estuary of the River Camel.

Working south from the boundary with Devon, past Morwenstow where Stephen Hawker, the eccentric vicar wrote of smugglers, wreckers and dissenters in the early nineteenth century, the cliffs are continuous until Bude Haven is reached.

**BUDE** was the northernmost outport of Padstow, the best place to bring in a small ship for many miles. Bude or Bewd had its own ships by the sixteenth century and probably much earlier, but they were small smacks bringing in coal and other essentials for the isolated villagers of Bude and Stratton and the surrounding farms: 'Bude, an open sandy bay, in whose mouth riseth a little hill, by every sea flood made an island, and thereon a decayed chapel; it spareth road only to such small shipping as bring their tide with them, and leaveth them dry when the ebb hath carried away the salt water.' That was Carew's description.[1]

Bude faces due west into the prevailing winds, and a large sea with an uninterrupted fetch of 2,000 miles from America rolls into Bude Haven making the approach spectacular and for long periods impossible; but by the end of the eighteenth century there was a small partly sheltered harbour drying out at low water. The farming area behind Bude was poor acid moorland, until it became known that the spreading of beach sand on the land had a very beneficial effect as it contained lime in the high shell content. Transporting the sand inland was expensive and laborious; because of the lack of roads, and the rugged nature of the coastline, the sand had to be carried in the panniers of pack horses and mules, a system which applied throughout the whole of the north coast. In the late eighteenth century several canal schemes were proposed for Bude, principally as a means of carrying the sand inland, but every possibility of attracting other canal traffic was explored. It is often forgotten that the River Tamar rises and flows less than five miles inland from Bude and thence south to Plymouth, and it was even suggested that a canal from Bude could join the Tamar and form a route from the Bristol Channel to the English Channel.

In 1819 construction of a less ambitious canal was started which included construction of a breakwater on the south side of the harbour out to the Chapel Rocks, and a sea-lock 114 ft long and 33 ft wide, leading to wharves and basins with various facilities including warehouses and lime kilns.[2] In 1823 the sea-lock became operational and trade grew considerably. Although coal and culm and general goods remained the most important cargoes, building materials greatly increased in importance and limestone from Wales and Devon (with more culm for the kilns) appeared in large quantities to compete with the beach sand. Imports of guano and phosphate also appeared. A high proportion of the ships left Bude in ballast. By 1875 Bude was importing rails and sleepers for railway construction which in turn greatly reduced the viability of the port and especially its canal which finally went out of business in 1902.

The first breakwater, completed in 1823, was largely washed away in a storm in 1838, but the carefully built, massive structure which was put in its place in 1839 remains to this day.

It is worth dwelling on the difficulties of navigation at Bude, as similar conditions affect most of the places mentioned in the following pages. A vessel arriving from Wales, say, with coal would approach Bude, if the wind and sea were not excessive, and heave to off the port. Despite a tidal range of up to twenty-eight feet at spring tides, there are only a few days in the month when, for an hour or two each side of high water, there is sufficient depth over the cill of the sea-lock to bring in a laden ship. The vessel waits until a flag is hoisted on shore to indicate sufficient water. Then the master has to make up his mind immediately whether the wind will allow him to sail safely into port. If the wind is from the East there may be calm seas, but it is unlikely that he will attempt to beat up the comparatively narrow channel; if the wind is from the North or South, he should be able to reach in safely; if the wind is from the West, as it generally is, then the seas are thundering in too. But if the wind is from the West, or South-West and moderate, then the master would probably choose to make for the lock, with his heart in his mouth as he approached Chapel Rocks, acutely conscious that he was relying on the force of the wind to give him steerage way as he entered the shallower water where the big seas got steeper, and the man at the helm had to use more and more of his strength to keep her on course. If the wind dropped at that stage, the ship was in great danger of broaching or of being driven off course onto the rocks. If not, she would sail on safely into the comparatively calm waters behind the breakwater, where sails had to be furled smartly and a boatload of hobblers would be ready to take her lines and help her into the lock.

If the conditions were unsuitable for entering Bude, then the ship would probably sail off northwards to anchor under the shelter of Lundy Island until things improved, quite likely a week or two later.

Masters had to be equally careful leaving Bude; they could get some help out from the hobblers, but unless they could see their way clear to gaining a substantial offing, they ran the risk of being driven back inshore.

The Acland family were very influential in Bude throughout the nineteenth century; one of their many contributions was the preparation by Arthur Acland (with the help of Mr Goman, the harbourmaster) of a special set of tide tables predicting the depth of water at lock gate for various conditions.[3] Arthur Acland also built an iron cross on the rocks on the north side of the harbour, the level of the horizontal arms being at half tide level.

But the difficulties of trading to and from Bude were not only navigational, as witness the following petition of 1792 which B. Dudley Stamp of Ebbingford Manor, Bude, has been kind enough to make available:

*To the honourable the Commissioners of his Majesty's Customs:*

The Petition of the undersigned Lords & Ladies of Manors Freeholders Merchant Traders Masters of ships and others concerned humbly sheweth That the Trade of the Harbour or Creek of Bude in the County of Cornwall has of late Years very much increased particularly in Export of Corn, Oak, Bark, Timber, etc. and would still more increase but for the disadvantages & difficulties hereinafter mentioned.

That the said Harbour of Bude is situate on the North Coast of the County of Cornwall and at present within the limits of the Port of Padstow from the Custom house of which it is nevertheless distant forty Miles.

That the Master of Ships arriving at or sailing from Bude aforesaid are therefore under the necessity of going fourscore miles by bad roads to Enter — or clear out their ships which is a peculiar hardship and constant source of great Trouble and Expense and exposes their vessels and cargoes to the Hazard of being cast on shore and lost (which has frequently happened) the said Harbour of Bude very wide and without Pier or Quay not being a place of safety but with certain winds and when the contrary winds prevail it becomes highly dangerous unless vessels put to sea immediately which they cannot do during the absence of their Master in going to and returning from the Custom house at Padstow which cannot be effected under two or three days.

That this circumstance is a cheque and Burthen upon the Trade and Industry of your petitioners the removing of which will be highly advantageous to a great number of his Majesties Subjects particularly in the North West of the County of Devon and the North East of the County of Cornwall and will also tend to the advancement of Agriculture and Commerce and to the increase of Coasting Trade of the Kingdom. Bude aforesaid being one of the very few Harbours for a long range of Dangerous and rugged Coast (extending from Bideford in Devon to Padstow in Cornwall) at which Vessels can with any safety touch.

Your petitioners upon this Occasion naturally look to your Honours as the Constitutional Fosters and Guardians of Trade, being well assured of your Honors uniform wish to free Commerce every unnecessary Shackell.

Your Petitioners presume with all Humility to submit to your Honours consideration the following Plans Either of which if carried into execution would afford them great relief without subjecting the

The ketch CERES unloading at Bude in 1934 and celebrating her 125th birthday. She is behind the massive breakwater on the left, and has fenders out to enter the sealock at the next highwater.
*Terry Belt Collection*

Revenue to the smallest Expense viz to extend the Limit of the Port of Bideford so far to the Westward as to comprehend the said Harbour of Bude which is distant from the former only twenty-four miles on a good Road and there being a great number of Officers in your Honours Service at Bideford than the present Duty of that Port requires to establish two of the said officers one as a deputy or pro-Collector and the other a deputy or pro Comptroller to dispatch the Coast Business at the said Harbour of Bude and to return their Accounts to the Collector and Comptroller of Bideford or to order such one or more officers with like power from Padstow or some of the creeks within said Port (where also are more than the present Trade requires) to act as above mentioned at Bude.

Your Petitioners are very far from intending to dictate to your Honours upon this Occasion but only suggest what occurs to them as the most advantageous and frugal method of removing the Inconvenience they labour under — humbly praying your Honours to take their Case into consideration and afford them such Relief as to your Honours shall seem fit.

| At Bude 1792 | (Signed) |
|---|---|
| | L. Stafford |
| | L. Carteret |
| | Sir Francis Bassett |

A Treasury Warrant dated December 13th, 1850 reduced the jurisdiction of Padstow so that it extended from Perran Sands to Dizzard Point, and on the same date the port of Bideford was extended south to Dizzard Point, thus transferring Bude from Padstow to Bideford. Ships which did not belong to Bude until after 1850 are therefore not dealt with in this book (unless they had some other Padstow affiliation).

**CRACKINGTON HAVEN**, about six miles south-east of Bude is a sandy bay to which in summer smacks used to bring limestone and coal for a kiln once the farmers had removed most of the beach sand: they often obtained export cargoes of slates from local quarries. To the navigational risks described for Bude must be added the dangers of having to beach the vessel on an open beach, with rollers from the west pounding the hull on a hard bottom, and making it difficult to get the vessel off after unloading, and impossible in winter.

**BOSCASTLE** lies another five miles down the coast, one of the most romantic little harbours imaginable.

When the de Botterell family, Norman followers of William the Conqueror built their castle overlooking the River Jordan, they caused to be created a classic model of a feudal village. The Jordan stream joins the River Valency and together they run into a tiny natural harbour, the only landlocked natural harbour between Padstow and Appledore. From the beginning, Boscastle looked after itself; with waterwheels, millers, a pottery, boat and ship-building, lime kilns, malting house, smithy, warehouses, etc. Although an outport of Padstow since records began, Boscastle in a very real sense has written its own history. Initially known as Bottreaux Castle, Botrizcastell and Boascastle, there were many other variants before Boscastle became the accepted name. She has had her own ships since the earliest surviving port records of the 1560s, bringing coal from Wales and necessities from Bristol, and exporting the produce of local farm, quarry and mine, principally slates and some manganese and iron ore. These and general trades, together with limestone from Wales for the kilns, grew until the building of the local railways in the 1890s after which the harbour gradually reverted to be used by local fishermen with only an occasional coal cargo coming ashore.

Despite the twisting entrance channel in past Meachard islet and the protection of Penally Point, there can be a heavy swell into this

The inner harbour at Boscastle with the ketches BROTHERS and BLUEBELL.
*David Clement Collection*

harbour, and if the wind is strong from the West for any length of time, as it is for most of the winter, then a heavy slow groundsea finds its way in and makes it dangerous to lie alongside or in shallow water. A jetty (on the south side of the entrance) was built at the instigation of Sir Richard Grenville in 1584. The present quay and harbour wall were built in 1740, and the outer breakwater on the north side was added about 1820.

Despite these improvements the swell continued to penetrate into the inner harbour throughout its heyday in the mid-nineteenth century, and enormous coir warps were used to steady the moored vessels. When conditions were bad, ships would prefer not to moor alongside the rough quay, but instead they would lie in the inner harbour but some distance away from the quay, made fast to permanent ground moorings, with large warps stretched taut fore and aft. That helped to reduce the pounding on the bottom, and they would then discharge and load over the side when the tide was out, using pack horses, mules or later, horse drawn carts, exactly as if they were on one of the open beaches such as Crackington Haven.

Although a single ship brought about 200 tons of timber to Boscastle from North America, the normal size of cargoes was less than 100 tons. Even in calm weather it was not easy to take sailing ships into and out of Boscastle, and every device was used including horses towing along the quay, lines from buoys in the fairway, kedge anchors, warps to blocks and rings in the cliffs (some of which can still be found), but most of all, reliance was placed on hobblers (or hovellers), that is longshoremen in gigs or smaller rowing boats who towed the ship in the desired direction and handled lines. In addition to all that, expert sail handling was needed to take advantage of every slant of wind without being driven onto the rocks which were never more than a few feet away. The ability of hobblers to manoeuvre the ships was probably the key factor restricting the size of vessels using the port.

The story has been told[4] of a vessel owned by Sloggett & Roseveare, Boscastle merchants, which met a French privateer when nearly home. The captain set all possible sail for the harbour entrance and the privateer, convinced that the Cornishman was simply running himself ashore, sailed home empty handed. Doubtless the lookout on Willapark had alerted the hobblers, otherwise the Boscastle ship might well have run herself ashore! Roseveare and Sloggett were partners in ownership of several ships, but the two most likely candidates to take part in the story were LYDIA, a 46 ft sloop built at Bideford in 1791 and the brigantine MARY, herself a French prize condemned in 1800. She was 53 tons, and 50 ft long and lasted until broken up in 1851.

The following excerpts from the *West Briton* refer to one of the later trades through Boscastle harbour:

*22nd November, 1861.* The shipping trade at this port [Boscastle] has considerably improved of late, owing to vast quantities of iron ore being brought from Trebursye, two miles from Launceston, where it is said there are inexhaustible quantities. The manager, Mr Martin, talks of having steam engines to convey trucks of ore on the common roads, and has engaged a private road and other premises on the north side of the harbour, of Messrs. Rosevear & Sloggett, for that purpose, thereby avoiding the sharpest incline on all the road; but some people say it will never do for this hill & dale country, whose roads have so many short angles.

*7th March, 1862.* Cornwall's First Traction Engine
An engine & two iron carriages capable of carrying seven tons each arrived at Treburseye from Lincoln (Taplin & Co.). Transport was from Lincoln to Tavistock by rail & there assembled & by road to the mine (3½ days), there being trouble with the piston. It weighs 10 tons. The engine will travel Treburseye to Boscastle with ores and back with coal.

It completed its first journey to Boscastle on April 17th.

The engine spent much of its time under repair and was viewed with suspicion, causing horses to bolt and setting light to the clothes of a farm worker. It was too large and unwieldy for the local roads, but the iron ore trade continued using wagons with large teams of horses, but not on the scale suggested by the press.

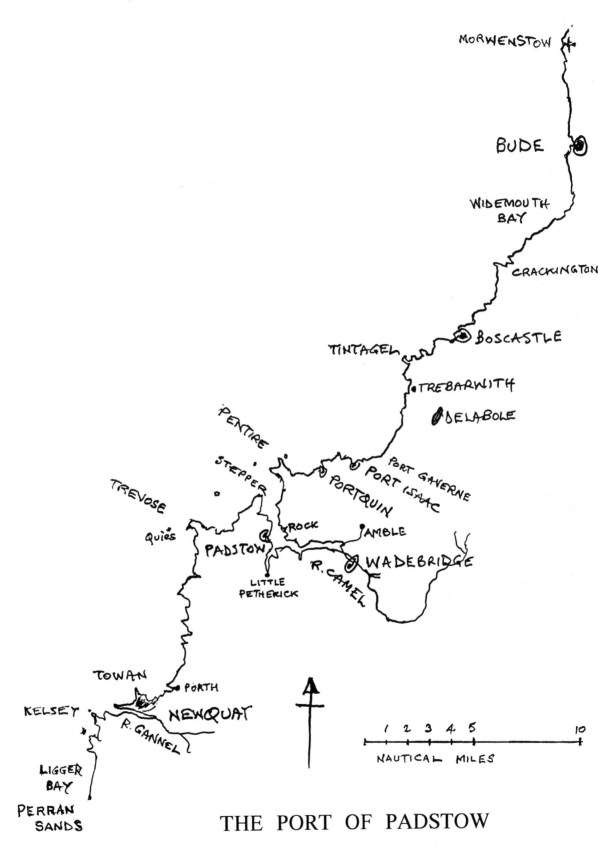

MORWENSTOW

BUDE

WIDEMOUTH BAY

CRACKINGTON

BOSCASTLE

TINTAGEL

TREBARWITH

DELABOLE

PENTIRE

PORT GAVERNE

PORT ISAAC

STEPPER

PORTQUIN

TREVOSE

ROCK

AMBLE

QUIES

PADSTOW

WADEBRIDGE

R. CAMEL

LITTLE PETHERICK

TOWAN

PORTH

KELSEY

NEWQUAY

R. GANNEL

1 2 3 4 5 10
NAUTICAL MILES

LIGGER BAY

PERRAN SANDS

# THE PORT OF PADSTOW

PERRAN SANDS TO MORWENSTOW

The last really significant event in Boscastle harbour occurred in 1941 when a floating mine came in with the tide and blew up the breakwater. The National Trust took note of the deterioration in the harbour resulting from the damage, and repaired it in 1966. The harbour remains enchanting.

If the natural formation of landlocked Boscastle harbour be regarded as unusual, then the choice of men to use the next 'outports' of Padstow is even more unusual.

**BOSSINEY HAVEN** and **TINTAGEL HAVEN** are mere clefts in the high cliffs about three miles west and south of Boscastle, and yet smacks and ketches beached in these clefts to bring necessities to the locals, and took on board export cargoes of slates. In the case of Tintagel, exports of slates from Delabole and other quarries continued into the twentieth century.

**TREBARWITH STRAND** south of Tintagel and much closer to Delabole was a more heavily used landing place despite facing directly west onto the Western Ocean. Here trains of mules and packhorses carried goods up from the beach (which is totally covered at high water) and brought slates down to be loaded into the beached smacks. Later a cart track was hewn out of the native rock.

Delabole has been famous since 1600 or earlier for the quality of its slates. The nature and scale of the industry can be judged from the following advertisement which appeared on July 10th, 1840:

To be sold by public auction . . . at the West Delabole Slate Quarries in Tintagel, a very large quantity of ready-made slate, flooring stone, slabs, window sills, tram-roads, incline planes, whims, whim chains and other machinery erected and used for working the several quarries called Basil Hole Quarry, West End Quarry, The Gibbet Quarry, Point Hole Quarry, Providence Quarry and Drya Quarry. The stock of slate and flooring comprises about 600,000 ready-made slates and rags and from three to four thousand feet of flooring and slabs of the following description: Duchesses, Small ditto, Countesses, Small ditto, Ladies, Small ditto, Doubles, Singles, Queens, Rags, Scantle Slabs and Flooring with about 30 dozen of Collar Stones. The machinery consists of three excellent whims, a valuable machine for cutting slate and floor stone, a boat, about 4,500 feet of whim-chain, four iron buckets, crabs and rollers, two incline planes, upwards of 500 yards of tram-roads, tram waggons and their machinery erected for loading vessels, etc.

But mining and quarrying in this area was by no means limited to slate. Antimony, lead, copper and iron ores were mined and loaded away from the local ports and beaches.

Until the railway came, **PORT GAVERNE** was the main loading point for Delabole slate, especially when, at the start of the nineteenth century, the 'Great Slate Road' was built from Delabole down to the Port Gaverne beach. Waggons drawn by teams of oxen and horses then took the place of the mules and packhorses which previously brought the slates and distributed imports. But it was still back-breaking work, much of it undertaken by the local ladies, to transfer the sharp slates from the wagons to the holds of the waiting ships, when straw or hay was sandwiched between the slates to reduce breakage.

Another advertisement demonstrates that it was not only slates which were exported:

TREORE ANTIMONY MINE, PORT GAVERNE, 18th September, 1884

The lease, engine, pump and mining plant of the above mine is offered for sale by Private Contract. The mine is working and intending purchasers can inspect the rich lodes now open by application at the mine.

Particulars from Mr William Paynter jun. Fore Street, Wadebridge.

Port Gaverne is better sheltered from the prevalent westerlies than places like Trebarwith, but there was still great difficulty and risk in beaching ships and getting them off safely after unloading and loading. The ships' own ground tackle was not enough, and there were permanent arrangements of ropes and chains to offshore rocks and anchors to assist the process of warping off. But the hobblers' boats were there to help, and often needed to tow the vessel a few cables offshore before a slant of wind gave her safe way towards a proper offing.

**PORT ISAAC** and Port Gaverne together formed the most important centre for the pilchard fishery in North Cornwall until Newquay came to the fore in the nineteenth century. Both places had seine companies and pilchard cellars but there was only a tiny village at Port Gaverne whereas Port Isaac was the local centre of population, as it is today.

The Great Slate Road to Port Gaverne reduced the number of vessels trading into Port Isaac proper in the nineteenth century, but there were still market boats and smacks and schooners bringing coal and salt and barrel staves, and exporting herring and pilchard. Port Isaac is more sheltered than Port Gaverne, and since Elizabethan times a pier has improved on nature to reduce the swell. The breakwaters of today were not built until the present century. Port Isaac, like Polperro and other places in Cornwall, has settled down to making a quiet living from inshore fishing and tourism.

**PORTQUIN** lies two miles west of Port Isaac as the crow flies. It is a narrow creek with cliffs both sides, with an entrance quite difficult to pick out from seawards and protected by the Cow and Calf rocks. It is just possible to anchor a single small vessel in the creek with bow and stern anchors. There would not be swinging room on a single anchor.

Yet Portquin sent its own ships to Wales for coal in the sixteenth century, and its inshore fishing fleet supported a village of about one hundred inhabitants, (with the help of employment in local mining and agriculture), and there were large fish cellars and a seine company all financed in 1803 by Rawlins, Norway and Billing, three of the principal merchants of Padstow and Wadebridge.

Many of the dozen or so cottages which can still be identified have been empty since the nineteenth century and the tale is told that the men of Portquin were lost in their fishing boats in some disastrous gale (some put the date as early as 1697, others as late as 1830). There are many variations to the story but whilst fishermen drowned, and continue to drown, there is no record of any such disaster.

It seems certain that the decline of the pilchard and herring fisheries in the nineteenth century and the closing of the small mines led to emigration to the New World and a gradual decline in the population. The fish cellars have been converted into holiday accommodation.

**ROCK** and the outports in the estuary of the River Camel, or Crooked River as it was also known, are the next to be considered.

From Portquin the cliffs continue westwards without a break past the Rumps and Pentire Point into Padstow Bay. Although smacks undoubtedly beached themselves at Pentire Haven and Pentireglaze Haven (at the North end of what is now Polzeath beach) to land coal and lift lead ore from the Pentire mines, and smacks also served Trebetherick by running themselves ashore on what is now Daymer Bay, it is not until Rock and Porthilly are reached opposite Padstow that permanent landing facilities are encountered. Of these landing places only Rock can aspire to outport status.

These days there are mooring buoys off the village of Rock at which small craft can stay afloat at all states of the tide, which is

The SS DUNRAVEN and several sailing vessels show how active the quays at Wadebridge became at high water spring tides. *c.* 1902.
*Nigel Coombes Collection*

River Camel, Wadebridge.

helpful to yachtsmen and fishermen, but in the last century at low water, there was only a tiny rivulet running down from Black Rock. The ferry from Padstow to this Black Rock was already in existence when the Duchy of Cornwall was formed in the fourteenth century and it was known for many years as the Black Rock Ferry. The village must have derived its name and its original *raison d'être* from the ferry and the rock.

Smacks delivered coal to Rock into the twentieth century, and barges brought building materials until the Second World War.

**WADEBRIDGE** is in a more important category; perhaps it should be termed an in-port of Padstow rather than an outport, but small ships have been getting up the river to Wadebridge for hundreds of years, and lying alongside the quays.

In 1833 the steam mineral railway from Wenford to Wadebridge was opened, second only to the Stockton to Darlington railway, and the next year it was extended to Bodmin.[5] The second steam railway in the world was an important boost to the port of Wadebridge; granite, iron ore, and later china clay and other minerals were exported, and imports included coal, nitrates, groceries, timber, rails, limestone and hardware: but most important was the transporting of sand from the estuary to the inland farms to improve the soil.

A plan of Wadebridge made in 1840 shows the thirteen spans of the famous bridge, then, working downstream on the left bank, a marsh, the Subscription Town Quay, Railway Quay and Dock, a public slip, and Sir W. Molesworth Quay. On the right bank, next to the bridge, 'Town Quay, C. P. Brune Esq.' Then Mr R. Symons' garden, Mr Norway's quay, Mr Fox's quay, landing place and, finally, Mr T. Martyn's quay. The plan indicates a proposal to build a jetty out 130 feet into the river from Martyn's quay, to increase the depth alongside from 8½ ft to over 12 ft at high water spring tides.

So Wadebridge was a busy port and became busier as the railway system was progressively developed so that in the 1860s iron ore from several small mines and increased quantities of china clay were brought from Bodmin Moor to the quayside.

Granite for the Eddystone Lighthouse was dressed on the quay at Wadebridge 1878-82 and then shipped to a yard near Plymouth. Granite was also supplied for Tower Bridge and doubtless for numerous less famous purposes.

In 1898 the railway link between Launceston and Wadebridge was completed, and business hummed; but when the railway line was finally extended to Padstow and opened in 1899, fewer ships found it necessary or desirable to go on up to Wadebridge. Between the wars there was the barge traffic described elsewhere, and occasional ketches with coal or building materials. These days the boat yards are busy building and maintaining yachts and small fishing vessels and a sand dredger may be seen occasionally, but Wadebridge no longer handles cargo.

Two other loading points on the left bank above Padstow were **Penqueam** and **Pinkson Creek**. The slate quarries at Penqueam were worked throughout the nineteenth century. They produced thin leaves for roofing, but softer and with less lustre and not so durable as the slates of Delabole. Pinkson Creek was surrounded by various small mines and quarries. Both had fallen into disuse and were cut off by the railway construction along the estuary in the 1890s.

**LITTLE PETHERICK.** The one other landing place within the Camel estuary worthy of mention is a village which lies at the head of a creek two miles south of Padstow. Smacks and ketches traded up Little Petherick creek, past the 'seamills' whose wheels were turned by the release of water impounded at high tide; the THOMAS & ELIZABETH was one of the last. But after construction of the railway bridge across the mouth of the creek in 1898, the low headroom restricted the traffic and it tailed away to nothing.

The remaining outports of Padstow lie to the southwest: sail out of the estuary on the early ebb tide, turn to port past Stepper Point,

* Claims have been made that other railways and tramways had the distinction of being second only to the Stockton to Darlington line.

Newquay's loading facilities with the three-masted schooner MARY WIGHTON.
*Royal Institution of Cornwall*

and coast towards Trevose Head. After a very inhospitable length of cliffs, Trevone and then Harlyn Bay appear. On the west side of **Harlyn Bay** a small quay close under Catacleuse cliffs was built about 1794 by Henry Peter Esquire of Harlyn, and this was used by the Catacleuse Sein Company, which had a cellar nearby, and also by smacks serving the villages of Harlyn and St Merryn.

**NEWQUAY** was Padstow's most important outport. To reach it round Trevose Head, with its lighthouse which was not built until 1847 despite numerous shipwrecks in the vicinity, steer south past Park Head, and sail on until about eight miles south of Trevose.

There were several Domesday settlements in the Newquay area taking advantage of the streams, the climate, the fishing and the comparatively sheltered coves, but the name Newquay is slightly newer than, for instance, the New Forest, since it dates back only to 1439 when the Bishop of Exeter granted an indulgence for the construction of a new quay. One Edward Arundell bequeathed £20 to repair the quay in 1586. This was on the site of the present North Quay of Newquay harbour. From such early days until well into the nineteenth century, small ships traded to Newquay, just as they did to Bude and other outports, by coming in at high water and

unloading and loading at low water with the help of pack-horses and later waggons.

That was the *modus operandi* at **Porth**, (on the northern outskirts of present day Newquay serving the old village of St Columb Minor), and up the **Gannel** (to the south of Newquay serving Crantock) as well as in Harbour Cove itself where the quay offered additional shelter.

Then in 1832, at the start of the railway age, Newquay started to move with the times. The Lord of the Manor spent £1,000 on harbour improvements, including the south quay, which turned Harbour Cove into a better protected harbour, although some awkward swell still penetrated and of course it dried out at low water. Next came mine tramways and railways which greatly increased the ability of Newquay to export iron ore and china clay. In 1836, Joseph Thomas Treffry, a great Cornish industrialist, became Sheriff of Cornwall and that same year extended his mining interests to North Cornwall and Newquay in particular. Squire Treffry made further improvements to the harbour. Iron ore was brought in waggons and stored in hoppers arranged so that ships could be loaded through trap doors down chutes.

The schooner HETTY sails into Newquay; a difficult manoeuvre even at the best of times. *Newquay Old Cornwall Society*

The HETTY, by then a ketch, loading one of the last cargoes of china clay at Newquay soon after the First World War. *Royal Institution of Cornwall*

In 1849, Treffry's sloop MODEL loaded the first thirty tons of lead ore from Treffry's East Wheal Rose mine, making use of Treffry's railway to the harbour.

His most ambitious scheme, to build a harbour of refuge safer to enter than Padstow, was started in 1848. Excavation was to form a channel through Towan Head, with breakwaters at each end, between which ships could lie in safety whatever the weather. Small wonder that a schooner built the next year at Newquay was named TREFFRY. But unfortunately he died in 1850 and the scheme was abandoned.

Nevertheless his mining and harbour investments had been sound, and trade increased. The harbour became the property of the Cornwall Mineral Railway Company — and later of the Great Western Railway. In 1874 the Fowey to Newquay railway was opened for goods traffic, terminating on the new jetty in Newquay harbour much as it exists today. Passengers were brought in for the first time in 1876.

A constant succession of sailing vessels brought coal and fertilisers and general cargo and departed with china clay, iron ore and other minerals, as well as grain from the surrounding farms. Several memoirs mention a November gale in 1854 or 1855 when there were twenty-one ships in Newquay harbour, the largest number ever recorded, but it was the norm in the second half of the nineteenth century for four ships to be loading, and for others to be waiting to take their place at the loading berths.

Various factors combined to cause the decline of Newquay as a commercial harbour. The small Cornish mines gradually closed down: the completion of the railway network took the trade elsewhere, largely to the south coast ports where steamships could stay afloat at all states of tide.

The steam coaster from Par Harbour could offer delivery of 800 tons of china clay in the Mersey on a definite date. The schooner from Newquay could offer 120 tons of clay, but might have to wait for a week or more for the Northwest wind to change before she could even set sail: but she could still be tolerated as long as her freight charges were sufficiently low. So the decline was gradual.

The Great Western Railway kept the harbour repaired until it was handed over to the local authority, Newquay UDC, in 1929, but the last cargo outwards had been in 1921 when the ketch HETTY loaded china clay, and the last incoming cargo was in the following year when the ketch HOBAH brought bagged manure and left in ballast for Appledore.[5]

Newquay has also been moulded by fisheries and holidays. Newquay and Port Isaac were the greatest centres of the seine fishery for pilchard in North Cornwall, and the numerous seine companies provided much employment and prosperity until the decline in the closing years of the nineteenth century. But already the holiday trade was on the increase, and Newquay has expanded in the twentieth century to become much larger than Padstow or Wadebridge, largely to provide for holiday makers and retired people.

The statutory limits of the Port of Padstow extend along the coast for another four miles or so to the southwest beyond Newquay, ending at Perran Sands, but Porth, Newquay and the Gannel are the last outports.

In the details of the ships of Padstow, their owners and crews, mention will often be found not only of the outports, but also of the villages and settlements they served, as set out below:

The ketch VIXEN sailing into Newquay with hobblers' boat in attendance. The fish cellars are in the foreground.
*Newquay Old Cornwall Society*

| Outport | | Hinterland |
|---|---|---|
| Bude | | Stratton |
| Boscastle | ) | Hallworthy |
| Port Gaverne | ) | Delabole, Camelford |
| Port Isaac | ) | St Teath, St Endellion |
| Portquin | | Trelights |
| Rock | | St Minver |
| Wadebridge | | Egloshayle, St Breock |
| Padstow | | |
| Porth | ) | St Columb Minor & Major |
| Newquay | ) | Indian Queens |
| Gannel | | Crantock |

It is notable that Padstow, whose very isolation turned her into a supplier of ships and mariners, lacks the hinterland served by her outports. In the heyday of Padstow's shipping activity, before the railway reached the harbour, the tonnage of cargo handled at Padstow itself was only a small proportion of that handled at the outports.

The cutter PORTH in the 1880s beached at Porth, one of Padstow's minor outports. The cart-tracks show that her cargo of coal has already been collected.
*Royal Institution of Cornwall*

# 4 EARLY SHIPS

*A Shipman was ther woned fer by West . . .*
*Hardy he was and wise, I undertake;*
*With many a tempest hadde his berd be shake:*
*He knew wel alle the havens as they were*
*From Gotland to the Cape de Finistere,*
*And every creke in Bretagne and in Spaine:*
*His barge Ycleped was the MAGDELAINE . . .*

Chaucer, *The Canterbury Tales*

---

### 'A Creke of the Port of Plymouth & Ffoye'

IN the Public Record office in Chancery Lane, London, some 'port books' for Padstow survive covering the period 1565 to 1719, and throughout this time, Padstow was for Customs' purposes 'a creek of the Port of Plymouth & FFoye'. Many of the books are missing and others are totally illegible, but they provide a very adequate picture of the trade patterns of the times. They also provide the names of the ships and their masters, and the size of their cargoes, but virtually no other particulars of the vessels themselves.

The port books are almost entirely a list of ships and goods in the following typical form:

'Entries inwards' – or *Intra*.

'In ye THOMAS & SARAH of Padstowe, Edward Madock Mr (i.e., Master) from Norway . . . ' a list of cargo follows, possibly with 'subsidies' or customs' duties, or perhaps the following:

'In his maj. warehouse at St Merryn, 98 cow hides salv'd from the CHARITY of Limerick being wrackt in this port.'

The exports are termed 'Entries Outwards', or in the early years Extra, and include some details, for instance:

'In ye JUST of Padstowe, Henry Allen Mr, for Lisbone, Peter Swymmer Md.' followed by a list of cargo which would often include some thousands of Helling Stones, or Hilling Stones, which were the famous roofing slates quarried locally, or a number of 'barrells of herrings english taken.'

Other papers list vessels to which 'coastal cocquets' were issued, that is to say permits which had to be carried and presented on request.

It is in some cases impossible to be certain about the identity of particular vessels since it becomes probable or certain that there was more than one vessel with the same name. Another peculiarity is that ships with the same name and the same master are described in one voyage as being 'of Padstow' and a month or more later as being 'of Portisick' or, less commonly, 'of Botreaux Castle': unless that were done in a random manner (like much of the spelling of the time) it seems possible that the phrase 'of Portisick' refers to the last port she sailed from: that is to say, for example, that the ANN 'of Portizick' sailed last with a cargo of Delabole roof slates from Port

Isaac and returned from, say, Crosick (i.e. Croisic in S. Brittany) with a cargo of French salt, to be described as the 'ANN of Portizick' delivering salt to Padstow, she would next perhaps be described in the port books as 'the ANN of Padstowe with a cargo of Tyn slabbs for Bristoll'.

The ships of other major ports such as Bristoll, Swanzey or Beddeford are always described as being of their home port; it is only the ships of Padstow which are periodically ascribed to the various outports of Padstow in the port books of Padstow, and it is only an unconfirmed theory that they were ascribed to the outport they last or generally sailed from.

In some of the seventeenth century port books, I was glad to find a figure (in various dog-latin codes) of the burden, or burthen, of the various ships, that is to say the 'deadweight tonnage' in today's terms. Unfortunately further examination showed that in almost every case the burden tonnage was exactly equal to the number of Chalders of 'Coles' (London measure) brought by the ship on that particular voyage, and the figure was often about half the tonnage of exports ('Copper Oar' etc.) taken off by the same ship at the next sailing.

By comparing the cargoes of the same ship, as recorded in the port books, the following approximation can be reached for measures in the Bristol Channel in the seventeenth or eighteenth centuries:

1. Chalder of coal (London measure) approximated to 1.8 tons of 'oar'; or, 5.4 thousand Hilling Stones (roof slates); or,
2. Weyes of Salt.

Part cargoes of all categories seem to have been quite common. The amount of cargo carried by a given ship did not seem to vary consistently with the seasons of the year. It is possible that the limited amount of cargo available was shared out between the waiting ships; but a more pressing requirement was, perhaps, the exact nature of the points at which loading and unloading took place. A cargo of coal to be unloaded on the beach at Trebarwith (which is only exposed at half tide) might be limited to the amount which could be unloaded over one low tide, as it would be extremely hazardous for the ship to stay longer on the beach, and any remaining cargo would keep her aground longer and increase the danger of pounding on the hard beach as the tide flooded and the surf rolled in. In contrast a ship could dry out in safety alongside the quay at Padstow with a full cargo, and if necessary take several days to unload. But the difficulties of land transport throughout this whole period were such that these small vessels had to take the risk of beaching themselves in remote coves to deliver coal to a hamlet, and take away the local products of farm, mine and quarry.

How should we see the world through the eyes of a Padstow mariner in 1565, the year of the oldest surviving Port Book of Padstow? The preceding decades had seen numerous wars with France, Scotland and other countries, and equally numerous makings of peace. But wars were the business of kings and princes rather than of ordinary folk and mariners. News of war and peace travelled so slowly that it was often out of step with the state of affairs, and the affairs of State.

In the previous centuries, the coasts of Biscay, Brittany and Normandy had all been in fief to the kings of England, whilst the more northerly coasts of France, as far as the Scheldt estuary, had been even more firmly attached, being a Royal Domain of England: so there were many traditional links with France. The wine trade with France was strongly established on a large scale.

In 1564 the Netherlands revolted and started war against their Spanish oppressors, and England backed the Dutch and drifted towards the open conflict with Spain which came in 1587.

The great discoveries of the Americas and the East and West Indies were being followed by the exploitation of these lands, with Spain and Portugal in the vanguard with papal blessing. But the hardier mariners of France, England and the Netherlands were putting to sea in greater numbers and seeking their fortunes near and far. The Elizabethan era was under way.

Nevertheless one would expect the very small ships of Padstow to be about their humdrum business, and so they were. The 'customer and comptroller' and the 'searcher' books of the period, Michaelmas 1565 to Easter 1566, list several small boats from Mombles (Mumbles) 'bringing coal to Paddistowe', the BASTIAN de Portyzyke (Port Isaac) 5 tons — Jones Master from Temby; other Padstow ships being the MARRY or MARY de Bottrizcastell of 10 tons, Willym. Bridgman Master, and PERAN de Padstowe, 20 tons, Richardus Laurens Master.

The searcher's book Michaelmas 1565 to Easter 1566 also includes the arrival of the MYSERECORDYE (*Misericordia* meaning compassion) of 45 tons burden, Bartholomew Pearce the master, the WHIT DOVE de Hambourge, 24 tons burden, the BASTIAN de Marane (Marans) 31 tons burden and the JESSUS de Lubyck.

I was slow to realize the significance of this last name, but I finally connected her with a drawing of her from the Pepys Library at Cambridge which led me to her fascinating history. She was bought

JESUS DE LUBECK
1565

by Henry VIII from Lubeck merchants in 1544 and was included in the State lists of King's ships through the subsequent reigns of Edward VI (1547-1553), Mary I (1553-1558), and on into the Elizabethan age. She measured 700 tons burden, the same as the more famous MARY ROSE, and apart from the HARRY GRACE A DIEU, they were the biggest ships in Henry's fleet. One suspects that a Lubeck galleon or carrack bought by King Henry VIII would be more burdensome than an average King's ship, and would certainly not be under-measured, and her length was probably not much more than 100 feet and her beam about 45 feet. Nevertheless, the 1548 list of the Navy[1] notes that she was manned by 300 soldiers, mariners &c, had eight brass pieces of ordnance and sixty-six of iron. It seems probable that many of the iron pieces were small swivels and portable arquebuses, and the poor soldiers can have had standing room only!

In 1562 one John Hawkins made an experimental voyage to Guinea and thence with slaves to the West Indies, where he was able to make profitable trade with the Spanish settlers. He returned to England with shiploads of hides, with ginger, sugar and pearls, and although he was cheated out of some of his goods by the Inquisition and King Philip of Spain, he had opened the trade route to the West Indies.

Queen Elizabeth was impressed and not only took shares in his next voyage, but also lent him her JESUS of Lubeck. He sailed in October 1564 and there is a full account of his adventures in Hakluyt. With the JESUS went the SALOMON, 140 tons, TIGER, 50 tons and SWALLOW, 30 tons 'being all well furnished with men to the number of one hundredth threescore and tenne'. The crew of the JESUS was much reduced for habitability on a long expedition and also, of course, to make room for the slaves. The voyage was less peaceful but just as successful as the first, and he came home via Florida and the Grand Banks, and 'with a good large winde, the 20th September (1565) we came to Padstow, God be thanked, in safetie, with the loss of twentie persons in all the voyage and with great profit to the venturers of the said voyage, as also to the whole realme, in bringing home both golde, silver, pearles and other jewels great store'.

Queen Elizabeth was pleased for John Hawkins to mount a third adventure, in command of the JESUS and other ships, and this time accompanied by his young kinsman, Francis Drake. They set sail in October 1567 and all went well until a Spanish fleet caught up with them in Mexico, and the JESUS was lost after a desperate fight. But Drake and Hawkins escaped, and together continued to singe the King of Spain's beard for almost thirty years.

Careful examination shows that the full Hawkins entry in the Padstow port book was as follows: 'JESSUS de Lubyck 90 tons burden, John Lovell of Saltash master, from the Indies with diverse merchandise, John Hawkyns of Plymouth Gent., a warrant dated 1 day of Oct.'

If Hawkins had been wrecked on the Doom Bar, the course of world history might have been quite different.

Reverting to the domestic affairs of Padstow, in the following year, 1567, several additional vessels are listed, including CLEYER (Clair ?) de Porquine (Portquin) and MARIE de St Collumbe, so Padstow and its outports of Port Isaac, Portquin, Boscastle and Newquay (St Columb) were all operating in the sixteenth century. Bude is first mentioned in 1616 when the SAYJOUR and SPEEDWELL are listed. That must have been a desperately dangerous port to work from before the harbour works were constructed.

By the year 1600, the port books make clear that Padstow ships were trading to 'Biskay' ports, including St Abastian and in particular Buddeaux (Bordeaux) and Bayon, Bretagne (Brittany) ports with St Mallows to the fore, and in the Channel ports as far up as Gent.

Trade with Yeareland (Ireland) was prominent including Corke, Dublyn, Watherford, Waxford, Gaalewaye, Lymbricke and Youghal, but unfortunately the records have not survived covering the period from 1599, when the English expedition to Ireland started, to 1601, when the Irish (together with their Spanish allies then in Ireland) surrendered.

An interesting arrival in November 1593 is the LYON of Rochelle, burden 30 tons, John Labue Master, from Newfoundland, the first English colony in America, founded just ten years earlier by Sir Humphrey Gilbert.

The most numerous vessels calling at Padstow were the even smaller craft of the Bristol Channel ports, including Milford, Swanzey, Temby (or Tinbie), Newporte, Carmarthan, Appledore, Beddeford, Barnstaple, Bristowe, Croydon (sic) and Gloucester.

In the sixteenth century appear entries from ports such as Minsterworth, Northam, Elmore, Croswicke, Framylode and even Tewkesburie, in other words, the fore-runners of the trows of the River Severn were trading from their individual villages: in later years this trade was rationalised and a regular 'market boat' from Bristol took the place of almost all such local traders in mixed goods.

In the early years of the seventeenth century, Padstow trade with France and Ireland (and more especially Wexford) flourished. The trade with Ireland was of the nature of a primitive packet service, although much timber and tallow was brought to Padstow. Padstow's trade with the continent consisted mainly of importing wine and iron from Spain, wine and *salis baie* (Bay salt) from France, and manufactured goods from the Low Countries. In return, Padstow was able to provide herring and pilchards, precious slabs of tynn and some agricultural produce. The herring and pilchards were mostly caught locally and described as 'english taken' and thus duty free and reserved for English ships by the navigation laws, but barrels of Irish herring were also re-exported. The export market in the first-class roofing slates, which later was to become such a mainstay, had evidently not been developed by 1600, nor had the china clay trade started.

A small vessel of Crosick (Croisic) in South Brittany arrived in 1602, and that appears to have been the start of a long and happy association with that port which, in many ways, resembles Padstow in appearance and activity. For many years thereafter, ships of Padstow went every year to Croisic. As time went by, the outward cargo was generally many thousands of hilling stones (roofing slates), and the ships usually brought salt back from Croisic but also brandy and rozin pitch. Come to think of it, it's probably the hilling stones which cause the buildings of Croisic to remind one of Padstow, although the wild scenery and seas of Brittany have much in common with Cornwall, as do the fiercely independent people.

So Padstow was playing its humble part in the expansion of English trade in the first half of the seventeenth century, a period when the expeditions of Raleigh and others were followed by the sailing of the MAYFLOWER in 1620, and the colonisation by the English of New England and many of the islands in the West Indies. The might of Spain was challenged wherever it was to be found. Churchill, in his *History of the English-Speaking Peoples* had this to say of conditions at sea:

It is well to remember the ordinary seaman who sailed in ships sometimes as small as twenty tons into the wastes of the North Atlantic, ill-fed and badly paid, on risky adventures backed by inadequate capital.

These men faced death in many forms — death by disease, death by drowning, death from Spanish pikes and guns, death by starvation and cold on uninhabited coasts, death in the Spanish prisons. The Admiral of the English fleet, Lord Howard of Effingham, spoke their epitaph: 'God send us to sea in such a company together again, when need is'.

The Trinity House papers include a statement in 1617 that the Turks had captured more than 300 English and Scottish ships in recent years. In 1619, Sir J. Killigrew petitioned the King for a lighthouse at the Lizard point, but eventually Trinity House commented that 'it is not necessary or convenient to erect a lighthouse there, but *per contra*, inconvenient, having regard to pirates and enemies whom it would direct to a safe place of landing.'

Baltimore in Ireland was one of Padstow's trading ports, and in 1631 Barbary pirates from Algiers raided the town and carried off 1,500 of the inhabitants in chains. The pirate fleet was then chased by fifteen small vessels from Niewport and Ostend (ships from both ports being frequent traders to Cornwall and Ireland) who brought them to action off Cape Finisterre, rescuing a number of the Irish prisoners who settled happily in Belgium. The rest of the captives were taken to Algiers. When subsequently, the British government raised a ransom for them, they were not best pleased.[2] That incident throws light on conditions at sea - and in Ireland - at the time.

In 1626, Captain Bonython at Pendennis Castle reported to Sir John Coke that there were 'divers Turkish men-of-war upon these coasts'. A kinsman near the Lizard had boarded a ship laden with Rochelle salt to find no man in her, and her chests broken open and rifled; some Turks seen the previous day may have taken the men and such pillage as they saw fit.

King Charles II gave comprehensive orders to captains of merchantmen regarding pirates. The section applicable to the small ships of Padstow was as follows: 'If the master of any English ship or vessel of less than 200 tons burden shall yield his ship unto any Turkish ship, pirate or sea-rover (not having at least double his number of guns) without fighting, every such master shall be lieable to all and every penalties in this Act contained.'

The penalties included being banned for life of command of any English ships.

It seems probable that Padstow ships and men were involved in the expeditions to help the Huguenots in La Rochelle in 1625-1627, but no details have been found. Rochelle, Ile de Re and Marans were all destinations for Padstow ships.

In 1640 darkness descended as far as the port books of Padstow were concerned — and as far as many Loyalist Cornishmen were concerned, and there are no records until 1660. Trade must have been seriously disrupted by the Civil War in which Cornwall was strongly Royalist, and painfully subjugated by the ruthless Roundheads, but subsequently, in 1649, it seems certain that shipping from Padstow to Cork and Waterford would have been kept busy supplying Cromwell's cruel Irish campaigns. When surviving records were resumed in 1660 there was much increased shipping of coal from Wales to Padstow and the outports, especially from Swanzey which must have already become a major coal mining centre. There were perhaps the following reasons for the increase in the coal trade; Cornwall, especially North Cornwall, is not a good place to grow timber. The Cornish oaks up the valley of the Camel curve away from the prevalent westerly winds and any tree within a mile or two of the sea shows signs of being burnt by the salt spray. Whilst there were gnarled spinneys where grown frames and knees could be selected for limited wooden shipbuilding, the supply of timber for building and firewood was soon exhausted. The land was being cleared for agriculture. Even unpromising acres near the sea were brought into production to feed large families, and the large families themselves made possible the clearing of millions of rocks and stones off fields which were previously untillable, and the building of the thousands of miles of dry-stone walls or hedges as they are known locally. So there was less firewood than before, and more people to keep warm. Finally, the mining and metal industries were on the increase and although it was not until about 1790 that steam started to be used on a large scale for pumping and winding, coal was already required in increasing quantities for smelting and other industrial processes. On the industrial scene, despite almost constant wars with the Dutch and with France, Ireland and Spain, together with permutations and combinations of all four, Padstow's ships extended the destinations of their voyages by the end of the seventeenth century to include, amongst many others, Jamaica, the Canary Islands, Norway, Oporto (often reported as Port-o-port), Leghorn, Fyall, Alicante and Bilbao. In addition, there were increasingly visits to and from Dantzick, Amsterdam and Christiania, although it is probable that some of the more exotic arrivals were surprised to find themselves on the north coast of Cornwall.

In those days, any ship sailing thousands of miles from the West Indies or New England faced potential difficulties in the Western Approaches. With primitive charts, inaccurate compasses and no proper means to gauge their speed through the water, they often had difficulty in finding the entrance to the English Channel. Chronometers were not available until the eighteenth century, so there was no way of establishing the ships' longitude accurately. Much reliance had to be placed on noon sights of the sun with quadrant or cross-staff which allowed fairly accurate calculation of the ship's latitude. If the ship could be sailed due East along latitude 49° 40' North, or thereabouts, she would pass safely south of the Scilly Islands, and could run for a considerable distance to the East before turning North and identifying the South coast of England in relatively safe circumstances, and proceeding thence to her destination, be it London or Amsterdam. But pity the Master whose ship ran in from the Atlantic before a westerly gale in thick weather, with no opportunity of taking a noon sight for a week or more. If he heaves to, he will make no progress and the lengthy voyage will be prolonged indefinitely; if he runs on, he may end up, as many did, on the rocks of Ushant or Scilly, or even near Padstow, as happened to a few. The one other available assistance to navigation was to sound the depth of water with a deep sea lead; but to find bottom in fifty or more fathoms as was necessary to establish soon enough whether the ship was approaching land, was a major operation beyond the means of all but the largest and best manned ships, and in those days the knowledge of actual depths was rudimentary; in any case if soundings revealed shallow water in thick weather, with the ship running on before the wind, the master seldom knew which way to turn to avoid disaster.

## The Trade Pattern, Seventeenth and Eighteenth Centuries

By the end of the seventeenth century a trade pattern had been established which remained basically unaltered for many years, except when disrupted by war. Its intensity is impossible to assess due to incomplete records, but Padstow could expect the arrival of ships from foreign ports about once a week, from Ireland about once a week, and there would be a market boat from Bristol about once a week. Small coasters and colliers would arrive at the rate of about

one every other day, some of them competing with the regular market boats but most of them bringing coals and taking away ore or helling stones.

Dealing more fully with the coastal imports, coles were of course predominant; about 10% to 20% were described as 'culme' which I have seen variously translated as anthracite or colliery waste. It tended to originate from Milford more than from Swansea.

The surviving 'arrivals' records for 1694 appear to be complete enough to allow an overall assessment with the following results:

| | |
|---|---:|
| Colliers of Padstow (incl. outports mainly Port Isaac) | 40 |
| Colliers of Clovelly (an unusually large number) | 35 |
| Colliers of Swanzey | 12 |
| Colliers of Oystermouth (previously Mumbles) | 6 |
| Colliers of Bideford | 3 |
| Colliers of Truro, Neath, Elfracombe, Fowey & Bristol together | 8 |

Number of arrivals:   TOTAL:   104
Average cargo about 17 chalders

The weight of a chalder of coal varied with location and date. A Newcastle chalder was often over 2 tons, whereas a London chalder was seldom much more than 30 cwt (1.5 tons). I believe the Bristol Channel chalders, despite being described as London measure, were just under 2 tons, and therefore that Padstow and outports imported just about 3,000 tons of coal in 1694, mostly from Swanzey, but also from Neath, Milford, Lanelly and Tenby. It is impossible to know whether that was a typical year.

David Thomas in *Old Ships and Sailors of Wales* reckoned 27 cwt. of coal per chalder loaded from Swansea in 1709, and using that assumption, my 3,000 tons per annum would be reduced to 2,400 tons. But the measures of the time were inaccurate and variable, and it may even be that fewer tons were measured at the loading ports in Wales than were unloaded in North Cornwall.

At first it seemed extraordinary that Cardiff, which was already established as a principal port, is not mentioned once in the many thousands of entries. The explanation must be that the coal mines were not close enough to the port of Cardiff, that is until the coming of the railways.

It is difficult to follow the fortunes of any one particular ship after so many years, but this much can be said: it is rare to find the same ship arriving with coal from Swanzey less than one month after her previous arrival. This rate of delivery compares, I understand, very unfavourably with rates further up the Bristol Channel, but it should be remembered that ships bound for Padstow (of which about half probably had to be discharged eventually on the beaches of the outports) had to wait for reasonably settled weather before daring to arrive at their final destination.

The Welsh colliers often brought some butter and cheese, especially from Swanzey, but general supplies came with the regular market boats from Bristol. For instance on 17th April 1704, PLAINE DEALING arrived with:

. . . lead 1 Tun, Ironmongery wares 3 Tuns, Grindstones 1 Tun, 34 caskets of bottled syder, 6 small caskets of english spirits, 6 cwt Linen, 2 cases glas, english made white salt, 6 boxes candles, 2 doz wool cards, 4 small casks oyle, 1 cwt. copper manufactures, grocery wares, cheese, tobacco, empty bottles and dressed leather.

Rock salt arrived from Liverpool occasionally. Another Bristol ship brought 'sope, hoops, cheeses, groceries, hopps, chairs, hatts, tallow, sadlers wares and tobacco.'

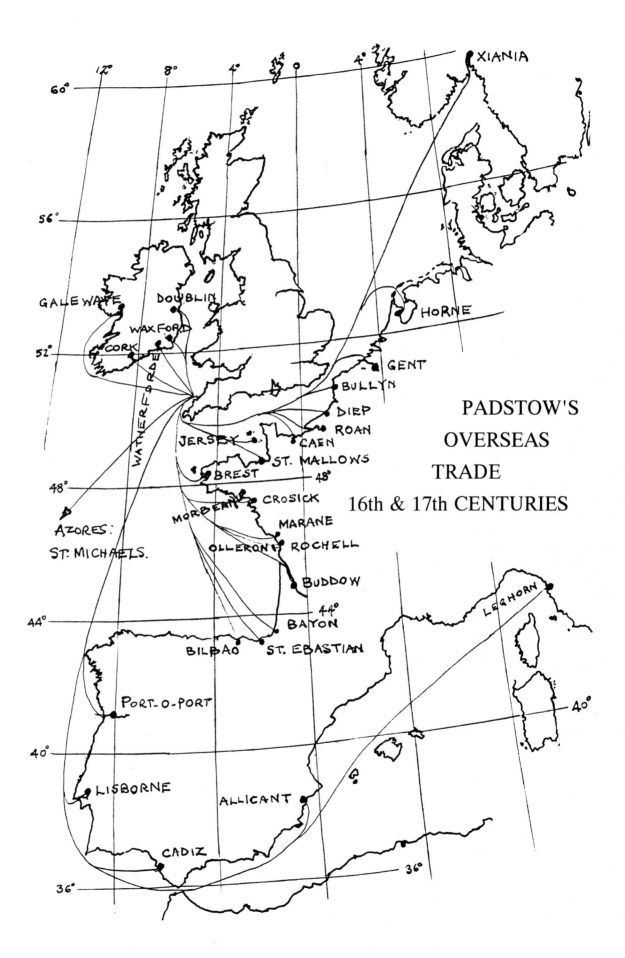

PADSTOW'S
OVERSEAS
TRADE
16th & 17th CENTURIES

At first I found it difficult to explain the importation to Padstow, several times a year, of up to 7 tons of 'Tobacco Pipe Clay' from Barnstaple, often accompanied by Bideford and Barnstaple earthenware: but I was fortunate to make the acquaintance of Alison Grant who, together with her book *North Devon Pottery, The Seventeenth Century* was able to explain that Tobacco Pipe Clay was merely the name of a high quality white clay mined near Torrington. At Bristol it was used for making tobacco pipes (hence its name) and in sugar refining, but it had other uses in potteries, for slip (i.e., decorative mixtures) and glaze. With potteries known to have been operating in Boscastle and Padstow, the trade is explained.

Coastal Exports were almost as varied. By 1660 the export of helling stones was the mainstay, and continued to be so into the twentieth century. The best quality stones came from Delabole and were loaded into beached vessels at Boscastle, Trebarwith and Port Gaverne (which counted as part of Portizick), but there were several other quarries and ships were loaded at Bude, Tintagel and on quite a large scale further up the River Camel than Padstow from quays which were later destroyed to construct the railway from Wadebridge to Padstow.

The small size of the local vessels is emphasized by an export certificate of 20th August, 1684 for the SUCCESS HOY of London, for '140 thousand Hilling Stones'. The hoy was the humblest Thames coaster, fore-runner of the Thames barge, yet able to lift two or three times the cargo of the Padstow ships of the time.

In addition to slates, there was the export of lead, slabs of tin, lead ore and copper ore often 'mixed with mundick [iron pyrites]'. Swanzey was, even in those days, the destination of most of the 'copperoremen' but others went to Bristol and Neath. Sometimes mundick formed a cargo in its own right.

The export of farm produce was less regular. After a good harvest, wheat and barley were exported over the following twelve months (so there were adequate barns and warehouses). Occasionally though, wheat was imported and in greater quantities than needed for seed.

The following are typical coastal exports:

*Padstow: Coast Cocquets Outwards; Lady day Quarter 1711*

JOHN OF TRURO, J. Birdwood Mr, for Bristol, 2 Blocks quantity 4 tons wt of tyn. 14 tons copper oar.
INDUSTRY of Padstow, H. Sussex Mr, for Bristol tyn, pewter, 10 thousand hilling stones, 3 tons wet and dry fishes, sheep skyns, beeswax, 2 casks shruff brass, 5 old brass potts, bullocks hair.
CHARLES of Padstow, Wm. Billing Mr, for Bristoll [a similar mixed cargo, but including '8 hogsheads train oyle', which must surely refer to pilchard oil, not whale oil as was the later usage].

Bone ashes and soap ashes, and cowhides in the hair were also sent to Bristol. (The ashes were, I believe, used in the manufacture of glass.)
On 19th January, 1715, the PETER GALLEY of and for Bristol departed with: '60 barrells herring english taken, 30 bundles sheeps pelts, 4 parcels broken glass, 1 tun wrought pewter, 27 bushels malt Winchester measure, 3 boxes bullocks tails, 1 cask reformed sugar, 15 blocks tyn, 2 small bundles linen returned, 1 cwt old brass pots, 1500 herrings in tals (dyslectic salt ?), 1 tun codfish, 200 livres sterling money'.
Other ships about then took to Bristol similar cargoes, including also '2000 bullocks horns, codd and ling, 3 packages of coney skins, 6 bundles sheep pelts, 1 bundle flax, 3 maunds english cyder, 12 blocks coined tyn and pewter plates'. Quantities of wine and brandy

sometimes feature 'recovered from wracks in this port' which might have been a convenient way of laundering smuggled goods.

Foreign trade was distorted by the Navigation Laws, reintroduced by Cromwell, which laid down that English goods should be carried in English bottoms, and that foreign ships could only bring goods from their own country. Thus a Norwegian ship bringing softwood from Xania (Christiania) had no hope of a return cargo. Foreign ships were, however, allowed to buy supplies (many of the records are marked 'supply only') and one suspects that surreptitious trade was carried out in that way, as well as by normal smuggling. Certainly the Navigation Laws made it necessary for Padstow ships such as HOPEWELL, 30 tons, to find their way to Norway and bring back sparrs and deales (planks), and that became a regular part of the pattern; but Norwegian ships continued to trade to main centres, such as Dublin, and in 1710 we find the CATHERINE of Milford arriving at Padstow from Dublin with Norway deales and 10 barrels of tar, presumably a part cargo trans-shipped for Padstow.

It seems that there were numerous relaxations of the Navigation Laws to suit the political situation, and certainly in the 1690s, when England and Holland were allies, there was an influx of Dutch ships which were at the time considered to be the élite trading ships of Europe, and which loaded away cargoes of hilling stones several times as large as the Padstow ships could manage. But the Dutch ships tended not to come back for more and they may have found the navigation in North Cornwall somewhat nerve-wracking.

Looking in more detail at the overseas imports, the trade in Spanish iron, and in Spanish and French salt continued despite the availability of English salt from Cheshire which came from Liverpool or via the Severn. Salt came from Oleron and Bayonne as well as Croisic and Saint Ebastian. The foreign salt was often split into so many weys 'for the fishery' and so many 'for the country'; perhaps the duty had to be paid on imports for use inside the country, but not for curing fish to furnish an important export. That was certainly the case in the early nineteenth century when bulk salt for fish curing was exempt from a heavy tax on salt.

Cargoes from St Mallows consisting of honey, wine, brandy, soaps, oakham, Vittroy canvas, dewlaps, and nuts remind one of Masefield's Cargoes and of the 'Quinquireme of Ninevah' rather than the 'Dirty British Coaster'! French and Spanish wine and brandy continued to arrive officially as well as unofficially.

Imports from Ireland were more down to earth; bacon, butter, tallow, hides, candles, frize (or freeze, a cheap woollen cloth), tymber, including clapboards, staves, laths and trannails; sheeps pelts and herrings. All arrived from Waxford, Wicklow and Doublyn. 'Great cattle' and sheep were imported from Youghal in 1680 and the Irish of course continue to export such livestock to this day.

Also in 1680, Padstow started to benefit from the English colonies, and a cargo arrived from Jamaica bringing logwood, sugar, elephants' teeth and 'ffusticke'! Homecoming vessels picked up Canarys wine and Madeira in increasing quantities.

It will be noted that amongst other things the imports clearly supported a ship-building industry at Padstow including, as they did, pitch, oakum and canvas from France, iron from Spain, timber and treenails from Ireland, and masts, sparrs and baulks from Norway, together with the famous 'Swedish iron' which lasts for ever. Copper, brass and lead were readily available locally.

Exports overseas were more difficult. As in the home trades, the hilling stones were the mainstay; the tin, copper ore and other minerals had ready markets at home. Herring and pilchards were a real asset, but Padstow's share was a drop in the bucket when measured against the rest of the kingdom. So the Padstow ships sailing to Europe took their hilling stones and supplemented them with limited quantities of locally woven English broadcloth, and more of the much cheaper freeze, re-exported from Ireland. The ships of Padstow brought the essentials back to Padstow and made life possible and bearable in this isolated part of Cornwall; they were brave and enterprising but through no fault of their own, small and inefficient, and they never could succeed in creating enough wealth to break out from Churchill's description of the English seventeenth century sailors as being 'badly paid on risky adventures backed by inadequate capital'.

## The Early Ships of Padstow

Clearly, for this book, the most important features of this chapter should be the particulars of the ships themselves. Alas, they remain shadowy images with many unknowns.

You will find in Chapter 5 details of the service of over 200 Padstow vessels which appear in the port books between 1565 and 1719, but there is almost no firm knowledge of where they were built, how they were rigged, what their dimensions were, nor what was their fate, except in a very few cases.

The vessels were small, very few being above 50 tons burden. The average burden of the ships in the Appendix to this chapter are as follows:

| Portquin | Bude | Port Isaac | Boscastle | Padstow |
|---|---|---|---|---|
| 8 tons | 14.5 tons | 19.5 tons | 21 tons | 27.2 tons |

That is not a surprising result. Tiny Portquin must have sent open boats to Wales for coal in the early days; Bude amounted to almost nothing until the harbour was built, and the others are not far apart, although the largest ships, naturally enough, tended to belong to Padstow.

The hunt for evidence of the particulars of these vessels has been interesting. The Antique Collectors Club has published its magnificent *Concise Catalogue of Oil Paintings in the National Maritime Museum* (1988) and one of its best features is a series of helpful indices, including the Alphabetical Index of Named Vessels, Chronological Index of Named Vessels (but the relatively few paintings before 1720 are virtually all of warships or, at the very least, East Indiamen), Index of Named Persons, Index of Dated Events (both alphabetical and chronological), Index of Named Places (including one nineteenth century painting of Bude harbour), Indices of Major Collections, Acquisition Numbers and Item Numbers. I have omitted the Index of Vessel Types, which was the most helpful to my quest: by seeking out cutters, luggers, smacks and sloops, I was quickly guided to the works of Charles Brooking (1723-1759) and Dominic Serres (fl, 1783-4) which show convincingly that, in the eighteenth century, small fore-and-aft rigged vessels were not limited to the royal yachts and Dutch types so beloved of painters and historians.

The histories of the development of English sailing ships which I have read seem to start with the seals of the cinque ports, and so far as small vessels are concerned, move straight to the revenue cutters and the royal yachts already mentioned. Thereafter they are able to deal with relatively well-documented local types (such as Mounts Bay driver, or Cardiff pilot schooner) very often without being able to pinpoint the origins of the species. Even in recent years, North Cornwall has not produced such specific local types of ship or boat.

Another helpful publication is Archibald's *Dictionary of Sea Painters*, also published by the Antique Collectors Club. My remarks refer to the enlarged 2nd Edition published in 1989. There are numerous reproductions of paintings, apparently chosen for their artistic merit rather than the historical importance of their subjects and, as a result, there are more examples of small workaday ships than usual. Two works in particular have caught my eye. Simon de Vlieger (c. 1600 - 1653) painted a series of coastal and estuarial scenes in Holland, including *A squally day in a Dutch estuary*. Here, in the mid-seventeenth century, is a gaff-rigged sloop sailing with all the features of that handy rig which lasted well into the twentieth century, including a running backstay set up on the weather quarter to reduce the strain on the rest of her gear. And she is really making up well to windward, with the headsail sheeted inside the shrouds, and displaying the aerodynamic slot between her two sails so beloved of designers of the mid-twentieth century! The Dutch flag at the peak of the gaff should be streaming straight towards us — but that's where the artist is allowed his licence.

*A squally day in a Dutch estuary* by Simon de Vlieger (c. 1600-1653). An early fore-and-aft rigged sloop on the port tack.
*National Maritime Museum*

In contrast is a painting of the same time by Pieter de Zeelander, mid-seventeenth century, entitled *An English hooker off the Dutch coast*. The term 'hooker' or 'howker' covered a variety of modest sized types from Scandinavia to France, often two masted (as in the case of the Swedish 'hukar'). The vessel in the painting has a burdensome hull with relatively high freeboard and plenty of sheer. Her mainmast is amidships and carries a single large square-sail. There is a small foremast stepped right forward also with a single square-sail, and a small bowsprit, or rather a small spar projecting forward of the stem. It seems to me that the purpose of this spar must have been to carry a bowline from the foresail when close hauled.

In 1679, a Frenchman, Jean Jouve, published an album of designs of different types of vessel to be seen in the harbours, ports and rivers from Nantes to Bayonne. The album contains over seventy perspective drawings of different types from the 200-300 ton flutes of Bayonne and Bordeaux, some of them built in Holland, and the ship-rigged *terreneuves* of Nantes, already taking large crews to bring

AN ENGLISH HOOKER, MID-17th CENTURY
After a painting by PIETER DE ZEELANDER

D. A Mornac sur la Rivière de Sendre il y a des barques de 15 jusqu'à 50 T. qui portent du sel a Bourdeaux , Bayonne et Espagne. Les plus grandes sont montées de 5 hommes.
E. Une barque de Nantes de 19 T. qui vient de Bretagne chargée de bled et autres marchandises et qui retournera chargée de vins montée par 3 hommes et un garçon.
F. Au Port des Barques (la Rivière de Charante) il y a des barques de 12 jusqu'à 25 t. pour pescher et porter leur poisson à la Rochelle, Rochefort ou Bourdeaux. [Most of the single masted vessels in the album are lighters or river barges, but here is a seagoing vessel, as large as most of the Padstow ships of the period, with a single square sail. She has a light spar holding the weather leech forward. This spar, known in Cornwall as a Vargord, was a standard fitting in Cornish luggers of the late eighteenth and nineteenth centuries. It appears to me that the line above and parallel to the foot of the sail indicates not a bonnet but a line of reef points, so that a reef could be taken in or let out from the deck without lowering the sail. A bonnet would have required an extra pair of sheets not shown in the drawing to be kept permanently taut.]
G. Une barque de Maran depuis 30 jusqu'à 90 T.

back salt cod from the Grand Banks, down to the humblest barges and chaloupes on the Charente and Garonne rivers. But it is the small seagoing vessels which interest us in the present context. Their descriptions follow:

A. Une barque de Bayone dont il y en a plusieurs depuis 12 jusqu'à 60 T. montées de 5 ou 6 hommes.
B. Une barque de Gironde depuis 12 jusqu'à 30 T. qui vont aux costes de Normandie, de Portugal et d'Espagnes montées de 4 à 5 hommes. [This vessel is fully decked with cargo hatches visible and ratlines in the mainmast shrouds.]
C. Une barque de Bordeaux depuis 15 jusqu'à 50 T. qui naviguent dans les costes de Bretagne etc. montées de 3 hommes. [These are demanding waters, but she would expect to put in every night with such a small crew].

Maran is inland from La Rochelle, and Padstow ships went there for salt and wine. I included this drawing to show just how small and simple a full rigged ship can be (although she does boast a yard under her bowsprit). Is it too far-fetched to suggest that the KESTLE FRIGGETT of Padstow in the 1670s might have been of a similar rig? Her unusual name does suggest a rig unusual to Padstow.

With a second mast stepped right forward it was perfectly possible to sheet the foresail as shown in drawing E when running before the wind. However, with the wind on or forward of the beam, it became progressively more difficult to get the sail to fill, and the spars projecting forward of the stem in the drawings A, B and D were steeved steeply up so as to be at the right level to take bowlines from the weather leech of the foresail.

Drawing C has no such spar, but instead what appears to be a small bumkin projecting near the stem. If this bumkin could be moved to either side of the bow it could be used to take the sheet from the weather clew of the foresail when sailing close to the wind. Experiment would probably soon show that a fixed bumkin near the centreline of the vessel was just as effective, providing a taut weather leech; so, lo and behold, the lugsail rig has been invented.

It is surprising that such a comprehensive survey of the whole Biscay coastline of France in 1679 shows not a single boom or gaff. Some of the squaresails on the smaller craft may have been embryonic lugsails, but otherwise the only departure from square rig was the lateen mizen to be found on most of the large three masted vessels of the period. There wasn't even a sprits'l rigged boat to be found on the rivers.

With the ancient trading and cultural connections between Cornwall and Brittany and Biscay, it seems certain to me that the sixteenth and seventeenth century ships of Cornwall fitted generally into the pattern of Jean Jouve's album, and not the budding fore-and-aft rigs of the Low Countries. I find Basil Greenhill's words in *The Merchant Schooners* most convincing:

The technology of the seventeenth and eighteenth centuries limited the size of the fore-and-aft rigged vessel. Neither the rope, nor the iron fittings, nor the simple mechanical aids, such as blocks, were good enough to stay a tall single part mast, or to set and control a big gaff sail, even if it had been possible to make a well-setting sail with the fabrics and techniques available.

The Dutch were, to my mind, a special case. They were acknowledged to be the aristocrats of maritime trade at the time; their sheltered estuaries and inland waterways provided relatively smooth water, and considerable incentive to develop a rig which could point as close to the wind as possible. To sail down a canal, you must be able to fetch the required course, or you cannot sail at all. Their well built shallow draught vessels were exceptionally beamy, which reduced the difficulty of staying the mast, their leeboards gripped the water in the same way as later proved so effective in the Thames barge, and the relatively smooth water reduced the difficulty of controlling gaffs and booms.

The argument can also be developed from the Cornish viewpoint. I have been becalmed in a lumpy sea off the North Brittany coast in a heavily rigged gaff cutter, when it was important for us to make progress with every puff of wind on a broad reach. The slatting of the boom, gaff and sails, as the vessel rolled, was almost unbearable, and the wear and tear on all our gear was obviously much worse than in a gale of wind. Naturally we rigged boom guys and preventer tackles, but were sorely tempted to lower all sail and lash down tight. Had I been an eighteenth-century Cornishman, I would have reverted to a well braced square rig for my next ship. (Had I been a twentieth-century Cornishman, I would have fitted an engine!)

So I have convinced myself that the Padstow ships of the sixteenth, seventeenth and eighteenth centuries were all square rigged on one, two and only exceptionally three masts, with an occasional main topmast and tops'l in the larger two and three masted vessels. But I know of no single painting or drawing of a named vessel to offer as confirmation.

As to their hulls, the drawings of Jean Jouve all indicate frames at close centres, and although some of the very small craft in his album are clinker built, all those I have selected (and all the larger vessels without exception) are of carvel construction. Most of the types are square sterned, but the single-master F might be described as a double-ender, or by the Cornish expression, two-bowed. The bows are, of course, bluff, and the hulls are wide with a beam of about one-third of the length, but all show an increase in draught towards the stern, and a carefully developed run aft.

Of the types I have reproduced, A appears to have open holds like a Severn trow, F to be half decked like many fishing boats, whilst all the others are fully decked, with cargo hatches and poops raised one whole or one half deck. All have little deadrise and are obviously intended to beach or take the ground as a matter of course. Indeed, most of the drawings were done with the tide out, and show the entire hull.

The late Edgar Marsh in *Sailing Drifters* surmised that the carvel construction of Cornwall's wooden vessels might be traced back (via the Phoenicians) to the Old Testament, wherein Ezekiel refers to caulkers (who would be required for carvel and not clinker built ships). But he went on to emphasize the connections with Breton and Latin influences, which favoured carvel construction.

One very practical point surely is that the clinker built vessels of the Thames and East Anglia, or of the Low Countries, could settle into their mud berths without damage, whereas the ships of the Westcountry, as of Brittany, whether beaching to unload coal at Port Gaverne or drying out in some exposed fishing haven, were subjected to pounding on a hard and often stony or rocky bottom twice a tide, and carvel planking was less vulnerable in such circumstances than the sharp edges and uncaulked overlaps of the clinker build.

It may be noted that all the ships types reproduced are described in the original French language as 'barques'. Apart from the port books, the principal sources of information for seventeenth-century shipping in North Cornwall are the surviving Maritime Surveys carried out in 1626 and 1629. Those surveys were ordered by the Lord High Admiral so that the Council of War could know what resources were available to reinforce the Navy, and in theory they included the number of mariners, sailors and seafarers together with their names, ages and dwelling places, and also the numbers, strengths and burthen of all ships and barques belonging to each port and haven, 'as well as those that are there at this present as of those that are abroad'. In practice the surveys can be shown to be incomplete and inaccurate (for example many of the sailors are listed as being ten years younger in 1629 than they were in 1626), and although the barques named in the surveys occur in the port books, so do many others which are not included in the surveys. The burthen or burden tonnages vary considerably.

Todd Gray has edited the surveys, and written an introduction. They were published by the Devon & Cornwall Record Society and Todd Gray in 1990 under the title *Early-Stuart Mariners and Shipping; The Maritime Surveys of Devon and Cornwall 1619-35*. I am grateful for permission to copy the passages relevant to Padstow and outports in this chapter.

Reading the 'Book of Naval Muster Returns 1628-'9' (an appendix in Gray's book) which presumably resulted from such a survey, it is noted that the vessels from the large south coast ports such as Plymouth, Stonehouse and Dartmouth, are all described as 'ships and pinnaces': Plymouth had fifty-six such, with burdens from 160 to 20 tons, and Dartmouth ninety-two from 200 to 20 tons. Whereas the vessels of St Ives, Boscastle and Padstow are all described as 'barques': St Ives has three varying from 45 to 20 tons, Boscastle four from 30 to 12 tons, and Padstow three from 26 to 16 tons.

According to Jacques Vichot of the Musées de la Marine, the term barque, although of course generic, was applied in France in the Middle Ages and subsequently particularly to vessels of modest size engaged in coasting and fishery. It seems that the same was true of Cornwall in the seventeenth century.

One final matter of interest in the survey of 1626 (see the end of this chapter) is that whilst Padstow had lists of masters, sailors and fishermen, and the parishes of St Columb and those covering Port Isaac, Boscastle and Tintagel also had sailors and/or fishermen, the return for the Parish of Egloshayle and St Breock consists of 29 bargemen, which is just sufficient to outnumber the 28 masters and sailors of Padstow! The Parish of Egloshayle and St Breock contains Wadebridge, so even in those early days barges must have been used extensively to distribute goods along the banks of the River Camel and its small creeks and tributaries. It seems likely that many if not most of the masters and sailors were away at sea when the survey was carried out, whereas the bargemen were readily available to be recorded.

Over the period covered by the old port books (1565-1719) the number of Padstow ships which can be said confidently to have existed at any one time increased as follows:

| | | |
|---|---|---|
| Date 1605 | 12 ships | |
| Date 1635 | 14 ships | |
| Date 1675 | 25 ships | |
| Date 1710 | 32 ships | |
| Date 1718 | 37 ships : | rough average 24 ships. |

Some of them were very short lived, and it is not possible to make any accurate calculation as to their life expectancy.

If one takes the period covered by the books as 155 years, less twenty missing (1640-1660), i.e. 135 years, and the average number of ships at any one time as twenty-four, then as there are about 200 Padstow ships listed in the books, their average life would be about 135 times 24 divided by 200, that is about sixteen years. If that figure seems high, it should be remembered that some ships with very short lives will not have appeared in the surviving books. On the other hand, a significant proportion of Padstow vessels were prizes or bought from or sold to other ports, in which cases the life indicated by the books would be less than the actual total life. The small Padstow ships must have been massively built; they were quite often rebuilt; and they were used much less intensively than their successors in the hectic commercial years of the nineteenth century; perhaps sixteen years is on balance a reasonable life expectancy.

Doubtless some of them survived as barges in the Camel estuary when their seagoing days were over. They were all small enough to penetrate up the creeks of the estuary to Little Petherick and villages above Wadebridge, provided they worked their tides, but their beam may have made them unsuitable for some of the narrower inlets such as that which led up to the village of Chapel Amble.

By 1700, changes were beginning to occur in the rigs of ships large and small. An English merchant in Madeira[3] provides us with the types calling there, including Westcountrymen, in letters he sent to his London offices.

*12th Febuary, 1701.* A Topsham pink put into the road, bound to the Canaries.
*20th Febuary, 1701.* A small ketch from Ilford Comb with herrings . . . to return with malvasias.
*24th October, 1701.* The Catherine sloope, New Yorke'
*13th January, 1703.* Here is come from Nevis a sloope and a brigantine and a sloope from St Christophers; a sloop from Boston with provisions and two New England ketches from Tercera with wheat.
*28th August, 1704.* Since our last has been despatched two small Bermudas sloops for Barbadoes with about 80 pies of wine.
*6th January, 1705* . . . a small West Country barke bound for Barbdoes.

*26th. January, 1706.* Ann Gally, Capt. Hinde with an loading of corne Plimouth . . .
*6th Febuary, 1709* . . . the Elizabeth Pink of Biddiford.

Several doggers and numerous galleys belonging to Bristol are mentioned.

'Brigantine' and 'Brig' appear frequently, but never plain 'Brig'; it is difficult to escape the conclusion that the term Brig was originally short for Brigantine, but sailors and scholars love to argue about the differences between Brigs, Jackass Brigs, Hermaphrodite Brigs and Brigantines and they doubtless meant different things to different men.

Of more immediate interest for Padstow is the inclusion of barques, galleys, pinks, ketches and sloops amongst the west-countrymen calling at Madeira.

**BARQUE.** As we have already seen, barque was a general term for a vessel of moderate size and embraced all the larger ships of North Cornwall in the 1620s.

**GALLEY.** The trading galleys of Bristol and Plymouth in 1700 seem to have been armed ships of between 100 and 400 tons measure.[4] They were fast sailing ships, with large crews, pierced for oars, which were designed and allowed to sail independent of the convoys organised by the Admiralty, and although some of them doubtless completed their crews from the broad-shouldered seamen of Padstow[5] they were too large to be Padstow ships.

**PINK.** Pinks are more difficult. The fishing pink of the seventeenth century was often a beamy double ender with a square sail on a single mast. Before he died about 1684, Gerrit Batten painted pink[6] just such a vessel but with a small foremast close to the stem with its own small square foresail, very similar to vessel 'E' in Jean Jouve's 1679 survey. Later, as pinks got bigger and the fore-and-aft rig gained acceptance, the term pink-sterned came into use to describe a high, narrow, pointed stern, and the Americans developed the long-lived 'pinky' schooner, with masting remaining as described in Batten's painting, but with purely fore-and-aft sails. Some Padstow ships probably looked very like vessel 'E' above, and one may speculate that squaresails became lugsails over the years, and later developed into the fore-and-aft rig we know so well.

**KETCH.** Like all the foregoing types, the ketch was a square rigged vessel until towards the end of the seventeenth century. The type is seldom mentioned in *The Bolton Letters,*[3] and nothing like it appears in Jean Jouve's work, wherein all the two masted vessels have a small foremast, not a mizen. When large iron mortars became available for use at sea in the late seventeenth century, the navies of England and France quickly produced ships to mount them. In the almost universal three-masted warship, the rigging got in the way of the mortar bombs, so the foremast was dispensed with and the unbalanced appearance of the resulting ship is shown in the sketch of a French 'Galiote à bombes'; the English 'bomb ketch' was very similar. I have not found examples of the ketch rig predating the bomb ketch, although some Dutch galliots might be termed ketches. The mercantile versions of the ketch rig mentioned in *The Bolton Letters* would surely have stepped their mainmasts further forward.

**SLOOP.** The numerous references to 'Sloops' in *The Bolton Letters* leave no doubt that they are not referring to sloops-of-war (a relatively large square-rigged type), but they are recording the appearance on the scene of a large number of small single-masted traders. It is interesting to find reference in 1704 to Bermuda sloops, when here in the closing years of the twentieth century, the vast majority of our yachts are Bermudan sloops!

There are numerous definitions of the sloop, cutter and smack rigs, but all are agreed that a sloop has one mast, with a fore-and-aft mainsail, and a triangular staysail set on the forestay. The sloop may or may not have a triangular jib set out on a bowsprit which may be fixed or running. Some authorities would say that this second triangular sail at the bow turns the sloop into a cutter. A running bowsprit is one which can be unshipped and brought inboard; a feature which was particularly useful in small crowded Westcountry harbours.

**SMACK.** A smack (often a fishing smack) might have any one of a number of rigs, but the very sloops we are interested in, which beached themselves at the outports of Padstow, were also called smacks.

Early sloops (like cutters and ketches) retained square top-sails on their masts, and their boomless mainsails were set on standing gaffs, and brailed up to gaff and mast when not in use, but throughout the eighteenth century the use of fore and aft sails became more and more general in the small ships trading in the Bristol Channel and elsewhere.

In his wonderful book, *Sailing Drifters*, already mentioned, Marsh included some contemporary accounts of life aboard the Cornish fishing luggers of the nineteenth century.

Aids to navigation were primitive. A chart was seldom if ever carried. Yet the 'old man' was seldom at a loss for his position, relying on a traverse board which recorded by the insertion of pegs into selected holes, how many half hours had been sailed on a particular course. [Other pegs indicated the speed for each hour of the watch.] Thus the helmsman kept a score of how many glasses - hour glasses - the lugger had sailed on any point during his watch and at what speed. Occasionally the master took a squint at the board and conjectured the boat's position, and could take her from Cornwall to the North Sea and home again, whilst it is on record that one ancient reached Australia with only a traverse board to aid his navigation.

Early foghorns were made from conch shells' and by obtaining echoes from cliffs in thick fog they found their way along the coast and its estuaries. Conch shells were superseded by bullock horns, and eventually by tin trumpets and 'bull-roarers'.

Cooking arrangements were primitive often consisting of a hearth made from a hollowed-out piece of granite, or a small box filled with clay and stones.

All these remarks (apart from reaching Australia) must have been doubly applicable to the Padstow traders of the sixteenth and seventeenth centuries.

So, with compass, conch shell, lead line, traverse board and common sense, the early mariners of Padstow found their way from Norway to Gibraltar and home again, aided only by an occasional notebook recording the observations of their precursors.

I will end this section with some words of Edgar Marsh: 'Yes, life was hard in those days, but it bred men who lived to a ripe old age, were self-reliant, fearless and staunch as the oak from which their boats were built.'

## Francis Basset's Survey of Mariners and Ship: 1826 and 1629

### THE FOLLOWING TWO LETTERS PRECEDED THE 1626 SURVEY:

*To the right honourable my master the Duke of Buckingham his grace*

May it please your Grace

Your commands bearing date the 11th of July, for the taking [of] a muster of the Mariners & Fishermen on the North Coast of Cornwall, came not to me until the last of that month. I have exactly, & with as much speed as might be, performed that duty, and have returned (unto Mr Nicholas) a perfect list of them to be presented [to] your Grace. There is not any ship either in or belonging to any of those ports, only three small barques no way capable of ordnance, the biggest not being above twenty ['forty' crossed out] tuns. I know not of any thing worth presenting your Grace but most humbly crave to be enabled by your gracious commands to manifest the duty due, from the humblest of your Grace's servants.

[signed] Francis Basset
Tehidy [Tehidie] this 10th of August 1626

*For Edward Nicholas esq. my right worthy friend at York House at the sign of the gate in the Strand, London*

R[eceived] 27 August 1626 Mr Francis Basset
Vice-Admiral of the north of Cornwall.

Worthy Sir

I received on the last of July, a command from my Lord (which bore the date the 11th of that month) for the taking of a muster of all the Mariners and Fishermen within the jurisdiction of my Vice-Admiralty, which with all the speed that might be I have effected, and return you ['at' crossed out] present a perfect list of them, and beseech you present it my Lord, with my letter enclosed. Sir, you have [been] most friendly, infinitely obliged me by preserving me in my Lords good Grace, which appears to me from himself. Believe me Sir there is not any thing in the world I more desire than to be commanded by him, and to do him service, which in all I can I will ever faithfully manifest, and trust so to serve him, and thank you as you shall not repent you of such favours done unto me. Upon all occasions wherein you shall think me capable of my Lord's command, I beseech you let me receive them: and wherein so poor a man may do you service, rest assuredly you shall readily command.

Your most affectionate friend to serve you,

[signed] Francis Basset
Tehidy [Tehidie] this 10th of August 1626

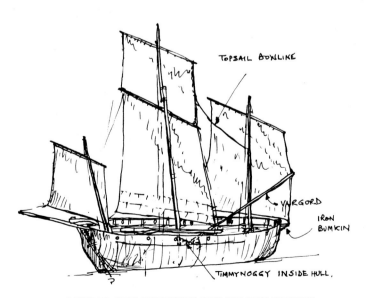

MODEL OF MOUNTS BAY LUGGER 'EMILY'

## THE SURVEY OF 1626

*A list of [illegible] Mariners, Sailors and Fishermen belonging unto the port of Padstowe [Padstow] in the county of Cornwall taken (by Francis Basset esq. Vice-Admiral of the North parts of the said county of Cornwall) the first of August 1626*

### MASTERS

| | Age | | Age |
|---|---|---|---|
| Jeffrey Cornish | 60 at sea | Innego Dyer | 60 at sea |
| Edward Harris | 60 at sea | Walter Kettowe | 48 at sea |
| John Norman sen. | 61 | John Norman jun. | 27 at sea |
| Morgan Phillipps | 40 at sea | Peter Quint | 40 at sea |
| Benjamin Skoute | 40 at sea | William Willson | 40 at sea |

### SAILORS OF PADSTOWE [PADSTOW]

| | | | |
|---|---|---|---|
| Nicholas Androw | 23 at sea | James Bennett | 40 at sea |
| John Bone | 24 at sea | John Burdwoode | 40 at sea |
| John Cornishe | 24 at sea | Bennet Dandey | 28 at sea |
| Philip Dyer | 26 at sea | John Edwards | 30 at sea |
| Erasmus Glover | 40 at sea | Richard Glover | 35 at sea |
| Gregory Hodge | 30 at sea | Richard Jewells | 30 at sea |
| Henry Peter | 24 at sea | Henry Quinte | 18 at sea |
| John Richard | 30 at sea | John Sare | 40 at sea |
| John Tippett | 40 at sea | John Welshe | 26 at sea |

### FISHERMEN OF PADSTOWE [PADSTOW]

| | | | |
|---|---|---|---|
| Edward Edwards | 60 | John Garred | 40 at sea |
| William Gilbert | 57 | Henry Moyle | 58 |
| Walter Perkin | - | John Saundry | 45 |
| Reginald Scarbroke | 36 at sea | | |

### FISHERMEN OF THE PARISH OF ST MERRIN [ST MERRYN]

| | | | |
|---|---|---|---|
| Henry Jley | 26 | Henry Jley jun. | - |
| John Rawlin | 22 | John Roberts | 35 |
| John Tom | 30 | | |

### FISHERMEN OF THE PARISH OF ST COLLOMBE THE LOWER [ST COLLOMB MINOR]

| | | | |
|---|---|---|---|
| Charles Beard | 55 | John Cocke | 35 |
| Christopher Deane | 31 | John Emott | 26 |
| Robert Emott | 80 | William Emott | 23 |
| Christopher Kestell | 47 | Humphrey Olde | 23 |
| John Richard | 50 | Richard Robert | 30 |
| Nicholas Warren | 50 at sea | | |

### FISHERMEN OF THE PARISH OF CRANTOCKE [CRANTOCK]

| | | | |
|---|---|---|---|
| Goyen Cocke | 66 | Philip Harrie | 44 at sea |
| John Hockin | - | Bennet Michell | 63 |
| John Scovren sen. | 52 | John Scovren jun. | 46 |
| John Scovren minor | 20 | Thomas Scovren | 20 |
| William Typpett | 53 | Bennet Wills | 35 |

### FISHERMEN OF THE PARISH OF CUBERT

| | | | |
|---|---|---|---|
| Saundrie Dellbridge | 60 | John Emott | - |
| James Oates | 48 | | |

### FISHERMEN OF THE PARISH OF ST MINVER

| | | | |
|---|---|---|---|
| Oliver Ball | 34 | John Hickes | 33 |
| William Hickes | 60 | Richard Ivy | 35 |
| John Jackett | 63 | Robert Jackett | 35 |
| John James | - | Walter Jeffrie | 40 |
| Anthony Jenkin | 58 | Ambrose Marke | 48 |
| Mathew Morrice | 54 | Nicholas Olver | 34 |
| Raphe Olver | 60 | Otes Pope | 18 |
| George Shoale | 60 | Humphrey Stile | 29 |
| Nicholas Stile | 24 | | |

### FISHERMEN OF THE PARISH OF ELLION [ST ENDELLION]

| | | | |
|---|---|---|---|
| John Aunger | 46 at sea | Ralph Billinge | 60 |
| Richard Billinge | 16 | John Bray | 60 |
| Nicholas Browne | 30 at sea | Richard Browne | 62 |
| John Browning jun. | 20 at sea | John Browning sen. | 70 |
| | | ['at sea' crossed out] | |
| Richard Carveth | 37 | John Chevalle | 40 at sea |
| Thomas Collen | 23 | Ferdinand Collinge | 35 at sea |
| Robert Davies | 50 at sea | Nicholas Emott | 68 at sea |
| Thomas Emott | 30 at sea | Richard Forde | 20 at sea |
| Raphe Gey | 40 | Thomas Gey | 30 at sea |
| John Gilbert | 65 | Christopher Grigg | 50 at sea |
| Francis Grigg | 46 at sea | William Grigge | 40 at sea |
| George Hicks | 45 | William Hickes | 35 |
| | | ['at sea' crossed out] | |
| Humphrey Jackett | 27 | John James | 50 at sea |
| Thomas James | 50 | George Jefferie | - |
| Oliver Moyle | 60 at sea | Christopher Olver | 26 at sea |
| John Olver | 20 at sea | Nicholas Parson | 20 at sea |
| John Pearse | 60 at sea | John Rowe | 45 |
| Anthony Stone | 61 | John Tom | 27 at sea |
| William Trefry | 24 at sea | William Trefry | 20 |
| John Trenden | 25 at sea | Thomas Trenoden | 50 at sea |
| John Triplett | 23 at sea | sen. | |
| Robert Wills | 44 at sea | John Waye | 60 at sea |

### BARGEMEN BELONGING TO THE PARISH OF EGLOSEALE [EGLOSHAYLE] AND ST BREAGE [ST BREOCK]

| | | | |
|---|---|---|---|
| Joseph Beare | 55 | Simon Billinge | 27 |
| Thomas Billinge | 20 | John Bligh | 38 |
| John Cawlinge | 54 | John Cocke | 70 |
| Thomas Cocke | - | John Corke | 38 |
| Frances Couch | 40 | Edward Ede | 56 |
| Humphrey Grosse | 34 | Nathaniel Hambley | 40 |
| Jacob Hellson | 56 | John Launder | 40 |
| John ['Hatc' crossed out] Hitchens 48 | | | |
| Hugh Lawrence | 42 | Richard Pearse | 30 |
| Bartholomew Phillipp | 32 | Stipio Preler | 28 |
| John Scott | 60 | Clemens Simon | 42 |
| Richard Skinner | 40 | James Skrout | 57 |
| Henry Sleepe | 40 | John Trerubie | 55 |
| John ['Trega' crossed out] Tregathen 70 | | | |
| Walter Trerubie | 56 | Christopher Wolfe | 35 |
| Henry Woode | 24 | | |

### THE PARISH OF BOTREAUX CASTELL [BOSCASTLE]

the Sailors and Fishermen did not appear

| | | | |
|---|---|---|---|
| Philip Joeile | - | Edward Joslen | - |
| William Popham | - | Bawden Tincke | - |
| John Tincke | - | William Tincker | - |
| John Tubb sen. | - | John Tubb jun. | - |
| Roger Tubb | - | Charles Stephen | - |
| William Stephen | - | Richard Warren | - |

### THE PARISH OF TINTAGELL [TINTAGEL]

The Sailors and Fishermen did not appear

| | | | |
|---|---|---|---|
| John Browne | - | Thomas Browne | - |
| John Hender | - | John Hender | - |
| Thomas Hender | - | John Lavers | - |
| John Parson | - | John Robins | - |
| Richard Robins | - | Richard Tincke | - |
| William Tincke | - | Hercules Weyles | - |
| Clemens Wickett | - | | |

BARQUES BELONGING UNTO THE PORT OF PADSTOWE [PADSTOW]
Morgan Phillipps owner of a barque called the GEORGE of 28 tons.
Morgan Phillippes owner of an other barque called the FORTUNE of 28 tons.
Peter Quinte owner of the HARRIE of 40 tons or there abouts.

## THE SURVEY OF 1629

*A List of the names of all the Mariners, Sailors and Fishermen within the north part of Cornwall: their names, of what parish, their profession, their age*

BOTREAUXCASTELL [Boscastle]
1 barque 30 tons Edward Josling, owner.
1 barque 12 tons William Stephens, owner.
1 barque 26 tons John Tubb, owner.
and 1 barque 25 tons Roger Tubb, owner.

PADSTOWE [Padstow]
1 barque 16 tons Mr John Prideaux, owner
1 barque 16 tons John Norman, owner
1 barque 26 tons William Rommoe of Penryn [Perine] owner.

### CRANTOCKE [Crantock]

| | Age | | Age |
|---|---|---|---|
| *Sailor* | | | |
| Philip Harrise | 40 | | |
| *Fishermen* | | | |
| John Michell jun. | 30 | John Skovern sen. | 48 |
| John Skovern | 36 | Thomas Skovern | 28 |
| William Skover | 27 | William Tippett | 54 |
| Bennet Wills | 67 | | |

### LOWER ST COLLUMB St Columb Minor

| *Sailors* | | | |
|---|---|---|---|
| Charles Beard | 55 | Christopher Castell | 50 |
| Christopher Davye | 32 | John Emmett | 34 |
| Thomas Emmett | 16 | William Emmett | 23 |
| John Hendra | 50 | Thomas House | 22 |
| James James | 17 | John James | 30 |
| Humphrey Ould | 27 | John Richard | 50 |
| Richard Roberts | 30 | Francis Sare | 17 |
| Nicholas Warren | 50 | | |

### ENDELLIAN [Endellion]

| *Mariner* | | | |
|---|---|---|---|
| Roger Davys | 50 | | |
| *Sailors* | | | |
| John Anger | 40 | Ralph Billing | 54 |
| Richard Billing | 20 | Thomas Billing | 16 |
| Christopher Brea | 20 | William Browne | 30 |
| Ferdinand Collen | 30 | Thomas Colline | 27 |
| Joseph Collins | 34 | Robert Davye | 40 |
| Thomas Denman | 45 | Thomas Emmett | 30 |
| William Emmett | 20 | Christopher Grigge | 50 |
| William Grigge | 40 | Thomas Guy | 30 |
| John Hickes | 52 | Humphrey Jackett | 32 |
| John James | 40 | Thomas James | 40 |
| George Jeffery | 47 | Gilbart Jeffrey | 15 |
| Christopher Olliver | 30 | John Olliver | 26 |
| Richard Olliver | 20 | Nicholas Parson | 19 |
| Edward Poulstagg | 30 | Thomas Renoden | 20 |
| Anthony Stone | 60 | John Tom | 25 |
| ['Anthony Trebell' crossed out] 60 | | | |

| William Trefy | 30 | Arthur Triplett | 25 |
|---|---|---|---|
| John Triplett | 35 | John Waye | 50 |
| *Fishermen* | | | |
| William Browne | 50 | John Browninge | 25 |
| Richard Carveth | 38 | John Colline | 20 |
| Richard Couch | 18 | John Dea | 18 |
| John Grigge | 22 | Ralph Guy | 40 |
| George Hickes | 43 | William Hickes | 40 |
| Thomas Oliver | 16 | John Parker | 18 |
| John Rawe | 50 | William Trefry | 21 |

### ST MYNVER [St Minver]

| *Sailors* | | | |
|---|---|---|---|
| William Hickes | 56 | Mathew Morishe | 50 |
| John Style | 55 | | |
| *Fishermen* | | | |
| Oliver Ball | 34 | John Hicks | 31 |
| Richard Ivye | 40 | John James | 60 |
| Walter Jeffrey | 40 | Ambrose Marke | 50 |
| Anthony Myllard | 55 | Nicholas Olliver | 33 |
| Oatts Pope | 24 | George Shoale | 60 |
| Humphrey Style | 30 | Nicholas Style | 27 |

### BOTREAUXCASTELL [Boscastle]

| *Mariners* | | | |
|---|---|---|---|
| Edward Joslinge | 55 | William Stephens | 46 |
| John Tubb | 46 | Roger Tubb | 30 |
| *Sailors* | | | |
| John Avery | 25 | Thomas Avery | 30 |
| John Brure | 26 | Humphrey French | 23 |
| Richard James | 40 | William James | 25 |
| Erasmus Quinte | 18 | John Quinte | 20 |
| John Salter | 32 | | |

### PADSTOWE [Padstow]

| *Mariners* | | | |
|---|---|---|---|
| Thomas Barrett | 40 | Walter Kittowe | 40 |
| Peter Quinte | 36 | William Wilson | 40 |
| *Sailors* | | | |
| Nicholas Androw | 26 | Henry Quint | 22 |
| John Beale | 34 | Robert Riffell | 20 |
| James Bennett | 40 | Henry Rissell | 50 |
| John Bond | 25 | Henry Roch | 24 |
| Nicholas Bone | 60 | John Sandry | 55 |
| Nathaniel Bullock | 30 | John Swymmner | 21 |
| John Cornishe | 30 | John Tippett | 50 |
| Robert Cornishe | 23 | Nicholas Tippett | 20 |
| John Denn | 20 | John Welch | 32 |
| Philip Dyer | 25 | William Weste | 40 |
| Roger Edmund | 22 | John Edward | 40 |
| *Fishermen* | | | |
| Edward Harrise | 60 | Gregory Hodge | 40 |
| John Bordwood | 34 | Richard Morishe | 23 |
| William Jelbert | 20 | John Norman | 30 |
| Richard Jeles | 48 | Michael Parken | 25 |
| William Jels | 40 | Henry Peeter | 22 |
| John Richard | 36 | William Peeter | 18 |
| William Sandry | 20 | John Peter | 20 |
| John Sard | 50 | Erasmus Speare | 20 |
| John Speare | 20 | Richard Trelathde | 55 |

The above extracts covering Padstow and outports have been taken, with Todd Gray's kind permission, from his *Early Stuart Mariners and Shipping*.

# 5 SHIPS, 16th TO EARLY 18th CENTURY

*I have seen old ships sail like swans asleep . . .*

James Elroy Flecker

The information for this chapter is taken principally from surviving Port Books, 1565-1719. Customs records provide earlier dates for some vessels.

**ABIGAIL (ABBIGAIL)** of Padstow, 1687-'8
    William Luggier (Lugger) Mr
Traded to St Maloes, bringing back 3 Ells of Vittroy Canvas, Soapes in ten half-chests, Dewlaps, and 1¾ tonnes of French Wine unfill'd. (Unfill'd or unfild meant undefiled, pure, unadulterated, unwatered.)
**ADVENTURE** of Portizick, (also of Padstow occasionally), about 20 tons burden, but may have been lengthened *c.* 1710 as cargo increased up to 33 tons thereafter. 1692-1719
    John Aunger (Anger) Master 1692-'97
    Nicholas Aunger Mr 1694, 1705, 1709, 1713
    Jame Aunger Mr 1697
    Anthony Aunger Mr 1703, 1711, 1716, 1717
    Michael Aunger Mr 1705
    Arthur Aunger Mr 1705
    Anthony Hicks Mr 1707
    John Grigg Mr 1708
    Joseph Aunger Mr 1716.
**ADVENTURE** of Botreaux Castle, burden about 15 tons, 1703-'4
    John Martin (Martyn) Mr 1703
    James Cann? 1704
**AMITY (AMMITY)** of Padstow, burden 20 tons, 1665-'6
    Robert Harris Mr 1665
    John Browne Mr 1666
Traded to Dublin, Youghal, Watterford.
**ANGELL** of Padstow, burden 12 tons, 1575
A single entry inwards from Bristol, 13th March 1575
**ANN (ANE)** of Padstow, burden 8 tons, 1577-'80
    Wm Tooker (Tucker) Mr 1577
    Richard Carne Mr 1580
**ANN (ANNE)** of Padstow, burden about 40 tons, 1674-'97
    Thomas Merryfield Mr 1674
    Richard Dunn Mr 1674-'79
    Wm Kittow Mr 1679-'84
    Wm Dunn Mr 1687, 1696
    Wm Pearce Mr 1687
    John Dunn Mr 1689
    Thos Oliver Mr 1694
    Warden Wakeham Mr 1695
In various trades: Wheat to Liverpool, Barrells of White Herrings and Red Herrings from Wexford.
**ANNE (ANNA, ANN. AN)** of Padstow, burden 26 tons, 1629-'39
    Nathaniel Bullock Mr 1629
    Henry Quint Mr 1630-'3
    Peter Quint Mr 1633
    Thos Barrett Mr 1637
    John Burdwood Mr 1638-'9.
Traded to France, Ireland and Holland.

**ANNE CONTENT** of Padstow, burden 18 tons, 1601-'2
    William Jollyfe Mr
Traded to Ireland.
**ANNE & ELIZ.** of Padstow, burden about 25 tons, 1719-?
    Wm Triplet Mr 1719
**ANTHONY (ANTONY)** of Padstow, burden 8 tons, 1533-'68
    Corke Mr
**ARTHUR & MARY** of Padstow, burden about 40 tons, 1686
of Botreaux Castle, 1687
    Samuel Cornish Mr 1686-'7
**BASTIAN** of Portyzyke, burden 5 tons, 1565
One of the earliest entries.
**BETTY** of Portizick, burden about 25 tons, 1692-1712
(also frequently of Padstow)
    Arthur Triplet Mr 1692
    Nicholas ffrench Mr 1692
    John Sussex Mr 1695
    Roger Hose Mr 1695
    Walter Trefry Mr 1698-1701
    Wm Martyn Mr 1703, 1706, 1708, 1712
    John Wakeham Mr 1703-'4
    Joseph Trevethan Mr 1704-'6
    George Rowe Mr 1705
    Matthew Hender Mr 1711
Burden increased to 40 tons by 1708, presumably by lengthening.
**BETTY** of Botreaux Castle, burden about 15 tons, 1705-'9
    John Martyn Mr 1706
    Zacharias Deane Mr 1707-'8
    Lawrence Romick Mr 1709
**BLESSING** of Padstow, burden 16 tons, 1620-'5
    William Burkes? Mr
**CATHERINE** of Padstow 1692-'7
    Nicholas Collins Mr 1692
    Samuel Pascoe Mr 1697
She traded with Beddeford (Bideford), bringing, with other items, several tons of tobacco pipe-clay to Padstow every year.
**CATHERINE** 22nd June, 1713. Entered by Capt. John Tonkin; formerly called the GANGER (GAGNER) of St Malo, being a prize taken by the said Capt. Tonkin and condemned in Her Majesty's Court of Admiralty and valued at £40 'as of his oath'; probably the same as the following:
**CATHERINE** of Padstow, burden about 12 tons
    Thomas Broad Master
which brought coal from Wales later that same year, 1713.
**CHANCE** of Padstow, burden 16 tons, 1620
    Benjamin Stout Mr
Traded to France.
**CHARITY** of Padstow, burden 18 tons, 1660-'88
    John Row Mr 1660 (possibly earlier)
    William Mitchell Mr 1688
Traded to Brittany in times of peace.

(Entered once as LOVE & CHARITY, later as CHARITIE)

**CHARLES** of Padstow, burden about 30 tons, 1708-'18

    Bernard Stephen Mr 1708

    Thos Hicks 1710

    William Billing 1711

    William Rivers 1711-'12

    Ralph Billing 1713

    Christopher Walcombe 1717-'18

    Thos Broad 1716

Regularly brought coal from Swanzey and Neath, and sometimes carried copper oar, blocks of Tinn, hogsheads of traine oyle barrels of herring, pewter plates, beeswax, etc. as exports to Bristoll.

**CHRISTOPHER**, burden 10 tons, 1575-'82; an entry in 1575 reads: 'Extra [i.e. outward bound] in le Christopher de Botreauxcastell, decem doll.'

    Wm Osburne est. Mr (Master).

**CLEMENT** (CLEMENCE) of Padstow, 1579-1606

    John Brown Mr 1579

    John Joste 1583

    Reede & Jenkin Bowen 1605

May have been lengthened about 1600, as burden increased from 18 to 23 tons.

**CLEYRE** (CLEYER) of Porquine (Portquin), burden 5 tons 1567-'8

    Wm Reede Mr

Brought coal from Swanzey. (There are very few references to Portquin).

**CONCORD** of Padstow, burden about 50 tons, 1712

    Thomas Oliver Mr

On 9th September, 1712, CONCORD cleared for Dunkirk carrying 111,000 Helling Stones (i.e. roofing slates). That is her sole entry in the surviving port books. She may have proved to be too big for the Padstow trades of the time. Thomas Oliver was back as Master of PROVIDENCE by 1715.

**CORONATION** (CARNATION), burden about 35 tons, 1696-1713

    Warden Wakeham Mr 1696

    William Kittow Mr 1697-'8

    Nicholas Robins Mr 1703-'13

In her early years traded to Ireland taking slates and malt, and bringing back herrings, Freeze and Tallow, but later she was in the coal trade largely from Lanelly, Tynby and Swanzey.

**DELIGHT** of Padstow (of Gannell in 1684), 1660 or earlier — 1686. Burden about 40 tons (perhaps less in early years).

    John Parson Mr 1660

    Robt Harris 1668

    Thos Row 1684

    John Rogers 1883

    John Courtis 1885

    Wm Lugger 1886

In 1684 cleared for Port-o-Port with herrings, and entered in from Oporto — evidently the same place.

**DELIGHT** of Padstow, burden about 25 tons, 1719-?

    John Garland Mr 1719

**DELLEN** (DELLIEN, DELYNGE, DELLYEN) of Padstow, 1543-'75, burden 25 tons 1553, burden 20 tons 1568, burden 50 tons 1575

    Robertus Sare & Henricus Peyne Masters 1567-'8

    (Robert Sayer & Henry Payne)

    John de Lyle Mr 1571

    Wm Tucker Mr 1575

Traded to Bretayne (Brittany) and Galeway (Ireland).

**DESIRE** of Padstow, burden about 35 tons, 1660-?

    Erasmus Randell Mr 1660

Brought coal from Swanzey.

**DESIRE** of Padstow, burden about 12 tons, 1704-'5

    Wm Martyn Mr 1704-'5

**DESIRE** of Padstow, burden about 40 tons, 1706-'8

    Thomas Oliver Mr 1706-'8

These could be one, two or possibly three vessels: all brought coal from Swanzey.

**DOVE** of Padstow, burden about 20 tons, 1679-'94 also of Portizick, 1703-'19

    Thos Merryfield Mr 1679-'86

    John Eddy Mr 1684

    Wm Lugger Mr 1686

    Joseph Harris 1694

    Richard Wedge Mr 1703-'5

    John Sleeman Mr 1705

    Thomas Hides Mr 1707

    George Rowe Mr 1708

    Thomas Andrew Mr 1708

    John Aunger Mr 1711-'18

    Rules ? Broad 1719

Traded to St Sebastins, bringing back Spanish Salt: to Castna, Oporto, Dunkirk, Crosick, Ostend, Morliauy (Morlaix) St Martyns, St Mallo, also Bristol Channel ports, especially in later years.

**EDWARD** of Padstow, burden 14 tons, 1670

    Humphrey French Mr

**EDWARDE** of Porquine (Portquin), burden 11 tons, 1579

    Thomas Will Mr

Sailed for Milford 27th April, probably to fetch coal.

**ELIZABETH** (ELZABETH, etc.) of Padstow, burden 28 tons, 1575-'91

    Nicholas Carne Mr 1575

    Michael Walker Mr 1579-'81

    Jo Phillips Mr 1591

    Tomas Phillips Mr

    Walker traded to Bordeaux,

    Jo Phillips to Wexford

**ELIZABETH** (ELIZA) of Padstow, burden about 25 tons, 1660-1711 of Botreaux Castel, 1690

    Arthur Triplet Mr 1660

    Warren Neale Mr 1664

    Wm Perkins Mr 1665

    Richard Dunn Mr 1668

    John Triplett Mr 1670-1673

She traded to Watterford and Wexford taking 30,000 slates at a time and returned with Tymber, bacon, tallow, candles and Freeze. In the eighteenth century, she brought many coal cargoes from Neath and Swanzey.

**ELIZA'TH & ANNE** of Port Isaac, burden about 30 tons, 1718-?

    Enoch Davis Mr

Brought 16 chalders (London) of coales from Neath, Michaelmas Quarter 1718.

**ELIZABETH & JAMES** of Port Isaac, 1716-?

There is a solitary note of a vessel of this name bringing back French salt from Crossick (Croisic) in 1716.

**ELIZA & SUSANNA**, burden about 30 tons, 1718-?

    Ina Garland Mr

Brought 16 chalders (London) of coales from Swanzey in the Ladyday Quarter, 1718.

**ELLYN** (ELLEN) of Padstow, burden 20 tons, 1571-'9

    Thomas Croker Mr

ELLYN of Portizick, burden 7? tons, 1598
  Thomas Tremaine Mr
ENDEAVOUR (INDEAVOUR, etc.) of Padstow and of Portizick, burden about 15 tons, 1670-'91
    Wm Billings Mr 1674-'83
    Rd Billings Mr 1680, 1684-'6
    Thomas Billing Mr (recorded at Barnstaple)
Regularly brought 10 chalders (London) of Coales or Culme to Padstow and outports.
ENDEAVOUR (ENDEAVOR, etc.) of Padstow and Portizick, burden about 20 tons, 1692-1718
    Wm Roberts Mr 1692
    Chas Mitchell Mr 1693-'7
    Rd Billing Mr 1696-'7
    Jn Sleeman Mr 1699
    Joseph Trevethan Mr 1700-'1
    Warden Wakham Mr 1700-'1
    John Mitchell Mr 1703-'18
    Anthony Cleverden Mr 1708
    Peter Bryant Mr 1711
    John Olver Mr 1714
The Mitchell family took her to the Welsh coal ports; the other masters traded in her to Ireland, Brittany and North France.
See also INDEVOUR.
EXCHANGE of Padstow (also of Portizick), burden about 40 tons, 1680-'97
    Philip Corkram Mr 1680-'97
    Thos Olver Mr 1682-'92
    Wm Doune Mr 1688
Traded to Dublin, St Anderas (Santander), Dunkerke, Swanzey, Norway, Diep, St Mallo, Burdiaux (Bordeaux), Crozick (Croisic), Milford, Bridgwater and Waterford, largely in charge of Phillip Corkram who must have been one of Padstow's most enterprising navigators.
FALCON (FAULCON) of Padstow, burden about 60 tons, 1715-'17
    Thomas Maddox Mr
Brought up to 30 chalders (London measure) from Swanzey, one of the largest cargoes recorded to date in a Padstow ship (see JUST and PEACE).
FFRANCES of Botreaux Castle, burden 8 tons, entered 28th March, 1598
FFRANCIS of Porthcezick and of Padstow, burden 16 tons, 1637-'8
    John Triplet Mr 1637-'8
FORTUNE (FFORTUNE) of Padstow, burden 11 tons, 1603
    Richard Browne Mr 1603
FRIENDS ADVENTURE of Padstow, burden 30 tons, 1695-1719
    Leonard Nicholas Mr 1695
    (or Nicholl, Nichols) Mr 1705
    John Dunn Mr 1705-'8
    John Parker Mr 1708 & 1713
    Wm Parker Mr 1709-'12 (or Parkin) 1711
    Thomas Olver 1711
    Wm Gummer 1716-'17
    Ralph Billing 1717-'18
    James Roberts 1717-'19
Traded widely in Europe. In 1700 took Tyn, lead and Irish tallow to Rochell. In 1704 her cargo to Bristoll included Calve skins, Tyn, Copper Oar, Helling Stones, old Brass, 2 Hogsheads Sope ashes, 4 pieces damnified Muscovados sugar, (salvage in casks).
FRIENDS ENDEAVOUR of Padstow, burden about 30 tons,

1702-'19 or later
    Thos Rickards Mr 1704
    Richard Billing Mr 1703
    Ralph Pearce Mr 1704
    Michael Carveth Mr 1704
    John Pearce Mr 1707-'8
    Ralph Pearce Mr 1709-'16
    James Roberts Mr 1716-'19
First described in customs house records 18th March, 1702, as FRIENDS ENDEAVOR, English built, Thomas Rickards Master, from Morlaux (Morlaix?) with French salt. Presumably, the reference to 'English built' is to dispel any suspicion that duty might be payable on the vessel itself. Perhaps she had been recaptured from the French at some stage, as the phrase 'English built' occurs rarely in the records.
  A typical cargo (to Bristol) consisted of 10 tons of Tyn and twenty thousand Hilling Stones (slates), and less typically in 1719, 29 tons of Wooll.
GABRIELL of Portissickee, burden 6 tons, 1568
    Henry Tubbe Mr
GABRIELL of Portizick, burden 13 tons, 1603
    Eilliam Emmett Mr
GENET, see JENET
GEORGE
Towards the end of the sixteenth century Padstow suffered an epidemic of ships called GEORGE. The entries in the port books are given below to demonstrate how difficult it can be to identify separate vessels:
GEORGE of Padstow, burden 14 tons, 1553
GEORGE of Padstow, burden 12 tons, 1570
    Glen Mr
GEORGE of Padstow, burden 16 tons, 1570
    John Dellick Mr
GEORGE of Padstow, burden 10 tons, 1575
    Wm Richards Mr
GEORGE of Padstow, burden 17 tons, 1575
    Jacob Dellicke Mr
GEORGE of Padstow, burden 46 tons, 1575
    Wm Sandrie Mr
GEORGE of Padstow, burden 30 tons, 1577
    John Dellicke Mr
GEORGE of Padstow, burden 31 tons, 1579
    John Braye Mr
GEORGE of Padstow, burden 30 tons, 1580
    Jacob Braye Mr
GEORGE of Padstow, burden 50 tons, 1582
    Jacob Braye Mr
GEORGE of Padstow, burden 12 tons, 1591
    John Ash Mr
GEORGE of Portizick, burden 12 tons, 1591
    Raphe Moille Mr
GEORGE of Padstow, burden 11 tons, 1591
    John Harrye Mr
GEORGE of Portizick, burden 20 tons, 1591
    Raphe Moyle Mr
GEORGE of Padstow, burden 13 tons, 1593
    George Reede Mr
GEORGE of Portizick, burden 13 tons, 1602
    Moyle Mr
GEORGE of Padstow, 1608
    Moyle Mr

GEORGE of Padstow, 1617

GEORGE of Padstow, 1620

GEORGE of Padstow, burden 8 tons, 1620
> Edward Harris Mr

GEORGE of Padstow, burden 20 tons, 1620
> Morgan Phillips Mr

GEORGE of Padstow, burden 20 tons, 1626
> Morgan Phillips Mr

Strangely enough, there has been a complete absence of ships named GEORGE at Padstow ever since.

GIFT (GUIFT) of Padstow, burden 20 tons, 1630
> John Tippett Mr

GIFT of Boscastle, burden 10 tons, 1660 (or earlier)-1675
> Andrew Basse Mr 1660-'75

A small smack which seems to have traded from Padstow and Boscastle taking typical exports (slates, etc.) and bringing back general cargo and potter's clay.

GOOD LUCK of Padstow, burden about 30 tons, 1693-'4
> Warden Wakeham Mr 1693-'4

Apparently short lived, at least at Padstow.

GOODFELLOWSHIP of Padstow, burden 18 tons, 1601
> Henry Harris Mr

Trading to Ireland.

GOODWILL of Padstow 1712-'13
> A. Triplett Mr

Nothing more is known of this vessel.

GRACE of Padstow, burden 18 tons, 1601
> Hughe Reede Mr

Probably the same vessel as GRACE of Bude.
> Matthew Small Mr reported in 1611.

GRACE of Boscastle, burden about 30 tons, 1660-'92, (or earlier) of Padstow, (1670)
> Humphrey French Mr 1660-'74
> Wm James Mr 1678-'81
> John French Mr 1684-'7
> Wm Hames Mr 1687
> Giles Heard Mr 1690-'2

It was surprising to come across the modern rendering 'Boscastle' in 1660, to be followed by several variations of Botreaux Castle, Boudreaux Castle, etc. Principally involved in the coal trade from Welsh ports.

GRACE of Botreaux Castle, burden about 20 tons, 1709-'11
> Jethro Martin Mr 1709-'11
> Joshua Martin Mr 1711

GREGORY of Padstow, 1697
> Richard Randle Mr

The arrival of this vessel on the 11th October, 1697 from Liverpool is recorded. She brought 1120 bushells of white salt, and quantities of cheese and earthenware.

HANNAH (HANAH) of Padstow, 1701
> William Roberts Mr

On 2nd August, 1701, this vessel sailed for Diep (Dieppe) carrying 45,000 slates. At least eight other ships took slates from Padstow to Diep that summer, and others went to Dunkirk, Rotterdam, Ostend and St Mallo. No more is known about the HANNAH.

HAPPY RETURN (HAPIE RETURNE, etc.) of Padstow, burden about 35 tons, 1681-1701, of Bude 1686
> Wm Kittow Mr 1681
> John Ballard Mr 1686
> Thomas Peirce Mr 1694-'7
> (or Pearce, or Pearson)

> Thomas Hicks Mr 1701

In 1694 she entered inwards with 30 tons of Pott clay and bricks made of Pott clay, from Newnham, and departed with 30 tons of copper oar mixed with Mundix (often spelt Mundick).

HAPPY RETURN of Botreaux Castle, burden about 30 tons, 1716-'18
> Thomas Carter Mr 1716-'18 (or later)

An active collier: possibly the same vessel as last after long unexplained absence.

HAPPY RETURN of Portissick, burden about 20 tons, 1717-'19 or later
> Michael Millard Mr 1717 (or later)
> Nicholas Millard Mr 1718
> Richard Millard Mr 1719

An active collier.

HARRIE (HENRY) of Padstow, burden 40 tons, 1605-'33
> Rodger Paul Mr 1605
> John Quint Mr 1620
> Peter Quint Mr 1626
> Edward Harris Mr 1633

These two names (HARRIE, HENRY) are shown to be the same vessel in the *Maritime Survey* of 1626 taken in conjunction with the port books. Trading to France and Ireland.

HONNOR of Padstow, burden 23 tons, 1593
> John Goodall Mr

Trading to Bayon (Bayonne).

HOPE of Padstow 1682-'5
> Henry Butler Mr 1682-'3
> Richard Clemens Me. 1683
> John Burrow Mr 1685
> Michael Farley Mr 1685

Traded almost exclusively to Spain and France. Typical cargo to St Abastian (San Sebastian) 130 barrells herring, English taken, 150 douz. glass bottles, returning with Spanish salt.

HOPEWELL of Padstow, burden 50 tons, 1637
> Henry Quint Mr

From France with 35 weyes of salt. A single entry in a period in which few records survive.

HOPEWELL of Padstow, burden about 30 tons, 1679-'98
> John Kittow Mr 1679-'86
> Rd Olver Mr 1683
> Henry Harris Mr 1686-'7
> Wm Kittow Mr 1692
> John Beoridge Mr 1698

Traded to Rotterdam, Newport (Nieuwport), St Andera (Santander), Dunkerk and London, which last was an extremely rare destination for Padstow ships. In 1685 brought deales from Norway and 40 weyes of salt from Morbean (Morbihan). In 1686 she went to Dublin, St Mallow and Bullyn. (Boulogne).

HOPEWELL of Padstow, burden about 10 tons, 1703-'7
> Pedler Mr 1703
> John Speare Mr 1704-'5
> Anthony Olver Mr 1707

Traded to Wales for coales.

HOPEWELL of Padstow, burden about 25 tons, 1712-'18

Prize, *ex* GIFT OF GOD, owner Thos Martyn who bought her for £60.
> Thomas Martyn Mr 1712-'15
> Wm Billing Mr 1717
> Thos Billing Mr 1718

Traded to Wales and France.

**INCREASE** (ENCREASE, etc.) of Padstow, burden about 18 tons, 1709-'17

     Ralph Savage Mr 1711-'17

     John Savage Mr early 1717

Most of her voyages were with general cargo between Padstowe and Bristoll acting as a market boat. Ralph Savage moved from her to the SWAN in 1718 so she may have been sold or lost.

**INDEVOUR** of Padstow, 1684-?

     John Aunger Mr

Brought groceries etc. from Bristol, but may well have been the same vessel as the ENDEAVOURE of Padstow and of Portizick.

**INDUSTRY** (INDUSTRIE, etc.) of Portizick and of Padstow, burden about 40 tons, 1682-1719

     Wm Mitchell Mr 1682

     Wm Nicholl Mr 1683

     Hugh Row Mr 1683

     Wm Billing Mr 1684-1700

     Richard Billing Mr 1693-'4

     Rhos Olver Mr 1695

     Anthony Oliver Mr 1696

     John Aunger Mr 1700-'1

     Wm Billing Mr 1701

     Jn Sussex Mr 1703-'6

     Henry Sussex Mr 1708-'19

Traded to Port-o-Port as well as frequently bringing 25 chalders of coales and also butter from Swanzey. In 1686 she brought Deales, Sparrs and firewood from Norway. She continues to feature frequently until 1718 (or later possibly, in absence of records).

**JANE** (JUNE, JAN, JONE, JOAN) of Padstow, burden about 28 tons, 1687-'97

     Richard Harris Mr 1687

     Joseph Harris Mr 1692-'7

Brought 16 chalders of coales.

**JENET** (JENAT, JONAT?) of Padstow, burden 18 tons, 1568-'71. The first entry reads JENAT of Padstow xviii doll.

  John Delicke Mr a (to) Bristowe (a spelling of Bristol not found later). The maestro's name later appears as John Dirrike, and in 1571 as Johanus de Lick.

A smack trading in the Bristol Channel.

**JESUS** of Bodscastell, burden 18 tons, 1593-1601

     George Quinte Mr 1593

     William Kneebone Mr 1601

Traded to Cork and elsewhere in Ireland. Kneebone had special authority and credit to trade in Monster (Munster).

**JOAN** (JOANE) of Padstow, burden about 28 tons, 1687-'96

     Richard Clemens Mr 1687

     Wm Hender Mr 1687-'90

     Robert Denbowe Mr? 1696.

**JOANE** of Bodrex (Botreaux Castle), burden 16 tons, 1638

     John Tubb Mr

To Bristoll with wheat and malt.

**JOANE** of Boscastell (sic), 1660

     Geo. Redmore Mr

Brought 9 chalders, coales. Might be same vessel as last.

**JOHANNA** of Padstow, also of Portizick, burden about 25 tons, 1696-'8

     Walter Trefry Mr 1696-'7

     Richard Billing Mr 1697

In the coal trade during the short period she features in the Port Books.

**JOHN** of Padstow, burden 27 tons, 1553

     Robert Sare (later Sayer?) Mr

**JOHN** of Padstow, burden 26 tons, 1575-1600

     Jacob Quinte Mr 1575

     Gabriell Sherman Mr 1579-'80

     John Quinte Mr 1591-'3

     Henry Quint Mr 1593

     George Quint Mr 1593

     Wm Joliffe Mr 1602

     Wm Kneebone Mr 1605

     Wm Browne Mr 1608

Traded to Sansebastian (sic), Ireland (Youghall). Gabriell Sherman later owned the Bristol Privateer MARY.

**JOHN** of Padstow (and of Botrixcastell), burden 10 or 12 tons, 1582, 1578-1633

     Brianus Harry Mr ((Brian Harris) 1578

     Wm Daaer ? Mr 1579

     Jacob Martyn Mr 1579

     Thomas Martyn Mr 1582

     John Triplet Mr 1598

     Bowden Kittow Mr 1602

     John Norman Mr 1620-'9

     Walter Kittow Mr 1630-'3

**JOHN** of Botreaux Castell, burden 20 tons, 1605

     Edward Joslyne Mr 1605

Lisborne and Ireland.

**JOHN** of Padstow, burden about 25 tons, 1614-'38

     Wm Wilson (Willson) Mr 1614-'17

     Walter Kittow Mr 1617

     Christopher Bray Mr 1637-'8

Traded to Lisbon and Ireland but in closing years was in the Bristol Channel trade, typically taking wheat and barley to Bristol, and bringing back deales, nailes and other general goods.

**JOHN** of Botreaux Castle, final burden about 30 tons, 1674-'85

     John Fuge Mr 1674-'83

     Joseph Fuge Mr 1684-'5

Principally in the coal trade but occasional voyages to St Aanderas (Santander) and Roan (Ruan or Rouen?) Once took 20 chalders. May have been lengthened about 1683.

**JOHN** of Padstow (also of Portizick), final burden about 30 tons, 1673-'94

     Thos Billing Mr 1673

     Thos Skinner Mr 1674

     Warden Wakeham Mr (or Walkam) 1674-'94

     Wm French Mr 1684

     Jn Triplet Mr 1687

     Wm Martyn Mr 1692

     Richard Oliver Mr 1694

May also have been lengthened as cargo loads increased in later years.

**JOHN** of Padstow, burden about 50 tons, up to 30 chalders, 1697-1701

     Henry Harris Mr 1697

     Nyot Doubt Mr 1698

     Thos Richards Mr 1699

     Wm Doubt Mr 1699-1701

Several times to Norway for softwood and iron.

**JOHN** of Portizick 1703-'13

     Thomas Emmett Mr 1703-'13

     Wm Tripet Mr 1713 ?

Coastal trade to Bideford with general cargo.

**JOHN** of Padstow, burden about 15 tons, 1708-'11, (reported to be of Truro, 1711)

    John Burwood (Birdwood) Mr 1708-'11

    John Parsons Mr 1709

A small coaster.

It is less than certain that the correct details have been allotted to each of the vessels named JOHN and it is distinctly possible that there are too many separate vessels listed above.

**JOHN & GREGORY (GRIGORY)** of Padstow, burden 20 tons, 1674-'94

    John Corkram Mr 1674-'81

    Jn Brewer Mr 1682

    Wm Kittow Mr 1684-'5

    Jn Doubt Mr 1685-'6

    Gregory Parkin Mr 1687

    Richard Bose Mr 1687

    Nicholas French Mr 1692

    Richard Oliver Mr 1692

**JOHN & HENRY** of Padstow, burden about 20 tons, 1709-'14

    John Pearce Mr 1709-'13

    Christopher Welcomb Mr 1710

    Henry Thomas Mr 1714

Mixed trading, mainly in the Bristol Channel.

**JOHN & MARY** of Padstow, burden about 25 tons, 1709-'19

    Jn Parsons Mr 1716-'17 (or later)

    Nicholas Trevillian Mr 1717-'18

    William Gummer Mr 1718

    Nicholas Trevethan Mr 1719

Engaged in the Bristol Channel trades, coal and general cargoes.

**JOHN & RICHARD**, 1710

    A mistaken entry for RICHARD & JOHN q.v.

**JOHN & THOMAS** of Padstow, 1686

    Francis Mouni Mr

An isolated entry. It seems most likely that she belonged not to Padstow but to some other port.

**JOHN & WILLIAM** of Portizaack (also of Padstow), burden about 20 tons, 1713-'19 (or later)

    William Triplet Mr 1713-'15

    John Triplet Mr 1716-'19

    M. Triplet Mr 1718

Although she carried occasional cargoes of coal from Wales, the Triplet family kept her largely as a 'constant coaster' carrying general cargoes to and from Bristol.

**JOHN BAPTISTE** of Botrixcastell, burden 10 tons, 1575

    Jacob Oseborne Mr

From Bristoll, 10th April, 1575

**JOLLYEN** of Padstow, burden 11 tons, 1569

    Garry Leyger ? Mr

A single entry.

**JONAS** of Padstow, burden 20 tons, 1637-'8, 1670

    Nicholas Warren

    Mr John Fuge, 1655-'70

Carried wheat and barley to Bristol.

**JOSIA** of Padstow, 1704

    William Martyn Mr

Mentioned only once in the Port Books when she arrived from Liverpool with 2,331 bushells of rock salt. That was a very large cargo for Padstow and she may have been sold elsewhere thereafter.

**JUST**

A French prize condemned High Court Admiralty 23rd October, 1710, with prize goods transferred to warehouse at Padstow. The vessel itself was 'entered by oath of Peter Swymmer, 23rd February

in Lady day Quarter 1712.

    Richard Broad Mr 1712

    Thomas Hicks Mr 1713

    John Pearce Mr 1713

    Henry Allen Mr 1714

    Whitson ? Mr 1716 (last entry found)

On 9th September, 1712 the JUST prize 'made free', sailed for Dunkirk with 100 thousand Hilling stones. The figure 110 in one entry may refer to her burden tonnage which tallies with a cargo of 2,269 bushels of Portugal salt which she brought home from Lisbone in 1714, before going to Christiana for timber. The following year she was on the banks of Newfoundland trading salt and fish, and in 1716 back to Norway. She was Padstow's largest ship for many years.

**KATHERINE (KATHEREN)** of Padstow, burden 14 tons (elsewhere given as 8 tons), 1580-'2

    Tubbe Mr

**KATHERINE** of Padstow, burden 18 tons, 1681

    Thomas Ben Mr

One entry only found.

**KESTLE FRIGGETT (KITTY? FRIGGETT)** of Padstow, burden read as 14 tons, 1674-'5

    John King Mr 1674

On 17th September, 1674, she was entered inwards from St Martins (near La Rochelle) with 12 weys of French salt. The merchant's name appears to be James Kestle, which would support but not wholly explain the first version of her name.

**LANSDOWN (LANDOWN, LANSOWN)** of Padstow and of Boas Castle, burden about 20 tons, 1717-'19

    John Oliver Mr 1718

    John Williams Mr 1718-'19

A Bristol Channel coal trader.

**LAURELL (LAWRELL, etc.)** burden about 35 tons, of Padstow 1682-'8 and of Botreaux Castle, 1684

    John Brewer Mr 1682-'4

    Richard Olver Mr 1685-'7

    Samuel Cornish Mr 1685

She carried about 24 Chalders of coal and culme from Milford and other Welsh ports, and traded to France.

**LETITIA (LATITIA, etc.)** of Padstow, burden about 30 tons, 1684-'7

    Andrew Emmett Mr 1684-'7

This short-lived smack joined a small fleet of such vessels carrying helling stones and cloth to Crozick (Croisic) in South Brittany, and bringing back salt and pitch.

**LOVES INCREASE** of Bewd (Bude), burden about 15 tons, 1704

    John Haile Mr

One of the few Bude ships preceding construction of the lock and canal.

**LOYAL ANN (LOYALL ANNE, etc.)** of Padstow, 1715-'19 (or later)

    William Triplet Mr 1715-'19

General trader, France and Bristol Channel.

**MAGDALENE (MAGDALYNE, MAUDLYNE)** of Padstow ? burden 15 tons, 1601

    William Mitchell Mr 1601

Only featured in the Port Books for one year - but managed to have three different spellings in that short time. Irish trader.

**MARE (MARIE)** of St Collumbe, burden 14 tons, 1569

    John Pollard Mr

The only ship in the Port Books ascribed to St Columb.

**MARGARET (MARGERET)** of Botrixcastell & of Padstow, burden 10 to 18 to 24 tons, 1579-1603

   Thomas Martyn Mr 1579

   John Burdwood Mr 1582-'91

   John Harris Mr 1601

   William Talbott Mr 1603

Starting with a tiny sloop trading to Gloucester, the next phase, still only 18 tons, saw trading to Brittany and beyond, and in 1602 a final increase in tonnage to 24. Whilst they could be two or even three different vessels, the continuity and lack of overlap suggest successive lengthening of one ship.

**MARLBOROUGH** of Padstow, one entry only, 1715

   George Toman Mr

from Bristol with general cargo, Lady Day Quarter 1715.

**MARTEN** de Padstow (sic), burden 7 tons, 1569

   William Gravellyn Mr

**MARY (MARRY)** of Botriycastell (Bottrizcastell) and of Padstow, burden 10 tons, 1566-'80

   Willyam Bridgman Mr 1566

   John Bennet Mr 1580 (1582 Padstow)

   William Dyar ? Mr 1580

The vessel captained by Bennet was a separate and larger one, 28 tons.

**MARY** of Porthcesick (Port Isaac) burden 10 tons, 1638

   Thomas Emmett Mr

**MARY** of Padstow, burden about 20 tons, 1660-'9

   Mathew Grigg Mr 1660

   Abraham Stephens Mr 1668

**MARY** of Padstow, 1694 and of Portizick, burden about 20 tons, 1713-'18

   Richard Olver Mr 1694

   John Parsons Mr 1705

   Richard Broad Mr 1707-'9

   Richard Billing Mr 1711-'14

   James Trefry Mr 1715-'16

   J. Person (Parsons ?) Mr 1717

   James Trefry Mr 1718

   Richard Billing Mr 1718

**MARY** of Bewde (Bude), 1711

   Joseph Rundle (Randell ?) Mr

Arrived from Neath 21st July with 4 chalders of coal. One of very few early Bude vessels.

**MARY** of Padstow, 1718

   Richard Richards Mr

Left for Diep (Dieppe) 9th May with 18 thousand Helling stones. A small enough cargo to suggest that she may be the same vessel as the last.

**MARYGOLD (MARY GOULD, etc.)** of Padstow, burden 20 tons, 1579-'80

   Wm Tucker Mr 1579

   Jacob Braye Mr 1580

**MARYGOLD (MARY GOULD, etc.)** of Padstow, burden about 45 tons, 1696-'7

   Edward Madock Mr 1696-'7

One of the larger Padstow colliers of the time. May have been bought from Clovelly.

**MATHEWE** of Padstow, burden 10 tons, 1575

   Jacob Billin (Billing ?) Mr

Despite the burden tonnage given, she apparently brought in 10 tons of iron and 14? tons of pitch from France in the same entry.

**MATHIAS** of Botreaux Castell, burden 20 tons, 1625

A single entry *intra* from Ireland.

**MAYFLOWER** of Bewd ?, burden 20 tons, 1633

   John Tippett Mr

A single entry marks her return from France 7th June, 1633.

**MAYFLOWER** of Padstow, burden 22 tons, 1660 (or earlier)-1675

   Michael Kittow Mr 1660-'75

   Michael Rendle Mr 1670

**MAYFLOWER** of Padstow, burden 10 tons, 1703-'13

   John Parsons Mr 1703

   Richard Billing Mr 1704-'5

   Joseph Harris Mr 1707

   William Hender Mr 1708-'10

   Samuel Pasco (Paschoe) Mr 1709-'12

Traded widely but ended up on the regular run to and from Bristol with general cargo. While Billing was Master, the ship was as often described as 'of Truro' as 'of Padstow'.

**MERCHANT** of Padstow, burden about 35 tons, 1700-'3

   John Dunn Mr 1700-'3

**MYCHELL (MICHELL, MIGHELL)** of Padstow, burden 60 tons, 1579-'83

   John Triplet Mr 1579-'83

   Jacob Triplet Mr 1580

A large ship (for Padstow) trading to Rochell and Bourdeaux. In 1580 she brought in 24 tons of Salis Baye (presumably bay salt, obtained by enclosing brine in lagoons and awaiting evaporation).

**MYNION (MINON)** of Portizick, burden 6 tons, 1591

   Richard Wail Mr

A small enough vessel for only her more important cargoes to be entered. She sailed for Bristoll carrying Pilchard Traine which was, presumably, the fish oil obtained from the pilchard fishery, although the term 'train oil' was later applied to whale oil.

**NATHANIELE (NATHANIELL)** of Padstow, burden about 15 tons, 1699-1703

   Peter Major Mr 1698

   John Wakeham Mr 1703

Traded to Brittany despite her small size.

**NICOLAS** of Padstow, burden 9 tons, 1543-'71

   Benedict Mason Mr 1543 (1533?)

**NIGHTINGALE** of Padstow, burden about 55 tons, 1715-'18, or later

   John Gummer Mr 1715-'17

A large vessel for Padstow bringing up to 29 chalders of coal.

**ORANGE TREE** of Padstow, burden about 30 tons, 1684-'5

   Richard Olver Mr

   Nicholas Kemp Mr

Brought brandy and 'Plaistʳ. of Parris' from St Abastian and took hilling stones to Dunkerk.

**PADSTOW** of Padstow, burden about 35 tons, 1716

   Ralph Parsons ? Mr

One entry only found.

**PADSTOW MERCHANT (PADSTOWE)** of Padstow, burden about 60 tons, 1679-'96

   Richard Dunn Mr 1679-'86

   Wm Dunn Mr 1686-'92

   Nicholas Warren Mr 1688

   John Dunn Mr 1696

Traded widely with Spain and France and in the Bristol Channel.

**PATIENCE** of Padstow, burden 30 tons, 1620

   William Wilson Mr

   (single entry)

**PEACE** of Padstow, burden about 60 tons, 1682-'86

Michael Furger Mr 1682
Thomas Wills Mr 1682
John Betty Mr 1684
Jonathon Symons Mr 1684
John Sussex Mr 1684-'5
Richard Clement Mr 1685
John Burrows Mr 1686

Ireland, France and Spain were among her destinations. Credited with a cargo of 40 chalders (London) of coal in 1684, the largest coal cargo recorded in the port books up to 1719.

**PEACE** of Padstow, burden about 25 tons, 1712
John Sloman Mr

This single entry for an apparently smaller vessel suggests that this might be a second PEACE, or perhaps a first entry of the PEARL which follows, also with John Sloman as Master.

**PEARL** (PEARLE, PEARLL etc.) of Padstow, burden about 25 tons, 1713-'16
John Sloman Mr 1713-'16
John Sleeman Mr 1716

A busy Bristol Channel collier, but also carrying exports of copper ore, etc. from Padstow.

**PEARL** of Newkey, burden about 25 tons, 1715
Barnet Billing Mr

Probably the same vessel as the last. The only mention of Newkey (Newquay) for many years in the Port Books.

**PEGGY** (PEGY, PEGGEY) of Padstow, burden about 10 tons, 1705-'17
William Billings Mr 1705-'8
John Oliver Mr 1705, 1707
John Paschoe Mr 1711-'13
Martin Lobb Mr 1715-'17

A small vessel bringing 5 or 6 chalders of coal from Swanzey, and probably landing it at remote coves.

**PELLICAN** (PELICAN) of Padstow and Portizick, burden about 25 tons, 1696-1703
Nicholas Robins Mr 1696-'7
John Parsons Mr 1797
Ralph Billing Mr 1703

A collier trading to Swanzey.

**PERAN** (PEREN, PERYNE) of Padstow, Oner (burden) 26 tons, 1553-'75
Richard Laurens Mr 1566
Laurens St John Mr 1575

A final entry in 1575 includes 'le PEREN de Bristoll, St John est Mr' so she may have been sold to Bristol, or the scribe may have muddled Laurens and St John.

**PERIL** of Padstow, burden about 20 tons, 1717
George Morris Mr

This rather unlikely name only appears once (in 1717) but in absence of records may have had a long and safe life after that. Might be another version of PEARL.

**PETER** (PEETER) of Padstow, burden 6 tons, 1557-1601
It is difficult to decipher her Master's name when she was trading to Bristoll in 1577; William Woter ? Walter Towne ? Her Master's name in 1591 was Talbert. In 1601 she, or another of the same name, arrived from Watherforde (Waterford) with 15 tons (note increase) of beames and barrell staves. By then the Master's name was William Enibone which I take to be the later Kneebone clan.

**PHILIP & MARY** of Padstow, burden about 20 tons, 1715
John Trefry Mr

She sailed for Dunkerk in June 1715 with 44,000 hilling stones, and

that is the first and last we hear of her.

**PLAIN DEALING** (PLAINE etc.) of Padstow, burden 35 tons, 1687-1705
Richard Brewer Mr 1692-'7
Thomas Pearce Mr 1693-'4
Richard Pearce Mr 1702
Ralph Pearce Mr 1704-'5

First mentioned as bringing brandy and salt from Brittany, she soon settled down to the Bristol Channel trades, bringing in as much as 24 chalders of coal, and exporting copper oar and tyn. Her last appearance in the books was on the November 22nd, 1705.

**PRIMROSE** of Padstow, burden 10 tons, 1679-1712
Lawrence Romick Mr 1705-'9
Gilbert Reynolds Mr 1711-'12

In 1708 she loaded with 8 casks of Trayne Oil, 10,000 Hilling Stones and 7 tuns of block tyn for Bristoll.

**PROSPERITY** (PROSPERYTY) of Padstow, burden of about 45 tons, 1660-1705
William Basse ? Mr 1660
Bassen ? Mr 1674
William Kittow Mr 1675
Michael Kittow Mr 1685-'95
John Sussex Mr 1687
Walter Wakeham Mr 1696
Thomas Oliver Mr 1697-1705

She traded to Swanzea, Boulogne, Dublin, Dunkerk, Crosick, Liverpool, Bristol, Diep, and doubtless many other places, and must have been one of the most enterprising and successful Padstow ships of the period.

**PROSPEROUS** of Padstow, burden 10 tons, 1705-'12, also of Portizack, 1708
Arthur Triplet Mr 1705-'8
John Triplet Mr 1709-'11
Edward Bussacott Mr 1711
John Pratt Mr 1712

The PROSPEROUS was a coaster almost invariably carrying 6 chalders of coal or general cargo, and probably based at Port Isaac much of the time.

**PROSPEROUS ENDEAVOUR** of Bewde (Bewd), burden about 7 tons, 1711-'13
Joseph Rundle (Randle) Mr 1711-'12
Jasper Hawkins Mr 1713
Jasper Randle Mr 1713

Her small size and short life illustrate the dangers of trading to Bude before the lock and harbour were built.

**PROVIDENCE** of Padstow, burden about 12 tons, 1668-'74
John Corkram Mr 1668-'74

**PROVIDENCE** of Padstow, and of Boudreaux Castle occasionally, burden about 20 tons, 1684-'98
Thomas Mitchell Mr 1684
Richard Clees (Cleys?) Mr 1686-'95
George Rowe Mr 1688
John Sussex Mr 1693
Nicholas Robins Mr 1694-'96
John Potter Mr 1698

Capable of voyages to St Abastian for iron and Norway for deales, but spent most of her time hauling coals from Wales.

**PROVIDENCE** of Portizick 1703 and of Padstow 1703-'11
Anthony Oliver Mr 1703-'9
John Triplet Mr 1711

**PROVIDENCE** of Padstow, burden about 20 tons, 1709-'19

Thomas Hicks Mr 1709
Thomas Thomas Mr 1711-'12
Chas Mitchel Mr 1712
Clement Morris Mr 1713-'18
Abraham Clearke Mr 1719

Especially under Thomas Thomas, she was a Bristol trader bringing salt and general cargo. Her cargo capacity appeared to increase to about 35 tons by 1715.

**PROVIDENCE** of Padstow, burden about 40 tons, 1715-'18

Thomas Oliver Mr 1715
John Parsons Mr 1715
Roger Spear Mr 1716
William Palmer Mr 1718 ?

The name PROVIDENCE is perhaps less confusing in this context than GEORGE (q.v.), but a PROVIDENCE arrived from S. Antonio in April 1718, Wm Palmer Master, with 10 tons of Spanish iron and 60 barrels of small nales, and it must remain doubtful to which of the above (if any) this report refers.

**PROVYDENCE** of Bautreaux Castle, burden 40 tons, 1684

John Benoke Mr 1684

**PURDUE TROW** (PURDUR TROVE, etc.) of Padstow, burden 25 tons, 1617

Morgan Philips Mr

This vessel is of interest in that it appears to be the only reference (by name) to the Severn Trow type of vessel in these early Port Books.

**RECOVERY** of Padstow, burden 16 tons, 1668-'90, and of Portizick, 1683-'89

John Rawe (Rowe?) Mr 1668-'82
Nicholas Dunn Mr 1674
John Row Mr 1684-'87
John Richards Mr 1687

By 1687 she could carry 21 chalders of coal and may have been lengthened.

**RECOVERY** of Padstow, burden about 40 tons, 1718-'19 and later, probably

William Arthur Mr 1718
John Doubt Mr 1718
Nicholas Trevethan Mr 1719

Carried 70,000 slates to Dunkerk, and brought 25 chalders of coal, as typical cargo.

**RETURN** of Padstow, burden 36 tons, 1696

Lawrence Rennick Mr

One entry only: sailed with 36 tons copper oar, December 1696. Might be HAPPY RETURN.

**RICHARD & JOHN** of Padstow and of Portizick, burden 30 tons, 1692-1712

John Richards Mr 1692-1712
Thomas Pearce Mr 1697
Joseph Trevethan Mr 1707

For twenty years John Richards brought general cargo to Padstow from Bristol and returned with produce of mine and farm. Occasionally when incentive offered, she reinforced the work of the colliers or entered the export trade, for example taking 30,000 slates to Ostend.

**RICHARD & MARY** of Padstow, burden 35 tons, 1687-1718 and of Portissick, 1694-1712, and of Boscastle, 1716

Richard Oliver Mr 1687-1715 (Oliver often spelt Olver)
John Oliver 1693, 1707, 1712-'18
Humphry Bemock Mr 1713 (Benoke ?)
Christopher Millard Mr 1713

John Parsons Mr 1716

Richard and John Oliver (with occasional relief masters) had a record even more impressive than John Richards of the RICHARD & JOHN; they regularly traded to Bristol for thirty years (and possibly longer) bringing the necessities of life to Padstow and the outports, entering other trades when good opportunities presented themselves.

**RICHARD & THOMAS** of Padstow, burden 12 tons, 1660-'82 and of Botreaux Castell, 1680-'82

John Browne Mr 1660 and/or
George Browning Mr 1660
Thomas Oliver Mr 1668
Hugh Row Mr 1678
John Brewer Mr 1680

A vessel which, like the previous two, brought various goods from Bristol but probably to the smaller outports and beaches rather than to Padstow itself.

**RICHARD & WILLIAM** of Botreaux Castle, burden about 40 tons, 1684

James Hallet Mr 1684

On 19th March, 1684, she arrived with 24 chalders of coal. No other details are known.

**ROGER** (RODGER) of Padstow, burden 22 tons, 1630-'5

Walter Kitowe Mr 1630
Harris Mr 1635

On 15th July, 1635 sailed for Ireland with Barley Mault, perhaps with a view to improving the quality of the poteen.

**SARAH** of Padstow, burden 18 tons, 1662

Justinian Rosengrave Mr

Reported carrying iron from Bideford.

**SARAH** of Padstow, burden 25 tons, 1696-'7

John Sussex Mr

She features for only two years and in one of the best recorded periods, so the chances are that she was lost after a short and very active life.

**SAVIOUR** (SAVJOUR) of Bude, burden 18 tons, 1616, and of Padstow, 1615, and of Botreaux Castle, 1620

Richard Yeo Mr 1616
Edward Joslyn Mr 1620

Traded to Ireland and France despite her small size.

**SOCIETY** of Padstow, burden 50 tons, 1715-'18 (and probably thereafter)

Richard Parkin Mr 1715
Henry Allen Mr 1715
William Parker (and Parkin) 1715-'18

Her destinations from Aurndell (Arendal in Norway) to Haverdegras (Le Havre ?) illustrate the development of commerce in Europe following the Treaty of Utrecht in 1713.

**SPEEDWELL** of Bude, burden 15 tons, 1617, and of Padstow, 1617,

Richard Yeo Mr 1617
John ? Mitchell Mr 1617

**SPEEDWELL** of Padstow, burden 26 tons, 1630-'7

John Norman Mr 1630-'7
Richard Morish Mr 1637

She traded exclusively to various Irish ports, taking such goods as Hilling Stones and Mault Barley, and bringing back tymber, cloth, herrings and tallow.

**SPEEDWELL** of Padstow, burden about 15 tons, 1674-'92

Edward Parsons Mr 1674-'5
John Parsons Mr 1680-'7
Michael Clements Mr 1687-'8

Until 1686 this vessel fits the description 'Constant Coaster', trading regularly to Bristol and the ports in South Wales. Then it appears that she was lengthened, her burden doubled to about 30 tons, and she concentrated on the coal run.

**SPEEDWELL** of Padstow, of Portizick and of Botreaux Castle burden about 10 tons, 1703-'18 (or later)

> Arthur Triplet Mr 1703-'18
> John Martyn Mr 1704
> Jethro Martyn Mr 1705
> John Triplet Mr 1705-'18
> Nicholas Harper Mr 1707
> George Heale Mr 1707-'8
> William Whitefield Mr 1707

Judging by the multiplicity of masters, more than one vessel is involved in 1703-'8 but it is impossible to separate them. By 1709, Arthur Triplet was carrying larger cargoes, such as 32 tons of lead oar, so their vessel had probably been rebuilt. Arthur and John then shared her until 1718 or later.

**STRONGBOW** of Bautreauxcastle, burden about 40 tons, 1684

> Samuel Cornish Mr

She only gets one mention in the Port Books, bringing in 24 chalders of coal (London).

**SUCCESS** (SUCCESSE etc.) of Padstow, burden 20 tons, 1674-'86

> John Quinton Mr 1674
> Anthony Gregory Mr 1675
> Anthony Parsons Mr 1675-'80
> William Hendry (or Hender) Mr 1679-'86

A Bristol Channel trader.

**SUNDAY** (SONNDAY etc.) of Bodreauxcastell, burden 15 tons, 1569-'75, and of Padstow, 1575

> William Jones Mr 1575
> Thomas Brett Mr 1575

It was impossible to interpret some details of these entries.

**SUPPLY** of Padstow, burden about 45 tons, 1693-1709

> Grigory Parkin Mr 1693
> Warden Wakenham Mr 1696
> Joseph Harris Mr 1697-1701
> Trevethan Mr 1703
> Thomas Pedler Mr 1704-'9

Under Joseph Harris she traded widely visiting *inter alia* Diep, Dunkerk, Ostend: Thomas Pedler kept her almost exclusively in the Swanzey coal trade.

**SWALLOW** of Padstow and of Portizick, burden about 15 tons, 1703-'15

> John Hicks Mr 1703-'8
> Arthur Olver Mr 1711
> Anthony Oliver Mr 1711-'15

A small coaster trading to Neath, Swanzey, Bristol, Bideford, etc.

**SWAN** of Padstow, burden about 25 tons, 1718-'19 (and probably thereafter in absence of records)

> Ralph Savage Mr 1718
> John Savage Mr 1718-'19

**SWANN** (SWAN etc.) of Botreauxcastell, burden 18 tons, 1617-'60

> Richard Tubb Mr 1637
> Baldwin Tinke Mr 1660
> John Beale ? Mr 1660

There is also an isolated mention of a SWANN in 1675

> Richard Oliver ? Mr

**TALLENT** (TALLANT, TALLENTE, etc.) of Padstow, burden about 35 tons, 1660-1708

> Robert Harris Mr 1660

> Walter Ansley Mr 1665
> Nyatt Doubt Mr 1674-1700
> Nicholas Waren (Warren ?) Mr 1685
> Joseph Harries Mr 1685-'90
> Warden Veale Mr 1693
> Wm Kittow Mr 1694
> John Doubt Mr 1695-1708
> William Doubt Mr 1697

Traded extensively with Ireland, France and the Low Countries, as well as bringing up to 23 chalders of coal from Wales. A long adventurous life.

**TEN BROTHERS** of Padstow and of Portizick, 1693-'6

> Abell Pascoe Mr 1694
> Thomas Paschoe Mr 1696
> Richard Pascoe, recorded in Barnstaple
> Simon Pascoe, recorded in Barnstaple

Her few entries give no figure for tonnage but the indications are that she was very small indeed, bringing in a few miscellaneous items from Bideford.

**THOMAS** of Padstow, burden 35 tons, 1583

> William Tucker Mr

**THOMAS** of Boutreaux Castell, burden 16 tons, 1608

**THOMAS** of Padstow, burden 12 tons, 1630-'9

> Erasmus Glover Mr 1630
> James Bennett Mr 1630
> Edward Harris Mr 1639

**THOMAS & JAMES** (JAME, JANE) of Padstow, burden about 30 tons, 1674-'97

> Thomas Olver Mr 1674-'80
> Arthur Triplet Mr 1682
> Clement Hoskins Mr 1696
> William Billings Mr 1697

In the days before names were emblazoned on ships, and when many of the entries relied on word of mouth from distant outports, it is not surprising that there were wide variations in the recorded names of ships.

**THREE BROTHERS** (also written 3 BROTHERS) of Padstow, burden about 25 tons, 1682-'91

> Anthony Parsons Mr 1682-'5
> Andrew Emmett Mr 1684
> Clem Hoskins Mr 1691

Traded to St Andera (Santander), Oporto, St Valrey and Crozick, and later in the Bristol Channel.

**TRINITIE** (TRYNYTYE etc.) of Padstow, burden 10 tons, 1568-'72

> Wm Derstoll Mr 1568
> Bryan Garry (?) Mr 1570
> Thomas Telmes Mr 1572

**TRINITY** of Padstow, burden about 25 tons, 1660-'87

> Richard Oliver Mr 1660
> John Browning Mr 1685
> Anthony Oliver Mr 1669-'75
> Hugh Row Mr 1682
> George Row Mr 1687

Mostly in the Bristol Channel trades.

**TRINITYE** de Boatescastell, burden x tons, 1582

> Robertus ? Steven ? Mr de Glour (Gloucester)

**TRUE LOVE** (TRUELOVE, etc.) of Boscastell, burden about 25 tons, 1660 or earlier

> Warren Beale ? Mr
> John Frost Mr
> John Symons Mr

John Brewer Mr
John Beale ? Mr
All listed as masters in 1660, so probably more than one vessel!
**TRUE LOVE** of Padstow and of Portizick, burden about 30 tons, 1715-'19 (or later)
  Thomas Emmett Mr
  John Garland Mr 1715
Typically carried Hilling Stones to Penzance, there loading copper oar for Bristol, then general cargo for Padstow.
**TRUELOVE** of Padstow, burden about 15 tons, 1699-1703
  Richard Broad Mr
**TRYALL** of Padstow, burden about 30 tons, 1694
  Henry Harris Mr 1694
On 25th February, 1694 she sailed for Bristol with 80,000 Helling Stones, 1,000 weight of Pewter and 108 Ellms!
**TRYNITIE** of Portizick, burden 6 tons, 1591
  Richard Will ? Mr
**TRYNITY** of Padstow, burden 20 tons, 1611-'37, of Botreaux Castle, 1620, and of Porthciesick, 1637
    William Stevens ? Mr
    Warren Skinner ? Mr 1620
    William Payne Mr 1637
See also TRYNITIE and TRINITY.
**TWO BROTHERS** of Padstow, burden about 20 tons, 1707-'19, of Botreaux Castle, 1713-'19
    Ralph Peirce (Pearse) Mr 1707
    Laurence Rouminick Mr 1711
    Jethro Martyn Mr 1713-'17
    Thomas Oliver Mr 1717
A collier generally carrying 12 chalders of coales or culme.
**TWO BROTHERS** of Padstow, burden about 35 tons, 1717-'19 (or later)
    Ralph Pearse Mr 1717-'19
This vessel must be separate from the previous (despite the Master's name) as she arrived almost simultaneously in September 1717, and with a 33 ton cargo.
**TWO SISTERS** of Botreaux Castle, 1715
    Jethro Martyn Mr
A single entry. It seems almost certain that this should be TWO BROTHERS.
**UNION**
In 1712 large quantities of contraband were seized at Padstow in a vessel of that name, but there is no information about the fate of the vessel herself. The following entries may refer to the same vessel:
UNION of Padstow, burden about 35 tons, 1713-'18 (and possibly later)
    Henry Thomas Mr 1713-'18
    Pearce Mr 1717

George Row Mr 1718
Traded to Callis (Calais ?), Dunkirk, Crossick, Guernsey. Despite taking occasional coal cargoes, she could be said to specialise in the French trade, and her visits to Guernsey, etc. may indicate an interest in the wines and spirits trade which is not necessarily reflected in her manifest.
**UNITIE** of Padstow, burden 20 tons, 1593-'4
    William Rusell ? Mr
Arrived from Cork in September and left for Rochell.
**UNITIE** of Padstow, burden about 40 tons, 1687-1710
    Joseph Harris Mr 1687
    Wm Doubt Mr 1688
    John Doubt Mr 1688-1700
    (Nyet) Doubt Mr 1692-1710
    Henry Harris Mr 1698
    Richard Randall Mr 1700
Continental trader.
**UNITIE & GRACE** of Padstow, burden 30 tons, 1593
    George Horne Mr
Arrived from Rochell.
**WILLIAM** of Padstow, burden 14 tons, 1603
    Henry Horne Mr
An isolated entry.
**WILLIAM** of Padstow, burden about 40 tons, 1693-'6, and of Portizick, 1694
    William Martyn Mr 1693-'5
    John Mitchell Mr 1696
This Bristol Channel collier arrived with widely differing quantities of coal and culme, viz. 24 chalders, 8 chalders, 12 chalders, 10 chalders. Perhaps she unloaded part cargoes *en route*, at Clovelly for instance.
**WILLIAM & MARY** of Padstow, burden about 35 tons, 1708-'19 (or later)
    John Parsons Mr 1708
    John Parkin(s) Mr 1715-'18
    Joseph Trevithan Mr 1716-'18
    John Parker Mr 1717-'19
    William Billing Mr 1718
These vessels, like those of a later generation, tended to start their careers in the demanding foreign trades, but in middle age to be relegated to the local work in the Bristol Channel.
**WILLIAM & THOMAS** of Portizick, 1695
In September of that year, Arthur Triplet, Mr, brought her from Bideford with a small general cargo, which included tobacco and pipe clay. It is surprising that there is no other mention of her in what is one of the best recorded periods, but perhaps she was very small and not usually used as a freight carrier.

NORSEMAN *c.* 1100          Conjectured appearance of early ships.          HOOKER *c.* 1600

# 6    CAMEL ESTUARY BARGES

THE barges of the Taw and Torridge, of the Dart, Tamar and Fal, have been studied thoroughly and there are some interesting publications about them. Such eminent authorities as Basil Greenhill and David MacGregor have pointed out the distinctive double-ended schooner rigged barges of Padstow and the river Camel, as illustrated in early photographs, but as far as I know, nobody wrote about them or described their features before the last of them disappeared from the scene. All we have to go on are some newspaper reports, some photographs and a few fading memories.

As detailed in Chapter 4, the Maritime Survey of 1626 listed twenty-nine bargemen of Egloshayle and St Breock, that is bargees whose livelihood was to navigate barges within the estuary of the River Camel.

The Gascoyne Map of Cornwall (1699) shows only Padstow on the whole estuary as a town with streets, but the following settlements are named, working downstream, and would clearly have been served by barges: Pendavey, Wadebridge, Trevilling, Trewornan, Amble, Treguna, Penquean, Ponskin, Tregena, Trevelver, Halwyn, Little Petherick, Trebetherick. Although Wadebridge is clearly more important than the other places mentioned by virtue of its position and bridge, it only has a very few buildings and is not in the same league as Padstow. Bodille (now Porthilly) and St Enodoc churches are shown and there were farms associated with these already ancient chapels. There are records of barges trading to and upstream of Wadebridge and also to Amble and to Little Petherick, and without a doubt they went to all the riverside farms and settlements, including a dozen and more mines and quarries when they were active. The construction of the causeway carrying the railway along the left bank of the river from Wadebridge to Padstow cut off most of the old landing places, but by that time, at the end of the nineteenth century, the mines and quarries were largely closed. Of the settlements shown on Gascoyne's map listed above, all appear (and with almost the same spelling) on today's Ordnance Survey maps, with one exception: Ponskin was later known as Pinskin, and appears on today's maps only as Pinkson Creek; there were iron and copper ore mines on that inlet and seagoing vessels as well as barges used to load in the creek before the railway was built.

Gilbert's historical survey of 1817 says of Wadebridge 'There are commodious cellars and timber yards with good anchorage for boats and barges which come up daily from Padstow and supply the inhabitants with goods.'

Gilbert also leads us to another connection with barges, that is to say canals: 'The distance from the navigable part of the Fowey to the River Camel does not exceed five miles, and even in this short distance there are several small streams, sufficient to feed a canal cut through this narrow isthmus . . . The advantages which a union of these two rivers would produce must be obvious to all and therefore need not be particularized here.' He was, in fact, vainly repeating dreams of earlier years. There was a public meeting in Bodmin in 1793 with Sir William Molesworth in the chair which voiced the advantages of a canal to join the Rivers Fowey and Camel, and civil engineers George Bentley and Thomas Bolton reported on various alternative schemes the following year. The famous civil engineer Sir John Rennie commented in 1796 favouring a canal from Wadebridge

to Bodmin which would take sand from Padstow to spread on land near Bodmin, and coal for Bodmin town, in 15-ton barges which could return with minerals for export; but he could see no future for through traffic to Fowey on a canal so close to Lands End.

Nevertheless, that did not stop Marc Isambard Brunel (the father of Isambard Kingdom Brunel) from proposing in 1825 a thirteen mile Padstow-Fowey ship canal, including a tunnel near Lanhydrock! That was the very year he started construction of the famous Thames tunnel between Rotherhithe and Wapping, on which his son also worked, before his vast works for the Great Western Railway and the steamships GREAT WESTERN, GREAT BRITAIN and GREAT EASTERN. Like son, like father: the scale of work necessary to drive a tunnel at Bodmin capable of carrying sea-going vessels between Padstow and Fowey would have daunted anyone except possibly the Cornish miners and quarrymen: perhaps it is fortunate that it daunted the financiers and nothing came of the scheme. Instead, the Bodmin to Wadebridge Railway opened in 1833 and 1834 along lines favoured by the earlier canal schemes (and thereby avoided gradients).

Meanwhile the barges of the Camel continued to trade in the estuary. Little is known of their construction, but to get up to Wadebridge on a daily basis on one flood tide they must have been propelled by sail and sweep, and to get alongside there at neap tides, they would have shallow draught. Those that went on up through the bridge at Wadebridge, or traded to Amble under Trewornan Bridge, must have lowered or unshipped any masts, and were probably towed the last mile or so by horse or man power.

With twenty-nine bargemen listed in 1626, there were probably about half-a-dozen 15- or 20-ton barges, plus a few smaller ones. It is not known to what extent seagoing vessels reached Wadebridge in those early days, but the completion of the mineral railway from Bodmin certainly increased the exports of iron ore, granite, and in due course of china clay, and facilitated the import of coal from Wales and the transport of sea sand from the estuary to the poor inland farms. Lime was also imported, burnt and taken inland, and slate and timber were brought in. As seagoing vessels could only get alongside at Wadebridge at spring tides, and even then, depending on their draught, with part cargoes, there was a regular need for the barges to carry all the water-borne commerce at times of neap tides, and to lighter cargo out of ships bound for Wadebridge at Padstow during spring tides, and also to complete their cargoes at Padstow, when they had come down river from Wadebridge with part cargoes. This activity tailed off once the railway was extended to Padstow in 1899, and as road transport improved, the barges lost all but one type of freight and that was sand, gravel and stone.

When John Rennie was commenting on the canal proposals in 1796, he recognised the value of the shell sand near Padstow which was already being spread on local land to improve its fertility, and he saw it would be a useful cargo to Bodmin. It continued (and continues) to be available in vast quantities, and for many years barges from Padstow grounded themselves on a suitable sand bank in the estuary on a falling tide and as soon as the sand was uncovered, their crews performed the back-breaking task of shovelling a load of sand into the barge using the traditional longhandled shovels. As the tide came in, the barge floated off and

A schooner-rigged barge off Rock, June 1906.          *Photo J. C. Burow*

was sailed to Padstow (or possibly to some other landing place in the estuary) for unloading.

Great knowledge and judgment of the tides was needed for all these barging operations. In catching the tide up to Wadebridge, an intimate knowledge of the unbuoyed and changing channel was essential to avoid running aground early on: and if you started too late, the last mile or two had to be won against the first of the ebb stream, with prodigious expenditure of effort. If a sand barge grounded itself too soon on the sand bank, once loaded with sand it failed to float off at the next high tide. That might not just mean financial loss and frustration; if the wind went round into the wrong quarter, it might mean danger of being pounded and eventually swamped by the seas at the following high tide.

The mariner and the bargee knew his tides, not so much from the Admiralty tide tables, but more as a farmer knows the seasons.

Spring tides do not, of course, occur only during the spring, but at fortnightly intervals throughout the year, reaching their peak two days or so after new moon and full moon. That much is common knowledge, but how many people know what every bargee and coasting seaman knew, that high water spring tides are always at the same time at any given port? Padstow is a seven o'clock port because high water spring tides always occur a few minutes before seven o'clock (Greenwich mean time).

We are told by Gilbert that barges arrived at Wadebridge daily. The winds in the Camel valley are fluky, and although the flood tide runs strongly at Padstow, it tails off to nothing much as Wadebridge is approached. At spring tides then, the pilot and the bargeman must

wait until there is an adequate depth of water just above Padstow, and can then set out on the six-mile journey to Wadebridge. Low water at spring tides is, of course, exceptionally low and he would have to wait almost until half tide before sailing from Padstow. If he could fill his sails most of the way, then three hours should suffice to take him to his berth alongside the quay at Wadebridge, ready to settle on the mud as the tide ebbed. Consider then the situation in deep winter. It is necessary to set out from Padstow at about 4 a.m. in pitch darkness up the unbuoyed channel in order to arrive at Wadebridge around high water. That sounds rather daunting, but the alternative is to set sail at about 4 p.m. in failing light in order to berth at Wadebridge at 7 p.m. in total darkness! It is surprising that no anecdotes have survived about this dilemma, but I suspect that the bargemen got up early, ran aground fairly frequently on the rising tide, came off after some delay and were grateful for the gift of daylight when they reached Wadebridge.

The larger barges were unusual in being rigged as fore-and-aft schooners and I reproduce a photograph showing one of them dried out off Rock in 1906. She has a gaff-rigged mainsail and foresail, and a single headsail set on the forestay which runs to the stem head. The mainsheet is rigged down from the end of the boom to a large iron ring which is attached to the sternpost in such a way as to allow the tiller freedom of movement. The hull is double-ended but beamy and shallow, with a little deadrise and apparently a hard chine at the turn of the bilge. The staying of the masts is in the simplest possible fashion, and the winch on the foredeck suggests that the boom of the foresail could be used as a derrick for handling cargo. These schooner barges are visible in the background of several photographs of Padstow taken in the late nineteenth century, and they are all double-ended and some of them appear more sharply pointed than the one illustrated here, although that may be an optical illusion. As far as can be discovered, no drawings of the lines of any of them has been found, if indeed they ever existed.

Even less is known about the smack-rigged barges of the estuary, one of which is illustrated loading sand near St Georges Well between Padstow and Harbour Cove. Like the schooner barge, she appears to be double-ended and quite unlike any of the Taw and Torridge barges described by Alison Grant and Barry Hughes in *North Devon Barges*. Her hull lines look similar to the schooner.

Since the Second World War sand-winning operations have been carried out by the suction dredgers described in chapter 18 and also at low water by modern earth-moving machinery.

The Camel barges are almost totally anonymous. There were several reports of incidents with barges in the nineteenth century newspapers, the following being typical:

*Royal Cornwall Gazette*, 2nd September, 1898
At Padstow yesterday a barge manned by N. England and W. Prior was carrying road stone from the quarry at Stepper Point to Padstow Quay for the use of Padstow Urban District Council. After taking in a cargo the barge hauled off into deep water in the Narrows when she shipped water and sank . . .They took to their boat which was drawn under by the sinking barge. Gigs from Hawkers Cove coast guards and

HELEN PEELE, the lifeboat, rescued them both. The weather was fine but the barge was a total loss in deep water.

In December 1805 a press report recorded the death by drowning of a bargeman, Thomas Beer of St Kew, bound for Amble from Padstow, and another later report referred to a man being knocked overboard by the mizen boom of a barge. Although the photograph of the schooner-rigged barge reproduced here plainly has an aftermast larger than the foremast, at least one has been spotted with the aftermast rather shorter than the foremast, so the reference to a mizen boom does not necessarily indicate the existence of a ketch-rigged barge of some basically different type.

None of these reports mentions the name of the barge, and the presumption must be that they were mostly un-named; they were certainly unregistered, except for a few old seagoing hulls used as barges in their final years.

When liquidators disposed of William Stribley's assets in November 1879, they included at Yard South Quay, 'The big masted barge' 32 tons, plus a 30-ton, a 20-ton and a 15-ton barge.

In 1991, taxing the memories of Tom Morrissey, Alf Orchard and other Padstow men produced the following vignettes of mostly twentieth-century Camel barges:

**BEATRICE CAROLINE**, ON 85826. A Fowey ketch built at Falmouth in 1886. Bought by Wm. S. Martyn of Wadebridge who unrigged her and used her as a barge on the Camel. Gone from the

Loading sand into a smack-rigged barge near St George's Well.     *Royal Institution of Cornwall*

Mercantile Navy List by 1932, but still to be seen as a floating hulk into the 1950s.

**BEAUMARIS**, a wooden motor barge built in the 1920s by Steve Brabyn and owned by him. She had wheel steering, an open hatch and carried about 40 tons.

**CHARLOTTE, ON 47233**. A 62-ton ketch built in 1863 at Kingston (Shoreham) Sussex by May and Thwaite but owned by James Jenkin of Newquay 1880, and bought from him by John Neal of Padstow in 1884 who registered her at Padstow in 1889 and owned her until he died in 1922. Thereafter David W. Davies, (also spelt Davis), owned her as he did ELIZABETH and WILLIAM & EMMA, using her as a barge until her remains were left in Cant Cove. Register note says 'broken up in 1924'.

**DARING**, an old Port Isaac lugger which was used as a barge at Wadebridge, owned by Bill Beare. She used to collect fresh water gravel from the river at Sladesbridge and take it to Wadebridge presumably for use as a concrete aggregate.

**DRUNKEN JANE**, a barge of 25-30 tons capacity owned by Parkyn and operated between Padstow and Rock. Presumably a nickname.

**EBENEZER**, a smack-rigged barge which replaced GRAND TURK. Her remains are said to lie in Porthilly Cove.

**ELIZABETH, ON 10886**. This Bridgwater ketch (built as a schooner in 1854) spent her declining years (1920-1930) registered at Barnstaple in the gravel trade. Her managing owner was David W. Davis of Wadebridge whither she was often towed with 100 tons of road stone.

**FLYING SCUD**, a schooner barge with the same owners as GRAND TURK.

**GENESTA, ON 91327**. A Harwich boomie barge built by Vaux in 1886. After an adventurous life she was used as dumb timber lighter between Padstow and Wadebridge and then was moored as a houseboat off Porthilly, opposite Padstow in the late 1940s and in due course left her bones in the graveyard in Cant Cove.

**GRAND TURK**. The remains of this barge were rescued from the sand at Rock in 1977 by Roy Davis, the well-known local diver, and taken to the Charlestown Shipwreck Centre to form the centrepiece of a diving display. Subsequently the Centre has been reorganised and only a few of the timbers of the barge are to be seen.

**ISABELLA, ON 62772**. Built as a schooner at Freckleton by P. Rawstrone in 1872, and converted to ketch rig soon after 1900, this vessel was registered first at Preston and then at Gloucester. Her first connection with Cornwall was being owned by Joshua Cowls of Porthleven in 1933, but soon after that her registration was closed, and she was used as a barge on the Camel following in the footsteps of ELIZABETH. Later she became a houseboat for Lady Frazer at Rock and eventually finished up in the graveyard at Cant Cove.

**JESSIE, ON 78968**. This 22-ton smack was built as a barge by Billing at Wadebridge in 1876. Fairly soon thereafter she was registered at Truro and owned successively by Robert Dixon and Samuel Ingram, both of Truro. Believed converted to a lighter, 1908.

**MARCO POLO**. Only her name is remembered.

**RICHARD & SARAH**. There were three Port Isaac RNLI lifeboats called RICHARD & SARAH all of them self-righting pulling boats. One of them was fitted with a Kelvin slide-valve engine and used as a barge in the Camel, owned by Parkyn.

**THE BIG MAST BARGE**. Already mentioned as one of shipbuilder Stribley's assets.

**THE SABBATH-BREAKER**, Capt. Pollard. The Pollard family were masters of several Padstow ships, none of which could be described as a barge. Various Cornish vessels were nicknamed Sabbath-Breaker (often for being launched or working on a Sunday) including this barge of which nothing more is known.

**THE WADEBRIDGE & PADSTOW PACKET**, John Cradoe's ferry. Nickname for a barge which plied regularly between Padstow and Wadebridge.

**WILLIAM**. Remains at Seamills in Little Petherick Creek are said to be of the barge WILLIAM last used in connection with Padstow harbour construction in 1933.

**WILLIAM & EMMA**. This vessel was built by Francis Hawke & Sons at Stonehouse, Plymouth in 1880 as a cutter-rigged 'outside' barge and registered in 1889 at Plymouth (ON 95138). At that time her registered tonnage was 19, but in 1900 she was re-registered at Falmouth and soon after that she was presumably lengthened as her tonnage increased to 27 and she became ketch rigged. By 1924 she was owned by David W. Davis of Wadebridge, like ELIZABETH, and presumably used for similar purposes. She is remembered as barge built and taking stone from the Stepper Point Quarry.

Three other Tamar barges carry their way into this book by virtue of being owned for part of their careers in Padstow outports:

**JESSIE**, (ON 78087 but 78069 also found), was built by R. Hill & Sons at Plymouth in 1878. (The National Maritime Museum monograph No.46 on Shipping and Trade on the Tamar has her registered in 1868, but I believe it must have been 1878 as her official number was not reached until about then). She was a square sterned, cutter-rigged smack 54.4 ft long, credited with 35 ton cargoes in the Tamar area. She was bought by Alexander Stephens of Porth (near Newquay), in 1892, and used by him to bring coal in the traditional way from Wales to be unloaded by beaching as close as possible to the customer. Unfortunately she was lost — with sixty-four tons of coal, according to some reports — on the Nancy Rock, Park Head, near Trevose, in 1893. Sixty-four tons seems an impossibly large cargo for her, but perhaps she had been lengthened and then lost before the changes found their way to the register.

**JOHN HEDLEY** was a larger vessel, 65 ft long, built at Netstakes, Gunnislake by E. Crocker & Sons in 1866. She was built as a smack but converted to ketch rig in 1874, which might suggest an intention for her to engage in outside trade; and about that time Richard Roose of Port Isaac became her owner, with Richard Triplett of Plymouth as her manager, and Capt. Cowling of Port Isaac owning some shares in her. In 1897 the Rooses of Port Isaac sold her to William Philip of Padstow and the next year she was sold to John Westcott of Plymouth who used her as a hulk.

**VOLUNTEER**, (ON 65148) of only 24 tons, was built at Plymouth in 1864 and although the Mercantile Navy Lists 1872-1875 show her as owned by William Symons of Tintagel, (within the Padstow limits), it seems most likely that she spent her entire life in the Plymouth area until broken up in 1926.

As well as the barges, rafts of timber were sometimes quanted up to Wadebridge, generally needing two flood tides to complete their journey.

# 7 THE SIX-OARED GIGS

ON Saturday 7th September, 1991 took place the Great River Race through London, by then a well established event initiated by the Company of Watermen & Lightermen of the River Thames. There was a Chinese dragonboat, a Hawaiian outrigger, a curragh, 118 entries all told, all rowing, sculling or paddling their craft from Richmond to the Isle of Dogs. Those freemen of the Company of Watermen & Lightermen who were not more actively engaged were able to watch the event in comfort from an excursion vessel, and many of them agreed that, apart from the Company's own shallop, the six-oared Cornish Pilot-Gigs stole the show.

The entries included RHOS from Roseland, SOCOA from Cadgwith, SOWENNA from Mevagissey and TEAZER from Padstow. The WILLIAM PETERS from the Scilly Isles and others had appeared on an earlier occasion.

It is true that mention of Cornish gigs today turns one's mind to the races and regattas in which they take part so magnificently; but they were not designed for pleasure. In the late eighteenth century, the mariners of Cornwall competed to offer services to vessels approaching their shores. The first boat to reach a ship might put a pilot aboard, or help her come to a safe anchorage, or prevent her from entering dangerous waters. Other duties might include delivering orders, bringing messages, mail or men ashore, or taking samples, say of a grain cargo, on behalf of the merchants. The requirement was for the fastest possible seaboat capable of living in the turbulent seas of the area, and the answer was a lightly built gig about 30 ft long but less than 5 ft in beam, with 6 oarsmen on 6 thwarts and a steersman, or coxswain, and capable of stepping a mast and setting a lugsail when the wind served; there was often a small mizzen as well.

The Peters family of St Mawes, who built their first gig in 1790, and continued to build them into the twentieth century, set the standards and developed the design. The gigs were built of young, well-seasoned, narrow-leafed elm, with planks only ¼ inch thick. They are clinker built with lovely lines, and capable of flexing in a seaway without leaking. The toughness of the gigs and their crews is illustrated by the many voyages which were made to Brittany for brandy and lace in these open boats! They were virtually invisible when there was a big sea running, and if a revenue cutter should by chance close one of them, the gig merely had to pull to windward and the cutter had no hope of seeing her again. The speed through the water naturally depended on conditions, but their ability to cover a mile at over nine knots has been carefully verified.

It is the Peters family tradition that their first order for a six-oared gig was placed by a gentleman in holy orders, and that she was destined for Padstow. The late Roger Gillis, who did so much to revive interest in the six-oared gigs, thought that she was most probably the first Padstow lifeboat.

If that were the case, then the second Padstow lifeboat, and the first Padstow gig to be identified by name was the MARINER'S FRIEND and the following details have been obtained from the records of the 'Padstow Harbour Association for the Preservation of Life and Property from Shipwreck'. She was built in 1827, by Richard Tredwen of that famous Padstow clan, having been designed by David Williams, the Inspecting Commander of the Coast Guard who collected subscriptions for her. She was 23 ft long with a beam

of 6.5 ft, so although described as a six-oared gig, her oarsmen must have sat on three thwarts, not six. She cost £50 and was taken over by the Padstow Harbour Association in 1829, being housed at Hawker's Cove, and serving until 1855 when she was declared unworthy of further repair. Cyril Noall and Grahame Farr describe her as being built by John Tredwen, and rowing four oars. Quite likely she was built by Richard in John's Yard, and in the course of her long and hectic life she may well have modified to row four or six oars at different times: or there may have been a second boat.

But the early lifeboats have diverted us from the story of the true six-oared gigs. The Padstow estuary doubtless employed numerous able small craft in the eighteenth and early nineteenth centuries, but it was the men of outport Newquay who were better placed to go 'seeking' and it was for them that the Peters family built their famous six-oared NEWQUAY in 1812. After that came a whole succession of gigs, the names of some of them lost for ever. Newquay had TREFFRY and DEFIANCE in 1835. There have been two or even three TEAZERS: the first was built as ZOE TREFFRY, renamed TEAZER at Newquay and sold to form the roof of a chicken house in the first world war: another was built at Rawle's Padstow yard which also had the VIXEN for the yard's use. The Padstow gigs ARROW and STORM performed gallant services on the Doom Bar in 1859. The names of gigs at Boscastle and Portquin have been lost whilst of several Port Isaac gigs only the names of CORSAIR and TOM SAYERS survive. The *West Briton* reported:

*7th May, 1841.* On Wednesday evening Mr W. Withell, shipbuilder of Padstow and seven of his men, after leaving their work, took their gig and rowed to the island of Newland (West of Rumps Point) in search of gulls' eggs. On getting back into the boat the lift of the sea hove her on a projecting rock, and the tide immediately falling eight or ten feet she upset and with much difficulty five saved themselves by getting on the island, but James Docton, son of Mr Docton, printer, and John Brenton were drowned. The former has left a wife and one child, and the latter a wife and four children to lament their untimely loss. The boat was dashed to pieces and the other six persons remained on the island for some hours calling for help, till a vessel came by which took them off and landed them safely.

*11th Febuary, 1848.* Lost on 6.12.1847, from the barque *Marchioness of Abercorn*, of Londonderry, about 70 miles from Cork towards Lands End, two carvel-built boats, viz: long boat, abt. 26 ft long x 8¾ ft wide, decked with main and fore hatchway in the deck. Pinnace, about 23 ft long, stowed in the Long Boat; paint drab inside and out except bottom of red. Also on 3rd February, 1848, off Trevose Head, two six-oared gig boats and oars. One painted black with white streak, name DAUNTLESS of Padstow, Thomas Carter; the other painted outside green, with white bottom, length 28 ft breadth 4 ft 9 ins inside painted yellow with red bottom. Should the said boats or either of them have been picked up, the parties will please give information of the same to the Receiver of Admiralty Droits, Padstow or Messrs R. and J. Tredwen, and they shall be handsomely rewarded.

The Newquay regatta on Midsummer day, 1857 featured hurling, a race for ship's boats over one and one-half miles, a gig and punt chase, and the band of the Royal Miners Artillery, but the regatta started at 3.30 p.m. with a race for six six-oared gigs over seven miles, for three prizes, which were won by TREFFRY (first, of

Newquay), CIRCE (second, of Truro) and DOVE (third, of Newquay). The other three gigs were GIRL I LOVE, NEWQUAY and ARROW.

In the active period of shipbuilding in Padstow, every yard had its gig. Captain Rawle's VIXEN has been mentioned already, whilst CONSTANCE was attached to the Dennis Cove site, and PEACE at the old Lower Yard. HERO was Cowl's in the 1860s-1880s; on 21st September, 1882 she rescued the crew of the ketch ALBERTA.

The TEAZER was normally housed in the davits opposite the Customs House. In June 1884 at the Padstow regatta, the TEAZER won first prize for working gigs with a Port Isaac crew. There was a heated dispute as to whether the boat or the crew made the difference, and a gentleman offered a £5 prize to the winners of a race over five miles with the Padstow crew in TEAZER, and the Port Isaac men in HERO. The HERO beat the TEAZER by two minutes.

In the June 1886 Padstow regatta there were three gigs, DOVE (Billing, Newquay), TOM SAYERS (Brewer, Port Isaac) and CONSTANCE (Tom Cowl, Padstow): CONSTANCE broke an oar in getting under way at the start. That regatta also included a race for 'Yachts below five tons' including FAIRY (Williams, Newquay) SOUTHENER (sic) (Moore) and NOVELTY (Rawle).

It is worth copying the main events of the Newquay regatta, held on 19th August, 1887 from the published programme:

## NEWQUAY REGATTA 19th AUGUST, 1887

| | | | *Master* | |
|---|---|---|---|---|
| *RACE I* | | Yachts not exceeding 28 ft keel Time allowance 30 seconds per ft | | |
| (1st) | JAMIE | | Mabley | 19'3" |
| | SILVER QUEEN | | H. Brown | 20 |
| (3rd) | FAIRY | | W. Williams | 19 |
| | LILIAN | | N. House | 18 |
| (2nd) | ALARM | | Brabyn | — |
| *RACE II* | | Lug-sail fishing boats | | |
| (2nd) | OCEAN GLEANER | | Bunt | |
| (1st) | PROSPEROUS | | Clemens | |
| | BEATIE | | Hockin | |
| | KATE | | Hoare | |
| | WHITE WINGS | | Billing | |
| | REFORM | | Brown | |
| | TEMPERANCE | | Pappin | |
| | PRIDE OF THE OCEAN | | Pappin | |

Padstow's six-oared gig TEAZER on the jetty next to the operating machinery for the new gate to the inner harbour.

| | *RACE III* | 2nd cl. Fishing Boats, any rig, not exceeding 20 ft keel | |
|---|---|---|---|
| | LIZZIE | | Carter |
| (1st) | MABEL | | Hicks |
| | JUMBO | | Tinney |
| | WILLIE | | Carter |
| | QUEEN | | Matthews |
| | ELIZABETH JANE | | Trebilcock |

| | *RACE IV* | Six-oared Gigs | Coxswain |
|---|---|---|---|
| (2) | TREFFRY | | Prout |
| (1) | DOVE | | Billing |
| (3) | NEWQUAY | | Carter |
| (4) | TEAZER | | Bunt |

*RACE V*        Four-oared Gigs

BESSIE
CLEMENS
and several other boats

*RACE VI*        Gentlemen Visitors Punt Race

*RACE VII*       Gig & Punt Chase — time 20 mins.
Also, swimming matches in the harbour

In the regattas of the 1890s the names CONSTANCE, TEAZER, TREFFRY and DOVE recur in the six-oared gig class. In the first half of the twentieth century, the gigs only played a minor role and almost disappeared, but 1953 saw the start of a great revival led by Roger Gillis and the Newquay rowing club. They went to the Scilly Isles and bought the old SLIPPEN, GOLDEN EAGLE (Bryher) and BONNET (Tresco) and carried out major renovations in Padstow and Newquay. In 1954 these three, together with NEWQUAY, DOVE and TREFFRY, rowed the first six-gig race at Newquay since 1857, and three of the six took part in both races! In 1955 they returned to the Scilly Isles and bought GIPSY (St Agnes), ZELDA (Tresco) and SHAH (St Agnes). Stephen Brabyn and Donald McBirnie, Padstow shipwrights, performed miracles of renovation, and then Tom Chudleigh started building new gigs in St Mary's, including three using the surviving moulds from TREFFRY of 1838, and these new gigs were named ACTIVE, GOOD INTENT, and UNITY, which may be recognised as the names of old Newquay seine companies. By 1988 there were 27 six-oared gigs in Cornwall and the latest, the SPECULATION, of Newquay, also built by Chudleigh, was off to 'Douarnenez 88', the great Exposition of traditional vessels over in Brittany. By 1991, the number of gigs in existence had increased to thirty-nine and the construction of new

Start of ladies' gig race off Newquay, June 1988. The gigs include the WILLIAM PETERS, ROYAL, SPECULATION, ENERGY and GOOD INTENT.                                    *Simon Culliford*

gigs was under way at Padstow itself, with Peter Reveley having built DASHER for Padstow Gig Club, CAPE CORNWALL for Cape Cornwall Pilot Gig Club, and CORSAIR for Port Isaac Gig Club.

List of the 6-oared gigs of Padstow and Outports of which the names have survived:

| Padstow | | Newquay | |
|---|---|---|---|
| ARROW | 19th C. | ACTIVE | 1974 |
| CONSTANCE | 19th C. | BONNET | c.1830 |
| DASHER | 19th C. | DEFIANCE | 19th C. |
| DASHER | 1989 | DOVE | 1820 |
| DAUNTLESS | 19th C. | GIPSY | 1858 |
| GAZELLE | 19th C. | GIRL I LOVE | 19th C. |
| HERO | 19th C. | GOLDEN EAGLE | 1970 |
| PEACE | 19th C. | GOOD INTENT | 1975 |
| RESCUE | 19th C. | NEWQUAY | 1820 or 1812 |
| RIVAL | ? | SHAH | 1873 |
| STORM | 19th C. | SLIPPEN | c.1830 |
| TEAZER | 19th C. | (ex BERNICE) | |
| TEAZER | 1988 | SPECULATION | 1987 |
| VICTOR | 19th C. | TEAZER | 19th C. |
| VICTORIA | 19th C. | (ex ZOE TREFFRY) | |
| VIXEN | 19th C. | TREFFRY | 1838 |
| WARSPITE | 19th C. | UNITY | 1978 |
| | | ZELDA | 19th C. |

| Port Isaac | |
|---|---|
| TOM SAYERS | 19th C. |
| CORSAIR | 19th C. |
| CORSAIR | 1991 |

With unregistered craft as old as these, there is much uncertainty as to who built them and when, and several different versions are given in the books and articles referred to in the Bibliography. The longevity of the old gigs is undoubtedly due to the excellence of the original workmanship, the care with which timber was chosen and seasoned, and the purity of the copper used for fastenings. They have not been pampered; some of the old gigs still being used were carrying out daring rescues in the Scilly Isles a hundred and fifty years ago! On the other hand, some of the recent reconstruction jobs have been very considerable, leaving little of the original structure in place.

The Thames Great River Race is an interesting procession through smooth water. Not all the competitors would agree with that description but the contrast with rowing a triangular course in the open sea off Newquay or even in the Camel estuary off Padstow is startling. Any craft making its way through the water has a life of its own, but to watch these slender gigs, driven by oarsmen or quite often these days oarswomen, snaking their way through the seas, visibly flexing, has a special fascination.

Ladies' Newquay gig championship, 1987. *Ralph Bird Collection*

# 8 REVENUE CUTTERS & SMUGGLERS

THE first serious attempts to establish a seagoing revenue service were made in the reign of Charles II in the second half of the seventeenth century.

Although there were taxes to pay on imported goods, the principal smuggling activity was the export of wool mainly from the eastern counties of England by 'owlers' who were fleecing the Crown by not paying the export duty.

Some of the first detailed references to smuggling are to be found in the Padstow port books, and the following are perhaps worth reproducing in full to show the style of such records.

### PADSTOW GOODS & MERCHANDIZES IMPORTED FROM 26TH DEC. 1710 TO 25TH DEC. 1711.

Jany 20th. In ye MANCELL GALLY of Bristoll Paule Portlock Mr. from Gibraltar 3 casks qt 400 galls Spanish wine, 500 lemons.

March 29th. In ye warehouse, seized by ye officers and admitted to entry, Ord$^t$ of Court of 12th Feby last Geo Robinson & Co M$^d$: 34 Casks Irish Tallow.

May 17. In ye warehouse seized by ye officers in ye REBECCA sloop, condemned in y Exchq$^r$ ... 23rd April last ... Hubbard & Co M$^d$: 320 gallons of French Brandy va 80cw. One Hogshead French Clarret unfilled.

October 19th. In ye WM. & MARY of Milford John Moy M$^r$ from Dublin, Wm. Montgomery M$^d$. Two thousand six hundred Norway Deales.

In ye UNITED HEART of Llanelly Griffith Morrish Mr. from Dublin, Wm. Montgomery M$^d$ 15cw Norway Deales (1,500).

Goods & Merchandizes exported do do Nill

Robt. Quarme
Compt$^r$

---

Padstowe      Entries Inwards      Lady Day Quarter

Feby. 6, 1711. In her maj's warehouse salved out of the ST PEDRO of Bilbao, Matthew Delazama Mr for Cork. Edward Brown M$^d$ 20 Tons Spanish Iron.

Feby. 12th 1711. 10 tons ditto.

Feby. 23rd 1711. The JUST prize 110 (Tons ?) by oath of Peter Swymmer M$^d$.

Feby. 27th 1711. In her maj's warehouse, seized in the SUCCESS and prosecuted h. my. Exchequer del'd by Warr & O. Chambre Corker M$^d$ 3 Hogsheads tobacco q$^t$ 1741 (pounds ?) 4 Hogsheads of ffrench Clarret q$^t$ 183 gallons. At 20 yards freeze, 6 casks brandy q$^t$ 163 gallons .. 4¾ barrell staves.

---

In her maj's warehouse seized in the UNION del'd by warrant & order Symon Trogea M$^d$ 7 Hogsheads ffrench clarret q$^t$ 281 gallons 1 hogshead tobacco, .. 68 gallons clarret & white wine 167 gallons brandy, 32cw candles 1 M. hoops 50cw soap.

Total Entries Inwards Lady Day Qu. 1712
Entries Outwards Ditto Qu. Nil.

That last was an unusually exciting quarter for Padstow including as it does, salvage from a Spanish wreck, the inward arrival of a new prize (probably a Frenchman) followed by the seizure of contraband

in the SUCCESS and the UNION. And all this 'ffrench' brandy coming in during the War of the Spanish Succession which was not ended until the Treaty of Utrecht in 1713.

In the Customs and Excise archives is an unpublished book containing the names and particulars of all the revenue cruisers 1671-1928: it does not include the small yawls and boarding boats, but all larger vessels of which the names survive, are believed to be recorded.

Until the end of the seventeenth century, it was apparently the practice to name many of the revenue cutters after the ports from which they operated: thus in 1674 there is mention of a MARGATE smack, of Margate, a GRAVES END smack and a QUIN-BOROUGH smack. The first mention of Padstow comes in 1698 by which time there were PLYMOUTH, FOWEY, PENZANCE, PADSTOW, ILFRACOMBE and BRISTOL serving in the Westcountry. Most of these vessels, including the PADSTOW, were sloops and her instructions were to cruise from Lands End to Bideford.

No details have survived of her crew and armament, but a few years later such a sloop might have had a master or master-surveyor, ten men and one boy. In 1730 a small sloop carried '6 musquets, 4 pistols, 6 cutlasses and 2 swivels' (i.e. small canon mounted on swivels on the bulwarks).

Fowey, the nearest south-coast port to Padstow, was a hive of activity, and many of the family names of Fowey smugglers, mariners and revenue men tally with those of Padstow. Some of the Padstow port books of the seventeenth century show almost as many Fowey ships as those of Padstow. There was an ancient ferry from Padstow upriver (but helped by the flood tide) to Wadebridge and beyond, leaving little more than a ten-mile walk via the ancient churches and hostelries of Bodmin, before taking a boat down the Fowey river to Foye, as it was often spelt. Doubtless young seamen looking for a ship often took that route, and it seems more than likely that, on occasion, ponies and pack-horses took the same lanes and paths with brandy and baccy. Bodmin could be avoided if necessary by taking a track slightly to the East across the moor, where the descendants of those animals still range far and wide to find grazing today.

William Rawlings of St Columb was a friend and correspondent of Lord Dartmouth, the President of the Board of Trade[1] and in letters of 1765 he describes how one of his servants met at night near Padstow a cavalcade of sixty horses each carrying about one-and-a-half hundredweight of tea. John Knill who was Mayor of Padstow in 1767 was reputed to be a busy free trader.[2] Rawlings described the smuggling from Scilly as notorious, and said that much wine was brought from Lisbon and sold for a little more than half the ordinary price. 'The captains themselves smuggle large quantities and connive at their men doing the same, not allowing them sufficient wages whereon to live without it'. In later correspondence in 1775 he stated that the excise vessel off Padstow, instead of chasing, had been chased into the port by a large Irish vessel which by way of bravado fired seven guns at the mouth of the harbour and hung out a flag in triumph, and then sailed to Newquay where smugglers and excise officers were on excellent terms, to discharge her cargo. It was not uncommon for a hundred horses to be awaiting the arrival of a cargo at Newquay nearly every day of the week.

From C. S. Gilbert's *Historical Survey of the County of Cornwall* 1817 and 1820, we learn that William Rawlings of St Columb, gent. married 16th September, 1755 Catherine Warne and later settled in Padstow, a very successful merchant. One son William became Vicar of Padstow and another, Thomas, succeeded him in the business, married 1783 Margery Price, was High Sheriff 1803, and a most respectable county magistrate and Deputy Lieutenant of the county. Gilbert states bluntly (in 1817) that the commerce of Padstow is in the hands of the Rawlings. By then the commerce was somewhat more respectable, no doubt.

After the PADSTOW already mentioned, the only cruising cutters actually based at Padstow were as follows: SPEEDWELL, 57 tons, a lugger crewed by six men, and declared unfit for service 6th September, 1781 and SHARK, a 'temporary cruiser' spending time at Barnstaple and also Padstow. She was commanded by William Matthews with a mate, eleven men and one boy 1804-'5.

Graham Smith in his book *Smuggling in the Bristol Channel* recalls how, when the SHARK was based in Padstow in March 1805, she captured the Fowey lugger DART off Clovelly, and took her back to Padstow where her cargo of spirits, tobacco and pepper was auctioned. She herself was condemned and taken into the Customs service, being renamed BUSY.

SPEEDWELL was a traditional revenue cutter name; a fine example with that name was built (like many others) by John Gely at Cowes in 1797. Her dimensions were 77 ft 9½ ins length, 57 ft 7 ins on the keel. Beam 25 ft 4 ins, depth of hold 10 ft 9 ins: she was 197 tons and armed with twelve 18-pounder carriage guns and two six-pounders. She was commissioned 9th January, 1798, John Hopkins in command. According to the builders' list she had a crew of sixty, but the Customs records give forty-four and one boy. Her station was at Milford and she patrolled from Holyhead to Lands End, including the Bristol Channel. Her rig was listed as lugger, but when she was sold to the Royal Navy in 1806 she was described as a gun-brig, becoming HMS LINNET; as such she was captured off Madeira on 25th February, 1815 by the French frigate GLOIRE. It is interesting to note that naval records leave no doubt that LINNET was the same vessel as SPEEDWELL, but give her dimensions as 86 ft by 22 ft.

John Hopkins also commanded the STAG which took her place at Milford, then yet another SPEEDWELL in 1813-1815, so he must have visited Padstow over a long period.

After the SPEEDWELL was declared unfit for duty in 1781, it appears that the adjacent stations at St Ives and Ilfracombe were instructed to cover that section of the north coast of Cornwall. The BRILLIANT (30 tons) and DOLPHIN (26 tons) were based at St Ives in 1784, but by 1797 a new DOLPHIN had been built, of 139 tons, 14 guns with a crew of 32 men, and her cruising station was from St Ives to Padstow, around Scilly, and from Lands End to Helford. Nevertheless, the only relevant seizure to be found was by the excise cutter FERRET based at Milford. She captured the Padstow sloop SUCCESS near Ilfracombe in 1789 and found her to be carrying 'over 1,000 lbs of manufactured tobacco and nearly 300 lbs of snuff', all packed in bladders ready for sinking at a prearranged spot off the coast.

In November 1808 'the Padstow cutter SPEEDWELL' rescued the crew of the Quiberon transport INTEGRITY of North Shields as she was driving ashore off Constantine, and piloted in a Hanoverian galliot; it is not known whether SPEEDWELL was a revenue cutter,

but there is no SPEEDWELL in the surviving Padstow ship registers.

Padstow will also have seen the WASP, a 44½ ton cutter with four carriage guns and four swivels and 'small arms in proportion'. Her Master-Surveyors were Robert Adams in 1790, Constantine Philip Henvill in 1793 and James Sarman in 1794, and the rest of her crew consisted of mate, cook and eight men. She patrolled from Scilly to Padstow and Hartland Point and a Letter of Marque was issued to her on 17th February, 1793.

Ilfracombe was a regular station for cutters and the RACER and the RESOLUTION were off the coast in the late eighteenth century, giving way to DOVE, HARPY and HAWKE in the early nineteenth century. When the merchant cutter GAZELLE was registered at Padstow in 1846 she was described as a former revenue cutter, but no earlier name was given, and she was perhaps too small to feature in the surviving revenue lists of the time. GAZELLE had been built at Leith in 1835 and was sold at Padstow on 16th December, 1846 to Richard and John Tredwen. Her personal particulars were 35 ft length, 11.7 ft beam, 6.6 ft depth and she was only 16.5 tons (new measurement). John Reynard was her Padstow master, but the following year she was sold to John Paynter of St Ives, who re-registered her there in 1849.

The last direct connection between revenue cutters and Padstow came in 1863 when John Willmett launched a 'revenue smack' at the Dennis Cove yard. Her name is unknown, and it seems probable she was a small vessel for local use.

It is not surprising that the ships of the smugglers are less well documented than those of the revenue service. Smuggling was perhaps less active on the north coast of Cornwall than the south, as indicated for instance by the records of Roscoff in Brittany which was a prime loading port for brandy and other goods. In 1832 the following arrivals were reported there: from Plymouth 5, Dartmouth 4, Fowey 3, Coverack 3; Cowes, Lizard and Falmouth Road had two apiece. That record was towards the end of a very profitable era of trade. There were even cases of undecked galleys bringing cargoes from France.

But the Isle of Man and some of the Irish ports were also smuggling and distribution centres, and for long periods the vast majority of the population, even including the Royal Navy, saw no justice in huge taxes on such items as liquor, silks and tea, so there was more scope for smuggling on the north coast than appears from merely studying the atlas.

The case of the 50-ton sloop JUBILEE built at Bideford in 1809 may be indicative of the general state of affairs. Her ownership and registration see-sawed between Fowey and Padstow; her owners and masters were members of such famous families as Giles, Pollard, Hawken, Gurney, Carter (King of Prussia Cove) and Webb, and her final registry at Fowey ends with the prosaic note: '1835 Seized for smuggling and broken up at Padstow.'

Lundy Island was a secure base for pirates and smugglers from an early date. Its closest connection with Padstow came in Tudor times, when John Peers of Padstow, a famous pirate, became its uncrowned king for a few years. But it remained an important smuggling depot until towards the end of the eighteenth century.

The Bristol Channel pilot cutters were viewed with great suspicion by the Revenue Service. The pilot cutters went 'seeking' westwards from Bristol, Swansea and Cardiff for weeks at a time, in order to be the first to meet homeward-bound ships and put their pilots on board them. If unsuccessful, the cutters would often put into Padstow for stores, and there were many friendly connections made over the years. Several Bristol pilot cutters were built at Padstow, including the GEM and the VICTOR of 1845, the HENRY and EIRENE both built by R & J Tredwen in 1851, and the SAMUEL and SWIFT, both by John Tredwen Jr in 1860.

The masters of merchant sailing ships were often also the owners or part-owners of their ships, and it was also often the custom that they could carry some cargo on their personal account. The Honourable East-India Company retained its highly professional masters by allowing them the fringe benefit of bringing home goods from the East in their ships; for many years the allowance was up to 20 tons of such goods, and the profits to the captain were often very substantial.

Consider, then, what profitable arrangements could be made between a Bristol pilot cutter backing and filling quite legitimately off Trevose Head and the captain of, say, a homeward-bound Bristol West Indiaman loaded with rum. A pilot is put on board, after which as night falls the cutter makes for Padstow for a night's rest at anchor and to replenish supplies. Off Pentire Point she has the luck to fall in with a Port Isaac inshore fisherman, and picks up some really fresh sea bass. By next morning where should the excisemen start searching? Perhaps some arrangements like that account for the siting and naming of Old Jamaica Inn in the middle of Bodmin Moor.

Tobacco was doubtless obtained in similar ways from the 'plantation traders' of Bristol and Liverpool as they came in through St George's Channel to pick up a pilot.

Well-substantiated stories of smuggling abound in Cornwall, and a good many books have been published on the subject. Those looking for news of Padstow and its outports will be disappointed at the paucity of references.

The cliffs of Morwenstow, and the associated saga of cruel Coppinger, the ruthless pirate and smuggler, are just outside the area covered by this book, and it is just as well as his various dark deeds are as difficult to substantiate as Arthurian legend, despite happening as recently as the late eighteenth century.

Boscastle was said to be a smuggling centre, but I have found no evidence to support the statement. There are many caves and tunnels and headings and old shafts along the coasts near Padstow, but the caves are natural and the man made excavations easily explained by the endless mining activities which started before Phoenician times, and continue in fits and starts even today. On the other hand, there are rumours of an old tunnel from Pentire Glaze farmhouse; and a secluded and amazing cave, almost sealed by a landslide, near Pentire Point is known locally as Coppinger's cave, so who can say?

A REVENUE CUTTER WITH

A LARGE CREW . . .

COULD REDUCE HER RIG

FOR WINTER CRUISING . . .

OR SET A CLOUD OF CANVAS FOR THE DOWN-WIND CHASE

# 9 THE EIGHTEENTH-CENTURY SHIPS

AS I concluded earlier, there were about thirty-seven Padstow ships in 1718, and all that is known about them is included in the alphabetical list of early Padstow ships (Chapter 5).

There then followed a long period, for which there is no surviving official information. *Lloyd's Register of Shipping* was the outcome of a committee formed in 1760, and the oldest surviving edition (very likely the first published) covers the years 1764-'6; but the little ships of remote Padstow are not to be found in the register until the closing years of the century, and even then only two or three of Padstow's larger ships are listed.

It became compulsory for all British ships of over fifteen tons to be registered at their home port custom house in 1786, but none of the eighteenth-century Padstow registers have survived, and many of the first twenty years of the nineteenth century are missing.

Fortunately, we are in a position to set down an accurate list of all the ships on the Padstow register in 1792. The following is taken from an official annual list of every British registered ship that year.

| Year & No. of Reg. | | Name | Tons | 94ths of a ton | Men & Boys |
|---|---|---|---|---|---|
| 1786 | 1 | LIBELLA | 37 | 23 | 3 |
| | 5 | PATSEY | 51 | 47 | 4 |
| | 7 | ENDEAVOUR | 31 | 24 | 3 |
| | 9 | FRIENDSHIP | 31 | 47 | 3 |
| | 10 | PADSTOW | 36 | 47 | 3 |
| | 11 | NEPTUNE (Prize) | 24 | 47 | 2 |
| | 12 | ELIZABETH | 43 | 70 | 3 |
| | 13 | OWNER'S DELIGHT (European Built) | 55 | 74 | 4 |
| | 15 | JOHN & MARY | 44 | — | 3 |
| | 16 | INDUSTRY | 35 | 47 | 3 |
| | 17 | ROBERT & MARY | 35 | 71 | 3 |
| 1787 | 1 | SALLY | 29 | 70 | 3 |
| | 2 | WILLIAM & MARY | 36 | 24 | 3 |
| | 4 | PROVIDENCE | 34 | 47 | 3 |
| | 5 | PEGGY (Prize) | 35 | — | 3 |
| | 10 | POLLY | 35 | — | 3 |
| | 11 | BROTHERS | 41 | 70 | 3 |
| | 12 | CORNISH OAK | 37 | — | 3 |
| | 13 | WILLIAM & MARGARET | 51 | 71 | 4 |
| 1789 | 1 | JENOPHER | 48 | — | 4 |
| 1790 | 2 | EAGLEBUSH | 61 | — | 4 |
| | 3 | MARY | 57 | — | 4 |
| 1791 | 1 | BETSEY | 31 | 70 | 3 |
| | 2 | ST MICHAEL | 24 | — | 3 |
| | 4 | PRINCE EDWARD | 29 | — | 2 |
| | 5 | LYDIA | 34 | — | 3 |
| Total | | 26 SHIPS | 1021 Tons | | 82 |

A number of questions and comments arise from these figures. What happened to the missing numbers, eg. registration numbers 2, 3, 4, 6 and 8 in 1786? Doubtless some were wrecked and others sold to other ports, but some might, for instance, have been lengthened and re-registered at Padstow with revised particulars in 1791. We know from other sources that No.6 of 1787 was PILOT and was sold to St Ives in 1790.

1786 was the first year of the compulsory registration of vessels over 15 tons and some ships did not get back to their home port until 1787, so both these years have an unusually large number of registrations, together covering all extant ships. But we cannot say that Padstow had as many as thirty ships in 1787 because some of the missing numbers of 1786 may have been re-registered in 1787, or lost later in 1786.

The measurement of tonnage was 'builder's measure', later called 'old measure'. Measurement was evidently not particularly accurate either at Padstow or elsewhere. It will be noted that in every case the 94ths of a ton are either 23, 24, 47, 70 or 71, i.e. they are the clerk's interpretation of ¼, ½ or ¾ of a ton, and that applies to the prize 'made free' by the Admiralty as well as the locally measured vessels. Until the compulsory registration came into force in 1786, *Lloyd's Register* only gave the tonnage of ships to the nearest ten tons (or occasionally to the nearest five tons for very small vessels).

The shipwrights of Padstow were certainly not producing a steady stream of new vessels with none listed as registered in 1786, and only one in 1789. They may have been building some fishing vessels which were too small to require registration.

The 'number of men and boys usually employed' is clearly the minimum. Most of the vessels of which we know the rig from other sources were sloops, but the CORNISH OAK was a 37-ton brig with a crew of three! One can picture a small, beamy decked boat with a foremast well forward, carrying a single square sail, and a mainmast with mainsail and main topsail; there was probably no fore and aft canvas. That same list includes small sloops of Bridgetown, Barbados, for example, which 'usually employed' eighteen men; they must have been sailing with warlike intentions.

A similar list has survived for the following year, 1793, with the following changes in the Padstow fleet: OWNER'S DELIGHT, ROBERT & MARY, PROVIDENCE and ST MICHAEL are no longer listed, but the following are added:

| Registered at Padstow | | Name | Tons | 94ths | Men & Boys |
|---|---|---|---|---|---|
| 1792 | 1 | LAMB | 114 | — | 8 |
| | 2 | THREE FRIENDS | 35 | — | 3 |
| | 3 | SALLY | 18 | — | 1 |
| | 4 | APOLLO | 33 | — | 3 |
| | 5 | ANN | 52 | 47 | 4 |
| | 6 | GOOD INTENT | 22 | — | 2 |

The changes resulted in the following totals: 28 ships, 1,086 & 4/94ths tons British built, 59 & 47/94ths tons Prizes, 92 men or boys.

The totals (including prizes) for some other ports were as follows:

| | Ships | Tons |
|---|---|---|
| Aberystwyth | 104 | 3,333 |
| Barnstaple | 80 | 6,773 |
| Beaumaris | 332 | 13,522 |
| Bideford | 57 | 3,756 |
| Bridgwater | 32 | 1,822 |
| Bristol | 307 | 43,851 |
| Cardiff | 22 | 874 |
| Cardigan | 244 | 6,601 |
| Chepstow | 34 | 2,336 |
| Exeter | 157 | 13,444 |
| Falmouth | 48 | 5,004 |
| Fowey | 52 | 2,374 |
| Liverpool | 584 | 92,098 |
| London | 1,861 | 374,223 |
| Looe | 12 | 594 |
| Milford | 103 | 4,078 |
| Padstow | 28 | 1,140 |
| Penzance | 33 | 2,143 |
| Plymouth | 114 | 6,442 |
| St Ives | 34 | 1,751 |
| Scilly | 11 | 267 |
| Swansea | 116 | 6,304 |
| Truro | 10 | 667 |
| Weymouth | 115 | 6,102 |

Liverpool was already twice as important as Bristol in 1793, and London's supremacy was firmly established. It is more surprising to see the large numbers of vessels registered at the Welsh ports. Despite the relatively small size of the Welsh ships, there are nearly 35,000 tons of Welsh shipping listed, as compared with 31,000 in Devon and 14,000 in Cornwall, and that without including Chepstow in Wales.

The abstract of the totals from the 1793 list is as follows:

The number of Padstow ships trading declined from about thirty-seven in 1718 to twenty-six in 1792. The earlier ships averaged about thirty tons burden (or burthen) whereas the twenty-six of 1792 had an average measured tunnage (or tonnage) of thirty-five. Just as today the deadweight tonnage of a ship (the actual weight of cargo, etc.) exceeds the measured gross tonnage, so in the eighteenth century the burthen (the weight of cargo) exceeded the measured tonnage, although it is difficult to say by how much. One might judge that the Padstow ships of 1792 had an average burthen of 50 tons, and therefore a total carrying capacity of 26 x 50 = 1,300 tons, whereas the total capacity in 1718 had been about 37 x 30, say 1,100 tons. The capacity of Padstow's ships had increased by less than a fifth over the period, and that was a much more disappointing performance than appears at first sight, because the same period saw the birth of the industrial revolution along the banks of the River Severn and the Bristol Channel, with a tremendous surge in shipping activity. What little we know about the Padstow ships of the eighteenth century is to be found in:

a) the alphabetical list of early Padstow ships, Chapter 5

b) the official annual lists of 1792 and 1793 already reproduced in this chapter

c) the list of ships that survived into the nineteenth century, in the Appendix.

There are, however, a few additional ships to which references have been found which help to fill the gaps:

BETSY of Porth, John Hughes master, loaded 300 bushels of coal at Great Forrest Canal, Wales, in 1771.

DOVE, of Padstow, Nicholas Diamond master, loaded coal at the mouth of the Kidwelly Canal in 1773.

DUKE OF YORK, of Boscastle, Henry Parnell master, did the same in 1771.

HAWK. In 1744 this 70 tons sloop sailed as a privateer with eight guns and ten swivels. Although Bristol owned, her master Henry Sussex, is believed to have been a Padstonian, and she sailed with a large Padstow crew.

MARY HARRIOTT. In 1770 an entry in St Columb Minor church register refers to Peter and Susanna Clark being drowned from this vessel near New Key.

## 1793 Totals

| | British Built | | European | | Prizes | | Men & Boys Usually Employed |
|---|---|---|---|---|---|---|---|
| | No of Ships | Tons | Ships | Tons | Ships | Tons | |
| England | 10,227 | 1,101,012 | 44 | 15,249 | 362 | 70,349 | 87,569 |
| Jersey | 77 | 5,902 | — | — | 14 | 947 | 728 |
| Guernsey | 90 | 6,334 | 1 | 106 | 6 | 610 | 513 |
| Man | 177 | 4,477 | — | — | — | — | 866 |
| Plantations | 1,568 | 89,724 | 12 | 858 | 165 | 12,734 | 8,380 |
| Scotland | 2,096 | 153.858 | 12 | 2,380 | 35 | 6,036 | 13,401 |
| Ireland | 1,152 | 63,588 | 14 | 2,661 | 27 | 3,318 | 6,730 |
| Total: | 15,337 | 1,424,897 | 83 | 21,254 | 609 | 93,994 | 118,286 |

Grand Total: 16,079 ships, 1,640,145 tons.

**NANCY**, of Padstow, Nicholas Diamond master, loaded coal at Kidwelly Canal in 1771.

**NEWKEY**. A ship of this name was reported to be trading to Ireland in 1774; the master's name was Ley.

**RICHARD**, of Padstow, Simon Peter Palmer master, noted in 1764 that she arrived in Tenby for coal.

**SEAFLOWER**, a Padstow sloop, foundered off Pwll Du (on the Gower coast) on Sunday, 7th July, 1776. Her master, Thomas Retallick, was buried in Oxwich churchyard.

**SUCCESS**. A Padstow sloop of this name was captured by the excise cutter FERRET in 1789.

**TWO SISTERS**, of Padstow, a sloop of 50 tons burthen, George Hawker master, was wrecked near Whitford Point (on the Gower coast) carrying Delabole slates in 1804.

**UNION**, of Padstow, William Billing master, was piloted to Great Forrest Colliery in Wales by Henry Phillips in 1765.

**UNION**. A brig, John Trick master, was captured by the cutter BLACK PRINCE off St Genny's on 23rd July, 1779 when sailing from Boscastle for Bristol. (There is no certainty that she was a Padstow ship).

**WASP**, of Padstow, Stephen Webber master, a privateer, shared in the capture of the PRINCESS OF ORANGE in 1782.

**WILLIAM & JAMES**, of Padstow, Botellick master, was piloted to Great Forrest Colliery in 1766.

The author and his friends have hunted for other Padstow ships of the eighteenth and early nineteenth centuries. He would welcome any additional information.

The end of the eighteenth century found Padstow self-sufficient as ever, but increasingly well-equipped to expand with the British mercantile marine to meet the challenge of the Napoleonic wars, and the trade and commerce which followed. The capacity of the shipyards was about to increase, output from the farms and mines was rising, and the maritime families of North Cornwall produced a rapidly increasing number of enterprising seamen. To talk of Padstow's golden age of sail would be sentimental and misleading, but the real days of sail at Padstow were about to begin.

COLLIER *c.* 1700

WE do not know who built the early ships of North Cornwall. Of the two hundred or so Padstow ships of the sixteenth and seventeenth centuries doubtless some were bought from other ports, and some were prizes, but there is no reason to doubt that these small vessels were largely built locally.

In the eighteenth century, it is suggested elsewhere in this book that Padstow, to some extent, suffered a setback in maritime activity because of the success of the world traders of Bristol, and the coal exporters of Wales. Thus the 'constant coasters' of Bristol and the colliers of Wales could meet the needs of the good people of Padstow in exchange for the local products of mine, quarry and farm more efficiently than the little ships of Padstow of the sixteenth and seventeenth centuries which had to hunt far and wide for the necessities of life.

*Lloyd's Register* of 1776 has been analysed (Goldenberg *The Mariner's Mirror* Nov. 1973) to tabulate the places where all the British built vessels in the register had been built; thus Appledore 6 ships, Barnstaple 17, Bideford 30, Bristol 114, Chepstow 17, etc. Ilfracombe, Falmouth, St Ives and Torbay are also mentioned. At that date, these places built sloops and brigs (and in the case of Bristol, snows and ships) but not a single schooner was recorded. More to the point, there was no mention of Padstow. It could be argued that the very remoteness of Padstow and the small size of her vessels meant that they did not appear in *Lloyd's Register*. To a degree that is doubtless true, but nevertheless the *Register* does, for instance, list nine sloops built at Barnstaple, of only 50 tons average, so it is at least certain that Padstow was not an important shipbuilding centre or there would have been some equivalent entry in *Lloyds*.

Clive Carter provides us with the first named Padstow shipbuilder in his book *Cornish Shipwrecks* when he mentions the brig CORNISH OAK, built at Padstow in 1782 by John Bone, and lost in November 1801 (Boyd, Master).

The *Universal British Directory* for 1798 lists the following as shipwrights of Padstow: Richard Martin, Thomas Pearce, Thomas Pope, R. Tredwin and M. Withell.

In 1804 a survey was made of all the Westcountry shipbuilders to see if they were adequate to meet the Napoleonic threat. Although very few naval vessels were constructed in Cornwall, the yards were deemed adequate to meet the local demand for merchant vessels. The survey referred to the following as being shipbuilders of Padstow: M. Withel, John Williams, John Brabyn, Thomas Pearce, G. Sloggett, G. Rame, John Tredwyn. Thereafter the newspapers and the ship registers between them provide the names of the builders of almost all the ships built at Padstow (and later at some of the outports), and allow the construction of the yard lists given in this chapter.

The Tredwen family (spelt Tredwyn above, and Tredwin occasionally) must be the greatest shipbuilding clan Padstow has ever possessed, and because the exact site of their yards is known, they are a good starting point round which to sketch the overall picture. First, to dispose of a distraction let it be said that, so far as is known, there is no close connection with Richard Tredwen, the Cardiff shipbuilder who had a yard on the Glamorgan Canal and built nearly twenty sloops, schooners and brigantines between 1830 and his death in 1857. It is quite likely that he came from Chepstow

where, in 1819, the brig MARY was built by one Purchas and one Tredwen. But is it mere coincidence that the MARY was built for Neville Norway, the well-known Padstow merchant and shipowner, and remained in the Padstow register until sold to London in 1830?

John Tredwen was one of the Padstow shipbuilders in 1804 and although missing ship registers prevent us from knowing his output until 1812, he was thereafter the most prolific and successful Padstow builder, being responsible for at least fifty vessels by 1845. It seems highly likely that he built the AGNES in 1809, the first schooner built at Padstow; he certainly built the second, SUSAN in 1813. By 1835 he was constructing his comprehensive ship yard and ship repair facilities when, for some reason, a legal action was brought against him holding that he was encroaching on the rights of the Admiralty by carrying out construction 'below the low water mark'. He went to London (a considerable expedition) and eventually was fully vindicated, indeed praised by the Admiralty and encouraged to complete his designs. Padstow gave him a tremendous welcome on his homecoming with the firing of guns and the ringing of bells: we are not told whether or not the 'Obby Oss' took part in the celebrations.

In 1839, the Admiralty Hydrographer carried out a survey of Padstow and its approaches, and a large continuous stretch of foreshore and land upstream of the small Padstow basin, as it then was, is labelled 'Mr Tredwen's Freehold'. The plans show much more construction of docks and quays on Tredwen's land than for the whole of the rest of Padstow.

He, John Tredwen, went from strength to strength with his yard producing famous sloops, smacks, cutters, dandies, schooners, polacres and brigs. Typical of the newspaper reports of the time is the following in the *West Briton*, 14th June, 1839:

On Wednesday last, the schooner *Falmouth Packet*, Peter Christian master, was launched from one of Mr Tredwen's slips into his extensive ship-dock at Padstow, after being lengthened 10 ft in the midships and altered from a cutter to a Schooner. She is copper to the bends, and fitted out as a yacht, the expense not being limited. Wm. Glasgow Esq. of Green Bank, Falmouth, is the owner and she is intended for the fruit trade, in his own account.

or the following from *Mitchell's Maritime Register*, (referring to his son's work):

*Padstow 22nd June, 1857* — Launched this evening from the building yard of Mr John Tredwen a fine schooner of about 180 tons burthen named the FLORENCE NIGHTINGALE, the property of Messrs. Hooper of Newquay and intended for the coasting trade. Also at the same time from the same yard, a ketch-rigged vessel of about 200 tons burthen named SUNSHINE, the property of the builder and likewise intended for the coasting trade.

It seems that the last vessel attributed to John Tredwen Sr was the Bristol pilot cutter GEM completed in 1845, perhaps for the Gilmore family of Pill who certainly owned her later. Meanwhile in 1841 Richard Tredwen appears on the scene as the builder of the sloop TEMPERANCE and in 1843, R. & J. Tredwen (that is Richard and John Jr) take over the running of the whole yard.

The FLORENCE NIGHTINGALE
leaving Venice. Commander T. Teague
*Newquay Old Cornwall Society*

Richard built up a tremendous reputation, both for his gallant personal participation in life-saving work, and for his skill in salvaging ships which others expected to be abandoned. Here is a list of some of his achievements:

1833. Salvaged the FLORA and took her to Padstow for repair.
1834. The sloop MARY ANN of Padstow (Carter, Master) went ashore on rocks in the Gannel estuary. Tredwen got her off and into Padstow.
1836. Tredwen raised the schooner CATHERINE which had sunk at the entrance to Falmouth, and towed her to St Mawes.
1843. The brig TOWAN of Cork was disabled off Padstow, and Richard Tredwen boarded her and beached her successfully (for this he was awarded a medal by the Royal Humane Society).
1845. He rescued the sole survivor from the wreck of the snow WILLIAM PITT at Padstow as she was being pounded to pieces on the Doom Bar.
1848. The MARCHIONESS OF ABERCORN (a barque built in Quebec in 1837) went ashore off Crantock beach. Tredwen got her off, bought and repaired her, and in August she sailed from Padstow with emigrants to Quebec, Padstow's largest ship up to that time (875 tons, new measure).
1848, also. Salvage of the brig AMETHYST at Porthcothan.
1850. Salvage of the OCEAN at Mawgan Porth.
1854. Saved the crew of the schooner SARAH from the Doom Bar in his shipyard gig. The schooner's anchors had dragged and eventually her cables parted and she was being driven into the surf to become a total wreck.

He was described as a gallant, scientific gentleman.
In 1853 his name disappeared from the shipbuilding firm, but the construction of ships continued undiminished under the banner of John Tredwen Jr until 1871.
In the *West Briton* of 13th July, 1860 appeared the following advertisement:

*To be let*: all those very extensive Shipbuilding Yards, Graving Dock, Timber Ponds, & Premises erected and occupied by the late Mr Tredwen, and now in the occupation of Mr John Tredwen. The premises are 5 acres in extent, with a river frontage of upwards of 1000 ft, and comprise three building yards, capable of building five vessels; a wet and dry dock of over 300 ft x 120 ft for repairing vessels; and two extensive timber ponds, the whole bounded by massive stone walls with 30 ft entrance gates. The premises are replete with every convenience (for continuing trades of shipbuilding and repairing, boat-building, sailmaking, block-making, smithery, cooperage and timber, coal, lime and iron trades). There are large sheds for the protection of workmen in inclement weather, boat loft, sail loft, rigging loft, and store-room, cooper's shop, block shop, four-forge smith shop, large iron cellar, nail cellar, paint cellar, tar cellar, and pitch house, a roomy office overlooking the premises, a commodious dwelling house of nine rooms besides scullery, pantry and dairy, a stable, gig house, barn, straw house, laundry, beer cellar, wash house, pump, stone tank, greenhouse, flower garden, two walled gardens, and about an acre of the very best land. On these premises has been carried on a very extensive and lucrative business, (established for the past 70 years) and offers a rare opportunity for a spirited builder. Application may be made to Mr Richard Tredwen, the Proprietor, Trevone, Padstow.

John (Jr) seems to have remained the 'spirited builder' for another eleven years, although the number of new ships completed which reached a peak of seven in 1860, tailed off to about two per annum from 1866 to 1871.
The advertisement gives an excellent account of the facilities required for wooden shipbuilding in the nineteenth century, although it does not deign to mention the saw pits, nor was the neighbouring rope-walk included.
The advertisement also indicates that the business started in 1790, although that may have been the date of the first shipbuilding on the site by some earlier proprietor.
Most of the Padstow shipbuilders were also ship owners and none more than the Tredwen family who over the years had an interest (and generally a substantial interest) in at least seventy-eight ships. They can be placed in various categories: some were built on speculation and sold later, some were retained in ownership until the client could pay for them, others as has been indicated already, came into ownership as the result of being salvaged and repaired; but the family also acted as ship owners independent of their building and repairing activities. They had an eye for a ship and a nose for a trade, and, for instance, were quick to buy up old North American-

built ships of large capacity when the Cornish mines went into recession and emigration became the order of the day.

Martin Withell (or Withiell), first noted in 1798, built the brig BRITANNIA in 1803, and four ships including a brig by 1820, and doubtless others not attributed to him in these early years. He is last heard of in Piggott's Directory of 1823, in which he and the other pioneer shipbuilder George Sloggett, are both listed with the address 'South Quay'. That is to say, they were sandwiched between the Tredwen property and that small basin which comprised the port of Padstow at the time and is now the enclosed inner basin. George Sloggett built the sloop ANNE in 1809, followed by nine other sloops, and then was followed by his son John Sloggett in 1834, who built three more sloops, ending with BOSCASTLE in 1838. John Brewer built a couple of sloops in the 1830s and Thomas Withiell (a generation after the activities of Martin) three more. These minor builders ought perhaps be classified as shipwrights with an ability to build a small ship when opportunity offered.

In 1830, Thomas Carter started his shipbuilding career by launching the CHARLES PHILLIPS sloop and thereafter he launched a ship a year until 1849, and then two more in 1854. He was followed by John Carter and then Edwin Carter, their last vessel being the schooner TREBISKIN in 1859. The Carters mostly built sloops, smacks and luggers with an occasional schooner. On the 1839 Hydrographer's plan, 'Mr Carter's Shipyard' is marked downstream of Padstow, in the location later known as the Lower Yard. The plan also shows 'The Quarry Boatyard' between Carter's and Padstow. The following extract from *Mitchell's Maritime Register* gives the flavour of the times:

*11th March, 1857.* There was launched from the yard of Mr Carter this evening a fine schooner of about 180 tons burthen named GAZELLE, the property of Messrs Dusting & Co. of Penzance and intended for the Mediterranean trade under the command of Captain Thomas Dusting.

At Dinas Cove, upstream of Mr Tredwen's Freehold, it was possible to launch a ship into a 'pool' of deeper water clear of the Town Bar and to lay out a slip in the cove which enabled larger ships to be built. Here, in 1855, shipowner F. H. Thomas made history, as recorded in the *Royal Cornwall Gazette*, by launching the only full-rigged ship to be built at Padstow.

PADSTOW, *31st August* — Last evening Mr F. H. Thomas launched from Dinas Cove in this port, a very fine vessel of about 800 tons burthen, named the *Morning Star*. Preparations had been made to launch her on the evening of the 29th, but owing to some defect in her ways, and the subsidence of a portion of the ground underneath, she refused to move. These defects having been remedied, the launch was successfully accomplished last evening at a few minutes after six o'clock. This vessel is believed, with, it may be, one or two exceptions, to be the largest ever built in Cornwall, and we think her model will prove to be a triumph in the science of shipbuilding very gratifying to her builder, who has not previously had any connection with the business, but who laid down the vessel for himself and a respectable body of co-owners. She is 150 ft long over all, her beam 21½ ft, fore-rake 9 ft with a very beautiful bow and stern — the latter elliptic. Internally the stern is sharper than the bow, and from the great length and beautiful water line, it is confidently anticipated that she will sail very fast. The draughts etc. are the joint work of Mr Thomas and his foreman builder, Mr John Cowl, who has most zealously carried on the work to a successful issue. The good feelings of the inhabitants were shown in a most unmistakeable manner; and on ascertaining that the vessel could not be moved on Wednesday evening, Mr Carter and Mr S. Bennett, ship-builders, both sent their men, and gave their own assistance in

making the necessary arrangements for launching last evening. After the vessel was hauled into dock, an excellent supper was set out in a loft in Mr Thomas' premises, where 100 persons sat down, and enjoyed themselves; and under cover of the shed below, 50 of the youngsters sat down to a similar treat. After supper was over, and the room cleared, music was called in, and dancing kept up with spirit for several hours. We trust this beautiful vessel will not disappoint the expectations of the owners, and that she will prove a source of both profit and pleasure to them.

Mr Thomas must have been a most persuasive entrepreneur to convince the hard-headed investors of Padstow to join him in this venture, but he pulled it off and, as well as acting as her managing owner for world-wide trade, he built six smaller vessels in the following four years. Later he became Lloyd's surveyor at Falmouth.

In 1861 John Henry Willmett (sometimes Willmott) started shipbuilding, and the following year John Stribley. There is conflicting evidence as to where exactly they built their ships. By then the Carters had stopped building at the lower yard, and the small vessels Willmett and Stribley built until 1864 could have been built there. Several ships were credited to Stribley in the ship registers but to Willmett in the surveyor's reports, which supports the idea that they shared one yard for a time.

In 1863 James Willmett took over the firm and at the Dennis Cove yard where Thomas had built the full-rigged ship MORNING STAR a decade before, he built three schooners and then, in 1865, the large and most unusual barque POMARON, built to Henzell's patent and to Lloyd's special survey. Her history is given in a separate chapter. At the time it was put about that other similar ships were to follow, but in July 1865 Willmett was declared bankrupt, and in the following two years W. F. Willmett built three small ships in the Dennis Cove yard, presumably carrying on the business, of which no more is heard thereafter.

John Stribley continued strongly until 1876, building a whole string of schooners and barkentines — such as the EMPRESS OF CHINA who left her bones in Australia. He was followed briefly by William Stribley whose last ship was the three-masted schooner JULIA in 1879. His assets were sold after his death that same year.

Meanwhile, by 1873, John Cowl (who had helped Thomas design and build MORNING STAR back in 1855) had established himself at the lower yard which proceeded to produce a dozen schooners and half-a-dozen smaller craft. William Cowl was said to be the chief carver of figureheads for Padstow built ships through this busy period. John himself died in December 1882, but the firm carried on as John Cowl and Sons. By that time the building of wooden merchant sailing ships in the Westcountry was coming to an end, and the *Royal Cornwall Gazette* on 1st April, 1885 advertised for sale John Cowl's shipyard and one partly built vessel. The firm carried on with the same name, completing the last two-masted schooner built at Padstow, the AMARANTH in 1886 and surviving as a repair yard capable of building small craft. The slip was still usable after the Second World War.

Captain Charles Rawle came late to shipbuilding, setting himself up at the Higher Yard (no longer known as 'Mr Tredwen's Freehold') in 1874. Rawle also had the Dennis Lane rope walk which was conveniently sited close to his yard. John Harvey ran the other Padstow rope walk which was by the mill pool behind the churchyard. Both were marked clearly on the Admiralty survey of 1839. Rawle's yard turned out a series of lovely schooners including MARY WATERS, FAIRY KING and PRIDE OF THE WEST, and the larger barkentine ROSALIE (later named JEANNE and then PIERRETTE). But the end was in sight; in 1889 he completed the

PRIDE OF THE SOUTH shows off the lovely lines of Rawle's later schooners
somewhere in the Low Countries. *c.* 1900. She is dressed overall for some long-
forgotten event.          *National Maritime Museum*

three-masted schooner MILDRED, the last sailing vessel of any size
built at Padstow, and of course the construction of the Wadebridge
to Padstow railway was to start not long afterwards, which meant
the demolition of all the shipyards except the lower yard (John
Cowl & Sons) and an old deserted slip downstream at St George's
Well (where the schooner THOMAS & ELIZABETH had been
built in 1842).

The activities of the Bennett and the Brewer families, and of one
or two other families, will be found in the Yard Lists in Chapter 10.
Looking at these lists one is struck by the importance of family life
in Padstow shipbuilding. Scarcely a shipbuilder is named without his
son or his brother succeeding him.

According to many people Padstow was not the most salubrious
of towns; indeed the following excerpt is taken from the report of
an inspector of the Board of Health dated 1851:

The town is without sewerage, very damp, at times ill-supplied with
water — an unusually large proportion of the houses are without
conveniences and there are pig-sties in many of the most crowded back
premises. Some of the houses are built under a steep hillside or cliff,
others are within reach of occasional flood tides, and others are built
upon the margin of a mill leat, the waters of which being contaminated
with sewage, are offensive and unhealthy.

And the work in the shipyards, blacksmiths shops, rope walks and
in the surrounding farms, mines and quarries was hard and
unremitting, but down on the waterfront the tides cleansed the
foreshore twice a day, the sailing ships arrived from and set out for
endless destinations, and there was the buzz of the sawyers at work
and the noise of the caulking mallets, and the distinctive smell of
timber and tar. The craftsmen of Padstow must have been strongly
wedded to the building of wooden sailing ships. Working in wood
is a highly skilled and satisfying craft. They imported the best timber
from all over North America and Europe, and kept going long after
many others had changed to iron and steel. John Brabyn was one of
the shipbuilders named in the survey of 1804; Stephen Brabyn was
the shipwright who carried out the extremely skilful task of
renovating the Cornish six-oared pilot gigs for Newquay and
Padstow over 150 years later.

## Shipbuilding in Padstow's Outports

In the great surge of shipbuilding in Britain in the mid-nineteenth
century, wooden ships were being built and launched in endless tiny
nooks and crannies around the Westcountry, and the outports of
Padstow were no exception. The yards close to Newquay were the

most prolific, providing more than forty vessels from smacks to schooners between 1840 and 1880.

There were four shipyards in or near Newquay and their locations are shown on the sketch map on p.68. Since the Clemens family built more ships than any other, and worked at three of the four yards, the story of shipbuilding at Newquay can be told by building it around their activities.

In 1838 Thomas Clemens, who had been an apprentice shipwright at Padstow, laid out a small yard two miles up the River Gannel, near Tregunnel. The following year he launched the cutter CAROLINE and the sloop JOHN & MARY. The river was narrow near the site of the yard, reducing to a small stream at low water. Accordingly it was necessary to launch the ships broadside on at high water spring tides. In 1842 he completed the schooner LADY OF THE LAKE, and in 1851 he lengthened the schooner LIBERTY which had been built at Ilfracombe in 1838.

Meanwhile, at Newquay harbour itself the South Pier had been built in 1832, and when Squire Treffry further improved the harbour and repaired the North Pier in 1841, it became possible to repair and build ships at what was called the Quay Yard in sheltered conditions within the harbour. Thomas Clemens' two sons, John and Martin, had charge of the yard and in 1849 completed their first vessel, the schooner TREFFRY, doubtless named after the industrialist who had made the yard possible. She was followed in 1851 by the schooner TOWER, and that same year they carried out major repairs to the smack MARYS & HELENA. The following year they built the smack GEM, and in 1854 the schooner KATE. Two years later, after completing the schooner ELIZABETH JANE, they vacated the Quay Yard and laid out a new berth at what became known as the

Island Cove Yard. This was perched up on a bank which had been formed over the years by ships discharging their ballast in the shelter of the Island off Killacourt. There, in 1856, they started building the schooner TREGUNNEL, but almost immediately she suffered gale damage, so they moved her to their father's old yard at Gannel and completed her in 1858.

John Clemens then took over the Gannel yard, and with Richard Clemens built the EMMA JANE. He next built three schooners solely in his own name before handing over the business to his two sons, Thomas and John, who built a dozen schooners between 1867 and 1879, and finally the ketch TRIUMPH in 1881. To complete the story of the Gannel yard, it continued to produce some small craft, and in 1907 T. Clemens built the 7-ton auxiliary yacht POPPY with a paraffin motor for a Paignton owner.

Meanwhile from 1857 until 1860, the Quay yard had been taken over by one Richard Tredwin of Eothen and formerly of Cardiff. The Cardiff shipbuilder of that name is reported to have died in 1857[1] so perhaps this was a son of the same name. Martin Clemens returned to the yard in 1860 and mainly kept busy with repair work on ships in the harbour; but in 1865 he built the schooner KITTIE for Richard Martyn Clemens, and in 1867 the FOREST DEER, for W. Hicks, J. Solomon and others. Later, Martin moved to Fowey and T. and J. Clemens operated from the Quay yard but no further ships were built. Eventually John also left for Fowey, leaving Thomas to carry on with his sons Albert and Richard.

At Porth, over a mile northeast of Newquay harbour, there was a place suitable for building ships in a sheltered corner of the beach where the stream runs down to the sea. Here in 1818, W. Withell built the 44 ft long sloop PORTH. It was not until 1857 that

The tiller-steered TREGUNNEL waiting for a loading berth at Newquay, c. 1895. Her topsail yard is braced tight around and her lower yard is cockbilled ready to lay alongside.
*National Maritime Museum*

The schooner LOUISE being prepared for her
launch into the Gannel in February 1877.
*Terry Belt Collection*

LOUISE in 1947, abandoned near Falmouth.
*National Maritime Museum*

This primitive representation of the schooner GLENDORGAL might be thought to exaggerate her clipper lines, but comparison with the photograph of the PRIDE OF THE SOUTH proves that neither sheer nor rig need have been accentuated.
*Royal Institution of Cornwall*

Martyn & Lewarne built the next ship at Porth, the schooner GLENDORGAL followed by the smack LITTLE JANE in 1858.

Joseph Osborne, shipwright, re-opened the Island Cove yard in 1868 and built the small smacks RESOLUTION and VIXEN, and in 1871 the schooner CONQUEST. His final launching there in 1872 was notable: the steam launch JANE was the only steam vessel ever built in Padstow or the outports, and the last vessel built at Island Cove. Osborne then moved to Porth and built the smacks AGNES LOUISA in 1875 and another PORTH in 1877. In 1880 he completed the schooner LADY JANE and the yard closed down.

At Port Isaac, Port Gaverne and Boscastle, all ancient settlements, it seems certain that ships were built in small numbers in the very early days, but no records remain. However, details are fairly complete for the nineteenth century and Port Isaac and Port Gaverne together built nine small vessels, and Boscastle another eight or so, but three of them too small to be registered. Port Isaac and Port Gaverne were dominated by Warwick R. Guy, who owned the shipyards and most of the ships.

Bude, or Bewd, featured in the Padstow port books of 1616 and trade over the bar to the river mouth was carried on with great difficulty. Only one ship is recorded as built at Bude before the canal and harbour works started in 1819, and that was the brig MARY completed by William Barrow in 1813. Thereafter trade increased, and shipbuilding recommenced in 1826 when Thomas Bound launched the sloop FRIENDS three years after the opening of the Bude canal. Being of 26 registered tons, her burthen was probably about 50 tons, the same as the canal barges which may well have occupied the same building berth. Although Bude was an outport of Padstow only until 1850, the full list of ships built at Bude is given in the yard list up to 1904 so that the full career of Stapleton's yard there is covered.

Ward Jackson wrote in his excellent book about Fowey[2] of rather more than 1,000 vessels with Cornish connections in the Mercantile Navy List 1879. 129 are shown as having been built in Fowey: next come Falmouth and Padstow with 119 apiece. If, however, one adds the ships built in outports, it is clear that port of registry Padstow came from behind in the race to build wooden ships in the nineteenth century and became the biggest shipbuilding centre in the county, and the Tredwen family who built about 130 ships between 1812 and 1871 deserve the lion's share of the credit.

A balanced account of nineteenth-century shipbuilding in Cornwall is available from The Cornwall Maritime Museum database. The following table shows the number and tonnage of ships built in selected two year periods within the three principal shipbuilding ports of registry.

|          | 1825-'26 | 1855-'56 | 1875-'76 |
|----------|----------|----------|----------|
| Fowey    | 30/2,586 | 2/222    | 5/839    |
| Padstow  | 9/410    | 15/1,776 | 12/1,356 |
| Falmouth | 2/105    | 2/137    | 17/1,860 |

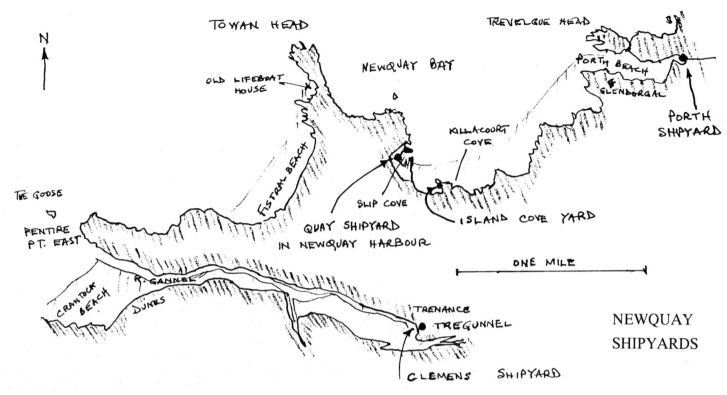

The ketch THOMASINE & MARY, wrecked in 1926. She was one of only half a dozen ships built at Boscastle and she carried the tall topmast popular in North Cornish ketches to the bitter end.

*Royal Institution of Cornwall*

The schooner CORNISH LASS wrecked off St Agnes, 6th January, 1896. There was a later CORNISH LASS, a ketch built at Penryn, which served the Benedictine monks on Caldy Island for many years.
*Royal Institution of Cornwall*

In 1825 Fowey and its strong outports built on their capacity which had been built up during the Napoleonic wars. In the 1850s, Padstow, thanks to the drive and enterprise of John Tredwen who had created a large-scale modern wooden shipbuilding centre, took a surprising lead, but by 1875 Falmouth was already showing the ability to survive as wooden shipbuilding tailed off. Ten years later, wooden shipbuilding in Cornwall had virtually ceased, but the construction of small iron and later steel ships at Falmouth kept the wolf from the door well into the twentieth century.

## The Twentieth Century

In the first half of the twentieth century there was virtually nothing but repair work and a little boat building at Padstow. Cowl had the lower yard for a time and Bill Lindsey carried on some boat building also near the brick building. When he built the 25 ft motor boat SAINT SAVIOURS in 1952 for service as the ferry to Rock, he completed the first British registered ship built at Padstow since 1904. But the renaissance came slowly and unexpectedly. In 1964 Derek Kelsall and Pat Patterson started designing and building trimarans at Wadebridge as the Multi-Hull Construction Co. Ltd. They had very considerable success and more will be found about these remarkable vessels in the chapter on yachts.

In 1973 the small motor fishing vessel SALLY ALLSORTS was built and her entry in the Mercantile Navy List is as follows:

| | |
|---|---|
| *Official No.* | 362398 |
| *Name* | SALLY ALLSORTS |
| *Type* | Motor Fishing Vessel |
| *Port & Year of Registry* | Falmouth, 1974 |
| *Where & when built* | Bodmin, 1973 |
| *Material* | Steel. Reg. tonnage 13 net, 19 gross |
| *Owner* | Vickers Oceanics Ltd P.O. Box 6 Barrow Shipbuilding Works Barrow-in-Furness, Cumbria |

So Bodmin may not be a port, but it is in the hinterland of Padstow, and is the site of the building of the first British registered steel ship ever built in the hinterland!

Steel shipbuilding really got under way when Brian Chapman built his JUBILEE QUEEN at Wadebridge in 1977. Here was a motor vessel of 99 gross tons with a certificate for 254 passengers. Furthermore, her building demonstrated that small welded steel ships could be built efficiently without the back-up of a large shipyard. Shipbuilding is an assembly job and now more than ever, most of the expenditure goes into engines, ground tackle, life saving equipment, radar, radio, navigation equipment, etc., none of which need be made in or near the shipyard.

There was a lengthy gap between the building of JUBILEE QUEEN in 1977 and the real start of systematic steel shipbuilding.

The AMANDA off Newquay during the First World War. She is apparently lying to a light anchor with sails set. Judging by the people on her foredeck, this might be for a family occasion; that would be in keeping with what we know of her long life.
*National Maritime Museum*

A & J Marine of Padstow completed the steel motor fishing vessel GIRL DEBRA in 1989. She cannot be described as beautiful in the traditional sense: she was designed by Denis Swire as a 'rule-beater' with the object of being as large and powerful as possible, but with a registered length of less than 10 metres, thereby acquiring greater freedom under EEC regulations. Her dimensions are 38.5 ft overall x 17 ft beam x 8 ft draught, figures which look more appropriate for a Roman grain ship than a modern fishing vessel! She has a bulbous bow, and a 300 h.p. Volvo diesel engine driving a propeller inside a Kort nozzle for greater propulsive efficiency. She was built for skipper David Driver of Seaton, which gives her Exeter registry and the fishing number E 444. Her launch was recognised as a great occasion at Padstow. The three-masted schooner MILDRED had been completed in 1889 and GIRL DEBRA, in 1989, was the largest ship built at Padstow for 100 years, with a launching displacement of 38 tons. She was immediately followed in 1990 by the near sister ALIZE, BM 127, built for Brixham owners and rigged as a 'mini beam trawler'. Her dimensions were similar, but she had a 300 h.p. Cummins oil engine. The third vessel of the class, BOY DOMINIC, H 11, was also completed in 1990 for owners at Hull.

In 1991 A & J Marine completed their fourth ship, the beam trawler STEPHANIE B, FD 78, for Fleetwood owner Brian Bond. She is a larger vessel, 14 metres long overall and with a waterline length of 12.9 metres x 5.95 beam x 3.43 moulded depth. She measured over 51 tons displacement at launch and 65 tons on departure.

It is to be hoped that this successful series of steel ships marks the secure re-establishment of shipbuilding at Padstow.

Meanwhile at Rock and Wadebridge, there had been rapid development of moulded Glass Reinforced Plastic (GRP) boats. One of the complications of this method of construction is to decide where the vessel was built. For instance, in 1970 the GRP aux. yacht DE MARNI had her hull moulded at Topsham, but building and fitting out was completed at Rock. The motor crabber GIRL RACHEL has Plymouth Rock after her name, not because she was made out of that particular material, but because her hull was made at Plymouth by Skentelbery, but she was completed by G. B. Smith & Son of Rock, who build boats there under cover up to 44 ft long.

Two firms at Wadebridge have emerged in particular as leading builders of small GRP fishing vessels, Port Isaac Workboats and Chapman & Hewitt. Since 1987 they have produced an increasing number of boats large enough to appear in *Olsen's Almanack*, and therefore in the yard lists which follow this chapter. Both firms are selling boats not only all around Great Britain, but also on the Continent. A typical recent completion was the RIPTIDE, J 145. Built by Port Isaac Workboats for Jerseyman Norman Renouf, she has an offshore 125 moulded GRP hull, length overall 42 ft x 16 ft 6 ins x 3 ft 3 ins draught, displacement 10 tonnes, and twin Iveco diesel engines each 350 h.p. giving 24 knots. She works 1000 lobster pots twenty-five miles south-west of Jersey and is also netting for cray fish and turbot. She has a galley, six berths, a colour sounder, two Decca navigators, three VHF radios and a Cellnet telephone. To those who are old enough to remember, she looks like a small motor torpedo boat!

On the yachting front, an interesting company was formed in Wadebridge in 1980. Oceancraft, run by Les Savage, built the

A revival of shipbuilding at Padstow:
GIRL DEBRA E444 in June 1989.

Ebbtide range of steel ocean-going cruising yachts designed by Alan Pape. Les Savage's greatest difficulty was to show a potential customer a completed boat — they were almost invariably in distant waters. He moved the operation to Malpas on the Truro River in about 1985.

Cornish Crabbers Ltd have become well established at Rock and Pityme and there always seem to be some of their boats on moorings or on the move at Rock. They are in effect GRP replicas of the traditional Cornish gaff cutter rigged crabber, but the modern construction is much lighter and they are constructed as shallow draught hulls with centreboards. The 29-ft long crabber has a draught of only 2 ft 5ins but increases to 4 ft 8 ins with the centreboard down. This makes her very handy for estuarial cruising although clearly she is capable of much more ambitious voyaging. The development of the firm was rapid. A group of enthusiasts formed Westerly Boats Ltd at Rock in 1960. They built brilliant racing dinghies, sailed them brilliantly, ran a sailing school, and hired out boats, and by 1967 were successful enough to move to Pityme and start production of crabbers and also various other classes on a substantial scale.

North Cornwall Marine were advertising the Tamarisk '24' traditional gaff rigged cutter, and subsequently the Tamarisk '29' on somewhat similar lines in the late 1970s. Their address was St Columb Industrial Estate. Offshore Marine (SW) of Camelford supply GRP hulls of various kinds.

The GRP age has, on the face of it, thrust additional responsibilities onto naval architects, especially in hull design. In the past a boat builder or naval architect could learn gradually by experience how to improve his designs, but now, once the die is cast, once the mould has been made, any mistake will be reproduced in any number of sister ships. If the penalties of failure have increased, one hopes that the benefits of success are also greater. A high

proportion of recent Padstow fishing vessels have been designed by the Cornish naval architect Garry Mitchell. By the end of 1991 he was credited with having about 1,500 fibreglass vessels moulded to his designs, and he has developed an international reputation. One of his recent involvements has been in the major rebuilding of the whole of Iran's fishing fleets.

It may be that his success has less to do with theory and test tanks (neither of which I'm sure he despises) than with his upbringing in the Mitchell family, with his father Percy, the master builder at Portmellon, who built over three hundred wooden boats in his career including VIKING (25 ft), ST ENODOC (21 ft), SHELDUCK (15 ft), KINGFISHER (15 ft), CURLEW (15 ft), WINNIE (26 ft), KITTIWAKE (15 ft), MELODY (20 ft), I & N (21 ft), LADY MARY (28.5 ft), CHOUGH (22 ft) BUCCANEER (40 ft), SUPERB (21 ft), and three un-named ferries (two at 22 ft, one at 32 ft) all for Padstow and outports, and the CORNISH QUEEN (40 ft) which came to Padstow after a spell at St Ives. A few of these craft are dealt with elsewhere in this book as they are British registered ships. Others are small fishing vessels, excursion vessels and 'toshers', that is mackerel boats about 20 ft long with a cuddy and a protected steering position forward, a large working well with the engine or engines under a wooden casing amidships, and a mizen aft.

But boats and boat building cannot be dealt with in any detail in this book. The pilot gigs are a noble exception and merit a separate chapter. The immemorial oyster dredgers of the River Fal deserve a mention, and here is the place for it. They claim to be the world's last fleet of oyster dredgers working under sail alone, and they do so to keep the local byelaw which is designed to avoid over fishing. The summer races of so-called Falmouth working boats are largely between boats which no longer dredge, but behind the scenes there is a work-a-day fleet kept for the actual dredging.

The three-masted schooner JULIA lost with all hands in 1931, engineless to
the last.                                    *David Clement Collection*

SCHOONER-RIGGED CAMEL BARGE
showing attachment of mainsheet to sternpost,
leaving tiller unobstructed

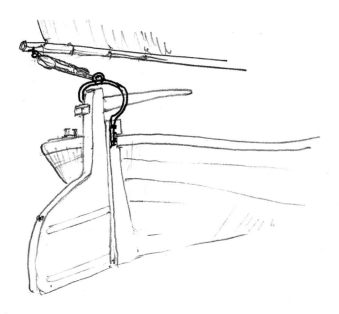

There are two reasons for looking at this fleet. In the first place,
one of the boatbuilders who contributed most to the fleet of
beautiful gaff cutters was one Stephen Brabyn whose yard was in
Calenick Creek off the Fal. He built cutters from 1890 to about
1905, and he also built Edward Allcard's famous transatlantic yacht
TEMPTRESS. Many times in preparing this book I have been
surprised by coincidences, only to find that they are not
coincidences, but family connections. Can it be that the Brabyn
family whose ship and boatbuilding at Padstow has already been
mentioned also operated at Calenick? Incidentally, another branch
worked at Looe — or is that just another coincidence? The other
reason for mentioning the oyster dredging is that two of the fleet
were built at Newquay. The PHANTOM and SUNNY SOUTH
were both built as pleasure boats 25 ft x 8 ft 3 ins x 4 ft, and a third
slightly smaller boat, HONOUR, worked as such at Newquay,
having been built at St Ives by Painter. The Painters (or Paynters)
were yet another example of boatbuilding and shipbuilding becoming
a family tradition. As well as building at St Ives they also had yards
at Amlwch in Anglesey and at Kilkeel, County Down, and were
responsible for the distinctive Cornish shape of many of the two-
masted luggers of the type known as nickeys which were to be
found up and down the Irish Sea.

# Yard Lists, Padstow and Outports 1782-1992

| DATE | | THE PADSTOW YARDS | | | | DATE |
|---|---|---|---|---|---|---|
| | BUILDER UNKNOWN | JOHN BONE | | | | |
| 1780 | Gibraltar Bg. | — | | | | 1780 |
| 1782 | Three Brothers Cr. | Cornish Oak Bg. | | | | 1782 |
| 1783 | Elizabeth Sp. | — | | | | 1783 |
| 1785 | William & Margaret Sp. | — | | | | 1785 |
| 1790 | Charles Sp. | — | | | | 1790 |
| 1792 | Three Friends Sp. | — | | | | 1792 |
| | Ann Sp. | — | | | | |
| 1795 | Betsy Sp. (lengthened) | — | | | | 1795 |
| 1796 | Susan Sp. | — | | | | 1796 |
| | Jeremiah Sp. | — | | | | |
| 1797 | Habbacot Bg. | — | | | | 1797 |
| 1799 | William Sp. | — | | | | 1799 |
| 1801 | Industry Sp. | — | | | | 1801 |
| | Maria Bg. | — | | | | |
| | William Bg. | — | | | | |
| | Union Sp. | — | | | | |
| 1802 | Prince Edward Sp. | — | | | | 1802 |
| 1802/3 | Betsy Bg. | **MARTIN WITHELL** | **JOHN TREDWEN** | **GEORGE SLOGGETT** | | 1802/3 |
| 1803 | — | Britannia Bg. | — | — | | 1803 |
| 1807 | Defiance Sk. | — | — | — | | 1807 |
| | Lisbon Packet Bg. | — | — | — | | |
| 1809 | Agnes Sr. (1st Sr.) | — | — | Anne Sp. | | 1809 |
| 1812 | — | Nanscow Sp. | Unity Sp. | — | | 1812 |
| 1813 | — | — | Susan Sr. | — | | 1813 |
| 1814 | — | John & Sarah Sk. | — | — | | 1814 |
| 1816 | Jane Sp. | — | Philippa Sp. | — | | 1816 |
| | Padstow Cr. | — | — | — | | |
| | Valentine Sp. | — | — | — | | |
| | Tryall Cr. | — | — | — | | |
| | Charlotte Sp. | — | — | — | | |
| 1817 | — | Alan Bg. | Hannah Sp. | — | | 1817 |
| 1818 | Industry Cr. | — | Star Sp. | John & Hannah Sp. | | 1818 |
| 1819 | — | — | Commerce Sr. | — | | 1819 |
| 1820 | Susan boat | Grace Sr. | Ceres Sr. | Venus Sp. | | 1820 |
| 1821 | — | — | Lanson Castle Sp. | Sheba Sp. | | 1821 |
| | — | — | Thomas & Nancy (Polacre Sr.) | — | | |
| | — | — | | — | | |
| 1822 | One & All Sp. | — | Alice Sr. | — | | 1822 |
| | — | — | Albion Sp. | — | | |
| 1823 | — | — | Enchantress Lr. | — | | 1823 |
| 1824 | — | — | Ann Maria Sp. | Thomas Sp. | | 1824 |
| 1825 | — | — | Valency Sp. | Nelly Sp. | | 1825 |
| | — | — | Penally Sp. | — | | |
| | — | — | Pendarves Sp. | — | | |
| 1826 | — | — | Delabole Sr. | Susan Sp. (Rose on boat-1820) | | 1826 |
| | — | — | Affo Sp. | Sir R .R. Vyvyan Sp. | | |
| | — | — | Marys & Helena Sp. | Star ? Sp. (Rose upon) | | |
| 1827 | — | — | Mariner's Friend L-B | Providence Sp. | | 1827 |
| | — | — | — | Margaritta & Esther Sp. | | |
| 1828 | — | — | Bude Packet Sp. | — | | 1828 |
| | — | — | Another Hull? | — | **THOMAS CARTER** | |
| 1829 | Nancy Sp. | **JOHN** | Symmetry Sr. | Orb. Sp. | — | 1829 |
| | — | **BREWER** | Mary Sp. | — | — | |

| DATE | | THE PADSTOW YARDS | | | | DATE |
|---|---|---|---|---|---|---|
| 1830 | — | Jane & Margaret Sp. | Sprightly Sp. | — | Charles Phillips Sp. | 1830 |
| | — | — | Rose Sk. | — | — | |
| 1831 | — | — | Primrose Sk./Sr. | Despatch Sp. | Daria Louisa Sp. | 1831 |
| | — | — | Ocean Bg Sr. | — | — | |
| 1832 | — | — | Saint Stephens Sp. | — | Secret Sp. | 1832 |
| | — | — | Brothers Sp. | — | — | |
| 1833 | — | Mary Sp. | Aid Sp. | — | Monarch Sp. | 1833 |
| | — | — | John Sp. | **JOHN SLOGGETT** | Caurinus Sp. | |
| 1834 | Intrepid Sp. | — | Charles Sp. | Rosamond & Jane Sp. | Samuel & Elizabeth Sp. | |
| | — | — | Mary Sr. | — | — | |
| | — | — | Harriet Sp. | — | — | 1834 |
| 1835 | — | — | Racer Sp. | Traveller Sp. | Favorite Sp. | 1835 |
| | — | — | Mary Ann Sr. | — | Ann & Elizabeth Sp. | |
| 1836 | — | — | Sarah Sp. | — | — | 1836 |
| | — | — | Iris Sr. | — | — | |
| | — | **THOMAS WITHELL** | Trevaunance Sp. | — | — | |
| 1837 | — | | Kate Sp. | — | — | 1837 |
| | — | — | Lord Porchester Sp. | — | | |
| 1838 | — | Belle Sr. | Marshall Sr. | Boscastle Sp. | Marina Sr. | 1838 |
| | — | — | Briton's Queen Sr. | — | — | |
| 1839 | — | — | Celerity Sr. | — | Canadian Sp. | 1839 |
| | — | — | Nautilus Dy./Sp. | **R.& J. TREDWEN** | — | |
| 1840 | Elizabeth Mary Sr. | Bess Sp. | — | — | Albion Sk. | 1840 |
| | Mary Jane Sr. | Sir Wm. Molesworth Sp. | — | — | — | |
| 1841 | — | Cornish Lass Sr. | Bedwelty Sr. | Temperance Sp. | Catherine Sp. | 1841 |
| | — | ex Excel (temp. name) | — | — | Zephyr Sr. | |
| | — | — | — | — | Ruth Sk. | |
| 1842 | Thomas & Elizabeth Sr. | **PHILIP RAWLE** | Millicent Sp. | — | — | 1842 |
| 1843 | (at St George's Well) | Rose Sr. | Cottager Sr. | Conservator Sp. | Ebenezer Lr. | 1843 |
| 1844 | Bottreaux Castle Sp. | Spring Sp. | — | Lady Mona Bg. | Jennifer Sp. | 1844 |
| | — | — | — | Alert Sp. | — | |
| | — | — | — | Ada Sp. | | |
| 1845 | Albion Sp. | — | Gem Cr. | Vesta Sp. | Paul Pry Lr. | 1845 |
| | — | | — | Victor Cr. | Elizabeth Lr. | |
| 1846 | Enterprize Sr. | **S.J. BENNETT** | — | Hope Sr. | Welcome Lr. | 1846 |
| | — | **& BROS.** | — | — | Grace Lr. | |
| 1847 | Victoria Sp. | — | — | Rose Sr. | Medora Sr. | 1847 |
| | — | — | — | Ellen Jane Sr. | Honor Lr. | |
| 1848 | — | Louise Sr. | — | Delabole Sr./Sk. | — | 1848 |
| | — | — | — | Agnes Sophia Sr. | — | |
| 1849 | — | — | — | Camalan Sr. | Frank Lr. | 1849 |
| 1850 | — | — | — | Ceres Sp. | — | 1850 |
| | — | — | — | Emblem Sr. | — | |
| | — | — | — | Active Sr. | — | |
| 1851 | Favourite Sr./Bn. | — | **J. TREDWEN JR.** | Henry Cr. | — | 1851 |
| | — | — | — | Eirene Cr. | — | |
| | — | — | — | Florist Bg. | — | |
| 1852 | — | Rebecca Lang Sr. | — | Infanta Sr. | — | 1852 |
| 1853 | — | — | Saint Petrock Sr. | — | — | 1853 |
| | — | — | Billow Sr. | — | — | |
| | — | **E. T. BENNETT** | Fayaway Sr. | — | — | |
| | — | — | Truro Sr. | — | — | |
| 1854 | — | Lenora Sk. | Emily Sr. | **F. H. THOMAS** | Betsey James Sr. | 1854 |
| | — | **S. J. BENNETT** | Phoenix Sp. | — | Ellen Frances Sr. | |
| | — | — | Mary Sr. | — | **JOHN CARTER** | |
| 1855 | — | Jane & Sarah Sk. | Aurora Bg. | Morning Star S. | Volutina K. | 1855 |
| | — | Queen of the West Sr. | Cornwall Sr. | (with J. Cowl) | — | |
| | — | — | Alma Bn. | — | — | |

## THE PADSTOW YARDS

| DATE | | | | | | DATE |
|------|---|---|---|---|---|------|
| 1856 | — | Mary Jane Sr. | Sarah Ann Sr. | Bessie Sk. | — | 1856 |
|  | — | — | Edith Sr. | Pet Sr. | — |  |
|  | — | — | Cornubia Sp. | — | — |  |
| 1857 | Star of St Agnes Sr. | — | Maria Sr. | Lizzie May Sr. | Gazelle Sr. | 1857 |
|  | Telegram Sr. | — | Florence Nightingale Sr. | Lizzie Grace Sr. | — |  |
|  | — | — | Sunshine K. | — | — |  |
| 1858 | Jessie Bg. | Constance Sr. | Edith Sr. | — | — | 1858 |
|  | Lucretia Sk. | — | Ocean Queen Bn. | — | — |  |
|  | — | — | Fawn Sp. | — | — |  |
|  | — | — | Comet Sp. | — | **EDWIN CARTER** |  |
| 1859 | — | — | Louise Sp. | Bessie Jane Sk. | Edwin Sk. | 1859 |
|  | — | — | Eliza Ann Sr. | — | Thomas Sk. |  |
|  | — | — | Beatrice Sr. (pro tem name for Clodagh?) |  | Trebiskin Sr. |  |
|  | — | — | Clodagh Sr. | — | — |  |
|  | — | — | Amphitrite Sr. | — | — |  |
|  | — | — | Maria Louisa Sp. | — | — |  |
| 1860 | — | — | Mary Simmons Sr. | Cilicia Sr. | — | 1860 |
|  | — | — | Swift Cr. | — | — |  |
|  | — | — | M.D. Sarah Sr. | — | — |  |
|  | — | — | Morfa Mawr Sr. | — | — |  |
|  | — | — | Volunteer Sr. | — | — |  |
|  | — | — | Samuel Cr. | **JOHN HENRY** | — |  |
|  | — | — | Collina Cr. | **WILLMETT** | **SLOGGETT** |  |
| 1861 | — | — | Camelford Sr. | Prince Alfred Sk. | Alarm Sk. | 1861 |
|  | — | — | Alice Jane Sr. | Willie Sk. | **JOHN STRIBLEY** |  |
| 1862 | — | — | Penpoll Sr. | Mary Kellow Sr. | Caroline Phillips Dy. | 1862 |
|  | — | — | Volunteer Sr. | Amelia Sr. | (Lloyds gives Willmett) |  |
|  | — | — | Albion Sk. | Little Racer Cr. | — |  |
|  | — | — | Selina Ann Sr. | Peace Dy. | — |  |
|  | — | — | Atalanta Sr. (pro tem name for Mary James?) |  | — |  |
|  | — | — | Julia Sr. | — | — |  |
|  | — | — | Mary James Sr. | — | — |  |
| 1863 | — | — | Tremenhere Sr. | Revenue Smack | Tretherras Sr. | 1863 |
|  | — | — | Mary Eliza Sr. | **JAMES WILLMETT** | (Farr gives Willmett) |  |
|  | — | — | Rose of St Agnes Sr. | **Dennis Cove Yd.** | Annie Sr. |  |
| 1864 | — | — | Ariel Bn. | Mary Phillips Sr. | (Lloyds gives Willmett) | 1864 |
|  | — | — | Annie Sr. | Lizzy (Lizzie) Sr. | — |  |
|  | — | — | Ann Williams Sr. | — | — |  |
|  | — | — | Giles Lang Sr. | — | — |  |
| 1865 | — | — | Hannah Sr. | Ton Mawr Sr. | Alberta Sk. | 1865 |
|  | — | — | Janie Morcom Sr. | Pomaron Bk. | — |  |
|  | — | — | Mary Seymour Sr. | **W. F. WILLMETT** | — |  |
| 1866 | De Lank Cr. | — | Wonder Sr. | **Dennis Cove Yd.** | Janie Barfield Sr. | 1866 |
|  | — | — | J.T.A. Sr. | Edith Morgan Sr. | — |  |
|  | — | — | — | Minnie Sr. | — |  |
| 1867 | Star of Gwent Cr. | — | Princess of Wales Sr. | Amanda Sr. | Lizzie Sk. | 1867 |
|  | — | — | Ann Walters Sr. | — | J.C.A. Sr. |  |
| 1868 | — | — | Lizzie Sr. | — | Souvenir Sr. | 1868 |
|  | — | — | Water Nymph Sr. | — | J.K.A. Sr. |  |
| 1869 | — | — | Gipsy Queen Sr. | — | Sappho Bkn. | 1869 |
|  | — | — | Ida Elizabeth Sr. | — | — |  |
|  | — | — | Janie Vivian Sr. | — | — |  |
|  | — | — | Adelaide Bn. | — | — |  |
| 1870 | — | — | Flower of the Fal Sr. | — | Lizzie Male Sr. | 1870 |
|  | — | — | Gipsy Maid Sr. | — | Janie Sr. |  |

| DATE | | | THE PADSTOW YARDS | | | DATE |
|---|---|---|---|---|---|---|
| 1871 | — | — | Jane Francis Bg. | — | Water Lily Sr. | 1871 |
|  | — | — |  | — | Lily Sr. |  |
|  | — | — | **JOHN COWL** | — | Elizabeth Drew Sr. |  |
| 1872 | — | — | **Lower Yard** | — | Bessie (Rebuilt) Sr. | 1872 |
|  | — | — | — | — | Emily Ellen Sr. |  |
| 1873 | — | — | Peace Sr. | — | Ingrid Sr. | 1873 |
|  | — | — | Mary Coad Sr. | — | — |  |
| 1874 | — | — | Corsair Sr. | — | Empress of China Bkn. | 1874 |
|  | — | — | — | **CHARLES RAWLE** | Fortunate Sr. |  |
| 1875 | — | — | Agnes Strout Sr. | Mary Waters Sr. | Jessie Sr. | 1875 |
|  | — | — | Hesperus K. | — | — |  |
| 1876 | Milicent Mary Cr. | — | J.K. Allport Sr. | Eliza Annie Sr. | Hopeful Bkn. | 1876 |
|  | AER Cr. | — | — | Susie May Sr. | — |  |
|  | Phyllis Cr. | — | — | — | **WILLIAM STRIBLEY** |  |
| 1877 | — | — | Emma Sr. | — | Clara Sr. | 1877 |
| 1878 | — | — | Janie Sr. | Fairy Flower Sr. | Kathleen Sr. | 1878 |
|  | — | — | Katie Sr. | Fairy King Sr. | — |  |
| 1879 | — | — | Fairy Glen Sr. | Rosalie Bkn. | Julia 3m. Sr. | 1879 |
| 1880 | — | — | Laura Emma Sr. | Pride of the West Sr. | — | 1880 |
| 1881 | — | — | Katie Sr. | Pride of the South Sr. | — | 1881 |
| 1884 | — | — | Bessie Cr. | — | Eleanor & Jane Sr. — | 1884 |
| 1886 | — | — | Amaranth Sr. | — | — | 1886 |
| 1889 | — | — | — | Mildred 3m. Sr. | — | 1889 |
| 1890 | — | — | E.L.C. Cr. | — | — | 1890 |
|  | — | — | Winnie/Jimbet Cr. | — | — |  |
| 1894 | — | — | — | Gipsy Cr. Yt. | **J. EDYVANE** | 1894 |
| 1901 | — | — | — | — | Bluebell Cr. Yt. | 1901 |
| 1903 | — | — | Silver Spray Cr. Yt. | — | — | 1903 |
| 1906 | Molly B. Cr. | — | — | — | — | 1906 |

| DATE | **PADSTOW** | **WADEBRIDGE** | DATE |
|---|---|---|---|
| 1842 | — | Mary Josephine Sr. (Builder Unknown) | 1842 |
|  | — |  |  |
| 1876 | — | Jessie (built as a Barge by Billing) | 1876 |
| 1952 | St Saviour's (Ferry) (Builder Wm. Lindsey) | — | 1952 |
|  |  | — |  |
| 1962 | Gaviota N. MFV | — | 1962 |
| 1965 | — | Trident I ) Trimarans by | 1965 |
|  | — | Triptych ) |  |
| 1966 | — | Toria ) Multihull | 1966 |
| 1967 | — | Trifle ) | 1967 |
| 1968 | — | Tanith ) Construction Co Ltd | 1968 |
| 1969 | — | Cornish Clipper) | 1969 |
| 1970 | — | De Marni, Yacht (at Topsham & Rock) | 1970 |
| 1973 | — | Sally Allsorts MFV (at Bodmin) | 1973 |
| 1977 | — | Jubilee Queen Pass. (Chapman) | 1977 |
|  | — | Jolly Robber Yt. (at Rock) |  |
| 1979 | — | Bethney Mary MFV | 1979 |
| 1985 | — | Our Belle Ann MFV (Chapman & Hewitt) | 1985 |
| 1987 | — | Girl Rachel MFV (at Plymouth & Rock) | 1987 |
|  | — | Prue Esther II MFV (Chapman & Hewitt) |  |
| 1988 | — | Lisa Maria MFV | 1988 |
|  | — | Nikki, D. MFV |  |
|  | — | Orcades II MFV (Chapman & Hewitt) |  |
|  | — | Curly Greenslade MFV |  |

| DATE | PADSTOW (cont) | WADEBRIDGE (cont) | DATE |
|---|---|---|---|
| 1989 | **A&J MARINE** | — | 1989 |
|  | Girl Debra MFV | Red Rhum MFV |  |
| 1990 | Alize MFV | Betty Louise MFV (at Rock) | 1990 |
|  | Boy Dominic MFV | Phoenix MFV (Chapman & Hewitt) |  |
|  | — | Equinox (Chapman & Hewitt) |  |
|  | — | Riptide MFV |  |
|  | — | Tristar MFV |  |
| 1991 | Stephanie B. MFV | Celtic Victor MFV | 1991 |
|  | — | Hurricane Diving Tender |  |
| 1992 | Dart Princess Pass. | — | 1992 |

## PADSTOW OUTPORTS

| | GANNEL | NEWQUAY QUAY YARD | PORTH & ISLAND COVE, NEWQUAY | PORT ISAAC, PORT GAVERNE BOSCASTLE | BUDE | |
|---|---|---|---|---|---|---|
| 1806 | — | — | — | Hope Bn. (Boscastle) | — | 1806 |
|  | — | — | — | (Builder not known) | **W.M. BARROW** |  |
| 1813 | — | — | **WITHELL** | — | Mary Bg. | 1813 |
|  | — | — | at Porth | — | — |  |
| 1818 | — | — | Porth Sp. | — | **THOMAS** | 1818 |
|  | — | — | — | — | **BOUND** |  |
| 1826 | — | — | — | — | Friends Sp. | 1826 |
| 1828 | — | — | — | — | Enterprize Sp. | 1828 |
|  | — | — | — | — | **CHAS. CARTER** |  |
| 1835 | — | — | — | — | Lady Acland Sr. | 1835 |
|  | — | — | — | — | **STAPLETON** |  |
| 1836 | — | — | — | — | Affo. Sp. | 1836 |
| 1837 | **T. CLEMENS** | — | — | **H. SANDRY** | Victoria S. | 1837 |
|  | — | — | — | at Port Isaac | — |  |
| 1839 | Caroline Sk. | — | — | Mary Stephens Sp. | **ROBERT** | 1839 |
|  | (launched as John | — | — | — | **STAPLETON** |  |
|  | & Mary) | — | — | — | — |  |
|  | — | — | — | **JOHN LAKEMAN** | — |  |
| 1842 | Lady of the | — | — | at Port Isaac | Mirre Sk. | 1842 |
|  | Lake Sr. | **J&M CLEMENS** | — | — | Velocity Sp. |  |
| 1847 | — | — | — | Echo Sp. | — | 1847 |
| 1849 | — | Treffry Sr. | — | **BENNETT** (Pt. Isaac) | — | 1849 |
| 1850 | — | — | — | Bessy Jane Sr. | — | 1850 |
| 1851 | Liberty Sr. | Tower Sr. | — | — | — | 1851 |
| 1852 | (lengthened) | Gem Sk. | — | **STEPHENS** | — | 1852 |
| 1853 | — | — | — | Sylph Sk. (Port Isaac) | — | 1853 |
| 1854 | — | Kate Sr. | — | Victoria Sk. (Pt. Gaverne) | — | 1854 |
| 1855 | — | **J&M CLEMENS** | **T. R. AVERY** (Boscastle) | — | — | 1855 |
|  | — | — | **Island Cove Yard** | Thomasine & Mary Sk. | — |  |
| 1856 | — | Elizabeth Jane Sr. | Tregunnel | (Ex Ann temp. name) | — | 1856 |
|  | — | — | — | (started) | — — |  |
| 1857 | **J&M CLEMENS** | **R. TREDWIN** | **MARTIN &** | Pet Sk. | Elizabeth Scown Sr. | 1857 |
|  | (from Cardiff) | LEWARNE (Porth) | — | — |  |  |
|  | — | — | Glendorgal Sr. | — | — |  |
| 1858 | Tregunnel Sr. | Trevaunance Sk. | Little Jane Sk. | Lily of the Valley | — | 1858 |
|  | (completion) | — | — | **GEORGE** (Boscastle) | — |  |
|  | — | — | — | Ellen Vair Sr. | — |  |

| DATE | GANNEL | NEWQUAY QUAY YARD | PORTH & ISLAND COVE, NEWQUAY | PORT ISAAC, PORT GAVERNE BOSCASTLE | BUDE | DATE |
|---|---|---|---|---|---|---|
| 1861 | Emma Jane Sr. | — | — | Caroline Goodyear Sr. | Sir T.D. Acland Sr. | 1861 |
| | **J CLEMENS** | — | — | (ex Annie Bottreaux | — | |
| | — | — | — | temporary name) | — | |
| 1863 | Driving Mist Sr. | **M CLEMENS** | — | — | — | 1863 |
| 1865 | Edith Sr. | Kittie Sr. | — | — | Ellen Martin Sr. | 1865 |
| 1866 | SMC Sr. | — | — | — | —— | 1866 |
| | **T&J CLEMENS** | — | **JOSEPH OSBORNE** | — | — | |
| | — | — | **Island Cove Yard** | — | — | |
| 1867 | Ocean Belle Sr. | Forest Deer Sr. | — | — | — | 1867 |
| 1868 | Fairy Queen Sr. | — | Resolution Sk. | — | — | 1868 |
| | Happy Return K. | — | — | — | — | |
| | (lengthened) | — | — | — | — | |
| | Josephine Dy (rebuilt) | — | — | — | — | |
| 1869 | Rippling Wave Sr. | — | — | — | — | 1869 |
| 1870 | — | — | Vixen Sr. | — | — | 1870 |
| 1871 | TEJ Sr. | — | Conquest Sr. | — | — | 1871 |
| 1872 | Fairy Belle Sr. | — | Jane Sl. | — | Annie Davey Sr. | 1872 |
| 1873 | William Martin Sr. | — | **J OSBORNE** (Porth) | — | — | 1873 |
| 1875 | Mary Peers Sr. | — | Agnes Louisa Sk. | — | — | 1875 |
| 1876 | Fairy Maid Sr. | — | — | — | **CARTER** | 1876 |
| 1877 | Louise Sr. | — | Porth Sk. | — | Jessamine K. | 1877 |
| | Leila Sr. | — | — | — | **STAPLETON** | |
| 1878 | Lottie Sr. | — | — | — | Agnes Sr. | 1878 |
| 1879 | Guiding Star Sr. | — | — | Surprise Sk. | — | 1879 |
| 1880 | — | — | Lady Jane Sr. | (Mitchell also named | — | 1880 |
| 1881 | Triumph K. | **NEWQUAY** | — | as builder) | **HENRY** | 1881 |
| | — | (exact site | — | — | **STAPLETON** | |
| 1907 | **T. CLEMENS** | not known) | — | — | Agnes K. (Lady | 1904 |
| | Poppy Aux. Yt. | — | — | — | Acland rebuilt) | |
| | — | **STAFFIERI** | — | — | — | |
| 1975 | — | Symmetria Cr. Yt. | — | — | — | 1975 |
| 1988 | — | — | — | Barcris MFV | — | 1988 |
| | — | — | — | (reported built | — | |
| | — | — | — | Port Isaac) | — | |

In addition, the following vessels were built by **WARWICK R. GUY** at Port Gaverne. Agenoria Sk 1858, Telegraph Sk 1859, and Electric Sk 1863 (McOwen also named as builder of Electric).

*Abbreviations in Yard Lists*:

| | | | |
|---|---|---|---|
| Bg | Brig | MFV | Motor Fishing Vessel |
| Bkn | Barkentine | Pass. | Passenger Vessel |
| Bn | Brigantine | S. | Ship (full rigged) |
| Bk | Barque | Sk. | Smack |
| Cr | Cutter | Sl. | Steam Launch |
| Dy | Dandy | Sp. | Sloop |
| K | Ketch | Sr. | Schooner |
| L-B | Lifeboat | 3m Sr. | 3 Masted Schooner |
| Lr | Lugger | Yt. | Yacht |

# 11 HENZELL'S PATENT

*Farewell and adieu to you fair Spanish ladies,*
*Adieu and farewell to you ladies of Spain.*
*For we're under orders for to sail to old England,*
*And we may never see you fair ladies again.*

Chanty

---

*LLOYD's Register* 1862 includes the following vessel: 'HENZELL'S PATENT, Brig. 227 tons, built at Newcastle in 1861 by Henzell, Owner, I. Sewell. Vessel belongs to Shoreham and is trading Newcastle to France. A1 for 5 yrs Expl. [presumably meaning Experimental].'

Thomas Smith Henzell, a Newcastle shipwright, was granted a patent on 29th October, 1856, and as far as is known, the brig named HENZELL'S PATENT was the only vessel built to his patent until the barque POMARON was built at Padstow. His patent is reproduced hereafter.

The brig HENZELL'S PATENT had the dimensions 117.0 ft long, 26.5 ft beam, 12.8 ft depth. These figures say much about her design; a typical brig of the time of her length and beam would have had a tonnage of about 350 and a depth of about 17.5 ft. Alternatively, a brig of her tonnage would normally have had approximate dimensions 95.1 x 23.2 x 14.6. Henzell was trying to design a ship which would have more cargo space and carry a greater weight of cargo on a shallower draught than would other ships of her measured tonnage. With her shallow draught and flat bottom she would be ideal for trading over shallow bars and taking the ground, but she would make too much leeway when sailing to windward; therefore she needed to be equipped either with centreboards or leeboards, both of which were in common use on smaller craft. Instead, one of the principal features of his patent was the fitting of a set of what he called floats. These were placed along each side of the ship, miniature keels, protected in timber casings, which could be lowered or raised on chains. They were not centreboards but 'sideboards' which therefore did not intrude into the hold space.

Henzell recognised that his long hull would be subjected to additional hogging and sagging stresses because its depth was abnormally small: therefore he devised 'double diagonal' planking through bolted top and bottom.

He and his Shoreham client used her and showed her off to the full. She traded to the continent and around the British Isles. Bristol was her survey port in 1864. Unfortunately *Lloyd's Register* for 1864 has the word 'wrecked' posted beside her entry, and we hear no more of her.

Meanwhile a London owner, Frank Barry of Adelaide Place, London Bridge, had seen potential value in Henzell's patent. He may or may not have known of the development of huge square rigged sailing barges which was going on that very year at Sittingbourne, but he was able to get favourable terms to have a barque built by James Willmett at Padstow to Henzell's patent and to Lloyd's Special Survey.

In due course the following report appeared in the *Royal Cornwall Gazette*, April 1865:

LAUNCH AT PADSTOW — On Thursday evening a fine barque was successfully launched from the ship-building yard of Messrs Willmett. She is stated to be the largest ship ever built at Padstow, and is intended to carry 800 tons. She is constructed on new principles, and is a remarkably fine specimen of marine architecture. We understand that other ships of the same size and character are now being built at this yard.

She certainly was not the largest ship built at Padstow as the MORNING STAR, built on the same slip ten years earlier, was larger in every dimension and measurement. Nor were other vessels of the same type under construction. Sadly the cost of building a novel type of vessel to Lloyd's Special Survey had been underestimated and James Willmett was declared bankrupt two months later.

Her survey dated 22nd March, 1865 is endorsed with her launch date, 12th April. All her fastenings were of copper or yellow metal; the only iron in the hull was in breasthooks and knees. Her frame had been completed on 16th September, 1864, the beams had been fitted in November and she was completed 'before the plank be painted or payed' in March 1865. She had one long boat and two others: her three bower anchors each weighed 16 cwt and she also had a 5 cwt stream anchor and two small kedges; she was classified A1 for eight years, (seven for the quality of materials with an extra year for copper fastenings). She was barque rigged, and if the sails listed in her survey are to be trusted she had a single topsail on her foremast and double topsails on the mainmast. The hull was built of red pine (including beams and side timbers) with the following exceptions: floors of beech and hack (i.e. hackmatack); rudder of oak; keels of American elm (but keelsons of red pine). The stem and sternpost of English oak, and the deadwood of English elm. Clearly the shipbuilders of Padstow relied heavily on the port's trade with Quebec. The outer planking was four inches thick, the inner, three inches. At the time of survey she was felted with 1¼ ins king pins, zinc nails. *Lloyd's Registers* show her to have been coppered the following year.

The surveyors had difficulty in filling in the standard forms as POMARON's novel construction was not catered for: for instance the standard form allowed for a vessel to be 'sheathed', by which was meant an additional skin of planking built on outside a completed hull normally to strengthen a weak hull, but sometimes to protect a hull from ice damage. When the shipbuilders of the New World started sending a flood of cheap ships back to Britain in the eighteenth century, the vested interests in the home country demanded that they should be sheathed before being awarded a 'classification' in *Lloyd's*, and with some justification as they were sometimes hurriedly built and planked with unsuitable softwoods. Thus POMARON is described as 'sheathed', by virtue of her 'double diagonal' construction; the word sheathed appeared on the standard form and the surveyor could not cross it out because the inner diagonal planks were indeed sheathed by the outer diagonal planks.

She had three bilge pumps (one of iron and two of lead) and an iron windlass.

Her name indicates that her owner had already decided on her trade. Captain John Cotton stood by her final weeks of building and rigging, then sailed her up to Liverpool to pick up a general cargo for Villa Real on the south coast of Portugal, and for Pomarao, a mining village twenty miles north up the Guadiana River which forms the frontier between Spain and Portugal. Cotton was a Gloucestershire man, born in 1828: he obtained his master's certificate (No. 5330) at Bristol in 1851 and was in his prime by 1865. He took her out of the Mersey, dropping his pilot at the Bell buoy, the outer limit of compulsory pilotage. It was necessary to beat to windward out into the Irish Sea, and then the routine passage to Pomarao was undertaken, to be repeated dozens of times in the years to come, south-southwest for over six hundred miles down St George's Channel, west of Land's End and across the Bay of Biscay to landfall at Cape Vilano or Cape Finisterre. With prevalent westerly winds it was sometimes possible to fetch this course all the way with the wind from the starboard side, but quite often they were becalmed in the Bay for two or three days and the wind was more variable near the Spanish coast. If the chronometer was at all suspect they would keep well to the west until latitude 43° North was reached, then run into the land to get a new point of departure.

In summer the northeast trade winds would carry them down the west coast of Iberia in great style, but they took care to keep several miles offshore to avoid the massive lines of fixed fishing nets which the Portuguese built out from their beaches. In winter, this part of the voyage was more difficult as the northeast trades were further south, and the winds off the Portuguese coast tended to be south and west, requiring windward work with some of Henzell's patent floats in the lowered position to act as keels. Then turn to port round Cape St Vincent of blessed memory and past Lagos with its towering battlements, and Faro, then turn to port again and head towards the shallow waters of the Rio Guadiana. In summer this last leg of the voyage would be fast sailing with the strength of the NE trades undiminished, but blowing offshore so the ship was in relatively smooth waters.

The Admiralty Pilot warns about moving sandbanks, nets and fish traps off the approaches to Rio Guadiana. 'The channels and banks in the vicinity of the bar are subject to constant change as a result of gales and the freshets which come down the river in winter'. So mariners from Padstow might almost have felt at home! 'The tidal streams are moderate except during floods which frequently occur in winter, when the rate is greatly increased and discoloured reddish water extends a considerable distance to seaward of the bar; the entrance should not then be attempted.'

The lower reaches of the Guadiana form the boundary between Portugal and Spain, and there are old forts in evidence near the river mouth.

Pomarao is no less than 22 miles up the river, and marks the upper limit of navigation for oceangoing vessels. Vessels still go to Pomarao for copper ore, but in 1865 iron ore was also exported. In early days, sailing vessels would have had to work the winds and the tides to get up to Pomarao and doubtless needed every trick of the trade from dredging to kedging, but by the time the barque POMARON arrived, they may have had the help of a steam tug.

The return to Liverpool (or occasionally to Newport, Monmouthshire) was easier in winter than in summer. In winter it tended to be southerly and westerly winds all the way home: in summer the trade winds which were so helpful on the outward leg made it necessary to stand out far into the Atlantic in a northwest direction before picking up the favourable west winds.

The POMARON stayed in this trade all her life, making about one round voyage a month, taking out coal or general cargo and returning with iron ore or copper ore. In 1869 Captain C. T. Vaughan took over from John Cotton and in 1870 it was Captain Thompson. Watts became her master in 1872 and was still in command on 15th December, 1874 when the London steamship TOSKOFF, sailing from Marianopole for Falmouth, came upon the POMARON about twenty miles west of Ushant looking like the proverbial half-tide rock. Heavy weather had damaged her sails and rigging and had washed away bulwarks and stanchions. The hull had probably been strained by heavy ore cargoes, for as well as ore there was three feet of water in the hold. The TOSKOFF was able to take off the whole crew and the POMARON was left to her fate.

But Henzell's patent was not a complete failure. A giant flat-bottomed sailing barge had been built to suit the requirements of trading up the Rio Guadiana, with shallow draught and able to take the ground safely and comfortably. She had brought home nearly 10,000 tons of ore every year for over nine years, surviving everything the Bay of Biscay had to offer in the way of wind and weather.

The only ships which might be compared with the POMARON were the giant sailing barges built by George Smeed at Sittingbourne as coastal colliers:

At least the Smeed yard was building these giant barges in a fashion familiar to their shipwrights. They were simply scaling up the Thames sailing barge (including leeboards in most cases), and giving it a sensible sea-going rig. None of them was classed at Lloyds except SARAH SMEED, the smallest of them.

In contrast, the POMARON was built to Lloyd's demanding standards by men who had never seen a ship of that shape or type, with novel features, and she obviously cost more than anticipated. It is a shame that more capital was not available to build sister ships with improvements and perhaps economies. It is also to be regretted that no photographs of the ship have been found, nor reports on the functioning of the patent 'floats'.

| Built | Name | Cargo in Tons | Dimensions | Feet | | Rig | Fate |
|-------|------|---------------|------------|------|------|-----|------|
| 1865 | POMARON | 800 | 131.5 | 29.1 | 13.9 | Barque | Lost 1874 |
| 1865 | ELIZA SMEED | 500 | 140 | 27.8 | 13.2 | Barkentine | Sold & lost c. 1882 |
| 1866 | GEORGE SMEED | 770 | 156 | 30.5 | 15. | Barkentine | Sold 1879 & lost by 1884 |
| 1868 | ESTHER SMEED | 800 | 166 | 31.0 | 16.9 | Barque | Lasted until 1878 |
| 1872 | EMILY SMEED | 750 | | 13.3 | 25.8 | 13.3 | Barkentine | Lasted until 1934 as a lighter |
| 1874 | SARAH SMEED | 650 | 125.7 | 25.7 | 11.3 | Three-Masted Schooner | Lost 1882 |

# A.D. 1856 . . . . . . N° 2541.

## Construction of Ships or Vessels.

LETTERS PATENT to Thomas Smith Henzell, of South Shields, in the County of Durham, Shipowner, for the Invention of "IMPROVEMENTS IN THE CONSTRUCTION OF SHIPS OR VESSELS."

Sealed the 14th April 1857, and dated the 29th October 1856.

PROVISIONAL SPECIFICATION left by the said Thomas Smith Henzell at the Office of the Commissioners of Patents, with his Petition, on the 29th October 1856.

I, THOMAS SMITH HENZELL, of South Shields, in the County of Durham, Shipowner, do hereby declare the nature of the said Invention for "IMPROVEMENTS IN THE CONSTRUCTION OF SHIPS OR VESSELS," to be as follows:—

These improvements in the construction of ships or vessels are designed for the following purposes:—

Firstly, to effect a very great saving in the cost of building or constructing the ship or vessel, together with increased strength; secondly, to enable the ship or vessel, to carry more cargo, according to the registered tonnage, and with a less draught of water, than vessels of the usual construction; thirdly, to dispense entirely with the use or necessity for ballast.

In the first place, the ships or vessels are built almost entirely of straight timber; the bottom of the vessel is flat, but slopes slightly upwards at the stem and stern. There are three keels. The centre or midship keel is quite

---

2    A.D. 1856.—N° 2541.    *Provisional Specification.*

*Henzell's Improvements in the Construction of Ships or Vessels.*

straight, and the space between it and the bottom of the vessel at stem and stern is filled in with dead wood. The side keels are curved at each end to the desired form of the bow and run of the vessel, being the only curved pieces in the vessel, excepting the side keelsons, which necessarily take the same curve and the deck beams. The midship and sister keelsons are quite straight. The floor timbers run transversely, and the inside and outside planking longitudinally, with a diagonal planking. The side timbers are quite straight and vertical, with diagonal planking, the inner and outer planking crossing in opposite directions. The planks are bolted to the side keels and keelsons and to the deck clamp, and, running up the whole height of the vessel to the upper rail, afford an immense increase of strength to the vessel.

The vessel is also furnished with side floats, which can be hove up and down, so as to give less or more hold upon the water, as may be desired, without increasing the immersion of the hull by means of ballast, and also offering much less resistance than vessels of the ordinary construction.

SPECIFICATION in pursuance of the conditions of the Letters Patent, filed by the said Thomas Smith Henzell in the Great Seal Patent Office on the 28th April 1857.

TO ALL TO WHOM THESE PRESENTS SHALL COME, I, THOMAS SMITH HENZELL, of South Shields, in the County of Durham, Shipowner, send greeting.

WHEREAS Her most Excellent Majesty Queen Victoria, by Her Letters Patent, bearing date the Twenty-ninth day of October, in the year of our Lord One thousand eight hundred and fifty-six, in the twentieth year of Her reign, did, for Herself, Her heirs and successors, give and grant unto me, the said Thomas Smith Henzell, Her special licence that I, the said Thomas Smith Henzell, my executors, administrators, and assigns, or such others as I, the said Thomas Smith Henzell, my executors, administrators, and assigns, should at any time agree with, and no others, from time to time and at all times thereafter during the term therein expressed, should and lawfully might make, use, exercise, and vend, within the United Kingdom of Great Britain and Ireland, the Channel Islands, and Isle of Man, an Invention for "IMPROVEMENTS IN THE CONSTRUCTION OF SHIPS OR VESSELS," upon the condition (amongst others) that I, the said Thomas Smith Henzell, my executors, administrators, by an instrument in writing under my, or their, or one

Specification.　A.D. 1856.—N° 2541.　3

### Henzell's Improvements in the Construction of Ships or Vessels.

of their hands and seals, should particularly describe and ascertain the nature of the said Invention, and in what manner the same was to be performed, and cause the same to be filed in the Great Seal Patent Office within six calendar months next and immediately after the date of the said
5 Letters Patent.

NOW KNOW YE, that I, the said Thomas Smith Henzell, do hereby declare the nature of my said Invention, and in what manner the same is to be performed, to be particularly described and ascertained in and by the following statement in writing, and on reference to the accompanying
10 Drawings, that is to say:—

My improvements in the construction of ships or vessels are designed principally for the following purposes:—

Firstly, to effect a very great saving in the cost of building or constructing the ship or vessel, together with increased strength; secondly, to enable the
15 ship or vessel, to carry more cargo, according to the registered tonnage, and with a less draught of water, than vessels of the ordinary construction; and, thirdly, to dispense entirely with the use or necessity for ballast.

In the first place, the ships or vessels are built almost entirely of straight timber; the bottom of the vessel is flat, but rises slightly upwards at the stem
20 and stern. There are three keels. The centre or midship keel is quite straight, and the space between it and the bottom of the vessel at stem and stern is filled in with dead wood. The side keels are curved to the desired form of the bow and run of the vessel, being the only curved pieces in the vessel, excepting the side keelsons, which necessarily take the same curve (both of
25 which, however, will set or bend sufficiently with straight timber), and the deck beams and top rail or covering board. The midship and sister keelsons are quite straight. The floor timbers run transversely, and the inner and outer floor planking longitudinally, with a diagonal ceiling. The side timbers are quite straight and vertical, with diagonal planking, the inner and outer
30 planking crossing in opposite directions. The planks are bolted to the side keels and keelsons, and, running up the whole height of the vessel to the upper rail, afford an immense increase of strength to the vessel.

The vessel is also furnished with sliding side keels or floats, which can be hove up and down, so as to give less or more hold upon the water, as may
35 be desired, without increasing the immersion of the hull by means of ballast, and also offering much less resistance than vessels of the ordinary construction.

In the illustrative Drawing accompanying these Presents, Figure 1 represents a side view of a vessel constructed according to my Invention, and drawn to a

4　A.D. 1856.—N° 2541.　Specification.

### Henzell's Improvements in the Construction of Ships or Vessels.

scale of about one-eighth of an inch to a foot; and Figure 2, a plan view of the lower flat of the vessel, showing the light and load water lines and the upper rail; Figure 3 is a half end view, the left-hand half representing the after end, and the right-hand half the fore end of the vessel, shewing the lead
5 of the side timbers. The lines set off are intended to combine large carrying properties with more than an average speed, but the latter may be increased by finer lines and a greater depth of dead wood. $a$, $a$, represents the centre or midship keel of the vessel, which, as usual, is quite straight; $a^\times$, $a^\times$, in Figure 2, is the centre keelson; $b$, $b$, is the stem post, and $c$, $c$, the stern post;
10 $d$, $d$, is the dead wood forward, and $e$, $e$, is the dead wood aft; $f$, $f$, are the side keels, which are curved to the desired form of the bow and run of the vessel, and are also curved slightly upwards towards the stem and stern; $g$, $g$, are the side keelsons, which take the same curve as the side keels. The outer line of the side keelsons in Figure 2 also represents the light water line, and the
15 line $h$, $h$, the load water line. $i$, $i$, are the sister keelsons, which are straight in plan view, and $k$, $k$, shews the line of the top rail or covering board; $l$, $l$, is the rudder, and $m$, $m$, the cutwater; $n$, $n$, represents the bowsprit, and $o$, $o$, the deck stringer; $p$, $p$, are the transverse floor timbers. The floor planking is not shewn in the Drawing, but is intended to run longitudinally with a
20 diagonal ceiling. The side timbers $g$, $g$, are quite straight and vertical, and the side planking is diagonal, the outer planking $r$, $r$, running in one direction, and the inner planking or ceiling shewn by the dotted lines $s$, $s$, running in the reverse or opposite direction, so that they cross at right angles, or nearly so, as shewn at the bow of the vessel. The whole of the ends of the outside
25 planking rabbit into and are bolted to the side keel, leaving about four inches of solid keel below to caulk and protect the plank ends. The side timbers $g$, $g$, step on the side keels, and dowel or rabbit into the floor ends, and run up to the upper rail or covering board. The deck beams are placed athwart ship, and step on the deck stringer $o$, $o$, into which the ends are dowelled and bolted
30 vertically. The deck planking runs diagonally and butts against the plank adjoining the coamings, and the ends may be bolted vertically on to the deck stringer and beams, thus avoiding the use of knees, *if desirable*. $t$, $t$, are the sliding side keels, which are enclosed in a casing $u$, $u$, outside the diagonal planking, and run in grooves $v$, $v$, being hove up and down as required by
35 means of the chains $w$, $w$.

Having thus described the nature and object of my said Invention of improvements in the construction of ships or vessels, together with the manner of carrying the same into practical effect, I would remark, in conclusion, that I claim as my Invention the general construction and arrangement of ships or vessels, as shewn in the annexed Drawing, and above particularly described.

In witness whereof, I, the said Thomas Smith Henzell, have hereunto set my hand and seal, this Twenty-second day of April, in the year of our Lord One thousand eight hundred and fifty-seven.
5　　　　　　　　　THOˢ S. HENZELL. (L.S.)

LONDON:
Printed by GEORGE EDWARD EYRE and WILLIAM SPOTTISWOODE,
Printers to the Queen's most Excellent Majesty. 1857.

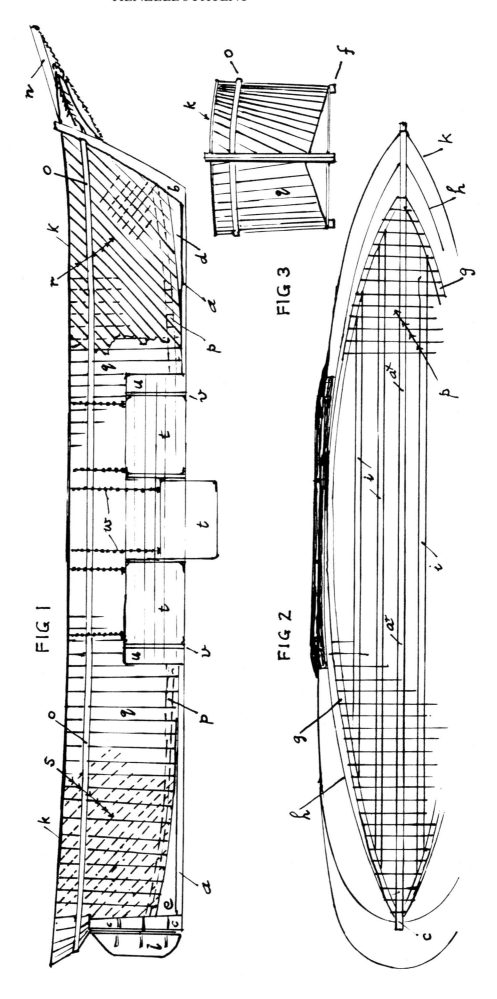

FIG 1

FIG 2

FIG 3

# 12 EMIGRANT SHIPS AND SQUARE RIGGERS

## Emigration

THE emigrant trade was of considerable importance to Padstow. At least thirty different substantial ships, many of them too big to come alongside at Padstow, sailed direct to North America and other destinations carrying up to 300 passengers each, some of them making several voyages (the EAGLE made nineteen). Twenty of them were Padstow ships, built, registered or owned in Padstow.

People remember Padstow as a schooner port, but here is a considerable fleet of passenger carrying square-riggers which not only worked out of Padstow, but also sailed from other west-country ports such as Plymouth, Truro, Falmouth and Bridgwater.

Cornishmen are to be found all over the world, many of them the descendants of skilled miners; the process of emigration started several centuries ago, and continues today as the fluctuating price of minerals causes prosperity or poverty in mining communities. The Napoleonic wars left Cornwall as the most important metalliferous mining centre of Europe, but in the 1840s cheap South Australian copper became available, followed by lead and copper from the Great Lakes and silver and lead from Mexico. That was enough to coin the phrase 'the hungry forties' in Cornwall, and when the copper market collapsed again in 1860, a second wave of emigration got under way. Emigrant ships sailed from Padstow in the nineteenth century until the 1860s; after that, emigration continued but largely by steamship from the bigger ports.

A typical sailing bill read as follows:

### EMIGRATION TO UPPER CANADA

The First Ship for Quebec
The well known Bristol built Brig
**JOHN AND MARY**
Burthen 450 Tons     James Oliver master
Positively Sailing on the 25th Instant
Persons desirous of emigrating will find this a
favourable opportunity, etc. etc.
For particulars apply to the Captain on board or to
J. TREDWEN, the Proprietor
Padstow, 8th March 1844

The fares charged in the 1830s were generally between £3 and £6, but steerage passengers were expected to provide their own food and cooking arrangements. A few years ago, the *Western Morning News* published the experiences of Jabez Brown of Bude who emigrated to Canada at the age of nineteen in 1848. He and his father walked to Stratton and caught the carrier's van (which most people these days would think of as a local stage coach) to Rock. There they took the Black Rock ferry to Padstow, and Jabez was handed over to Captain Easthope of the barque CLIO as a cabin passenger. They set sail from Padstow on 11th April and three days later had to alter course for Ireland because of a serious leak and choked pumps. The many miners on board threatened 'to rise' unless the ship headed for land. Luckily the leak was less serious than first thought, and the pumps were cleared and CLIO resumed her westerly course. On 29th April she was hove to in a gale. A few days later, at a market on board, beef was sold for 5½d. per pound, sugar 4½d., butter 12d., raisins 6d., all per pound. By 8th May they were in fog on the Grand Banks and later surrounded by ice. On 17th May they were off Cape Breton Island with their royals set in brilliant sunshine and with fourteen ships in sight. After pilotage and quarantine they were off Quebec on 29th May, just in time to see the city on fire (with 1,600 houses burnt down and over 200 lives lost). From Quebec it was steamer to Montreal, another to Kingston and Lake Ontario and yet another to Port Hope, his destination, having taken fifty-seven days from Padstow.

The CLIO sailed at least a dozen times from Padstow to Quebec between 1840 and 1850 and made other voyages from Truro and Mopus (Malpas). She carried 'upwards of 300 emigrants', so her contribution to the settlement of Upper Canada, (now the rich country of Southern Ontario), was considerable. Her particulars and an outline of her history are included in the Appendix, (as are those of the other Padstow owned emigrant ships), and it will be seen that she was one of the largest at 513 tons (new measurement), and 117.7 ft long with a maximum beam of 26.6 ft; a large ship for her day, but in twentieth-century terms, her dimensions are those of a tug or a small trawler rather than a transatlantic passenger ship for 300 passengers. CLIO's crew list from an earlier 1842 voyage survives as follows:

| Name | Age | Born at | Rank |
|---|---|---|---|
| Thomas Brown | 47 | Tintagel | Master |
| Frederick Jenkins | 25 | Crantock | Mate |
| Richard Philp | 22 | Portquin | Second Mate |
| Nicholas Bunt | 47 | Port Isaac | Cook |
| Francis Hayne | 26 | Lellissick | Seaman |
| William Thomas | 32 | Port Isaac | Seaman |
| John Browne | 25 | Boscastle | Seaman |
| Nicholas Bunt | 27 | Port Isaac | Seaman |
| James Hayne | 18 | Port Isaac | Seaman |
| Andrew Prater | 23 | Crantock | Seaman |
| Henry Trebilcock | 32 | Padstow | Seaman |
| Thomas Williams | 23 | Stratton | Ordinary Seaman |
| William Tremayne | 23 | Sticker | Steward |
| Edward Thomas | 18 | Boscastle | Seaman |
| Henry Lobb | 20 | Tintagel | Seaman |
| William Coppledick | 18 | St Teath | Apprentice |
| Thomas Garland | 18 | Boscastle | Apprentice |
| William Nichols | 16 | Boscastle | Apprentice |
| William George | 14 | St Teath | Apprentice |

The document gives the dates they joined the ship (in March 1842)

The brig DEW DROP built in 1820.

*Malcolm McCarthy Collection*

The sloop MARY built at Padstow in 1833.

*Private collection*

Plate 1

LEANDER was built at Sunderland in 1850.

*Malcolm McCarthy Collection*

EMPRESS OF CHINA in the South Seas.

*Maritime Museum of Tasmania*

Plate 2

and when they left (in general July, 1842 when the ship got back to Padstow), discharged; but opposite the names A. Prater, T. Williams, T. Garland and W. Nichols appear the words '23rd May, at Quebec. Ran away.' The ship took her time loading a lumber cargo for Padstow and on 11th June, 1842, the following are added to the crew list:

| Name | Age | Born at | Rank |
|------|-----|---------|------|
| Henry Lapham | 26 | Connecticut | Seaman |
| Bomard Francis | 23 | Kaorarovski | Seaman |
| John Beverly | 21 | Yarmouth | Seaman |

They made up her complement for the return to Padstow.

CLIO sailed from Padstow again for Quebec on 1st August and arrived back in Padstow 14th November, 1842. CLIO's owners at the time were the Avery family, with strong Boscastle connections. Even so it is surely surprising to find the whole crew, except the steward, were born in the outports of Padstow, but less surprising to see what a high proportion of them belong to families whose names keep recurring in this book right up to the present day.

The CLIO featured in the *West Briton* on 16th April, 1847:

On Tuesday last the barque CLIO lying at Cove in Padstow harbour with upwards of 300 emigrants on board for Quebec, being under sailing orders, some of the passengers came up to the town to buy provisions etc. for their voyage. When about to return, two tradesmen William Brabyn and William Rawlings took nine of them in a rather small boat, and there being much billow in the river, the boat on her passage to the ship upset and they and five passengers were drowned. Brabyn has left a wife and four children and Rawlings a wife and six, totally unprovided for.

That same year a series of newspaper reports gave a clear reason for the surge in emigration: 'Food Riots at Wadebridge. Hundreds of quarrymen from Delabole and elsewhere entered the town when corn was being loaded into a vessel. They were given bread but came back the next day in force with bludgeons etc. but fortunately there were no serious incidents.'

Such distress was widespread in Cornwall due to the depression in mining and agriculture.

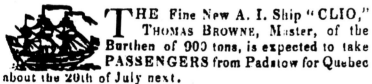

THE Fine New A. I. Ship "CLIO," THOMAS BROWNE, Master, of the Burthen of 900 tons, is expected to take PASSENGERS from Padstow for Quebec about the 20th of July next.

Apply at Mr. AVERY'S Offices, in Padstow or Boscastle.

Boscastle, June 17, 1840.

Other emigrant ships sailing from Padstow, roughly in chronological order were:

SPRING FLOWER, the barque registered at Padstow in 1827 and sailing in April that year for Miramichi. She had berths for 180 emigrants on outward passages and brought home timber and sometimes grain. She sailed to New York, Restigouche and Quebec as well as Miramichi, and carried emigrants from 1827 until 1844 or later, under captains Brown, Symons and Key. As with CLIO, the Avery family had a major shareholding in SPRING FLOWER until

she was sold to North Shields in 1859. At one time, in 1836, she and DEW DROP were both in the tiny harbour of Boscastle simultaneously taking on emigrants.

ELIZABETH. A ship of this name sailed from Padstow to Quebec in 1830 with 184 emigrants, chiefly farmers and tradesmen.

A vessel named MIRAMICHI (presumably the Glasgow barque of 582 tons built at Portland, New Brunswick in 1829) is reported to have sailed from Padstow but no date has been confirmed. (Hicks Collection : unconfirmed)

ECONOMIST. Captain Moon. A ship of this name sailed from Padstow to Quebec with 230 emigrants in 1832 probably the Plymouth barque which had been built on Prince Edward Island in 1829. She sailed more than once, taking up to 200 emigrants at a time.

VESSELS FOR SALE.

FOR SALE by AUCTION, at Padstow, on FRIDAY, the 24th of January next, by Six o'clock, at the HOTEL, on the Quay, kept by Mr. RAWLINGS,

TWO NEW SMACKS,

60 and 90 Tons burthen, not named; the brig "DEW DROP," 300 Tons; and the smack "LOUISA," 55 Tons, at sea.

On the day following, on the NORTH QUAY, at Ten o'clock, the Stores, Sails, Rigging, Cables, Anchors, Plank, Timber, &c., of several shipwrecked Vessels.

Apply to Mr. P. RAWLE, jun.; or to Mr. THOMAS CARTER, Padstow.

Dated, Padstow, December 28, 1844.

DEW DROP. Built as a snow, Captain Michael Wade of Tintagel brought this long-serving Padstow brig from Hull as managing-owner, but later she was owned by Tom Avery of Boscastle and sailed from there as well as Padstow from 1833 until 1852 with emigrants to Quebec, St John's (New Brunswick), New York and Miramichi. Her crew were eleven or so strong and masters included Edwin Key, Ralph Brown, T. Rickard and J. Burke.

LOUISA. On 31st March, 1834 Captain William Old took charge of the Bristol full-rigged ship LOUISA at Padstow and sailed for Miramichi with emigrants. She was 411 tons, length 105.8, breadth 30.3, height between decks 6.1 ft. She had been built at Workington in 1810 with 'one deck and a half deck'. That indicates that there was a deck below the main deck along the after half of the ship which could be used as accommodation: any emigrants in the forward half of the ship would be living on planks and straw placed on top of the ballast and cargo. Her owner, Davis Hewson of Bristol, accepted her back from William Old on 13th August at Padstow whither she had returned with a cargo of lumber.

The 200 ton barque IPSWICH, described as an emigrant ship, was hauled off the Doom Bar in 1836, and is reported to have sailed from Padstow for Quebec on 27th June, 1838 with Captain Lakeman in command.

JOHN AND MARY. This brig, the subject of the sailing bill quoted earlier, worked from 1839 to 1844 between Padstow and Quebec, for instance sailing with 108 passengers on 16th April, 1841. She was sold to Quebec owners in 1844 and lost sight of. Her particulars are, of course, in the Appendix.

## FOR QUEBEC,

THE BRIG "JOHN and MARY," now lying in Mr. TREDWEN's DOCK, *Padstow*, will take a FEW PASSENGERS, and positively sails on the 20th of March. As every accommodation to afford comfort will be made, this will be an excellent opportunity for Persons intending to Emigrate, more particularly as the "Clio's" term of four years' standing allowed by Lloyds, having some time since expired, and is now expunged from their books; and the "JOHN and MARY" having been regularly surveyed by Lloyd's Surveyor, stands high, which united with the meekness and ability of the Captain, it is hoped will command a preference.

Application to be made to Mr. TREDWEN, or the Captain on board.

Dated, Padstow, February 13, 1844.

The snow **VOLUNA** is well covered in the appendix. In 1839 she traded Padstow-Pugwash (Nova Scotia)-Padstow-Gloucester-Quebec-Gloucester-Padstow-Quebec-Padstow and she was regularly billed to sail with emigrants from Padstow for Quebec thereafter. In 1857, her owners were fined £20 for allowing her to sail without a mate on board, and on 31st May that same year she was wrecked on the rocks off St Agnes Island in thick fog, having sailed from Falmouth the previous day for Quebec.

The barque **BELLE** of 1840 was either built for Norway & Co. of Wadebridge, or bought by them soon after completion. In April 1842 she is reported to have taken 264 passengers for Quebec. Later that year 71 named emigrants signed a testimonial to her captain George Brewer and she went on taking up to 140 passengers into the 1850s.

The barque **MARCHIONESS OF ABERCORN** had a brief spell as an emigrant ship with Edwin Key as master before being lost in 1849.

Although the barque **DAEDALUS** was not reported in the newspapers as an emigrant carrier until 1850, she had been owned by T. L. Seaton and registered at Padstow since 1844 and she was taking emigrants to Quebec when sailing from Falmouth, Plymouth and Portsmouth as well as Padstow until about 1860. She normally had a crew of nineteen all told.

The brig **EAGLE**, M Parnall master, was advertised to sail from Padstow for Quebec on 6th April, 1847. This was the first of her many voyages from Padstow.

**JANE LOWDEN** was yet another barque built in Canada and owned by T. L. Seaton. She was unusual among Padstow ships in trading to the Black Sea, but her chief trade was to Quebec with emigrants and back with timber, both from Falmouth and Padstow.

She was one of eight lumber-laden ships which were caught in a violent storm on 20th December, 1865, returning to Europe from the St Lawrence River. Her crew of seventeen took to the rigging when the storm struck, but the JANE LOWDEN was blown over on her beam ends and they were washed away. Eight struggled back and lashed themselves to the hull. When the waterlogged vessel righted herself days later, they had to take to the rigging again where they died one by one in the following days. Captain Casey was rescued by the Dutch barque IDA ELISABETH of Rotterdam on 23rd January, 1866, the sole survivor of 160 men on the eight ships; it is reported that he only weighed 48 pounds when rescued, but he survived, and even recovered sufficiently to be able to walk a little.

The ship **INTREPID** is adequately covered in the Appendix.

The **MORNING STAR**, the only full rigged ship built at Padstow, was well suited to carry emigrants, having two decks. Her cost was more than the capital resources of Padstow could bear, and she had numerous shareholders in St Issey, Bodmin, St Teath, St Tudy, Camborne, Truro, Rock and even Manchester. She is reported to have taken emigrants from Padstow, but since she traded to India, the West Indies and Australia as well as North America, their destination is uncertain.

A ship called **MARGARET** is also reported to have taken emigrants, but it is suggested that the vessel was more probably the

Padstow emigrants were often rowed over for a final service in St Michael's Church, Porthilly, before sailing for the New World.

MARGARITA (see Appendix) in view of R. Easthope and T. Key taking command of her in the 1850s. She was lost in the Gulf of Mexico in 1860.

ALCHYMIST. This barque built on Prince Edward Island in 1828 had an adventurous life before transferring from Falmouth to Padstow registry in 1855. She was taking emigrants from Restronguet and other Westcountry ports in the 1830s. In June 1844, Captain Hill wrote confirming her safe arrival at Quebec from Padstow after encountering contrary winds and icebergs. In May 1845, the arrival of the barque ALCHYMIST direct from Ichaboe with about 260 tons of guano was reported. Ichaboe is an island off the coast of Great Namaqua Land, S.W. Africa, and was at the time a source of inferior guano. The trade was hazardous; a British crew had been captured and killed by Moorish pirates in 1844. Thomas Littlefair Seaton was her Padstow owner from 1855 to 1868 when she was sold foreign. His regime was emigrants out and lumber home, and the emigrants would be thankful that there were no guano cargoes involved.

MALAKOFF, UNION, COLUMBUS and CYRUS. These four vessels, none of them Padstow ships, have been listed as sailing from Padstow with emigrants, but it has not yet been possible to identify them with any certainty. (Hicks Collection)

In June 1866, reporting yet another slump in mining, the *West Briton* reported: 'UNPRECEDENTED EXODUS. Emigration to America, California, Nova Scotia, Australia and New Zealand. According to the gloomy prospects, unless the spirit of emigration is kept up, the distress will be greatly increased.'

As well as those of the ships already mentioned which continued trading, another group of ships took part in the 1860s.

Some of the interesting history of the barque SIR CHARLES NAPIER is covered in the Appendix but, in addition, she is credited with carrying supplies to the Crimea and bringing back various old cannon to adorn Prideaux Place in Padstow, and under Captains Broad and Mabley, she took emigrants to Quebec in the 1860s. In 1945 there were old salts at Padstow who could remember her being laid up in Dennis Cove each winter, then fitted out in the spring and off to Quebec for a load of timber. That routine continued through the 1870s until she was sold to the Norwegians in 1881.

The brig JESSIE, built at Padstow, was smaller than the other emigrant ships, but commanded by J. Tippet through the 1860s, she traded transatlantic and took emigrants on occasion.

The barque ALBERT (ON 25430) joined the Padstow fleet in 1864, the STORM (ON 53006) and the ZARAH (ON 11543) in 1866, and the activities of all three are to be found in the Appendix. Bread riots threatened in Cornwall as late as January 1868, so these latecomers found passengers to the New World, as the brigantine ADELAIDE (ON 58295) is reported to have done on completion by John Tredwen Junior in 1869.

Padstow's experience with iron and steel hulls was consistently unfortunate, and the last of her emigrant ships demonstrates the point. The iron full-rigged ship ENGLAND'S GLORY, 787 gross tons, was completed by W. Pile & Co., the famous Sunderland yard, in 1869 for Smith & Co. of London and E. Moon of Plymouth. She was chartered to the New Zealand Shipping Co. and with Moon as captain sailed to Port Chalmers in 1870. About 1874, Moon became managing owner and William Knight of Padstow took over as captain. In 1876, another New Zealand charter took her out from London to Auckland in ninety-eight days port to port; a fair-weather passage. By 1881, with Knight still in command, she was registered at Padstow and had been reduced to Barque rig. She left London for

The figurehead of the ship ENGLAND'S GLORY now in Southland Museum, New Zealand.

Nelson and Bluff in New Zealand on 10th May, loaded with 380 tons of railway iron and a general cargo. Off the Cape of Good Hope the iron began to work and shift. Frantic efforts were made to wedge it into place but without success, so she bore away for Mauritius where the cargo was discharged and re-stowed. Three weeks after arriving at Mauritius she was able to sail to Nelson, where most of the general cargo was unloaded, then on slowly down the stormy west coast of South Island where she was forced to heave to in a heavy gale. The iron started moving again, so she ran for the Foveaux Straits and sheltered in the lee of Stewart Island. The next day, 7th November, she sailed on towards Bluff Harbour, picked up her pilot, failed to gather steerage way at a critical point, and grounded on the rocks at Look-out Point. The swell was sufficient to thump her up and down on the rocks until she was holed, filled and fell over on her side, a total wreck. Captain Knight and his crew had been able to launch their boats and land at Bluff after a fruitless voyage of six months. ENGLAND'S GLORY had no emigrants on board when she was lost, but her remains rest just about as far away from Padstow as it is possible to get on the surface of the earth.

The organization of the emigrant trade was far from haphazard. Conditions may have been primitive and crowded by today's standards, but there were government regulations and they were generally obeyed and there was little mortality. Many of the ships had relatively old and lightly built soft wood hulls, but they were far from being the floating coffins of some novels. They were surveyed and repaired and some of them were 'doubled', that is had an extra layer of planking built onto the outside of the hull to strengthen it. Ashore the organization had to be complex, requiring the equivalent of a network of travel agents and the ability to provide supplies for relatively large numbers of people. The well-established merchants of the Norway and Avery families were in a position to play a leading role, and also to provide ship-owning capital: the Tredwen family, whilst more local to the town of Padstow, also contributed, and of course gained considerably from all the shipwork.

Another requirement was for experienced well-qualified deepwater masters and mates, eventually with full square-rigger Board of Trade certificates. Robert Easthope was born at Cork and Tom Seaton at Whitby, but they soon progressed from being the masters of Padstow emigrant ships into the position of respected local owners. The Mably and Langford families were already well established locally, (Thomas Langford was the surveying officer for Padstow 1814-1831) and, together with the Browns, Symonses and Keys, they provided many masters and mates and, to some extent, shareholders.

BARQUE 'BELLE', 1840. Reconstruction

## The Other Square-riggers

As described in earlier chapters, until the fore-and-aft rig was developed in the eighteenth century, virtually all Padstow's ships were, technically, square rigged. Looking quickly through *Lloyd's Register* for 1780, there are what later generations would consider to be strange anomalies in the rigs. The brig BETSY, 45 tons, built at Quebec in 1764: the sloop LOVELY PEGGY, 160 tons, built at Dublin 1775. We would expect the tonnages to be reversed a few years later. Next to the LOVELY PEGGY appears the ship LOVELY NELLY, 160 tons, built at Dublin 1775, a three-masted full rigged ship no bigger than a sloop, built at the same time!

In the nineteenth century the advantages of the various rigs came to be more fully understood. The craft with fore-and-aft rig, that is cutters, sloops, ketches and schooners, tended to be small vessels with a small number of relatively large sails. They only required small crews and were handy for coastal and short sea work. The square-rigged vessels, that is ships, barques, barkentines, brigs, snows and brigantines, tended to be larger vessels with larger crews. The square rig allowed the sail area to be split up into a greater number of sails, so that they were each of a handy size even in a very large ship: the square rig really came into its own for long downwind ocean passages.

There were endless exceptions to the general assessment given above. Small British schooners traded to Newfoundland whereas the coal trade from Newcastle-upon-Tyne to the Thames was largely in the hands of brigs. The huge American fore-and-aft schooners were as large as the largest full rigged ships (and had steam winches to handle their huge sails).

For hundreds of years, many of the larger vessels required large crews to defend the ship against corsairs and other enemies, so as in naval vessels there were plenty of men to climb aloft and handle square sails. Throughout the nineteenth century, as the economic pressures came on and the need for defence diminished, it became necessary to have rigs which could be handled by smaller crews. Thus full rigged ships were modified into barques, barques became barkentines and schooners were re-rigged as ketches, in each case to enable the crew to be reduced somewhat.

The Appendix includes details of all Padstow's nineteenth century square-riggers (along with all other rigs): the next few pages list the larger ones, other than the emigrant ships already dealt with, and the POMARON which is the subject of a separate chapter.

The same owners and masters who participated in the emigrant trade naturally tended to be involved with the other big blue-water ships of Padstow. Thus the Easthopes bought the small full rigged ship HARRIET SCOTT in 1851; she was converted to barque rig and traded to North America until she was lost in 1854. The following year they registered the larger ship CARTHAGE of mysterious origin, lost in 1861. In 1859 they bought the WINDSOR, the only Padstow ship to exceed 1,000 tons, and finally in 1862, the LADY SALE, another Canadian-built full rigged ship.

John Tredwen owned ROYAL ADELAIDE in 1869 and shared AURORA with John Cory, who owned THE KILDARE and JOHN HENRY when he was still a Padstonian. ROSALIE, built at Padstow in 1879, was briefly registered at Cardiff as owned by James H. Cory before being sold foreign.

John Stribley had the barques BREADALBANE and LOTA (and numerous smaller vessels). William Geake owned the famous barkentines LYDIA CARDELL and WILLIAM GEAKE (and the smaller three masted schooner JANE SLADE).

That leaves a few other square-riggers to be listed, each with different owners; the barque ALAN, the ship CORNUVIA, the barkentine COUNTESS OF DEVON, the barque LEANDER, the barkentine LILE, the brig, later barkentine, MARIE SOPHIE, Mear's barque OCEAN SPRITE, the barque RUBY which Williams had altered to barkentine rig, the barque SAUGEEN and Bellamy's brig TRY AGAIN. The HOPEFUL and EMPRESS OF CHINA are dealt with later in the chapter.

So far, forty-four Padstow square-riggers, all over 230 gross tons, have been mentioned (and a few emigrant ships which sailed from Padstow without being built or owned there). Sadly, examining their histories, it is surprising to find how many of them were lost soon after becoming Padstow ships.

## SHIPS LOST WITHIN SIX YEARS OF ACQUISITION

| Name | Built In | Padstow owned | Loss |
|---|---|---|---|
| Alan | 1858 Austria | 1870 | Wrecked 1873 |
| Albert | 1847 Nova Scotia | 1864 | Wrecked 1869 |
| Aurora | 1855 Padstow | 1855 | Wrecked 1861 |
| Breadalbane | 1849 Nova Scotia | 1855 | Lost at sea 1859 |
| Carthage | Unknown | 1855 | Lost 1861 |
| Countess of Devon | 1873 Plymouth | 1905 | Lost 1905 |
| England's Glory | 1869 Sunderland | 1880 | Wrecked 1881 |
| Harriet Scott | 1836 Quebec | 1851 | Lost 1854 |
| Hopeful | 1876 Padstow | 1876 | Wrecked 1880 |
| Lady Sale | 1843 New Brunswick | 1862 | Lost 1867 |
| Marchioness of Abercorn | 1837 Quebec | 1848 | Lost 1849 |
| Marie Sophie | 1879 Elsfleth | 1898 | Lost 1902 |
| Royal Adelaide | 1831 Quebec | 1869 | Wrecked 1872 |
| Storm | Unknown | 1866 | Stranded 1871 |
| Windsor | 1850 Quebec | 1859 | Aband'ed at sea 1866 |

Thus one-third of Padstow's biggest sailing ships were lost within six years of coming under Padstow ownership, and if one considers the nine foreign-built vessels above, they were on the average 16½ years old when bought by Padstonians, and were lost on the average between three and four years later. Those are rather grim statistics, and it is possible to see some of the factors which brought them about, including the shortage of capital at Padstow, the acumen which saw the advantage of buying large, cheap ships of limited life when the relatively short periods of mass emigration occurred and, finally, the salvaging and rebuilding of ships wrecked on the Cornish coasts which produced some bargains which were too tempting to be passed up.

## The Australian Connection

John Stribley built the beautiful barkentines EMPRESS OF CHINA and HOPEFUL at the Dennis Cove yard in 1874 and 1876 respectively. It was not long before the EMPRESS OF CHINA was registered in Hobart, Tasmania, and she made a great impression there. I found two paintings of her displayed in Hobart Maritime Museum, and the best account of her loss is given in Harry O'May's *Wrecks in Tasmanian Waters*:

The EMPRESS OF CHINA was a splendid little wooden barque [sic] of 250 tons built at Padstow, England in 1874 and owned by Facy and Fisher of Hobart. She made many smart trips between inter-colonial ports and sailed from Geelong for Hobart on 28th December 1888. When off Albatross Island she ran into thick fog. Captain Chaplain took in all light sails and posted the Bo'swain on the look-out. At 2.45 am on the 31st land was reported on the lee bow. The helm was put down and the head sheets let fly but all efforts to save her were too late. She struck the Black Pyramid Rock about seventeen miles west of Hunter Island.

All hands got away in the boat with a compass and a few provisions. They sheltered under the lee of the rock till the fog lifted. Then they returned to the spot where the barque had struck but she had disappeared. The castaways landed on Cape Grim at 5.30 pm on 1st January 1889. Hobart shiplovers were distressed when they heard of the loss of the 'Little Empress' as she was called by her many admirers.

The Stribley family (and at times their bank manager) held the ownership of the HOPEFUL for a few years before Williams of Truro took her, but in 1880 her registry was transferred from Padstow to Sydney, New South Wales, the owner being R. Philp of Townsville. Can it be mere coincidence that she and her near sister went out to Australia in 1879-1880? The Philps of Padstow were well-known shipowners for generations: was there kinship with Robert Philp of Townsville, Queensland? If so, then here is another enterprising Padstow shipowner, because the barkentine HOPEFUL was his first vessel, and he and James Burns founded the famous Australian shipping and trading firm, Burns, Philp & Co. Ltd with its huge fleet and a trading empire all over the South Pacific. But Robert Philp was born in Glasgow in 1852 so the connection with Padstow is probably limited to the vessel itself. Immediately after her arrival in Australian waters, disaster struck. 'The barkentine HOPEFUL dragged her anchors near the mouth of Liverpool Creek, Cardwell, Queensland on 12th January 1880 and drove ashore. Her remains were purchased by Mr Philip of Cardwell for £250.' So runs the entry in *Australian Shipwrecks* Vol 3, and it agrees with the official report of her loss (c. 2906 1881). Her Padstow registry closes with the note '12th April, 1880, Stranded near S. Burnard Island, New South Wales'. Is that a second stranding? If so, she survived them both and traded for Burns Philp in the Coral Sea for five years before they sold her in 1885.

Queensland became a separate colony in 1859, reinforcing the likelihood that there was a second episode in New South Wales. Her felt and yellow metal were renewed in April 1880, but that might be either the culmination of a major repair following a January stranding, or Mr Philp (Philip?) taking advantage of a docking following an April stranding.

But her ultimate fate remains a mystery; J. A. Curtis of Sydney owned her 1885-7, and then she was 'sold foreign'. The final intriguing entries in *Lloyd's Registers* 1890-1892 describe her as a lorcha with un-named Chinese owners. A lorcha has been defined as an eastern trading vessel with a European type of hull, and a Chinese junk rig for ease of handling by native crews, employed in the nineteenth century by European companies, often in the opium trade. It can be said with some confidence that the HOPEFUL was the only lorcha built at Padstow.

A third barkentine, the Bideford registered FLYING SCUD, owned for a time by John Ennor of Newquay, was registered at Ramsey, Isle of Man, by Thomas Corlett c. 1887. He sailed her out to Australia in 1890, and changed her registry to Sydney, New South Wales. No more is known.

A somewhat similar situation arose earlier when the schooner OSPREY, built at Leith in 1842, 66 tons, and registered at Padstow 1850-1853, then subsequently at Glasgow, disappeared from our ken. Or did she? In 1884, a schooner named OSPREY was registered at Sydney, New South Wales, and for the first time given an official number, 49299. It was known that she had been built at Leith, but the date was not known. She was measured to be 64 tons. It seems probable that the OSPREY was the vessel previously registered at Padstow and Glasgow, and it would be interesting to know how the intervening years had been spent. *Australian Shipwrecks*, Vol 3, contains the following entry: '1897. On 1st and 2nd June, during wild and stormy weather, the coastal traders ABILITY, BELL BIRD, FAVOURITE and OSPREY were driven ashore near Forster, NSW and could not be refloated. The OSPREY was a schooner of 64 tons on dimensions 72.0 x 16.1 x 9.2 ft'. These are compatible with the measurements on the Padstow register.

Earlier in this chapter the emigrant ships ENGLAND'S GLORY

and MORNING STAR were mentioned as trading to the antipodes, and there is one last emigrant ship to deal with. The NAUTILUS, 82 tons, was built at Padstow in 1839 by John Tredwen. He passed her to his kinsman Charles Tredwen in 1849 and she traded from Liverpool to Tampico. Charles and some friends decided to emigrate to Australia in his small schooner and they invited a Captain Robert Brown to take command, as he was experienced in trading to the Far East. Brown was a versatile man who had been a shipwright as well as a sea captain. He had designed and built the schooner yacht ACHELOUS at Ilfracombe in 1852 which sought to improve upon the lines of the famous AMERICA which had beaten all comers at Cowes the previous year. ACHELOUS was extraordinarily successful and joined the Royal Yacht Squadron, being renamed GOLIATH despite being less than fifty feet in length. Brown was clearly taken with the idea of sailing a schooner only 10 ft longer than his yacht to Australia, for he accepted, and in January 1854

took over the NAUTILUS at Liverpool. The voyage was a success and in due course, what may have been Padstow's smallest emigrant ship, arrived in Port Phillip Bay. Robert Brown returned to Devon and Charles Tredwen settled his family in Melbourne and commanded his NAUTILUS in the coastal trade, but not for long, because on 15th January, 1856, she was wrecked on a remote beach near Cape Liptrap, Victoria on a voyage from Melbourne to Westernport for stone. Leaving Captain Tredwen and one woman passenger on the wreck, the crew of four managed to cross the coastal ranges reaching Port Albert after three days. There they were suspected of being escaped convicts until they produced a letter from their captain requesting assistance.

As a final postscript, the 1866 *Mercantile Navy List* includes a CORNWALL of Melbourne of 29 tons owned by Richard Tredwen of Williamstown (near Melbourne), Victoria.

Barkentine COUNTESS OF DEVON.
*The Newquay Old Cornwall Society*

# 13 THE ROARING DAYS OF SAIL
## The Nineteenth Century

### The Shape of the Ships

AT the start of the nineteenth century the Padstow fleet consisted of about thirty small vessels, sloops, cutters and brigs. One of the factors influencing changes of hull and rig was the substantial number of prizes 'made free' during the Napoleonic wars. For example, of twenty-two ships registered at Padstow in 1814 and 1815 (the first surviving Padstow registers) nine were foreign prizes with French and Scandinavian origins.

The first schooner known to be in the Padstow fleet was the REVENGE, foreign built in 1794 and owned in Padstow by 1801. It seems likely that it was the influence of her and others like her which led to the building of the first schooners at Padstow which were, as far as we know, the AGNES (1809), SUSAN (1813), COMMERCE (1819) and the GRACE and CERES (both 1820). The polacre schooner THOMAS & NANCY of 1821 was the only other

schooner built before 1825, after which the schooner rig rapidly increased in popularity.

Another rig which reached Padstow in the shape of prizes was the ketch. The SALLY ANN, built in Prussia in 1799, was owned by Rawlins of Padstow by 1809. *Lloyd's Register* shows her to be a ketch, but she is also described as a galeas. The EDWARD *ex* HOFFNUNG was registered at Dover in 1813 and Padstow in 1816 and her name suggests a similar origin. But the ketch rig did not catch on at Padstow for many years, and it never superseded the schooner rig to the extent that it did in other Westcountry ports. VOLUTINA (1855), SUNSHINE (1857) and HESPERUS (1875) were the only three ketches built at the Padstow yards; TRIUMPH was the only ketch built at Newquay, and none was built at Bude until it had ceased to be an outport of Padstow.

The polacre (or polacca) THOMAS & NANCY was the only

The schooner GIPSY MAID at Padstow c. 1905. Note railway buffers at end of quay on the right.          *Terry Belt Collection*

vessel of that rig built at Padstow, but the CAMEL and the PETER & SARAH were two others of great interest which came to be owned at Padstow. The CAMEL was built at Ragusa, and the term 'polacca' was originally used to describe a three masted Mediterranean type. Polacre basically means pole masted, that is having no topmast as a separate spar. The PETER & SARAH was built at Bideford where the polacre brigantine was a popular rig. They were known locally as 'muffies', a corruption of herm-aphrodites! MARGARET (ON 29837) was reported to be an hermaphrodite when owned in Newquay in the 1870s.

. The following table lists the rigs of vessels built at, or belonging to, Padstow as listed in *Lloyd's Register* (and supplements):

| Rig | Year 1851 | Year 1871 |
|---|---|---|
| Ship | — | — |
| Barque | 4 | 3 |
| Brig | 7 | 2 |
| Snow | 1 | — |
| Brigantine | 4 | 4 |
| Schooner | 51 | 77 |
| Ketch | 2 | — |
| Smack | 20 | 5 |
| Cutter | — | 6 |
| Sloop | 2 | — |
| Dandy | — | 1 |
| Total | 91 | 98 |

Although the comparison between the two years is somewhat deceptive, this tabulation does demonstrate the increasing predominance of the schooner rig. The smallest Padstow vessels in the 1851 register were ADA, 35 tons, and ST STEPHEN, 28 tons after lengthening, whereas the smallest in 1871 were WILLIE, 41 tons, and VELOCITY, 45 tons. There were well over 100 vessels built or owned in Padstow by 1871, but *Lloyd's Register* was progressively losing interest in vessels of small size. Most of the smacks listed in 1851 were still in existence but unlisted in 1871. By 1891, with very few exceptions, vessels had to measure at least 100 gross tons to be included in *Lloyd's Register*, so much of the Padstow fleet was omitted.

The 1851 edition reveals the extent of the practice of lengthening Padstow's small ships, many of the operations being carried out at Tredwen's dockyard.

| Name | Built | Rig | Length'd | Rig after lengthening |
|---|---|---|---|---|
| ALERT | 1844 | Sloop | 1851 | Ketch |
| CELERITY | 1829 | Schooner | 1848 | Schooner |
| ELIZABETH | 1839 | Schooner | 1850 | Schooner |
| LIBERTY | 1838 | Smack | 1850 | Schooner |
| MARY JOSEPHINE | 1842 | Schooner | 1851 | Schooner |
| OCEAN | 1831 | Brigantine | 1851 | Schooner |
| ST STEPHEN | 1832 | Smack | 1839 | Smack |
| SAMUEL & ELIZABETH | 1834 | Sloop | 1848 | Schooner |
| VESPER | 1837 | Schooner | 1839 | Schooner |

Further details of all these vessels will, of course, be found in the Appendix. The VESPER was lengthened only two years after being built; perhaps advantage was taken of a docking to repair major damage.

The 1871 edition of *Lloyd's Register* includes ten lengthened Padstow vessels, as follows:

| Name | Built | Rig | Length'd | Rig after lengthening |
|---|---|---|---|---|
| ALBION | 1862 | Smack | 1869 | Schooner |
| BESSY JANE | 1850 | Schooner | 1872 | Schooner |
| CATHERINE | 1841 | Sloop | 1863 | Schooner |
| CONSTANCE | 1858 | Schooner | 1870 | 3 mast Schooner |
| FAVOURITE | 1851 | Schooner | 1864 | Brigantine |
| FAWN | 1858 | Smack | 1860 | Smack |
| LITTLE RACER | 1862 | Cutter | 1865 | Schooner |
| ROSE | 1843 | Schooner | 1855 | Schooner |
| TREBISKIN | 1859 | Schooner | 1868 | Schooner |
| VESPER | 1837 | Schooner | 1839 | Schooner |

Only the VESPER survives from those lengthened in 1851, or earlier. Although built as a schooner, FAVOURITE was altered to brigantine rig before lengthening. FAWN was re-rigged as a two masted dandy some years after lengthening, and others changed rig later in life.

Of the 91 Padstow ships listed in the 1851 *Lloyd's Register*, 24 of the largest were trading to foreign countries, including 8 in the emigrant and timber trades to Quebec and New York State, 7 to the Mediterranean, 2 to the Baltic, and 3 to the near continent. The other four ships were the brig FLORIST for the River Plate, the schooner LOUISE for Galatz on the Black Sea, the brig LADY MONA for Arica, Chile, probably on some mining enterprise, and the brigantine RANGER for Charleston, South Carolina. Eight of these were actually sailing from Padstow, principally in the Quebec and Mediterranean trades. With only two exceptions, the square riggers were in the transatlantic trades, and the schooners were in the European and Mediterranean trades. Of these 24 ships, Lloyds lists only 7 as yellow metalled, and 4 as sheathed with zinc, leaving a number trading to the Mediterranean and tropical waters apparently without sheathing against marine borers.

By comparison, in 1871, 27 foreign traders are listed, but only 2 were trading to North America, with the emigrant trade coming to an end; 12 were for the Mediterranean, 4 for the West Indies, 4 for South America, and the rest for Western Europe. Only 4 of these were actually sailing from Padstow; it could be said that Padstow ships were no longer serving Padstow, but instead, in the coasting as well as the overseas trades, they were simply units of the British Mercantile Marine, earning their living wherever freights offered. They were also better protected against borers: 18 were yellow metalled, 3 were coppered, 4 were zinc sheathed, and the FAWN was protected with union metal, a patent alloy. The only two unprotected ships were trading to Spain.

In 1871, it was no longer true to say that the square riggers traded transatlantic, and the schooners did not. A new breed of powerful schooners built by Tredwen and Willmett were trading to the West Indies and South America, and the barque POMARON and the brigs JESSIE and JANE FRANCIS were trading to Iberia.

The various rigs are demonstrated in a series of reconstructions of Padstow ships to be found at the end of this chapter. The terms 'brigantine' and 'barkentine' (or barquentine) have caused much confusion. A barkentine was often described as a three-masted brigantine in custom house registers, and as *Lloyd's Register* did not record the number of masts of a vessel until 1875, and then only sporadically, many barkentines are listed as brigantines in *Lloyd's Register* and elsewhere. Brigantines are sometimes described as 'square rigged on foremast, schooner rigged on mainmast' in early registers, but some early schooners had square topsails on their mainmast, so the exact rig remains doubtful. The term 'schooner-brig' sometimes occurs on the Padstow, St Ives and Penzance registers. A number of Scottish schooners (DEVERON, DUNDARG and KINNAIRD for example) were bought by Padstow owners and promptly described as brigantines, to the extent that one suspects they were different names for the same rig, much as the Germans often called a brigantine *Schonerbrigg* and a barkentine *Driemastschoner*.

Schooners themselves had many variations of rig. The early schooners with square topsails on both masts have already been mentioned, but many of the early westcountry coasting schooners only had one square sail, a square fore topsail.

Those trading further afield often had a longer fore topmast and set a topgallant sail above the topsail. After about 1865, the normal practice was to rig schooners with an upper and lower fore topsail in place of the deep single topsail, thus reducing the size of sail for ease of handling.

The topgallant schooner, both two-masted and three-masted, remained in widespread use until the end of the sailing ship era. One of the reasons for the popularity of this rig was that it enabled a master with a 'fore-and-aft certificate' to trade worldwide. In the last quarter of the nineteenth century there were many schooner masters with 'fore-and-aft certificates' who had little or no opportunity of qualifying for the 'ordinary master's certificate' which would have allowed them to take command of a square-rigged vessel such as a brig or brigantine.

Another schooner variation concerned the rigging of the bowsprit. Almost all the smacks, cutters and sloops registered at Padstow had 'running bowsprits', that is to say, the bowsprit could be unshipped and run inboard to avoid the vulnerable projection forward which was particularly liable to damage when, for instance, loading coal in a congested dock. So when the first schooners were built at Padstow, some of them (the SUSAN for instance) had running bowsprits. However, as the schooner rig developed, the standard rigging became more complex and the unshipping of the bowsprit was seen not to be worthwhile, entailing as it did striking the foretopmast or arranging temporary stays. But there were exceptions: in 1866 the running bowsprit schooner RACER was built for William Luke, a Charlestown merchant; in the days when the tiny basin at Charlestown was full of vessels, it can be imagined that this ability to unship the bowsprit might make all the difference between being able to get in or having to wait outside!

## Surveys

Although there is virtually a total absence of drawings of the hulls of sailing vessels built at Padstow, the results of numerous Lloyd's surveys are preserved and tell us much about them. For instance, the coasting smack MARYS & HELENA, built by John Tredwen in 1826, was surveyed at Padstow in 1841. As she had not been examined for five years, the survey was *de novo*, taking nothing for granted.

She measured 48.3 x 16.0 x 8.5 ft. Her frames were 18½ ins apart, so with 8 ins floors and 7ins foothooks there was a gap of only 3½ ins between the timbers of each frame from bilge to bilge. The moulded thickness of the frames tapered from 8 ins for the floors to 5½ ins for the top timbers. The deck beams were 8 x 7½ ins, the keel 8½ x 9½ ins, the keelson 10½ x 11½ ins and there was a false keelson 10 x 10½ ins.

The outside planking was 2 ins thick, increasing to 2¾ ins for the bilge planks, and 3½ ins for the wales. The inside planking (ceiling) was also 2 ins with 3 ins for the bilge planks.

The entire frame was of English oak, as was all the outside planking apart from the keel and bottom which were American elm. The inside planking was of American oak to the bilges and English oak above. The decks were of yellow pine (American yellow pine was almost invariably used for decks at Padstow).

Iron bolts were used throughout, 1 ins diameter for the keelsons, 7/8ths ins for transoms and hooks, 5¾ ins dia. at stem, deadwood, deck beams, etc. and 5/8ths ins dia. elsewhere. With through bolting from inside to outside planking, the hull became an almost solid oak structure at least 10 ins thick below the waterline and well over 1 ft thick at the bilges.

She had four jibs, two foresails, one mainsail and one gaff topsail and was 'well found in light sails'. There were two bower anchors, one stream and two kedges, all of sufficient weight, seventy-five fathoms of ¾ ins chain, and various cables and warps from 6 ins to 3 ins size. Her equipment included one boat, one windlass and one wooden pump.

Mr Broad, the surveyor, went on to detail various repairs which had been carried out, to recommend classification of the vessel, and to sign for receipt of his ten shilling fee.

The tiny smack TEMPERANCE, built in 1841, had only marginally smaller scantlings, retained 2 ins outer planking, but had 1½ ins rather than 2 ins ceilings. The VICTORIA, built at Port Gaverne in 1853, had even bigger timbers leaving a gap of only 2 ins between adjacent frames, and thicker planking.

The drawing of a typical cross section indicates where the various timbers named in the surveys are to be found in the vessels' structure.

Turning now to the surveys of schooners, one would expect the scantlings to increase proportionally with the tonnage, to provide roughly the same factor of safety (though at some critical length or size of ship, additional strengthening would clearly become necessary). However, with English oak frame timbers seasoning at the yards for several years before use, with floors and foothooks already sized at 8 ins or more for the smacks, and with so little space left between adjacent frames, it was certainly not a simple matter to build a schooner twice the size of a smack simply by doubling the strength of each individual member. Instead the process was evolutionary with only a moderate increase in the scantlings, and with the achievement of some greater strength in other ways, such as using better materials, insisting on 'greater shifts' in timbers and planking (or, in other words, keeping the butts in adjacent timbers further apart), and providing additional fastenings. In any case, the schooner traded less to the most exposed beaches than the smacks, so it could be argued that they were less subject to the most severe wear and tear.

Here are the figures for the schooner BEDWELTY built by John Tredwen in 1841 for comparison with the MARYS & HELENA, surveyed the same year. The schooner measured 63.1 x 18.3 x 11.4 ft. Her frames were 21½ ins apart, so with 10 ins floors and 9¼ ins foothooks, there was a gap of only 2¼ ins between the timbers of each frame. The moulded thickness of the frames tapered from 11 ins for the floors to 4¼ ins for the top timbers. The deck beams were 10 x 9 ins, the keel 10 x 10 ins, and the keelsons 11½ x 19 ins.

The outside planking was 2½ ins thick, increasing to 3½ ins for bilge planks and 4 ins for wales. The inside planking was also 2½ ins, with 3¼ ins for bilge planks.

In the smack, the alternate frames were not bolted together whereas in the BEDWELTY they were described as well bolted together. The types of timber used were the same in both vessels, except that the bottom planking of the schooner is described as American white rock elm, and there was American red pine for the waterways.

Iron bolts of 1/8th in. to 5/8ths in. diameter helped to ensure that the hull was a virtually solid structure at least 13 ins thick below the waterline and over 15 ins thick at the bilges.

Being a new ship, the BEDWELTY's survey gives us a list of her sails which is undoubtedly a complete suit and no more. Two standing jibs, one fore-topmast staysail, one fore-staysail, one foresail, one fore topsail, one mainsail, one main topsail. She had a list of ground tackle similar to the smack, one long boat and one other boat. Mr Broad was of the opinion she was entitled to be classed A1 for twelve years and he signed for receipt of a £2 fee.

Bear with me now for one more survey, that carried out during the building in 1878 of the famous Padstow schooner KATIE by Cowl & Sons for Thomas Jenkin of Newquay.

The KATIE measured 85.5 x 23.0 x 10.8 ft. Her register tonnage was 99.48 (BEDWELTY was 86 reg. tons by the same method of measurement). There are two points to be made from these measurements. First, it is no coincidence that KATIE was just under 100 registered tons since that gave her exemption from various charges, including compulsory pilotage at Liverpool and other ports: in the second place, note that the tonnage divided by length x breadth x depth for BEDWELTY was much greater than the equivalent figure for KATIE: in technical terms, KATIE had a much lower block coefficient. Both schooners were intended for coastal service. BEDWELTY was designed, like the smacks, to carry the maximum amount of cargo within the traditional blunt-ended hull, but the KATIE, whilst no great flier, was closer to what had become the Cornish tradition in schooner building which was that they should be fast, and rather light-framed compared with the rest of the country; Basil Greenhill writes of Cornish schooners in general, 'They seemed to be designed for speed and sailing qualities even at the cost of earning power'. Sailing qualities were particularly important on the north coast where the ability to escape from a lee shore was essential.

To draw the comparisons with BEDWELTY, KATIE's frames

## TYPICAL CROSS SECTION OF A NINETEENTH-CENTURY PADSTOW SAILING VESSEL

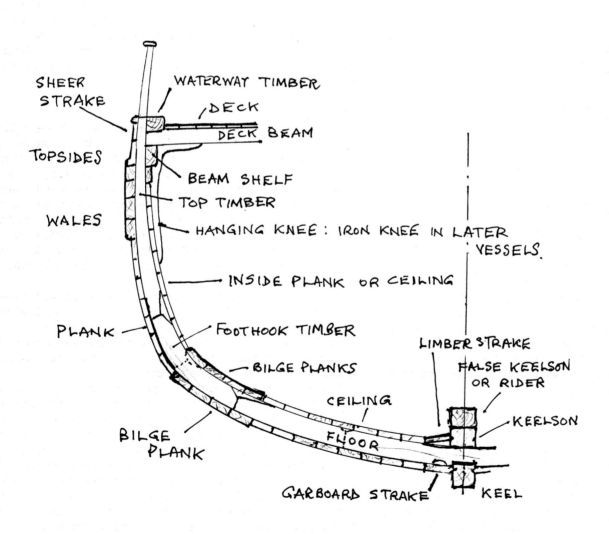

were 20 ins apart, so with 8½ ins floors and 7½ ins foothooks, there was a gap of 4 ins between the timbers. The moulded thickness tapered from 10 ins for the floors to 5 ins for the top timbers. The deck beams were 8½ x 8½ ins, the keel 10 x 13 ins and keelsons 12 x 8½ ins and 12 x 18 ins.

The outside planking was 2½ ins increasing to 5 ins for bilge planks and 4 ins for wales. The inside planking was also 2½ ins, with 4 ins for bilge planks. The frames were all bolted together up to the gunwale. The frames, stem, sternpost and rudder were all oak, largely French oak as supplies of English oak were becoming scarce. The keel and bottom planks were elm, but all the rest of the planking, inside and out, and also the keelsons was of pitch pine, a marvellous timber, workable, tough, long-lived, the heaviest of all softwoods, whose only shortcoming was that resin tended to collect on the tools. The decks were of yellow pine.

The butts in the foothooks were separated by at least one-sixth of her breadth, and in the hull plank, butts were at least 5 feet apart. The fastenings were of yellow metal, with some galvanised iron at deck level and for fastening iron knees, etc.

The sails of a new schooner were now so well established that the surveyor merely noted, 'one suit complete'. She had two bower anchors each weighing 5¼ cwt, and one stream and one kedge anchor, each little more than one hundredweight.

She carried one longboat. Her scuppers were closed, and she had hanging ports in the bulwarks to free the deck of water.

The surveyor, William Bowden, concluded with the following 'General Remarks':

This vessel is well built with all new material of the best quality . . . also fastened and salted in accordance with the Rules . . . I am of the opinion that she merits the favourable consideration of the Committee to be classed 12 A as contemplated, viz.
  9 years under Table A
  1 year under the mixed material rule
  1 year for yellow metal fastening, and
  1 year for salting with about eight tons of salt.
  12 A.

His fees comprised: Entry Fee £2, Special Fee £5.13s.0d. Certificate 2s.6d. Travelling Expenses £7.10s.0d.

The Committee duly assigned her the classification A1 for twelve years. In the event, she lasted ninety-four years.

Commenting on KATIE's survey, the scantlings of this 85 ft schooner built in 1878 are remarkably similar to those of the 48 ft smack MARYS & HELENA built in 1841! The biggest difference is that the plank thickness had increased from 2 ins to 2½ ins. A structural engineer or a naval architect might calculate that the maximum sagging or hogging stresses in a hull 85 ft long would be more than three times those in a 48 ft hull, varying as the square of the length, or worse. It may have been the lack of such calculations which allowed the Cornish yards to develop their reputation for light construction, speed and sailing qualities. Alternatively their success could be put down to careful evolution and excellent workmanship.

The method of establishing the twelve year classification is interesting. The 'mixed material rule' came into play when some timbers listed as '12 year material' were used as well as the '9 year material', on which a vessel's nine year hull classification was based. This concession, like the year for yellow metal fastening and the year for salting was a very practical inducement to use good materials and workmanship. By the 1870s it was common practice to pack rock salt between the frames to prevent or delay the onset of rot in the wood. Eight tons of salt seems excessive, amounting as it does to about 4% of the cargo capacity of the schooner. But at least it would somewhat reduce the amount of ballast needed for unladen passages.

To study the Lloyd's surveys is to realise how carefully they were carried out: the laborious dismantling of timbers to reveal conditions underneath, the testing of three links of every chain to destruction, the complaints of warps and cables not being sufficiently long (a frequent shortcoming), the timing of visits to the yards to make inspections at different stages of construction.

As well as the different types of timber already mentioned, greenheart was sometimes used for sheerstrakes, and American white oak or hackmatack (larch) for planking, especially in the second half of the century.

A great deal of the inspection work was to check the general standards of workmanship and various phrases recur. The Plymouth surveyor was wont to report, 'this is a good built vessel, the frames is square and free from sap.' The Falmouth man's style was, 'This vessel have been about 18 months in building; the frame, transoms, hooks and knees is well grown to the form, the plank well seasoned and well fastened, near all the tree nails passing through the ceiling'. Some vessels after repairs were pronounced, 'in fair condition and fit to carry a dry and perishable cargo'.

The system seems to have worked to warn underwriters effectively. On 15th December, 1837 the barque GOVERNOR DOUGLAS of Miramichi was surveyed 'in the pier at Padstow', and the report included the following: 'This vessel got ashore in this harbour in July last and strained and became hogged very much on the starboard side, nearly all the plank fastenings of which have been driven out and require major repairs'. Sure enough, *Lloyd's Register* 1838 notes under her entry, 'Damage repairs 1837. Wants additional fastenings'.

## Ownership

For the purposes of ownership, a registered British ship is divided into sixty-four shares 'in the said ship and in her boats and appurtenances'. It is a truism that the small sailing vessels of the nineteenth century were financed by the sale of shares to large numbers of people; the butcher, the baker, the candlestick maker, and also very frequently, the ship's master; and Padstow was no exception. In the Appendix, giving the history of the individual ships, full details of ownership (as revealed in the customs house registers) have been given in only a very few cases, otherwise many volumes would be needed to record transactions, but most Padstow family names have been noted.

At the start of the nineteenth century Padstow was such a poor place that only a few prominent families such as Avery, Rawlings, Norway, the Carters at St Columb, and the Martins at Boscastle had the ability to take part in the ownership of ships, apart from a few small smacks owned by their masters, or by even more isolated communities such as Portquin or Porth.

As the century progressed and the universal penny post was followed by the telegram, the organisation of shipping changed radically in home waters. The tempo increased, and it became essential for the master to keep in touch with a managing owner to plan the next freight and, if possible, the one after that. The resulting increased prosperity spread through Padstow, Port Isaac, St Columb and Newquay, and the butcher, the baker, the candlestick maker — but also the banker, the chandler, the sail-maker, the doctor, the fish merchant, the farmer and many others — were buying shares in the numerous vessels under construction.

As described in the chapter on shipbuilding, the shipbuilding families were themselves major shipowners, Tredwen and Stribley in particular. One of the interesting features of Tredwen's ownership is the series of joint ownerships between John Tredwen Jr and John Cory. The Cory family had lived at Poundstock (between Bude and Tintagel) since the seventeenth century or earlier. John was born in 1822 and went to sea from Padstow. In 1854 he was able to buy and take command of the ketch MILLICENT, but he soon moved ashore and from 1855 until 1870 he and John Tredwen Jr had a joint venture owning at various times thirty-two shares each of the ALMA, AMPHITRITE, AURORA, EDITH, JANE, MARY ELIZA and three successive vessels named VOLUNTEER. In addition, Cory had a minor interest in the smack CONSERVATOR, and owned all sixty-four shares in the barques JOHN HENRY and THE KILDARE before he and his family moved to Cardiff in 1872. In Cardiff he still owned THE KILDARE and JOHN HENRY, and in the 1880s, BELLE OF THE PLYM and EZEL, and in due course a large fleet of ocean-going steam colliers.

In 1876, *Lloyd's Register* gave the names of forty owners (managing or nominated) with addresses in Padstow or the outports, owning seventy-four ships of over 8,300 net tons. The list follows in alphabetical order:

| Owner & Address | Name of Ship | Net Tonnage |
| --- | --- | --- |
| W. S. Allport, Padstow | CORSAIR | 121 |
| Bennett & Co., Newquay | DRIVING MIST | 79 |
| Richard Brewer, Padstow | JANIE VIVIAN | 92 |
| E. O. Broad & Co., Padstow | GIPSY MAID | 89 |
| | GIPSY QUEEN | 95 |
| | JOHN & JENIFER | 65 |
| | SIR CHARLES NAPIER | 514 |
| Henry Buse & Co., Padstow | IDA ELIZABETH | 74 |
| | PIONEER | 124 |
| J. Casey, Port Isaac | LIZZIE MAY | 86 |
| T. Clemens, Newquay | BERTHA | 102 |
| Joseph Grigg Coad, Port Isaac | MARY COAD | 99 |
| | SOUVENIR | 97 |
| J. Crocker, Newquay | WILLIAM MARTYN | 93 |
| W. M. Darke, Newquay | LOUISA | 138 |
| J. P. Dunstan, St Columb | AMANDA | 87 |
| | UNITY | 126 |
| | WATER NYMPH | 61 |
| J. M. Fishley, Port Isaac | LITTLE RACER | 73 |
| | VOLANT | 112 |

The sloop-rigged smack CONSERVATOR at Lynmouth c. 1883. *Terry Belt Collection*

| Owner | Ship | Tons |
|---|---|---|
| Wm. Geake & Co. St Col. Maj. | CONQUEST | 68 |
| | JANE SLADE | 140 |
| | LYDIA CARDELL | 225 |
| | SILVER STREAM | 152 |
| W. R. Guy & Co. Port Isaac | BESSY JANE | 79 |
| | ELECTRIC | 73 |
| | VOLUNTEER | 83 |
| B. M. Harvey, Padstow | COURIER | 128 |
| | LILY | 70 |
| J. Hawke Jnr & Co. Pt Isaac | HESPERUS | 77 |
| | MARY SEYMOUR | 149 |
| J. Haynes, Port Isaac | VOLUTINA | 78 |
| W. Hicks & Co., Newquay | FOREST DEER | 68 |
| | RGD | 68 |
| J. Hockaday, Delabole | TEAZER | 50 |
| R. Hoskin, St Kew | CONSTANCE | 149 |
| A. Hutchings, Padstow | ALBERTA | 52 |
| | WATER LILY | 71 |
| Hutchings & Knight, Padstow | BELLE OF THE PLYM | 96 |
| T. Jenkin & Co., Padstow | AMELIA | 70 |
| | HENRIETTA | 99 |
| | INGRID | 99 |
| | MARGARET | 79 |
| | MINNIE | 87 |
| N. Lewarne, Porth | WESTERN STAR | 75 |
| T. Martyn, Wadebridge | TREBISKIN | 60 |
| W. Martyn & Co., Crantock | PENPOLL | 55 |
| T. May, Port Isaac | PRINCESS OF WALES | 121 |
| Wm. C. Phillips, Port Isaac | EMMA & AGNES | 109 |
| | LIZZIE MARY | 97 |
| | MILDRED | 100 |
| F. Prideaux Snr, Padstow | ALBION | 57 |
| S. Prout & Co., Port Isaac | NEW CORNWALL | 75 |
| T. G. Prout, Newquay | INFANTA | 63 |
| J. Richards, Port Isaac | OCEAN QUEEN | 121 |
| R. Roose, Port Isaac | JOHN HEDLEY | 60 |
| Jn. Stribley, & Co., Padstow | ANNIE | 71 |
| | EMILY ELLEN | 97 |
| | JKA | 60 |
| | JOHN WESLEY | 98 |
| | LIZZIE | 56 |
| | LIZZIE MALE | 107 |
| | LOTA | 472 |
| J. Strout, Port Isaac | AGNES STROUT | 130 |
| | CILICIA | 90 |
| | EDITH | 81 |
| Tonkin & Co., Newquay | OCEAN BELLE | 67 |
| J. Waters, Port Isaac | MARY WATERS | 100 |
| Edwin Williams, Port Isaac | ANN WILLIAMS | 134 |
| Wm. B. Williams, Newquay | EMMA JANE | 56 |
| | FAIRY BELLE | 90 |
| | FAIRY MAID | 100 |
| | FAIRY QUEEN | 85 |
| Henry Wilson, Padstow | CORNUVIA | 799 |
| Total | 74 vessels of | 8,323 net tons |

The list does not include the many ships built at Padstow for owners elsewhere, nor, of course, the many small vessels not listed in *Lloyd's Register*. Nor does the list of owners include the hundreds of shareholders with interests large or small in one or more vessels.

In the last quarter of the nineteenth century the managing ownership of the Padstow shipping became more concentrated into fewer fleets. The Allport family of Padstow, Tavistock and Plymouth owned increasing numbers of sailing coasters into the twentieth century, with William S. Allport acting as principal manager until after the Great War. He was one of the most faithful supporters of the Padstow ships, but eventually had to give up the struggle. In 1904 he was the prime mover, and the principal provider of money to have the three-masted steel schooner DORIS built at Cock's yard at Appledore, a noble attempt to bring Padstow shipping into the twentieth century. Alas, she was wrecked in 1907. The most remarkable feature of the Allport family is that in all their maritime activities, no evidence has been found that any member of their family spent time at sea.

William Phillips of Port Isaac owned and managed schooners on an increasing scale and in 1884 decided to move to St Austell. John Cory had gone to Cardiff to export coal to the world, but Phillips, faithful to his schooners, went to St Austell to concentrate on the china clay trade, mostly to the Mersey, which had the advantage of a return cargo of coal being readily available. This book therefore deals with all his ships up to 1884, and after that such of his fleet as were built or registered at Padstow.

The Williams family at Newquay are remembered for their five handsome schooners FAIRY BELLE, FAIRY FLOWER, FAIRY GLEN, FAIRY MAID and FAIRY QUEEN, but they also owned a dozen others — two dozen if other branches of the family are included. A sixth schooner, the FAIRY KING, was retained in ownership by her builder, Charles Rawle, on completion in 1878 and sold away to Watchet four years later.

Seventeen schooners were owned and managed by John Ennor of Newquay between 1883 and 1906, but since *Lloyd's Register* of 1890 makes reference to John Ennor Senior, it is possible that father and son of the same name were involved. That is one of numerous family relationships which make it difficult to sort out the labyrinth of ownership details in the nineteenth century. Instead, Chapter 14, 'The Principal Seafaring Families and their Ships', consists mainly of a list of ships attached to each family name. It is then a relatively simple matter to refer to a particular ship's details to discover what more is known about the ownership.

Christopher May, of the Port Isaac family, has been kind enough to provide an abbreviated family tree showing that in one branch of the family there were nine master mariners, three of them named Thomas, two named Robert, and at one time five of them brothers! Two dozen ships which they owned or captained have been traced, taking care to avoid connections with another branch of the May family at Par. The Port Isaac Mays had marriage connections with the families Moyse, Bate, Coad, Couch, Clements, Rowe and Phillips, all of Port Isaac, (all of which feature in the chapter on seafaring families) as well as with other Padstow and Newquay families.

Any boy being born into such a community in the nineteenth century would find it difficult not to follow the sea; there were plenty of opportunities for a willing lad, and his parents would have the reassurance of knowing that he was not sailing with strangers. Another advantage for a young man in the small ships of Port Isaac was that, with such small crews (roughly half composed of mates and masters), promotion came quite rapidly for those who deserved it.

The Sloggett family require special mention and it might have appeared as well in the shipbuilding chapter as here. The family seat was at Tresloggett in St Mabyn parish in the time of Edward III and

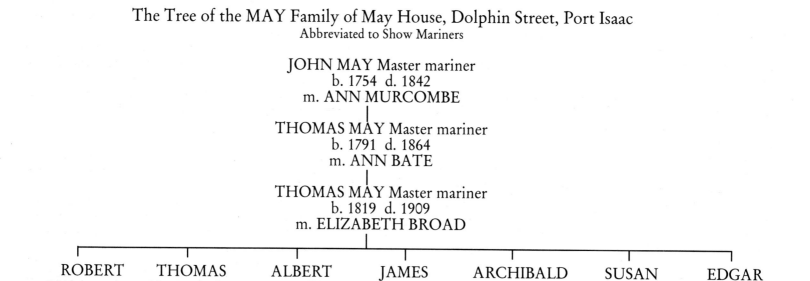

The Tree of the MAY Family of May House, Dolphin Street, Port Isaac
Abbreviated to Show Mariners

JOHN MAY Master mariner
b. 1754  d. 1842
m. ANN MURCOMBE

THOMAS MAY Master mariner
b. 1791  d. 1864
m. ANN BATE

THOMAS MAY Master mariner
b. 1819  d. 1909
m. ELIZABETH BROAD

| ROBERT | THOMAS | ALBERT | JAMES | ARCHIBALD | SUSAN | EDGAR |
|---|---|---|---|---|---|---|
| Master mariner | Master mariner | Master mariner | Master mariner | Master mariner | b. 1867 | b. 1869 d. 1956 |
| b.1841 d.1948 | b.1856 d.1929 | b.1859 d.1946 | b.1861 | | | |

ROBERT
Master mariner
b. 1889  d.1950s

earlier; over the centuries there were branches of the family at Padstow, Boscastle and Lanteglos, all in the Padstow hinterland. (This Lanteglos by Camelford is not to be confused with the place of the same name near Fowey). By the nineteenth century the family had married into the Prideaux, Hawker and Carew families, had branches widespread throughout the British Empire and had some very distinguished members. In the early part of the nineteenth century the Boscastle merchants, Sloggett and Rosevear (led by William Sloggett) owned a fleet of smacks, and the Padstow branch, headed by George, built and owned a similar fleet in which George's son, John, was an active master.

When the shipbuilding died out, the Padstow branch moved on to pastures new. Aaron stayed on and commanded and owned a series of schooners, but before that, Thomas, a grandson of George, the shipwright listed in 1804, had become a Naval Architect and moved to Cardiff as a Board of Trade surveyor. His son George became a well-known naval architect and marine engineer. He carried much responsibility in the Cambrian Steam Navigation Co. Ltd, being superintendent of a substantial fleet of ocean going steam colliers, but first in 1892, at the age of 26, he mounted his own shipping venture by purchasing the old French brig VOLZY which one suspects had run into trouble in the Bristol Channel. He registered her at Padstow and had her altered to ketch rig. He spread his risk by selling thirty-two shares to Arthur and William Hutchings which was as well, for she foundered a few months later off the Isle of Wight with a cargo of cement from London for Dartmouth. Perhaps it was that experience which led him to be a marine superintendent and consultant rather than a shipowner. The family tradition continues to this day, with Jolyon Sloggett, born 1933, also a naval architect and marine engineer, an eminent consultant to the marine and offshore industries.

### Iron and Steel

Over 920 vessels are included in the Appendix, and only eight of them are not built entirely of wood (apart from fastenings and a few iron knees).

In 1865 the Hooper family of Newquay went to Harveys of Hayle to have the brigantine MARIA built. Her survey notes 'some iron deck beams', which is not surprising as Harveys were expert foundrymen and ironworkers already building iron steamships and mining equipment. What is surely surprising is that on no other occasion did the shipowners of Newquay go to Harveys, just a few miles down the coast. MARIA, later a barkentine, had a long and prosperous career until sunk by U-boat in the Great War.

In 1866, A. and D. Mackay of Padstow took delivery of the smack CLYDE, 60 tons, built for them by Charles Connell on the Clyde. She had a wrought-iron frame which was planked with German oak. *Lloyd's Register* noted 'experimental construction; biennial survey'. Charles Connell's yard went on to build more famous ships for a further one hundred years before becoming a part of Upper Clyde Shipbuilders. So an outside influence introduced composite construction to the seafarers of Padstow, but it seems they were not particularly favourably impressed.

The iron full-rigged ship CORNUVIA, built at South Shields in 1869 by Readhead (another yard which survived for a century), was never registered at Padstow, but her first owner H. Wilson was from Padstow so she must count as the first iron Padstow ship. ENGLAND'S GLORY, built the same year by Pile at Sunderland, came to be the first iron vessel actually registered at Padstow in 1881, when W. Knight, who had been her master for some years, took over managing ownership.

It is quite probable that neither of these large iron ships ever visited Padstow; so when John Phillips of Port Isaac bought the iron schooner CAMEO in 1889, altered her to ketch rig and registered her at Padstow, she was quite likely the first locally owned iron vessel to enter the Camel!

By then the Padstow yards had closed. Although most Padstow owners were content to buy second-hand wooden ships, John Hawken went to Martenshoek in Holland in 1893 and arranged for G & H Bodewes Gebroeders to build him the iron ketch SAINT PETROC, 98 gross tons. F. Conway commanded her until she went missing in 1900.

The short-lived schooner DORIS, Padstow's first steel ship built in 1904 and lost in 1907, has already been mentioned, but her principal owner, William Allport, persevered and in 1911 he bought a second steel three-masted schooner, the MARGARET MURRAY, keeping her until 1918.

The incidence of iron and steel sailing ships at Padstow can thus be summarised as two small composite vessels, two iron ships which may never have visited Padstow, two iron ketches and two steel schooners. Padstow had expert blacksmiths, but lacked all the other specialised tradesmen needed for the building and maintenance of iron and steel ships. Any major hull maintenance or repair work meant paying out good money to 'foreigners'. That ran counter to the philosophy of Padstow and was good and sufficient reason to discourage the ownership of such ships in Padstow and the outports.

## Losses

Working through the histories of the nineteenth-century sailing vessels of Padstow, the months in which 512 of them were lost have been established. These were all accidental losses by stranding, collision, foundering, burning, being abandoned or going missing. Various other terms are used, such as 'shipwreck', 'running aground' and 'breaking up', or just 'lost'. They have all been included and the losses plotted month by month.

The results are perhaps not unexpected, but they do demonstrate quite dramatically the dangers of winter weather. The losses for the six months April to September inclusive are less than half the losses for October to March, and that is in spite of a Cornish tradition not to sail in December, especially in the early years of the century with the smaller smacks often laid up for a winter season from December to February.

Not included above are ten vessels sunk by U-boats in the Great War. At first sight, the loss of ten vessels may not appear too severe in the face of 512 vessels lost from other causes, but in fact it was a deathblow to the remnants of Padstow's nineteenth century fleet, and although her maritime trades continued to serve the fishing fleet which visited Padstow every year, the trades and facilities required for sailing vessels disappeared.

Graphic descriptions of wreck and rescue can be read in the several books on the subject listed in the Bibliography, and any spell of bad weather was likely to result in reports in the *Western Morning News* and the *Royal Cornwall Gazette* dealing with loss and damage. As an example, the *Gazette* on 23rd October, 1875 carried the following:

### PADSTOW

Intelligence was received at Padstow on Monday that Nicholas Penhaligon, Wadebridge, was washed overboard and drowned from the schooner ALBION, of Padstow, Prideaux master, during her passage from Swansea to Charlestown. Deceased, who was of about 19 years of age, was engaged in fixing the side lamps at the time of the occurrence.

A SMACK ABANDONED. The smack LENORA, of this port, Bennett master from Wadebridge, for Porthleven, with granite, encountered a heavy gale on Saturday, and about nine p.m. she carried away her boom, which caused her to heel over and fill with water. This

## LOSSES OF 19th-CENTURY PADSTOW SHIPS
## MONTH BY MONTH

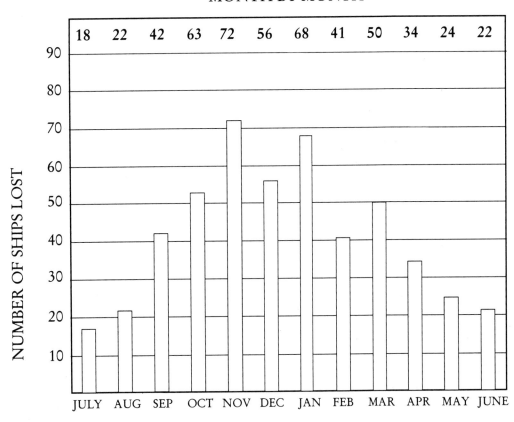

| 18 | 22 | 42 | 63 | 72 | 56 | 68 | 41 | 50 | 34 | 24 | 22 |
|----|----|----|----|----|----|----|----|----|----|----|----|
| JULY | AUG | SEP | OCT | NOV | DEC | JAN | FEB | MAR | APR | MAY | JUNE |

was eight miles west of the Brissons. The master, man, and boy, forming her crew, landed in their boat at St Ives on Sunday morning at three o'clock, and a fishing boat was shortly afterwards dispatched from St Ives. The crew succeeded in boarding the smack about daybreak, and afterwards took her into Hayle, where she arrived at seven p.m. The LENORA was of 40 tons register, and belongs to Mr William Bennett of Merryn.

Board of Trade enquiries were another source of shipping news, and the following also appeared in October, 1875:

### THE LOSS OF A PADSTOW VESSEL

A Board of Trade enquiry was opened last week at Greenock into the circumstances attending the collision between the FLYING SQUALL of Glasgow, and the schooner SMC of Padstow, whereby the latter was sunk and three lives lost. The court was composed of Mr Grieve, MP, and Mr Ross, the nautical assessors being Captains Castle and King. Mr Alex Blair appeared for the Board of Trade, Mr McLean for the master of the FLYING SQUALL, and Mr Young of Glasgow for the owners of the SMC. Mr Blair, in opening the case, said the collision occurred about three miles off Cambrae Head in the Frith [sic] of Clyde. The FLYING SQUALL was coming up the Frith [sic] of Clyde on the evening of the 12th of August, steering NE by N., having another tug in tow. About twenty minutes past twelve when off Cambrae Head, the wind being NE and blowing a fresh breeze, a red light was observed. The SMC was about forty yards from the steamer, when a green light suddenly appeared, whereupon the helm of the steamer was put to starboard and the engine was stopped. The vessels were too near, however, to avoid a collision, the result being that the captain, his son and the cook of the Cornish vessel were drowned. For the disaster the FLYING SQUALL men assert that the SMC was responsible, while the survivors of the SMC attribute the blame to the crew of the FLYING SQUALL. The first witness examined was Wm. Reid, master of the FLYING SQUALL, who said that the lights of the steamer were all burning fully when the collision occurred. He considered there was no

danger of a collision until the schooner starboarded her helm. Other witnesses connected with the steamer corroborated this evidence. James Smith, one of the crew of the SMC stated that on the night of the accident, he had placed the lights of the schooner in the fore rigging. From the time they were lighted until the schooner went down the lights burned brightly. Witness stated that the captain of the schooner was an excellent seaman, and bore a good character. He also gave it as his opinion that it was impossible for those on board the schooner to know on which side the steamer intended to pass, so frequently did it go from one side to the other. The inquiry was adjourned.

The following is included as typical of numerous fulsome press reports of vessels lost in the Padstow area:

### TOTAL WRECK AT NEWQUAY

The Cutter GLEANER of Padstow, the property of Mr Frank Bray, merchant, of that town, captain Mr Ivey, put to sea (with a part cargo of grain, bound to Padstow to complete her burthen), between 12 and 1 o'clock this morning, under most favourable circumstances, the sea at the time being calm, with a fair breeze from the NNE, but within two hours she was on the rocks and before four this morning had become a total wreck. The circumstances of the mishap appear to be these. The vessel had taken a tack from the neighbourhood of Trevelgy Head in a North Westerly direction, when off Towan Head she was about to tack for the second time in a North Easterly course for Trevose Head when she misstayed, and was being carried by the tide, which was just at its full, in dangerous proximity to the rocks off this jagged piece of coast line, so picturesque to the admirer of natural beauty, but hideous to the distressed mariner, when the crew cast their anchor, and took to their boat. This it appears was accompanied with very considerable danger. The captain's wife was on board and she was first put adrift in the boat in charge of the cook, the boat being attached to the vessel by a painter, she was naturally very nervous and became exceedingly excited, rendering the boat almost unmanageable, and they were in imminent danger of being swamped, in which case it is more than probable that

The topsail schooner GAVENWOOD was wrecked on the Manacles on a wild November night in 1917.
*Terry Belt Collection*

The JOSEPHINE started life as a French lugger.

*Private collection*

MARY SEYMOUR was built at Padstow in 1865. A painting by James Garde of Padstow.

*Malcolm McCarthy Collection*

Plate 3

The EMILIE, registered at Padstow in 1890, had been built in Norway in 1866.

*Private collection*

GOLDEN CHANCE near Stanley in the Falkland Islands in 1980.
She is now on the International Register of Historic Ships.

*John Thompson Collection*

Plate 4

all lives would have been sacrificed. This catastrophe, however, was mercifully avoided, and in the end the captain and mate were successful in embarking in the boat and pulled round to the harbour where they landed and went at once in quest of assistance. The vessel must then have went to a speedy doom, for on the arrival of the rescue party it was found that the cable had parted and the vessel had been carried by the tide over the Cribbar Rocks in a deep basin full of water situate at the extreme North Westerly point of the Towan Head, known as the 'Cribbar Drang', quite surrounded with jagged slate rocks, and was fast breaking up. All hopes of saving her were at once abandoned. The crew were unable to save even their clothing. The cargo which consisted of grain, chiefly in bulk, must be totally lost. A strong rescue party are now engaged in saving so much of the wreck as is possible but the extent of the salvage cannot be much as it is impossible to extricate the sheltered bark from her perilous position. The GLEANER was built at Truro about 13 years ago and became the property of Mr Bray through purchase about 2 years since. She was looked upon as a superior class vessel, her total tonnage was about 75. She was, we believe, fully insured in the Padstow Marine Insurance Association.

14th March, 1889

There were no dramatic storm conditions involved, but the wind was from the NNE, making it difficult to beat out of Newquay Bay. Until she missed stays, they were doubtless taking what advantage they could from the tidal eddies near the rocks to help them on their way: that left them in a vulnerable position when she lost steerage way. When there was a heavy ground swell and a strong tidal stream, a lack of wind could be more dangerous than a gale of wind!

Hobblers wait in their boat to assist the MARY WATERS to her berth. *Terry Belt Collection*

Reports from the *Western Morning News* describe how other typical casualties occurred:

*21st September, 1882.* The Ketch ALBERTA, entering Padstow with a strong NE wind on Tuesday evening, ran into a schooner anchored in the Pool without lights it is said. She carried away the schooner's jibboom and lost her own mizenmast. The ALBERTA ended up ashore at Chapel Point with a large hole in her bottom, and if the storm

continues she will probably become a total loss. Her crew were taken off by the gig HERO (John Cowl & Sons).

*30th October, 1882.* The loss of the ketch VICTORIA with all three of her crew on Friday night was reported. She was bound from Newport for Wadebridge. Her hull was seen drifting on Dunbar (Doom Bar). Christopher Beer (her master) and William French were both Padstow men; the former leaves a widow and three children and the latter's wife is approaching confinement, The third member of the crew was from Boscastle. The vessel's owner was Captain Lobb of Port Isaac.

*3rd February, 1883.* The ketch MILLICENT (Pinch master) Swansea for Padstow with culm, missed stays and ran aground near the pilots' houses in Hawker's Cove. She came off on the flood tide and is now at the town but making water. The MARY JOSEPHINE (Pollard master) anchored near Newland Island, having lost her sails. The lifeboat ALBERT EDWARD under the experienced command of coxswain William Webb took off all three of her crew, but was able to put them back on board later. The vessel was brought to the town quay yesterday morning.

Captains' reports form another source of information, and here is one from Captain Male of the schooner MARY JANE of and from Padstow for Liverpool, which struck a bank midway between the Formby and Crosby banks, and settled down into the sand.

Left Padstow 3rd February, 1858. On 4th, 6.30 p.m. passed over the bar at the entrance to the Victoria Channel, Liverpool, the wind WSW squally, strong and rather hazy. Saw and recognised the lights and kept the lead going. 6.45 passed the Formby lightship and shaped the course SE When about halfway between Formby and Crosby lights, the lead still being kept going, got a cast of 6 fathoms. The next cast which followed immediately afterwards the man called out 'No water' when the ship struck heavily, there being much sea on. The tide was about half ebb and as it receded she became fast. One of the bower anchors was placed out astern with a view to preventing her driving further on the bank on the flood tide. Soon after the flood had made the boat was got out for any purpose it might be required for. As the tide rose the vessel again became very uneasy and laboured and struck very heavily, the sea making a fair breach over her. Two seamen were in the boat alongside for the purpose of taking care of her, a portion of the effects of all hands having been put into her as they expected they would have to leave the vessel. Found the water over the cabin floor and was about to leave when the boat broke adrift leaving the master and mate on board. There was too much tide and sea for the boat to return and the master and mate were obliged to take to the rigging for the preservation of their lives. At high water the vessel's deck was at least 8 ft under water. At daylight of the 5th they were able to descend to the deck where they found everything washed away and the hatches blown up. At noon the wind had moderated and they were taken from the wreck by a waterman's boat and at the same time, assisted by another boat took from the vessel various sails and stores and landed at Liverpool about 3 p.m. On the following day some other rigging and stores were recovered and when I last saw the vessel on the 7th she appeared to be settling down in the sand with very little appearance of being saved. The two seamen informed me that after the boat broke adrift they made the best of their way to the Mersey. In doing so the boat shipped a sea and fearing it would go down they threw all the clothing they had in her overboard and thus all was lost. They succeeded, however, in getting alongside an American ship that was at anchor near the Rock lighthouse, where they remained for the night.

The MARY JANE was one of many Padstow ships which took china clay from Cornwall to Liverpool and brought back coal. The schooner KINNAIRD, owned by Allport of Padstow in the early years of the twentieth century, was another. On 5th and 6th November, 1911 the Holyhead steam lifeboat DUKE OF NORTHUMBERLAND 'saved her crew of 4 and assisted to save

The schooners VIA and PRIDE OF THE WEST are Both seen off Dover. Note the different shapes of their squaresails; VIA's upper topsail has been cut from the mainsail of a Barry pilot skiff. PRIDE OF THE WEST has a baggywrinkle on her topping lift to reduce chafe on the mainsail.                                    *David Clement Collection*

vessel'. Unfortunately, on 20th December, 1911, the very next month, the KINNAIRD was lost in collision off Holyhead, sailing from Runcorn with coal for Charlestown, Cornwall. The Holyhead lifeboat DUKE OF NORTHUMBERLAND between 1893 and 1921 served an extraordinary number of Padstow ships, including SARAH, BALLINBREICH CASTLE, GIPSY MAID, HARMONY, OLIVE BRANCH, FAIRY MAID, JANIE, MARIAN and HETTY, as well as KINNAIRD herself. This remarkable performance must be partly coincidence, but it also shows the predominance of the trade to the Mersey. The steam lifeboat (there were only six built for the RNLI all told) must have reminded the Padstow men of their own steam lifeboat, the JAMES STEVENS No.4 and of her tragic loss after only one year of service, as compared with the DUKE OF NORTHUMBERLAND's lengthy career at Holyhead during which she saved over 250 lives.

Elsewhere in the book the loss of Padstow ships in places as far away as the antipodes has been described, but that by no means completes the story. In the Appendix will be found many casualties in distant seas. For example, the barque ALAN was at Pernambuco in 1872 when the captain and all but one of her crew died of yellow fever. All we know of the loss of ELIZA ANN is the brief note in the port register 'wrecked at Gallipoli 8th Feb. 1867'. A similar note on MARGARITA's entry reads 'Lost in the Gulf of Mexico 27th April 1860', whilst the schooner T. E. J. after seven years active Mediterranean trading 'foundered near Corsica 23rd April 1878'.

The loss of the brig AURORA was more controversial. She left London on 6th December, 1860 with general cargo for Trieste and Venice. The note on the Padstow register reads 'Wrecked on Torre Rinaldo 14th March 1861', but there was more to it than that. She successfully delivered her cargo and left Venice for home with a cargo of wheat on 6th March, 1861. For the following week she suffered a chapter of accidents before running aground near Brindisi, in the hands of a band of Italian fishermen. At the subsequent enquiry her captain lost his ticket for running her ashore and abandoning her, causing her loss unnecessarily. The crew with one exception, testified that the captain was often under the influence of drink.

## The Surviving Trades

Towards the end of the nineteenth century, with British shipyards producing large numbers of iron and then steel ships powered by compound and then triple expansion steam engines, the smaller sailing vessels of Padstow were better placed than some to retain their viability. Their running costs were low and they could trade far up shallow rivers whether to Waterford or Wadebridge, delivering the relatively small quantities of freight needed in small communities. They thought nothing of beaching themselves in exposed havens to unload into carts and wagons.

They were in existence, having been built in preceding decades, so no capital investment was needed to keep them running. Furthermore, as the steam coaster captured the major coal trades in the Irish Sea and elsewhere, and the steam puffers came to serve the Western Isles, large numbers of Scottish schooners came onto the

Capt. W. G. Clemens was master of the BESSIE (ON 67266) for many years and died of old age in command of her.
*Royal Institution of Cornwall*

market at very reasonable prices to act as replacements when Cornish vessels were lost.

There were still plenty of highly competitive shipwrights, blacksmiths, sailmakers and ropewalks readily available at Padstow and elsewhere to maintain sailing vessels.

One surviving account of trade in the last quarter of the nineteenth century was written by Captain Sydney Bate, who was born in Port Isaac on 8th October, 1857 and brought up in Padstow and Rock. His father was a master mariner, and captain of the schooner PET. He joined his brother William's schooner TREBISKIN and worked his way up to be master of the same PET. She was an interesting ship, built at Pugwash, Nova Scotia in 1857 as a tiny schooner, but registered at Padstow that same year. In 1878 she was lengthened and converted to ketch rig and Sydney and his elder brother Stephen were both masters of her after that.

Sydney married Miss Janie Bunt of Port Navas and subsequently took command of his father-in-law's 62-ton ketch WATER LILY (ON 45226, registered at Falmouth). From this point, the story is told in his own words:

Our first voyage was from Port Navas to Dublin with granite. We made a fast passage, unloaded, took in ballast and sailed for Garston where we arrived the following afternoon. Here we loaded coal for Capt. Bunt, my father in law, who had a coal business in Port Navas, where we exchanged it for a load of kerb stones for London. Here we took on dog biscuits for Bristol, but were obliged to put into Padstow on the way, weatherbound. Eventually we got away and reached Bristol without mishap. From there to Newport to pick up coal for Port Navas.

We had a rough passage especially round Land's End, but after taking shelter in Penzance for several days we reached home safely.

It being winter, we stopped running for a couple of months, when we again fitted out and took a cargo of granite coping to Newcastle. We had a record voyage, leaving Port Navas on Thursday, and were back in three weeks, despite being caught in a gale of wind and having to shelter in Harwich Harbour for several days.

Going North through Yarmouth Roads we encountered the impressive sight of four to five hundred sailing ships, which had been taking shelter, setting sail again after the storm. About thirty miles north of here, the wind shifted from Sou'west to Nor'west and began to blow very hard. Very soon most of the ships started to turn back to the roads again, being in ballast and unable to make any headway when the wind shifted.

We had a very rough night, but the next morning the wind veered to the Sou'west and we had a good trip to Newcastle. We discharged next day, took on a cargo of coal and sailed in three days for Port Navas. We had a fine fair Northerly wind and on getting outside the Bar, we set our square sail and carried the fair wind all the way to the Dodman. It was a lovely fast passage and we reached Port Navas exactly a week from the time we had arrived at Newcastle.

We did the whole round trip of 1200 miles, despite our setbacks, including discharging and loading in exactly three weeks.

Having discharged our coal at Port Navas, we took on kerb for London, and from there we loaded cement for Gloucester. I called in home on the way round, and took Janie, my wife, on board for a trip to Gloucester. She greatly enjoyed going up the Gloucester Canal. There is a magnificent Cathedral of which we had a bird's eye view of the outside from the ship, and crossed the Severn to Lydney, Monmouthshire. Here we loaded coal for Port Navas.

Reaching home safely, we discharged part of the cargo on Helford Beach for my wife's uncle Capt. T. Bunt, taking the remainder home to Port Navas.

We next loaded grain for Maryport and having discharged, loaded pig iron for Pembrey, close to Llanelly. We experienced a very heavy gale on our passage to this place, which carried away our main-gaff. We fixed the gaff and set a close reefed mainsail, but in running over Llanelly Bar

ALLPORT'S 'BESSIE', BUILT IN 1875

our gaff topsail sheet got fouled in the end of the gaff, so I ran up the rigging, slid out on the peak halyards and cleared the sheet. The pilot was at the tiller. My word! It was a risky bit of work for had the vessel gybed I would have been flung into the sea. There was a heavy sea running at the time but sailors do not consider risks when an emergency situation arises.

When we got in we discharged and reloaded with coal for Messrs Freeman and Sons of Penryn. We had a nice passage home and then loaded granite coping for London. This we discharged at Putney Bridge but to get there we had to unstep two of our masts and lay them on the deck, so that we could be towed up under the London bridges by a small tug. Afterwards we were towed to Hay's wharf where with the aid of a crane we restepped our masts. We towed down to Northfleet, near Gravesend, where we took in a cargo of cement, and at the lower reach of Gravesend we took in 40 tons of Powder for Dublin. We had a rather rough voyage there for we were caught in a southeasterly gale in St. George's Channel. We arrived all well, discharged and proceeded to Garston, Liverpool, in ballast, where we took on coal for Port Navas. I am speaking now of the year 1881, and when we arrived at Garston we found that the QUEEN OF THE CHASE with my father in law Capt. William Bunt in command, had just arrived from London with a cargo of ore. We loaded our coal for home and sailed some days before QUEEN OF THE CHASE which was also taking on coal for Merthen Hole in the Helford River. We reached home safely.

About a fortnight later, I handed over WATER LILY to the mate, who had been on the ship a long time. I then took command of QUEEN OF THE CHASE.

She was built in Falmouth by James Mayn for Pope and Co., and lengthened in 1862 to 98.02 tons. The Popes ran fast fruit ships as well as other cargoes and she had been in both the Mediterranean and also the Newfoundland trades. Captain Bunt of Port Navas bought her between 1886 and 1890.

We loaded kerbing at the lower quay, Port Navas, for Dover. The wind was blowing hard from the East and so we waited a few days till it changed to South West and I made up my mind to sail. It was in the afternoon and my wife had read in the papers, that a gale was predicted from America to sweep across the Atlantic, so she did not want me to set off. I had made up my mind to do so, and we left Helford on the Thursday afternoon in the latter part of September. The next day about 5 p.m. we were caught in the predicted gale off St. Catherine's Point, Isle of Wight.

The gale struck us all of a sudden. We were running with single reefed sails, when without warning the wind veered North and struck the ship with great force carrying away the jibboom, boom, jib and all the gear attached, which all fell into the sea. The main sheet carried away and the main boom swung out and hit the after shroud of the main rigging. I immediately put her head to wind and lay to, urging the crew to cut the wreckage adrift before the jibboom could knock a hole in our bow.

Whilst we were in this predicament, a large steamer proceeding down Channel, altered course and came close to us. The Captain, through a megaphone, asked if we required any help. I replied, that so far we were in no danger as our vessel was not making any water. I thanked him for approaching so closely to find out if we needed assistance.

After a couple of hours, we got the wreckage free and keeping the QUEEN OF THE CHASE hove to, we had our tea, which included a blackberry pie, which my wife had made for us to take to sea.

We remained hove to till midnight, when the gale moderated somewhat. I then sailed her under close reefed canvas to Dover, which we reached on Sunday without further trouble.

At Dover we loaded cement for somewhere on the Medway and then sailed for Liverpool again with a further cargo of cement. When we were off Newhaven in Sussex, the ship was caught in another very heavy Nor'westerly gale and we had to run to Dungeness roads for shelter. At midnight the wind backed and blew strongly from the south'ard and before long it veered and blew hurricane force from WSW.

Both cables were out to their full extent and we had them shackled to the mast. A Dutch pilot boat was blown clean out of the roads. The next morning I beheld a vessel completely disabled, sails blown away being driven helplessly before the gale. After a couple of days, the wind subsided enough for us to resume our passage westward. We put into Portland for the night.

We left the next day, but after a few hours the wind blew very hard from the East and as she was making water, we decided to put into Falmouth for repairs. She was beached on Boyer's Cellars and the shipwright found that she needed some caulking. We left the next day and reached Land's End. Thirty-six hours later we reached Liverpool and discharged cement.

Describing another occasion on which he had had to cope with mountainous seas and a shifting cargo, he tells how they managed at last to reach the entrance to Port Navas creek where his father in law was just hauling his nets with a load of herring. Capt. Bunt said he was most surprised to see them as he had given them up for lost. QUEEN OF THE CHASE was the only vessel out of nearly three hundred which had reached her destination. All the rest had either put in for repairs or been lost. 'My wife was agreeably surprised to see me', he said. She had been asking her father where he thought they had gone.

He told the story of how once on a course for Queenstown, Ireland, he was called hastily on deck to find a large barque coming straight for them. As he took avoiding action she followed him, so, suspecting the officers were at dinner leaving an apprentice in charge, he fired a gun. Immediately an officer appeared on deck, took the necessary evasive action and knocked the apprentice to the deck.

At this time Captain Bate had his wife and eldest son (aged six weeks) on board. This incident and some subsequent rough weather upset them and they were sea sick.

There is no doubt that competition from steam led to improvements in the small sailing vessel. Take the ketch TRIUMPH as an example. She was built by T. & J. Clemens at Newquay in 1881, the last ship ever built there, but beautifully built, with an elliptical stern, and rigged for deep water, setting a squaresail and raffee topsails. Much has been written about the small schooners which traded across the Atlantic, such as the Western Ocean Yachts of Portmadoc, but here is an even smaller ketch which did the same.

Captain R. J. Hockin was her master, and owned sixteen of her sixty-four shares. Details of his last voyage as master in 1885 may be taken as typical. Articles were signed at Newport and she sailed for Cadiz with coal. Thence she took a cargo of salt to Black Tickle, an isolated fishing settlement in Newfoundland. It took some time to collect a cargo of codfish before she delivered it to Plymouth. From Plymouth she sailed with fire-bricks and fire clay for London. In the Thames, disaster struck: she was run down and sunk on 22nd November, 1885 in collision with SS RENOWN of Newcastle. Her crew survived, the underwriters paid up for a total loss, and in due course R. J. Hockin had an increasingly leisurely job as harbour master at Newquay.

But that was not the end of the TRIUMPH. In the words of Oliver Hill's contemporary notes 'she was rose again and hailed from London'. Edwin Gill of Rochester became her owner, and she was re-registered first at London, then Jersey and finally London, without change of ownership. Captain J. H. Waters of Faversham, who had her for a time for Gill, thought that 'she was too heavily built and dead in the water, and sluggish in a seaway', but then he was used to big, lightly built East coast barges which seldom, if ever, took the ground in rocky Westcountry harbours.

The final sad news of TRIUMPH is to be found in LLOYDS WAR LOSSES: The First World War: 'Missing, since leaving Briton Ferry 3rd November, 1915 for Landerneau with coal.' That was the epitaph of many a small sailing vessel in those dark days.

A less digestible description of the patterns of trade can be obtained from surviving cargo books, and two which have not been previously published describe the activities of small Port Gaverne smacks, one for the period 1902-4 and the other 1912-13. The two should be examined separately, so different is the modus operandi:

### EXTRACTS FROM CARGO BOOK
### OF A PORT GAVERNE SMACK 1902-1904

| Passage | To | Cargo | Sailed | Arrived | Days |
|---|---|---|---|---|---|
| | | | 1902 | | |
| Newport | Bude | Coal | Nov 18 | Nov 19 | 1 |
| Bude | Cardiff | Sand 20T. | Dec 8 | Dec 13 | 5 |
| Cardiff | Wadebridge | Copperas & Coal | Dec 22 | Dec 25 | 3 |
| | | | 1903 | | |
| Padstow | Newport | Ballast 30T. | Feb 4 | Feb 5 | 1 |
| Newport | Arthurs'n Waterford | Coal | Feb 15 | Mar 14 | 27 |
| Arthurs'n | Newport | Ballast 9T. | Mar 31 | Apr ? | — |
| Newport | Bandons Quay | Coal 96T. | Apr 8 | Apr 14 | 6 |
| Bandons | Portsm'th | Oats 540qrs. | May? | ? | — |
| Portsm'th | Glasgow | Steel Scrap 100 T. | ? | Jun 25 | — |
| Glasgow | Frogmore | Coal 94T. | Salcombe | July 13 | — |

### EXAMINED AT SALCOMBE JULY 13th, 1903

| Salcombe | Totnes | Light | July 31 | Aug 1 | 1 |
|---|---|---|---|---|---|
| Totnes | Ipswich | Umber 100T. | Aug 12 | Aug 21 | 9 |
| Ipswich | London | Light | Sept 2 | Sept 6 | 4 |
| London | Torquay | Cement 100T. | Sept 10 | Sept 16 | 6 |
| Torquay | Shoreham | Cracked Stones 97½T. | Oct 2 | Oct 10 | 8 |

| | | | | | |
|---|---|---|---|---|---|
| Shoreham | Swansea | Steel Scrap 101T. | Oct 18 | Nov 6 | 19 |
| Swansea | Malpas | Culm 100T. | Nov 18 | Nov 20 | 2 |
| Malpas | Devoran | Light | Nov 26 | Nov 26 | ½ |
| Devoran | Swansea | 550 barrels Arsenic 106T. | Dec 1 | Dec 22 | 21 |
| | | **1904** | | | |
| Swansea | Exmouth | Coal 99T. | Jan 20 | Jan 23 | 3 |
| Topsham | Fowey | Manure | Feb 21 | Feb 22 | 1 |
| Fowey | Bristol | China Clay | Mar 7 | Mar 12 | 5 |
| Bristol | Newport | Light | Mar 19 | Mar 20 | 1 |
| Newport | Youghal | Coal 100T. | Apr 12 | Apr 18 | 6 |
| Youghal | Bristol | Oats 945 bbls. | May 17 | May 18 | 1 |
| Bristol | Newport | Light | May 25 | May 25 | ½ |
| Newport | Castle-Townsend | Coal 102T. | May 30 | Jun 6 | 7 |
| Castle T. | Leap | Light | — | — | — |
| Leap | Crosshaven | Part cargo, Scrap iron | — | — | — |
| Crossh'n | Glasgow | Scrap iron | — | — | — |
| Glasgow | Mevagissey | House coal 97T. | — | — | — |
| Mevagissey | Par | Light | Aug 27 | Aug 27 | ½ |
| Par | Penarth | China clay 100T. | — | — | — |
| Penarth | Plymouth | Steam coal 100T. | | | |
| Plymouth | Hayle | Wheat 446½ qtrs. | — | Oct 13 | — |
| Hayle | Cardiff | Sand 104T. | — | — | — |
| Cardiff | Penzance | Coal 101T. | Oct 29 | Oct 30 | 1 |
| Penzance | Newland | Light | Nov 4 | — | — |
| Newland (probably Newlyn) | Cardiff | Stones 55T. | Nov 5 | Nov 10 | 5 |
| Cardiff | Hayle | Steam coal 96T. | Nov 17 | Nov 20 | 3 |

In the period 1902-1904, the smack carried twenty-nine useful cargoes in twenty-four months. Three men shifted roughly 2,800 tons of material within an area as far north as Glasgow, as far east as Ipswich, and as far west as Bandon's Quay. She sailed forty-one passages, the shortest taking half a day, the longest (from Newport to Arthurstown) taking twenty-seven days. The average passage time was 5.3 days. It is not possible to analyse time spent in port, which might have been necessary for a dozen different reasons. The overall impression, however, is of a smack being worked hard, with no lengthy winter lay-up, and willing and able to carry all manner of cargoes including those needing a clean, dry vessel.

Christmas and New Year 1902 (and the whole of January) were spent at home (Padstow). On 22nd December, 1903 she arrived in Swansea, and stayed until 20th January, 1904. The probability is that her captain and mate got a friendly passage home for a Christmas holiday, leaving the youngest member of the crew to look after her at Swansea.

## EXTRACTS FROM CARGO BOOK
## OF A PORT GAVERNE SMACK 1912-1913

| Passage | To | Cargo | Sailed | Arrived | Days |
|---|---|---|---|---|---|
| | | | | **1912** | |
| Newport | Slade (Ilfracombe) | House coals 103T. | May 16 | May 25 | 9 |
| Slade | Newport | Sand ballast 24T. | Jun 3 | Jun 6 | 3 |
| Newport | St Ives | Large house coal 100T. | Jun 11 | July 6 | 22 |
| St Ives | Newport | Light | ? | July 25 | ? |
| Newport | Padstow | Large house coal 100T. | July 30 | Aug 4 | 5 |
| Padstow | Newport | Sand ballast | Sept 13 | Sept 15 | 2 |
| Newport | Padstow | Large house coal | Sept 19 | Sept 20 | 1 |
| Padstow | Pt. Talbot | Sand ballast 8T. | Oct 4 | Oct 5 | 1 |
| Port Talbot | Padstow | Steam coal 99T. | Oct 10 | Oct 12 | 2 |

Layed up at Padstow from 12th October, 1912 until 12 March, 1913

| | | | | **1913** | |
|---|---|---|---|---|---|
| Padstow | Newport | Sand 36T. | Mar 12 | Mar 15 | 3 |
| Newport | Solva (near Milford) | Manure 100T. | Apr 2 | Apr 9 | 7 |
| Solva | Newport | Sand 21T. | Apr 21 | Apr 24 | 3 |
| Newport | Bally-cotton | House coal 100T. | May 4 | May 19 | 15 |
| Bally-cotton | Newport | Light | May 23 | May 25 | 2 |

By comparison, the smack working in 1912-1913 has a very limited role. Apart from an isolated voyage to Ballycotton, her activities are limited to South Wales and the north coast of Cornwall. Apart from a chance load of manure, she carried only various grades of coal as cargo: only seven useful cargoes in a complete year. Fourteen passages, seven of them light or in ballast, the shortest being of one day's duration, the longest taking twenty-two days (beating west from Newport to St Ives). The average passage time was 5.8 days. Having unloaded (generally in North Cornwall), there appears to have been little urgency for her to return to Wales for another coal cargo. Apart from sand as ballast, there appears to have been no cargo available for the passage from Cornwall to Wales. The Cornish mines had closed. All-in-all, the performance of this smack in the twentieth century appears to have been remarkably similar to that of a typical Padstow collier of the sixteenth or seventeenth century, as described in Chapter 3, except that export cargoes from Padstow were no longer available.

The most important difference from the 1902-1904 log is that the vessel was laid up at Padstow for no less than five months, October to March.

A full cargo of sand was taken from Hayle to Cardiff in 1904. Sand ballast was easy to arrange at Padstow so when thirty tons or more of sand ballast were taken to Newport, there may well have been a market for it on arrival.

It would be interesting to know how the master decided whether to sail 'light' or 'ballasted', and how much ballast to ship. In the 1902-1904 book the only 'light' passages are short and in sheltered waters. On the other hand, in 1912 the smack sailed from St Ives to Newport apparently without ballast, and similarly in 1913 Ballycotton to Newport. The master might have been influenced by settled southwesterly weather (in May and June), by a shortage of ballast, by a shortage of money, or by a combination of all three.

## Nineteenth Century Rigs

The following notes and definitions are in explanation of the series of sketches of the different rigs found in Padstow ships in the nineteenth century. The opportunity has been taken to illustrate the

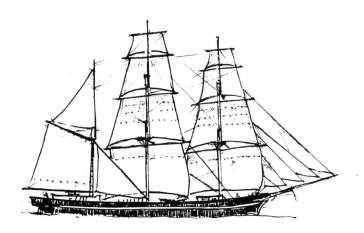

BARQUE SIMILAR TO THE 'SAUGEEN' OF 1856

FULL RIGGED SHIP.
AN IMPRESSION OF 'MORNING STAR', 1856

appearance of specific vessels for which other satisfactory illustrations have not been found.

1) A full-rigged ship has three (or more) masts and is square rigged on all of them. The MORNING STAR was the only full-rigged ship built at Padstow.

2) A barque has three (or more) masts and is square rigged except on the mizen (or aftermast). The barque BELLE had a false stern gallery and painted gun ports. These features were originally intended to give the appearance of being important and heavily armed, but became decorative in the same way as some later passenger steamers had two or three funnels when they required only one. SAUGEEN of 1856 was more utilitarian.

3) A barkentine (or barquentine) has three (or more) masts and is square rigged only on the foremast. The HOPEFUL has the following sails on her foremast, working up from the deck: the foresail, the fore lower topsail, fore upper topsail, the fore top gallant and the fore royal. That is in contrast with the two preceding vessels which had foresail, foretopsail, a fore topgallant and fore royal. In the 1860s it became common practice to split the topsails into upper and lower topsails by introducing an extra yard, thus reducing the size of the largest sails in the ship, and making it possible to reduce the size of the crew.

4) A brig has two masts, both square rigged. The ALAN was a beamy apple-bowed cargo-carrying brig.

BRIG 'ALAN', 1817. Reconstruction

BARQUENTINE 'HOPEFUL', 1876

A SNOW SUCH AS THE 'EAGLE', 1839

BRIGANTINE 'SHEPHERDESS' BUILT 1865.
after a painting by H. P. JENSEN

5) A snow is a brig with the following refinement: a 'trymast' is fixed close abaft the mainmast so that the spencer (or spanker); i.e. the fore-and-aft sail on that mast, together with its gaff and mast hoops could operate without interfering with the mainmast rigging. In the early part of the nineteenth century a true snow, like the EAGLE, had no boom for the spencer. The EAGLE has a boat hung from her stern, which is an indication that she was built in North America.

6) The term brigantine covers several different rigs of two masted vessels, but in the late nineteenth century it meant square rig on the foremast and fore-and-aft on the mainmast; the SHEPHERDESS is an example.

7) The polacre brigantine PETER & SARAH is so termed because her foremast is a single timber and her foretopsail is 'set flying', simplifying the running and standing rigging when compared with a normal brigantine.

8, 9, 10, 11) A schooner is a vessel with two or more masts, with the foremast not higher than the mast abaft it, and with fore-and-aft sails on all masts. Fore-and-aft schooners (like ELIZABETH DREW, as illustrated) have no square sails.

POLACRE BRIGANTINE 'PETER & SARAH', 1853

'ELIZABETH DREW' AS A FORE-AND-AFT SCHOONER
IN HER OLD AGE.

TOPGALLANT SCHOONER 'FLOWER OF THE FAL', 1870

TOPSAIL SCHOONER 'EMILY', 1873

Topsail schooners have square topsails on the foremast (or in some early cases of two-masted schooners, on both masts). Some clipper schooners, like FLOWER OF THE FAL, had square topsails and topgallant sails, and some even sported a 'royal' above the topgallant, but while the term 'topgallant schooner' has achieved some recognition, all these rigs are often covered by the term 'topsail schooners' as opposed to 'fore-and-aft schooners'.

Of the four schooners illustrated, the EMILY was the coastal work-horse, with a single square topsail (if she had been larger, that sail might have been divided into lower and upper topsails); the FLOWER OF THE FAL was the aristocrat designed for the transatlantic and mediterranean trades with square topsail and topgallant; the LYDIA CARDELL, previously a deepwater barquentine had been rigged down to a schooner to reduce crew (but still retained square lower and upper topsails and topgallant), and the ELIZABETH DREW in the 1920s had a diesel engine (often referred to as the iron topsail), and had all her yards removed from the foremast 'to reduce work upstairs', making her a fore-and-aft schooner. Her patched sails tell their own story.

THREE-MASTED SCHOONER 'LYDIA CARDELL', 1873
AS RE-RIGGED AT ARKLOW, 1903

GALEAS KETCH SUCH AS 'SALLY ANN', 1809

KETCH 'TRIUMPH', 1881

12, 13) As to ketches, the SALLY ANN illustrates the introduction of the rig to Padstow waters and the TRIUMPH shows it
in its final and finest form.

14, 15) That leaves the small fry; first the luggers represented by
ENCHANTRESS and EBENEZER. The former had a vargor (a
strut keeping the foresail taut to windward) and both had their
mizen masts offset so as not to foul the tiller. Small craft like these
were often half-decked. Originally the ENCHANTRESS had been
an open boat, but when she was 'rose upon' (that is enlarged and
converted) by John Tredwen in 1823, she measured 17 tons and had
to be registered.

LUGGER 'EBENEZER', 1843. Reconstruction

THREE-MASTED LUGGER
SUCH AS 'ENCHANTRESS', 1823

SMALL SLOOP WITH HAGBOAT STERN
SUCH AS 'KING'S FISHER', 1816

CUTTER 'SWIFT', BUILT 1860.
A BRISTOL PILOT SKIFF

16) The sloop KING'S FISHER is the only vessel in the Padstow registers described as having a hagboat stern, and it is far from certain what was meant by the term by 1831 when she was registered. In the eighteenth century, sterns were described (for customs documentation, for instance) as square, round, pink, lute or 'hackboat', but there were only a few of the last three categories. Chapman's *Architectura Navalis Mercantoria* of 1775 includes drawings of a hagboat with curved timbers radiating out around the sternpost to give an enlarged stern to which the American term 'fantail' seems appropriate. The sketch of the KING'S FISHER attempts to show the resulting stern on a very small vessel, but the exact shape remains uncertain. One of the factors affecting the rig of the KING'S FISHER when she was built was the attempt by the government to limit the speed of small vessels so that they could not escape from the revenue cutters.

The revenue cutters had a large sail area made possible by having long fixed bowsprits and privately owned sloops and smacks were not allowed to have such bowsprits. Hence the relatively short running bowsprits of the sloops and smacks of Padstow early in the nineteenth century.

17) The word 'cutter' was used in Cornwall to describe the use of the vessel rather than the rig. It was largely applied to pilot cutters and revenue cutters and later to cutter-rigged yachts. The sketch of the pilot cutter SWIFT is based on an old photograph and she was typical of the numerous Bristol Channel pilot cutters.

18) Sloops or smacks such as the THOMASINE & MARY were essentially cargo carriers with beamy burdensome hulls. By coincidence, the sketch of THOMASINE & MARY bears a strong resemblance to that of the SWIFT, but the broadside view hides the fact that the first has a beam equal to almost half her length, whereas the pilot cutters had a beam of less than one third of their length. It is possible, also, that Chidgey's painting of the THOMASINE & MARY was somewhat flattering.

SMACK 'THOMASINE & MARY', 1855.
after a painting by THOMAS CHIDGEY

# 14 THE PRINCIPAL SEAFARING FAMILIES AND THEIR SHIPS

EVERY time a name appears in Chapter 5, it marks in effect the appointment of a man to be master of a North Cornish ship. I have found 537 such appointments in the port books of Padstow between 1565 and 1719 that can be firmly allotted family names, and they include about 160 different family names. Many of the names were only mentioned once or twice, whereas the following families were very dominant : Oliver (29 mentions), Triplet (22), Harris (22), Martin (17), Parsons (15), Kittow (14), Pearce (14). Thus 25% of the ships' masters were provided by seven families and, by continuing the process, it is established that 50% of the masters were provided by twenty-four families over the period of 155 years.

Many of the families lived in Padstow but others were spread from Bude to Newquay and inland to Wadebridge. The Aungers, Rowes, Billings and Trevethans were largely based in Port Isaac, as were the Martins (or Martyns) in Boscastle. Boscastle was also the stronghold of some smaller clans, such as the ffrenches, Kneebones and Tubbs. There were Randells (Rundles) at Bude, as there still are today.

The maritime surveys of the 1620s (see Chapter 4) confirm how local most of these families were, and give additional credence to the general conclusion that the ships of Padstow and the outports remained largely in the hands of influential local families throughout all these early years. During the period covered by the old port books, over two hundred Padstow ships have been identified: more than fifty of these were in the hands of seven families, and the vast majority of the remainder were in the hands of smaller local clans.

If we take the family names of those owning or taking command of Padstow ships in the nineteenth century, and look back to the Maritime Surveys of 1626 and 1629, we find the following families on both lists: Allen, Avery, Barrett, Beer, Bennett(s), Billing(s), Bray, Brown(e), Carveth, Cock/Cook, Couch, Dav(e)y, Eddy/Ede, Edmund(s), French, Guy, Hambley, Harris, Hicks, Hockin(g), Ivey, Jenkins, Jewel, Kitto(w), Mitchell, Oats, Old, Oliver, Parker, Peters, Phillips, Pope, Prideaux, Quinte, Randall, Rawlin(g)s, Richards, Roberts, Stephens, Tabb/Tubb, Tippett, Tom(s), Tref(f)ry, Warren, West, Wills, Wilson, Wood.

There are forty-eight family names of which two thirds also occur as masters in the port books 1565-1719.

The Maritime Surveys list 140 different family names for those connected with the sea in Padstow and the outports, so it could be argued that about one third of those families connected with the sea in the 1620s went on to produce ship owners and ship masters in the nineteenth century. Such an argument would be totally invalid today, as reference to any telephone directory, and consideration of the high mobility and large numbers of families of the same name such as Smith would make clear, but until the nineteenth century mobility was much less, and in the surveys of the 1620s many of the families listed above were to be found in Padstow but not in other ports of the southwest, so it seems likely that of the Padstow mariners of the 1620s, something like one quarter produced descendants who owned or captained Padstow ships in the nineteenth century.

On the other hand, some very prominent Padstow ship owners of the nineteenth century are absent from the maritime surveys and the port books 1565-1719. The families Allport, Bate(s), Burt, Dark(e), Ennor, Harvey, Hawken, Hutchings, Knight, Mabley, May, Parnall, Sloggett, Stribley, Trebilcock and Tredwen all owned and captained large numbers of Padstow ships in the nineteenth century, but there is no mention of them in the earlier maritime surveys and port books. Other families, the Cory family in particular, appeared in Padstow in the nineteenth century records, but moved away to become major shipowners elsewhere.

The Padstow Trefry family was the only one of that name mentioned in the maritime surveys of the 1620s in the whole of Cornwall and Devon, so Padstow can surely claim to have had a part in the origins of the Treffry dynasty of the nineteenth century with its widespread interests in mining, railways and shipping, including the development of Newquay, although they were mainly based on the south coast.

## Family Names of Owners and Masters of Padstow Ships and Ships they Owned or Commanded, 1800-1900

Limited where possible to those with North Cornish connections. Principal sources: *Lloyd's Registers, Mercantile Navy Lists, Padstow Ship Registers* and *Olsen's Fisherman's Nautical Almanack*. Dates after ships' names indicate date of build, not date of family interest, and are only included to avoid confusion with other ships of the same name. Families with only one or two vessels have generally been omitted. Various different spellings have been combined, e.g. Jenkin(s)/Jenkyn(s).

*: name appears in the Maritime Surveys 1626-1629 (Chapter 4)
†: name appears as Master in Padstow Port Books 1565-1719.

The owners of twentienth-century vessels will not be found in this list unless the family name was already included for the nineteenth century. Many of the owners of fishing vessels are mentioned in Chapter 17. Individual members of families may be identified by following the fortunes of their ships in the Appendix, and if necessary in the original sources. It must be appreciated that families with the same surname are not necessarily relations.

### A

**Abbott.** Catherine 1829, Commerce 1819, Eagle 1839, Frances Ann, Hannah 1817, Maria 1824, Sarah 1836

**Adam(s).** Alberta 1865, Hope, Mary Seymour 1830, Padgy, Prince Alfred, Thomas 1797, William 1789

**Allen.** * † Fairy Flower, Fairy King, Treffry

**Allport.** Agnes Ellen, Agnes Strout, Annie Harris, Ariel 1864, Bessie 1875, Corsair, Courier 1869, Dalusia, Daring 1859, Doris 1904, Galatea 1868, Henry Edmonds, Ida Elizabeth, J K Allport, Janie 1878, Jessie 1858, Kinnaird, Lily 1871, Lord Devon, Lottie 1878, Margaret Murray, Maria 1857, Marian, Rare Plant, Sam Slick, Sly Boots, Teazer, Veho

**Avery.*** Albion 1822, Amelia 1820, Ariel 1864, Boscastle 1793, Brutus 1835, Caroline (c.1800), Catherine 1842, Charlotte 1830, Clio 1838, Dew Drop 1820, Dundarg 1830, Edward (Prize), Fair Trader,

Favourite 1835, Friends Goodwill, Industry 1778, Industry 1809, Intrepid 1834, Jennifer 1845, John & Mary, Le Gustave (later Cornwall), Lily of the Valley, Loftus, Louisa, Maria 1824, Monarch, Orb, Pet, Phillippa, Pomona, Rebecca, Sophia 1810, Spring, Spring Flower, Thomas and Nancy, Three Brothers 1850, Venus 1820, Zephyr

**B**

**Bake(r).** Our Jinny 1920, Mary (b.France), Anna Maria 1824, Diligence 1796

**Bamfield/Banfield.** Mary 1816, Mary Ann 1803, Mayflower 1866

**Barrett.** * † Elizabeth 1805, John & Mary, Mary (in 1798), Sisters, Stucley, Wild Pigeon

**Bate(s).** Agenoria 1858, Aid 1833, Bee 1846, Bessy Jane, Breeze 1837, Camalan 1849, Electric, Elizabeth Hampton, Emily 1873, Industry 1893, Lenora 1854, Liberty 1838, Lizzie 1867, Lizzie Mary, Mary 1840, Mirre, Nadir, Patra, Pet, Pendarves, Rob the Ranter, Salamander, Sprightly, Talbot, Tamar, Trebiskin, Vesper, Volunteer 1861, Yacht

**Battershill.** Corsair 1874, Lizzie Male, Pride of the South

**Beer.** * Affo 1836, Belle of the Plym, La Noroise 1962, Les Pleiades 1962, Sprightly, Victoria 1847

**Bellamy.** Albion 1822, Betsy 1819, Briton's Queen, Collina 1860, Conquest 1871, Criterion, Elizabeth 1839, George Canning 1827, Letitia 1835, Nanscow, Penally, Tamar, Valency 1825, Vesper

**Bennett(s).** Agnes Louisa, Atlanta II 1988, Bess 1840, Bessie 1871, Driving Mist, Flora 1843, Florence Nightingale, Fly 1817, George Canning, Glendorgal, Ingrid 1873, Lady Jane 1880, Lenora 1854, Lizzie Grace, Louise, Mayflower 1866, Peace 1873, Porth 1877, Royalist, Sir William Molesworth, Western Star

**Billing(s).** Albion 1822, Alert 1888, Breeze 1837, Brothers 1839, Clyde 1866, Daria Louisa, Duck 1810, Ebenezer 1804, Friends Goodwill, I & N 1956, Jessie 1878, Johann Carl, John (Prize), John 1865, John & Matilda, Lady of the Lake, Le Hereaux, Louisa & Rachel, Padstow 1789, Pete 1966, Philippa, Po, Pomona, Porth 1877, Providence 1827, Tamar, Three Brothers 1800, Young Benjamin

**Bird/Burd.** (see also Burt)

**Birt.** (see Burt)

**Blake.** Delabole, Janie Louise, Teazer

**Boase.** † Spring Flower, John & Jenifer, Mary 1829, Sir Charles Napier

**Brabyn.** Jane (Prize), Manwella (Yacht)

**Bray.** * † Ann 1792, Annie 1873, Antagonist, Gleaner 1875, Habbacot 1787, Mary 1813

**Brenton/Brinton.** Caroline 1874, Courier 1869, Eclipse 1819, Emma 1877, Hannah 1865, Henrietta 1872, Jane & Sarah 1872, Larch 1841, TMP

**Brewer.** † Albion 1822, Carthage, James & Ann, Jane & Margaret, Janie Vivian, John & Hannah, Leander 1850, Lizzie May, Marina, Mary 1833, Mary Jane 1840, Nanscow, Providence 1807, Ralph, Sisters 1807, Sir William Molesworth, Thomas & Elizabeth, Unity 1812, Via

**Briant/Bryant.** Caroline 1839, Ceres 1850, Hope 1806, Phoenix

**Brinham.** Ivy May, Julia Ann 1972, Prada, Prevail

**Broad.** Gipsy Queen, Jane Lowden

**Brokenshaw.** Hope 1827, John & Hannah, Mary (c. 1806), Patsey, Sir William Molesworth, Standard

**Brown(e).** * † Bottreaux Castle, Bulla, Clio 1836, Dew Drop 1820, Driving Mist, Elizabeth Hill, Emma 1877, Glendoveer, Henrietta 1872, Hetty 1877, John & Hannah, Kate ( FV c. 1880) Katie 1881, Kings Fisher 1816, Lily 1880, Lisa Maria 1988, Lota 1861, Lydia, Mary & Elizabeth, Mary Selina, Mirre, Myvanwy, Nautilus,

Northern Lass 1955, Pet 1856, Port Isaac Kestrel, RGD, Rose 1843, Seraphina, Sir R. R. Vyvyan, Spring, Spring Flower, Titania 1865, Tullochgorum, Venus 1820, Volunteer 1860

**Bryant.** (see Briant)

**Bullman.** Daedalus 1835, Voluna

**Bunt.** Bertha reg. 1870, Heatherbell, John & Hannah, Mary Wighton, Ontario, Resolution, Sprightly, Talbot, Three Sisters, Water Lily 1863, Willie 1861

**Burgess.** Boscastle 1838, LMA (MFV)

**Burk(e)(s).** † Boscastle 1838, Briton's Queen, Dewdrop 1820, Penally, Pictou, Racer, Rose 1843, Spring, Towan

**Burt/Birt.** (see also Bird) Agnes Strout, Alan 1817, Alpha 1877, Ariel 1864, Bacchus 1967, Betsey (prize), Britannia 1803, Camella 1975, Edward (prize), Fairy Belle, Ida Elizabeth, Morning Dawn 1970, Nanscow, Penally, Royalist, Samuel & Elizabeth, Sea Fox 1982, Star, Trevose of Newquay 1986, WJC, Welcome

**Burton.** Amaranth 1873, Amaranth 1886, Lizzie Mary

**Buse.** Edith 1856, Ida Elizabeth, Lord Porchester, Maria Louisa, Mary (Prize), Pioneer, Southerner

**C**

**Cardell.** Tretherras, Victoria 1847, Water Nymph

**Carne.** † Catharine 1853, Plymouth 1863

**Caroline** (Prize), Charles 1834, Fanny 1827, Jane & Margaret, Pet 1856, Thomas & Elizabeth

**Carter.** † Albion 1822, Amelia 1820, Belle 1838, Bessie 1871, Caroline 1839, Cornish Lass 1841, Daria Louisa, Edwin 1859, Elizabeth 1839, Elizabeth Jane, Ellen Frances, Enchantress 1823, Fanny 1827, Florence Nightingale, Flying Scud, Friends Goodwill, Happy Return 1814, Intrepid 1834, Jeremiah 1796, Jubilee (in 1834), Lizzie 1864, Mary (Prize), Mary Ann 1927, Mary Peers, Medora, Porth, Princess Charlotte, Rippling Wave, Sarah 1858, Spring, Tamar, Thomas 1859, Towan, Tower, Trebiskin, Tregunnel, Unity 1783, Valency 1838, Victoria 1853

**Carveth.** * † Alan 1817, Kate 1837, Millicent, Unity 1812

**Casey.** Ida Elizabeth, Lizzie May, Maria Louisa, Southerner

**Chalk.** Breeze 1838, Delabole 1848, Despatch 1831, Mary Ann 1827, Sir William Molesworth, Susan 1826, Three Sisters, Tower, Unity 1812, William & Jane

**Chapman.** Aspire 1961, CBKF, Earl St Vincent, Eliza 1826, Glenmore 198-, Harvest Reaper 1955, Henry Holman, Incentive IV 1958, J.K. Allport, Jean Howard 1980, Jubilee Queen 1977, Lottie 1878, Louisa 1860, Pilot Star 1960, Quiet Waters

**Chappell.** Elizabeth Mary, Georges 1847, Ocean Queen 1858, Royalist, Tower

**Chegwidden/Chigwidden.** Amelia, Ann 1792, Edith 1865, Glendoveer, Hetty 1877, Janie 1878, Lotus 1842, Louise, Reaper, Shamrock 1835

**Clemens/Clement(s).** Active 1784, Advance 1876, Bertha (reg. 1870), Bessie 1871, Camilla 1853, Carrie 1878, Clara 1877, Edith 1865, Elizabeth Davey, Fly 1815, Kittie 1865, Leila 1877, Look Out 1858, Louisa 1868, Lord Porchester, Maid of Mona, Margaret Hobley, Maria 1801, Mary Barrow, Miranda, Nancy 1829, Peter & Sarah, Rosamond Jane, Susan 1820, Susan Vittery, T & J, Tariff, Tom Henry, Tower, Try Again, Vitula, Whim

**Clemon.** Ballinbreich Castle, Emma 1877

**Coad.** (Pt.Isaac)/**Coode.** Camwood, Mary Ann 1827, Mary Coad, Meta (Truro connect.) Myvanwy, Petra, Prince Alfred, Rob the Ranter, Souvenir, Swift 1871, Trusty (in 1905), Victoria 1853, Voluna

**Cobaldick/Cobbledick.** Sophia 1810, Voluntina

**Cock/Cook.** Caroline (Prize), Clementina, Galatea 1868, Harmony 1814, Hind 1862, Industry 1778, James & Sarah, James & Ann, John

Barwise, Lark 1791, Osprey, Pomona, Rhoda Mary, Rosamond Jane, WJC, Why Not

Collin(g)s. Bertha (reg. 1870), Busy Bee, Trinity Buoy Yacht

Conway. Ballinbreich Castle, St Petroc

Cook. Aunde, Fairy Queen, Ruby, Sisters

Corsell. Albion 1845, John & Hannah, Tamar

Cory. Alma 1855, Amphitrite 1869, Aurora 1855, Belle of the Plym, Conservator 1842, Edith 1856, Ezel 1873, Jane 1802, John Henry, Mary Eliza, Millicent, The Kildare, Volunteer(1), Volunteer(2), Volunteer(3)

Couch. * Affo 1826, Aid 1833, Alfred 1865, Amelia 1820, Annie (FV lost 1904), Betsey 1819, Catharine 1872, Clara 1879, Comet 1858, Conservator 1842, Constance 1858, Deveron 1871, Fayaway, Fortunate, Friends Goodwill, George Canning, Georgiana 1820, Industry 1809, Jane 1816, Letitia 1835, Louise, Louise & Rachel, Mary (Prize), Mary Barrow, Millicent, Our Girlie 1921, Penally, Telephone, Unity 1863, Volunteer 1860

Courtenay. Annie 1864, Bessie Jane, Betsey 1789, Charlotte 1830, Dispatch 1810, Eaglebush, Emma 1813, Saunders Hill, Susan 1825, Willie 1861

Courtis. (see Curtis)

Cowl. Emma Jane 1861, Prince Edward

Crocker. Busy 1836, John Henry, Lord Devon, Louise, Maldon, Mary Seymour, Plymouth, Tullochgorum, William Martyn

Cundy. J K Allport, Miranda, Padstow 1789, William 1789

Curtis/Courtis. Devonia 1836, Friends 1787, Mary 1813

D

Daggua/Duggua. Conservator, Loftus, Ranger

Dark(e). Alarm 1849, Alarm 1861, Amelia 1820, Blue Bell (reg.1860) Canadian 1839, Favourite 1835, Frances Ann, Friends Goodwill, Hope 1827, Lotus 1842, Louisa 1868, Mary Josephine, Nancy 1829, Pomona, Rose 1847, Vitula

Davey/Davy. Bude Packet, Eleanor 1816, Friends 1787, Hope (Prize), Lady Acland, Lanson Castle, Lord Porchester, Mary 1829, Primrose 1831, Prince Regent, RGD, Satyr, Sisters, Star, Susan 1820, Susan Vittery

Davies/Davis. † Charlotte 1863, Dasher 1815, Elizabeth 1854, Louise, Salamander, Three Brothers 1800, Zephyr

Deacon. Ezel 1873, Louisa 1860, Mary Eliza

Dingle. Ballinbreich Castle, Bottreaux Castle

Drew. Bude Packet, Emma (c. 1850), Star 1818

Duggua (see Daggua)

Dungly. Chrisande 1940, Elizabeth 1819

Dunstan. Amanda 1807, Annie 1859, Clara 1877, Julia 1870, Kathleen 1878, Joseph R Pym, Lotus 1842, Royalist, Sunbeam, Unity 1863, Water Nymph, Willie 1865

E

Easthope/Easthorpe. Carthage, Clio 1838, Harriet Scott, Lady Sale 1848, Margarita, Voluna, Windsor

Edmund(s). Ballinbreich Castle, Janie 1878

Ellery. Fly 1815, John & Jenifer, Kate 1854, Orb, Orwell, Rosamond Jane, St Saviours

England. Fayaway, James & Ann, Lizzie May, Margaret & Esther, Polo 1972, Primrose 1831, Tamar, Tristan

Ennor. Agnes Cairns, Bessie 1871, Camellia 1877, Cavalier 1871, Clara 1879, Elizabeth Davey, Ethel 1876, Flying Scud, Frederick William, Maggie, Ocean Queen 1868, Royalist, Sarah 1858, Spark, Titania 1865, Tom Henry, William Martyn

Evans. Auspicious 1916, Grey Flamingo 197-, Hannah Christine 1990, John & Hannah, Mattanja 1990, Phoenix, The Kildare, Windsor

F

Fishlay/Fishley. Despatch 1810, Isabel, Little Racer, Maria 1824, Porth, Volant

Found (Bude). Victoria 1837, Marina, Sir R R Vyvyan

French. † James & Sarah, James & Ann, John (Prize), Jollivet, Unity 1783

G

Geach/Geake. Conquest 1871, Dick & Harry 1876, Jane Slade, Lydia Cardell, Silver Stream, William Geake

George. Boconnoc, Julia 1879, Willie 1865

Giles. Anne 1809, John 1788, Jubilee 1809, Porth, Sarah 1836, Thomas & Harriot

Gill. Aid 1833, Catherine Auld, Ethel 1872, June (Yt), Pursuit, Tregunnel, Triumph 1881, Vesta, Winlay

Gould. John & Mary, Mary (Prize), Mary (Prize), Nelly 1825, Penally, Teazer, Telephone

Greenway. Ceres 1811, Star 1818

Gurney. Jubilee 1809, Pink

Guy. * Agenoria 1858, Betsey Jane, Despatch 1837, Echo 1847, Electric, Harmony 1868, Ida 1873, James & Ann, Louisa 1860, Maria 1824, Mary Stephens, Scout, Sprightly, Surprise 1879, Sylph, Telegraph, Telephone, Volunteer 1861

H

Haines. (see Haynes)

Hallett. † Alert 1849, Bee 1846

Hambley/Hameley. * Ann & Elizabeth 1826, Mary 1877, Rose 1843, Thomas 1824, Treore, Venus 1820

Hames. † Agnes Louisa

Hancock. Anne 1768, Boy Malcolm 1973, Catherine 1843, Magnet

Harding. Mary Ann 1803, Nanscow, Windsor

Harris. * † Breeze 1837, Catherine 1843, Conservator 1842, Elizabeth & Maria, Endeavour 1788, Maria 1865, Sea Lark, Sir William Molesworth, William Harries, William Martyn, Willie 1865

Harvey. Amazon (PS), Bessie 1875, Camalan 1849, Comet 1842, Courier 1869, Ebenezer 1804, Elizabeth 1845, Gem 1852, Hebe 1847, Iris 1836, Jane & Margaret, John & Mary 1827, Jubilee 1809, Lafrowda, Lily 1871, Lord Devon, Magnet Packet, Mary 1816, Mary Ann 1827, Mary Jane 1840, Mary Seymour, One and All, Onward, P M Willcock, Planet, Queen Adelaide, Rhoda Mary, Sly Boots, Susan 1813, Thomas & Elizabeth, Three Brothers 1802, Treore, Veho, Villiers

Hawke. Ada 1844, Aeolus 1852, Hesperus 1875, Lily 1871, Mary Seymour, Peace 1862, Peace 1873

Hawken. Albion 1845, Archie 1887, Cornet 1842, Cornish Lass 1841, Dasher 1815, EGT, Energy 1853, Hope 1827, James & Ann, Jane & Margaret, John & Hannah, Larch 1841, Laurina 1845, Liberty 1838, Magnet Packet, Nautilus, St Petroc, Sir William Molesworth, Villiers

Hawker. Earl St Vincent

Hawkey. Georges 1847, Louise, Satyr, Susan Vittery, Try Again, Whim

Hawkins. † Jeremiah 1796, Primrose 1831, Rosamond Jane

Haynes/Haines. Alarm 1861, Ceres 1850, Clara 1879, Clio 1838, Harmony 1868, Louisa 1860, Phoenix, Sir R R Vyvyan, Tullochgorum, Voluntina, William & Jane

Heard. † Affo 1836

Heatherington/Hetherington. Anne 1768, Ceres 1820, Jane 1818, John 1788, Mary Ann 1803, Providence 1827, The Kildare

Hellyer. Carthage, Industry 1809, Pet, Rose 1843, Thomasine & Mary

Henwood. Ada 1848, Camellia 1877, Flower 1812, Lizzie/Lizzy

1864, Mary Barrow, Reaper, Rippling Wave, Trevannance

**Hicks.** * † Brothers 1832, Caroline (Prize), Forest Deer, Frances Ann, Gannel 1826, Infanta, Jane & Sarah 1829, Jeremiah 1796, Johnson & Elizabeth, Loftus, Margaret Murray, Maria 1824, Marshall, Mary Ann 1879, Mary Kitty, Mary Josephine, Ocean Belle, Pomona, RGD, Rosamond Jane, Ruby, Samuel & Elizabeth, Symmetry, Three Sisters, Three Brothers 1800, Tretherras, Victoria 1847

**Hill.** Pasco, Telegraph, Telephone

**Hockaday.** Clyde 1866, Delabole (SS), Prince Alfred, Teazer

**Hocken/Hockin(g).** * Affo 1836, Ariel 1864, Bee 1846, Bessie 1875, Bessie reg. 1872, Blessing 1788, Busy 1836, Caroline 1839, Cottager, Devonia 1836, Eclipse 1819, Emilie 1866, Emily 1873, Enchantress 1823, Ethel 1876, Frederick William, Friends 1787, Frolic 1813, Hind 1862, Jasper 1884, Jeremiah 1796, John 1788, Josephine, Julia 1879, Kittie 1865, Lady Agnes, Lenora 1854, Les Pleiades 1962, Louisa, Louise, Lydia, Maria 1841, Marie Louise, Maru, Mirre, Ocean Queen 1868, Pilgrim, Primrose 1831, Prince Edward 1786, Rebecca 1814, Shamrock 1870, Shamrock 1835, Sir R R Vyvyan, Superior 1834, TEJ, Tariff, Triumph 1881, Wanderer, Water Nymph, Why Not, William Geake

**Honey.** Alice Jane, J.M.S., P M Willcock, Penally, Village Belle

**Hooper.** Bee 1846, Bessie reg. 1872, Catherine 1869, Florence Nightingale, Maria 1865, Mirre (Bude connection), Model, Rebecca (Bridgwater connection), Reviresco

**Horsewell/Horswill.** Churchill 1816, Conservator 1842, Criterion, Elizabeth Mary 1840, Ellen Jane, John & Mary 1783, Mary 1833, Mary Ann 1803, Nanscow

**Hosken(s)/Hoskin.** Active 1784, Camalan 1849, Catharine 1842, Caurinus, Eastern Maid, Favourite 1835, Gannel 1826, Georgiana 1824, Giles Lang 1864, Isabella 1856, Jennifer 1845, Le Hereaux, Lile, Lucretia, Maid of Mona, Maria 1824, Maria 1841, Millicent, Rebecca Lang, Samuel & Elizabeth, Temperance, Wanderer

**House.** Amanda 1867, Annie 1859, Britannia (lost 1864), Elizabeth & Maria, Hind 1862, Kathleen 1878, Liberty 1838, Royalist, Unity 1863

**Hutchings.** Ada 1844, Alberta 1865, Amazon (PS) Belle of the Plym, Briton's Queen, Brutus 1835, Brothers 1832, CBKF, Cambria, Charlotte 1830, Conservator 1842, Deveron 1871, Endeavour 1788, English Girl, Ezel 1873, Flower 1812, Frances 1889, Hebe 1847, Lenora 1854, Louisa 1860, Mary Kitty, Nanscow, Ocean Queen 1858, Providence 1827, Queen of the West, St Stephens, Sally Ann 1799, Superior 1834, Telegraph, Thomas & Elizabeth, Viola 1872, Volzy, Water Lily 1871, Welsh Belle (Falmouth)

**I**

**Inch.** Fame 1816, Iona 1865, Rival

**Ivey.** * Fly 1817, Gleaner 1875

**J**

**Jacka.** Advance 1876, Maid of Mona, William Henry

**Jago.** Alice Jane 1865, Annie 1864, Janie Banfield, Lord Porchester

**James.** † Breeze 1838, Camelford 1861, Caurinus, Celerity, Friends 1826, Lafrowda, Maria c. 1840, Mary James, Millicent, Primrose, Red Jacket, St Petrock, Sisters, Telephone, Thomas & Mary, Vesper, WJC

**Jenkin(s)/Jenkyn(s).** Agnes & Sophia, Alfred 1865, Amelia 1862, Bertie 1877, Carrie 1878, Charlotte 1863, Elizabeth & Maria, Emma 1877, Flora 1843, Glendoveer, Henrietta 1872, Hetty 1877, Ingrid 1873, Janie 1878, Johnson & Elizabeth, Kate 1854, Katie 1878, Katie 1881, Lottie 1878, Louisa, Lydia, Margaret, Mildred 1875, Minnie, Pandora of Polruan (Yacht), Pride of the South, Pride of the West, Puzzle, Queen of the Isles, Rhoda, Rita, Sally, Sarah Ann, TEJ (St

Ives), TPC (Boscastle), Treffry, Unity 1863, Vixen, Westfa, Williams

**Jermyn.** Eclipse 1819, Mary 1833, Providence 1807, Rising Sun

**Jewel.** * Lord Devon

**Jones.** † Charles 1834, Isabella 1872, Royalist, The Saint, Tom Henry

**Jordan/Jorden.** De Lank, St Petrock

**K**

**Keat.** Hero 1872, Janie Vivian 1869, Lord Devon

**Kemp.** † Atlanta 1983

**Kernick.** Janie 1878, Welsh Belle

**Key.** Aurora 1855, Belle 1838, Brutus 1835, Dewdrop 1820, Florist, Marchioness of Abercorn, Margarita, Morning Star 1855, Rose 1843, Spring Flower

**King.** † Ceres 1811, Jubilee 1809, Viking X 1964

**Kitto/Kittow.** * † Pete 1976

**Knebone/Kneebow.** † Leila 1877

**Knight.** Albert 1847, Anne 1768, Ariel 1864, Belle 1838, Belle of the Plym, Betsy 1819, Ceres 1820, Champion of Wales, Crimson Arrow 1976, Courier 1869, Ellen Jane, England's Glory, Fame 1810, Infanta, Jane 1818, John & Mary, John & Matilda, Le Hereaux, Maria 1824, Mary (in 1797), Marys & Helena, Mary Jane 1840, Nautilus, Orb, Pascoe, Philippa, Primrose 1831, Saugeen, Susan 1820, Villiers

**Kunze.** Earl St Vincent, Margaret & Esther

**L**

**Langford/Longford.** Alarm 1861, Elizabeth 1839, Jane Lowden, Mary 1840, Valency 1838, Zarah

**Lewarne.** Glendorgal, Guiding Star 1879, Little Jane 1858, Mayflower 1858, SMC, Western Star

**Lewis.** Ceres 1811, Fairy Belle, Rising Sun, Viola 1872

**Libby.** Agnes Ellen, J K Allport

**Lobb.** † Adelaide 1869, Jainnie (FV), Mary Maria, Orion, Puzzle, Sir William Molesworth, The Saint, Victoria 1847, William Harries

**Longford** (see Langford)

**Lovering.** Anne 1768, Friends Goodwill, Providence 1827

**M**

**Mabley/Mably.** Caroline 1839, Catherine 1829, Eagle 1839, Hebe 1847, John & Jenifer, Le Hereaux, Mary 1833, Mary Kellow, Princess Charlotte, Republican, Rhoda, Sir Charles Napier, Spring Flower, Storm, Telegram, The Kildare, Three Sisters

**Mager.** † **Major** Kinnaird, Sea Lark, Teazer, Triumph 1881

**Male.** Annie 1864, Bessie Jane, Charlotte 1830, Donna Maria, Lizzie Male, Mary Jane 1856, Viola 1872

**Marshall.** Cornwall (Prize), Harmony 1815, Providence 1827, Sprightly

**Martin** †/**Martyn.** Agnes Louisa, Albion 1822, Alan 1858, Amelia 1820, Beatrice Caroline, Breeze 1838, Brothers 1839, Caurinus, Ceres 1804, Charlynne II 1963, Despatch 1837, Dick & Harry 1786, Eliza 1826, Fly 1815, Gannel 1826, Glendorgal, James & Sarah, James & Ann, John & Matilda, John Barwise, Kate 1857, Lady Jane 1880, Lane 1791, Little Jane 1858, Mary & Elizabeth, Marys and Helena, Mary Josephine, Monarch, Penpoll, Pet 1856, Peter & Sarah, Porth 1877, Ranger, Resolution, St Stanislas, St Stephens, Susan 1825, Swift 1871, Three Brothers 1800, Trebiskin, Vixen, WJC

**Matthews.** Belle of the Plym, Ebenezer 1869, Enterprise 1840, Gipsy Maid, Gipsy Queen, Henry Holman, Isabella 1856, John & Jenifer, Lafrowda, Lizzie May, Pet 1856, Sarah 1852, Satyr, Whim

**May.** Ann Williams, Caroline (c. 1800), Charlotte 1830, Charlotte 1863, Comet 1858, Florence 1869, Harriet 1834, Hope 1826, Jane 1802, Jane Francis, Lizzie May, Maria 1865, Mayflower 1866, Nadir, Orcades II 1979, Princess of Wales 1867, Rebecca 1866, Revenge (in 1804), Sappho 1869, Sarah 1858, Shepherdess, Susie May, Traveller,

Victoria 1853

**Maynard.** Edith 1858, Nimrod

**Mayne.** Le Hereaux, Margaret 1861

**Meluish.** Bessy Jane 1850, Betsy 1786

**Merrivale.** Henry Edmonds

**Metherill.** Hannah 1817, Maria (in 1838)

**Mitchell.** * Alfred 1865, Bessy Jane, Catherine 1869, Caurinus, Diligence 1796, Echo 1847, Electric, Hope 1826, Jehu 1835, John & Hannah, Lily 1871, Lydia, Mary Stephens, Rose 1847, Sylph, Tremenhere

**Morcom/Morcomb.** Charlotte 1830, Glendoveer, Jane & Margaret

**Morton.** Champion of Wales, John Barwise, Rebecca, Rosamond Jane

**Moyse(s).** Ann Williams, Comet 1858, Enterprise, Louisa *c.* 1791, Marys & Helena, Mayflower, St Stephens, Swift 1871, Yeoman's Glory

**N**

**Nance.** Hope (Prize), John & Hannah, Peace (Prize), Pink, Swallow, Tregunnel (Cardiff), Villiers

**Neal(e).** † Agenoria 1858, Ceres 1809, Charlotte 1863, Clyde 1866, Commerce 1828, Hesperus 1875, Jane 1802, Peace 1873, Peace 1862, Prince Alfred, Wild Pigeon

**Nicholl(s).** † Aid 1833, Camilla 1853, Daedalus 1835, Ebenezer 1804, James & Ann, Lord Porchester, Malpas Belle, Porth, Sarah Anna, Southerner, Star of Gwent, Tamar

**Norton.** Champion of Wales

**Norway.** Belle 1840, Constance 1858, Mary 1819, Mary Josephine, Rebecca, Samuel & Elizabeth, Treore

**O**

**Oatey.** Fanny 1827, Gem 1852, Ranger

**Oats.** * Vesta

**Odgers.** Dick & Harry 1786, Spriggan 1976, Thomas & Mary

**Old.** * Breeze 1837, Three Brothers 1800

**Oliver.** * † John & Mary 1827

**Osborne.** † Breeze 1837, Conquest 1871, Conservator 1842, Criterion, Earl St Vincent, Fairy Queen, Infanta, Jane (SL), London 1825, Lucretia, McGregor (FV), Marys & Helena, Ocean Queen 1858, Pink, Tamar, Trevone 1901, Victoria 1847, Vixen

**P**

**Painter/Paynter.** Auspicious 1916, Avail 1899, Crimson Rambler 1915, Industry 1893, Ivy May, Perilla 1914, Prevail 1895, Saunders Hill 1818, Williams

**Palmer.** † Traveller

**Pappin.** Active 1784, Busy Bee, Diligence 1875, Glendorgal, Glendoveer, Mary Annie, SMC, Thomas 1859, Tom

**Parker.** * † Betsy 1819, Despatch 1831, Edward (Prize), Jane & Margaret, Sir R R Vyvyan, Star, Susan 1820

**Parnall/Parnell.** Albion 1822, Catherine 1829, Ceres 1820, Commerce 1819, Cornish Lass 1841, Dalusia, Eagle 1839, Frances Ann, Intrepid 1851, Jane 1802, John 1788, John & Hannah, John & Sarah, Maria 1824, Mary 1819, Mary Josephine, Morning Star 1855, Nautilus, Porth, Rebecca 1814, Retford, Sarah 1836, Sir R R Vyvyan

**Pasco(e).** † Caroline 1839, Cavalier 1871, Clementina, Edward (Prize), George Canning, Henrietta 1872, Infanta, Le Hereaux, Lord Porchester, Orb, Regent, Rosamond Jane, Susan 1825 (Truro), Talbot, Welsh Belle, Young Benjamine

**Paynter.** (see Painter)

**Penalegan/Penhaligan.** Agnes Cairns, Hebe 1847, Maggie

**Peters.** * Agnes Ellen, Mary Ann 1827, Patsey, Rosamond Jane, Sir William Molesworth

**Petherick.** Ceres 1811

**Pethybridge.** Clementina 1847, Samuel & Elizabeth, Thomas & Elizabeth

**Pettigrew.** Caroline *c.* 1800, Hannah 1817, Harriet 1834

**Phillips.** * † Amaranth 1873, Amaranth 1886, Bessie Jane, Cameo 1876, Caroline Phillips, Edward (Prize), Emily 1861, Emma & Agnes, Emma Jane 1861, Florence Vivian, Fortune 1626, Friends Goodwill, George 1626, Happy Return 1801, Harmony 1868, Hope 1826, Janie Louise, Lizzie 1867, Lizzie Mary, Louisa & Rachel, Malpas Belle, Mary 1873,1840, Mary Phillips, Mildred 1875, Mildred 1889, Olive Branch, Pendarves, Pursuit, Rose 1830, Seraphina, Sheba, Temperance,Thomas & Mary, Tower, Ulelia, Valency 1838, Vesta, Village Belle, Wild Wave 1974, Williams

**Philp.** Caroline 1839, Ceres 1850, Eliza 1861, Elizabeth Hampton, Friends Goodwill, Intrepid 1851, Jane 1818, Laura Emma 1980, Robert Cottle, Unity 1812, Valency 1838, Vesta, Wonder (Fowey)

**Pollard.** † Alan 1817, Breadalbane, Britannia 1803, Hawk 1744, Intrepid 1851, Jubilee 1809, Mary (in 1809), Mary Josephine, Try Again, Union 1801, Unity 1812, Vesta

**Pope.** * Amelia 1820, Boscastle 1793, Brothers 1832, Charles 1834, Ellen Frances, Janie 1870, Lizzie 1868, Mary Phillips, Rebecca, Red Rose, Samuel & Elizabeth

**Power.** Anne 1768, Anne 1809, Champion of Wales, Hope (Prize), James & Ann, Unity 1812

**Prideaux.** * Albion 1862, Bess 1840, Bessie 1856, Charlotte 1830, Hope 1827, Mermaid 1789, Nancy 1784, St Stephens

**Prout.** Anne Davies, Charlotte 1830, Cicerone, Fruit Girl, Infanta, Sarah Fox, Susan 1820

**Q**

**Quinte.** * † Harrie 1626

**R**

**Randall.** * †/**Rundle.** * † Countess of Devon, Mountblairy, The Saint

**Rawle.** Bertha reg. 1870, Clio 1838, Fairy King, Pet, Pride of the South, Pride of the West, Rhoda, Spring, Windsworth

**Rawlings *//Rawlins.** Alice Jane 1865, Betsey 1789, Clio 1838, Earl St Vincent, Edward (Prize), Emma 1813, Giles Lang 1864, Ida Elizabeth, James & Ann, Jane 1790, Jane & Sarah, Jessie 1858, John 1788, Maldon, Mary Ann 1803, Nanscow, Padgy, Padstow 1789, Sally Ann 1799, Saunders Hill, Stag, Susan 1813, Thomas & Harriot, Thomas 1797, Trinity Buoy Yacht, William 1789

**Raymond.** Albion, Peace 1815

**Read/Reed.** † Ada 1876, Amphitrite 1859, Cottager, One and All

**Remeck/Remick/Rennick** † Dundarg, Emily 1861, Ida 1873

**Reveley.** Che Sara Sara 1971, Elizabeth Shaun 1971, Ystwyth

**Reynolds.** † Amelia 1862, Annie 1859, Diligence 1835, Edith 1858, John Wesley, Spring Flower, Tom Henry

**Richards*//Rickard.** † Anne 1809, Bessy Jane, Boscastle 1793, Briton's Queen, Caroline (Prize), Caroline 1874, Catharine 1842, Ceres 1820, Dew Drop 1820, Emma Jane 1861, Fame 1810, Frances Ann, Friendship 1793, Hope (in 1850), Jane 1816, Joseph R Pym, Kate 1837, Kinnaird, Le Gustave (later Cornwall), Louisa, Lucretia, Margarett, Mary 1833, Mary Kitty, Nadir, Ocean Queen 1858, Padstow *c.* 1801, Penally, Pendarves, Price, Providence 1827, Rebecca, Rose 1843, Samuel & Mary, Sprightly, Spring Flower, Thomas & Elizabeth, Thomas & Nancy, Union 1801, Unity 1812, Valentine 1816, Water Lily 1871

**Ridgman** (Bude). Nancy 1829

**Riley/Ryley.** Bess 1840, Hope 1827, John Barwise, Lizzie Grace

**Roberts.** * † Tamar 1807, The Saint, Vitula

**Robinson.** Mary Wighton, Plymouth 1863, Stag

**Rogers.** † Cornish Chough 1972, Orb 1829

**Rosevear/Rosevere.** Affo 1826, Boscastle 1838, Bottreaux Castle, Briton's Queen, George Canning, Hannah 1865, Hope 1806, Jane 1815, Letitia 1835, Lydia, Mary (Prize ), Mary (Prize), Newquay 1847, Peace 1862, Racer, Valency 1825

**Rowe.** † Ada 1844, Amaranth 1866, Annie 1859, Grace 1820, Kate 1857, Loftus, Lovely Cruizer, MCB, Our Belle Ann, Prince Edward 1786, SRJ (MFV), Talbot

**Rundle.** (see Randall)

**Russell.** † Cornish Queen 1964, Susie Jean 1990

**Ryley.** (see Riley)

**S**

**Sargeant/Sargent/Sergeunt.** Leander 1850, Marguerite, Unity 1812

**Seaton.** Alarm 1861, Alchymist 1828, Belle 1838, Ceres 1850, Daedalus 1835, Industry 1809, Jane Lowden, Jennifer 1845, Lutha, Phoenix, Voluna, Volutina

**Ships.** Aeolus 1852, Ariel 1864, Boconnoc, Caurinus

**Skinner.** † Fayaway, John & Susanna, Maria 1824, Mary Stephens, Volunteer

**Sleeman.** † Brothers 1832, Elizabeth 1783, Endeavour 1788, Frolic 1813, Idea, Ingrid 1873, Jane 1802, John 1788, Mary (Prize), Queen of the Isles, Rose 1847, Secret, Trevaunance

**Slogett/Sloggett/Slugett.** Briton's Queen, Jane 1816, Jane 1818, John & Hannah, Lancashire Lass, Lydia, Mary (Prize), Morning Star, Nelly 1825, Providence 1827, Superior, Tamar 1807, Thomas 1824, Traveller, Valency 1825, Venus 1820, Volzy

**Steer.** Jennifer, London

**Stephens** * † Bessy Jane, Engineer, John 1835, Jeremiah 1796, Jessie 1878, Johann Carl, John & Susanna, John 1865 & 1835, Louise, Mary Stephens, Mary Walters

**Stevens.** Echo 1847, Emma 1813, Minnie, Padstow (c. 1804), Peace 1815, Puzzle, Thomas & Mary

**Stout.** (see Strout)

**Stribley.** Ada 1844, Alberta 1865, Annie 1859, Annie 1864, Archie 1887, Bess 1840, Bessie (reg. 1872), Breadalbane, Caroline (Prize), Charlotte 1830, Dispatch 1810, Elizabeth & Mary, Emily 1854, Emily Ellen, Emma Jane 1861, Gurine, Hopeful 1876, Ingrid 1873, Intrepid 1851, JKA, Jane 1802, Janie 1870, Jessie 1858, John Wesley, Joseph R Pym, Larch 1841, Lizzie 1867, Lizzie Grace, Lizzie Male, London 1825, Lota 1861, Margarita, Mirre (Barnstaple connection), Ocean, Plover, Ralph, Rebecca, Royalist, St Stephens, Souvenir, Tretherras, Unity 1812, Valency 1838, Water Nymph, Willie 1861, Ystwyth

**Strout/Stout.** † Affo 1826, Agnes Strout, Boscastle 1838, Bottreaux Castle, Cilicia 1860, Edith 1858, Ferret 1827, J.C.A., Letitia 1835, Penally, Racer, St George, Why Not

**Sussex.** † Hawk 1744

**Symons.** † Britannia 1803, Gannel 1826, Jane 1806, Providence, Rosamond Jane, Spring Flower, Susan 1825

**T**

**Tabb/Tubb.** * † Active 1825, Annie 1859, Breeze 1837, Caurinus, Conservator 1842, Emily 1873, Georgiana 1824, Henry Edmonds, Lizzie 1867, Lydia Cardell, Maria 1857, Millicent, Planet, Rare Plant, Republican, Trebiskin, Windsworth

**Teague.** Caroline 1839, Elizabeth & Maria, Flora 1843, Happy Return 1801, James & Samuel, Lydia, Rosamond Jane

**Tebbett/Tippett.** * † Active 1825, Clementina, Jessie 1858, Larch 1841, Nautilus, Sally, Sir William Molesworth, Sunbeam, Valency 1838, Villiers

**Thomas.** † Amelia 1820, Ann Williams, Anna Maria 1824, Boscoppa, Busy Bee, Cilicia 1860, Delabole 1826, Diligence 1796, Doris 1904, Frederick William, Guiding Star 1875, Hannah 1817, Harriet Scott,

James & Sarah, Janie Vivian, Josephine, Lafrowda, Lizzie Grace, Lottie 1878, Margarita, Mary Annie, Mary Barrow, Morning Star 1855, One and All, Pet 1856, Surprise 1879, Telephone, Three Wishes 1972, Treffry, Tregunnel, Triumph 1881, Unity 1783, Water Nymph, Welcome

**Tom/Toms.** * Lady Jane 1880

**Torman.** (see Tummon)

**Trebilcock/Trebill** 1626. Camellia 1877, Ceres 1804, Che Sara Sara 1971, Clara 1879, Constance 1858, Frances Ann, Frederick William, Gannel 1826, Guiding Light 1985, Kate 1854, Mary & Elizabeth, Meta, Peter & James, Treffry, Tullochgorum, Water Nymph, William Henry, Willie 1865

**Tredwen/Tredwin/Tredwyn.** Aid 1833, Albert 1847, Albion 1862, Alma 1855, Alice Jane, Amphitrite 1859, Anne 1809, Aurora 1855, Betsey (Prize), Busy 1836, Camalan 1849, Ceres 1809, Ceres 1820, Charles 1834, Charlotte 1830, Comet 1858, Conservator 1842, Cornubia 1856, Dasher 1825, Delabole 1848, Ebenezer 1804, Edith 1856, Elizabeth & Maria, Elizabeth 1805, Ellen Jane, Emma Jane 1857, Endeavour 1788, Fayaway, Flora 1843, Florist, Friends 1787, Frolic 1813, Gazelle 1835, Hannah 1817, Happy Return 1841, Ida Elizabeth, Iris 1836, Jane 1802, John & Matilda, John & Mary 1827, Kate 1837, Letitia 1835, Lord Porchester, Louise, Lutha, Marchioness of Abercorn, Margam, Margarita, Maria Louisa, Marshall, Mary (Prize), Mary (Prize), Mary Eliza, Nadir, Nautilus, Orb, Pascoe, Peace 1815, Penally, Primrose 1831, Princess of Wales 1867, Rebecca, Rosamond Jane, Royal Adelaide, St Stephens, Sisters 1807, Storm, Sunshine, Tamar 1807, Test, Three Sisters, Traveller, Villiers, Volunteer (1), Volunteer (2), Volunteer (3), William & Jane

**Tregaskes.** (Bude) Stucley, Wild Pigeon

**Tremain(e).** † Ann 1792, Betsy 1819, Criterion 1834, Edwin 1859, Nanscow

**Tremeer/Tremere.** Brutus 1835, Three Brothers 1800

**Trethewey.** Boscoppa, Devonia 1865, Guiding Star 1879, Margaret Murray, Resolution, SMC, Sea Lark, Western Star

**Tubb.** (see Tabb)

**Tucker.** † Ballinbreich Castle, Bude Packet, Charlotte 1830, Eleanor 1816, Lady Acland, Lanson Castle, Mayflower of Camelot 1900, Sally Ann 1803, Viola 1872

**Torman.** †/**Tummon.** Charles Phillips, Edwin 1859, Kittie 1865, Lark 1791, St Stephens

**V**

**Veale.** Janie 1878, Maria 1865, Mary 1829, Jane Slade, Sheba

**Vivian.** Active 1825, John & Mary, Talbot (Falmouth)

**W**

**Wade.** Belle 1838, Camelford 1861, Dew Drop 1820

**Walters.** Ann Walters, Electric, Mayflower 1806 (Looe connection)

**Ward.** Dawnbreaker, Girl Barbara, Industry 1809, TPC (Boscastle)

**Warden.** (see Worden)

**Warne/Warren** * †/**Wearne.** Betsey (Prize), Betty Louise 1990, Bootlegger 1968, Louise, Superior 1834

**Waters.** Bessie Waters, Clyde 1866, Comet 1842, Mary Waters

**Watts.** Caroline (Prize), JKA, John & Hannah, Trustful (1971), Viola 1872

**Webster.** Anne 1768, Lady of the Lake, Thomas & Mary

**Wedlake/Wedlock.** Anna Maria 1824, Delabole 1826, Iris 1836, James & Sarah, Symmetry

**West.** * Janie 1870

**Whitefield/Whitfield.** † Friends 1826, Lady Mary 1836, Louise

**Whitford.** Caroline Phillips, Louise, Sir William Molesworth, Tretherras

**Wilce.** Fairy Flower, Lutha

**Williams.** † Alberta 1865, Ann Williams, Charles Tucker, Edith 1858, Emma 1877, Emma Jane 1861, Fairy Belle, Fairy Flower, Fairy Glen, Fairy Maid, Fairy Queen, Gavenwood, General Burgoyne, Glendoveer, Hetty 1877, Katie 1881, Lizzy 1864, Look Out 1858, Lord Porchester, Margaret Murray, Margarita, Mary Kitty, Mountblairy, New Parliament, Padgy, Peace 1815, Red Rose, Rosamond Jane, Ruby, Stag, The Saint, Thomas & Elizabeth
**Willmett.** Caroline (Prize), Caroline Phillips, Dispatch 1810, Valency 1838
**Wills.** * Alberta 1865, J.K.Allport

**Wilson.** * † Agnes 1812, Ariel 1864, Belle 1838, Cornuvia, Earl St Vincent, Harmony 1815, James 1847, Margaritta & Esther, Margarett, Swallow
**Withell/Withiell.** Britannia 1803, Elizabeth in 1811, Hope 1827, Jane 1818, Louisa, Unity 1783
**Worden/Warden.** Breadalbane, Doris, Elizabeth Hill, Galatea 1868, Marco Polo, Marian, Sly Boots, Southerner, Veho, Viola 1872
**Y**
**Yeo.** † Agnes 1809, Alice 1822, Ann 1792, Florist, Harvest Reaper 1955, Thomas & Nancy

Newquay Harbour in 1894, with the three-masted schooner MARY WIGHTON nearest camera.          *Royal Institution of Cornwall*

# 15  THE LIFEBOATS

*To go with the old grey Widow-Maker?*

## R. Kipling

AS trade expanded after the Napoleonic wars, so did the loss of life and property caused by shipwreck around the British Isles. In 1833 there were 24,385 registered British ships totalling 2.6 million tons, and the average number of ships lost per annum was just over 600. By 1840 there were 28,692 British ships of 3.3 million tons, and the number of ships lost in 1842 remained just over 600. About 1,500 lives were lost each year, and the average seaman could expect to have his ship lost under him one or more times in the course of his working life which started at the age of twelve or so and ended when it ended. These statistics were collected for parliamentary committees.

With one in forty ships being lost every year, not many of the little ships of Padstow survived to be broken up or abandoned in old age. Rather they were successively repaired and rebuilt until finally they were lost.

The RNLI provides additional statistics. In 1866, no fewer than 1,860 ships were lost around the coasts of the British Isles, causing the loss of about 900 lives: but the RNLI had that year saved 1,600 lives. Unlike the earlier figures these include foreign ships and small, unregistered fishing boats. The loss of 900 lives is surprisingly small, when a hundred or more might be lost in one moderately sized emigrant ship; however, not only the lifeboats but also the coastguards and rocket brigade were engaged in rescue work and becoming increasingly effective.

The loss rate gradually improved but the 1879 Mercantile Navy List gave the following analysis of a total of 315 ships which dropped out of the register whilst the new edition was in preparation. Sold foreign 31, wrecked 63, stranded 35, lost 46, broken up 45, abandoned 15, lost by collision 14, missing 11, foundered 25, burnt 3, condemned 9, other causes 18. Some of these descriptions do not make it clear whether the ship's life was ended accidentally or intentionally, nevertheless only about one ship in three was surviving to be condemned or broken up or sold to foreigners.

## Padstow Lifeboats

Padstow is a lifeboat station with one of the proudest and most gallant histories in the country. The gigs were making daring rescues before the term 'lifeboat' had been invented, and their crews had such skill and faith in their craft that they did not take easily to the idea of performing rescues in the shorter, clumsier, more heavily built early lifeboats encumbered with rubbing strakes, corks and aircases.

The first true lifeboat at Padstow appears to have been the MARINER'S FRIEND built by John Tredwen in 1827. When the Padstow Harbour Association for the Preservation of Life and Property from Shipwreck was formed on 11th November, 1829, they took her over and housed her at Hawker's Cove: but their philosophy was that prevention of shipwreck was better than cure

and they placed capstans on Stepper Point next to the Narrows with hawsers ready to be taken out to ships that lost steerage way. They built the Stepper Point daymark, buoyed the channel and built houses for pilots at Hawker's Cove so that they were always to hand. They also organised teams with rocket apparatus, and revised the sailing directions for vessels entering Padstow.

The people involved in forming this historic Association deserve to be recorded. The Patron was the Rev. Charles Prideaux-Brune (the manorial proprietor of Padstow and Padstow Penkevil), the trustees were John Paynter Esq. and the Rev. W. Rawlings (the vicar of Padstow). The committee chairman was Captain Julyan, RN and the treasurer, H. P. Rawlins, Esq. It is surely no coincidence that in 1830 the Corporation of Trinity House of Deptford Strond appointed the first six Padstow pilots as follow: Henry Bird, Benjamin Davies, Holland Hutchens, Thomas Knight, John Trebilcock and Simon Stribley.

The first RNLI lifeboat arrived in 1856, a specially designed fast six-oared boat named ALBERT EDWARD after the Duke of Cornwall, who contributed £25 towards her cost, and she was kept in the Harbour Association's house at Hawker's Cove.

These early lifeboats around the coast of Cornwall had to cover many miles of coast, and the first news of a wreck was often received from some distant beach or cliff-top watcher. Depending on the wind and tide, it might be impossible for the lifeboat to leave harbour and proceed to the wreck by water. Carriages were therefore kept on which to transport the lifeboat to a launching point as close to the wreck as possible and there were many hectic journeys through the Cornish lanes in wild weather. In some cases the final voyage to the wreck was only a matter of yards, but none the less demanding for that, going out from some beach through the thundering surf to a vessel impaled on nearby rocks. In such circumstances even the men of the pilot gigs could see the merit of a heavily built boat, with flotation equipment, as they were pounded mercilessly on the ground in the trough of every roller.

In the case of the Padstow lifeboat, a carriage was kept at Hawker's Cove, and another one at Polzeath so that she could, in northerly weather, be rowed to Polzeath in sheltered water, and thence transported to rescues in the Portquin and Port Isaac area. That ceased to be necessary in 1869 when the Port Isaac lifeboat station was established.

The ALBERT EDWARD gave good service and saved thirty-eight lives, but it was decided that a ten-oared boat would be even better and in 1864 a 32 ft self-righting boat took her place but was given the same name.

British lifeboats for many years could be divided into those which were self-righting after a capsize, and those which were not. The boats were given self-righting qualities by building them with narrow beam, but with large high volumes of buoyancy at bow and stern. If they were capsized by a breaking wave, the flotation at bow and stern caused them to roll back into the upright position. The oarsmen were to some extent protected from the weather by the huge fo'c'sle and poop, but these erections caught the wind, making windward work and manoeuvring difficult. In contrast the boats which were not self-righting had to be given wide beam and a heavy keel to reduce the risk of capsize. It was heavy work to row them in light winds, but there were advantages in gale conditions and the beamier boats had more space for survivors. Some lifeboats were (and are) able to shed their keels to work in shallow water, or escape from various predicaments.

It is not surprising that the self-righting types were favoured for the Padstow stations because of the breaking seas on the bar, as will be seen from the list of boats which served there (to be found at the end of this chapter).

Books have been written about rescues carried out by the Padstow boats, and it is only possible to mention one or two celebrated examples here. On 29th December, 1865 the West Indiaman JULIET, a Greenock barque, bound from Demerara for London with rum and sugar, had been driven to the north of Land's End by a SW gale. That evening she had to drop both anchors to avoid being driven onto the rocks below Roundhill on Pentire Point, pitching and rolling in heavy seas, with her ensign half lowered to signal distress. In a classic rescue, the ALBERT EDWARD sailed downwind across Padstow Bay, anchored close ahead of the barque, and veered down alongside her stern. By the grace of God and split second timing, the seventeen men from the JULIET jumped one and two at a time safely into the lifeboat, Captain Drummond, of course, being the last. That was the easy part of the rescue. There were now thirty men in a 32-ft boat plunging up and down close alongside the JULIET with mountainous waves breaking on the rocks close astern of them, and a full gale doing its best to set them there. Willing hands pulled them back clear of the wreck towards their anchor; a few square feet of sail were set; the anchor was broken out and brought aboard. Coxswain William Hills decided that to land on Polzeath beach in that surf was certain death, and to sail downwind round Pentire Point to Port Isaac in darkness, with visibility reduced by spray, was almost equally dangerous, so they had to pull at the oars for long hours into the teeth of a full gale to reach the shelter of the Narrows and Hawker's Cove. The JULIET later dragged her anchors and broke up on the rocks.

On 6th February, 1867 occurred the first Padstow lifeboat tragedy: the boat was about to make an emergency beaching at Polzeath when she was rolled over and over in tremendous surf, staying bottom up for about five minutes before being washed ashore undamaged. The crew were less fortunate, being thrown out close to rocks below Trebetherick. Eight were saved from the surf but five were drowned or battered to death, leaving four widows and eight orphans.

But there were plenty of volunteers to take the places of those lost, and they all retained faith in the ALBERT EDWARD and indeed later that same year, on 8th December, they carried out a particularly daring rescue of the crew of the TELEGRAPH of Padstow from the Doom Bar.

The second ALBERT EDWARD went on to save a total of 112 lives before, in 1883, the crew were persuaded to accept a more modern design which was also self-righting and ten oared but 34 ft long. The funds for this lifeboat were presented by Mr R. A. Preston whose yacht ARAB was totally wrecked on the Goodwin Sands on 24th October, 1882. He and eight others were saved by the lifeboat BRADFORD and the paddle tug AID. He expressed his gratitude by providing Padstow's lifeboat, the ARAB, which served with the same distinction as her forbears for seventeen years, saving seventy-five lives.

By 1897 the first steam lifeboats were being built for the RNLI and the Padstow committee recommended that North Cornwall would benefit considerably from such a vessel based at Padstow, as there had been several occasions when even superhuman efforts by oarsmen had failed to overcome the combined strength of wind, sea and current. The RNLI concurred, and in February 1899 the JAMES STEVENS No.4 arrived on station.

Just over one year later, late at night on 11th April, 1900 Padstow's second and greatest lifeboat disaster occurred. The Lowestoft smack PEACE AND PLENTY had sought shelter from a strong WNW wind under Stepper Point and anchored in the Narrows. That evening the wind got up and the smack was too close to the Doom Bar. The lifeboats ARAB and JAMES STEVENS No.4 were both launched. The ARAB was searching for the smack in the terrible seas on the bar when one exceptional breaker crashed over them, washing eight men overboard and breaking or washing away nine of their ten oars. Luckily the eight men were able to scramble back into the boat. Coxswain Brown burnt a distress flare and they decided to let the ARAB drop back slowly towards the Greenaway shore where they knew of a cleft in the rocks which might give them a chance of survival. They allowed the anchor to drag slowly, using their few spare oars to guide her and finally cutting the anchor cable so that the surf would carry her in. The ARAB was a total wreck but all thirteen men were able to scramble ashore over the rocks.

The JAMES STEVENS No.4, seeing the distress flare set off to help. With her greater draught it was always going to be a risky venture, and Coxswain David Grubb took her out into the deeper water of Hell Bay before turning East towards the other vessels. Disaster struck as she was making the turn. She was capsized by a freak sea, flinging the seven deck crew into the sea but leaving four in the engine room battened down below. Three of the seven were washed ashore more dead than alive, but survived; the other eight left four widows and fourteen children. The surf drove the battered steel hull into a cave where it was found at low tide the next morning, a cruel coffin.

To complete the story of that dreadful night, the PEACE AND PLENTY was also swept onto the Greenaway rocks and the Trebetherick Rocket Brigade saved five of her crew of eight with great difficulty.

Consider the events of that night through the eyes of Padstow folk. It was already dark when the rockets summoned the lifeboat crews. Crowds followed them nearly two miles across the fields to Hawker's Cove and watched them set out. Then nothing but an occasional flare, and later the realisation that twenty-four of the best men in the small community were missing. Finally, in the early hours, survivors from the ARAB were ferried back across the river from Rock with the news that at least some of the crew of the JAMES STEVENS had survived. A false hope for the families of eight of them. Then finally, the next morning, hundreds of people crossed the estuary to search the pitiful remains amongst the rocks and dispel any lingering hope.

The advent of the JAMES STEVENS No.4 had initiated a procedure of having one lifeboat at Padstow housed at Hawker's Cove, and a second boat permanently afloat on a mooring nearby, which was continued in various combinations for many years. The ARAB was replaced by a modern 36 ft ten-oared self-righter fitted with drop keels and water ballast tanks; this boat, also named ARAB, reached Padstow in September, 1901, taking over the boathouse, the 'No.1 Station'. The 'No.2 Station' was equipped at the same time with the unique RNLI tug HELEN PEELE,

The steam lifeboat JAMES STEVENS No 4 rounding Stepper Point, setting out for her first service, 4th April, 1899. Pentire Point in background.
*Courtesy RNLI*

(described in the steamer chapter), and the large twelve-oared, self-righting lifeboat EDMUND HARVEY, 42 ft long.

The No.1 lifeboat was principally for local service whereas the No.2 lifeboat, towed by the HELEN PEELE, could carry out distant services, including assisting ships in distress well offshore. The three of them which arrived in 1901 worked in gallant harmony for 28 years, saving 187 lives between them and providing much other comfort and assistance. The arrival of the HELEN PEELE in 1901 coincided with an important change in the shipping scene. In the twenty years 1880-1900, the lifeboats of Padstow assisted 23 sailing vessels and 1 steamship. In the first twenty years of the twentieth century, they assisted 27 sailing vessels (including a yacht for the first time) and 18 steamers. In the next twenty years (1920-1940), they assisted 12 steam, or motor powered vessels, 3 small fishing vessels which may or may not have had engines, and 1 sailing vessel. In turn then, we have the traditional pulling and sailing lifeboats dealing with sailing vessels in local waters, then the surge in steamships in the early twentieth century (emphasised by the HELEN PEELE's ability to assist them well offshore) and then after the Great War, the demise of the sailing ship, and a great reduction in the number of services required.

All three lifeboats were involved when, on 28th February, 1928 the Norwegian steamer TAORMINA, 1,335 gross tons, Port Talbot for Lisbon with coal, sought shelter in Padstow from a WNW gale. In those wind conditions, the sea breaks right across the estuary, and it was approaching low water: but the TAORMINA's master had no choice. She was leaking badly and her boats had already been smashed by mountainous seas, so he made for Padstow and ran her onto the Doom Bar. The HELEN PEELE and EDMUND HARVEY tried to reach her, but there was insufficient water; so the lighter ARAB was manned, and set out for the steamer under oars, fighting her way over the bar, a thrilling sight in the last of the daylight, anchoring to windward and veering down alongside the steamer, whose entire crew of eighteen were safely rescued.

The ARAB's crew of thirteen, the coxswain, helmsman, bowman and ten on the oars, were the youngest ever to man a Padstow lifeboat, and seven of them had never been out on service before, largely because no service had been required of the Hawker's Cove boat since 1921, an unprecedented interval and an indication of the changing conditions. This rescue was a splendid finale to the era of the pulling lifeboats of Padstow.

The SS TAORMINA was a listing wreck with eight feet of water in her holds the next day, but the weather was kind and it was possible to salvage her a few weeks later.

### Motor Lifeboats

The RNLI started experimenting with motor driven lifeboats well before the Great War, but they had reliability problems and it was necessary to devise means of propulsion which did not have exposed propellers vulnerable to damage on rocks or other obstructions. By 1929 motor lifeboats with jet propulsion were well established, and the HELEN PEELE, EDMUND HARVEY combination was replaced by the 61-ft twin screw Barnett lifeboat PRINCESS MARY, the largest lifeboat built up to that time. She was to prove herself immensely seaworthy and well able to look after the offshore services as well as some of the more distant coastal requirements.

In 1931, the pulling boat ARAB, as old as the century, was sold and the No.1 Station, the boathouse at Hawker's Cove, also received its first motor lifeboat, the single screw 35ft 6ins JOHN & SARAH ELIZA STYCH, inheriting the ARAB's duty to serve ships in the estuary and neighbouring waters. She was in action for the first time in January 1933, searching for a missing singlehanded fishing boat in rain and darkness and a southwesterly gale. Eventually she saved the man and the boat from the shallow waters of Daymer Bay.

At 2 a.m. on 23rd January, 1939, the PRINCESS MARY was sent out to help a small steamer making distress signals off Trevose Head.

Padstow Lifeboat Day c. 1910. The second ARAB making excursions from the Customs House.          *Malcolm McCarthy Collection*

The worst gale for several years was blowing her towards Stepper Point. She turned out to be HMS MEDEA, an old minelayer originally built as a monitor to bombard German positions in Belgium in the Great War. She had broken loose from the Hull tug SCOTSMAN which had been towing her to Wales to be broken up. The lifeboat herself was damaged by heavy seas and by the time she got close to the MEDEA, they were both drifting over the Doom Bar in great danger. An exceptional sea did further damage to the lifeboat and put all the electrical equipment out of action, and the coxswain had no alternative but to put to sea and wait over five hours in atrocious conditions before the rising tide allowed a safe passage back to her moorings. Meanwhile, the MEDEA ended up perched on the rocks near Trebetherick. Three of her running crew of four were rescued by rocket apparatus and breeches buoy; some of her bottom plating can be seen to this day.

The increasing complexity of lifeboats meant that surveys, major overhauls and repairs could no longer be carried out at the various lifeboat stations around the coast, and temporary lifeboats had to be provided increasingly frequently. There were other reasons for temporary lifeboats: in 1938 the JOHN & SARAH ELIZA STYCH was transferred to St Ives as their lifeboat had been wrecked, and a reserve pulling boat, the DOCEA CHAPMAN, took her place at Hawker's Cove, the last Padstow lifeboat without a motor.

In 1940 the motor lifeboat JHW replaced the DOCEA CHAPMAN which was sold and converted into the small Padstow fishing vessel GIRL MAUREEN (PW 112). So Padstow faced the war years with two modern motor lifeboats, the JHW and PRINCESS MARY, and they were soon to be assisted by the air-sea rescue launches of the Royal Air Force, as described in another chapter. Numerous launches were required in the war, the main demands resulting from crashed aircraft and the survivors of convoy battles well offshore. The PRINCESS MARY was well suited for this long-range work and many was the night and day she spent at sea with the thankless task of looking for possible survivors, and finding only wreckage or bodies or nothing. Nevertheless she saved thirty-three lives during and just after the war, the last ten in a particularly gallant rescue from the old Straits Steamship Co. liner KEDAH which broke loose from her tug, the EMPIRE SILAS of Bristol, whilst on her way to be broken up. The KEDAH rescue took place off St Agnes Head, and the lifeboat got back to Padstow in damaged condition in the early hours of 13th August, 1946 after over seven hours at sea in 'almost impossible conditions'.

Movements of the Doom Bar were reducing the depth of water at Hawker's Cove, and although lifeboats were kept there until 1962, and, indeed the lifeboat BASSETT-GREEN saved six lives in 1955 and 1956, it was the other lifeboat, PRINCESS MARY (and her successors), permanently moored and able to get to sea at most states of the tide, which carried out almost all services and in 1962 the Hawker's Cove station was shut down.

In 1952 the PRINCESS MARY was sold out of the RNLI service, and promptly continued her distinguished career as the motor yacht ARIES R. (q.v.) Her successor was the 52 ft JOSEPH HIRAM CHADWICK, a powerful twin engined boat drawing less water and therefore more able to operate at low tide. In 1961 her permanent mooring was moved nearer the quay into the patch of deep water downstream of the Town Bank, and served by her boarding boat the WILLIAM MYATT, she gave good service until 1967.

The continuing silting up of the estuary made the mooring off Padstow unsatisfactory and it was decided to build a new station in one corner of Mother Ivey's Bay on the east side of Trevose Head. The construction was a major undertaking including the 240 ft long launching slipway, the longest in the British Isles. Even the access path down the cliffs was a considerable achievement. The new station became operational in October 1967 and the brand new Oakley class 48 ft 6 ins self-righting lifeboat JAMES & CATHERINE MACFARLANE was winched up the slipway and housed in the new building, ready to be launched at any state of tide, wind or sea. The new station is five miles from Padstow but with modern communications and a Landrover, the crew reckon to assemble at the boathouse in just over one quarter of an hour. Summer holiday traffic can be a problem but in summer the vast majority of emergencies are dealt with by the inflatable inshore rescue boats. This Oakley-class lifeboat, and all subsequent classes are self-righting, but not by virtue of high flotation boxes at bow and stern like the earlier self-righters: instead the self-righting element is provided by keeping the high superstructure watertight so that when capsized it provides an enormous flotation force to bring the boat back to the upright position. As a result of this feature all the latest RNLI boats look decidedly top-heavy, and they do capsize when caught broadside on by enormous breaking seas, but what would once have been a disaster is now almost a well-established routine and they right themselves in a few seconds.

In the following years this lifeboat, like her predecessors, carried out a whole series of rescues, one of the most dramatic occurring on Sunday, 17th July, 1977. The tiny 17-ft Bermudan sloop CALCUTTA PRINCESS, with a man, a woman and a dog on board, had lost her sails, had a rope around her propeller and the tide was taking her towards the rocks of Dinas Head, Trevose. The lifeboat was launched at 17.34 hours with the wind WSW near gale force. The casualty was soon spotted close to the rocks in a confused sea with waves up to 20 feet high, and the lifeboat was taken close enough to throw a rope to the yacht. The crew of the yacht were too exhausted to help and the rope promptly fouled one of the lifeboats' two propellers. A rope was soon connected to a cleat on the yacht's deck, but such fittings are not adequate for extreme conditions, and the cleat broke, one of the lifeboatmen losing half a finger as a result.

The wind and current were now driving the yacht and the lifeboat onto the Bull Rock, but the Coxswain took the lifeboat into position between the yacht and the sheer face of the rock, almost touching the rock and rising and falling about 20 feet; they passed a tow rope to the yacht which was eventually secured to her mast enabling the lifeboat to get under way and pull the yacht to safety. In calmer waters the crew of the yacht were safely transferred to the lifeboat and the humans treated for hypothermia and shock. A helicopter from HMS HERMES was standing by to take them to hospital, but the transfer was postponed until the lifeboat had returned to the slipway. All went well. Afterwards Coxswain Tony Warnock said that it was only the fierce backwash off the Bull which had prevented them from being dashed onto the rocks.

In mid-August 1979 a freak storm caught the 303 yachts taking part in the Fastnet ocean race strung out between Lands End and the Fastnet Rock off the Irish coast. Fifteen yachtsmen lost their lives and the Padstow lifeboat and twelve others spent a total of 186 hours on service, rescuing sixty people and assisting twenty yachts.

The MACFARLANE faced an even tougher task on 15th December that year. The wind had been blowing up to violent storm force 11 from the west since the previous day and by 06.00 hours had reached force 14 on the anemometer at RAF St Mawgan. The 1,800 ton Greek freighter SKOPELOS SKY was limping along the coast with a dangerous list and seeking helicopter assistance. The wind went NW and blew force 10, gusting to hurricane force 12 with rain squalls, and the seas were by far the worst ever seen by any members of the lifeboat crew. After going through every possible safety drill the MACFARLANE was launched at 09.25. Coxswain Trevor England shouted warnings to his crew at the approach of extra big seas, but soon gave up as extraordinary seas were continuous. With the help of the flood tide she caught up with the SKOPELOS SKY in Portquin Bay but at first was unable to communicate with her. Helicopters arrived but were also unable to get any reply from the freighter. Eventually the lifeboat established radio communication and asked the freighter's captain if he would anchor. The reply was that the weather made it impossible to man the foc's'le. One of the helicopters requested the lifeboat to stand by while he attempted to lift the crew. After three men had been lifted off, the helicopter's winchman hit the freighter's superstructure repeatedly and the pilot suggested the lifeboat go in for the remainder. The crew gathered aft but the lifeboat was rocketing up and down between the freighter's main deck and her propeller boss. After repeated attempts which somewhat damaged the lifeboat, the freighter's crew waved her away indicating that they would only abandon ship by helicopter. The freighter's master still had hopes of saving his ship but an attempt to anchor failed and she drifted closer to the cliffs. More men were lifted off by helicopter in the last of the daylight, leaving the master and one other on board. They were lifted off by a Sea King helicopter with searchlights moments before the freighter was wrecked on Doyden Point. The lifeboat had been standing by throughout in unimaginable conditions. The coxswain congratulated the Sea King and being unable to enter Padstow faced the task of rehousing her up the slipway in winds which had moderated to a force 9, strong gale! The launchers, despite being up to their necks in water at times, succeeded and she was rehoused and reported ready for service by 20.00 hours.

The JAMES & CATHERINE MACFARLANE (operational number 48.02) was the final refinement of the design of the traditional British double-ended lifeboat capable of operation in almost any conditions. She looked after 90 miles of coastline between that served by the St Ives lifeboat to the SW and the Clovelly station to the NE. In its search for improvements the RNLI was conscious that the traditional boats were, by modern standards, slow. Released from its house, the MACFARLANE travelled at ever-increasing speed down the launching slipway, finally hitting the water at 40 knots, but thereafter her two 100 h.p. diesels could only push her along at less than 10 knots. So the RNLI had set about developing 'fast afloat' lifeboat designs, drawing considerably on the expertise of the US Coast Guard, followed by a 'fast slipway' design which turned out to be ideally suited for the Mother Ivey's Bay slipway. The prototypes were built in 1982, and when they proved successful the first production boat of the 47 ft Tyne class was built in 1984 with operational number 47.003 and allocated to Padstow. So the JAMES & CATHERINE MAC-FARLANE went to the Lizard Cadgwith station, was later on display at Land's End, and was succeeded by the JAMES BURROUGH with two General Motors diesels each of 425 hp, giving her a maximum speed of over 18 knots. The naming ceremony did not take place until 15th April, 1985 in the presence of many notable people, including the donor, James Burrough's grand-daughter Miss Nickie Allan, and the station branch President, Peter Prideaux-Brune, Esq., 156 years after his ancestor had fathered the Padstow Harbour Association for the Preservation of Life and Property from Shipwreck.

At the time of writing the JAMES BURROUGH is still on station, her exploits appearing regularly in *The Lifeboat*, journal of the RNLI, which has faithfully reported the gallant services of British lifeboats since back into the nineteenth century.

At the last count the lifeboatmen of Padstow (and the shore rescuers within the port) had been awarded twenty-eight of the RNLI's silver medals.

## Newquay Lifeboats

Although rockets and other life-saving gear were stationed at Newquay earlier, it was not until 1861 that the first lifeboat, the JOSHUA, was stationed there. She rescued the crew of the schooner HEROINE of Milford in 1864, but the following year was found to be suffering from dry rot, of all things, and was replaced by a second JOSHUA. The later JOSHUA was involved in a strange episode in December 1869 when an Austrian barque, the SUEZ, was found anchored off Newquay in a severely disabled condition. The JOSHUA brought her crew of ten ashore and was preparing to help save the ship herself, only to be threatened by a riotous crowd who had great expectations of profitable wreck if the ship was allowed to drag ashore. Eventually, with the help of a Cardiff tug, the SUEZ towed round to Padstow only to suffer another gale, her crew being taken off this time by the Padstow lifeboat. The SUEZ was repaired at Padstow, bought by Padstow owners and renamed ALAN; some particulars of her later career will be found elsewhere in the book.

The JOSHUAs and their successors were, until 1895, taken by horse-drawn carriage to the most suitable beach and launched into the surf. That year a launching slip was built out on Towan Head, which allowed the boat to be launched straight into deep water, and later a house was built at the top of the slipway. This was the steepest slipway in the United Kingdom, and too steep for the boat to be hauled up, so the carriage was retained and after a service the lifeboat would land on a handy beach and eight fine horses would pull it back up to the house at the head of the slip.

As well as serving the local cliff-lined coasts, the Newquay lifeboat was better placed than the Padstow boat to reach steamers and sailing vessels some distance off the coast, and a series of gallant rescues were performed, resulting in the saving of ninety-eight lives between 1864 and 1908.

On 17th December, 1917 the Danish steamer OSTEN was disabled in a fierce NE gale and looked as if she would be driven ashore near Newquay. The lifeboat crew assembled but a newly appointed Coxswain declined to launch into the teeth of the gale. At that, former Coxswain Gill said he had been out in worse and called for volunteers. The following accompanied him: R. Trebilcock, J. Clemens, R. Pearce, F. Pearce, R. Woodward, J. Grigg, R. Tretheway, J. Hicks, S. Hoar, Capt. Hicks, and Capt. J. Pappin. The list is of interest because these family names recur constantly in the lists of masters and owners of nineteenth-century sailing vessels, and recur again today as the owners and skippers of Padstow and Newquay fishing vessels. The JAMES STEVENS No.5 was successfully launched to the cheers of a large crowd and set sail successfully. Shortly, however, a large sea knocked her off course and the succeeding wave put her on her beam ends with the water-filled sails preventing her from self-righting. Gill and Pappin had been washed overboard but eventually made land; the lifeboat drifted back under the cliffs and with gallant help from the shore all were rescued, some suffering from hypothermia and Clemens seriously injured. Meanwhile the ebb tide carried the OSTEN safely down channel and she was towed eventually to Falmouth and safety. Despite the failure to assist the steamer, the RNLI gave gallantry medals to Gill and Trebilcock. The lifeboat was too badly damaged to be repaired and was swiftly replaced by the JOHN WILLIAM DUDLEY, a boat of the same type.

In 1920 she was replaced by the ADMIRAL SIR GEORGE BACK which, like all her predecessors except the original JOSHUA, was a self-righting pulling and sailing boat with ten oars. The station was closed in 1934, the stated reason being that no horses were available to re-house the boat after a service, but there had been no effective service from Newquay for fourteen years, and by then Padstow had a motor lifeboat and those were two good, if more controversial, reasons for closing the Newquay station.

In March 1940 the motor lifeboat RICHARD SILVER OLIVER was stationed in the harbour at Newquay as a wartime measure, and like the Padstow boats had a harrowing time searching for ditched aircraft and the survivors of convoy battles until June 1945, when the lifeboat departed, having done much useful work and saved eleven lives.

Since 1965, inflatable inshore lifeboats have been based at Newquay. Their activities are covered on a later page.

## Port Isaac Lifeboats

With the schooners, ketches and cutters bringing coal and lifting slates from Port Gaverne, Boscastle and other neighbouring nooks and crannies, and with the fishing fleets of Portquin and Port Isaac, there was a strong case for a local lifeboat in the mid-nineteenth century. Port Gaverne was the best place for a boathouse by the beach, but too far from one of the closest knit seafaring communi-

ties in the country, Port Isaac. So the station had to be at Port Isaac. But where could the boat be housed? Already there was not even room ashore for the fishing fleet, which had to be taken round to Padstow for protection from winter storms. So the house had to be up a steep hill through the narrow winding streets of the town about 200 yards from the beach. Thereafter the most distinctive feature of the Port Isaac station was the launching procedure. Numerous helpers were necessary to manoeuvre the boat round the bends in the streets, touching the houses on both sides and leaving scars which can still be seen. Scores of men and women held onto tail ropes to prevent the weight of the boat on its carriage taking charge. The report in the *Western Daily Mercury* of the arrival of the first lifeboat tells how things were done in those days:

The life-boat arrived with gear at Bodmin Road Station on Tuesday 5th October, 1869. Here it was met by a team of eight horses kindly lent by the merchants of Wadebridge. At Bodmin she remained for an hour for the inspection of the inhabitants; from here it proceeded to Wadebridge for the night. Early next morning it left via St Minver and St Endellion with eight horses lent by farmers of St Endellion. At Trewetha, about a mile from Port Isaac, they were met to form a procession by Capt. Ward [Lifeboat Inspector], the local Committee, the Rev. Smith, Vicar of St Minver, a band, then the boat on her carriage bearing two flags. She contained the crew dressed in white frocks and red caps, holding aloft their oars, while the horses were decorated with ribbons. On arrival at the beach Capt. Ward gave an excellent speech to 2-3,000 people. After launching, rowing and sailing exercises, the boat was fastened to a vessel by means of tackle. She was then turned over with her crew, uprighting in less than a minute, and freeing of water in a few seconds.

The Newquay Lifeboat WILLIE ROGERS     *Private Collection*

The Newquay lifeboat was
launched down the steepest
slipway in the United Kingdom.
*Private Collection*

From 1869 until 1927 Port Isaac had successively three lifeboats all named RICHARD AND SARAH after generous donors, and all were ten-oared self-righters. They were of the usual length for ten-oared boats, but their beam was restricted to 7 ft 6 ins to allow them to squeeze between the houses. They carried out a series of rescues comparable in skill and gallantry to those carried out by the other boats on this ironbound coast, saving eighty-six lives.

Towards the end of the Great War the station was closed temporarily for the simple reason that every man who could pull an oar or hoist a sail was already at sea.

In the early 1920s the RNLI was able to buy old cottages and demolish them to build a new boathouse near the beach. Thus, in 1927, when a new lifeboat was provided, she was still a ten-oared self-righter but of 8 ft 10 ins beam.

The need for a lifeboat at Port Isaac diminished with the end of the slate trade and the motorisation of the fishing fleet and the station was closed in 1933 as the Padstow motor lifeboat could meet any remaining need.

Since 1966, Port Isaac has become one of the many new stations for an inshore lifeboat, of which more later.

Bude had an unnamed lifeboat presented by King William IV in 1837, the last year of his reign, when Bude was still within the limits of the port of Padstow. The boat was considered unsuitable for local conditions and was not much used, especially after she capsized in 1844, drowning two of her crew. She lasted until 1852 by which time Bude had become an outport of Bideford. With local trade almost non-existent, the Bude station was closed in 1923, but like Port Isaac, there is now an inshore lifeboat station there.

## Inshore Lifeboats

In the late 1950s it was noticeable that the vast majority of emergencies were caused not by traditional shipwrecks, but by pleasure boats, sailing dinghies, bathers in difficulties, holiday-makers cut off by a rising tide and other such accidents. The RNLI realised that the best answer to such calls was not a slow hurricane-proof

lifeboat with a large crew, but a small fast boat capable of reaching the scene in a few minutes. The Bretons led the way in the late 1950s and the RNLI followed swiftly, introducing its first inshore rescue boats in 1963. They were inflated neoprene boats with powerful outboard motors capable of over 20 knots. They were followed by the *Atlantic 21* Class of inflatables with rigid fibreglass bottoms capable of over 30 knots, and by 1970 there were 100 IRB stations and there were more 'effective launches per annum' by IRBs than by the orthodox lifeboats.

In 1972 the term Inshore Lifeboat (ILB) was substituted for IRB and the ILB has gone from strength to strength. One of the many factors leading to research, development and the improvement of such craft has been the offshore oil and gas industry around the UK, including in particular, operations in the North Sea and around the Shetlands where rescue craft have had to deal with weather conditions as bad as any to be found in European waters.

The change in the crews has been as dramatic as the change in the lifeboats. With a crew of two or three they have to combine the skills of a motor mechanic, communications expert, navigator, medical auxiliary, swimmer, snorkeller and diver, all additional to a high standard of basic seamanship.

ILBs have been stationed at Newquay since 1965 and at Port Isaac since 1967. There has been one at Bude since 1966.

In the 1980s it was surprising to find no ILB station at Padstow itself, but in the estuary in the summer months there were so many other craft — including safety boats for the board and dinghy sailors — that it must have been considered unnecessary to add one more. However, the increasing number of incidents in the estuary led to the opening of a new ILB station at Rock on 26th March, 1994 with ILB No.D.350.

The following report in the RNLI's *Lifeboat Journal* shows the wide variety of rescue work undertaken by inshore lifeboats.

### BULLOCKS OVER CLIFF

Port Isaac Honorary Secretary received a request from HM Coastguard at 1606 on 5th October, 1975, for the ILB to be launched to stand by teams attempting to rescue bullocks which had fallen down a cliff at Port Quin. The fight to save the animals had been in progress since late morning but, with the rising tide and worsening sea conditions, waves were now breaking over the rescuers and there was danger that they might be washed under by the ground sea. The ILB was launched at 1610 and stood by until all those taking part were off the cliff.

At 1148 Coastguard Port Isaac had received a report that 30 bullocks had stampeded over a 150' cliff. The Land Rover was on the scene at 1210 and found that the farmer's sons and two policemen were at the foot of the cliffs with the animals. Port Isaac Cliff Rescue Company (including four ILB crew members) arrived at 1255 and laid out cliff lines and stakes and took a hawser down over the cliff. Fifteen of the bullocks were killed by their fall, five were injured and were put down by the veterinary surgeon, leaving ten to be rescued.

At 1420 a helicopter arrived, but the pilot found that because of their position in the cove he could not lift the cattle. Ten minutes later the East Cornwall Mine Rescue Team, who had also been called, were rigging their hawser and frame and the lift began.

At 1720 one bullock swam out to sea. The ILB managed to get a line around its neck (Crew Member Harry Pavitt lassoed it at his first attempt), but it was not possible to tow the animal; released, it swam off again and was drowned.

In the end, five bullocks were successfully hauled to the top of the cliff, the others being overtaken by the incoming tide and severe ground swell. The ILB left the cove at 1807, when all the rescuers were off the cliff, and returned to station at 1818.

The Newquay ILBs have had an even busier time than the Port Isaac boats; between 1965 and 1990 there were 590 launches at Newquay saving 207 lives. The *Lifeboat Journal* gives the following example of a rescue. Sunday, 3rd August, 1986. Fine day with light WSW breeze. It was reported in the early afternoon that people had been cut off by the tide in Beacon Cove. A prolonged search failed to find anything:

It was 1545 and the lifeboat was bound for harbour when the message came through that someone had now reported seeing a body on Bedruthan Beach. It was not certain whether the body was in fact dead and the station honorary secretary therefore asked the lifeboat to investigate. Halfway there the lifeboat helmsman was informed over the radio that the casualty was indeed alive but badly injured.

On arrival the lifeboat was asked by an auxiliary coastguard to search south of Bedruthan Steps as the original informant was still unable to pinpoint the exact position of the casualty. The crew could find nothing and just as they began to search north of the steps they heard that the auxiliary coastguard had spotted some clothes on a rock on the shore side of Pendaves Rock.

The lifeboat headed for the clothes and, below them, lying on another rock was the injured man. He was only just above the waterline, semi-conscious and bleeding badly from severe head injuries. The lifeboat's line of approach was strewn with underwater rocks and Helmsman

Bailey therefore stopped both engines and tilted them while the lifeboat was paddled towards the rock where the casualty lay.

The crew climbed on to the rock, bandaged the man's head with field dressings, put a survivor's lifejacket on him and wrapped him in survivor's sheets. Then, carefully, he was lowered into the lifeboat, the task being made all the more difficult by the wash at the base of the rock.

With the survivor on board, the lifeboat was paddled clear of the underwater rocks. The engines were dropped and started, the helmsman manoeuvring into clear water to seaward.

The injured man was beginning to show signs of shock and Helmsman Bailey knew he needed hospital treatment as soon as possible. A helicopter was called and when it arrived a diver with a basket stretcher was lowered on to the lifeboat. The casualty was lifted into the stretcher and then winched back up with the diver to the helicopter which flew to Treliske Hospital. The lifeboat meanwhile returned to station where she was rehoused at 1713.

## Conclusion

I have dwelt at some length on some recent experiences with the main Padstow lifeboat and the ILBs in the outports.

These demonstrate that times have not got easier for the lifeboatmen. They now have better, faster boats, special protective clothing, radar, excellent radio communications, wetsuits, breathing apparatus, and a host of other modern technological aids, but as a result they are called upon far more frequently than in the historical days of the traditional lifeboat and, what is more, they now put to sea in conditions which are so bad that the traditional boat could never have been launched. They are required also to master electrical, mechanical and navigational skills which would have baffled their predecessors. Together with the helicopter crews they are skilled professionals who have to be ready to risk their lives to save others at any time of the day or night, and they do so without a second thought.

In recent years, the merchant fleet of the United Kingdom has ceased to be the greatest in the world and in the last decade or so has shrunk to become what informed people believe to be a dangerously small and neglected remnant: but the merchant fleet of the world has continued to grow and, paradoxically as far as the United Kingdom is concerned, more of its citizens risk their lives at sea than ever before — but in the shape of surfers, anglers, board sailors, motorboaters, scuba divers, yachtsmen, swimmers and even rock climbers and bird watchers!

The number of launches of RNLI lifeboats each year has soared from about 500 to nearly 5,000 and our need for this inspiring service is greater than ever before.

## PADSTOW LIFEBOATS

| Date | RNLI official number | Name | Length & Type (SR=Self-righting) | Construction | Fate, if known |
|---|---|---|---|---|---|
| 1827-56 * | — | MARINER'S FRIEND | 23' 4 oars initially | 1827 Tredwen, Padstow | — |
| 1856-64 * | — | ALBERT EDWARD | 30' Peake 6 oars | 1856 Forrestt, Limehouse | — |
| 1864-83 * | — | ALBERT EDWARD | 32' SR 10 oars | 1864 Forrestt, Limehouse | — |
| 1883-1900 * | 51 | ARAB | 34' SR 10 oars | 1882 Woolfe, Shadwell | wrecked on service 1900 |
| 1899-1900 | 421 | JAMES STEVENS No.4 | 56' steam | 1899 J S White, Cowes | wrecked on service 1900 |
| 1901-31 * | 472 | ARAB | 36' SR 10 oars | 1901 Roberts, Mevagissey | sold to become a coal barge, Scilly Isles |
| 1901-29 | 475 | EDMUND HARVEY | 42' SR 10 oars | 1900 Thames Ironworks, Blackwall | sold 1929: yacht TREVONE q.v. |
| 1901-29 | 478 | HELEN PEELE | 95'6" Steam Tug | 1901 Ramage & Ferguson, Leith | sold 1929: see Steamship Chapter. |
| 1929-52 | 715 | PRINCESS MARY | 61' Barnett (Motor) | 1929 S E Saunders, Cowes. | sold 1952: yacht ARIES R, q.v. |
| 1931-38 * | 743 | JOHN & SARAH ELIZA STYCH | 35' 6" SR (Motor) | 1931 Saunders Roe, Cowes. | Transferred to St Ives and wrecked on service 23.1.1939. |
| 1939-47 * | 738 | J.H.W. | 35' 6" SR (Motor) | 1931 J. S. White, Cowes | sold 1947: renamed FOLLIE then NAVETTE |
| 1947-51 * | 747 | STANHOPE SMART | 35' 36" SR (Motor) | 1931 Saunders Roe, Cowes | sold to Liberia 1951 |
| 1951-62 * | 891 | BASSETT-GREEN | 35' 6" Liverpool (Motor) | 1951 Groves & Guttridge, Cowes | sold 1969 now yacht AQUA NOMAD |
| 1952-67 | 898 | JOSEPH HIRAM CHADWICK | 52' Barnett (Motor) | 1952 J. S. White, Cowes | sold 1980, now named FORCEFUL |
| 1967-84 # | 989 | JAMES & CATHERINE MACFARLANE | 48' 6" Oakley (Motor) | 1967 Berthon Boat Co. Lymington | Sold 1988, now on display, Land's End |
| | | Operational No. 48-02 (there was an earlier lifeboat with the same name) | | | |
| 1984 # | 1094 | JAMES BURROUGH | 47' Tyne Class | 1984 Fairey Allday Marine | |
| | | Operational No. 47-003 | | | |

\* No. 1 Station — Hawkers Cove          # Trevose Head Station

## TEMPORARY PADSTOW LIFEBOATS

| | | | | |
|---|---|---|---|---|
| 1886 | 52 | ELIZABETH MOORE GARDEN (borrowed from Bude) | | |
| 1938-9 | 623 | DOCEA CHAPMAN | 34' SR 10 oars | |
| 1941 & 1956 | 719 | QUEEN VICTORIA | 51' Barnett, (Motor) | |
| 1946 | 648 | ELSIE | 45' Watson, (Motor) | |
| 1949 | 692 | MILBURN | 45' Watson, (Motor) | |
| 1963 | 729 | JOHN R WEBB | 45' 6" Watson, (Motor) | |
| 1967 | 754 | LLOYDS | 51' Barnett, (Motor) | |
| 1974/5/6 | 847 | GERTRUDE | 46' Watson, (Motor) | |
| 1980 | 822 | JESSE LUMB | 46' Watson, (Motor) | |
| 1983/4 | 926 | GUY & CLARE HUNTER | 46' 9" Watson, (Motor) | |

In 1994 the ILB station at Rock started operations with boat No. D.350.

## NEWQUAY LIFEBOATS

| Date | No. | Name | Length & Type | Construction | Fate |
|---|---|---|---|---|---|
| 1860-65 | — | JOSHUA | 30' Peake, 6 oars | 1860 Forrestt, Limehouse | |
| 1865-73 | — | JOSHUA | 32' SR, 10 oars | 1965 Forrestt, Limehouse | |
| | | JOSHUA was renamed JAMES AND ELIZABETH in 1871. | | | Sold 1888 |
| 1873-1892 | — | JAMES & ELIZABETH renamed JAMES & ELIZABETH 1873 | 33' SR, 10 oars | 1865 Forrestt, Limehouse as SABRINA, | |
| | | JAMES & ELIZABETH was renamed PENDOCK NEALE in 1875 | | | broken up 1892 |
| 1892-99 | 331 | WILLIE ROGERS renamed ALEXANDRA 1900 | 34' SR, 10 oars | 1892 McAlister | condemned 1903 |
| 1899-1917 | 426 | JAMES STEVENS No.5 | 35' SR, 10 oars | 1899 Roberts | wrecked on service 1917 |
| 1917-20 | 453 | JOHN WILLIAM DUDLEY | 35' SR, 10 oars | 1900 Thames Ironworks, Blackwall | Sold 1926 and renamed GULL |
| 1920-34 | 509 | ADMIRAL SIR GEORGE BACK | 35' SR, 10 oars | 1903 Thames Ironworks, Blackwall | Sold 1936 and renamed HERON V |
| 1940-45 | 794 | RICHARD SILVER OLIVER | 35'-6" Liverpool (Motor) | 1937 J. S. White, Cowes | Sold to Chile in 1963 |

The following ILBs have served at Newquay since 1965:
D55, D110, D38, D76, D73, D171, D192, D278, C511 (1984-1995) These inflatables required frequent repair and replacement in the first few years, but the costs involved are much less than with traditional lifeboats, and the latest ILBs have much longer lives than the pioneers.

## PORT ISAAC LIFEBOATS

| | | | | | |
|---|---|---|---|---|---|
| 1869-87 | — | RICHARD AND SARAH | 32' SR, 10 oars | 1869 Forrestt, Limehouse | Sold 1887 |
| 1887-1905 | 135 | RICHARD AND SARAH | 34' SR, 10 oars | 1887 Forrestt, Limehouse | Sold 1905, renamed FOAM |
| 1905-1927 | 334 | RICHARD AND SARAH | 34' SR, 10 oars | 1892 Forrestt, Limehouse | Sold 1927 |
| | | This RICHARD AND SARAH was formerly CHARLES WITTON stationed at Drogheda. | | | |
| 1927-33 | 662 | ERNEST DRESDEN | 35' SR, 10 oars | 1917 Saunders | Sold 1933: seen as yacht 1993 |

The RICHARD AND SARAH ex. CHARLES WITTON was sold by the RNLI in 1927 and returned to Ireland to be named successively BENAGHMORE, MAEVE and POOLBEG, under which name she was serving as a motor yacht on the Shannon in 1986. It is to be hoped she has since achieved her century.

The following ILBs have served at Port Isaac since 1967: D139, D257, D366 named PETER AND MOLLY TABOR

### Note on the numbering of lifeboats

Since 1887 all RNLI lifeboats have had an 'official number' allotted by the Institution. The boats were not registered as British Ships, and so had no British 'official number' as used elsewhere in this book. The tug HELEN PEELE (RNLI official number 478) was for many years the only exception as she was registered at Padstow on completion and given the British ON 84984.

In 1923 the Institution registered the 'RNLB THE BROTHERS' and she was given the British ON 147551. She had just been completed by J. S. White at East Cowes and it seems to have been a trial registration because in 1928 the Institution started to register all its motor lifeboats in London with the prefix RNLB to their usual name, and has continued to do so since then.

Every shipyard gives a hull number to each of its creations, and on lifeboats this number was usually cut into the wooden stem of the boat. Modern boats carry the hull number on a 'builder's plate' in the wheelhouse.

In recent years, the lifeboats have been given an 'Operational Number', for instance the JAMES AND CATHERINE MACFARLANE had her number 48.02 painted on both sides of her bow. That demonstrates that she was No.2 in the 48 ft Oakley class. Since 1988 new classes of lifeboat have been given metric lengths, so the 38 ft Mersey class lifeboat GRACE DARLING carries the number 12-16. These operational numbers made communications simpler and safer, as many lifeboats have long and complicated names.

Thus each modern British lifeboat has four different identification numbers:

> RNLI - Official Number
> British register - Official Number
> Builders - Hull Number
> RNLI - Operational Number

Pentire Point and Newland Rock in a moderate summer gale.

# 16 PADSTOW & THE ROYAL NAVY

*At Flores in the Azores Sir Richard Grenville lay . . .*

A. Tennyson

## Early Days

ADMIRAL Sir Richard Grenville lived at Stowe Barton just north of Bude and if this were a book about the men of North Cornwall rather than the ships, this chapter would be much longer. Gilbert's *Historical Survey of Cornwall* gives some other early examples.

Sir John Arundell, 'bred to the sea service', became a naval commander of the first rank and in 1379 repulsed the French fleet which had been hovering on the coasts of Devon and Cornwall. Not long after he was wrecked on the Irish coast and lost with upwards of 1,000 men. John, his son and heir, was a great benefactor to St Columb where he was buried. John was made a KB in 1399, and was a naval commander in Henry V's reign.

The Bligh family flourished in Cornwall from about 1500 and John Bligh, the father of Captain Bligh of HMS BOUNTY was born at Tretane, St Tudy.

Tresinger, at St Kew, was the seat of the Matthews family which produced Abedneys Matthews, Captain-General of the Leeward Islands in the mid-seventeenth century, and two Sir William Matthewses held the same post subsequently.

Edward Gurney, born near Padstow, served in William III's navy. He had command of HMS DEFIANCE in 1691, and then HMS BRISTOL. He died in command of her in the West Indies in 1694. And Padstow has continued to supply men rather than ships for the naval service ever since.

One of the first incidents directly involving a naval ship at Padstow was the wreck of HMS WHITING there on 15th September, 1816 as reported in *Lloyd's List* of 21st September. The WHITING was a large schooner of 225 tons builder's measure, 98 ft long and with a beam of 24 ft. She was armed with twelve 12-pounder carronades, the deadly short-range weapons invented and made by the Carron Iron Company in Scotland. The ship had previously been named ARROW and, as such, was captured from the Americans in the war of 1812. She ran on to the edge of the Doom Bar in thick weather but her entire crew of fifty men, including Lt. John Jackson in command, were unharmed. The wreck became a danger to navigation and had to be removed.

## The First World War

In the 1914-1918 war, Padstow first saw action when the U-Boats found it profitable to stop ships by gunfire off Trevose Head and then place bombs on board to sink them, and later when ships were sunk by torpedo or gun fire without warning, Padstow saw a procession of survivors and wreckage coming ashore. The following excerpt taken from *The Tides of War 1914-1918* by W. G. Neale shows the dilemma posed by the submarine menace and the ferocity of the war at sea even in the early years of World War I.

The Leyland Line's 1895 ARMENIAN of 5,754 tons net, 530 ft in length and with a speed of 14½ knots, had already made arrivals at Avonmouth on 11th April and 23rd May, 1915. In the early morning of 28th June, Captain Irickey on voyage from Newport News to Avonmouth with 1,422 mules was steering to pass ten miles north of Lundy when he was warned by wireless of submarine danger in that vicinity. He changed course south towards Trevose Head some fifty miles south on the Cornish coast near Padstow. Shortly before seven o'clock the U38 was sighted. After an attempt to ram the U38, Captain Irickey put on full speed towards Trevose and for an hour the ARMENIAN was pursued, shelled some fifty times, set afire and finally put out of action by explosion in the engine room. The ship lay helpless twenty miles from Trevose Head. The white flag was hoisted but shelling continued. Twenty-nine men including twenty American cattlemen were killed. The survivors took to the boats. The Captain first saw that the hatches of the lower hold were battened and other buoyancy measures taken. It took two valuable torpedoes to finish the ARMENIAN. A remarkable sight ensued. The ARMENIAN sank bow first with half her length reared vertically in the air. The survivors were rescued next morning and landed at Avonmouth. Captain Irickey was awarded the Distinguished Service Cross and three other men received the Distinguished Service Medal.

The Royal Navy responded by intensive coastal patrols to keep the U-boats submerged. Padstow was in Patrol, Area XIV which stretched from Hartland Point round Land's End to Looe, with headquarters at Falmouth, and other port facilities at Newlyn and St Mary's. By 1918 this area alone of the Auxiliary Patrol deployed 2 large armed steam yachts, 55 armed trawlers (each armed with 12- or 6-pounder guns), 14 MLs (Motor Launches) and 44 steam drifters, the MLs and drifters being armed mostly with 3-pounder guns. The MLs were of the standard type built in the USA and Canada, 550 of which had been delivered by the end of 1916. They were 80 ft long and were driven at a maximum speed of 19 knots by 440 b.h.p. petrol engines. Six of them formed the 'Newlyn Hydrophone Flotilla', and the rest were based at Falmouth. Photographs show MLs from both flotillas at Padstow but it is not thought that they were based there for any length of time, but rather that they called in there or went in to avoid storms when patrolling in the area.

So many of the seamen of Padstow and the outports were serving in the Navy and the Merchant Navy that it became impossible to muster adequate crews for the local lifeboats.

Five Padstow ships were taken into the Royal Navy during the first war. The motor fishing vessel PERILLA PW 37 was hired in September 1915 and remained in service as a patrol vessel (but not in the local area) until 1919. The RNLI tug, HELEN PEELE, was called up in August 1917, and distinguished herself in northern waters helping the fleet and carrying out various rescue operations for which she was naturally much better equipped than most other tugs. She returned to normal duties at Padstow in 1919. The local motor fishing vessel CRIMSON RAMBLER PW 229 was hired right at the end of the war for local patrol work, probably for dealing with mines which broke away from their moorings.

The fourth ship was the three-masted schooner VIOLA, and she

A flotilla of the Royal Navy's anti-submarine Motor Launches sheltering in Padstow *c.* 1918.          *Tony Pawlyn Collection*

was taken up and fitted out to become a fully commissioned naval vessel and to take part in what must surely be one of the bravest naval episodes. When the Germans started submarine warfare in 1914, it soon became obvious what a lethal weapon they had in their hands. There was no way of finding a submerged submarine, and in any case, no weapon to deal with the submerged submarine. Therefore it was decided to create a fleet of decoy vessels to offer themselves to be attacked by U-boats, to tempt the U-boats to surface to examine their victims or to sink them by gun fire, and once the U-boat was within range, to bring hidden guns to bear and sink the U-boat. Endless ingenuity was used to deceive the enemy: guns were hidden in various cunning ways; highly disciplined crews had to appear dirty and slovenly; 'panic parties' lowered boats and left the ship once the U-boat had been sighted to give the impression the ship was deserted. Once the deadly game was known by both sides, sometimes a second panic party was laid on to convince the enemy that the last man had left. Total secrecy was essential. The ships changed their names and their appearance at frequent intervals.

The decoy ships were known as Q-ships because at one time they had Q pendant numbers. They tended to be small, old and slow, both to leave the bigger and better ships to carry out their essential transport work, and to persuade the U-boat that they were sitting ducks, probably not worth the expenditure of precious torpedoes, but easy to sink by gunfire. They were of almost every type of ship from small tramp steamer through collier, coaster, motor smack, trawler to every rig of small sailing ship. Some of the trawlers towed

British submarines which were released to attack the U-boat at the appropriate time.

The VIOLA was a topsail schooner built at Appledore by William Pickard in 1872. In 1884 she was bought by J. H. Male and others and registered at Padstow. About 1904 William Hutchings became managing owner and she was re-rigged as a three-masted schooner with O. Watts as master. C. Tucker was master during the war during which she, like hundreds of other sailing coasters, spent much of her time taking coal and supplies of all sorts to France. In 1918 a group of such coasters were fitted out as Q-ships at Granton. VIOLA was judged to be strong enough to mount one 4 ins gun and two 12-pounders, a terrifying armament for a wooden schooner less than 100 ft long, and the additional hands must have made conditions very cramped below decks: nevertheless she was loaded with coal and sailed off to St Valery-en-Caux bearing the false name of VEREKER. She remained a Q-ship until the end of the war, sailing also under the name VIOLETTA but apparently seeing no action against U-boats.

After the war ownership passed to Edwin P. Hutchings and she was fitted with an auxiliary motor in 1920, but on 21st May, 1922, when taking a cargo of china clay from Teignmouth to Glasgow, having refuelled at Brixham, she grounded on rocks at Kennack Sands near The Lizard and broke her back. Evidently she survived in some form as a Mr Willows owned her in 1924, and Mrs Willows in 1925, but perhaps she was kept as a hulk. The registry closed 3rd February, 1926.

When the Q-ships started in 1915 there were only a few of them, but by the end of the war there were over 200 including warships specially constructed to look like unarmed merchant vessels. With hindsight Admiral Gordon Campbell, the most famous exponent of the technique, felt that a massive initial effort before the secret was out might have been much more effective, and might have strangled the U-boat offensive at birth; but it seems to me that preparations on a massive scale could not have been kept entirely secret, and such an effort might have been largely wasted. As it was, although the Q-ships only accounted for 7% of the U-boat losses, the knowledge that there were such dangerous decoys soon made it impossible for U-boats to approach ships with impunity on the surface, and as they were forced to remain submerged they were much slower and less effective.

The fifth Padstow ship to join the Royal Navy was the MARGARET MURRAY. She was a three-masted schooner built by the Grangemouth Dockyard Company in 1885 for London owners; her dimensions were 107.2 x 23.7 x 11.7 ft and she was that rarity amongst Padstow owned ships, a steel hulled sailing vessel. But then it was W. S. Allport who bought her from C. T. Bowring Ltd, the famous Newfoundland trading and sealing firm, in about 1909 and Allport in gallant efforts to maintain the Padstow fleet had already moved into steel ships in 1904, when he had the DORIS built at Appledore only to lose her sadly in 1907. The MARGARET MURRAY like the VIOLA was not taken up until 1918 and she served from 30th April, 1918 until 18th October, 1919. She is described in her naval role as an auxiliary schooner, and as her two-cylinder paraffin engine (of 29 n.h.p.) was not built until September 1918, she cannot have seen active service before the Armistice. She was, however, the very last word in Q-ship development, an innocent looking three-masted schooner with a hull strong enough to house her one 4 ins gun, her three 12-pounders and a depth charge thrower, which was doubtless added as her engine gave her the ability to manoeuvre close to a submerging U-boat. There is an Imperial War Museum photograph of her with her guns exposed, ready for action, and the guns look enormous on her small deck. One is reminded of the Duke of Wellington's dictum: 'I don't know what effect they will have on the enemy but by God they frighten me.'

After the war she was owned by the Brito France Shipping Co. Ltd of Blyth and in 1924, when bound from Blyth to Dartmouth with coal, she went ashore at Maasvlakte, being later refloated and towed to Maasluis to be sold to breakers.

HM RESCUE TUG 'ST MINVER' SERVED THE ALLIES 1939-1945
AS THE FRENCH 'ABEILLE 22'

## The Second World War

When Britain was threatened by invasion after the fall of France in 1940, to meet the threat of total war we became the most mobilised nation in history: there was scarcely an able-bodied man or woman who was not engaged in the forces, or ARP (Air Raid Precautions), the Land Army, the LDV (Local Defence Volunteers, later renamed the Home Guard) the Royal Observer Corps or one of a hundred other organisations.

At sea the mobilisation was even more complete. The convoy system was introduced almost immediately; the world's largest merchant navy had to be defensively armed and thousands of extra hands were needed at sea. Numerous ships, large and small, escaped from Hitler's Europe or were taken over without crews, and were then manned and managed by British companies. Admiral Rogers who had retired to Rock and helped to found the Rock Sailing Club, was off to sea again as a Convoy Commodore, like many other retired senior naval officers.

The threat of invasion in 1940 led to the formation of a sort of seagoing Home Guard. At Padstow, the Auxiliary Patrol was divided into the river patrol, and the so-called seagoing motor boats which were mostly fishing vessels. The river patrol consisted of the auxiliary patrol vessels STORM COCK, EILEEN, HARMONY, JMS, JUNE and MERRY FISH, and these small motor boats were known as Parkyn's Navy.

The seagoing flotilla in 1940 consisted of FORGET-ME-NOT, OCEAN PRIDE, OUR KATIE, PEEL CASTLE, ROSE BUD, TREVESSA and UNITED BOYS II.

As the threat of invasion passed, the number of craft needed for the RNPS (Royal Naval Patrol Service) was reduced but with the prospect of a long war other needs had to be met for the local defence of Padstow. One of the most soul-destroying but essential tasks was mine-watching. With German aircraft dropping magnetic and acoustic mines, the minewatching service both ashore and afloat had the duty of plotting any mine entering the water around the British Isles, so that it could be swept, if possible, before doing damage.

In September 1941 the build-up of naval personnel at Padstow led to the arrival of the Accommodation Ship WATCHWORD. She had been the French fishing vessel CONGEY, seized by the Royal Navy after the French surrender in 1940, when so many Frenchmen had to make the heart-rending decision whether to carry on the fight against the Nazis from the UK or to return to their families in Vichy France, without knowing to what extent Vichy France would become Hitler's puppet. The Royal Navy could not afford to allow any indecision and literally hundreds of French ships, large and small, ancient and modern, were boarded and taken over generally peacefully, but by force if necessary, in British or British-controlled ports, some to fight on gallantly with Free French crews, others (including WATCHWORD) to be manned by the Royal Navy.

Naval histories dwell on the British fleet's attack on the French fleet at Mers-el-Kebir in July 1940, and later on the dramatic scuttling of the French fleet at Toulon to prevent a most potent weapon falling into Hitler's hands, but they cannot describe the hundreds of minor dramas, equally devastating to those involved. We will never know what happened to the French crew of the little CONGEY in 1940, but she played her humble part in Padstow 1941-1943, and then went off to Plymouth to become a 'balloon tender' helping to maintain the barrage balloons which protected our invasion fleets, as they prepared for D-Day in Normandy, from low flying German aircraft. It is quite probable that something dramatic did happen to her French owners in the war, because it was not until 1946 that arrangements could be made for her to return to France.

Throughout the war two little grey steam drifters were based at Padstow. For most local people they symbolised the naval presence at Padstow as there was always one at sea and one in port. Much of the time their nominal purpose was to be safety vessels for the Fleet Air Arm who were flying from St Merryn and other airfields, but with the RAF Air-Sea Rescue launches available, the drifters were the tough seaworthy vessels which took it in turns to maintain a standing patrol off Padstow: they were the GOLDEN CHANCE and the PRESENT FRIENDS.

These little ships, like a thousand others, had little to protect them against air attack or surfaced submarines (they were not worth a torpedo): in 1940 it was rifles and a few sandbags around the wheelhouse: by 1942 it was 'plastic armour' around the wheelhouse and a World War I Lewis gun or two. There were also various strange devices which were intended to fire a rocket up above the vessel, dragging a long wire into the air which might then wrap itself around the attacking aircraft or, better still, get snarled up in its propellers. Like the Q-ships of the First World War, it may not have been the most efficient way of destroying the enemy, but it was improvisation at short notice, it was fairly cheap, and it must have been quite a worry for enemy pilots contemplating low level attacks on British ships. In the English Channel the patrol vessels were later given 20 mm Oerlikon anti-aircraft guns which were particularly satisfying guns to fire since a bright arc of tracer could be seen sweeping towards the enemy, but Padstow was lower priority and the Lewis guns sufficed to the end.

The patrol vessels spent endless weeks at sea, but there was some action: the PRESENT FRIENDS was bombed and machine-gunned by German aircraft just off Padstow on 30th April, 1941. On 4th May following that, the drifters helped a damaged Belgian ship, the MARIE-FLORE which had been bombed in a convoy battle; they escorted her into sheltered waters and helped with salvage and repairs. Convoy battles took place off Trevose Head as in the First World War, but with the active intervention of German aircraft. HMS BROCKLESBY, a 'hunt' class destroyer, shot down two of them off Trevose on 20th March, 1942.

GOLDEN CHANCE and PRESENT FRIENDS were a pigeon pair. They were both built at Lowestoft in 1914, typical wooden steam herring drifters about 85 ft long; they were both hired for naval service 1915-1919, tending anti-submarine nets; they both fished for Lowestoft companies between the wars and re-entered naval service in 1940, being released in 1946.

The Prunier Trophy was awarded annually from 1936 until 1966 for the biggest landing of silver darlings (fresh herrings) from a single shot of the nets brought to Lowestoft or Yarmouth. Although the fishing fleets competing in the autumn of 1939 had already been reduced by the requisition of ships for the navy, it was still the time of the so-called phoney war, and it was quietly decided to compete

for the trophy in the month of November, and PRESENT FRIENDS (LT 89) was the winner with a shot of 194½ crans.

After the Second World War, only a few steam drifters went back to fishing. Over a hundred had been lost in the war, and the more economical motor fishing vessels were taking over, but there were more exciting things to do. GOLDEN CHANCE was bought by the Colonial Development Corporation and ended up in the 1950s registered at Port Stanley in the Falkland Islands, where she was employed in the seal fishery. She is still largely intact as an abandoned hulk near Port Stanley and is now to be found in the *International Register of Historic Ships*. PRESENT FRIENDS was sold for £5,000 to ex-servicemen who planned to set off for South America and Australia in her in 1947. However, she sprang a leak off Land's End, was beached in the Helford River, then taken to Shoreham in a derelict condition and eventually broken up there in 1952.

Various other craft were involved in the naval work at Padstow in the Second World War. The small open motorboat KINGFISHER joined the river patrol in 1941 (later listed as KINGFISHER III presumably to differentiate her from other naval KINGFISHERs). She is believed to be the boat which survived the wreck of the barque ANTOINETTE, described in another chapter. The SILVER CLOUD II replaced the STORM COCK in the river patrol in 1944.

The MLs of the First World War have already been mentioned but in 1944 ML 215 was based at Padstow to be a target boat for aerial attack practice; she was of the famous Fairmile 'B' class, 112 ft overall length, with a maximum speed of 20 knots, powered by two 600 h.p. engines. ML 455, a sister ship, normally based at Falmouth joined her at Padstow for a time in 1944. Towards the end of that year, a motor launch of a different type was at Padstow; she was HDML 1457, a harbour defence motor launch, one of a large class, 72 ft overall and powered by two diesel engines each of 150 h.p. Her entry in the Admiralty list for Padstow has the note 'to be shipped abroad on completion'. This vessel had been built at Blackmore's yard at Bideford, and the implication must be that the final fitting out was done at Padstow. She ended up in the French navy in 1946.

Presiding over this naval activity at Padstow in World War II was none other than Admiral Gordon Campbell, VC, DSO who made his name in Q-ships in World War I. Having left the service in 1928 with so many honours and decorations, he may have felt disappointed not to be closer to the principal naval actions, but it is impossible to think of any man more able to win the respect of the independently minded seamen of Padstow.

By 1939 hardly any of Padstow's old schooners and ketches were left in commission, but one of them, the MARGARET HOBLEY,

HMS 'BUDE', 1941

HMS 'PADSTOW BAY'                                                    1946

was commissioned as a BBV (Barrage balloon vessel) from 1940 until 1944.

The steam drifter ADELE (built at Yarmouth in 1915), which was owned by the Padstow Fishing Co. Ltd 1929-1934, had been promptly hired by the Admiralty on completion and armed with a 6-pounder gun. HM Drifter ADELE tended anti-submarine nets, was renamed KINGFISHER still in the naval service in 1918, and returned to fish out of Yarmouth as ADELE in 1919. After her time at Padstow she was registered at Lowestoft, and her owner was George Tripp. In 1941 she again joined the Royal Navy and carried out harbour service until 1946. After that she fished until about 1960, being owned by Northern Trawlers Ltd and then Albert G. Catchpole of Kessingland, Suffolk.

The steam yacht MEDEA also took part in both world wars, as detailed elsewhere in this book.

HMS VULTURE was Padstow's most important contribution to World War II, but she wasn't a ship! An airfield had been built at St Merryn at the end of World War I, which was recommissioned by the Royal Naval Air Service in 1940 as HMS VULTURE (renamed HMS CURLEW in 1952).

So the ships were going and gone, but the men were sailing on, and the Admiralty appears to have recognised the contribution of Padstow and its outports in the naming of numerous warships, including the following:

**PADSTOW.** Two fleet minesweepers, one in the First World War later renamed PANGBOURNE, and one in the Second renamed ROLIKHAND when she was transferred to the Royal Indian Navy.
**PADSTOW BAY** (ex LOCH COULSIDE), a frigate completed in 1945.
**ST BREOCK, ST COLOMB, ST ENODER, ST GENNY, ST ISSEY, ST MABYN, ST MINVER, ST TEATH** and **ST TUDY** were all naval rescue tugs built for the First World War, as well as being towns and villages within the Padstow hinterland.
**NEWQUAY** was the name given to a fleet minesweeper under construction in 1918 but she was renamed NAILSEA on completion.
**TINTAGEL.** A First World War destroyer built by Swan Hunter.
**TINTAGEL CASTLE.** A handsome corvette which took part in the Battle of the Atlantic.
**TREVOSE HEAD.** A naval repair ship under construction in Vancouver in 1945, but completed as the merchant steamship TURAN.

It would be agreeable to be able to claim that HM Paddle Tug CAMEL was named for the river, but one of her consorts was the DROMEDARY.

In the 1970s a rather strange looking craft joined the fleet of the Royal Corps of Transport. The 72 ft MV TREVOSE was designed and built by REME, the Royal Electrical & Mechanical Engineers; she started work as a general service launch, but was transferred to be used for training. Some naval gentlemen have been unkind enough to maintain that she shows signs of having been designed by landsmen.

HMS 'TINTAGEL CASTLE', 1944

# 17　AIR-SEA RESCUE

## The Sea Shall Not Have Them

THE Second World War was without doubt the noisiest period in the Camel Estuary's history. Much of the noise was only indirectly connected with the war. For instance, airfield construction for the RAF Coastal Command required many thousands of tons of concrete aggregates, and the quarry on Stepper Point (which had been opened in the mid-nineteenth century with the object of removing the headland which had so disastrously blanketed the sails of ships approaching Padstow) was re-opened, and major blasting operations took place several times a day, with an endless stream of lorries carrying the crushed rock away. It was all used locally so none went by sea. Occasionally there was an even larger explosion when a sea-mine broke loose from its mooring and drifted ashore.

When the Home Guard finally got some ammunition, there were fierce marksmanship competitions on a rifle range improvised on St Enodoc golf course, on the St Minver side of the river.

From Rock to Trebetherick it was clear that a German invasion would have little difficulty in moving troops and vehicles inland over the beach and the low sandhills, so a large field of land-mines was laid, and protected by barbed wire to prevent casual casualties amongst golfers and others. Gun Point had a gun once more.

Polzeath beach had a tubular steel barrier built across it to prevent enemy landing craft from coming inshore: it made surf bathing quite tricky at high tide. Concrete 'dragons' teeth' appeared wherever it was thought a vehicle might try to get from the beaches to the countryside.

The noise of high-powered petrol engines invaded every nook and cranny, and not just from the numerous aircraft, but also from a small flotilla of fast motor launches quite unlike anything based previously at Padstow.

From the formation of the Royal Air Force at the end of the First World War until 1939, its marine branch was principally engaged in the development and operation of 'seaplane tenders' which served the flying boat squadrons around the coast and at overseas bases. A small dedicated band of officers and men (including Aircraftsman T.E. Shaw, better known as Lawrence of Arabia), worked on a range of tenders, pinnaces and armoured target boats, but it was only in 1939 that orders were placed for the first High Speed launches (HSLs) which were to form the backbone of the Air Sea Rescue (ASR) units which were based all around Britain and, indeed, all around the world. Apart from prototypes, there were the original British Power Boat Co.'s 'whalebacks' designed by Hubert Scott-Paine, and these were followed by several other types built in Britain and North America, mostly 67 ft long and powered typically by three Napier Sea Lion petrol engines of 500 h.p. each. Late in the war marine versions of the famous Rolls Royce Merlin (the engine of the Spitfire and the Hurricane) became available, as did the American equivalent Packard engine.

These engines all had certain common features. They were noisy, hot and required frequent attention and they all drank vast quantities of petrol. This combination of wooden boats and petrol engines, (which the air-sea rescue boats had in common with virtually all our naval coastal forces) was in theory a recipe for disaster in the shape of fire and explosion; but strict precautions

were taken, and although the risk must have contributed to the losses suffered from enemy action (and one-quarter of the ASR boats entering service 1939-1941 were so lost), accidental fire losses do not feature!

In theory, air-sea rescue generally worked as follows:

(i) The ditching aircraft gave its position by radio or the approximate position was given by another aircraft.

(ii) An ASR aircraft (generally a slow-flying Lysander or Walrus), took off to search the area of the ditching, looking for survivors.

(iii) An ASR launch was also despatched to pick up any survivors, often guided in by radio from the ASR aircraft.

Of course there was much more to it than that. First of all the aircrew required training and experience to ditch safely and escape from the aircraft. In 1939 our fighter pilots only had a Mae West lifebuoy, so they were about one-quarter as easy to find as a floating tea-chest, and there was a lot of flotsam about. Later they had dinghies, flares, dyes and coloured smoke to draw the attention of rescuers.

Once found, it was no easy job, even in a flat calm, to get a stunned, waterlogged pilot on board without doing him further injury. A scramble net was fixed over the side of the launch, and often members of the crew entered the water to assist those being picked up.

If the ASR search aircraft was a Supermarine Walrus, then numerous ditched aircrew had extra cause to be grateful: this extraordinary single-engined biplane amphibian flying-boat was designed by R. J. Mitchell, the same genius who designed the Spitfire. The Navy catapulted the Walrus from cruisers and battleships to act as a spotter plane, the eyes of the fleet; but in the RAF her role was ASR. Cruising at low altitude and at much less than 100 m.p.h., she was more likely than other types of aircraft to spot survivors in the water, and having spotted them, she would often land bravely in quite rough seas and pick them up. It was quite normal for the sea to be too rough for her to take off again, especially with the additional weight. But the men were safe, and an ASR launch would arrive in due course to escort the Walrus to safety.

In the North Sea and the English Channel, when the air war was at its height, ASR launches were posted to pre-arranged positions sometimes quite close to enemy coasts, so that the crews of damaged aircraft, struggling home, had a good chance of being recovered,

Off North Cornwall, aerial activity was somewhat less intense, but the need for Air-Sea Rescue services was soon realised.

Many convoys were routed through St George's Channel, between Cornwall and Ireland, and the swept channel through the extensive British minefields brought the ships within sight of Trevose Head. Coastal Command, flying mainly Ansons and Hudsons, had several local bases, the nearest at St Eval. Sunderland flying boats based on Milford Haven were often to be seen. The Fleet Air Arm had a land base at St Merryn.

HSL 2661 was built by J. Meakes
at Marlow using prefabricated units
produced by John I. Thorncroft & Co.
at Hampton. Trials May 1944.
*RAF Museum, Hendon*

Much flying training was carried out off North Cornwall, and towards the end of the war a large armoured buoy was moored off Port Isaac so that allied 'ship buster' aircraft could practise rocket attacks.

There was a great shortage of vessels suitable for ASR work at the start of the war, but in March 1942 a small unit was formed at Padstow with RAF St Eval as the parent station. The details are all to be found in the Public Record Office at Kew:

44 ASRMC (Air-Sea Rescue Marine Craft) Commissioned 3rd March, 1942. Flt. Lt. Garwood in command with F/O Stott and P/O Hoskin as masters. Pinnaces 97 and 98 were the stop-gaps, but they sailed for Tyree, Scotland, on 10th June, soon after the 60 foot Pinnaces 1228, 1229 and 1230 had arrived for duty, followed some months later by Pinnace 1234.

The daily log of the early months tells of endless training and liaison with Walrus and Lysander aircraft. Bomber crews were taken to sea for 'wet dinghy drill' to enhance their chances of survival if they ever had to ditch.

When the lifeboat house had been sited at Hawkers Cove it was because it was sheltered and there was sufficient water to launch the boat at all states of tide: once launched she was close to the open sea and the Doom bar. Although the depths of water were already somewhat reduced, the same factors led to the ASR base being established at the same place. However, there was scarcely room to lay out moorings for four boats, and it was touch and go whether or not they ran aground at low water spring tides.

The crews lived in typical temporary wooden hutments and the small number of officers worked watches to cover day and night. Rations, pay and transport were provided by RAF St Eval.

Writing of his time there, Flight Lieutenant (later Squadron Leader) Garwood noted the crews' frustration at the absence of aircraft crashes. 'I did explain to them that we should not wish aircraft to crash into the sea just for us to rush out and pick them

up, but it was action they wanted, not exercises.' One is reminded of the old Cornish prayer, 'Lord, we cannot desire for ships and sailors to suffer shipwreck, but if suffer they must, Lord, please guide them to run ashore near this church.'

But the frustration continued. One aircraft ditched and all three pinnaces were out until dawn next day; but the aircrew had drifted safely ashore in their dinghy, and made their own way back to base. 'Another day we were called out to a ditched aircraft and as we were about to pick up the crew, a Walrus amphibian aircraft landed and took the crew off, leaving us to pick up the dinghy and return, somewhat crestfallen to base.'

Flight Lieutenant Garwood was posted elsewhere at the end of 1942, but his insistence on a high standard of training was to pay dividends later.

Activities in 1943 included the following taken from the unit log:

. . . Searching for, and sinking floating mines (normally British moored mines which had broken loose in storms).

8.1.43 Assisted in D type dinghy sailing trials. Frequently at sea with more bomber crews.

6.6.43 Pinnace 1234 picked up body. ATC (Air Training Corps) cadets were given sea experience.

9.7.43 Fifty Americans arrived to learn how the British ASR system works. (They paid us the compliment of modelling their own organization of 'crash boats' on ours even to using Scott-Payne designed high speed launches.)

24.8.43 Searching for Flying Fortress crew. A/S co-operation with Walrus, Anson, Spitfire, Mosquito, Wellington and Lancaster aircraft!

Hove to off Trevose in heavy seas. (That entry must have been made in many ships' logs over several centuries!)

25.8.43 0515 hrs. Pinnace 1234 picked up three empty dinghies and one with seven survivors.

Ambulances, Padstow, 1410 hrs.

Pinnace 1228 continued search for four missing members of the Flying Fortress aircrew, but without success.

13.9.43 Pinnace 1228 on secret exercises with American technicians.

14.10.43 Pinnaces 1228 and 1229 sailed for Fishguard and joined another unit.

2.12.43 Pinnace 1230 sailed for Milford Haven and service elsewhere.

10.12.43 HSL 2641 arrived for service. (This 67-ft Thornycroft high speed launch could put out in even more atrocious weather than the 60 ft pinnaces, but she had a slightly greater draught and there was evidently insufficient water for her at Hawker's Cove at low tide.)

30.12.43 HSL moorings laid off quarry jetty for use on spring tides. (The less sheltered, disused quarry jetty was further out beyond Hawker's Cove, closer to Stepper Point, and closer to the flying rocks which sometimes followed blasting operations at the quarry.)

There were very frequent gale warnings through November and December, 1943 and January, 1944. Although strongly built, ASR launches are 'thin-skinned' compared with the traditional wooden craft which learned to survive off North Cornwall. Their low draught and high-sided hulls combined to make them surge around at anchor or at moorings unless moored at bow and stern.

Putting to sea around Stepper Point, they would go into the teeth of a westerly gale within a minute or two of getting under way. The seamanlike procedure would have been to reduce speed drastically going into a head sea, but the operational necessity was often to maintain maximum possible speed towards the search area. In such circumstances the boat would tend to take off from one wave and land on the face of the next and, at speed, water becomes a remarkably hard substance to land on. It was not uncommon for ASR crews to suffer injuries, as a result of the violent motion: their spines were particularly vulnerable.

These problems had been well understood by the designers of the HSL's, and they were given a deep V hull form at the bow so that, instead of slamming on a flat surface, the bow would enter the wave, getting more buoyancy as it bit deeper, and easing the motion. But the HSL had to have the ability to plane over the water rather than cutting through it, so much of the bottom had to be flat.

RAF Pinnace P 1230 at Hawker's Cove.
*RAF Museum, Hendon*

15.2.44 HSL 2641 rescued eight, plus one body from Liberator No.3 of 103 Squadron US Navy; co-operated with Sunderland flying boat 50° 35' N. 6° 09' W.

17.2.44 Pinnace 1234 stood by trawler ATLANTIC of Ostend.

23.5.44 HSL 2641 picked up two injured crew from a ditched Swordfish off the Gulland Rock. One other missing.

5.7.44 Engaged with Walrus and Warwick aircraft in search for Seafire pilot off Bude. (The Supermarine Seafire was the naval version of the famous Spitfire, modified to operate from aircraft carriers.)

31.7.44 HSL 2641 took Liberator survivors from a Walrus Amphibian which was unable to take off in heavy swell. (It seems likely that a wealth of seamanship and airmanship lies hidden in that sentence.)

31.7.44 HSL 2661 arrived from Fowey for duty.

7.8.44 All twelve crew of MV ARTHURTOWN arrived at Hawker's Cove in their ship's boat in thick fog. Their motor coaster had hit the rocks off Trevose Head then ran ashore in a sinking condition close to the Stepper Point daymark.

8.8.44 Landed fifty-five survivors from a ship on fire off Stepper Point. (This was evidently the result of a minor convoy battle, the ships being on their way to Normandy.)

14.8.44 The US Navy's tank landing ship LST921 was torpedoed and broke her back off Hartland Point. HSL 2661 brought wounded survivors back to Padstow; a Fairmile Motor launch of the Royal Navy rescued others. The LST did not sink but was towed to port and broken up.

5.1.45 Submarine torpedo attacks took place off Lundy Island.

7.1.45 Dumping obsolete ammunition at sea.

10.1.45 Pinnace 1234 sails for Newlyn and R.A.F. Mount Batten (Plymouth).

14.1.45 Called out to site of aircraft crash with two Walrus amphibians. Oil and wreckage. No survivors.

20/25.1.45 HSL 2641 dumping US ammunition at sea from RAF Davidstow (yet another wartime airfield, near Camelford. A Beaufighter Strike Wing from Davidstow helped to protect the invasion fleets on D-Day in June 1944.)

20.2.45 HSL 2661 drifted ashore on rocks at Greenaway Bay and was seriously damaged, remaining fast ashore. (Preparations for salvage were made over the following three weeks.)

8.3.45 HSL 2641 picked up two survivors from a Martinet near Trevose Head. (The Miles Martinet was a Fleet Air Arm target-towing aircraft.)

10.3.45 HSL 2641 recovered the body of a Corsair pilot. (The Chance Vought Corsair was probably the greatest carrier-borne fighter of the Second World War. Almost two thousand were built for the Royal Navy. They were powerful aircraft and difficult to manage from small aircraft carriers, and the casualty rate amongst trainee pilots was high.)

15.3.45 The patched-up hull of HSL 2661 was floated off the rocks at Greenaway Bay at high water spring tides, but subsequently sank and was abandoned.

15.3.45 HSL 2660 arrived to join the unit.

10.4.45 Making films of rocket-firing aircraft.

22.4.45 Two HSLs proceeded to assist torpedoed vessel. HSL 2641 was recalled, but HSL 2660 returned with eight survivors.

1.5.45 HSL 2670 attached to unit briefly as HSL 2641 under repair at Falmouth.

5.7.45 Airborne lifeboat taken to sea for exercises by aircrew of 282 Squadron. (The airborne lifeboat, in the design of which Uffa Fox had a hand, was carried by large Coastal Command aircraft, clamped to their underside, and could be parachuted down to survivors in the sea. It had sails and a small engine. Not many months later, a small flotilla of such boats provided exciting racing in the Camel estuary when little else was available immediately after the war.)

July '45 It was noted that the HSLs were non-operational at spring tides. The Doom bar was on the move and the water in The Narrows north of Hawker's Cove was getting progressively shallower.

31.8.45 HSL 2660 picked up one survivor from a crashed aircraft. In December the closing down of the base was under way.

22.12.45 HSL 2660 was delivered to Helensburgh.

3.1.46 Refueller 2066 was escorted to Appledore [having ferried fuel from the depot at Padstow railway station to Hawker's Cove for two years.]

30.1.46 HSL 2641 allotted to 238 Marine Unit. That was the final entry in the log of ASRMC.


Squadron-Leader Garwood can be proud of them. On my count they brought home over 83 survivors, and assisted in several other rescues.

In all theatres, three hundred Air-Sea Rescue launches of the RAF saved almost 14,000 lives in the Second World War.

The crews of the Air-Sea Rescue services were dedicated to saving human life and had the same outlook as lifeboatmen, but the High Command were probably more interested in other aspects. In the first place, highly trained aircrew were much more difficult to replace than aircraft. One of the reasons for the defeat of the Luftwaffe in the Battle of Britain was the large number of skilled aircrew lost by the Germans, whereas a good proportion of RAF pilots made it back to base, even after being shot down. Secondly, there was the effect of Air-Sea Rescue on morale. Virtually every

sortie by allied aircraft entailed flying over water, and the presence of a well-organised rescue service did wonders for the confidence and efficiency of our aircrews.

### Summary of ASR Craft which served at Padstow

*Rescue Craft*

| | | |
|---|---|---|
| Pinnace | P.97 | 1942 |
| Pinance | P.98 | 1942 |
| 60' Pinnace | P.1228 | 1942-43 |
| 60' Pinnace | P.1229 | 1942-43 |
| 60' Pinnace | P.1230 | 1942-43 |
| 60' Pinnace | P.1234 | 1943-45 |
| 67' Thornycroft | HSL 2641 | 1943-46 |
| Pinnace | P.50 | 1944 |
| 67' Thornycroft | HSL 2661 | 1944-45 |
| 67' Thornycroft | HSL 2660 | 1944-45 |
| 67' Thornycroft | HSL 2670 | 1945 |

*Auxiliary craft*

| | | |
|---|---|---|
| Marine Tender | 801 | 1942 |
| Refueller | 2066 | 1944-46 |
| RAF Mooring Vessel | GIRL JOYCE | 1944 |

In addition, Royal Air Force HSLs operated from Newquay for a time, including the following 68 ft 'Hants & Dorset' class launches: HSL 2627, HSL 2688 and HSL 2692.

The Fleet Air Arm at St Merryn at one time had their own safety vessel. Her presence was reported in 1944.

Needless to say, the RNLI Lifeboats based at Padstow and Newquay also kept up their gallant work throughout the six-year period of the war.

HSL 2670 on trials in the Solent in 1944.                    *RAF Museum, Hendon*

# 18  YACHTS AND SMALL BOATS

MOST histories of navigation picture man's first adventure afloat as a noble savage bravely setting out astride a tree trunk, using primitive paddles. If that was the first of the seven ages of man and the sea, then it was followed by the mysterious medieval mariner, the ages of discovery and sea roving, the golden age of sail, followed by the age of steam (and the motorship). In terms of seafaring, each development made the seafarer more and more remote from the sea itself, culminating in life in a huge mechanical steel box, living in what looks like a block of flats many feet above sea level, and almost never getting wet.

Yachting on a large scale developed along with the steam age. That was probably no coincidence: it seems likely that the Industrial Revolution produced prosperity on a scale which made leisure and resources available for such activities.

Padstow was not a natural yachting centre. The gentry from London and elsewhere might base their yachts at Cowes, Salcombe, Fowey or even Falmouth, but not on the north coast at Padstow. Even when internal combustion engines became commonplace, Padstow was too remote from home and from cruising grounds to become a yachting centre, and the dangers of navigation on that coast remained formidable.

The seamen of Padstow had a grim tradition of wresting a living from the sea, which did not make it easy to promote the joys of yachting. One of the favourite sayings to be found in the memoirs of seamen is that 'he who goes to sea for pleasure would go to hell for a holiday'. I have spent many happy weeks cruising in small wooden yachts which would certainly not measure up to the requirements of either the old Board of Trade or the present National Union of Seamen; my wife, I fear, has often thought of joining the Union.

Every year since 1888 the Royal Cruising Club has published a journal containing the logs of notable cruises. The early indices are full of cruises in home and European waters, but almost none on the north coast of Cornwall. After the Great War, Padstow starts to be mentioned. In 1920, F. Howard Sinclair sailed his newly purchased cutter VAITI from Belfast to his home in Dartmouth via Lundy and Padstow.

*13th July*. R. spent most of day trying to get engine to start. Towards evening it gave several consecutive revolutions and we were deluded into thinking the invalid convalescent.

*14th July*. SW by WSW Head wind, but day promised to be fine. Made first long board to 2 miles SW of Hartland Point, beating towards Padstow all the afternoon. The engine now declined to have anything to say to a spark and our turn to windward was a very poor bit of going. When darkness fell we held on for five hours on port tack towards NNW. The wind freshened and the seas became irregular and so steep that our progress must have been infinitesimal; it was a case of dodging breaking seas in the dark.

*15th July*. At dawn the weather was very thick and rain with squalls frequent, visibility generally bad (¼ cable). Suddenly about 7 a.m. land loomed in sight, and we made out Tintagel Head 8 miles to Eastward of Pentire Point. All day we pounded ahead. There was a very big ground swell on the coast and with an adverse tide we scarcely held our own,

but it was still daylight when we succeeded at last in weathering the Newland Islet and making close round Stepper Point (rendered unique by the direction painted in large letters on a board: 'Keep close to the rocks'). Unfortunately we had just missed the last of the flood and the race was beginning to sluice out when the high rocks kept us from getting the breeze. All we could do then was to drop anchor and wait.

R. took the dinghy to try and obtain some bread, of which we had been short since Lundy, and on his return shifted our anchorage a few cables' lengths further inside, just as far as possible without coming foul of a half-secured wreck which lay across the reputed navigable channel. When returning in the dark the dinghy came in contact with a newly-tarred rope stretched between the wreck and the rocks on shore. The words describing this outrage (used by the crew) were not beatitudes.

*16th July*. Our anchorage caused uneasiness to the foreman of a quarry on shore, who shouted that they could not proceed with their blasting until we moved. When the tide turned we beat in further to Hawker's Cove. Here the steam lifeboat and ordinary lifeboat occupy most of the deep water, having their moorings laid out with three anchors. It behoves anyone dropping his hook there to consider possible consequences. Our anchor fouled its fluke and in a heavy squall we drifted and dragged fast to leeward; our mainsail was ready to hoist, and with a couple of reefs and working jib we decided to make for the harbour proper, which was right to windward. We headed up very well indeed and were within sight of the tidal harbour entrance when the ebb became so strong that when the boat stayed by the time the next board was well begun, we realised that it was a losing venture, and VAITI's head was turned for our late anchorage close to the steam lifeboat.

*17th July*. Bar. 30. Beat up to Railway Pier at Padstow (finding that the harbour dries out), dropped anchor just outside the pier and about ½ cable distant. A three-masted Norwegian sailing craft went out, but returned later reporting the weather too much for her.

A Southampton tug has been here for three weeks waiting for more favourable weather. The whole navigable channel at Padstow is said to have greatly altered of late. However, if one keeps to the instructions at Stepper Point and on entering Padstow Bay hugs the shore on starboard all the way, a yacht is quite safe at anything over half-tide. Paid a visit to the boatbuilder's yard in Padstow. He had just finished a nice piece of work, a sixteen-foot yacht's dinghy.

*18th July*. Heavy rain in morning, wind WSW. At 9.30 a.m. it cleared when we left Padstow Pool. Outside fairly big seas were running, but as the uneven bottom around Trevose Head itself and its position on the coast is accountable for much of the troubled waters, we decided to push through in hope of more normal conditions further SW. Happily, when well clear of the headland, the forecast proved correct, the weather became much more comfortable, as VAITI rapidly opened up the various points to which we were just sufficiently close to make out the distinguishing features.

In 1927, S.R. Brown used Padstow as a harbour of refuge for his 6-ton Falmouth quay punt VALA.

*17th August*. Bar. 29.9. . . Wind light; kept on starboard tack; sighted land 2 p.m. As the barometer was falling fast and the sky was threatening, decided to make for Padstow, which we could fetch with the help of a short tack. 87 miles by log. We found no difficulty in entering with a flood tide, the ebb makes the danger; we clung close to

Stepper Point, and anchored in Hawker's Cove just inside the Doom Bar 7.30 p.m.

The sands shift continually. There used to be a passage past Hawker's Cove up to the town, now it is a cul-de-sac. This decreases the rush of tide and improves the anchorage. The deep water lies close to the shore; there is only room for a boat to swing clear of the rocks if the wind is on shore and she is not moored. We moored just ahead of the steam lifeboat[1] so felt safe.

*18th August.* Bar. 29.65. It blew hard from the SE in the night and the rocks looked very close at low water, but they are steep to; later the wind went round to SW and dropped; storm cone hoisted.

*19th August.* Bar. 29.9. Wind NNW, strong, sea rough, breaking heavily on the bar; ship lying quiet.

French crabber came in well reefed and anchored in fine style; the locals say she is very often here; five men in crew, all young and clean looking in red and blue trousers, etc. She is a fine boat with high bow and great beam drawing nearly ten feet, roller reefing mainsail, and no engine.

Explored coast on foot, and ate enormous Cornish teas.

*20th August.* Bar 29.32. Wind SW, approaching gale force; bright intervals. Walked along cliff to see the waves breaking on the rocks, and felt glad we were on land.

*21st August.* Bar. 29.7. Storm cone lowered. Wind SSW, moderate. Started 6.30 a.m. all plain sail; no bother with bar. Heavy swell outside; 7.45 a.m. wind increasing rapidly, and veering to WSW dead in our teeth; 8.30 a.m. had more than enough; nearest port to windward St Ives, so ran back to Padstow, anchoring 9.30 a.m.

Heavy swell from N. all day, causing breakers all over the harbour at low water; Hawker's Cove quiet, but the broken water within fifty yards of anchorage to the E. Storm cone hoisted again.

*22nd August.* Bar. 29.6. Wind SW strong, dropping by night.

*23rd August.* Bar. 29.9. Wind NW. Storm cone still hoisted.

8.30 a.m. Under way, wind light; crossed bar at low water. We did not keep close enough to the rocks, so bumped in the trough of the swell; quanted over with the spinnaker boom, only 8 feet of water close to the rocks, 20 yards distance about. The shallowest spot is just opposite the old hut where the capstans are for hauling in boats.

Commander R. D. Graham RN was one of the real stalwarts of the RCC. In 1930 he took his 7-ton cutter EMANUEL to Newquay and Padstow.

On the 15th [September] we sailed round the land inside the Longships. . . We anchored in St Ives Bay in 10 fathoms at 8.30 p.m. Weighing before dawn next morning we sailed to Newquay and secured alongside E jetty at 9.30 a.m. Here, as usual, the mate found friends. A considerable run comes into this harbour, and it is necessary to secure with two heavy hawsers bow and stern.

For our passage to Padstow it may be worth reproducing my log as written at the time.

*19th September.* Turned out at 2.45 a.m., called mate and started preparing for sea. As we had a leg[2] out and two heavy hawsers fore and aft this was a long job. Having got all ready the jib was hoisted and the forward ropes let go so that the yacht's bows swung round. Then slipping aft I hoisted the mainsail and we forged ahead, fouling some rowing boats moored to the quay. These we managed to push clear, and luffing we sailed through the entrance. This all sounds simple enough, but in the pitch dark with a considerable run coming into the harbour, was not quite so simple as it sounds. To add to our discomfort heavy rain began just before we slipped.

Outside we found the wind strong from the S. and increasing as we left the harbour. At times Trevose red light showed through the rain, but with EMANUEL tearing along under her full mainsail and rather out of hand, it was impossible to steer a compass course. A gybe was necessary, as the Quies rocks, a mile off Trevose, lay right on our course. It was impossible to judge our distance from Trevose, or to see more than a few yards ahead; so I told the mate to steer as near north as she could while I hastily shortened sail (I had judged it necessary to hoist the full mainsail as the wind had been light and fluky in the harbour). I lowered the foresail and put four turns in the mainsail (middle jib had been set). It was now blowing a heavy gale, and mate had all she could do to hold the EMANUEL to her course. Gradually rounding Trevose we hauled to the wind on the starboard tack. Day broke about 6.30 a.m. There was a surprisingly big sea considering that the wind was off the land, and I thought it as well to secure the mate with the fall of the main sheet. I hove-to for a few minutes to get a bearing of Trevose and to study the chart. Both of us, of course, were drenched, and I could get no wetter when I reefed the foresail to be in readiness, as I expected the jib to blow away.

When somewhat past Trevose weather cleared for brief intervals, and some minutes later Padstow entrance showed up clearly a couple of miles to windward.

At this moment the wind veered to WSW, so that only one short tack was necessary to clear Newland, whence the wind easing a trifle, we could fetch the entrance. Passing Stepper Point we had very short tacks to keep in the channel which, near LW lies close under the land. We missed stays once. The jib had been set foul of the forestay, and I could not bear to come to our anchorage just under the coastguard in such a slovenly state. Accordingly I hoisted the foresail and lowered the jib, but the latter fouled half-way as the mate put the helm down to go about. The jib taking aback prevented her head from coming into the wind. I pulled the jib down and, jumping aft to the tiller, just got enough way on her as her bowsprit almost overhung the rocks. With a fair chance EMANUEL never misses stays and round she came. In the excitement and relief, however, I carried on too far on the other tack and felt her touch on the sand, but she answered her helm, and after a few seconds pause the foresail took aback and we were off, with a flurry of sand showing in the water astern. . .

We anchored off Hawkers Cove a little astern of the lifeboat, and had a long job clearing up below as the cabin was full of spars, hawsers, etc. Also, the money drawer had upset, and the mate would not allow me to dry half our medicine chest, i.e., the roll of lint. . .

We got the kedge all ready for letting go and hung a sinker on the cable, veering to our extreme limit of 30 fathoms. Although the weather shore was but three cables distant, there was enough lop to cause EMANUEL to tug at her cable. I also put extra lashings round the mainsail to reduce windage. At 1.30 p.m. I am writing this log, rolling somewhat as the flood tide sheers us broadside to the lop. The south cone flies ashore. We had seen this last night, but thought it applied to the gale just passed.

We are very glad to be out of it, but if our cable parts I don't see how the kedge warp can hold us, and the sea may have the laugh of us yet. We sit and wait, the mate supremely indifferent. The breakers on the bar to leeward are a fine, but terrifying sight. I had let a couple of turns out of the mainsail to beat up the channel, and with the present wind it will be a job to reef and set the mainsail in time if cable parts.

My log ends here, and except for a few rough notes as to times, the remainder of our cruise is written from memory.

---

[1] The steam lifeboat was the RNLI tug HELEN PEELE, approaching the end of her long service at Padstow. In 1929 she moved to the Clyde and was converted into a yacht-tender.

[2] A wooden leg is often rigged when in harbours which dry out at low tide to prevent the vessel from falling over away from the quay.

As the afternoon wore on I became seriously anxious for the safety of the ship. With high water some slight swell came into the anchorage. Half a mile to leeward big rollers were tumbling on the bar in a foaming line of white. There was no reason why our cable should part, and evidently the anchor was not going to drag, but if either of these misfortunes should occur, particularly at night, we should have been on to the bar and broken up in quite a few minutes.

It was quite out of the question to lay out the kedge to windward. It seemed unwise to remain in the yacht for the night, and we were discussing landing on the rocks under the coastguard station. There was a spot a little astern of us, and thus to leeward, that I felt confident we could reach in the dinghy. Before we started to cast loose the boat I saw the coastguard semaphoring to us. Unfortunately I have forgotten this, though I still remember — more-or-less — the morse alphabet, and with the mate to prompt me from a signal card we managed to effect communication. We were first informed that we should be aground at LW. This was not the case, but the coastguard officer was evidently alarmed for our safety. There were some fishermen's boats hauled up on the shore, and I asked if he could get one manned to take us ashore. The reply was to ask if we would like the lifeboat manned for us. After some hesitation I agreed. In half an hour's time we saw the crew hurrying across the fields.

They put off in a small boat to the lifeboat and a few minutes later the latter slipped her moorings, and took us in tow and pulled us about 50 yards ahead of where we had dropped our anchor. I let go both anchors and the lifeboatmen took out a line to the shore. We were now securely moored in perfect safety, and incidentally slept soundly through the night. At midnight the glass touched 28.50.

We were detained at Padstow by wind and fog until the 23rd. We took the opportunity of visiting the lifeboat, a new twin-screw motor craft of the latest model.

By 1935, the RCC Journal's index begins with Aden and ends with West Indies and thereafter home waters are less in evidence than ocean passages.

The present scene on the Camel estuary could scarcely be in greater contrast to the scene in, say, the 1930s. Certainly in the summer months there are many more people on the water than at any time in the past.

On the top half of any tide in the summer you will see dozens of board-sailors skimming across the estuary, water skiers in action, classes of planing dinghies racing, Malibu boards off Newquay and Polzeath, snorkelling round the rocks of Pentire Point, plastic kayaks playing in the surf and scuba divers setting out for some coastal wreck in a powerful inflatable boat not unlike the inshore lifeboats which are ready to go to the rescue of anyone in trouble. Modern inventions and protective clothing have enabled us to develop a much more intimate relationship with the sea than was possible before the Second World War. Gone are the days when the sailor preferred not to be able to swim, since that would merely prolong the agony.

Since 1989, the inner harbour at Padstow has been turned into a floating dock so that vessels arriving or leaving within about two hours of high water can sail in or out, and those staying remain afloat at all times. This has made Padstow a more desirable destination for cruising yachtsmen, (and it seems, for commercial fishing vessels also) and the number of vessels using Padstow has increased dramatically. The old-timers doubtless feel that the town is in danger of losing its character and becoming a combination of Blackpool and Disneyland. Certainly the character of Padstow is changing fast but if there is noise and congestion, it is the fault of the wheeled traffic on land and not of the seagoing fraternity without which the place would be meaningless.

From the sailor's point of view, the ability to sail in and moor alongside and stay afloat in the shelter of the inner harbour must be compared with the experiences of the three visiting yachts described earlier.

The Rock Sailing Club was formed in 1938, and raced the Rock one-design 12-ft dinghies, gunter rigged with short masts so they could pass under the iron railway bridge at the mouth of Little Petherick Creek. Immediately after the war they raced in airborne lifeboats, but it was the influx of modern fast planing dinghies which really made the club take off. Since 1955 they have had the picturesque old warehouse on the quay at Rock as their headquarters. Also in 1955 the Padstow Sailing Club was formed, despite the comment by ancient mariners that the estuary was far too dangerous for such goings-on.

The Rock club has gone from strength to strength and has become an important venue for the national meetings of important classes such as Wayfarers, Kestrels, International Canoes and Hobie Catamarans. The Padstow Harbour Commissioners have not been slow to benefit from all this activity, as witness a notice at Rock which reads: 'PHC HARBOUR DUES MUST BE PAID ON SAILBOARDS'.

So sailing clubs thrive, but there is no yacht club. Perhaps the new marina-like facilities in the inner harbour at Padstow will lead to one.

In the yard lists at the end of the shipbuilding chapter will be found a series of trimarans built between 1965 and 1969 by the Multihull Construction Co. Ltd, personified by Derek Kelsall and Pat Patterson. These vessels made a special contribution to yachting and there is something special to be said about each of them in addition to the technical details in the list of yachts which follows. TRIDENT I was the first to be built and immediately made her mark by sailing out to Mombasa. She was sold to French owners in 1976 and it is impossible to follow her career thereafter, probably due to name changes which happen so frequently to sponsored racing yachts now-a-days. TRIPTYCH was next, a cruising trimaran designed by Piver, and cruise she certainly did, being owned successively in Grenada, West Indies and then in Rangiputa, New Zealand. Then in 1966 came TORIA designed by Kelsall, and she revolutionised the philosophy of multihull design and won numerous races later under the name GANCIA GIRL; then TRIFLE the winner of even more races, owned by Major-General Farrant. She was the first modern multihull to be in the Royal Yacht Squadron, but like TRIDENT I, sold to French owners, which is a compliment in itself because they have become quite dominant in long-distance multihull races. TANITH and CORNISH CLIPPER complete the remarkable series, both designed by Kelsall, as are all the others apart from TRIPTYCH.

## Padstow Yachts

The following list includes British registered yachts, built, registered or owned in Padstow (including outports) and other vessels found in *Lloyd's Yacht Register* or of special interest. Some of them have fishing numbers.

ALIE later MARU q.v.
AQUA NOMAD *ex* RNLB BASSETT-GREEN, ON 184445. Built 1951, Cowes, Groves & Gutteridge, Liverpool type motor lifeboat, 3 net tons, 35.5 x 10 x 7 ft, 2 x 20 b.h.p.. engines. Padstow No. 2 lifeboat 1951-1962, Poole 1962-'9. Sold 1969, renamed AQUA NOMAD in private ownership.

**ARIES R.**, *ex* RNLB PRINCESS MARY, ON 161304. Built 1929, East Cowes, Saunders Roe Ltd. Barnett type motor lifeboat, 15.71 net tons, 61.4 x 15.0 x 7.2 ft 2 x 80 b.h.p. Weyburn engines. Padstow lifeboat 1929-1952. Sold 1952 and renamed ARIES R. Twin screw motor yacht 2 x 6 cyl. Foden diesels fitted 1952, each 120 b.h.p.

In 1954 the ARIES R. became the first motor boat to cross the Atlantic both ways without the assistance of sails. She was well suited to face the rigours of the voyage because of her lifeboat design and service, during which time she saved 48 lives and assisted numerous vessels. C. Harcourt-Smith had her specially fitted out by Toughs of Teddington and with a crew of four she reached New York in 33 days and came back in 23. Her name is often given as plain ARIES.

**BLUE FALCON OF BUDE**, ON 359298. Built 1973, Littlehampton, 6 tons gross and net. Auxiliary fibreglass yacht. Registered at Padstow 1976. Owner Malcolm Deare.

**BLUE LOBSTER**, ON 302455. Built Emsworth 1965. A wooden auxiliary yacht of 4 net tons, 25.9 8.6 4.1. Registered at Padstow but owned in Yorkshire.

**BLUEBELL**, ON 84983. Builder unknown, but rebuilt 1901, Padstow by John Edyvane with sails by Courtenay. 5.68 net reg. tons. A cutter yacht 28.5 ft long, registered at Padstow, owned by Edward C. P. Sanford of St Endellion. Stranded Greenaway Rocks, 6th August, 1908.

**CAMELLA**, ON 359260. Built 1975, Waterlooville (Hampshire) by Westerly Marine. 5 net tons. Auxiliary Fibreglass Sloop Yacht, 26.0 ft long. Centaur class designed by Laurent Giles. Owner 1975 Col. Thomas Hardy CBE, MC, TD, DL, of Bingham, Notts; 1985 A. Burt, Wadebridge. Registered at Padstow.

**CORNEILLE** see MEDEA.

**CORNISH CHOUGH**, ON 342545. Built 1972, Pietarsaari, Finland. 10 net tons. A fibreglass motor yacht. Owner 1972, William J. Rogers of Newquay. Registered at Falmouth.

**CORNISH CLIPPER**, ON 335205. Built 1969 Wadebridge, Multihull Construction Co. Ltd. 10.52 net tons. A sloop-rigged fibreglass trimaran yacht. 37.0 ft x 20.6 ft depth 3.0 ft draught, with two outboard motors. Registered Fowey.

**DE MARNI**, ON 340371. Built 1970, Topsham & Rock. 2 net tons. A fibreglass auxiliary yacht. Registered Plymouth.

**DEOLI**, ON 166956. Built 1905, Porthleven, R. Kitto & Sons. 7.3 net tons. A wooden auxiliary twin-screw yawl-rigged yacht with two Bergius engines. Registered Padstow in 1938 when owned by Alex G. Hemsley of Rock, and still listed in 1976.

**DOZMARE**, ON 145661. Built 1899, Falmouth, T. Gray, rebuilt 1924 by R. S. Burt & Son. Altered 1927, Plymouth, by Hawke. Built as a Falmouth quay punt. A wooden cutter rigged aux. yacht fitted with an Ailsa Craig 4 cyl. engine in 1924 and 19 b.h.p. Stuart Turner in 1960. Rigged as a yawl at times. Registered, Padstow 1924 when owned by Francis Randolph Cyril Coleridge, gent. of Bodmin.

An American yacht with this name might be greeted with the response 'I'll bet she does', but in fact she is named after Dozmary pool of Arthurian legend on Bodmin Moor, which is at present a rather disappointing pond.

**FEU FOLLET**, later MARU q.v.

**FOLLIE**, later NAVETTE q.v.

**FRANGIPANI**, ON 184065. Built 1957, Brixham, J. W. & A. Upham Ltd. 4.45 net tons. Aux. sloop yacht. 8 b.h.p Stuart-Turner engine. Registered at Brixham. Listed here because of ownership by Nigel T. Tangye of Glendorgal Hotel, Newquay in the early 1960s (see also SPRAY OF GLENDORGAL).

**GANCIA GIRL** ex TORIA q.v.

**GAY SALAR**, ON 309495. Built 1968, Wallasea Island, Marina. Reinforced Plastics Ltd and Essex Yacht Builders Ltd. 9.99 net tons. Aux. ketch rigged fibreglass yacht designed by Laurent Giles, with 62 h.p. Perkins diesel. Registered Weymouth, owned in 1970s by D. A. Hayman of Newquay.

**GENEEN**, ON 145665. Built 1929, East Looe by A. Collins. 2.24 net tons. Auxiliary lugger yacht with 10 h.p. Brooke Marine engine. Registered at Padstow in 1938 by Frederick H. Cory of Chesham, Bucks.

**GIPSY**, ON 95737. Built 1894, Padstow, by Rawle. 18.93 reg. tons wooden cutter yacht. Registered at Fowey 1899 but not surviving World War I.

**GIRL EVA** built 1912 Porthleven, R. Kitto & Sons. 7 tons Thames measurement 1935, owned by R. W., P. A. S., and J. R. David. Home port Padstow (moved after World War II to Bosham, Burlesdon and Dartmouth). Wooden yacht rigged successively as yawl and auxiliary gaff ketch.

**GREBE II**, ON 164199. Built 1935, Gosport, Camper & Nicholsons Ltd. 3.75 net tons. Wooden auxiliary Bermuda sloop. Registered Portsmouth and included here because owned by Miles Bowker of Newquay in the 1970s.

**GULL** ex RNLB JOHN WILLIAM DUDLEY. Built 1900, Thames Ironworks. 3 net tons. 35.0 x 8.5 ft, self-righting lifeboat. Served as Newquay lifeboat 1918-1920. Sold 1926 and renamed GULL. Noted at Littlehampton in 1966.

**HERON V.** *ex* RNLB ADMIRAL SIR GEORGE BACK. Built 1903 Thames Ironworks. 4 tons, 35.0 x 8. 5 ft, self-righting lifeboat, served at Lizard 1903-1978 and Newquay 1920-1934. Sold 1936 and renamed HERON V. as yacht. Noted at Sharpness in 1972.

**IAGO**, ON 306381. Built 1964, Bergen, Norway by Lars Hausberg. 5.14 net tons. Wooden motor cruiser with 56 b.h.p. Parsons diesel. Registered in Brixham in 1964 and owned since the mid-1970s by Peter S. Delf of Padstow.

**JOANDEL**, ON 302451. Built 1960, Bideford by Blackmore & Sons. 15 net, 38 gross tons. A motor launch built for a London doctor and registered at Padstow. In 1963 she was transferred to Southampton by the Southampton Harbour Board and renamed SHB NEPTUNE. In the 1980s she was a private motor yacht on the Thames.

**JOLLIVET**, ON 336201. Built 1968, Plympton, 4 net tons. Fibreglass auxiliary yacht. Registered Falmouth 1969, owned since mid-1970s by James G. French, Newquay.

**JOLLY ROBBER**, ON 366925. Built 1977 Rock, 4 net tons, fibreglass yacht. Registered Portsmouth 1977.

**JUNE**, ON 145663. Builder unknown. 3 net tons. A wooden auxiliary ketch yacht 25.6 ft long with a 10 b.h.p. Brooke Marine petrol motor. Registered at Padstow in 1935 and was owned successively by L.H.L. Saunders of Trevone, N. Berry Gill, and T. G. Burgess of Camelford. *Lloyd's Yacht Register* describes her as a yawl, and the Padstow ship register describes her as whaler-sterned. JUNE served as an auxiliary patrol vessel in World War II.

**KALOMA**, ON 357345. Built 1972 at Littlehampton, 4 net tons. A fibreglass yacht registered at Padstow, and owned by A. M. Blood, Stratton, Bude.

**LADY CLARISSA**, ON 308638. Built 1969, Southampton, 3 net tons. A fibreglass yacht registered at Padstow.

**LADY CLARISSA II**, ON 335580. Built 1971, Nelson, Lancashire, 5 net tons. A fibreglass yacht registered at Padstow and owned initially by Dennis C. Townrow, St Issey.

**LINDSAY CHASE**, ON 166960, see STEPPER POINT.

**MANWELLA**, ON 162910. Built Littlehampton, W. Osborne &

YACHTS AND SMALL BOATS

Co., 3 net tons. A 25 ft wooden motor cruiser with a Buick 6 cyl. petrol motor, 20 b.h.p Registered at Littlehampton and then Plymouth but owned by Stephen B. Brabyn of Padstow after World War II.

**MARGUERITE**, built 1906, St Ives, W. Paynter. 7 tons Thames measurement. A wooden cutter yacht 26.3 ft long owned by A. St G. Sargeaunt of Padstow before World War I.

**MARIDA**, ON 334322. Built 1966, Looe, 4 net tons. Described in *Mercantile Navy List* as wooden yacht with motor. Registered at Falmouth, with fishing number FH 218 and owned (late '70s) by Richard A. Birch, Newquay. Perhaps better described as MFV yacht looking like a small tosher.

**MARU**, *ex* ALIE *ex* MIRANDA *ex* FEU FOLLET. Built 1893, Paimpol, L. Laboreur. 7 tons Thames measurement. A wooden cutter yacht 26.4 ft long of Plymouth, Falmouth and then (*c.* 1910) Padstow, at which stage she was owned by the Newquay shipowner R. J. Hockin.

**MEDEA**, ON 119160. Built 1904, Linthouse, Glasgow by Alex. Stephens & Sons Ltd. 57.17 net, 111.84 gross, 137 Thames measurement tons in 1904 and in 1964 when registered at Padstow. 109.7 x 16.7 x 9.4 steel screw steam yacht, schooner rigged.

MEDEA was built as a steam yacht for a Scottish laird by a famous Clyde yard, but in the First World War was taken into the French Navy and converted into the patrol vessel CORNEILLE or CORNEILLE I. She was given depth charges, a 75 mm gun and even an observation balloon. After demobilisation she entered the Royal Yacht Squadron in 1921, with her name MEDEA restored.

In World War II she joined the Royal Navy as a barrage balloon vessel in 1941; the following year she was handed over to the Free Norwegians and became a base ship for their submarines. After the war she was registered first at Colchester, then in 1964 at Padstow, owned by N. P. S. Millar, retired master mariner of Harlyn, and she became a familiar and graceful feature of Padstow harbour. In 1970 her register closed with the note 'sold to Sweden', but later that year she was bought by Americans, sailed to California and reconditioned. In 1973 she was handed over to the Maritime Association of San Diego, where she remains on display and in operation, the last steam yacht of her type in her original condition.

**MIRANDA** later MARU. q.v.

**MORVOREN**, ON 149517. Built 1927, Falmouth, R. S. Burt & Son. 4.12 net tons, wooden auxiliary yawl yacht, 32.0 ft long, with a 2 cyl. Thornycroft engine of 2 b.h.p. Owned in the 1970s by Henry A. Major of Newquay.

**NAVETTE**, *ex* FOLLIE *ex* RNLB JHW, ON 162591. Built 1931, Cowes, J. Samuel White, a self-righting motor lifeboat. JHW served at Lytham 1931-39 and Padstow 1939-47. Sold 1948 and converted into a ketch-rigged auxiliary yacht renamed FOLLIE and registered at Maldon, later renamed NAVETTE and registered at London.

**PANDORA** of POLRUAN, ON 335202. Built 1969, Woolston, Hampshire. 4 net tons, fibreglass yacht with motor, registered at Fowey but owned by Rae A. Jenkin, Delabole.

**POPPY**, built 1907, Newquay, Clemens. 7 tons Thames measurement. A wooden auxiliary lugger yacht 25.6 ft long, later rigged as an auxiliary cutter.

**PRIDE OF THE WEST**, built *c.* 1895. A Sennen Cove crabber taken over in 1936 by a Newquay yachtsman.

**SHB NEPTUNE**, ON 302451. see JOANDEL.

**SEA ANTELOPE**, ON 335579. Built 1971, Southampton, Seaglass Ltd and Southern Boatbuilding Co. Ltd, Woolston. 9.97 net tons. Fibreglass auxiliary cutter yacht, 36.0 ft long overall, with 42 b.h.p.

Mercedes-Benz oil engine. Registered at Padstow but with Mylor as home port.

**SHAMROCK**. On 6th September, 1903, the Padstow lifeboat saved the Padstow yacht SHAMROCK with three people aboard.

**SILVER SPRAY**, built 1903, Padstow, Cowl, 7 tons Thames measurement. Wooden cutter yacht, 29.9 ft long; fitted with Amanco 1 cyl. petrol engine in 1933. Home port was Padstow before World War I, then Plymouth. She survived World War II.

**SPRAY OF GLENDORGAL**, ON 307530. Built 1965, Falmouth, Falmouth Boat Construction Ltd, 6.85 net tons. Wooden auxiliary ketch yacht, 30.0 ft long with 4 cyl. Perkins oil engine 20 b.h.p. Registered at Falmouth; owned by Porth Markets Ltd (N. Tangye) of Newquay. Nigel Tangye, who had previously owned FRANGIPANI, travelled and wrote books about Cornwall in her.

**SPRIGGAN**, ON 184158. Built 1950, Woodbridge, 3 net tons, a wooden motor boat 22.4 ft long with a 4 b.h.p. engine, owned by Frank Odgers of Porth in the late 1970s.

**STAR OF GWENT**, ON 58245. Built 1867, Padstow, 15.52 reg. tons. Wooden cutter, 37.0 ft x 13.3 ft x 7.1 ft. Registered at Padstow 1867, owner Thomas Nichols, St Columb, gent. Re-registered Cardiff 1868, owner J. P. Lewis of Cardiff followed by other Cardiff owners. It seems likely that she was a pilot cutter type built as a yacht but used later by pilots. A wreck off Morte Point, 12th April, 1890 was listed as STAR OF GHENT, but seems likely to be her.

**STEPPER POINT**, ON 166960. Built 1960 Looe by H. Pearn & Sons Ltd. 9.39 net tons 37.0 (overall), 13.0 x 6.2. A wooden triple-screw motor cruiser with three General Motors diesels, built for J. C. F. Prideaux-Brune. She was registered at Padstow, and remained so when in 1962 she was sold to R. J. C. Motors of Sussex, and renamed LINDSAY CHASE. Sold to Ansamo SA of Panama 1965.

**STORMCOCK**. The Padstow yacht STORMCOCK was assisted by the Clovelly lifeboat 13th July, 1946. She is probably the vessel which served as an auxiliary patrol boat at Padstow in World War II.

**SYMMETRIA**, ON 364836. Built 1975, Newquay by P. Staffieri. 9.44 net tons. A wooden auxiliary cutter yacht 37.7 ft long. Registered at Falmouth and owned by Pepini Staffieri of Newquay.

**TANITH**, ON 308637. Built 1968, Wadebridge, Multihull Construction Co. Ltd. 10.52 net tons. A GRP sloop-rigged trimaran with an outboard motor registered at Padstow.

**TARION**, ON 334985. Built 1968, Littlehampton, David Hillyard, 16.78 net tons. A wooden auxiliary ketch yacht 42.0 ft in overall length, registered at Littlehampton and owned in late 1970s by Drs William and Anne Baird of Port Gaverne.

**TIR NA N'OG**, ON 145664. Built 1896 at Gorran, Cornwall. 8.68 net tons. 37.0 x 12.4 x 6.8. A wooden vessel registered at Padstow in 1935 as a Bermudan cutter and given a 2 cyl. Bolinder oil engine in 1937. She was owned by Bernard Deburca of Bodmin, but went to Scottish owners after the war.

**TORIA**. Built 1966, Wadebridge, Multihull Construction Co. Ltd. 42.0 x 22.7 x 7.0 draught 4.3 ft. A sloop-rigged centreboard trimaran with Padstow as home port which won the Round Britain race in 1966 and many others. Renamed GANCIA GIRL in 1970.

**TREVONE**, ON 145662, *ex* EDMUND HARVEY. Built 1901, Blackwall, Thames Engineering Co. Ltd, G. L. Watson design. 1.68 net tons. A twin-screw ketch-rigged motor yacht 41.8 ft long which served as Padstow sailing and pulling lifeboat until 1929 and was then converted and fitted with two Bergius paraffin motors. These were replaced by two Kelvin diesels in 1969. She remains registered at Padstow, but has had a series of owners elsewhere.

**TRIDENT I**, ON 308634. Built 1965, Wadebridge, Multihull

Construction Co. Ltd. 23.63 net tons. An auxiliary ketch rigged trimaran yacht with 47 b.h.p. Perkins oil engine. Registered at Padstow but home port Mombasa until sold to French owners 1975.

**TRIFLE**, ON 334876. Built 1967, Wadebridge, Multihull Construction Co. Ltd. 9.91 net tons. A GRP sloop rigged trimaran racing yacht registered at Poole until sold to French owners.

**TRINITY BUOY YACHT.** Built 1791 on River Thames, lengthened 1797. 118 tons. A snow owned by Rawlins in 1801 and trading Bristol-Wales. (*Lloyd's Register* 1801). The vessel is included in this section because she is (like JOSEPHINE) termed a yacht. Rawlins was an unusual name in 1801, but there is no certainty that it was the great Padstow family that owned her. A later TRINITY BUOY YACHT helped build the Bishop's Rock Lighthouse, but Trinity House have been unable to find any record of the eighteenth century ship.

**TRIPTYCH**, ON 320966. Built 1965, Wadebridge, Multihull Construction Co. Ltd. 75 net tons, 87 gross tons, 64 ft x 32 ft.

Wooden cruising trimaran. 'Empress' class designed by Piver. Registered in Ottawa and owned initially in Grenada, West Indies, and then in Rangiputa, New Zealand. Still listed thus in Canadian Government's List of Ships 1991, but it seems likely that, as with the British Mercantile Navy List, entries are sometimes perpetuated if no changes are notified by the owner.

**VIKING.** Built 1948 Port Mellon, Percy Mitchell. 14 tons Thames measurement. Wooden auxiliary yawl rigged yacht, 33.8 ft long. Home port Padstow, first owned by Harold Capes, Bodmin, then by Conway Clifford.

**WHIZZ-KID.** In recent times this 26 ft aux. sloop offered day sailing from Padstow, but she also goes further afield on sailing holidays, and has been seen in the Scilly Isles. Owner Ted Finch of Rock.

**WILMA P.J.**, ON 334350. Built 1966, Slagelse, 4 net tons. A fibreglass motor yacht registered at Falmouth, owned by Derek Hayman of Newquay.

*GALIOTE À BOMBE* OR BOMB KETCH

# 19  SEINE COMPANIES & FISHING VESSELS

*The Pilchards are come and hevva be heard,*
*The town from the top to the bottom be stirred.*

## Traditional

THE fishing vessels of Padstow, Portquin, Port Isaac, Port Gaverne, Boscastle, Bude and St Columb have put to sea for hundreds of years to meet local requirements.

There is a myth that the fleet from Portquin was lost in some dreadful storm, and the widows and children left the village uninhabited thereafter. Certainly most of the primitive cottages of Portquin were left to rot over a period of many decades, but no evidence has been found of the great calamity. Tragedies and losses have always accompanied the fisheries, and as will be seen, they continue today, but all the evidence is that the population of Portquin slipped away progressively as the pilchard fishery declined in the late nineteenth century, and as in the rest of Cornwall, emigration to the Americas was commonplace.

The seine companies of the pilchard fishery were one of the most distinctive contributions of Cornwall to the country's fishing industry. Their origins are lost in the mists of time, but by 1594 they were sufficiently important to feature in an Act of Parliament (35 Eliz. c. xi) and they continued to grow in importance until about 1875 after which, despite some good years, there was a steady decline.

Pilchards used to arrive off the Cornish coast in July, coming from the West; they are small fish of the herring family weighing less than half a pound. They came close inshore round Mounts Bay in July, but by September and October had worked their way along the North coast of Cornwall to Newquay and Port Isaac which were for centuries the principal pilchard ports of North Cornwall. The season was generally over by December. Sean or sein (and sometimes seine, according to the local custom) fishing was undertaken basically as follows. When shoals were seen approaching the shore 'the cry was raised' and the master seiner went to direct operations from the cliff top, or sometimes from a small gig called a lurker. He guided the seine boat (a beamy boat carrying the seine net) so that it encircled the shoal with the net. Another similar boat carrying the tuck-seine net and warps and ground tackle followed, and was indeed called the follower or vollyer. Together they manoeuvred the encircled shoal of fish into the shallow water with footropes on the seabed, and anchored it securely. Sometimes the tuck-seine net was needed to complete the encirclement, but its final purpose was to bail fish out of the captured shoal as required by the shore party. There were numerous variations and elaborations of this basic procedure. The fish could be kept alive in the encircling seine net for several days whilst the traditional 'bulking' treatment took place in the fish cellar. The cellar was partly filled with alternate layers of salt and fish, the whole 'bulk' being then pressed with heavy weights,

draining off oil and blood. The fish were then washed and packed in hogsheads (barrels) and pressed again. The oil, known as train oil, was sold separately. Some of the catches were smoked, especially those for export to Mediterranean countries where they were known as fumados or, in Cornwall as fermades.

In September 1860 the following advertisement appeared in the *West Briton*:

*For Sale at Port Gaverne*

The RASHLEIGH sean, consisting of two stop seans one tuck sean with tarpaulins, graspers, and mooring ropes complete. Also five boats, oars, spars, masts and sails. Washing trays, flaskets, salt maunds, press poles, bucklers and press stones, etc. etc. One hundred tons of Liverpool salt, together with the extensive and commodious cellars, leasehold, now held on two lives.

Graspers were, I believe, grapnel anchors; flaskets were the long narrow baskets carried by the fishwives who hawked the fish 'to the country'.

The *West Briton* reported on 7th November, 1845:

Newquay. On Sunday last 'the cry was raised'. The following seins had varying success: SPECULATION, ROSE, ACTIVE, FLY, GOOD INTENT, CONCORD, TOBY, UNITY. Several thousand hogsheads were caught. Many fish were sold to the country at about 2s.6d. per flasket.'

A flasket would hold about 300 fish weighing about 75 lbs, and the fishwives who bought them would have had the arduous task of crying their wares for several miles. Further reports from the *West Briton* follow:

*30th October, 1873.* The MOTHER IVEY's Company have again commenced to land fish from their seins. The CATACLEW Company's sein shot on Sunday afternoon, but missed the fish owing to being short-handed, ten of the seiner's crew (including the leading hands) declining to work on Sunday.

*20th October, 1890.* Pilchards are again making their appearance in the Bristol Channel after an absence of close on fifteen years. Fishermen on the Padstow hills and Mr Thomas Hellyer of Harlyn have lately seen acres of fish in the bays. Unfortunately, the seine fishing for these fish has long been abandoned at Padstow, but it is hoped that efforts will be made to secure some, as it would be a great help to the working classes in the winter.

But this influx of pilchards proved to be a flash in the pan, and the decline continued.

The following excerpt from the *West Briton*, 14th February, 1871 shows how steamers were already taking the bulk of the pilchard export trade but leaving the smaller ports to be served by sailing ships.

The only two cargoes of pilchards sent to the Mediterranean this season by sailing vessels were carried in the A1 clipper schooners belonging to Mr William Luke, merchant, of Charlestown. The MARIA LOUISE, 98 tons register, with 662½ hogsheads sailed from Newquay 29th December, 1870 and arrived at Naples 12th January, 1871. The running bowsprit schooner RACER, 61 tons register, with 442 hogsheads sailed from St Ives on the evening of 4th January and arrived at Genoa on 18th January, making the passage in the remarkably quick time of less than 14 days, believed to be the fastest passage for a vessel of her size on record.

Other local seine companies not already mentioned include HOPE, SPY, TETHY, TREFFRY and UNION, all of Newquay, VENICE and CAROLINE of Portquin, CAROLINE, FOX, GOOD INTENT, INDUSTRY, MARY, NEW, PROVIDENCE and UNION all of Port Isaac, and FOX and LIBERTY of neighbouring Port Gaverne. Boscastle and Harlyn had companies known, apparently, only by their location.

Cyril Noall in *Cornish Seines and Seiners* gives a history of the pilchard fisheries.

Although the decline in the seine fishery was swift (there was only one company left, at Newquay, by 1907), the drift fishery for pilchards which took place only slightly further off shore, remained viable into the twentieth century. In 1907 it was reported that 'the Mounts Bay ports have about 170 pilchard drivers [drifters] and there is a goodly fleet of about 60 at Port Isaac largely engaged in pilchard driving in the autumn.' The Port Isaac boats were small half-decked or undecked luggers; there was no room at Port Isaac to haul them out of harm's way in the winter storms, so once the pilchard driving was finished, they were taken round to Padstow to be laid up for the worst of the winter.

This same fleet of small luggers also partook in the autumn herring fishery off Padstow. Cornwall marks the southern limit of the herring's habitat, but the autumn fishery off the North Cornish coast was a well-established institution, which benefited greatly from the opening of the railways.

The *West Briton*, 28th October, 1897. Large herring catches at Port Isaac
Port Isaac Road Station (London & South Western Railway) was last week a scene of great bustle. One hundred and fifty tons of herrings were brought from Port Isaac by carts and wagons and sent to Exeter, Birmingham, London, etc.

It may be that the herring drifters from East Anglia, following the herring, discovered the other potential for fishing off North Cornwall and towards the end of the nineteenth century established what was to become Padstow's main fishing activity for many years, that is to say, the spring trawling for soles and other flat fish in what had previously been largely neglected waters. Every year there was an influx of boats from Great Yarmouth and, especially, Lowestoft into Padstow in the early spring, and joined by Brixham trawlers and others, they based themselves in Padstow for several months and trawled the inshore grounds from Hartland down to Newquay, catching roker, lemon sole, whiting and gurnard, but above all large quantities of soles.

The *West Briton* 24th April, 1890. On Friday last, the Trinity pilots stationed at Hawkers Cove, from the lookout house on Stepper Point, counted no less than 150 trawlers fishing between Trevose Head and Padstow Points. Some of them were within the three-mile radius, of which the fishermen both of Port Isaac and of Padstow do not approve. They consider that means should be adopted by someone in authority to stop them. On Sunday afternoon a still larger number were to be seen trawling from the St Merryn and Padstow cliffs.

At that date, almost all of those trawlers would have been sailing trawlers without an engine. The passage is of interest as it demonstrates the scale of the invasion, the helplessness of the local inshore fishermen, and the large scale flouting of the custom of not fishing on Sunday which caused riots and grievous bodily harm in some Westcountry ports. Probably many of these particular vessels were from Penzance, St Ives and Hayle, and could innocently land their catches later in the week.

The trade really got underway when the LSW Railway was completed to Padstow in 1899, and three trains a day took fish away for distribution all over England. By that time steam vessels were involved in the fishing, mostly steam drifters but equipped with beam trawls in place of drift nets. After the First World War, they were generally fitted out as drifter-trawlers, with otter trawls, but the large number of wrecks left after the war resulted in expensive loss of gear.

The annual migration to Padstow had many manifestations, for instance in 1907 Thomas Phillips of Kirkley, Suffolk, had a ketch-rigged smack built at Rye, and named her TREVOSE, and she was followed in 1909 by TREVONE for John W. J. Tucker of Lowestoft and in 1910 by PENTIRE. All three were of 46 registered tons built at Rye and registered at Lowestoft, although PENTIRE (according to the *Mercantile Navy List*) was initially registered at Liverpool. On 30th January, 1917 a U-boat surfaced about 20 miles off Trevose Head and sank a fleet of six sailing trawlers by bomb and gunfire, including TREVONE.

In 1910 the VIGILANT of Lowestoft disappeared when fishing out of Padstow. She had been built at Galmpton in 1893, 55 tons, and her managing owner was John Charles Shepherd of 83 Raglan Street, Lowestoft. A relief fund was raised for the dependents of her crew of five men, to which the inhabitants of Lowestoft and Padstow contributed.

By 1906-'8, the fish dock at Padstow was quite inadequate to service the trawlers, with the result that the enlarged railway dock was built. The spring trawling continued to expand between the wars, resulting in the busiest scenes ever in Padstow harbour, with as many as seventy trawlers (with many of their shore personnel in attendance) basing themselves there from January or February until May.

Unfortunately very few of these ships were Padstow ships, as they would not have been viable for the rest of the year.

*Olsen's Fishermans Nautical Almanack* has been published annually since before 1880, giving a full list of 'Fishing Steamers, Smacks and Boats of over 15 net [later gross] tons.' Before the First World War Great Britain had literally thousands of such vessels. In 1884 Hayle and St Ives had over one hundred smacks, Bideford had seven, and Padstow had none. The number of fishing vessels over 15 tons registered at Padstow is so small that it is possible to list them in full at the end of this chapter.

It is remarkable that Padstow, which relied entirely on sail for carrying cargo (probably more so than any other port) and never owned a full-blown steam or motor cargo vessel, at the same time never owned a single sailing fisherman of over 15 net tons even when the harbour was full of Brixham trawlers and Lowestoft drifters! The first Padstow vessel in *Olsen's* is the Motor Fishing Vessel INDUSTRY, PW55, which appeared in 1912, owned then by R. Currow and W. Bate and later by E. S. Painter, and all the subsequent vessels are engine-powered.

The advantages of the internal combustion engine were quickly realized by fishermen all around Cornwall. The inshore fishermen of Padstow and the outports spent their lives amidst the rocks and tidal streams of their iron-bound coast, where the wind is blanketed by cliffs when most needed, or strikes with near vertical violence in williwaws down the valleys when least expected. Even before the First World War petrol, paraffin and oil engines were being installed, and after that war the boatyards were busy fitting engines into any boats without them, and fitting second and even third engines into boats which already had them. These extra engines were for reliability rather than speed, although the ability to get the fish to market on time was as important as ever. Almost all the motorised luggers retained a steadying mizen sail as do many of the motor fishing vessels to this day.

Reverting to the various fisheries, and having dealt with pilchard and herring, mention must be made of the mackerel shoals. The spring mackerel fishery off western Cornwall has remained one of the most important fisheries of England for centuries, but the shoals, coming from the west, tend to travel along the South rather than the North Coast of Cornwall. The fishermen of St Ives do well at the mouth of the Bristol Channel, but from Newquay and Padstow there is less commercial mackerel fishing but these days a great deal of fishing for summer visitors.

From Padstow mackerel were caught in large quantities by 'whiffing', that is with hand lines lowered (preferably into a shoal of fish) with numerous hooks on snoods from the line. The hooks often carried feathers to attract the fish. These days many of the amateur angling fraternity apparently disdain such slaughter and prefer to fish with an expensive rod and a single hook even for mackerel, although they naturally prefer greater prizes such as sea bass.

The largest fish caught regularly from Padstow must be the porbeagle shark which provides a thrill for the sea angler but which is not, I believe, sought commercially. Some of the local men have an uncanny knowledge of where to attract a porbeagle with ground bait. Padstow has been in the *Guinness Book of Records* since July 1976 when Jorge Potier caught a porbeagle weighing 465 lbs off Padstow, a world record.

The uncertainties of fishing must be greater than the risks of farming, especially in our fickle climate. To the hazards of navigation in the difficult waters in the Bristol Channel must be added the risks of really bad weather such as gales, blizzards and fog. On some days the search for fish is unsuccessful; on others, the bottom can fall out of the market. Governments can fix and alter quotas and mesh sizes, pots can disappear, nets can be damaged or lost; foreign trawlers can trespass.

Obviously over-fishing and negligent fishing can damage stocks, and controls are necessary, however controversial they may be, but some recent research indicates that the coming and going of the herring, pilchard and mackerel around the coasts of Cornwall may be very dependent upon the exact temperature of the sea water.

Cod, haddock, ling and plaice are all cold-water fish and it has long been realised that Cornwall was at the southern limit of the herring, which is also essentially a cold-water species, and that the mackerel shoals preferred the warm waters of the south coast. It now appears that a climatic change in the temperature of the sea water of as little as one or two degrees may be sufficient to be decisive as to whether herring, mackerel hake or pilchard thrive off North Cornwall, and such changes may be due to cycles in the activity of sunspots. Since 1980 the waters have been getting warmer and some scientists claim to see the influence of 'global warming' superimposed on earlier oscillations.

The inhabitants of Cornish villages do not quite have the reputation of their Breton counterparts for 'farming' the coasts and waters, but nevertheless all sorts of fishing and farming activities go on almost unobserved. Cockles in quite large quantities were collected from the beds opposite Padstow harbour in the nineteenth century to the tune of fifty tons per annum, providing a living for quite a number of old men and women of Padstow.

Although the commercial sean or seine companies disappeared round the turn of the century, private beach seining continued, and as recently as the 1970s local farmers would meet mysteriously on occasional dark nights, and visitors on Polzeath beach would be astonished to see lines of heavily clad men (and maids) walking silently out into the cold surf, spaced out along the net, and then along and back in again in the hope and expectation of trapping fish on the flooding tide.

The *West Briton*, 22nd September, 1881. When fishing on Thursday near Cant Hill, in the river Camel, Messrs. J. & H. Cory of Cardiff who, with a friend are on a visit to Padstow, caught about 400 pilchards, 150 mullet, and several bass, soles, and plaice. Such a large number has not been taken in the Camel for many years, and this haul has induced old fishermen who had given up all hope of ever catching pilchards again, to look up their nets in the hope of profitable catches as in former years.

That was probably John Cory the shipowner who left Padstow about 1870 to make his fortune with steam colliers out of Cardiff.

The shellfish fishery has become progressively more important on the north coast of Cornwall. In earlier days anyone seeking shellfish working from open boats was well advised to fish in the sheltered waters of the south coast to the east of the Lizard. Today, with the high prices for crab, lobster and crayfish, and with modern materials and methods to overcome the difficulties of wind and weather, the hunt for shellfish on the north coast is much more viable. For the close inshore work the tendency is towards smaller, more powerful motor boats. Tiny Portquin, for example, which had a small fleet of open boats for centuries, and then for a time had nothing, now has a tractor, a trailer and a fibreglass boat which only draws a few inches of water but which carries two powerful outboard motors giving a speed of over 20 knots. When the tide and weather serve, one man can launch the boat in minutes and tend pots along several miles of coast within hours and be safely home with the catch.

The general tendency towards smaller, more powerful vessels is well illustrated by the list of the larger vessels at the end of this chapter, which starts with INDUSTRY, 27 net tons, 13 h.p. and ends with WILD WAVE, 2 net tons, 250 kilowatts, equivalent to 335 horsepower!

The hundreds of small Padstow fishing boats cannot be dealt with individually, but two at least should be recorded. In January 1895 the old barque ANTOINETTE of St John's, New Brunswick, was driven on to the Doom Bar. Her crew were all rescued by lifeboat, but she broke up and her remains were scattered around the estuary. The ANTOINETTE had been built in 1874 in Yarmouth, Nova Scotia, and twenty years had been too much for her old longboat, so on her final voyage from Canada in 1894, the ship's carpenter had

'KINGFISHER OF PADSTOW'
PW 206. 26TH AUGUST, 1948

The other small fishing vessel deserving special mention is GIRL MAUREEN PW 112. The RNLI lifeboats are so well built that even when they are considered unsuitable for further lifeboat service, they often have long and active lives as fishing boats or pleasure craft. The RNLI lifeboat DOCEA CHAPMAN was a 34 ft self-righting boat, pulling ten oars built by The Thames Ironworks, Blackwall, in 1911. She was stationed first at Withernsea, then Easington and eventually served at Padstow 1938-1939. She was then sold locally, renamed GIRL MAUREEN, converted into a motor fishing vessel and worked hard for another 40 years or so, being owned for much of that time by Tommy Morrissey. Finally she was sent to Lynmouth to become a permanent museum exhibit named LOUISA II in memory of Lynmouth's lifeboat LOUISA which carried out a rescue in 1899, the story of which must be told.

On 12th January it was blowing a gale and a large ship was reported drifting ashore off Fore Point, North Devon. In Lynmouth the roads were deep under water and the boat could not be launched. They took the boat on her carriage thirteen miles across Exmoor through the night, a route which included the 1 in 4½ gradient of Countisbury Hill and the 1 in 4 Porlock Hill rising over 1,400 feet. A horse and cart went ahead and men with shovels to widen the road where necessary. They started off with twenty horses and many helpers and the road lit by flares and lanterns, and despite a wheel coming off the carriage, they caught up with the advance party at Ashton Lane, which was simply too narrow. They dragged the boat through on skids and took the carriage a mile around on the moor. At the bottom of Porlock Hill they had to demolish an old cottage wall to get past. A large laburnum tree had to be felled. At 6 a.m. they reached the coast. They launched and found the ship FORREST HALL, and helped to save her and her crew, which entailed her being towed rudderless to Barry in Wales, and then them in their open boat being towed part of the way back to Lynmouth and rowing the rest of the way.

Other small fishing vessels are remembered for dramatic incidents, and their names crop up in the lifeboat histories. The Port Isaac lifeboat saved the local luggers CASTLE and JTK in November 1872.

built a handsome new longboat of Canadian elm and oak. The boat was driven ashore undamaged and became the Padstow fishing boat KINGFISHER in due course, being given the fishing number PW 206. Not knowing any of this, I sketched her in 1948 without doing justice to her rugged lines. Her white hull showed signs of an extra gunwale having been added, but she looked very smart with green boot topping. She lasted until 1960. She should not be confused with the more modern MFV KINGFISHER PW 189.

The Port Isaac boats CHARLES & JOHN, BELL, COLUMBIA and LITTLE WILLIE were towed home in February 1883. The HARRIET ANN of Padstow with two on board was saved by the steam lifeboat JAMES STEVENS NO.4 just four months before the

'GIRL MAUREEN 'PW 112          1976

The CHARISMA refitting at Padstow in August 1991. Despite her Ballantrae fishing number BA45 she is Newquay owned and fishes from Padstow

MA VIE PW 228 brings home her catch, with Newland Rock in the background. 1992.                    *Author's photos*

Plate 5

PEGANINA PW 134 in June 1991 with a large power block near her stem for line hauling. Lost off the Doom Bar 29th December 1992.

CHRISANDE gets a lick of paint in August 1991. She betrays her Danish origins in the shape of her whale back and the outline of flags on her bows. She foundered in 1994.

The beam trawler FLAMINGO in front of the Padstow Custom House in June 1985. She was lost in November 1989.

*Author's photos*

Plate 6

DILIGENCE PW 240 returns to harbour. July 1986.

*Author's photo*

KALON BREIZ PW 129 showing off her pots and her Breton lines at Padstow. June 1989.

*Author's photo*

Plate 7

The motor fishing vessel OUR FIONA MARY of Padstow was painted at Brixham by Gordon Rushmer.

Capt. Steers of Port Isaac was master of the ELFRIDA when she was painted by Reuben Chappell.

*Courtesy the late Christopher May*

Plate 8

tragic loss of the lifeboat and many of her crew in April 1900. FLOSSIE was in trouble off Port Isaac in 1913; that same year DIADEM and DREADNOUGHT were assisted by the Padstow lifeboat. Other small local fishing vessels helped by lifeboats were SWEET BRIER of Newquay, 1902, PORPOISE of Padstow, 1921, ONLY TWO of Newquay, 1934, GLADYS of Newquay, 1935, ST MINVER of Padstow, 1958, SUSAN ANN of Padstow 1959, MOONLIT WATERS, 1961, and DEO GRATIAS of Port Isaac, 1965.

In *Cornish Shipwrecks*, Clive Carter describes how in December 1900, Port Isaac was inundated by huge seas, with cellars flooded, gear destroyed and the luggers SCORCHER, AUDREY, AMARANTH and BOY WILLIE all wrecked. This catastrophe was followed by the loss of the KINDLY LIGHT overloaded with herring in December 1903, with four young fishermen and Captain Callaway drowned; and then in 1904 the ANNIE capsized off Castle Rock leaving only one survivor.

In 1917-1918 the losses to German U-boats became so great that an Emergency Rescue Boat scheme was set up to enlist the help of motor fishing vessels, and the SWEET PROMISE of Newquay and the WILLING BOYS of Port Isaac both served.

In 1921 the 38-foot lugger OUR GIRLIE was built at Appledore by R. W. Blackmore & Sons for Mousehole owners and fitted with an 'Atlantic' 2-cylinder paraffin engine. The Port Isaac fisherman, Charles Couch Thomas, and his wife Elizabeth bought her in 1925 and she was re-registered at Padstow with the following particulars: Official Number 145317, 6.22 tons net, 16.11 tons gross, dimensions 37.7 x 12.4 x 5.9 ft. Rigged as a lugger with two masts, elliptical stern and straight stem.

On 27th November, 1928 she was catching herring off the Mouls when the wind got up from the WNW, so she took in her nets and set out for Port Isaac. Almost immediately her engine failed and the wind took her in towards Kellan Head and the rocks off Portquin. The coast shelves quite steeply there and by the time their anchor held they were in shallow broken water, where the five of them spent a decidedly uncomfortable night burning flares and then anything else which would burn when soaked in paraffin! Because she failed to show up at Port Isaac in such severe weather, the RNLI tug HELEN PEELE went out looking for her, and she was picked up by searchlight at 6 a.m., and her crew rescued in the most gallant manner just before OUR GIRLIE was driven onto the rocks and destroyed.

That proved to be the last service of the RNLI tug HELEN PEELE, whose particulars are given in another chapter. The awesome history of the lifeboats of Padstow, Newquay, Port Isaac and Bude are not given in detail in this book because they have been so comprehensively covered in the 'Wreck and Rescue around the Cornish Coast' series (with Cyril Noall and Grahame Farr the authors for the North Coast) and the 'Cornish Shipwrecks' series, (with Clive Carter dealing with the North Coast). These books, illustrated with the magnificent photographs of the Gibsons of the Scilly Isles, and others, describe hundreds of shipwrecks and rescues, and impart some understanding of the hardships suffered by Cornish seafarers and the skills they required to keep body and soul together in years gone by.

Development of the fishing vessels in recent years is perhaps best covered by excerpts from the technical press.

The *Fishing News*, 8th February, 1985 contains a very detailed description of the new fibreglass crabber CELTIC MOR (PW 31) built by Baumbach and Sons of Hayle. Dimensions 38 ft x 13 ft 7 ins and 5 ft draught. Skipper Dungey, with a crew of three, was to work on the grounds off Newquay. The main engine is a Volvo Penta developing 110 s.h.p. which also drives a Hydroslave pot hauler and other hydraulic and electrical systems, including a fish-hold sprinkler to keep the catch fresh.

But most impressive to the older hands must surely be the electronic apparatus on this comparatively small vessel including Radar (with range marker and 16-mile guard alarm), sounder (dual frequency colour), Kelvin Hughes Navigator, and of course comprehensive radio equipment, and auto-pilot.

CELTIC MOR was to work two day trips from Newquay and the catch was expected to consist of brown crabs (60%) spider crabs (25%) and lobsters (15%).

The vessel's full name is CELTIC MOR of NEWQUAY, thus indicating that although she is registered at Padstow, she belongs to the outport of Newquay.

The *Fishing News*, 28th June, 1985, deals in similar detail with the wooden 39 ft crabber GUIDING LIGHT (PW 377) built by C. Toms & Son of Polruan for skipper Phil Trebilcock, whose family name will be found elsewhere in these pages as the Trebilcocks were owners and masters of many of Padstow's nineteenth-century sailing vessels. GUIDING LIGHT has a Gardner diesel engine and equipment basically similar to CELTIC MOR. The skipper's comments are significant: 'With good catches of shellfish on the north Cornish coast the fleet at Newquay has increased tremendously over the last few years . . . we have to search further afield and use more gear.' The article ended with the news that Newquay had six more vessels of about the same size on order.

The 1st December, 1985 issue of the *Fishing News* gives equally full particulars of REGINA MARIS (PW 57) designed, like GUIDING LIGHT, by Barry Mitchell and built by C. Toms & Son who clearly maintain the tradition of Cornish wooden building of excellent sea boats. 'REGINA MARIS is very strongly built forward and aft with her deadwoods being extra robust to resist the port's heavy groundswell. Her planking is 1¾ inch iroko on grown oak frames.' Newquay, of course, dries out at low water and that mention of the groundswell highlights the problem which occurs when a vessel is just afloat or just aground, and every wave lifts her and thumps her down onto the bottom.

On 27th June, 1986, the *Fishing News* reviewed the newly completed 40 ft TREVOSE of NEWQUAY (PW 64) built of oak and larch by Cann and Pender of Brixham for John and Michael Burt, and also designed by Mitchell, but unlike the others mentioned above she was designed for long trips, ray netting and ground netting, so she has the more traditional wheel-house aft layout with accommodation for four below decks.

The completion of TREVOSE of NEWQUAY also marked the completion of an investment of over £1.5 million in six new boats for Newquay, the three mentioned above and also TRELAWNEY OF CORNWALL (38 ft for Arthur Cain), PEARN PRIDE (36 ft for David Glaves) and LAMORNA (40 ft for Ron Eglinton). So the average cost of an inshore fishing boat of about 38 ft length in the mid-1980s was over £250,000.

Newquay made front page headlines in the *Fishing News* of 24th April, 1987: 'Vivier ship aground at Newquay. The 200 ton shellfish vivier ship ROSS ALCEDO dragged anchor and ran aground at Newquay while taking on spider crab and brown crab from local fishermen.' On falling neap tides she could not be got off for over a week. The valuable catch had to be taken away in vivier lorries. The ROSS ALCEDO (there is a photograph of her ashore) was built in Bilbao as an orthodox side trawler in 1973, but converted into a vivier ship — that is, one specially equipped to keep her catch or cargo alive. Her employment in 1987 was directly related to the £1.5 million investment in Newquay inshore fishing boats as she collected their crab catches and trans-shipped them to Spain. It is my guess that the lobsters were flown direct to Paris. She was owned in 1987 by Compania Transportes de Marisco SA of Panama, which company had (as agents) St Catherine's Fisheries of St Martin, Jersey, Channel Islands. So the Cornish entrepreneurial instinct, which found profitable connections with the Channel Islands in smuggling days, continues unabated.

In October 1987 the *Fishing News* had more general comments about Padstow. Cornwall Fishermen Ltd had handled white fish worth about £325,000 in nine months. The shellfish tanks capable of holding four tons of lobster and crayfish had never been full because of demand for these species. Prices varied from 70-90 pence per kilo for brown crab and up to £9.80 to £10.30 for crayfish. Padstow boats had poor results looking for spurdog fish in January, which turned boats towards turbot netting and wreck netting which produced holds full of ling and pollack. A & J Marine were about to open their new drydock, which would be able to slip vessels up to 85 ft long and which should be well used when the Brixham beam trawlers returnd the following year.

In February 1988 the 40 ft ATLANTA II was delivered by John Moor of Mevagissey to Newquay skipper Bennetts. Her hull is of 1 & 5/8ths inch iroko planks on 3½ inch grown oak frames, but she introduced a real novelty to Padstow, a bulbous bow. Such bows have been fitted to large tankers and cargo vessels for many years to reduce the resistance of the hull to forward motion, and increasingly they are to be seen in deep sea trawlers as they ease motion in a seaway and save fuel, but their application to small inshore vessels is more unusual and controversial. ATLANTA II was fitted out for wreck fishing initially; this entails pinpoint navigation and the placing of special nets close to wrecks, which used to be thought of as enemies of fishermen. One of the aids carried by ATLANTA II was the first Furuno colour plotter in the UK. This plotter works with any of the electronic navigator systems such as Decca, Satnav and Loran and can display, for instance, a chart of the North Cornish coast at a selected scale, on which can be shown or erased or recorded any special feature (such as a wreck). Course lines, event marks, way points, etc., can be drawn by a cursor in any one of seven colours and recalled or erased at will. This sort of apparatus, together with sophisticated sounding machines, has turned 'wreck fishing' into a viable operation.

The *Fishing News* of 15th April, 1988 carried another article demonstrating that Padstow fishermen have the initiative to seek new methods. Skipper Dungey, who only three years before had commissioned CELTIC MOR, now took delivery of POUL NIELSEN (GY 370), a reconditioned 65 ft netter built in Denmark in 1940 of oak on oak frames. Grimsby has had a fleet of these Danish 'anchor seiners' for many years, catching such valuable fish as turbot and monk fish; and with the resurgence of fishing from North Cornwall, local men are feeling the need both to join in and be prepared to operate further afield. POUL NIELSEN was renamed CHRISANDE (PW 108).

The CHRISANDE foundered nineteen miles north of Padstow in November 1994. Her crew of four were picked up by the Jersey beam trawler PIETERJE.

For many years races between commercial craft have taken place. There was of course the racing home with the tea from China to get the premium prices on the London market: the competitions between 6-oared gigs and pilot cutters were originally strictly commercial, to get the business, but subsequently became regatta fodder. The traditional races for sailing barges in the Thames estuary and similar races between fishing smacks appear to me to be more a day out for the lads, although enormous prestige descends on the winners.

The two most pointless types of race, I suggest, are tug races and motor fishing vessel races, especially trawler races. Tugs and trawlers are really steel boxes with engines inside them. Their 'free-running' speed is of some importance as it gets them to and from the real work they have to do, which is to tow either a ship or a net through the water. Their ability to pull hard at a steady speed is far more important than their free-running speed. But I have seen tug races enthusiastically received on the Great Lakes and in California, and annual trawler races are now a regular feature at several English ports.

The *Fishing News,* 18th September, 1988 carries a report on Newquay Race Day held on 8th September with all proceeds going to the RNLI, and the mayor of Newquay presenting the first prize to skipper Phil Trebilcock of GUIDING LIGHT, as ATLANTA II had cut inside a marker to avoid another boat. If one remembers how much Newquay relies on the tourist industry, and that thirty boats took part all inviting visitors on board, one begins to see the point of the exercise. The helicopter rescue team from HMS Culdrose gave a demonstration together with the Newquay inshore lifeboat as one of the several items before the race.

The *Fishing News* of 7th October, 1988 records the completion of ORCADES II (PW 364) for Port Isaac skipper Jim May by Chapman and Hewitt of Wadebridge. The 'superfast Lochin 38' fibreglass planing hull with twin Volvo engines producing 600 h.p. is capable of 28 knots for distant water potting trips, thus offering an alternative to the more traditional displacement hulls of the vessels previously described, which carry out the same function at a speed of 8 knots or so but with living accommodation on board.

But wooden boats continue to be built and in late 1990 Newquay skipper Philip Crosswood took delivery of TALLULAH, built of larch on oak frames by Charles Anderson of Berwick-on-Tweed. She measures 30 ft 6 ins overall with 11 ft beam and a draught of 3 ft 6 ins. Her principal tasks will be netting, potting and angling trips during the summer.

In recent as in earlier years there have been the inevitable losses associated with operating small craft in dangerous inshore waters. In January 1988 the 26-ft netter LAURA JANE, working out of Newquay, was lost at night close inshore when she was apparently swamped by freak seas, and her skipper Colin Taylor and Peter Thorpe were lost despite searches by two helicopters, the Padstow lifeboat, the Newquay inshore rescue boat and several local fishing vessels.

The loss of the FLAMINGO (PW 251) on 24th November, 1989 was quite different. She had been built in Holland as a small 'motorkotter' beam trawler, and in 1973 sold to Brixham fishing as GREY FLAMINGO (BM 25). By 1986 she was owned by David Evans of Padstow and acquired the fishing number PW 251. I remember seeing her with GREY FLAMINGO on the bows but FLAMINGO on the stern. Beam trawlers tow their trawls by warps rigged from the outboard ends of long booms rigged out to port and starboard so that the two warps are as far apart as possible, helping to keep the mouth of the net wide open and the whole paraphernalia at the correct angle relative to the trawler. The accident occurred when FLAMINGO's gear fouled that of FOUR SISTERS, another beamer, so that their two powerful diesel engines, instead of towing the trawls directly astern, were applying forces of several tons on one of FLAMINGO's warps, sufficient to cause her to capsize rapidly. There were two survivors but skipper Coutsoubos was trapped in the wheelhouse and drowned, and William Jenkyn, one of the crew, died of hypothermia after being found by helicopter.

Reference to beam trawlers or beamers these days has little connection with the original beam trawl of the nineteenth and early twentieth centuries which preceded the invention of the otter trawl, with its doors keeping the mouth of the net laterally open. Since the Second World War the beam trawl has been developed, particularly by the Dutch, into the most advanced method of catching flat fish.

The completion of PEARN PRIDE (PW 62) has already been noted. The following appeared in the *Fishing News*, 27th September, 1991:

Off north Cornwall last Saturday the netter PEARN PRIDE began to take water. She was steaming out to the grounds and was about ten miles off Padstow when skipper Conium sent out a Mayday call. A helicopter from RNAS Culdrose was scrambled and the Padstow lifeboat was launched to assist a nearby crabber/netter OUR BELLE ANN (PW 100) which sped to the scene.

Tim Conium tried to keep her afloat but he had to jump after his crew onto OUR BELLE ANN when a big swell rolled PEARN PRIDE over and she sank into 200 ft of water.

## Registration of Fishing Vessels

The Merchant Shipping Act 1894 required every fishing boat to be lettered and numbered and listed on a register. The ports of registry are the same as for merchant vessels, which in Cornwall are Fowey (FY), Truro (TO), Falmouth (FH), Penzance (PZ), St Ives (SS) and Padstow (PW), so the registered fishing boats of Padstow and the outports (principally Newquay, Port Isaac and Boscastle) have the letter PW followed by their fishing number, painted on their hulls on each bow and often on each quarter. These days they frequently also have the letters and numbers painted onto the top of the wheelhouse so as to be visible from aircraft.

The return for registered fishing boats for 1912 showed that Padstow had 151 registered boats, but we know from *Olsen's Almanack* that only one of them, the INDUSTRY was of more than 15 tons, and the vast majority were small open boats, a few of them having recently been fitted with early internal combustion engines.

In 1986 a list of Padstow registered fishing boats gave 186 vessels by name, twenty-four of them over 10 metres long, and eleven of them (over 15 tons gross) included in *Olsen's Fisherman's Almanack*, 1987. All but a few of the rest had at least one engine, and an increasing number of them had electronic, navigational, communication and fish-finding equipment and hydraulic equipment such as line-haulers and power blocks.

There appears to be no strict requirement for a boat to operate from the port in which it is registered or, to put it another way, no need to get a Padstow number when a boat is sold, or an owner moves to Padstow, and Addendum 2 includes a number of boats which have fished from Padstow for years carrying the fishing numbers of other ports.

By the same token I have seen boats with the letters PW in Plymouth, the Channel Islands and even moored amongst the yachts up the Hamble River. My faith in the fishing number system was further shaken in 1989 when I saw the motor boat MANTA PW 108 in Newquay, and then sailed round to Padstow to notice the ex-Danish shelterdecker CHRISANDE PW 108 moored alongside on the afternoon of the same day.

ADDENDUM 1

**Fishing Vessels over 15 Tons Gross Registered at Padstow
As Recorded in Olsen's Fisherman's Nautical Almanack**

| Date | Official number | Name | Fishing No. | Tons Net | h.p. | Built | Owner |
|---|---|---|---|---|---|---|---|
| 1912-24 | — | INDUSTRY | PW 55 | 27 | 13 | 1893 Porthleven | R. Currow & W. Bate S. Turrell then E. S. Painter *et al.* |
| 1915-25 | 119941 | PERILLA | PW 217 | 7 | 30 | 1914 Looe | E. S. Painter |
| 1916 only | 119942 | CRIMSON RAMBLER | PW 229 | 7 | 30 | 1915 E. Looe | E. S. Painter *et al.* |
| 1916-20 | — | OUR JANIE | PW 216 | 19 | — | — | W. E. Eddy W. J. Harris |
| 1917 only | — | GENERAL BOOTH | PW 37 | 20 | 15 | 1897 | W. L. Mullender R. Capps |
| 1918-20 | 119943 | AUSPICIOUS | PW 109 | 9 | 26 | 1916 E. Looe | C. Smith then E. Evans & W. S. Painter |
| 1921 only | 119945 | PREVAIL | PW 77 | 6 | 25 | 1895 Pill | E. Painter & Ch. Brinham |
| 1924-26 | 119944 | AVAIL | PW 59 | 6 | 25 | '99 Porthleven | E. S. Painter |
| 1924-37 | — | IVY MAY | PW 84 | 26/ 22 | — | — | E. S. Painter & Chas G. Brinham & G. Coyde |
| 1924 only | — | SUNSTAR | PW 98 | 21 | | — | C. H. Westcott |
| 1926-32 | — | VENUS | PW 184 | 21 | 10 | 1885 Mevagissey | W. Orchard |
| 1927-32 | — | BREADWINNER | PW 212 | 19 | — | — | E. Pink *et al.* |
| 1928-83 | — | ROSALIND * | PW 233 | 23 | — | — | P. B. le Patourel |
| 1930-34 | 137578 | ADELE ** | PW 3 | 42 | 33 | 1915 Yarmouth | Padstow Fishing Co. Ltd |
| | | | Not a single vessel was added from 1931 to 1960 | | | | |
| 1961-71 | 182063 | QUIET WATERS | PW 144 | 20 | 88 | '48 St Monance | Padstow Fishing Co. Ltd then David P. Chapman |
| 1965-68 | — | FRANCIS STEVENS | PW 223 | 22 | 90 | 1920 Porthleven | D. R. Carlton |
| 1967-73 | — | BACCHUS | PW 251 | 31 | — | — | John Burt *et al.* |
| 1968 only | — | FELICITY | PW 258 | 25 | — | — | Ian E. Lindley |

| Date | Official number | Name | Fishing No. | Net | kW | Built | Owner |
|------|------|------|------|------|------|------|------|
| 1969-83 | 308636 | MAYFLOWER OF CAMELOT | PW 1 | 17 | 38 | 1920 Looe | Elcrew Ltd then Julie M. Tucker |
| 1971-73 | — | TRUSTFUL | PW 49 | 22 | — | — | P. R. Watts |
| 1971 only | — | PRADA | PW 56 | 24 | — | — | John Brinham |
| 1972-79 | — | MARIGOLD | PW 73 | 15 | — | 1957 Girvan | D. P. Chapman |
| 1975 only | — | BRIGHTER HOPE | PW 119 (ex LK 241) | 22 | — | Flekkerfjord, Norway later DONATOO | Thos H. Litton |
| 1975-86 | 379572 | ST STANILAS | PW 149 | 17 | 160 | 1956 France | Jeffrey H. Martin 1976 then Geo. B. Smith |
| 1977-79 | — | DONATOO | PW 119 | 22 | — | ex. BRIGHTER HOPE | Thos H. Litton |
| 1977 only | — | GOLDEN MARIANA | PW 104 | 24 | — | — | M. Mackenzie |
| 1982 only | 378886 | JULANTE | PW 7 | — | 110 | '78 Northumberland | G. & J. Price |
| 1982- | 366341 | LA QUETE | PW 222 | 10 | 216 | '77 Poole | La Quete Ltd |
| 1984-89 | — | GIRL DEBORAH | PW | 24 | — | '45 Fife | M. Devlin |
| 1984- | 379575 | LA CONQUETE | PW 201 | 10 | 216 | '82 Poole | C. B. Richards then B. J. Hill |
| 1984-87 | — | PATHFINDER | PW 375 | 24 | 115 | '47 Peterhead | A. J. Conium |
| 1985-91 | 168638 | GIRL BARBARA | PW 6 | 10 | 80 | '46 Portavogie | D. Whittaker then Ian Maclean 1990 |
| 1985 only | — | PILOT STAR | PW 188 | 24 | — | '60 MacDuff | D. P. Chapman |
| 1986- | 366340 | GOLDEN HOPE OF PETROC | PW 28 | 14 | 150 | '64 MacDuff | G. F. & J. B. McBurnie |
| 1987- | 704688 | GUIDING LIGHT | PW 377 | 7 | 126 | '85 Polruan | P. W. Trebilcock |
| 1987-88 | — | HARVEST REAPER | PW 58 | 15 | — | '55 Fraserburgh | Robert G. Yeo |
| 1987- | 704690 | REGINA MARIS OF NEWQUAY | PW 57 | 9 | 255 | '85 Polruan | Barrie P. Ball |
| 1987- | 704694 | TREVOSE OF NEWQUAY | PW 64 | 8 | 95 kW | '86 Galmpton | C. J. & M. L. Burt then B. Prynn |
| 1988- | 712231 | CELTIC CRUSADER | PW 78 | 24 | 214 kW | '59 Camaret | Celtic Fish Newquay |
| 1988 only | — | GLENMORE | PW 144 | 25 | — | — | D. P. & N. P. Chapman |
| 1988 only | — | POLLYANN | PW 148 | 15 | — | '80 Newhaven | D. P. Blewett |

In 1990, the qualification for entry into Olsen's Almanack was altered to suit EEC regulations, and all vessels over 10 metres length are included. The power of their engines is now given in kilowatts and the length in metres. This change resulted in an influx of vessels into the Almanack (not all of which would have qualified under the old rule) as follows:

| Date | Official number | Name | Fishing No. | Net | kW | Built | Owner |
|------|------|------|------|------|------|------|------|
| 1990 | — | ATLANTA | PW 21 | 6 | 93 | '83 Southampton | Karl L. Kemp |
| " | — | ATLANTA II | PW 82 | 10 | 205 | '87 Mevagissey | P. J. Bennets |
| " | — | BOY JAMES | PW 70 | 22 | 83 | '52 Edinburgh | L. W. Waterhouse |
| " | — | BOSCASTLE PEGANINA | PW 289 | 7 | 122 | '79 Rye | D. H. Pengelly |
| " | — | BOOTLEGGER | PW 354 | 6 | 74 | '68 Molesey | T. L. Warne |
| " | 342586 | CHE SARA SARA | PW 26 | 5 | 89 | '71 Looe | D. M. Trebilcock |
| " | — | CELTIC MOR OF NEWQUAY | PW 31 | 6 | 85 | '84 Hayle | C. D. MacAffer |
| " | — | CHRISANDE*** | PW 108 | 18 | 145 | '40 Denmark | F. P. Dungey |
| " | — | CHARLYNNE II | PW 139 | 21 | 141 | '63 France | J. Martin |
| " | 361263 | GREY FLAMINGO*** | PW 251 | 28 | 171 | Holland | D. L. Evans |
| " | — | INVENTIVE IV | PW 114 | 23 | 153 | '59 Fife | D. P. Chapman |
| " | 390599 | JEAN HOWARD | PW 150 | 11 | 134 | '80 King's Lynn | N. P. Chapman |
| " | 713512 | KALON BREIZ | PW 129 | 39 | 160 | '59 Camaret | S. E. Amor |
| " | — | LISA MARIA | PW 128 | 3 | 231 | '88 Wadebridge | J. D. Brown |
| " | — | LADY B. GOOD | PW 165 | 9 | 59 | '48 Polruan | W. Chown |
| " | — | MCGREGOR | PW 141 | 5 | 29 | '62 Looe | R. A. Osborne |
| " | — | OUR BELLE ANN | PW 100 | 4 | 298 | Wadebridge | B.H. Rowe |
| " | — | ORCADES | PW 364 | 6 | 74 | '79 Porthleven | A. J. May |
| " | — | OCEAN BREEZE | PW 1 | 21 | 254 | '69 MacDuff | Julian James |
| " | — | SEA FOX | PW 2 | 7 | 100 | '82 Hayle | M. E. A. Burt |
| " | — | SARA JEAN | PW 58 | 15 | 82 | '55 Fraserburgh | A. D. Stevens |
| " | 364817 | SUSIE JEAN | PW 372 | 8 | 167 | '74 Falmouth | Diana Madge Russell |
| " | — | THREE WISHES | PW 7 | 3 | 114 | '72 Mevagissey | Geo. B. Marsh |
| " | — | WILD WAVE | PW 38 | 2 | 250 | '74 Poole | J. H. Phillips |

Subsequent entry

| 1992 | — | HANNAH CHRISTINE | PW 14 | 39 | 172 | '91 Zaandam | David Evans |

*Notes to Addendum 1*

| * | Lasted continuously until 1983 |
| ** | Padstow's largest FV |
| *** | Since lost. |

ADDENDUM 2

### Index of Fishing Vessels of Padstow

A list in alphabetical order which includes (a) the vessels covered in Addendum I for which this list serves as an index (b) vessels with Padstow owners although registered at other ports (c) vessels built at Padstow (or outports) and registered at Padstow or at other ports. The list attempts to cover all British Registered ships, even though some of them are very small.

All are motor fishing vessels except ADELE.

| ON | Name and Fishing Number | | Year and Owner |
|---|---|---|---|
| — | ADELE  see Addendum I, 1930  Steel Steam Trawler | | — |
| — | ALIZE  BM 127  Built Padstow 1990 by A & J Marine  Steel MFV | | Brixham |
| 379577 | AN MORDROS  PW 287  8 tons net. | First noted 1982 | F. J. Bealing |
| 366616 | ANN VIRGINIA  PW 59  12 tons net. | First noted 1986 | Previously reg. Dartmouth & Inverness |
| — | ASPIRE  BF 234  24 tons net. Built 1961, MacDuff | | 1976  D. P. Chapman, Wadebridge |
| — | ATLANTA  see Addendum I, 1990 | | — |
| — | ATLANTA II  see Addendum I, 1990 | | — |
| — | AUSPICIOUS  see Addendum I, 1918 | | — |
| — | AVAIL  see Addendum I, 1924 | | —. |
| — | BACCHUS  see Addendum I, 1967 | | — |
| — | BARCRIS  SD 15  Built Port Isaac 1988 3 tons net. 261 kW. | | Sunderland |
| 366333 | BESSIE VEE  PW 170  11 tons net, built 1974, Wicklow | | 1976  H. C. Winter-Taylor, Padstow later Aquaserve Diving Ltd |
| — | BETHNEY MAY  PE 359  Built Wadebridge 1979, 13 tons net 89 kW. | | Poole |
| — | BETTY LOUISE  PW 24  Built Rock 1990, 6.5 tons displacement 250 h.p. | | Terry Warne |
| — | BOOTLEGGER  see Addendum I, 1990 | | — |
| 166959 | BOSCASTLE BELLE  PW 132  5 tons net. Built 1960, Looe | | Dorothy E. Cotton, St Tudy. E. Stein, then Jn Murt |
| 302454 | BOSCASTLE LASS  PW 236  2 tons net. Built 1965, Looe | | 1965  W. R. Cotton, St Tudy, later owned in Salcombe |
| — | BOSCASTLE PEGANINA  see Addendum I, 1990 | | — |
| — | BOY DOMINIC  H 11  Built Padstow 1990-'1 by A & J Marine  Steel MFV | | Hull |
| — | BOY JAMES  PW 70  see Addendum I, 1990 | | — |
| 359256 | BOY MALCOLM  PW 111  5 tons net. Built 1973, Looe | | 1976  Michael Hancock, Camelford, then D. Glaves, St Columb |
| — | BREADWINNER  see Addendum I, 1927 | | — |
| — | BRIGHTER HOPE  see Addendum I, 1975 | | — |
| — | CELTIC CRUSADER  see Addendum I, 1988 | | — |
| — | CELTIC MOR OF NEWQUAY  see Addendum I, 1990 | | — |
| — | CELTIC VICTOR  M 1009. Built 1991, Wadebridge, by Port Isaac Workboats | | Milford |
| — | CHARISMA  BA 45  38 tons net. 268 kW. Built 1988, Eyemouth | 1991 | Barry Ball, Newquay |
| 379573 | CHARLOTTA  PW 362  2 tons net. | First noted 1982 | — |
| — | CHARLYNNE II  see Addendum I, 1990 | | — |
| — | CHE SARA SARA  see Addendum I, 1990 | | — |
| — | CHRISANDE  see Addendum I, 1990 | | — |
| 364894 | CHRISTIANA S  SH 225  22 tons net. 240 h.p. Built 1957, Holland | | previously of Scarborough |
| — | | | 1990  D. P. Blewett, Bodmin |
| 366334 | CRIMSON ARROW  4 tons net. Built 1976, Mevagissey | | Geo. Knight, Tingagel |
| — | CRIMSON RAMBLER  see Addendum I, 1916 | | S. Turrell |
| — | DAIRY MAID (believed to be subsequent to his ownership of INDUSTRY) | | T. Wilkinson & P. Ward |
| 379571 | DAWNBREAKER  PW 280  2 tons net. | First noted 1982 | A. Conium |
| — | DIADEM  INS 154  45 tons net. 112 kW. Built 1966, Buckie | | |
| — | DILIGENCE  PW 240  2 tons net. Built 1976, Charlestown | First noted 1982 | P. J. Friendship |
| — | DONATOO  see Addendum I, 1977 | | 1982  C. W. & C. F. Hubber, Newquay |
| 304840 | EARLY ON  E 238  3 tons net. Built 1965 Weymouth | | 1976  T. P. Reveley & |
| 337409 | ELIZABETH SHAUN  PW 159 ex ST INA  5 tons net. Built 1972, Polruan | | 1985  J. C. Murt |
| — | FELICITY  see Addendum I, 1968 | | — |
| — | FLAMINGO  see GREY FLAMINGO | | — |
| — | FRANCIS STEVENS  see Addendum I, 1965 | | — |
| 147053 | FREEMAN of St Ives. 8 tons net. Built 1920, Porthleven | | 1972  Elsie Bleakley, Newquay 1976  C. Cottrell, Bude |
| 302453 | GAVIOTA N  PW 200  2 tons net. Built 1962, Padstow | | 1966  M. Townsend, Port Isaac |
| — | GENERAL BOOTH  see Addendum I, 1917 | | — |
| — | GIRL BARBARA  see Addendum I, 1985 | | — |
| — | GIRL DEBORAH  see Addendum I, 1984 | | — |
| — | GIRL DEBRA  E 444  Built 1989 by A & J Marine  Steel MFV | | Exmouth |
| — | GIRL RACHEL  PW 77  Built 1987 Plymouth and finished Rock | | M & S Murt, Padstow |

| | | | |
|---|---|---|---|
| — | GLENMORE  see Addendum I, 1987 | | — |
| — | GOLDEN HOPE OF PETROC  see Addendum I, 1986 | | — |
| — | GOLDEN MARIANA  see Addendum I, 1977 | | — |
| — | GREY FLAMINGO  see Addendum I, 1990 | | — |
| — | GUIDING LIGHT  see Addendum I, 1987 | | — |
| — | HANNAH CHRISTINE  see Addendum I, 1992 | | — |
| — | HARVEST REAPER  see Addendum I, 1987 | | — |
| — | HEATHER LEA II  INS 15  23 tons net. 134 kW. Built 1950, MacDuff | 1990 | D. P. Blewett, Bodmin |
| 359251 | HUSTLER  PW 83  7 tons net. Built 1972 Mevagissey | | R. G. Paulton |
| 166958 | I & N (later PETE)  2 tons net. 7 h.p. Built 1956, Portmellen | 1956-1975 | W. N. Billing, Port Isaac |
| — | INCENTIVE IV  see Addendum I, 1990 | | — |
| — | INDUSTRY  see Addendum I, 1912 | | — |
| — | IVY MAY  see Addendum I, 1924 | | — |
| — | JMS  A Port Gaverne FV named after Joey Mathilda & Sam | | Joe Honey |
| — | JAINNIE  A Port Gaverne FV | | Wm & George Lobb |
| — | JEAN HOWARD  see Addendum I, 1990 | | — |
| — | JESSIE LOU  PH 344  17 tons net. 193 kW. Built 1987, Guernsey | 1990 | White Acres Holiday Park, Newquay |
| 137725 | JIMBET ex WINNIE q.v.  R 341, listed until 1976 | | Ramsgate |
| — | JOAN  A Port Gaverne inshore FV | c. 1880 | The Brown Family |
| 359254 | JULIA ANN  PW 97  5t tons net. Built 1972, Mevagissey | 1976 | Mark Townsend, Port Isaac |
| | | 1982 | A. Tarby, Padstow |
| | | 1984 | Rosemary Brinham Padstow |
| — | KALON BREIZ  see Addendum I, 1990 | | — |
| — | KATE  A Port Gaverne inshore FV | c. 1880 | The Brown Family |
| 366332 | KENZA MORVOREN  PW 133  8 tons net. Built 1974, Falmouth | | C. D. Moffat |
| 364633 | LMA (of St Ives)  5 tons net. | 1984 | P. C. Burgess, Newquay |
| — | LA CONQUETE  see Addendum I, 1984 | | — |
| — | LA NOROISE  BD 22  25 tons net. Built 1962, France | 1987 | John E. Beer, Wadebridge |
| — | LA QUETE  see Addendum I, 1982 | | — |
| — | LADY B. GOOD  see Addendum I, 1990 | | — |
| 366335 | LAMORNA OF NEWQUAY  6 tons net. | 1977 | R. A. Eglinton of Newquay |
| — | LAMORNA  SS 28  7 tons net. 94 kW. Built 1986, Mevagissey | 1990 | R. A. Eglinton, Newquay |
| — | LAURA JANE  PW 361  26 ft. Lost of Newquay January 1988 | | Colin Taylor |
| 397658 | LES PLEIADES  BD 182  26 tons net. Built in France | 1990 | John E. Beer |
| — | LILY  A Port Gaverne inshore FV | c. 1880 | The Brown Family |
| — | LISA MARIA  see Addendum I, 1990 | | — |
| 302452 | MCB  PW 182  4 tons net. Built 1961, Appledore | 1961 | John Rowe, Port Isaac |
| | | 1985 | G. A. Northey, Newquay |
| 366338 | MA VIE  PW 228  3 tons net | 1982-'9 | W. P. A. Cain |
| — | MARIGOLD  see Addendum I, 1972 | | — |
| — | MATTANJA  TH 106  32 tons net. 221 kW. Built 1960, Holland | 1990 | D. L. Evans, Padstow |
| — | MAYFLOWER OF CAMELOT  see Addendum I, 1969 | | — |
| — | McGREGOR  see Addendum I, 1990 | | — |
| — | MORNING DAWN  CN 252  25 tons net. Built 1970, Arbroath | 1990 | C. J. Burt, Newquay |
| — | MY TARA  SS 62  35 ft. Built 1990, Hayle | | Robt Broderick, Newquay |
| — | NIKKI D  SD 46  6 tons net. 261 kW. Built 1988, Wadebridge | | Sunderland |
| 161172 | NORTHERN LASS  5 tons net. Built 1955, Kilkeel | | — |
| — | OCEAN BREEZE  see Addendum I, 1990 | | — |
| — | ORCADES  see Addendum I, 1990 | | — |
| — | ORCADES II  PW 364  10 tons displacement. Built 1988, Wadebridge | | J. May, Wadebridge |
| — | OUR BELLE ANN  PW 100  see Addendum I, 1990 | | — |
| — | OUR FIONA MARY  PW 160  35 ft. 112 h.p. | | — |
| 145317 | OUR GIRLIE  PW 183  6 tons net. 26 h.p. Built 1921, Appledore | 1925-'8 | Chas Couch Thomas and wife Elizabeth |
| | | | C. J. & M. L. Burt |
| — | OUR JANIE  see Addendum I, 1916 | | |
| — | OUR JINNEY  Built c. 1920, Port Isaac | 1920-'30 | W. J. Blake |
| — | PATHFINDER  see Addendum I, 1984 | | |
| — | PEARN PRIDE  PW 62  5 tons net. 142 b.h.p. Built 1985, Looe & Padstow | 1989 | David Glaves |
| 359259 | PEGANINA  PW 134. 9 tons net. Built 1974, Charleston. Lost 1992. | 1976 | L. W. Stedman, Boscastle |
| — | PERILLA  see Addendum I, 1915. | | — |
| 166958 | PETE ex I & N q.v. | 1976 | A Kitto, Trevorne |
| 185651 | PETERJOHN  PW 211  6 tons net. 24 h.p. ('55). Built 1951, Looe | 1976 | M. N. M. Marr, Newquay |
| | | 1982 | A. Merrill, Wadebridge |
| — | PHOENIX  SY35  Lochin '33'. Completed 1990, Wadebridge  Creel boat for the Isle of Harris | | |
| — | PILOT STAR  see Addendum I, 1985 | | |
| — | POLLYANN  see Addendum I, 1988 | | — |
| 335582 | PORT ISAAC KESTREL  PW 206  5 tons net. Built 1972, Mevagissey | | Harold R. Brown, Port Isaac |
| | | by 1982 | G. Noall & G. Murt |

| — | PRADA  see Addendum I, 1971 | | — |
|---|---|---|---|
| — | PREVAIL  see Addendum I, 1921 | | — |
| — | PRUE ESTHER II  PZ 550  13 tons net. 373 kW. Completed 1987, Wadebridge | | Penzance |
| — | QUIET WATERS  see Addendum I, 1961 | | — |
| — | RED RHUM  OB 128  4 tons net. 238 kW. Built 1989, Wadebridge | | Tobermory |
| — | REGINA MARIS OF NEWQUAY  see Addendum I, 1987 | | — |
| — | RIPTIDE  J145  10 tons. 700 b.h.p. 24 knots. Built 1990, Wadebridge | | Jersey |
| — | ST INA  later ELIZABETH SHAUN q.v. | | — |
| — | ST STANISLAS  see Addendum I, 1975 | | — |
| 362398 | SALLY ALLSORTS  13 tons net. Built 1973, Bodmin  Steel MFV | | Vickers Oceanics, Barrow |
| — | SARA JEAN  see Addendum I, 1990 | | — |
| — | SEA FOX  see Addendum I, 1990 | | — |
| — | SHEILA PAT  PW 186  3 tons net. Built 1977, Falmouth & Portmellon | | Wm R. Cotton, St Tudy |
| — | SILVER CLOUD  BF 373  25 tons net. Built 1959, Berwick  Wood MFV | 1990 | N. Chapman, Wadebridge |
| — | SOLENT  later TRY AGAIN q.v.  Wood MFV | | — |
| — | STELLA MARIS OF NEWQUAY  PZ 518  8 tons net. 127 h.p. Built 1984, Polruan | | B. P. Ball, Newquay |
| — | STEPHANIE B.  FD 78  Steel MFV. 12 metres long. Built by A & J Marine | 1991 | Fleetwood |
| — | SUNSTAR  see Addendum I, 1924 | | — |
| — | SUSIE JEAN  see Addendum I, 1990 | | — |
| 186983 | TALISMAN OF LOOE  6 tons net. Built 1956, Looe  Wood MFV | 1972 | R. A. Eglinton, Newquay |
| — | TALLULAH  30.5 ft. Built 1990, Berwick | | Phil. Crosswood, Newquay |
| 342130 | TEKAPO  E 61  3 tons net. 52 kW. Built 1971, Exmouth | 1984 | Channel Fish Ltd |
| | | 1990 | P. A. T. Humphrey, Padstow |
| 379574 | THREE WISHES  see Addendum I, 1990 | | — |
| 364825 | THRESHER  FH 248  12 tons net. 240 kW. Built 1974, Mylor | 1990 | L. Polkinghorne, St Teath |
| — | TRELAWNEY OF CORNWALL  SS 83  6 tons net. 167 kW. Built 1985, Hayle | 1990 | W. P. A. Cain, Newquay |
| — | TREVOSE OF NEWQUAY  PW 64  see Addendum I, 1987 | | — |
| — | TRISTAR  39 ft. 320 b.h.p. Built 1990, Wadebridge | | Bridlington |
| — | TRUSTFUL  see Addendum I, 1971 | | — |
| — | TRY AGAIN  PD 366  50 tons net. *Ex* SOLENT. Built 1958, Buckie  Wood MFV | 1986 | A. Conium, Padstow |
| — | VENUS  see Addendum I, 1926 | | — |
| 308635 | VIKING X  PW 238  7 tons net. Built 1964 Havavik Bergen, Norway | 1966 | Geo. King, Newquay |
| — | WILD WAVE  see Addendum I, 1990 | | — |
| — | WINNIE  later JIMBET q.v. 12 tons reg. Built 1890, Padstow, Cowl, | | J. Payne, Ramsgate |

Padstow in 1920. Some of the guests from the Metropole Hotel will have been taken sailing and fishing in these smart little cutters. The PW 11 in the middle of the picture is named ROYAL HIGHLANDER.

## *Padstow Steam Vessels*

ONE might almost suppose that the seafarers of Padstow had sworn a secret oath never to pollute their waters with a steam engine. When one recalls that Cornish engineers led the world with their great steam-driven pumps, and that Harvey's of Hayle, just down the coast, were running steamships in 1831 and building iron steamers themselves soon after that, and that Cornishmen like Cory and Hain were making their fortunes by putting steam tramps to work from the Welsh coal ports just across the water; when one remembers all that, is it not extraordinary that of over 300 ships built in the Padstow yards until building ceased completely in 1906, not one had an engine of any kind?

In undated correspondence, apparently written in the 1850s and 1860s, there is reference to 'Captain Hutching's little steamer. . . running twice a day to Wadebridge, sixpence on deck and ninepence in the cabin'. A steam launch of less than fifteen tons would not have been registered, and unfortunately no name is known for what is almost certainly Padstow's first steamer. She may well have been taken over by William Stribley who was actively engaged in the trans-shipment of goods from Padstow to Wadebridge. At the bankrupt sale (which followed his death) in August 1879, four barges and one steam vessel were offered.

However, in 1872 the first steam vessel appears on the Padstow port register, the steam paddle tug AMAZON, ON 7299, built 1856 at Blackwall, Gateshead, Durham, 12 tons net 42 gross. 72.6 x 13.9 x 7.1 ft. A wooden clinker built round sterned vessel with 20 h.p. engine with a single cylinder 24¼ ins dia. and 4 ft stroke, made by Jonathan Robson of Blackwall. The AMAZON was the first tug to be built for John Batey, co-founder of Lawson-Batey Tugs Ltd, the company which dominates towage in northeast England today. She is registered as sloop rigged, and could probably set a loose-footed mainsail and one staysail from her single mast. She was transferred from the Newcastle to the Padstow register on 13th September, 1872, her owners being John Hutchings, captain, (42 shares) and Stephen Commons, engineer, (22 shares). It seems probable that this was the same Hutchings whose launch plied earlier to Wadebridge, and the more powerful AMAZON would be better able to handle the increasing numbers of ships and barges.

In 1884 she was re-registered, with Hutchings sharing ownership with seven others including Harvey and Allport, so it looks as if Captain Hutchings was needing the support of shipowners to maintain the towage service. In any case he must have been trying to make some provision for his retirement, which came in 1893 when the AMAZON was broken up, and her register closed on 6th December.

The yards of the River Tyne had a great reputation for producing wooden clinker-built paddle tugs like AMAZON. Three which spring to mind are the REAPER, TOM PERRY, and UNITED SERVICE of Yarmouth, the last lasting from 1872 to 1940. But there were dozens of others. Some, like MESSENGER, PILOT and STEPHENSON became the pioneer steam trawlers in later life. The MONARCH (built in 1833), PILOT and several others joined the famous Watkins tug fleet on the London River, and in holiday periods ran excursions such as sea trips from Margate, as did the RAPID from Bridgwater, the SAMPSON from Bristol and the AMAZON from Padstow.

The second steam vessel to be registered at Padstow was the steam launch JANE, ON 69451, 10 tons net, 16 gross. 46.8 x 12.7 x 5.3 ft depth of hold. She was carvel built of wood by Joseph Osborne at the Island Cove Yard, Newquay and was screw driven by a single cylinder engine made by Williams & Co. at the Perran foundry. She had an elliptical stern. Her completion was reported in the *Royal Cornwall Gazette* on 17th February, 1872 when she was described as a beautiful model, a steamer built for the drift fishing trade. The JANE was the only steam vessel to be built in the outports of Padstow. She was registered in 1873, with her builder retaining all 64 shares. Drift fishing was seasonal, and through the summer the JANE was largely used for pleasure trips. She must have been quite satisfactory for passenger work because in 1876 she was bought by Edward Handcock, transferred to the Falmouth register, and joined the fleet of the St Mawes Steam Tug and Passenger Co. Ltd. They gave her a compound engine and sold her to London owners in 1889. Her last port of registry was Swansea in 1896 and she was not listed in 1900.

The ferry from Padstow to Rock has operated since the Duchy of Cornwall was formed in 1337. Small boats sufficed until 1884 when the Rock and Padstow Steam Ferry Company was formed 'by popular demand', with a capital of £500 in £1 shares. A suitable steam launch was purchased, and carried 6,400 people in the three months to November 1884.

In the absence of local railways at the time, the horse-drawn coach services were being extended and improved and it was anticipated that a proper ferry service would increase both commercial and tourist traffic. A horse boat was built capable of carrying a wagon and horses which could be loaded, and towed by the steam launch when required.

In November 1884 a minor flaw in the boiler occurred, which was repaired at the foundry at Wadebridge for £50. Thereafter the ferry was often reported in the *Western Morning News*. In response to complaints it was stated on 28th January, 1885 that 'The horse boat is in perfect order and could at any time take horses, carriages and cattle across at either high or low water.' But the demand for the horse boat was trivial and finally on 3rd November, 1885 there was a report of the Valedictory Proceedings of the Rock and Padstow Steam Ferry Company at which, amongst other arrangements, Capt. C. Matthews consented to take charge of the steam launch until the dissolution of the Company. He was accorded a vote of thanks. So we have no details, not even the name, of the third Padstow steam vessel, which was finally sold by auction on 4th December, 1885, for £102.

Following the demise of the AMAZON, there was no Padstow registered tug, but towing duties were carried out by a steam vessel called PRINCESS MAY. In 1895 when she is first mentioned, there were five small steamers registered as PRINCESS MAY and

The best surviving photograph of the paddle tug AMAZON at Padstow, c. 1880. *Royal Institution of Cornwall*

doubtless others too small to be registered, as the future Queen Mary was a very popular figure. The two most likely candidates to have worked at Padstow are PRINCESS MAY, ON 99487, built at Hull in 1893 and registered at Bridgwater, and PRINCESS MAY, ON 102754 built and registered at Falmouth in 1894, and owned by the St Mawes Steam Tug & Passenger Co. Ltd. If the latter, she had an exciting life, being sold to the Port Elizabeth Harbour Board in 1903 and sailing out on her own bottom. In 1905 she was transferred to the Cape Copper Co. Ltd, Ookiep, Cape Colony and worked for them at least until 1932 when she was refused registration as a British ship as the company had American owners by then.

The Hockaday family (Job, John and others) of Delabole owned a series of schooners from the 1860s onwards, and in 1884 a part of the family moved to Newport and ventured into steamships. The SS DELABOLE, ON 01352, was built 1884 at Newcastle by W. Dobson & Co. Tons 244 net, 420 gross, 155.0 x 23.0 x 11.2 ft. She was built of iron and her single screw was driven by a 70 h.p. compound engine built by Wigham Richardson & Co. She was registered at Newport, owned by the Delabole Steamship Co. with F. S. Hockaday as manager. She is included here because of her name and because much of her capital must surely have come from Padstow and Delabole, but she was sold to Norwegians within two years and renamed RAPID. Her entry in *Lloyd's Register* of 1890 is posted 'sunk December 1889'.

Late in 1898 J. Samuel White of Cowes completed the steam lifeboat JAMES STEVENS NO.4 at a cost of £3,340. Her length was 56 ft, her beam 14 ft 8 ins and she displaced 31 tons. Her single screw was driven by a compound steam engine and she reached a speed of 9.3 knots. The RNLI provided two engineers and two firemen who came to live in Padstow with the boat; a comment both on the experimental nature of these steam lifeboats and on the lack of experience of boilers and engines at Padstow. Her tragic tale is told in another chapter, but her loss on 11th April, 1900 led directly to the commissioning of Padstow's next steam vessel.

All Padstow's steamers were of different types, but the RNLI tug HELEN PEELE was the only vessel of her kind in British lifeboat history. In the days when lifeboats were propelled by sail and oar, techniques were developed whereby steam tugs towed them to the scene of a wreck and then, for instance, paid out a warp as they

drifted downwind alongside a wreck in shallow water, and hauled them out after the rescue. After the disaster of 1900 in which the JAMES STEVENS No.4 and ARAB were lost, the Royal National Lifeboat Institution decided that such techniques were necessary at Padstow, and since no commercial tug was based there, a specially designed RNLI tug was ordered from Ramage & Ferguson of Leith, famous builders of special small ships. Her specifications were: HELEN PEELE, ON 84984, built 1901. 16 tons net, 133 gross, 95.5 x 19.6 x 10.7 ft with a raised forecastle 34 ft long, two compound steam engines by the builders, 55 r.h.p. 11 ins and 22 ins x 10 ins stroke. Registered at Padstow in 1901 as a steel, clench built, twin screw, elliptical sterned tug with two pole masts. (The description clench or clinker built merely refers to the lapping of the steel plates in the rivetted hull).

Some particulars of her gallant 28 years service at Padstow will be found in the chapter on lifeboats, but when she was sold and left Padstow for the Clyde on 22nd May, 1929, she started a second career.

She had been bought that month by John Turner of Tignabruaich, Argyle, who had her converted into a steam yacht and sold her that October to William Tattershall Whitely of London, who promptly became Baron Marchamley of Hartfield. She is reported to have gone up the Rhine to Switzerland, but the date of that voyage is uncertain. In 1931 she changed hands again, her new owner being Capt. Thomas Winter of Sevenoaks, Kent. On 8th February, 1834, the shipping journal *Fairplay* reported HELEN PEELE offered for sale, lying South America. *Lloyd's Yacht Register* and the *Mercantile Navy List* continued to list her for many years, but I suspect that Capt. Winter was not available to amend the entries. She was registered at Padstow throughout but her fate remains a mystery.

The only other steam vessels to be registered at Padstow were the fishing vessel ADELE (reg. 1929) and the steam yacht MEDEA (reg. 1964) and details are given in other chapters.

Thus in the whole era of steamships from, say 1830 to 1980, the Padstow registers contain only one paddle tug, one steam launch, one twin-screwed lifeboat tug, one steam drifter and one Edwardian steam yacht. Also worthy of mention have been one steam coaster (the DELABOLE), one un-named steam ferry, and one steam lifeboat (JAMES STEVENS No.4).

To complete what might be described as a rag-tag and bobtail of steam vessels, it must be recorded that the wreck of the schooner JANIE was towed to the River Mersey and fitted with a steam engine in 1918 to meet the needs of war as a steam lighter (see Appendix).

No seagoing cargo steamship has ever been built or registered at Padstow.

### The Packet Steamers

The steamers which most directly affected Padstow were not Padstow ships, but the packets which traded from Hayle to Bristol, which started calling at Padstow periodically, and later on the Wadebridge & Padstow to Bristol steamers owned by Pocketts of Swansea, a service which continued in one form or another until the first years of the twentieth century. Passengers tended to go by train after 1898.

The port books of the sixteenth and seventeenth centuries indicate that four or five Bristol to Padstow traders made five or six voyages per annum carrying passengers and general goods, and subject to the ebb and flow of war and trade, that arrangement and scale of trade continued well into the nineteenth century.

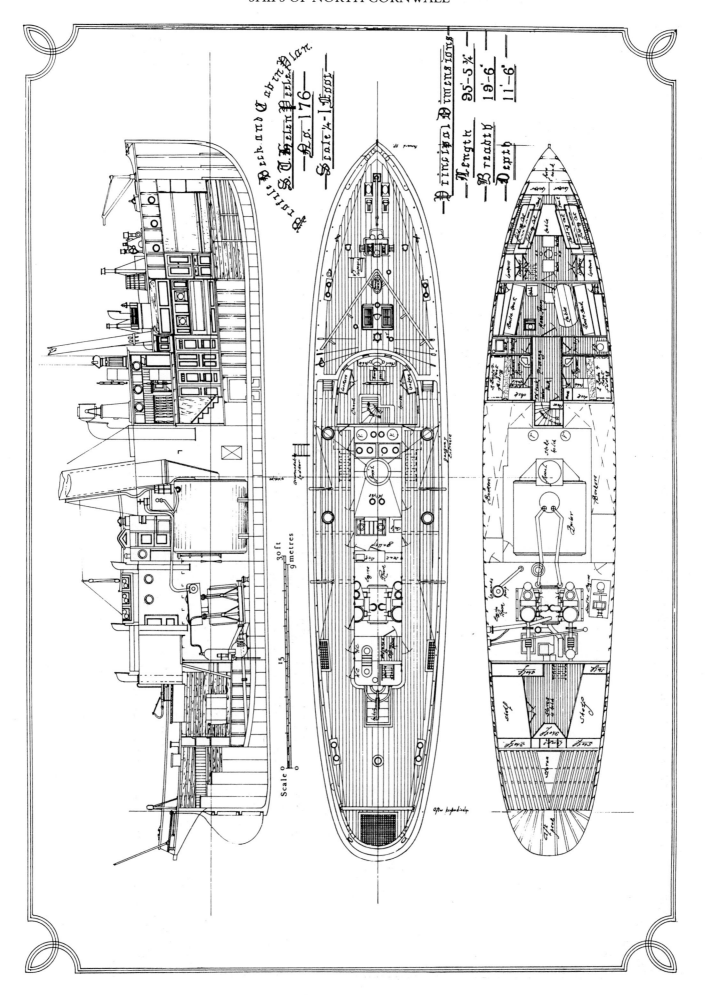

Profile plan of deck and cabin, HELEN PEELE.

*Philip Thomas Collection*

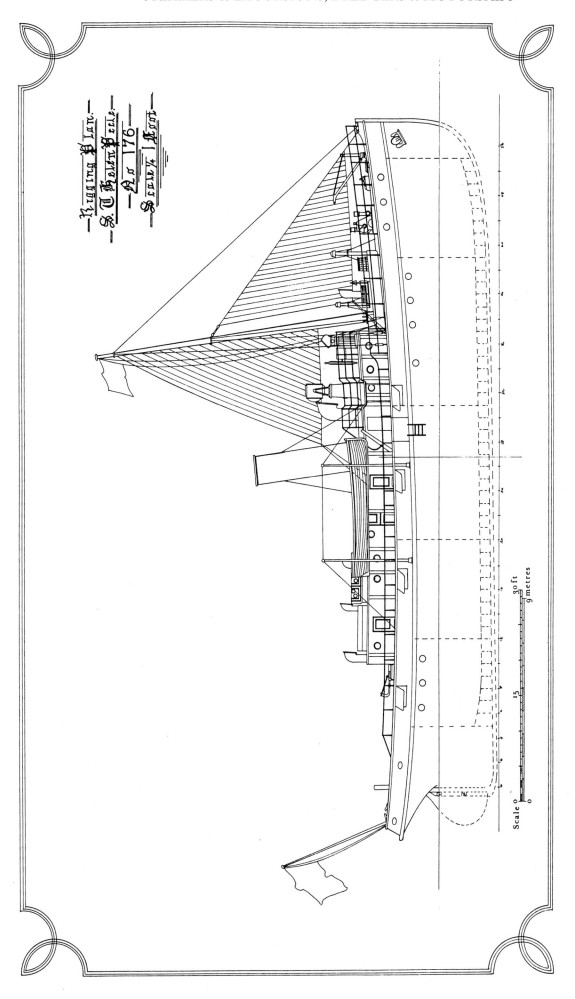

Rigging plan of the unique lifeboat tug HELEN PEELE.

*Philip Thomas Collection*

The first 'packet steamer' to make an impact on Padstow was the COUNTY OF PEMBROKE, 110 tons and her entry in *Lloyd's Register* 1834 gives under 'intended voyage' Bristol to Padstow. She had been built, 1831, at Bristol by Patterson and Mercer and bought in 1834 by Samuel Guppy of Bristol. In June 1834 she instituted a weekly service to Padstow, leaving Bristol on Tuesdays. It seems that the inhabitants of Padstow (and the Doom Bar) already had their antipathy to steam, and the service lasted less than a month. But in 1842, the Hayle Steamship Company, facing competition on the Hayle to Bristol run, initiated calls at Padstow by their wooden paddle steamers HERALD and CORNWALL. The HERALD was broken up about 1848 and the CORNWALL was replaced by the CORNUBIA, an iron paddle steamer built by Harveys at Hayle in 1858. Meanwhile the steamers of the rival Hayle and Bristol Steam Navigation Co. also visited Padstow, the BRILLIANT, QUEEN and ALBION, especially the iron paddle steamer QUEEN, built at Bristol in 1852 which was a regular visitor to Padstow until she was wrecked on Hartland Point in 1866.

Arrangements in the early years did not always work out, as witness the following item in the *West Briton*:

*Bristol. 22nd July, 1842.* The exhibition of the Royal Agricultural Society of England commenced on Wednesday 13th instant. From the facilities offered by the CORNWALL and HERALD, steamers on the one side, and the coaches on the other, a very respectable number of Cornish farmers made their appearance at the beginning of the exhibition. The BRILLIANT had given timely notice, by advertisement and otherwise, that she would call off Newquay by 7 o'clock, and Padstow by 8 o'clock, both of which places she passed at from 6 to 8 miles at sea, by which certain parties were not only disappointed but had to seek for other means of conveyance.

These Hayle packet companies faced increasing competition from the railways with the opening of the Saltash bridge in 1859. CORNUBIA went off to be a blockade runner in the American civil war in 1861, and the humble Padstow trade was taken over by the ships of James W. Pockett of Swansea. The Pockett steamers involved were the PRINCE OF WALES, (an iron paddle steamer built 1842 at Neath Abbey), HENRY SOUTHAN, (an iron screw steamer built 1845 at the same yard) and VELINDRA, (an iron paddle steamer built 1860 at Blackwall, London). These were all passenger-carrying packet steamers, the last being later more of an excursion vessel in which capacity she ran excursions to Padstow among other places. In 1872 the PRINCE OF WALES was running a service from Padstow to Swansea.

Pockett advertised a weekly service Bristol-Padstow-Wadebridge, but Wadebridge could only be served on spring tides and the service soon became fortnightly with the HENRY SOUTHAN normally filling the berth. With the passenger traffic being phased out, the cargo steamers COLLIER and DUNRAVEN took over towards the end of the century, although the paddler BRIGHTON also paid visits to Padstow: all these vessels were Pockett steamers.

Another cargo service worthy of mention was the regular arrival of the grey painted coasters of the Bristol firm Osborn & Wallis during the Second World War. Towards the end of the war they were more heavily armed than the naval patrol vessels which saw them in past Stepper Point and doubtless more liable to enemy attack. Lovering's handsome CORNEL provided a similar service from Cardiff.

In the twentieth century, steam coasters aplenty have come to Padstow, generally bringing coal from Wales, but the only passenger steamers have been excursion vessels sailing between Bristol, Cardiff, Swansea and the great holiday resorts such as Weston and Ilfracombe.

Pockett's paddle steamer BRIGHTON arriving at Padstow *c.* 1905.
*Nigel Coombes Collection*

The SS PAR of Fowey, built on the Clyde in 1902, approaches Padstow, passing Brea Hill. Steamers were still provided with auxiliary sails but they were seldom set. The PAR has one on each mast, all furled, and the crew are unrigging the sail on the mainmast to leave the gear free to handle cargo when she docks. The days of sail are virtually over.

## Excursion Steamers

In 1888 the brothers P. & A. Campbell transferred their Clyde-based paddle steamer business to Bristol, and successful excursions on a massive scale were carried on in the Bristol Channel area by their 'white funnel fleet'. It was not uncommon to see half a dozen excursion steamers moored at Ilfracombe, and places like Barry and Mumbles were well served. Padstow, being at the western end of the Bristol Channel, was not part of the regular excursion circuit but was visited several times a season, and there were also visits to Newquay.

There were breaks, of course, in both World Wars, and the paddlers, with their shallow draught, were converted into minesweepers and many were lost. After the Second World War, the excursion steamers lost their appeal to the general public and visits to Padstow became rare.

Now the PS WAVERLEY is our only surviving seagoing paddle steamer and her visits to Padstow are even more uncommon, but they are very well supported by old *aficionados*, and increasingly by a young generation to whom steam power is a novelty and a legend.

## Local Excursions

Apart from the AMAZON and JANE, no registered vessels played a part in the local excursion trade until after the Second World War. After the sale of the Padstow to Rock steam ferry in 1885, that link was carried on by a series of open boats propelled by oar and lugsail. The ferryman, Hodge Helbren, was drowned one winter's day in 1906 when a gust capsized the boat. That is said to be the only

fatality in the long history of the ferry. The Rawe family took over and a small motorboat was introduced in about 1913.

Between the wars, Steve Brabyn had three small motorboats working the ferry, ST ENODOC, ST SAVIOURS and AU REVOIR, and they took trippers around the estuary as well as doing the ferry work. In 1945 Bill Lindsey obtained the lease and his motorboats were ST MINVER, ST ENODOC (II), PETROCKSTOWE and ST SAVIOURS (II), the last three of which he built himself at Padstow. ST SAVIOURS, ON 166957, built in 1952, was the first British registered ship to be built at Padstow since 1906, and she was operated as an excursion vessel on occasion with a Board of Trade licence to carry 28 passengers.

In 1966 John England took over the ferry lease and had three boats specially built by Percy Mitchell of Portmellon. Later the Commissioners decided to run the ferries themselves and un-named boats were designated PHC No.1, No.2 and No.3 (a reserve boat). A new type of ferry with a hydraulically operated bow ramp, the BLACK TOR, entered service in 1994.

Local excursions in relatively small vessels rely on good weather and sheltered waters. Newquay and Port Isaac do not have the latter, so tend to offer fishing trips to hardy anglers. Padstow has the beautiful setting of the Camel estuary, sheltered waters, at least as far as the Doom Bar, and a fascinating coastline past Pentire Point and the Rumps to the Mouls Rock (dubbed Puffin Island for excursion purposes). The only disadvantage at Padstow is the lack of water at low tide. The excursion vessels and the ferries to Rock cannot get near the harbour at low water and intending passengers have to walk half a mile north to St Saviour's Point, and board from the beach. Excursions to Wadebridge have to be timed to take the flood tide up, and the ebb tide down again.

The following motor excursion vessels have worked from Padstow in recent years:

**BUCCANEER** A handsome wooden motor launch built 1964 at Portmellon by Mitchell for John England of Padstow, licensed for 70 passengers. Sold to North Haven Ferries, Poole.

**CORNISH QUEEN** An exact sister of BUCCANEER also built 1964 by Mitchell, but for St Ives owners. About 1986 R. D. and J. H. Paynter of St Ives sold her to R. A. Russell of Rock.

These two launches were 41 x 12 x 3 ft dr. larch on oak, with Kelvin engines.

**JUBILEE QUEEN**, ON 366337, built 1977 at Wadebridge. Tons 50 net 99 gross, 80 ft long. A steel motor vessel licensed to carry 254 passengers; built and owned by Brian T. Chapman of Wadebridge and registered at Padstow. Padstow's principal excursion vessel.

**PRIVATEER** A launch similar to BUCCANEER and also owned by John England until sold to North Haven Ferries, Poole. About 1986 she moved to the fleet of J. Harvey & Sons, Poole, and was renamed MAID OF SANDBANKS. Not listed by them after 1990.

**QUEEN OF CORNWALL** built 1970. A 49 ft wooden motor excursion vessel: an enlarged version of the BUCCANEER. She started her career at Padstow but in recent years has operated from Ilfracombe, carrying up to 75 passengers, owned by C. J. Barbeary.

**ST SAVIOURS**, ON 166957, built 1952 at Padstow by William H. R. Lindsey. Tons 4 net and gross. 25.2 x 7.5 x 3.6. A wooden motor launch with 18 h.p. engine. Rock ferry and excursions. Sold by Lindsey about 1973 to J. R. H. Wilson of Pulborough, Sussex.

**TRI-STAR**, ON 335582, built 1972 at Bideford by Bideford Shipyard Ltd. Tons 28 net 42 gross. 70 ft long. A steel twin-screw motor excursion vessel carrying up to 170 passengers. Owner Elizabeth A. England, Manager Arthur J. G. England of Padstow; owner changed to Padstow Boating Co. in 1983. Sold 1988 to Mackenzie Marine, Ullapool and renamed SUMMER QUEEN. Advertised for sale 1992.

In recent years powerful speed boats have taken passengers for short trips around the Camel estuary at high speed: their names include **007, JAWS, JAWS 2, CYCLONE, APOLLO, APOLLO 2,** and **APOLLO 3**.

The steel motor excursion vessel **DART PRINCESS** was built 1992 at Padstow by A & J Marine. She is 45 ft long and can carry 60 passengers. Her owner is Ken Lane and she is based at Paignton in South Devon. The newspapers described her as the largest passenger vessel ever built at Padstow — as the JUBILEE QUEEN had been built at Wadebridge.

## Dredgers

Since the 1950s there has generally been what looks like an old motor coaster in Padstow harbour, sometimes two, and they have indeed been old motor coasters, but converted into 'sand suckers', a specialised type of dredger.

The trade in 'sea dredged aggregates' has grown rapidly in recent years as public resistance has grown to the creation of sand and gravel pits on land. But the dredgings are not solely used for making concrete; sand is used for many industrial purposes. In Loch Aline, one of the prettiest anchorages off the Sound of Mull, is to be found the only current source in Britain of the beautiful white sand used for making optical glass. Grit is still spread on the roads. Different grades of sand are used for spreading on lawns, making abrasives, mixing into asphalt, children's playgrounds and many other uses. Even in the building trades, very fine sand is needed for the

manufacture of plaster, and fine loamy sand is used to make a workable cement mortar, whereas sharp sand made up of strong rock particles is needed if strength is required in mortar or concrete.

The shell content of the sand in the Camel estuary makes it particularly suitable for spreading on agricultural land.

Until the 1920s, the sand was won the hard way by shovelling into barges at low water. In the 1920s and '30s the motor lorries came into their own, and it was a simple matter to fill them with sand at low tide on the beaches on the Rock side of the estuary, and drive straight to the final destination. But suction dredging had already been invented and developed, and several companies were dredging sand in the Bristol Channel. The principles are simple: an open ended pipe is lowered to the channel bed; a powerful centrifugal pump sucks up sand and water, and spews it, often through a screen or riddle, into the hold; thus large stones and rubbish can be screened out and fall over the side: there are various refinements. The hold is a watertight box, sufficiently small so that even when it is full of sand and water, the ship still has adequate freeboard. Surplus water overflows from the hold back to the sea, taking with it in suspension some of the very fine dirt which might in any case have to be washed out later, depending on the customer's requirements. Many of the dredgers have another pump to deal with water drained from the sand once the hold is full.

The dredger returns to her berth where the sand is either grabbed out by crane, or pumped ashore, for sale or for further treatment.

In 1956 the Bristol firm Ashmead & Sons saw a future in sand dredging and tin dredging in North Cornwall. As far as Padstow is concerned this led to the formation of Ashmead (Padstow) Ltd and the arrival of the STOWMEAD at Padstow. Since then the following sand suckers have worked at Padstow or been managed from Padstow:

**BAYMEAD**, ON 169730, built 1944 at Rowhedge by Rowhedge Ironworks Ltd as the steel coastal tanker EMPIRE BOXER. Tons 139 net 340 gross. 146.8 x 23.7 x 9.3 with 395 b.h.p. oil engine by British Auxiliaries Ltd, Glasgow, owners C. Rowbotham & Sons. Renamed CHARTSMAN 1946. In 1966, sold to Coastal Prospecting Co. Ltd, and in 1967 port of registry changed from London to Bideford, vessel renamed BAYMEAD and converted to a suction dredger for tin dredging in St Ives Bay. Manager, D. C. Ashmead of Ashmead Management (Padstow) Ltd. It is believed that she was scrapped at Northam, Southampton in July 1974, but she remained listed in *Lloyd's Register* for many years thereafter.

**BLACK GEM**, ON 183357, built 1949 at Dartmouth by Philip & Son Ltd, tons 182 net 368 gross, 140.0 x 25.1 x 8.8 as the steel motor coaster WIMBORNE and registered at Poole, owned by John Carter Ltd. Sold 1968 to Anglo-Jersey Shipping Lines Ltd and renamed JERSEY CASTLE. Sold 1970 to Sand Supplies (Western) Ltd. Port of registry changed from Jersey to Bristol; renamed SAND GEM and converted into a suction dredger capable of lifting 350 tons of sand or aggregate. Sold in 1990 to Malcolm Carrington and Stephen Charles Smart, renamed BLACK GEM in 1981 and based at Padstow (although Bristol remained her port of registry). In 1985 her owners became David G. and Christine J. Williams of Hayle, trading from 1988 on as D G W Sand Co. Ltd. Broken up at Padstow 1990 by T. C. Fraser (Metals) Ltd.

**COEDMOR**, ON 180868, built 1946 at Faversham by James Pollock Sons & Co. Ltd as the Admiralty coastal lighter VIC 57. Tons 52 net, 147 gross. 80.0 x 20.0 x 9.5 with a compound steam engine 140 i.h.p. Owned by Ministry of Transport who sold her in 1948 to Arran Sea Transport & Supply Co. Ltd, Bute, renamed

ARRAN MONARCH. In a sense she was returning to her origins. When the Admiralty needed powered victualling lighters in the Second World War, it was decided that the best simple standard design which could be built of steel and handled easily was the 'Clyde puffer', dozens of which supplied the Western Isles with coal and other necessities. Despite being built at Faversham, VIC 57 was one of sixty-three such puffers built for the Admiralty. In 1953 she was sold to Wansborough Paper Co. Ltd, Watchet, and in 1960 to P. Herbert of Bude. Then in 1964 she was bought by Hollacombe Aggregates Ltd, Wadebridge, renamed COEDMOR, lengthened by Appledore Shipbuilders Ltd and converted into a motor suction dredger. In place of her compound steam engine which had been built at Beccles, she was given a Bergius Kelvin 6 cylinder diesel of 160 b.h.p., and powerful generators for the pumps. Her tonnage was increased to 91 net, 181 gross, and her length to 109.5 ft. The following year her owners became the Burry Sand Co. Ltd and Llanelly became her port of registry in place of London. In 1985 David and Christine Williams were owners, becoming D G W Sand Co. Ltd in 1988. Since becoming a dredger she has often worked in the River Camel.

**FIELD**, ON 183498, built 1949 at Poole by J. Bolson & Son Ltd. Tons 90 net 133 gross. 80.8 x 19.6 x 9.1. A steel twin-screw motor cargo vessel, she was built for the British Transport Commission and registered at Cowes, spending her time ferrying cargo to the Isle of Wight. Her owners changed to British Road Services in 1962. She was registered at Bideford in 1971 as owned by Herbs Ship Ltd, none other than P. Herbert of Bude, but the next year she joined the fleet of Ashmead (Padstow) Ltd. She served as a cargo barge and sand carrier until broken up in 1976.

COEDMOR at Wadebridge, 1877

**SAND SNIPE**, ON 303366, built 1961 at Poole by J. Bolson & Son Ltd. Tons 176 net 691 gross. 173.5 x 30.3 x 11.5. A steel motor suction dredger and sand carrier built for South Coast Shipping Co. Ltd and registered at Southampton. In 1988 she joined the fleet of the D G W Sand Co. and in due course worked much of the time from Padstow like others in the fleet. In 1990 she was reported to be taking calcified seaweed to Truro.

**SAND WYVERN**, ON 300671, built 1959 at Poole by J. Bolson & Son Ltd as the SAND GREBE. Tons 197 net, 531 gross, 675 deadweight. She was given two 6-cylinder Blackstone diesels, and was designed and built as a steel diesel electric sand suction dredger for the South Coast Shipping Co. Ltd, Southampton where she was registered. In 1973 Padstow became her port of registry and Wyvern Maritime Ltd of Padstow her owners. They renamed her SAND WYVERN. In 1977 she returned to Southampton owned by Westminster Gravels Ltd. In 1982 new owners Thomas J. Brown and others of Southampton renamed her SEA DRIVER. She remained on the Padstow register until broken up by L. de Ste. Croix in 1985.

**SANDIE**, built 1958 at Kallandso, Sweden, as the dumb barge WARGON V. Rebuilt as a motor vessel in 1970 and renamed SANDIE, of Baskarp, Sweden. In 1988 renamed SJOBJORN VIII, of Styrso, Sweden, a Swedish *sandsugningsfartyg* (i.e. sand sucker). In 1990 she was bought by the D G W Sand Co. and registered at Padstow, and renamed SANDIE: tons 87 net, 199 gross, 112.3 x 22.9 with a 6-cylinder Scania diesel of 220 kw. She was ready to start work in place of the discarded BLACK GEM.

**STOWMEAD**, ON 163394, built 1933 at Rowhedge by Rowhedge Ironworks Co. Ltd. Tons 168 net 377 gross, 179 net later. 135.0 x 25.1 x 11.4. A steel twinscrew coastal tanker with two Gardner 380 b.h.p. oil engines, named BEN HENSHAW, registered at London and owned by National Benzole Mixture Co Ltd. Sold in 1957 to the Channel Shipping Co. of London and renamed GRANTEZ, but passed almost immediately to Ashmead (Padstow) Ltd, registered at Padstow, and renamed STOWMEAD. Her conversion to a sand dredger was apparently not completed until 1959, but she worked out of Padstow until she ran aground near the harbour on 7th July, 1970, broke her back, was sold to a local demolition firm, Bird, and dismantled.

THE ADMIRALTY STEAM LIGHTER VIC 57,
LATER TO BECOME THE 'COEDMOR'

The BEN HENSHAW, later to become
STOWMEAD, from *The Motorship* and
author's collection

Plan of BEN HENSHAW from
*The Motorship.*

SEPTEMBER, 1933.

# A 350-TON COASTAL TANKER

## The "Ben Henshaw" for the Service of the National Benzole Co.

THERE was launched last month, from the yard of the Rowhedge Iron-works, Rowhedge, a small motor tanker for coastal service, to the order of the National Benzole Co., and named "Ben Henshaw." She is a twin-screw ship, and is capable of carrying 350 tons on a draught of 10 ft. 6 ins., comprising 300 tons of oil cargo and 38 tons of fuel oil in cross bunkers, in addition to 12 tons of fresh water and fuel oil.

The following are the main details:—

| | | | | |
|---|---|---|---|---|
| Length b.p. | ... | ... | ... | 135 ft. |
| Beam | ... | ... | ... | 25 ft. |
| Moulded depth | ... | ... | 12 ft. |
| Service speed | ... | ... | 9 knots |
| Engine power | ... | ... | 380 b.h.p. |

The hull is constructed on the transverse system and will carry light oil in bulk, the design providing for the fact that the ship will sometimes lie on the mud when loading and discharging. There is a forward hold, followed by four tanks to port and starboard, aft of which is the pump-room, with fuel bunkers between it and the engine-room.

The propelling plant consists of two five-cylinder Gardner two-stroke airless injection oil engines, of 190 b.h.p. running at 320 r.p.m., and in view of the service of the vessel, the funnel has a spark-arresting device. At the forward end of the engine-room is the main auxiliary, which is a Diesel-engine-driven generator, with an extended shaft and reducing gear, driving one of

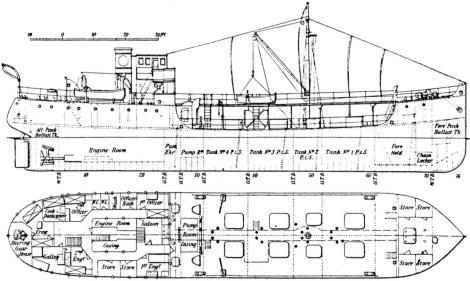

General arrangement plan of the "Ben Henshaw."

the cargo pumps in the pump-room through a shaft between the engine-room and the pump-room. There is a further generating plant, also driving an air-compressor and general service pump, and 55 Exide Ironclad batteries are installed for lighting when the generators are not in service. In the pump-room is a second pump, which is steam driven. An Oertz rudder is employed, and Reid's electrically assisted steering gear is utilized. The windlass on deck is coupled to an electric motor, this being flame-proof, as are the

generators and motors in the engine-room.

The accommodation is somewhat superior to that usually found on a vessel of this class. The cabins and saloon are in the poop with the captain's accommodation above the saloon. There is a cabin for a crew of four, and a separate two-berth cabin for the cook and donkeyman.

The four main tanks are subdivided by continuous longitudinal oil-tight bulkheads running fore and aft and extending to the main deck.

Two traditional Scottish built motor fishing vessels in Padstow, 1993, locally owned but retaining their Banff and Inverness fishing numbers. 1993.

*Author's photos*

Plate 9

Now that the inner harbour at Padstow is an enclosed floating dock, it is increasingly popular with yachts and fishing vessels that stay afloat at all states of the tide. The SY 222 on the boat in the foreground indicates that the GIRL IRENE is registered in Stornaway.

*Author's photo, 1993*

The inshore boats ATLANTA PW 21, TOPAZ PW 15 and JANINE PW 157 await fishing parties, anchored off Newquay in the July summer haze 1986.

*Author's photo*

Plate 10

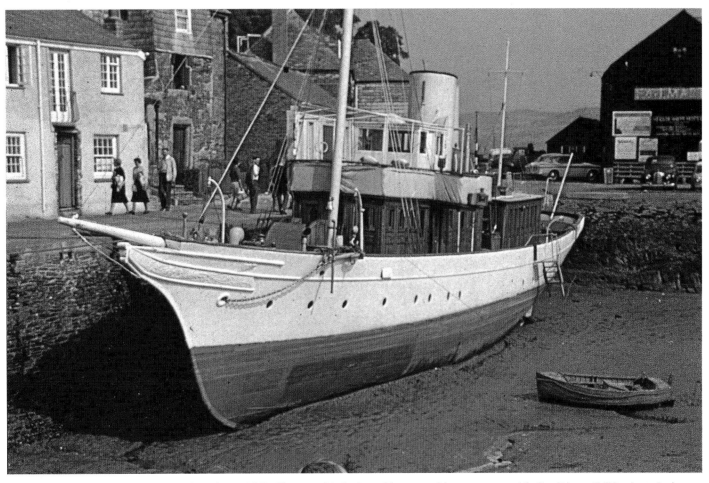

Captain Millars steam Yacht MEDEA in Padstow, 1962. She served in both world wars, and is now preserved in San Diego, California as the last Edwardian yacht of her type.

The arrival of the fast motorboats JAWS and 007 heralded a new type of excursion from Padstow harbour.

*Malcolm McCarthy, 1996*

Plate 11

The ferry arrives at Padstow from Rock. June 1993.

*Author's photo*

The suction dredger COEDMOR off Gun Point in the Camel estuary. June 1984.

*Author's photo*

Plate 12

**WESTMEAD**, ON 167351, built 1928 at Leiderdorp in the Netherlands by Gebr. Boot as the inland waterways motor tank barge DOMBURG (some references give DOMBERG). In 1938 Samuel Williams & Sons Ltd bought her, registered her at London and renamed her HARTFIELD. She measured tons 163 net, 202 gross, later 143 net 197 gross, 129.4 x 20.8 x 7.2 and for the next 23 years she was a familiar sight on the Thames, carrying molasses from the docks to the upper tidal reaches. Ashmead (Padstow) Ltd bought her in 1961, registered her at Padstow in 1962 and renamed her WESTMEAD. She was converted into a sand hopper with bottom opening doors — a useful adjunct to dredging operations — and worked for Ashmead as a hopper and a barge until 1973. She was then owned briefly by Herb Ship Ltd (P. M. Herbert) of Bude, and sold to T. W. Ward, who started dismantling her at Briton Ferry in September 1974.

That completes the fleet of larger Padstow dredges, but the following have also worked at Padstow either on isolated visits, or to assist in the construction and maintenance of the harbour.

**PETROC**, ON 366339. Tons 22 net, 41 gross. A small steel motor hopper dredger owned by the Padstow Harbour Commissioners in the early 1980s, which left with POLO about 1985 to work at Par Harbour.

**POLO**, ON 335578, built 1969 at Bideford by Bideford Shipyard Ltd. Tons 22 net, 41 gross. 50.8 x 19.6 x 5.8. A Padstow registered steel motor hopper barge owned by Arthur England.

**POLO II**, ON 359255, built 1972 at Bideford by Bideford Shipyard Ltd. Tons 29 net, 58 gross. A Padstow registered steel motor hopper barge owned by Harry Smale, Trakplant Ltd, Honiton.

SAND SNIPE in 1988

'STOWMEAD' BEING CONVERTED INTO A DREDGER AT PADSTOW, 17th JUNE, 1958

**POLO III**, ON 364563, built 1964 at Soby, Denmark by Soby Stalskibs. Tons 89 net, 150 gross (Danish) 101 net, 186 gross (Jersey register). 116.2 x 23.5 x 6.8 all after lengthening c.1970. A steel motor hopper suction dredger with two Scania diesels, 298 b.h.p., completed as the Danish AMANDA but renamed POLO III in 1975 when registered at Guernsey and owned by Geoffrey Smale, Honiton. Sold to Hull owners in 1981 and renamed HOOK SAND.

**SANDCHIME**, ON 303091, built 1952 at Renfrew by William Simons & Co. Ltd. Tons 61 net, 190 gross. 105.0 x 24.5 x 8.8. A steel grab dredger built with a triple expansion steam engine, which was replaced by a diesel engine by 1982. After government service in Scotland she was owned by Geoffrey Smale of Honiton in the late 1970s and by A. C. Riggall of Humberside since 1980. A grab dredger can clear out corners in docks and excavate all but the hardest materials for dock construction. SANDCHIME helped with the harbour works at Padstow in 1988.

**SARGIA**, ON 183687, built 1951 at Hull as the motor barge RENWICK and converted about 1968 into the Bristol sandsucker SAND OPAL. Tons 73 net, 115 gross. 95.2 x 17.8 x 8.1 sold in 1976 to Sarnia Marine & Shipping of Southampton, and renamed SARGIA. It is not known to what extent she worked at Padstow where she was to be seen in 1977.

BLACK GEM in 1989

## Motor Vessels

The largest Padstow motor vessels have been dredgers listed in the last few pages: before them the local excursion vessels were dealt with. The great majority of the motor vessels will be found in the chapter on fishing.

Precious few of Padstow's schooners and ketches were fitted with motors whilst in Padstow ownership. The master mariners of Padstow, Newquay and Port Isaac (who were also to a substantial extent the owners of the ships) saw little point in spending hard-earned money on auxiliary engines in the early years of the twentieth century, and Capt. Thomas May Jr, for instance, was firmly of the opinion that they were a passing phase which would not catch on. He ended up as a farmer, and no seagoing cargo motorship has ever been built or registered at Padstow.

The fishermen of Padstow were quick to take advantage of the internal combustion engine although their deep sea *confrères* eschewed engines of all kinds.

POLO II of Padstow, dredger of Westcountry ports, equipped for grab dredging and for trailing suction dredging.

# ENVOI

*Oh soon we'll hear the old man say*
*Leave her Johnny, leave her,*
*You can go ashore and get your pay*
*It's time for us to leave her.*

Chanty

---

## Tintagel Shipping Co. Ltd.

TINTAGEL and King Arthur's Castle fall within the limits of the Port of Padstow and Padstow ships loaded slates from Tintagel into the present century.

In 1989 the newly formed Tintagel Shipping Co. Ltd, a subsidiary of Inter Shipping with an address in Zurich, bought a huge steam turbine driven tanker, the OSA MERLIN (note the Arthurian connection) and renamed her TRADE RELIANCE. She sailed under the Cypriot flag (thereby presumably avoiding the relatively high cost of employing British mariners).

When the price of tankers rose substantially early in 1990, the Tintagel Shipping Co. sold her to BT Shipping Services, London, and she was renamed BT VENTURE and operated by the Oaklet Shipping Co. Ltd, Cyprus. She was scrapped in 1994.

TRADE RELIANCE had been built in 1971 in Japan as the KYOEI MARU but thereafter was named BLUE PHOENIX, MERLIN and OSA MERLIN. With a length of 315 metres, a breadth of 50 metres and a maximum draught of 19.3 metres, she greatly exceeded in size the largest passenger liners such as the Cunarders QUEEN MARY and QUEEN ELIZABETH. She could carry 215,000 tons of oil — a greater tonnage than all the ships of Padstow recorded in this book added together!

At first sight, this vast steel box with two powerful steam turbines appears as a dull commercial machine bearing no comparison to the little wooden sailing ships which traded with such enterprise over much of the world. But wait: in her short life, this tanker was heavily engaged in the Gulf Wars. She extracted several million tons of oil from the war zone, much to the benefit of the civilised world, she was twice set on fire by missiles, and was towed to Dubai for repairs with an unexploded missile on board. Her multi-racial crews have certainly not had dull lives, although they have doubtless suffered from the very short time such vessels stay in port, and the noisome drab and desolate nature of most oil terminals and refineries.

The twentieth century has seen the operation of 'Tintagel' ships change from sloop to supertanker, but the challenge, the enterprise, the dangers, the sweat, the immortal sea, and the fascination all persist.

# APPENDIX

## *The Histories of the Nineteenth-Century Ships*

HERE follows the history of all the sailing vessels known to have been registered or built or owned at Padstow since about 1800 in alphabetical order. The outports and hinterland of Padstow are included. Over 920 ships are listed.

In 1786 it became compulsory for each port to make a register of all decked vessels of 15 tons burthen or more. Copies were sent to London but a fire destroyed them in 1814, and only a few of the earlier registers survived in Cornwall. Some of the earlier vessels, then, lack proper documentation, and a few others may have been omitted altogether.

The tonnages given are marked (O) meaning old measure, or builder's measure, an arbitrary formula which did not adequately increase tonnage with depth of hull. In 1836 a new formula was introduced marked (N) for new measure. In many places the old measure was continued, sometimes along with the new for some years, and many old ships were never re-measured. The new tonnages tended to be less in the case of beamy coasters, but many deep-hulled ships were given an increase in tonnage. The Merchant Shipping Act of 1854 introduced a yet more accurate method of measuring the tonnages, each ton being 100 cubic feet of permanently enclosed space (as it remains to this day). After 1867, a reduction was allowed for living spaces, and the previous measurement was known as the 'gross' tonnage, whereas the reduced registered tonnage was termed 'net'. In this list some tonnages are marked 'reg.' either because they were measured soon after 1854 before the term 'gross' was used or because it is uncertain whether the tonnage given is net or gross. With other minor changes, a typical Padstow schooner had half a dozen different tonnages in the course of her life.

On the port registers tonnage in 'old tons' was given in tons and 94ths of tons, for example 54.32/94 tons. In 'new tons' it became tons and fractions in three thousand five hundredths of a ton, for example 102.2318/3500 tons, and since the 1854 Act it has been tons and hundredths of a ton given in decimal form, 64.58 for example. One of the many sources of discrepancy was that the last example might be copied as 64 tons, or more correctly given as 65 tons (to the nearest ton),

The Merchant Shipping Act of 1854 also introduced a new requirement that each registered British ship (anywhere in the British Empire) should be given an official number to be carved upon her main beam. The official number (ON) was to remain with her through all subsequent changes of name, ownership or registration, and is often the surest way of differentiating one ship from another.

The dimensions given are in feet and tenths of feet; when available they are taken from the Port Registers, or surveys, but in other cases they have been taken from *Lloyd's Register*. They represent length of hull, breadth, and depth of hold, but the exact methods of measurement of dimensions varied from time to time, so there are numerous anomalies.

Schooner means two masted topsail (or topgallant) schooner unless described in other detail. Almost all the Padstow-built schooners had square sterns and fixed 'standing' bowsprits, but details entered into registers and surveys were not always complete or correct.

All the ships listed were built of wood unless otherwise noted.

**A.E.R.** A small cutter of this name is reported to have been built at Padstow in 1876. (Hicks Colln.)

**ACTIVE** ON 25432, built 1784 at Poole, rebuilt 1824. Tons 52(O), 41(N). 47.5 15.0 8.8.

She started life as a sloop, but was schooner rigged after being rebuilt in 1824. Her registration was transferred to Padstow from St Ives in 1853, when she was bought by John Clemens and numerous others. Nicholas Hosken and Isaac Pappin were her Padstow masters.

In 1864 she was sold to W. Harris, Mevagissey and re-registered at Fowey. Finally she had Appledore owners and Bideford registration; gone by 1880.

**ACTIVE** ON 4457, built 1825 at Salcombe by John Evans. Tons 70(O) 54.08(N.1856). 54.9 17.9 9.1.

A schooner with a scroll head, she was initially a Plymouth coaster with Dartmouth and Salcombe given as home ports, but registered at Padstow in 1856 with Jos. Tippett owning her in 1856 and E. Tabb in 1857. She was lost at sea 8th December, 1858. Reg. closed 28th December 1858.

**ACTIVE** ON built 1850 at Padstow by R & J Tredwen. Tons about 100(O). No register has been found and it is possible that ACTIVE was a name *pro tem.* and that she was registered as EMBLEM. (c.f. ARCTIC).

**ADA** ON 22736, built 1844 at Padstow by Richard Tredwen and lengthened in 1866. Tons 35(N as built), 46(net. after lengthening). 46.6 14.1 7.5 as built; 48.2 15.5 7.4 after lengthening. Rigged as a sloop or smack until converted to a ketch on lengthening. Registered at Padstow 1844-1900, and owned successively by P. W. Hutchings, James Henwood of Little Petherick, T. Hawke of St Endellion, Stribley, and Rowe, generally with numerous minor shareholders. Her masters came mainly from the Henwood and Hutchings families. In 1900 she was sold to Bynon of Appledore and registered at Bideford. Lost at sea 14th May 1919 (note on reg.).

**ADA** ON 70484, built 1876 at Ulverston by Peet. Tons 115 net, 133 gross. 95 reg. (1928). 88.6 22.3 11 5.

A schooner which remained registered at Barrow throughout her long life but was owned in the 1920s in Polruan and Arklow until being laid up in the Gannel as a houseboat in 1928 owned by Thomas A. Reed of Newquay eventually became a floating museum.

**ADELAIDE** ON 58295, built 1869 at Padstow by John Tredwen. Tons 179 gross as built, 136 reg. (1906). 106.0 24.3 12.7.

A brigantine converted to schooner rig about 1916, she was built for C. Morris and registered at Fowey until 1924 when her owner Albert Benney transferred her registration to Falmouth. She was reported as a derelict at Penryn in 1934.

**ADVANCE** ON 75247, built 1876 at Garmouth by J. Geddie Jr. Tons 114 gross, 100 net. 89.2 21.5 10.4.

The ADA of 1876 laid up in the Gannel *c.* 1930.

A schooner registered at Peterhead, Kirkaldy and then Plymouth. She remained registered there in 1891 when Thomas Jacka of Newquay bought her, and when J. A. Clements, also of Newquay, took her over. She was wrecked at Scroby Sands on 23rd February 1913 when on passage from Hull to Teignmouth with coal.

**AEOLUS** ON 11673, built and registered at Cork in 1852. Tons 74 reg. 68.1 18.5 9.7.

A schooner with a scroll head, in 1857 she was re-registered at Padstow by William Ships who became her master, and John Hawke. She was abandoned at sea off Old Harry Rocks on 24th September 1883 when bound from London to Tralee with cement. The wind was West-South-West force 9, so she was probably seeking shelter in Studland Bay when overwhelmed by steep seas. Her crew of 4 were all saved.

**AFFO** ON 26786, built in 1826 at Padstow by John Tredwen. Tons 28(O), 20 (reg. 1875). 37.5 13.8 7.0.

A sloop which had an adventurous life taking coal and supplies to remote beaches. *Lloyd's List* reported her wrecked 15th August 1829, and again driven ashore at Boscastle 31st October 1837. Her Padstow owner was Rosvere (or Rosewarn) and members of the Bellamy, Strout, Couch and Rouse families were her masters before she was transferred to Bristol in 1843. She continued her old ways, being damaged again at Boscastle in 1872 and broken up in 1873.

**AFFO** ON 11623, built in 1836 at Bude by Stapleton. Tons 43(N), 37 reg. 49.8 16.5. 7.0.

This sloop was first registered at Bideford, but in 1848 John Hockin of Bude registered her at Padstow and appointed James Beer and later John Heard as masters. In 1861 her owner was Capt. William Goman, also of Bude, and her registration reverted to Bideford (of which Bude had become an outport in 1850). William was the son of John Goman, the Bude harbourmaster from 1830 to 1854. AFFO traded constantly to Bude. On 8th-9th December 1872

she was driven ashore under Hartland and lost with all hands, when bringing barley from Ireland.

**AGENORIA** ON 21379, built 1858 at Port Gavern by and for Warwick R. Guy. Tons 50 reg. 59.3 18.0 8.1.

She was lengthened in 1872 as her net tonnage became 65 for the rest of her life with dimensions 77.2 19.0 8.2. She was built as a smack (cutter rigged) but became a ketch after lengthening. J. Neal who had some shares was her master for many years, but in 1900, Mrs. Mary Bate of Port Isaac became owner, and H. Bate master.

On 10th August 1900 she was lost by stranding 5 five miles SSE of the Galloper lightship in the Thames estuary on passage Nieuport for Portsmouth with cement. Her crew of three were saved.

She was registered at Padstow throughout.

**AGNES** built 1809 at Padstow. Tons 60(O). 50.0 17.5 9.3. The first schooner to be built at Padstow, with square stern (like the majority of the sailing vessels built at Padstow) and standing bowsprit. Her entry in *Lloyd's Register* 1815 gives Master B. Harvey, owner Capt. & Co. (a normal entry when the master had even a small number of the 64 shares, but managed the ship's affairs). 2 guns. That year J. Yeo became her master and managing owner, and she was engaged in the home trades with Falmouth as her survey port. In 1829 the registration was transferred from Padstow to Swansea, and Mary Wilson of that port was her owner. In 1833 Thomas Richards of St Ives bought her and registered her there.

On 26th April 1845 she was thrown ashore on the quaintly named Man & His Man rocks about a mile off St Agnes Head. A gale was blowing and Capt. Richards and his crew were lucky to scramble on to one of the tall rocks, and eventually to be rescued by a passing schooner. The register was closed 5th May 1845.

**AGNES** ON 105246. The hull of LADY ACLAND (q.v.) which was rebuilt 1903 at Bude by Henry Stapleton. Tons 54 net, 67 gross, reduced to 45 net after installation of engine. 70.6 18.5 8.0.

Ketch rigged, she was fitted with an Invincible 40 b.h.p. semi-diesel engine probably in 1919, which was replaced by a 60 h.p. Widdop diesel in 1948. Her mainmast and other spars came from the wreck of the WILD PIGEON. The rebuilding was evidently of such a radical nature that the authorities treated her as a new ship and allotted a new Official Number.

Nicholas Tregaskes of Bude registered her at Bideford in 1904, and she remained a Bideford ship for the rest of her long life. Her ownership, however, was not static. The Tregaskes sold her towards

ADELAIDE as a brigantine.                    *Falmouth Art Gallery*

the end of World War I to the Cookson Barytes Co., Newcastle-on-Tyne, but Fred Wright of Braunton brought her back to the Bristol Channel in 1919 and ran her until 1955 when P. M. Herbert of Bude took her over, and she was still trading actively in the Bristol Channel.

Finally, in 1958, A. Barr of Argyll fitted her out, and sailed in her towards Australia, only to be wrecked in the West Indies, by which time some of her timbers had been at sea for 122 years.

**AGNES CAIRNS** ON 65787, built 1873 at Limekilns by Whitehead. Tons 136 net, 146 gross as built. 92.5 22.6 12.0.

A brigantine which was owned in Leith and then Aberystwyth until 1893 when John Ennor of Newquay registered her at Fowey, and had her re-measured at 98 net tons. He was followed as owner by his captain, Joseph Penaliggon also of Newquay who, about 1912, had her re-registered in Guernsey.

She was sunk by U-boat on 26th April 1917 eight miles NE of Alderney on passage Portsmouth for Guernsey with coal. The U-boat 'captured' her by sending the crew off in their boat, and then placing bombs on board. That was the most usual way of dealing with small ships to save torpedoes and shells as long as no escort vessels were in sight: a procedure which the Q-ships described in another chapter did much to discourage.

**AGNES ELLEN** ON 70504, built 1875 at Porthcawl by Martin. Tons 152 net (reduced to 128 later). 99.2 23.6 11.9. A schooner with a square stern and a female figurehead.

Henry Allport bought her from Welsh owners and registered her at Padstow in 1882. Under his masters W. Libby, J. Bowden and A. Peters, she became a regular trader between Runcorn and Cornwall. On 3rd January 1899 in a northwesterly gale, she was wrecked near Pen Brush Point on the Pembroke coast on passage Runcorn for Looe with coal. All six crew, including Captain E. Peters, were lost.

**AGNES LOUISA** ON 69461, built 1875 at Porth (near Newquay) by Joseph Osborne. Tons 62 net, 68 gross. 68.4 22.0 8.8. A smack with a semi-elliptical stern re-rigged as a ketch in 1881.

Her first owner was Martyn of St Colomb Minor but in 1887 the Bennett family of Porth bought her and J. Ham became master.

She was lost in the blizzard of 10th March 1891 off Lands End with all hands, Newport for Newlyn with coal.

**AGNES SOPHIA** built 1848 at Padstow by R & J Tredwen. Tons 53(N). 55.9 16.1 8.7. A coasting schooner owned by Jenkin and others, with W. Jenkin as master. Her register carries the note 'Lost at sea November 1853' but she appears in *Lloyd's Register* for several years thereafter.

**AGNES STROUT** ON 69460, built 1875 at Padstow by John Cowl. Tons 130 net, 138 gross. 94.6 23.5 11.5. A schooner with an elliptical stern (which was unusual in Padstow-built vessels other than fishing vessels), she was built for James Strout of Port Isaac, but managed by Allport & Sons at the time of her loss, when R. Burt was master. She was lost after collision with the German SS GEMMA off Dunwich on 15th January 1881, (not JEMMA as reported at the time).

**AID** ON 21115, built 1833 at Padstow by John Tredwen. Tons 31(O). 38.8 13.8 6.9 (1833).

A sloop rigged smack, changed to ketch rig in 1882. She was lengthened twice although her registered tonnage remained close to 31 throughout.

She was registered at Padstow throughout her life and her owners included James Nicholls of St Endellion, John Tredwen Jr and his widow from 1870 until 1888. Padstow masters included John Couch and Peter Follow in 1836, John Gill 1846, N. Bate 1850 and Samuel Bate 1853.

She was sold to W. Chapman of Weston-super-Mare in 1890 and foundered off Breaksea 13th July 1893, Bideford for Bridgwater with gravel. No lives lost.

**ALAN** built 1817 at Padstow by Martin Withell. Tons 88(O). 60.3 18.9 10.0. A brig regularly reported by *Lloyd's* in the home trades. She was wrecked at Padstow in November 1833, but salved. She was owned and captained by the Burt, Carveth and Pollard families of Padstow. In 1837 she was sold to St Ives, where her register bears the note 'Lost August 1837 on Stag Rocks off the Lizard'.

**ALAN** ON 62681, built 1858, *ex* SUEZ, of Austrian origin. Tons 359 net, 370 gross. 127.0 26.8 16.9. A barque registered at Padstow 1870, owned by Thomas Martyn merchant of Wadebridge, with E. L. Martyn as master.

In May 1872 it was reported that the master and all but one of the crew had died of yellow fever at Pernambuco; it is uncertain who was master at the time.

She was wrecked on Hog Island (Prince Edward Island Province) 25th August 1873 in a NW storm force 12 when bound from Montreal for Falmouth with maize. Seven out of her crew of 11 were drowned. The wreck was sold for $34. Captain Martyn and James Hawken survived.

Cornwall has more than its share of vessels of mysterious origin. This ship has also been reported as ALLAN, *ex* SOUETH. The number of foreign ships seeking to enter the English Channel was enormous, and quite a number became available to be bought in derelict or damaged condition. The most likely identity for this three masted barque is SUEZ, Captain Primudo, 348 tons, built at Lussin, her home port, in 1856, Austrian flag, and to be found in the French *Registre Maritime* in the 1860s.

**ALARM** ON 3875, built 1849 at Gloucester by William James Bebell. Restored in 1862. Tons 89 net, 101 gross when registered at Padstow in 1869. 69.8 20.0 11.9. A schooner first registered at Bristol and trading to Portugal.

William Martin Darke of Newquay bought her out-right in 1869, but she was lost in collision with the Portuguese schooner PROCTI DU RINU between Hut Point and Bull Point on 7th January 1874.

**ALARM** ON 29355, built 1861 at Padstow by Sloggett. Tons 48 reg. 59.2 17.9 8.5. A smack registered at Padstow and owned by Robert Langford and Seaton of Padstow, with W. Darke and J. Haynes as masters. Lost 3rd November 1862 (note on register).

**ALBERT** ON 25430, built 1847 at Windsor, Nova Scotia. Tons 463 reg. 122.9 28.2 18.4. A barque with a billet head bought from Bristol owners in 1864 by John Tredwen, merchant (32 shares), Jonathan Knight, mariner (20 shares) and Henry Bright, mariner (12 shares), all of Padstow, where they registered her.

She operated as an emigrant ship from Padstow, but she was wrecked at Bermuda 4th February 1869.

**ALBERTA** ON 53001, built 1865 at Padstow by J. Stribley. Tons 52(N). 59.8 18.9 8.6. A smack initially owned by John Stribley but soon sold to J. Hutchings (her master) and others. By 1871, T. Adams was master and saw her converted to ketch rig in 1873. In September 1882 she collided with an unlit schooner in the pool at Padstow and she ended ashore on Chapel Point with a large hole in her bottom. Her crew were taken off by Cowl's shipyard gig HERO. There were numerous shareholders throughout but by 1884 A. Wills of Wadebridge was the managing owner and master, and remained so until her loss on 12th March 1891.

She foundered 35 miles NNW of Seven Stones after collision with the Norwegian barque PIONEER whilst on passage Par for Gloucester with china clay. The wind was East force 9. One of her crew of three drowned. She was registered at Padstow throughout.

ALBION built 1822 at Padstow by John Tredwen. Tons 32(O). 40.5 14.0 6.8. A sloop rigged smack registered at Padstow.

First owned by Avery, then by Parnall and others, she had a multiplicity of Padstow masters including Pasco Billing, George Bellamy. G. Brewer, J. Raymond and J. Martyn, before being lost at Boscastle 11th June 1833. Her loss was recorded in *Lloyd's List* on 14th June and her port registration was closed, but she continued to appear in *Lloyd's Register* for a number of years, as has happened in a number of other cases.

ALBION built 1840 at Padstow by Thomas Carter. Tons 80(O) 64(N). 52.3 17.0 9.3.

This smack was registered at Falmouth with Martin and others as owners. In *Lloyd's Register* 1851 T. Jennings is master, G. Hill owner. Lost 1853 (note on register).

ALBION built 1845 at Padstow. Tons 12(N). 35.4 10.7 4.8.

This tiny sloop was registered at Padstow with John Hawken as owner and William Corsell as master. That same year she was sold to William Lowther of Neath.

The last note of her Padstow registry is that she had been raised and rebuilt at Port Talbot in 1851.

ALBION ON 29360, built 1862 at Padstow by John Tredwen. Tons 45(N). 59.4 17.5 7.8. Smack rigged. Lengthened in 1869. Tons 57 net. 74.5 17.5 7.8 (*Lloyd's*) and re-rigged as a schooner.

Initially her shares were split equally between builder and master F. Prideaux. Some time after lengthening, her owner became the same F. Prideaux Sr and her master F. Prideaux Jr.

She was wrecked on Long Sand in the Thames Estuary on 2nd June 1882, on passage Brussels for London with stone and two passengers who, with four crew, were all saved.

ALCHYMIST ON 19232, built 1828 at New Workington on Prince Edward Island. Tons 330(O). 103.1 26.7 19.0. Height in cabin decks 5'-7", with a full length male figurehead.

This barque was first registered in Falmouth when brought over from Canada, but in 1854 Wm. Stribley and Stephen Phelp (both Padstow families) were masters, and in 1855 she was registered at Padstow with Thomas Littlefair Seaton as owner and (briefly) master. Seaton remained managing owner, but Burrows and J. Rose were subsequent masters of this emigrant ship until she was sold to foreigners and the register closed 25th September 1868. More about her will be found in the chapter on emigrant ships.

ALERT ON 288, built 1844 at Padstow by R & J Tredwen. Tons 53(N) 47.6 14.2 7.6. A sloop rigged smack registered at Padstow in 1844 with H. Allett as owner and master. She was re-registered in London in 1848, lengthened and re-rigged as a ketch in 1851, and operated as a London and Margate coaster. Her register was closed by 1870.

ALFRED ON 52639, built 1865 at Flint by Michael Parry. Tons 73 net, 84 gross. 79.0 19.0 9.7.

A schooner with a male bust figurehead, owned in Chester until bought by Albert Jenkin of Newquay and registered at Padstow in 1893, with W. Mitchell as master.

About 1898 she was converted to ketch rig and by 1904 ownership was transferred to Samuel Couch of Port Isaac, for whom she sailed until 11th September 1910, when she was lost in collision with SS PINK ROSE of Liverpool three miles SE of the Runnelstone on passage Cardiff for Plymouth with coal.

ALICE ON 3303, built 1822 at Padstow by John Tredwen. Tons 61(O), 49(N). 52.2 17.0 9.1 as built. A schooner which was lengthened in 1854, increasing her tonnage to 86(N).

She spent her life coasting in the Irish Sea and southwest England, owned throughout by the Yeo family with her registration initially at Padstow but subsequently alternating several times between Bideford and Padstow. On 23rd November 1858 she was lost on Long Sand, on passage Porthcawl for Ipswich, Harvey master.

ALICE JANE ON 29684, built 1861 at Padstow by John Tredwen. Tons 80 reg. 74.4 19.5 9.2. A coasting schooner built for Hoskin of Plymouth and registered there until 1864. That year John Tredwen bought all 64 shares and she was registered at Padstow. Lost in collision off Dungeness 30th November 1866.

ALMA ON 19265, built 1855 at Padstow by John Tredwen. Tons 86 reg. 64.2 19.6 10.7. The ownership of this little brigantine was shared between John Tredwen and John Cory, two names to conjure with. Cory went on to become the famous owner of steam colliers at Cardiff. It is noted in the port register that ALMA was broken up in 1870.

AMANDA ON 58243, built 1867 at Padstow by Willmet at the Dennis Cove yard. Tons 87 net, 97 gross, later reduced to 80 net. 82.7 21.3 10.1.

A schooner but converted to ketch rig about 1929. She had a female figurehead and was registered at Padstow throughout.

Captain Henry House of Newquay had her built, and named after his daughter. Henry died in 1871 and in due course shares passed to his son Henry Jr who acted as master, as did Nicholas House later. Amanda House married Thomas Stephens, and in 1917 his brother Edward of Par and Fowey took 20 shares in AMANDA and became managing owner.

AMANDA sailed largely in the traditional trades between Cornwall and Wales, trading without an engine into the 1930s until abandoned in Pont Pill, Fowey, probably after Edward Stephens' death in 1935. By that time the Padstow register book was seldom if ever opened, and AMANDA continued to appear in the *Mercantile Navy List* until her register was finally closed in 1951.

AMARANTH ON 62118, built 1873 at Findhorn by Alec Anderson. Tons 145 net. 154 gross. 98.6 23.5 11.2. A round-sterned schooner with a female figurehead registered in Inverness until 1880 when she was bought by W. C. Phillips and her master J. Burton and registered at Padstow.

Sunk in collision with SS SAINT JACQUES of Havre on 26th October 1884 three or four miles E of Dungeness.

AMARANTH ON 84978, built 1886 at Padstow by Cowl & Sons. Tons 124 net, 140 gross. 94.3 23.4 11.7. Female figurehead, she is often said to be the last schooner built at Padstow and she was the last two masted schooner. MILDRED was the last, but she had three masts.

AMARANTH was built as a replacement to the ship of the same name for W. C. Phillips, and J. Burton survived to command her, followed by T. Rowe; she was registered at Padstow.

Phillips became a substantial owner of schooners and the list of Padstow ships would be longer had he not moved his home and headquarters from Port Isaac to St Austell in 1889.

AMARANTH was abandoned on 15th November 1905 after collision with Ashburner schooner JAMES & AGNES off the Lizard sailing from Preston for Calstock with coal.

AMELIA ON 3931, built 1820 at Penzance by Mathews. Tons 48(O), 57(N). 58.0 14.6 8.5. *Lloyd's Register* describes her rig as Sloop in 1832, Brig in 1841, Ketch in 1849 and Schooner in 1851! She was lengthened in 1848.

After 10 years at Penzance she was bought by Avery and others and registered at Padstow, J. Martyn, W. Dark, B. Carter, Weymouth, W. Thomas, Couch and Pope all serving as masters. Her registration gives her as a schooner.

On 5th January 1850 she was wrecked at Ilfracombe carrying coal and iron worth £130. There was a Board of Trade enquiry and the master, Thomas Avery, was reprimanded for attempting the entrance at night in fog. She was repaired but there is a note in the register 'presumed lost September 1858'.

**AMELIA** ON 29359, built 1862 at Padstow by Willmett. Tons 70 reg. 70.7 19.4 9.6.

A schooner registered at Padstow, and owned by Jenkin and others until 1883 and then by J. Reynolds Sr, T. Jenkin and Chigwidden were early masters, then J. Reynolds (Jr).

She sank after striking a rock off Longstone in the Farne Islands on 25th January 1887, having sailed from Elie in Fife for London with potatoes. Her crew of four were all saved.

**AMPHITRITE** ON 27275, built 1859 at Padstow by John Tredwen. Tons 73, later reduced to 63 net. 69.5 18.9 9.1. Like ALMA, this schooner started life owned equally by John Tredwen and John Cory, but Reed of Plymouth soon largely bought them out and she was registered successively in Plymouth (1860) and Preston (1872).

Her last owners lived at Kilkeel near which she was lost and the register closed 10th May 1911.

**ANN** built 1792 at Padstow, and believed registered there. Tons 52(O). Sloop rigged. Until 1798 she was owned by J. Lane and had masters J. Hole, James Yeo, Rouse and R. Yeo. Then she was owned by Bray, with masters J. Yeo, J. Champion and W. Chegwidden.

In 1807 one ANN was wrecked at Newquay, but if this one, she was repaired.

By 1812 this ANN was owned by Thomas Tremain who advertised her for sale.

J. Champion is said to have carved the figurehead of one ANN.

One ANN was a constant trader Bristol to Bude around 1795. One was a constant trader Bristol to Boscastle 1814-1818.

**ANN & ELIZABETH** ON 19205, built 1836 at Padstow by Thomas Carter. Tons 39(N), later 55 gross. 45.8 14.7 8.0. This sloop was registered at Padstow and owned by R. Hambly for all her thirty years, with J. Hambly as master.

She was lost at sea 8th December 1866.

**ANN WALTERS** ON 53170, built 1867 at Padstow by John Tredwen. Tons 159, reduced later to 126 net. 99.4 23.8 12.0. A powerful schooner built for Looe owners Walters and Hill and registered at Fowey, she entered the Mediterranean trade.

Ashore in the Humber on voyage London for Newcastle with loam she was sold as a wreck in 1893.

**ANN WILLIAMS** ON 47037, built 1864 at Padstow by John Tredwen. Tons 134. 90.9 21.8 11.8. This schooner was built for Edwin Williams of Port Isaac and registered at Padstow. He commanded her in the coasting trades, followed by G. Thomas and W. Moyse also of Port Isaac. The May family also featured in the ownership.

She was wrecked at the Black Dog near Aberdeen in a great storm on 5th-6th March 1881, and only one of her crew of seven survived.

**ANNA MARIA** built 1824 at Padstow by John Tredwen. Tons 45(O) 45.8 15.4 7.4. A sloop registered at Padstow and owned by Bake of Delabole. Her masters were N. Thomas, Richard Wedlock and Samuel Vine. Her register records 'Lost in 1829'.

**ANNE** built 1768 at Ipswich. Tons 32(O) 40.0 14.3 7.0. The first registration of this sloop at Padstow is missing, but from 1816 the Heatherington, Webster, Knight, Hancock and Lovering families of Padstow and the Power family of Boscastle were involved as owners and masters.

She was sold to Ilfracombe in 1826.

(*Lloyd's Register* did not recognise that ANN could be spelt ANNE until 1810, which complicates identification.)

**ANNE** built 1809 at Padstow by George Sloggett. Tons 38(O), 30(N). 42.6 15.3 7.6. (1835) Her first registration at Padstow is missing but in 1825 this sloop was owned and commanded by Martyn Richards, and subsequently owned by John Tredwen who had W. Giles, R. Power and F. Richards as masters. Lost in 1840 (note on register).

**ANNE DAVIES** ON 27605, built 1859 at Aberdovey by Jones. Tons 103, reduced to 91 net during Padstow ownership. 80.0 20.3 10.6. This schooner had a series of Welsh owners based successively in Aberdovey, Aberystwyth, Carnarvon, and Llanelly until bought by Robert Prout of Port Isaac and registered in Padstow in 1895.

Mrs Annie E. L. Herring of Padstow became her owner in 1912. She was broken up at Newquay and her register closed on 14th September 1914.

**ANNIE** ON 41643, built 1859 at Caribou, Nova Scotia. Tons 67 net, 71 gross, reduced to 54 net by 1900. 71.0 20.0 8.0. A schooner with square stern and billet head.

At first she was owned in Truro and traded regularly up the Tamar, but in 1866, William Stribley and Joshua Rowe registered her at Padstow. Dunstan and Reynolds also had shares, and E. Tabb and H. House were amongst her masters.

In 1892 she was sold to Bideford, where her register was closed 9th August 1926 with the note 'Vessel broken up'.

**ANNIE** ON 47035, built 1863-4 at Padstow by John Stribley (Port Register) or Willmet (*Lloyd's Survey*) at the Dennis Cove Yard (*R.C. Gazette*). Tons 83 reg. 74.0 20.6 10.2. A Padstow registered schooner with a 3/4 female figurehead, her 64 shares were held briefly by Humphrey Willyams, banker, but J. Courtenay soon became managing owner and Stribley took some shares back. Her master for a long period was J. Male; she was a coaster.

ANNIE was wrecked on St Tudwal's Island on 30th January 1877 and her crew of five were rescued by the Abersoch lifeboat MABEL LOUISA.

**ANNIE** ON 49954, built 1864 at Padstow by John Tredwen. Tons 78 reg. 74.5 19.2 9.2. A schooner with square stern, standing bowsprit and female figurehead, she was built for J. H. Trevithick of Hayle and registered at Penzance until 1881 when James Rogers, who had been her master, became managing owner and registered her at Hayle.

She was wrecked at Hastings on 15th August 1890.

**ANNIE** ON 67494, built 1873 at Ardrossan. Tons 45 net 49 gross. 63.3 19.3 7.3. This small round sterned schooner was Glasgow owned until detained by the Board of Trade at Arklow in January 1889 with allegations of defective hull and equipment. She was released to Bray of Padstow who repaired her, and had her registered at Padstow. Although she went to Cardiff owners soon after 1900, she remained registered at Padstow until broken up at St Ives and register closed 22nd March 1911.

**ANNIE HARRIS** ON 65301, built 1870 at Bideford by Johnson. Tons 148 net, 154 gross, later 117 net. 103.0 22.2 11.2. A brigantine registered at Bristol and trading to South America, but bought by W. S. Allport of Padstow in 1885. Whilst sailing from Swansea for Hartlepool with burnt ore she was lost by collision off Start Point on 18th July 1891.

**ANTAGONIST** ON 28955, built 1861 at Brixham by Samuel and John Dewdney. Tons 145.5 net and gross. 94.8 20.8 12.2. A schooner with square stern and female figurehead, she traded to the Mediterranean with Edward Vittery's fleet, registered at Dartmouth and then Brixham when Brixham became a separate port of registry in 1875. In 1880 she was bought by John Bradshaw, a shipbroker of Fleetwood and registered there, but he sold most of her sixty-four shares to Joseph Collins Cock of St Minver and other Padstow men. R. E. Bray is given as Master in 1881. Vessel wrecked December 1883 and Cert. of Registry lost with ship (note on the Fleetwood register).

**APOLLO.** On 10th January 1793, the APOLLO of Padstow was wrecked in Hell Bay (near Polzeath), leaving Padstow for St Ives with barley, Brewer master.

**ARCHIE** ON 84979, built 1887 at Plymouth by D. Banks & Co. Tons 63 net, 70 gross. 74.8  19.8  8.1. A Padstow registered ketch with a square stern, her owners were John Hawken, merchant, and others and her master H. Stribley. Suddenly, in 1896, the register changes the ownership to M. E. Wales of Punta Arenas, Chilian, and the following year 'sold foreign' register closed 29th October 1897. Can she have been Padstow's smallest emigrant ship?

**ARCTIC** The supplement to *Lloyd's Register* 1851 includes a section for 'New ships not registered' and there is an entry 'ARCTIC *pro tem.* with details of a brigantine built by Tredwen in 1850. The owner is given as Tredwen. The entry is over-printed Now Registered 'FAVOURITE' - see No.24 in Supplement. Evidently the vessel was built on spec. but the idea of launching a ship without a name was so unthinkable that she was christened ARCTIC *pro tem.* She soon became FAVOURITE ON 24934 and her temporary name was never mentioned again.

**ARIEL** ON 48961, built 1864 at Padstow by John Tredwen. Tons 178 gross. 102.7  23.2  12.8. A brigantine although described as a brig in her first survey and as a schooner elsewhere. She was registered at Plymouth and traded to Rio Grande for Ships & Co. In 1873 she was trading from Cardiff to the Mediterranean. W. S. Allport of Padstow bought her in 1875, and appointed C. Hocking, D. Burt, A. Avery and J. Smith successively to take charge of her. Plymouth remained her port of registry.

In April 1878 she hit a rock entering Par for china clay and was awash on her side off the pierhead. The locomotives of the narrow gauge mineral railway came to her rescue and hauled her upright.

ARIEL sailed from Dublin on 25th November 1914 with burnt ore for Cardiff, and was lost in a gale. A Manx newspaper of 15th January 1915 recorded that her figurehead had been washed ashore at Cranstal.

**ATALANTA** see MARY JAMES

**AUNDA** a seven ton sloop of Padstow. Cook master (too small to be registered), appears in the Bude port book in 1850.

**AURORA.** A schooner of that name was reported launched at John Tredwen's yard on 20th March 1855. It appears probable that she was soon renamed CORNWALL q.v.

**AURORA** ON 19269, built 1855 at Padstow by John Tredwen. Tons 288(N). 117.2  25.5  11.8. A brig with a break in the deck and a female figurehead. The 'break in deck' is the earliest noted on the register of a Padstow-built ship. Presumably it refers to poop and possibly foc's'le being raised ½ deck relative to the main deck. Registered at Padstow, she was owned on completion by Tredwen and seven others, and was one of the Padstow ships to trade (from Liverpool and London) without reference to the needs of Padstow. Her masters included E. Key and Thompson. AURORA was wrecked on Torre Rinaldo in the Mediterranean on 14th March 1861.

**BALLINBREICH CASTLE** ON 63070, built 1879 at Perth by Wallace. Tons 99 net, 111 gross. 84.0  21.7  10.6. A schooner with an elliptical stern which started life registered briefly at Perth, then Bideford, as Newfoundland trader. On 2nd January 1899 she sank at Holyhead and her crew of five were saved by lifeboat. But she was salved and bought by J. N. Clemow and others and registered at

Padstow in 1890, with masters W. Dingle, F. Conway, C. Tucker and S. Edmunds.

Her register end with the note 'Foundered 12th September 1919: crew landed at Youghal.'

**BANQUEREAU** built 1859 at Bayonne (Major Repairs 1866). Tons 118. Brick (Brig) of oak with iron fastenings.

This Bayonne brig owned by J. Bailac came ashore at Crigga in 1869 and was purchased by Capt. Thomas Clemens and renamed BERTHA q.v.

**BARBARA** a Norwegian barque bought in damaged condition by John Tredwen, repaired and renamed STORM q.v.

**BEATRICE CAROLINE** ON 85826, built 1886 at Falmouth. Tons 35 net. 59.4  17.5  5.7. This square sterned ketch was registered at Fowey throughout her life, and owned in Looe, and from 1918 to 1923 by Edward Stephens of Fowey, trading mostly along the south coast of Cornwall and Devon.

But in 1923 she was bought by William S. Martyn of Wadebridge. In 1931 he unrigged her to become a dumb barge on the Camel. She lasted as a floating hulk into the 1950s.

**BEAVER** built 1793 (or 1794) at Bideford. Tons 54 (O). Variously rigged as sloop, brig and brigantine.

This ship was almost certainly registered at Padstow for a time as *Lloyd's Register* 1796-1799 gives Padstow as her home/survey port, trading to Waterford. The port registers of the period do not survive. Her owner was W. Harvey and her master, Hockins. In 1909, the owner was Hawkins (Hockins ?) and master R. Vine, but she had moved to Cork. BEAVER was later based at Exeter (in the period 1815-1820).

**BEDWELTY** ON 20922, built 1841 at Padstow by John Tredwen. Tons 104(O), 86(N). 63.1  18.3  11.4. This coasting schooner was owned throughout her active life by the Todd family which had branches in Fowey, Padstow and Newport. She was registered at Fowey throughout.

*Lloyd's Register* for 1881 shows her owned by J. A. Trippett but adds 'now a hulk'.

**BEE** ON 13192, built 1846 at Appledore (Bideford) by William Clibbett. Tons 51(N) later 49. 51.6  17.6  7.7. A sloop rigged smack registered at Bideford when built, but at Padstow in 1848, then back to Bideford in 1861. Like other Bude vessels she was owned by John Hockin and Hooper and John Marshall and Hallett served as masters.

She was bringing a cargo of culm from Swansea into Bude in March 1880 when she was driven ashore and broke up. The crew were able to walk ashore.

**BELLE** ON 8646, built 1838 at Padstow by Thomas Withell. Tons 69(O) 59(N). 57.8  14.7  9.8. This schooner, registered at Padstow in 1838 with P. Wilson as owner and master, was an early example of a Padstow ship which traded without bringing goods to Padstow. She entered the Liverpool-Havre trade, but for her subsequent owners, Wade and Seaton and others, she soon settled down as a Padstow coaster, with Carter, E. Key and J. Knight as masters. BELLE was sold to Falmouth in 1855 and her register there notes 'Lost near Land's End, 5th February 1874'.

**BELLE** ON 13047, built 1840 at Low Lights, Shields. Tons 283(O) 320(N). 91.9  23.2  17.4. A barque with a sham gallery and a female bust as figure-head. BELLE was registered at London in 1841 and at Padstow in 1843, but her owners throughout were Norway (the old Wadebridge and Padstow family) and numerous shareholders in the Padstow area. *Lloyd's Register* confuse the issue by showing her port as W'bdge which normally signified Woodbridge but on this occasion can only refer to Wadebridge. Her masters were

The schooner
BELLE OF THE PLYM,
painted by A de Simone.
*National Maritime Museum*

successively Brewer of Padstow, J. Bisson of Jersey and J. Profitt. She traded London and Padstow to Quebec and elsewhere in North America.

In 1842 she carried a number of Wadebridge emigrants to Quebec and doubtless she carried others later.

Her register closes with the note 'Lost September 1859'.

**BELLE OF THE PLYM** ON 28123, built 1860 at Plymouth by Shilston. Tons 96 net 103 gross, later 78 net. 87.6 20.1 10.7 (Padstow Reg.) A schooner with elliptical stern and female bust as figurehead, she was initially owned by her builder and registered at Plymouth, trading thence to Hamburg and the Mediterranean. In 1873 she was registered at Padstow and, owned by Knight and Hutchings, continued in the continental trade. In the early 1880s, John Cory (by then a substantial Cardiff shipowner) owned her briefly, then James Matthews of Newquay and William Adams. On 1st August 1910 she was disabled in a gale off Padstow whilst taking fireclay from Plymouth for Glasgow and on 3rd August she was towed into Padstow and converted into a lighter for Cornwall Farmers Ltd. Register closed 4th October 1910.

**BERTHA** ON 62678, built 1859 at Bayonne, France. Tons 102 net 116 gross. 82.8 22.2 9.4. (10.8 after raising decks in 1873). A three-quarter length female figurehead was added in 1873. This brigantine previously named BANQUEREAU under French ownership, was registered at Padstow in 1870, being owned successively by G. Collins a St Columb solicitor, Charles Rawle of Padstow, Thomas Clemens of Newquay, and finally J. Bunt of Newquay who was also master. As was often the case there were many minor shareholders.

BERTHA was wrecked on 22nd October 1885 at Annalong when sailing from Carrickfergus for Ramsgate with granite. Wind ENE force 5. Crew of four all saved.

**BERTIE** ON 69406, built 1877 at Bridgwater by Carver. Tons 68 net 76 gross. 81.5 20.0 8.7. This ketch was registered at Bristol, but is included because Wm. A. Jenkin of St Blazey and Newquay was

master and managing owner in the mid-eighties, and he sold her to Edward L. Johns of Crantock.

**BESS** ON 19210, built 1840 at Padstow by Thomas Withell. Tons 59(O) 42(N). 48.4 15.0 7.8. BESS was a sloop rigged smack registered at Padstow and owned throughout by the Stribley family. As well as Stribleys, her masters included F. Prideaux, William Bennett and William Ryley. She was broken up in 1857.

**BESSIE** ON 19275, built 1856 at Padstow by F.H. Thomes. Tons 44 reg. 59.3 16.8 8.1. This smack was registered at Padstow in 1856, owned by Francis Prideaux, Master Mariner, 9 shares and by 13 others with one to ten shares each.

Lost off Hartland Point 28th September 1856 (note in register).

**BESSIE** ON 67266, built 1871 at Kingsbridge by Date. Tons 177 net 189 gross, later 149 net. 102.0 23.5 12.9. A famous three masted schooner by a famous builder, she was registered at Salcombe and started off in the Dartmouth to West Indies trade. By 1884 she was owned by J. Ennor of Newquay for whom W. G. Clemens was master for many years until he died aboard of old age.

In 1911 ownership passed to H. R. Bennett of Fowey and in 1916 to P. K. Harris of Appledore, but it was not until 1919 that she left the Salcombe register to be owned by the Anglo French Coasting Company of Manchester. By 1924 she was registered in Guernsey by Sarnia Shipping Co., St Sampsons, but wrecked in 1926.

**BESSIE** ON 62688. Date and place of build unknown. Rebuilt in 1872 at Padstow by John Stribley. Tons 43 net 48 gross. 71.0 16.5 7.4. This schooner 'appeared from nowhere' and judging by her great length relative to beam and to tonnage, she had unusually fine lines. Stribley himself owned her (with Hooper as master) but he died in April 1876 and she went to T. H. Hockin of Newquay, owner and master.

BESSIE is missing since leaving St Valery for Shoreham 18th January 1881 (note on register).

**BESSIE** ON 72553, built 1875 at Feock by John Stephens. Tons 93 net 116 gross. 89.6 22.2 11.4. A schooner with a semi-elliptical stern and three-quarter female figurehead. BESSIE was registered at Truro and owned in Devoran for her first fifteen years: then William S. Allport of Padstow added her to his fleet and kept her to the end.

She sailed from Rothesay Bay on 23rd October 1909 carrying Glasgow coal for Charlestown and went missing with her crew of five.

**BESSIE** ON 89181, built 1884 at Padstow by John Cowl & Sons. Tons 31 reg. This little cutter was registered at Cardiff and her successive Cardiff owners were William A. H. Harvey, John L. Harvey (who had her for thirty years), and finally, after the Great War, Mrs Annie Howells. BESSIE was out of register 1933.

**BESSIE JANE** ON 27272, built 1859 at Padstow by F. H. Thomas. Tons 41 reg. 55.1 16.6 7.8. Completed as a smack, she was registered at Padstow. At first John Male owned and commanded her, but from 1874 John Phillips of St Minver and John Courtenay of Padstow had shares, and Phillips was master. She became ketch rigged at some stage.

She foundered seven miles off Padstow bound from Newport to Padstow with coal on 18th October 1881. The wind was SE force 10 but all the crew survived. One wonders how.

**BESSY JANE** ON 21106, built 1850 at Port Isaac by Samuel Trevethon Bennett. Tons 82(O) 60(N). 57.3 17.6 9.1. Lengthened 1872 then tons 79 net 85 gross. 78.2 18.3 9.0. A schooner with female figurehead, registered at Padstow and owned initially by J. Stephens: with J. Meluish J. Richards and J. Bate as masters, she traded from Padstow to the Mediterranean and from Swansea to France. By 1866 she was owned, like many Port Isaac vessels, by Warwick R. Guy who kept her in the coasting trade until about 1895 when R. Mitchell, also of Port Isaac, took her over, having long been her master.

BESSY JANE was 'discarded 1907. Not to be used at sea'. Register closed 16th August 1909.

**BESSIE WATERS** ON 62684, built 1871 at Barnstaple by Westacott. Tons 51 net (later 54). 63.8 19.5 8.7. A smack with an elliptical stern registered at Padstow upon completion having been built for owner and master J. Waters of Port Isaac. He sold her to F. S. Peirce of Dover in 1874 but she was back in the Westcountry by 1891 with Barnstaple registry, and lost in a channel gale off Shoreham in December 1893.

**BETSEY** and **BETSY** were popular names, but *Lloyd's Register* insisted for many years that BETSY was the only permissible spelling! At one stage, however, when the competitor shipowners' 'red' register spelt it BETSY, the *Lloyd's* green books promptly decided that BETSEY was the only respectable version! It was not until 1845 that *Lloyd's* admitted both spellings and got them in the right order, so confusion is rife.

**BETSEY** prize, made free 1797 at Falmouth. Tons 47.5. 49.5 15.5 7.3. Sloop. Registered at Padstow 1807, owned by J. Tredwen, Thomas Burt and William Brokenshaw, her master. Broken up 1829 (note on register).

**BETSEY** built 1789 at Franks Quarry, Plymouth. Tons 32(O). 41.3 14.3 7.8. lengthened at Padstow 1795. Tons 43(O). 49.0 14.8 7.8. A counter sterned sloop registered at Fowey 1789, then at Padstow 1791, owned by Thomas & William Rawlings with Peter Courtenay as master. In 1815 she was re-registered at Whitehaven.

The Padstow register ends with the bald statement 'seized for smuggling'. A BETSEY of Padstow was reported wrecked near Maryport on passage Cork for Liverpool on 27th March 1815. That would fit in well with a subsequent registration at Whitehaven.

**BETSY** built 1786 at Southampton. Tons 55(O), a sloop, *Lloyd's Register* of 1790 has her trading London - Padstow and owned by her master, J. Melhuish.

**BETSY** built 1802 at Padstow. Tons 63(O). A brig for which no Padstow register has been found, and which had as survey ports, in succession, Dublin, Exmouth, Plymouth, Bristol and Newry. *Lloyd's List* reported the BETSY, Anderson master, Flint for Newry, wrecked near Poolwash, Isle of Man in a gale on 13th November 1836. Crew saved.

**BETSY** built 1819 at Bucklers Hard. Tons 32(O). 41.5 14.3 11.4. A sloop initially registered at Poole, but bought by Thomas Tremain of Padstow in 1823 and registered there in 1824.

She proved suitable for trading to Bude and the names of her masters are recorded Byley, Bellamy, Parker, Polloc, Knight and Couch. Lost at Walcheren 1st September 1833.

**BETSEY**. The wreck of a BETSEY at Padstow is recorded in *Lloyd's List* 17th December 1805, and another in the issue of 10th February 1807.

The wreck of a BETSEY at Padstow on 15th March 1815 is recorded in *Lloyd's List* 21st March 1815. These might have been any of the extant BETSEYs or BETSYs.

**BETSEY JAMES** (MNL) BETSY JAMES. The spelling difficulty continues. (St Ives Reg.) ON 22900. built 1854 at Padstow by Thomas Carter. Tons 74(N), 69 net later. 60.3 17.7 10.2 (Hayle Reg.) A schooner registered successively at St Ives, Hayle and then Penzance, she was essentially a coaster. She was lost in St Andrew's Bay 30th November, 1888.

**BILLOW** ON 13429, built 1853 at Padstow. Tons 121.2318/3500(N) 81.0 17.8 11.4. Schooner with standing bowsprit, square stern and female bust, carvel built. This coaster was registered at St Ives and owned by John Pool of Phillack nominated owner, and eight others including Phillip B. Spray the master, and George Millet Davis, Liverpool surgeon (12 shares; the only shareholder not living near St Ives).

Foundered at sea 17th or 18th November 1864 (note on register).

**BLESSING**. In 1789 this sloop was bought by Edward Hockin of Hartland Quay, in partnership with a Stratton (Bude) shipmaster. In 1795, there was a constant trader to Boscastle named BLESSING with one Bond as master. The supplement to *Lloyd's Register* 1801 includes BLESSING, J. Trick Mr, Sloop 32 tons, built Wales 1799, owner Lord Roll, trading Waterford, Plymouth. Note that J. Trick was also master of HABBACOT, another Bude trader of that era. This BLESSING recurs in *Lloyd's* until 1809.

Grahame Farr reports in *Shipbuilding in North Devon* that BLESSING, sloop 32 tons, was rebuilt at Bideford in 1802 and enlarged to 45 tons. Bideford registers show her as built at Cadoxton in 1788, and as she was registered at Cardiff in 1789, he concludes that various errors of date and tonnage occurred in *Lloyd's Register*.

It seems probable that all these references are to a single BLESSING which must be included in this list because of Bude ownership and which may well feature in the missing early Padstow port registers.

**BLUE BELL** ON 27278, built in France, date unknown, *ex* UNION. Tons 62 net 71 gross. 67.1 20.4 8.6. In 1860 William Dake of Newquay bought this French schooner which had stranded in Crantock Bay; he repaired and registered her at Padstow. In 1875 he sold her to Watchet owners, and in 1892 she passed to Melbourne Knight of Bristol who transferred her registration from Padstow to Bridgwater.

On 28th April 1892 she burnt off Dungarvan and subsequently foundered whilst on passage Portmadoc for Waterford with slates.

**BOCONNOC** ON 8641, built 1836 at Fowey by Marks and Rendle. Tons 37(N). 51.0 14.2 7.3. A sloop rigged smack registered at Fowey in 1836 and Cardiff in 1845, but brought to Padstow registry by William Skips (or Ships) of Port Isaac in 1851, lengthened to the dimensions given above and re-rigged as a schooner. Subsequent owners were Miller and Haynes, then J. George and J. Banbury of Bude. By 1900 she was owned in Newport but remained in the Padstow registry. She ended up with ketch rig. Broken up in 1912 (note on register).

**BOSCASTLE** built 1793 in France. Tons 42(O). Sloop rigged. Probably a French prize of which particulars would be found in the missing Padstow registers. By 1805 she was owned by J. Avery and was a constant trader to Boscastle 1810-1814. Her master included E. Attwell, F. Richards and Pope.

BOSCASTLE was lost with all hands off Aberthaw in February 1815, sailing from Boscastle for Bristol.

**BOSCASTLE** built 1838 at Padstow by John Sloggett. Tons 44(O) 30(N). 42.4 14.2 7.0. This sloop registered at Padstow, and owned by Rosevear with Burgess, Philip Burk and William Strout as masters, had an unusually short life.

She was broken up in 1843, perhaps because of being pounded on the hard bed of Boscastle harbour by the notorious ground swell.

**BOSCOPPA** ON 22396, built 1842 at Fowey by Marks and Rendle Tons 77(N) 72 (net 1866). 59.2 17.4 10.2 (1854). 63.6 19.4 9.8 (1859). Registered at Fowey in 1842, and in Padstow in 1854 where she is described as a schooner with a sharp stern and a male figurehead. The stern is unusual.

BOSCOPPA's Padstow owners were successively William Thomas (who commanded her), William Blackmore of Fremlington (who died in 1887) and John Butler. T. Trethewey was her master at one time. Blackmore converted her to ketch rig.

Cox of Appledore was her last owner and shortly after he acquired her, with D. Youngson as master, on 14th January 1888 she was wrecked on the South Tail of Bideford Bar, on passage Penarth for Fremlington with coal and one passenger.

She had a crew of five when first sailing from Fowey in 1842, and a crew of three when she was lost in 1888. Plus *ça change*.

**BOTTREAUX CASTLE** ON 19241, built 1844 at Padstow. Tons 56(O) 40(N), 37(net). 49.3 14.3 7.8 (1844). 50.8 15.7 7.7 (1859). The different dimensions in this and other cases are not caused by re-building, but by new detailed instructions for making tonnage measurements. A sloop rigged smack named after the ancient family seat from which the name Boscastle derived, she was registered at Padstow.

With owners successively Rosevear, J. Dyer, Francis Dingle and Jabez Brown, with several members of the Strout family as masters, she traded to Bude and Boscastle until 26th December 1879 when she was wrecked at the mouth of Boscastle harbour bringing in coal from Newport. The wind was SE force 9, so although she was in the lee of the cliffs, there would have been some fierce willawaws as she attempted the entrance. The crew of three including Master J. Sharrock, were rescued.

**BREADALBANE** ON 11749, built 1849-1850 at Pictou, Nova Scotia. Tons 480(O) 527(N) 467 reg. 121.2 28.6 18.8. A barque with a square stern and a scroll head trading Liverpool to Halifax until 1855 when she was registered at Padstow, where Samuel Pollard, a Wadebridge solicitor, briefly owned 64/64 shares before passing them to John Stribley, Padstow shipowner. He appointed W. Worden as master and she traded Bridgwater to North America, etc.

Her register ends 'Lost at Sea' and was closed 11th April 1859.

**BREEZE** ON 15911, built 1837 at Barnstaple by John Westacott.

Tons 60(O) 46(N). 47.4 15.3 8.3. A schooner registered at Padstow on completion and owned by P. Billing, her master, and others. In 1853 ownership passed to William Old and J. Osborne, and her masters were Thomas Bate, Joseph Harris, then E. Tabb. She traded between Wales and North Cornwall.

BREEZE was lost at sea 25th February 1857 (note on Register).

**BREEZE** ON 18386, built 1838 at Bideford by Evans and lengthened in 1849. Tons 72(O) 50(N). 51.3 16.0 8.3 (1838). Tons 61(N). 61.2 16.3 8.0 (1849 after lengthening). This schooner was also registered at Padstow on completion by Wm. Martyn (and others) of St Columb who remained her owner for her twenty year life. Her successive masters included W. James, Thomas Chalk, T. Stabbock and T. Chalk again.

She traded to Wales and Ireland and was lost at Ballyquinton, Strangford on 9th April 1858.

**BRISTOL TRADER** built 1806 at Clovelly by James Barrow. Tons 34(O). A sloop which specifically traded with Padstow and had as owner J. Barrow and as masters W. Bond and G. Stribling in the period 1807-1824.

*Lloyd's Register* gives a building date 1796, but as the vessel is not listed until 1807, and there is no local record of such a vessel being built in 1796, it seems probable that this vessel with Padstow connections was built in 1806, and quite likely her name would have appeared in the early missing Padstow registers. No further mention found after 1824.

**BRITANNIA** built 1803 (*Lloyd's Register*) in Padstow by Martin Withell. Tons 69(O). 54.5 18.3 9.3. A brig with a billet head registered in 1823 (first registration probably lost) at Padstow. Masters and owners included J. Burt, Pollard, Withell, James Symonds, Benoke and Banon. She was essentially a coaster. Lost near Ballycotton during gales 18th-19th December 1825.

**BRITANNIA.** The House family of Newquay briefly owned a schooner named BRITANNIA. *Lloyd's List* in February and March 1864 carried the following reports about the BRITANNIA of Cardigan, C. House, master.

a) On 15th February reported beached at Bedd Mannarch near Holyhead, Newquay for Runcorn with clay.

b) Run down and sunk 10th March by unknown vessel, probably American.

c) Established later that it was the schooner EMPIRE, Doolittle master, from Wicklow which had run down the BRITANNIA in Red Wharf Bay, Anglesey, before sailing on to Liverpool.

However, the *Royal Cornwall Gazette* on 25th March 1864 described how the BRITANNIA had been run down about 1.00 a.m. on 18th March by a coasting tug. Two of her crew had been drowned and the remainder clung to the mastheads until daylight and rescue. There were sixty ships named BRITANNIA at the time, and no record of House's ownership has been found, but the most likely candidate is the schooner ON 5698 built 1829 at Lawrenny, Milford Haven, lengthened 1850, 61 tons reg. and posted 'wrecked' in *Lloyd's Register* 1864-5.

**BRITON'S QUEEN** ON 3108, built 1838 at Padstow by John Tredwen. Tons 105(O) 93(N) 82(1859). 62.9 17.4 10.9. (1838). A schooner with a female bust registered at Padstow throughout.

Her early owners were Sloggett and Rosevear (of Boscastle) with Burke and Bellamy in command followed by James Richards and his Port Isaac family, but he moved to Calstock about 1870. Thomas Burman of Clovelly was the next owner (with numerous small shareholders), but by 1880 Arthur Hutchings of Padstow was master and owner, and remained so until her loss.

Wrecked on Bembridge Ledge on 29th September 1886 whilst on

passage Charlestown for Dieppe with china clay. She was salved, taken to Portsmouth and sold as a hulk.

**BROOKLANDS** *ex* SUSAN VITTERY q.v.

**BROTHERS** ON 11703, built 1832 at Padstow by John Tredwen. Tons 80(O) 1832, 84(O) 55(N) 1849. 55.3 18.6 9.3. Major repairs at Padstow 1837. Completed as a sloop rigged smack with running bowsprit and square stern. Registered at St Ives throughout. Converted to schooner rig 1843.

Her first owners were Hutchins and others including Sleeman of Padstow, her master. Hutchins became Hitchins in 1836 *Lloyd's Register* and M. T. Hitchins of St Agnes in the 1866 *Mercantile Navy List*, but her masters were G. Hicks of St Columb, Henwood and M. Pope. A Padstow coaster in all but register.

She was wrecked at Port Isaac 10th September 1835 but not totally lost. The August gale of 1852 wrecked a BROTHERS at St Agnes, probably her again, but she survived to founder at sea finally on 10th October 1870.

**BROTHERS** ON 19238, built 1839 at Township 13, Prince Edward Island. Tons 39(N). 49.0 14.7 7.6. A schooner with a male bust, she was registered at Bideford in 1840 but transferred to Padstow in 1854 with Martyn as owner, and T. Billing as master. By 1862 Billing was managing owner as well as master, and he continued to own her until she was broken up in 1881 (note on register).

**BRUTUS** built 1835 at Grand Rustico, Prince Edward Island. Tons 117(O) 105(N). 63.3 18.5 11.2. This schooner was registered on completion in Prince Edward Island by William Nicholls of Charlottetown, then sailed to England with a timber cargo and sold to Robert W. Avery of Padstow and registered there.

The following year she was trading to St Petersburg with William Tremeer as master. Edwin Key and William Hutchings followed in command, but she was shortlived, being broken up in 1844.

**BUDE PACKET** built 1827 (completed February 1828) at Padstow by John Tredwen. Tons 44(O). 44.2 15.5 7.4. A sloop registered at Padstow.

She was a constant trader to Bude, owned by W. Davey and Thomas Drew, with Drew, J. Tucker and J. Matherley noted as masters.

Lost February 1838 (note on register).

**BULLA** ON 68755, built 1873 at Jersey by Deslandes. Tons 80 net, later reduced to 75. 79.2 18.2 9.5. The schooner BULLA was owned and registered in Jersey until taken to Barnstaple registry in the late nineties. At the turn of the century her owner was Ernest Brown of Port Isaac, hence her inclusion in this list.

She subsequently had owners in Feock, Liverpool and Plymouth where she was converted into a lighter in 1928 and later abandoned in Hooe Lake.

**BUSY** ON 13139, built 1836 at Charlestown by William Pearse Banks. Tons 64(O) 43(N). 51.0 14.8 7.6. The sloop BUSY was registered at Fowey on completion but John Tredwen bought her 64/64 in 1847 and registered her at Padstow, and was her master for a time. He sold shares to N. Hocking and others, but retained an interest in her himself: later masters were Hocking, William James and J. Crocker.

BUSY was wrecked at Port Isaac in the 'ROYAL CHARTER Gale' on 25th October 1859. William Charles Mitchell of Port Isaac distinguished himself in the rescue of her crew and was awarded the silver medal of the RNLI.

**BUSY BEE** ON 91804, built 1885 at Plymouth by C. Gent. Tons 132 net 139 gross, later reduced to 112 net. 92.3 21.8 11.8. The schooner BUSY BEE was registered at Plymouth and owned by the builder for some years. In 1896 she was bought by D. Lauritzen of

Esbjerg and renamed NEIROS.

In 1902 she returned to the red ensign and was registered at Hull. In 1916, with the Newquay schooners earning good freights, Henry P. Thomas of Newquay bought her and T. Collings became her master, and G. Pappin is also noted as master.

On 16th October 1916, she was lost two miles West of Bude, having sailed from Newquay with china clay for Runcorn.

**C.B.K.F.** ON 83854, built 1881 at Falmouth by C. Burt. Tons 64 net 70 gross, later 56 net. 74.1 20.0 9.0. This ketch was registered at Falmouth until 1899 when William Hutchings of Padstow, who had already been in charge of her for many years, registered her at Padstow with fellow owners Charles H. Nurse and Robert Chapman, who by then was master.

Jim Nurse has researched details of her work and loss; sufficient here to record that on 21st June 1906 she was run down and sunk off Longships by SS TASSO on passage from Par with china clay for Weston Point. The two hands drowned but the master was picked up.

**CAMALAN** ON 13077, built 1849 at Padstow by R & J Tredwen. Tons 102(O) 86(N). 61.6 17.4 10.3 (1849). This schooner traded to the Mediterranean in her early years when owned by J. Tredwen and with R. Harvey and W. Bate in command. S. Hoskin of Port Isaac became managing owner and master through the 1860s but in the seventies and eighties she was owned in Appledore, disappearing from the registers by 1887.

**CAMEL** built 1801 in Ragusa. 195 tons (O) A polacca brig to be found in *Lloyd's Registers* between 1812 and 1823 trading to Malta and Antigua. An 1823 sailing report referred to her as the CAMEL of Padstow, but no register has been found. T. Bull was her master. Perhaps she was a prize in the Peninsular war.

**CAMELFORD** ON 42636, built 1861 at Padstow by John Tredwen. Tons 161 net. 99.5 22.7 12.2. This powerful schooner was built for deep water trade, and perhaps that is why she was registered at Liverpool. For the first ten years she was owned by Wade, with J. James in command, and traded to the Mediterranean and the West Indies. Robson owned her later, with J. Campbell as master.

She was wrecked on the Doom Bar on 7th March 1876 with a cargo of coal from Cardiff for St Lucia, so she kept her Padstow connection and her deep water trading to the end.

**CAMELLIA** ON 73910, built 1877 at Portsoy by Smith and Ritchie. Tons 91 net 98 gross. 76.4 21.1 10.0. A schooner with an elliptical stern and ¾ length female figurehead.

She was registered at Banff and sailed from Portsoy until 1885 when John Ennor of Newquay brought her south. W. Trebilcock was her first Cornish master, followed by Henwood who had her when she was lost.

She lifted a cargo of china clay from Fowey in September 1897 and on the 26th sank off the Lizard after colliding with SS MOSS ROSE of Liverpool. No lives were lost.

**CAMEO** ON 73852, built 1876 at Dumbarton by McKellar McMillan & Co. Tons 50 net, 55 gross. 63.7 18.0 7.5. This iron schooner of Glasgow registry is of note as being an early member of the fleet of Mr William Robertson who bought a coal barge on the Forth & Clyde canal for £10, and ended up owning a fleet of 45 steam coasters all named after precious stones. In 1889 she was bought (all 64 shares) by John Phillips of Port Isaac and registered at Padstow.

With him as master, she stranded on Atherfield Ledge on passage from Penzance for Woolwich with stone, 6th April 1890. Crew of three safe.

**CAMILLA** ON 27280, built 1853 at St Malo 'A Foreign Wreck'

The topsail schooner CARRIE killed both her Newquay masters.    *Newquay Old Cornwall Society*

(note on register). Tons 90 reg. later 78 net. 70.5  21.5  10.5. The schooner CAMILLA was registered at Padstow in 1860. Her owners were J. Nicholls of St Columb and others including her master T. Clemens.

Wrecked near Liverpool 3rd December 1872 (note on register). **CAMWOOD** ON 75516, built 1877 on Prince Edward Island by James White. Tons 125 net. 85.5  23.6  10.8. This brigantine like many others was built to bring a timber cargo to Britain where both cargo and ship were sold. CAMWOOD went to Liverpool and was registered there, but she soon had Westcountry owners, and in 1890 the Coode family of Port Isaac bought her. In 1892 she was registered at Padstow, Joseph G. Coode being managing owner.

CAMWOOD was lost in 1896.
**CANADIAN** built 1839 at Padstow by Thomas Carter. Tons 94(O) 70(N). 56.4  17.7  8.8. This large sloop rigged smack was owned by W. Darke, T. Rikard Avery and others during her short life with W. Darke and then James Darke as master. On 2nd July 1842 she was leaving Boscastle for France loaded with slates when a squall put her onto an isolated rock and she capsized.

She evidently survived that incident because a note on her register reads 'Lost April 1843'.
**CAROLINE** built in France, date unknown. Tons 87 and 115. This brig is to be found in *Lloyd's Registers* 1799-1805, owned by J. Avery and W. Avery and with J. Richards, W. May and J. Pettigrew. Clearly a Padstow ship whose register has been lost.

A French *corsaire* named CAROLINE was captured by HMS EMERALD in 1799.
**CAROLINE** ON 13089, built in France, date unknown. A prize condemned in the High Court of Admiralty 18th March 1813. Tons 56(O) 42(N). 38.34. Reg. 1861. The dimensions on the Padstow registers:

|  |  |  |  |
|---|---|---|---|
| 62.6 | 16.4 | 7.7 | (1813) |
| 49.3 | 14.4 | 8.0 | (1836) |
| 52.9 | 16.9 | 7.8 | (1861) |

Until about 1850 this remarkable schooner was owned by William Cock (often spelt Cook) and his family with Nicholas Bird, W. Hicks and J. Richards as well as members of the family in command. John Stribley, Willmett, and Andrew Watts the master mariner then took over.

She was lost off Trevose Head 11th October 1867 bringing coal from Newport towards Salcombe.
**CAROLINE** ON 11425, built 1839 at Newquay by T. Clemens. Tons 53(O) 40(N). 46.3  14.8  8.0. This smack was the first ship to be built in the Gannel yard. J. Carter Junior was her first master, but there were numerous shareholders and masters including Richard Hockin, George Pappin, T. J. Teague, William Philp, W. Carter, W. Pascoe and Seaton Bryant.

In 1862 her register changed from Padstow to Fowey, owner John Mabley of Pentewan, then to Bideford in 1867. She is out of the lists by 1870. 'Lost at Newport' is noted on the register without a date.

**CAROLINE** ON 68173, built 1874 at Bideford by John Johnson. Tons 158 net 166 gross, lower net tonnages later 107.1 22.5 11.6. CAROLINE was a three masted barkentine owned in Brixham until 1891 when she joined the considerable fleet owned or managed by W. S. Allport at Padstow. J. T. Richards and later A. Brenton acted as masters.

On 23rd January 1900 she was being towed out of Hayle bound for Cardiff with sand when she was grounded on the bar and was wrecked. The pilot and crew of six were saved. By then she was rigged as a three masted schooner.

**CAROLINE GOODYEAR** ON 43970, built 1861 at Boscastle by Hellyer. Tons 133 net 146 gross. This schooner was registered in London and traded Liverpool to the West Indies and Bermuda, Cardiff to South America, Bristol to the West Indies and so on. Her registration shifted to Teignmouth in 1874 and she was lost 14 miles SE of Bardsey on 15th January 1881.

**CAROLINE PHILLIPS** ON 29358, built 1862 at Padstow by John Stribley. Tons 64.28 reg. 67.5 19.4 9.3. The port register describes her as dandy rigged with two masts, and the official loss report calls her a ketch.

John Stribley, who owned all 64 shares when she was registered at Padstow, on completion promptly sold them to J. H. Willmett. That same year, he sold them to W. C. Phillips and others at Port Isaac, who ran her for the rest of her time.

She was lost on Mixen Sands on the night 23rd-24th January 1875 in a NW gale force 9, whilst on passage from Liverpool for Plymouth with a cargo of sugar scum.

**CARRIE** ON 78964, built 1878 at Sunny Corner, Truro, by Charles Dyer. Tons 94 net 104 gross. 85.6 21.8 10.4. CARRIE was a coasting schooner registered at Truro.

She was not a lucky ship, as witness the *Royal Cornwall Gazette* 16th February 1899: 'CARRIE of Truro arrived at Milford with the dead bodies of her captain and mate on deck. The captain was T. Solomon of Newquay who leaves a wife and five children; the mate was Alex Anderson aged 24.'

Apparently she was washed by heavy seas off St Anns Head and when the two hands Joseph Guswell and John Cundy came on deck it was to find the mate's body stuck in the port rail, and the captain washed into the after hold with his neck broken. The vessel was seriously damaged but they were able to run her into Castle Pill, Milford Haven.

Her loss was described in the *West Briton*, 26th March 1903. A telephone message was received at Penzance coastguard station from Newlyn saying she had struck the Runnelstone on Tuesday night. The crew of four took to their punt and drifted towards Porthwarra. The captain was washed out of the boat. As they approached the surf the remaining three jumped out of the boat to struggle ashore. Only Duncan Mackenzie climbed the cliff and saw nothing of the others.

The CARRIE was on passage from Newport for Par with coal. The lost were Captain Clemens, Newquay, Harry Barnecust of Par and the boy Gordon Stevens of Newquay.

**CARTHAGE** ON 27095, place and date of build unknown. Tons 545.73 (1855) 130.8 25.5 21.2. This full rigged ship, with two decks and a billet head, was registered at Padstow in 1855 with no indication of her previous history. Her owner was Richard Easthope (sometimes Easthorpe) with all 64 shares. He sold some to John Andrew of St Merryn, McDowell of Falmouth, V. Trayes of Cardiff, William Hellyar of St Merryn, John Brewer of Padstow and S. Carlile of London.

Easthope had captained ships in the Quebec trade and later owned shares in several large Canadian built square riggers trading to Mexico and South America as well as USA and Canada. Several of them appear in the list of Padstow emigrant ships, but not CARTHAGE despite her having the rare benefit of two decks.

Her Padstow register is little help, ending with the sentence: 'Lost in the St Lawrence River 11th May 1861'.

There was no CARTHAGE in *Lloyd's Registers* in any way compatible with this one. There was, however, a CARTHAGENIAN (sometimes spelt CARTHAGINIAN) of 564 new tons built at Quebec in 1840 by Edward Oliver. Her dimensions as built were 120.0 26.6 20.7. Her last appearance in *Lloyd's Register* is in 1849 with no home port given.

**CATHARINE and CATHERINE.** There is confusion in *Lloyd's Registers* and elsewhere as to the spelling of this name.

**CATHARINE** ON 11420, built 1833 at Fowey by Nickels. Tons 89(O) 69 net (1875), 60 net later. 59.7 18.6 10.1. A coasting schooner with a counter stern and woman's bust figurehead. Apart from a short spell at Par, she was registered at Fowey throughout, but in the early eighties she came into the ownership of Nicholas Tregaskes of Bude and after that of E. J. Rowse and her master M. Carne. They were both Newquay men, leading to her inclusion here.

She was lost at Mort Bay, Devon on 19th December 1890 (note on register).

**CATHARINE** or **CATHERINE** ON 19260, built 1842 at Padstow by T. Carter. Tons 66(O) 51(N). 48.4 16.5 8.7 as built. Lengthened 1863. Tons 82 net. 50.6 18.2 8.6 after lengthening. Sloop rigged when built, she was given schooner rig on lengthening. Avery owned her as a sloop followed by the Hoskin family of Port Isaac. They sold her to Swansea in 1863 and she was lengthened. She came back to Port Isaac, bought by William Couch Jr but was last listed about 1874.

**CATHERINE** ON 14138, built 1829 at Bideford by Thomas Evans. Tons 98 (O) 88(N). 62.8 19.5 11.2. A schooner with an unusual note that she was square rigged, on the Padstow Port Register. She was a coaster owned by Abbott and later W. Mably. Her masters included Parnall, T. Hicks and Mably who was drowned unfortunately when trying to salvage spars from a wreck on the Doom bar in February 1869.

CATHERINE was broken up in 1877 (note on register).

**CATHERINE** ON 19211, built 1843 at Kingston (Shoreham) by J. May and T. Thwaites. Tons 37(N). 50.0 13.2 7.3. This smack was registered at Padstow on completion, owned by William Hancock and used in the local trades, such as bringing coal from Newport.

Lost at sea 6th April 1858 (note on register).

**CATHERINE** ON 56405, built 1869 at Llyn Bwtri (Aberdovey) by John Jones, foreman. Tons 76 reg. 50 in 1900. 75.2 19.6 8.8. After serving as a schooner registered at Aberdovey and Aberystwyth, this vessel was bought by Thomas Mitchell Jr of Port Isaac, brought to Padstow and converted to ketch rig in 1891. Nine years later she was sold to Appledore owners and lasted into the early 1920s.

**CATHERINE AULD** ON 65065, built 1881 at Inverkeithing by R & D Ross. Tons 164 (1884) 142 (1892). 117 net at loss. 96.4 23.9 11.7. A brigantine with an elliptical stern. Built and based on the Forth, she was registered for a time at Barrowstowness which must be the harbour known now as Bo'ness. She was registered at Padstow in 1889, owned by James Skinner, a St Austell grocer, but the following year she joined the considerable fleet of W. C. Phillips of St Austell, who had moved there from Padstow. CATHERINE AULD remained registered at Padstow. She was last heard of when

CATHERINE (built in 1833) and
WESTERN STAR (on the right) at Newquay
in the 1880s.
*Newquay Old Cornwall Society*

sailing from Newcastle on 15th November 1893 with coal for Malpas and a crew of six.

**CAURINUS** ON 19250, built 1833 at Padstow by Thomas Carter. Tons 40(O) 28(N). 42.0 15.3 7.3 (1833). A sloop rigged smack registered at Padstow throughout and owned and commanded by J. Martyn, W. James, T. Hoskings, William Mitchell, William Ships and Henry Tabb.

Lost on the Wolf Rock September 11th, 1859.

**CAVALIER** ON 62109, built 1871 at Kingston, Elgin by W. Kinloch. Tons 86 reg. 80 net in 1892. 82.0 18.5 9.8. This schooner was registered at Lossiemouth briefly and then at Inverness for the rest of her life. She is included because John Ennor of Newquay owned her from about 1890 until about 1903, with W. Pascoe as master. Then she went to Cardiff owners but is not listed after 1905.

**CELERITY** built 1839 at Padstow by John Tredwen. Tons 64(O) 52(N). 50.5 15.0 9.0. Lengthened 1848. Tons 86(O) 69(N). 64.2 16.3 8.7. A schooner with fixed bowsprit, square stern and woman's bust. Although *Lloyd's Register* gives her as a sloop as built, the surveyor described her as a schooner in 1839. After lengthening she traded regularly to the Mediterranean and the Azores.

CELERITY was registered and owned in Penzance throughout. She was lost off Holyhead in December 1852.

**CERES** built 1804 at St Michael's Mount. Tons 43(O). 45.2 15.9 8.1. This small sloop was registered at Padstow in 1820, owned by William Martyn and others, with William Trebilcock as master.

She was wrecked at Northam Burrows, September 1829.

**CERES** ON 15580, built 1809 at Bideford by Henry Tucker. Tons 47(O) 35(N). 51.5 16.0 8.8. Earlier described as a cutter and a sloop, registered at Bideford; when John Tredwen registered her at Padstow in 1860 she had been re-rigged as a schooner, probably by him as he sold her on to Edward Neal, master mariner of Port Isaac a few months later in 1861.

Lost near Boscastle 13th January 1865 (note on register).

**CERES** ON 15560, built 1811 at Salcombe. Tons 57(O). 47.2 15.6 6.9. Lengthened in 1868. Tons 44 net. 65.2 17.7 7.2. Sloop rigged until lengthened when she became a ketch.

In 1830 she was registered at Dartmouth, and in 1837 and for the following 99 active years, at Padstow. King and others of Stratton owned her in 1837 with James Greenway as master. In 1841 William Lewis of Bude became owner and master. Then in 1852 she became the property of Henry Petherick of Bude whose family were to own her for 85 years. This is the famous CERES which sailed for 125 years and was reputed to have carried military stores to Spain during the Peninsular Wars. Indeed, she was originally built for the Spanish fruit and nut trade.

Captain W. W. Petherick took over from Henry in 1868 and had her lengthened that year: she was cut in half amidships and more than 15 feet added to her length, increasing her deadweight tonnage from 52 to 85 tons. It was generally considered bad practice to lengthen a wooden ship amidships as that was the point of maximum bending forces in a seaway and often coincided with relative weakness due to hatches, etc., but the job was obviously well done on CERES. R. Walter Petherick took over in 1884 and retired in 1930.

It would be impossible to recite all her adventures. On 27th November 1893 bringing coal from Newport, she was wrecked at Bude but her crew of three survived and she was 'got off against the odds'. Bude traders had more need than most for engine power and she was given an oil engine in 1913 supplied by the Turbinia Engineering Co. The engine was replaced in 1932 by one taken from the DODENTALJA of 36 b.h.p. In 1914, with the engine fitted, she arrived at Newport for a coal cargo only to be told that a steamer was arriving and of course had priority at the loading berth. Captain Petherick was able to point out that he too was a powered vessel and demanded, and obtained, the right to load first.

As a coaster she would take malting barley to the distillers in Scotland and Ireland, thence oats to the Channel ports, bricks or manufactures back to Bude, and so on.

In the First World War the engine was invaluable, enabling her to trade by following the coastline in waters too shallow for U-boats when most of the coasters were not allowed out, and she kept Bude and other ports supplied with essentials from Bristol.

W. Stainton, who had been successively boy, mate and assistant engineer in CERES, took over from Walter until his death in 1936. Mr A. Petherick had her for a few short voyages but was not on board when, on 24th November 1936, she foundered off Baggy Point, Devon.

Not many ships eluded both French privateers and German U-boats; no other vessel survived so many visits to Bude.

**CERES** built 1820 at Padstow by J. Tredwen. Tons 83(O) 64(N).

57.6  19.0  10.1 (1820 reg.). The rig of this vessel was variously described as a schooner, a brigantine and a schooner brig; the last in a *Lloyd's* survey of 1835. She was registered at Padstow and owned successively by Richards, W. Knight, Hetherington and R & J Tredwen. The first three were also her masters, and she may have ended in the hands of the Tredwens as the result of expensive repairs carried out in 1835.

After a life spent in the home trades, she was lost and the register closed 20th March 1848.

**CERES** built 1820 at Mevagissey by James Dunn. Tons 49(O). 49.3 16.0  9.0. This smack, only half the tonnage of the other CERES built in 1820, nevertheless started her life in the Mediterranean trade for owners which included John Cardell, and John Cardell the younger, both of St Columb.

She was registered at Fowey, moving to Scilly 1835, and was lost at sea 21st January 1838.

**CERES** built 1850 at Padstow by R & J Tredwen. 15 tons (N). 42.5 12.1  3.6, a sloop with a round stern. Being just over fifteen tons, this vessel had to be registered, as she was, at Padstow in 1850, owned half by Thomas Littlefair Seaton and half by John Dyer Bryant, both of Padstow. Stephen Phelp and James Haynes are both mentioned as masters. She was lost with a crew of four on 12 September 1853, her shattered hull being driven ashore at Trebetherick Point. Her dimensions suggest that she was either a yacht or a fishing vessel.

**CHAMPION OF WALES** built 1796 at Brixham. Tons 39(O). 44.5  15.1  7.1. This small sloop came to the Padstow register from Penzance and St Ives in 1823 to be owned by R. Power of Boscastle then William Knight of Padstow. In 1825 she was sold to Plymouth and the last of her in *Lloyd's Register* is in 1832 as a Topsham Coaster. Foundered 1833.

**CHARLES** built 1790 at Padstow, the Dinas Yard. The building of this 22 ton sloop is recorded but no register survives.

**CHARLES** built 1834 at Padstow by John Tredwen. Tons 47(O) 32(N). 46.8  15.7  7.6 (1834). This sloop traded to Wales and Bristol, owned by the Tredwens and with M. Pope and H. Burd as masters.

She was lost 22nd January 1847 (note on register).

**CHARLES PHILLIPS** ON 10912, built 1830 at Padstow by Thomas Carter. Tons 31(O) 21(N) 26 (net). 39.2  14.0  7.2. A sloop which took part in the Bristol trade to Padstow for William Phillips, James Retallick of St Wenn and Tummon until sold to Bridgwater in 1850.

In December 1871 she was in distress in Swansea Bay and her crew of three were rescued by lifeboat. But she survived until about 1880.

**CHARLES TUCKER** ON 14136, built 1839 at Swansea by W. Meager. Tons 80(O) 106 net, later 90. 80.6  20.4  10.3. This schooner was registered at Swansea, St Ives and then at Penzance, and it was not until 1890 that William Henry Williams of Newquay became her owner and she qualified to be included in this list.

She was converted to a lighter and her register closed 1892.

The schooner CHARLES TUCKER, owned by William Henry Williams of Newquay, and the Cardiff pilot cutter POLLY, drying sails in Clovelly.     *Royal Institution of Cornwall*

**CHARLOTTE** built 1816 at Padstow. Tons 34(O). This sloop was registered at Padstow until shifting to Bideford in 1922. She was lost 24th December 1830.

**CHARLOTTE** ON 5663, built 1830 at Plymouth. Tons 40(O). 41.2 13.7 7.5 (as built). Lengthened 1847. Tons 49 (1868). 51.7 15.5 7.1 (1856). 56.3 17.4 8.5 (1866).

CHARLOTTE came to the Padstow Register in 1836 and stayed there. Her owners and masters embrace almost all the largest maritime families of Padstow including Thomas Julian of Porth, A. Prout, John Sweet, J. Tredwen Jr, Anscott Hutchings, Francis Prideaux, J. Courtenay, John Male, S. Tucker of Tintagel, W. Avery, J. Stribley and J. May. She remained smack rigged despite being lengthened, and had many adventures.

On 6th December 1874, on passage from Cork to Falmouth with oats, she stranded at Wanson Mouth in Widemouth Bay in a westerly gale. Her crew of three and one passenger were rescued by rocket and breeches buoy.

**CHARLOTTE** ON 47233, built 1863 at Kingston, Sussex by May and Thwaite. Tons 62 net. 69.5 19.0 8.6. This ketch was first owned by William May of Shoreham, but by 1888 James Jenkin of Newquay bought her and he was followed by John Neal of Padstow who registered her there in 1889 and kept her going until after the Great War. Then David W. Davies of Wadebridge, who ran some of the barges on the Camel, took her and she was broken up in 1924 (note on register).

**CHURCHILL** ON 19604, built 1816 at Plymouth. Tons 69(O) 57(N). 56.0 17.1 10.1. An early schooner destined for the Mediterranean trade, she was registered at Yarmouth, Padstow, Truro, Plymouth, and Milford.

Her connection with Padstow was brief, for Nicholas Horswill owned her in 1822 but sold her to Truro the same year. She lasted until about 1860.

**CICERONE** ON 43566, built 1861 at Dartmouth by Kelly. Tons 154 gross net later 120. 99.5 22.0 12.5. She was built as a schooner and by 1890 rigged as a three masted schooner. Although registered at Dartmouth and Falmouth, by 1879 Francis Prout was her master and had an interest in her culminating in managing ownership.

She was lost in collision off the East Goodwin Lightship on 13th June 1905 whilst on passage from Fowey for Bo'ness with china clay.

**CILICIA** (**CICILIA** also found) ON 27277, built 1860 at Padstow by F. H. Thomas. Tons 90. 77.0 19.7 10.5. This schooner appears to have been built on spec. and owned by her builder for a few months before being sold to James Strout who ran her until her loss.

She has been missing since 13th November 1875 (note on register).

**CLARA** ON 77402, built 1877 at Padstow by William Stribley and yellow metalled at Quay Yard, Newquay by T. Clemens. Tons 100 net 114 gross, later 90 net. 84.8 22.3 10.6. This schooner was built for J. P. Dunstan of St Columb who retained ownership throughout. Her masters included M. T. Clemens, G. Trembeth and N. Clemens.

CLARA has been missing since leaving Tayport for St John's, Newfoundland with coal and with two passengers and five crew on 10th April 1892.

**CLARA** ON 72460, built 1879 at Bridgwater by Gough. Tons 86 net 95 gross, reduced to 63 net by 1928. 80.7 21.7 8.6 (as built). She was built for the Newfoundland trade and J. Haynes and H. Couch were masters in her early years. But her formal association with Padstow is brief, being limited to her ownership by J. Ennor of Newquay, 1889-'90.

In the course of her life of over fifty years she was registered at Bridgwater, Plymouth, Gloucester and Wexford, lasting in Ireland until about 1930.

**CLAUDINE** see COMET, ON 22198.

**CLEMENTINA** ON 15508, built 1847 at Appledore by Thomas Green. Tons 99(N) 90 net. 66.0 17.3 10.7 (reg. 1855). A brigantine with a break in the deck but, according to *Lloyd's Register*, schooner rigged for a period in mid-career.

CLEMENTINA was yellow metalled in 1848 and entered the Mediterranean trades until Pethybridge and Tippett, master mariner, bought her from Bideford in 1855 and registered her at Padstow; then John Pascoe, also of Padstow, became managing owner. She moved to St Ives in 1856 but Pascoe was managing owner again in the 1870s.

CLEMENTINA was lucky to survive to be broken up in 1885 after thirty-eight years of hard work.

**CLIO** ON 33034, built 1838 at Granville, Nova Scotia. Tons 473(O) 513(N) 487 net. 117.7 26.6 18.9. She was built of black birch, pine and oak and registered at St John on completion, a three masted barque. A few months later she was sold to Avery, the well-established Padstow merchant house, and in some ways she marks the zenith of Padstow shipping as a brand new deep water square rigger owned by Padstow, a full *Lloyd's* surveying port, trading from Padstow to Quebec and other North American ports, taking substantial numbers of emigrants and returning with prime timber for Padstow's expanding shipyards. Rawle and Easthorpe (master) took over from Avery and Brown (master) in 1845, but all went on as before until 1850 when the Doom Bar persuaded her people that she was too big for Padstow: she carried on as a Quebec trader, but sailing from Falmouth and Plymouth and even Gloucester. Her survey ran out in 1858 but Rawle & Co. remained the owners. In 1865 J. Moore of Stonehouse, Devon was her owner, and her register ends with the note 'Abandoned at Sea 3rd July 1866'.

**CLODAGH** ON 20789, built 1859 at Padstow by John Tredwen. Tons 119 reg. 83.3 20.7 11.2. This schooner was built for immediate 'export' to Waterford whither Padstow ships had traded for 500 years and more. She spent her life in the Irish Sea and British Channel ports and is gone from the registers by 1884.

**CLYDE** ON 53005, built 1866 at Glasgow by Connell. Tons 60 reg. 65.8 18.9 8.4. This large smack was built by Charles Connell, one of the pioneers of iron shipbuilding on the Clyde whose firm's final hull number was 512 for the handsome Ben line cargo liner BENSTAC in 1968. The smack herself is not without interest, being of composite (wood and iron) construction, like the clipper CUTTY SARK, which was built on the Clyde three years later. Her entries in *Lloyd's Register* are marked 'Iron frame, planked in part with German oak', and 'Experimental Construction, Biennial Survey'.

CLYDE marks a complete break with previous practice, being ordered by Padstow owners from a Clyde yard. That may be explained by her first owners being A. & D. Mackay of Padstow. They employed J. Waters as master. In 1870 ownership was spread with the Hockadays of Delabole taking a big interest and Edward Neal as master. He was washed overboard and drowned in the Portland Race in June 1872, and was succeeded by P. Billing.

CLYDE foundered off Hartland Point 29th September 1875 (note on register).

**COLLINA** ON 29351, built 1860 at Padstow by John Tredwen. Tons 47 net. 59.5 17.7 8.4. A cutter rigged smack registered at Padstow and owned by Bellamy and others of Boscastle. Her masters included J. Venning and Z. Callaway.

Burnt at Penzance 29th August 1871 (note on register).

**COMET** ON 13892, built 1842 at Guernsey. Tons 33(O). A smack with a semi-elliptical stern lengthened and restored in 1855 as a ketch, 58 tons reg. 66.8 16.7 8.2. This COMET was registered at Guernsey and then Southampton until the Padstow merchant John Hawken bought her in 1888.

She was supposed lost off Land's End about 3rd March 1881 with C. Harvey (master) and crew. She was on passage Padstow for Mevagissey with coal loaded at Newport.

**COMET** ON 22198, built 1858 at Padstow by John Tredwen. Tons 72 net 79 gross. 69.6 19.4 9.5. This large sloop was registered at Padstow by John Tredwen but soon owned by Ann Moyse of Port Isaac with J. Couch and May as masters. Charles Warne of Charlestown bought her in 1873 and she became a Fowey ship, but on 29th December 1874, sailing from Antwerp for Liverpool, she was damaged by ice, and her next appearance in the *Mercantile Navy List* is as a Sligo schooner *ex* CLAUDINE (Foreign name). It seems likely that she was re-rigged in Belgium and later sold to Sligo.

This COMET was wrecked at the entrance to Dartmouth on 9th November 1878, sailing from Sligo to London with oats.

**COMMERCE** see JANIE LOUISE

**COMMERCE** built 1819 in Padstow by John Tredwen. Tons 70(O). 55.2 17.8 10.0. Although described as a snow in *Lloyd's Register* of 1820, she was registered at Padstow as a schooner owned by Abbott with J. Parnell as master. In 1820 she was sold to Cardiff.

*Lloyd's List* for 5th February 1822 contains the news that she sank on Margate Sand on passage from Cardiff for London with iron. Captain J. Davis and his crew were saved. On the 12th February the Maldon fishing smack BROMLEY was wrecked on the hull of the COMMERCE.

**COMMERCE** ON 1526, built 1828 at Ipswich as a steamship of 36 tons (O). She appears in *Lloyd's Register* 1838 as a steamship of Gloster, 15 tons, owned by the Severn Steam Tug Company. At that early date she must have been a paddle-steamer. In the 1850s her entry in *Lloyd's* was as an unpowered sloop rigged 'flat' of 56 tons, having been 'almost rebuilt' in 1848. In 1858 she changed her home port from Gloster to Cardiff, and was measured at 49.62 reg. (gross) tons. 59.0 15.7 7.7, a sloop with fixed bowsprit, square stern and carvel built. In 1865 she was sold to Robert Neal of Padstow.

Her Cardiff register notes 'Lost 22nd August 1868'.

**CONQUEST** ON 62685 built 1871 at Newquay by J. Osborne at the Island Cove yard. Tons 68 net, 77 gross. 75.4 22.0 9.7. This schooner CONQUEST was registered at Padstow until 1900 and thereafter at Bridgwater. Her principal Padstow owners were Geake and M. H. Osborne and among her masters were J. Bellamy and M. Osborne. She was essentially a coaster.

Lost in Poole Harbour 21st October 1908.

**CONSERVATOR** ON 19216, built 1843 at Padstow by R & J Tredwen 'partly of old material'. Tons 31(O) 28(N). 48.7 13.2 6.8 (1843). This sloop rigged smack was registered at Padstow until 1858 and her owners and masters included her builders and Roger Duggua, John Cory (who shared her with John Couch Jr), A. Hutchings, Joshua Harris, Osborne, Tabb and Horsewell. She then moved to Aberystwyth, Beaumaris, and Carnarvon and became ketch rigged.

CONSERVATOR was lost in collision with the Italian barque CONCEZIONE in the Bristol Channel, January 1890.

**CONSTANCE** ON 19762, built 1858 at Padstow by S. T. Bennett. Tons 106 reg. 84.2 20.4 10.5. Lengthened in 1870. Tons 149 gross 99 net (1896). 108.2 20.4 10.5. She was built as a two masted schooner and given a third mast when lengthened.

There are two mysteries about this ship. Why was she registered successively at Padstow, Swansea, Plymouth and Falmouth when she was owned and commanded by men hailing from Padstow,

Newquay and St Kew? These men included Edward Norway, her first owner, W. Couch, Edwin and Richard Trebilcock and R. Hoskin who was her master for twenty years.

The second mystery is her loss and resurrection. On 17th December 1881 she was driven ashore on the Hayle bar seeking shelter when on passage from Newport for Santander with coal. Her crew and four pilots and extra hands were gallantly rescued by the Hayle RNLI lifeboat ISIS. The remains of the CONSTANCE's hull and gear were auctioned as being too damaged for repair. But she survived and her register was not closed until 1902 with the note 'vessel not to sail'.

A third mystery was solved in an article by William Beckett who sailed in her. How and why was her net tonnage reduced to 99 when the Trebilcocks took her in 1884? Apparently they moved the forward bulkhead aft one foot, thus increasing the allowance for crew accommodation without reducing her carrying capacity, as virtually all her home trade cargoes took her down to her marks without filling the hold. The object was to avoid the compulsory pilotage and pilotage fees for vessels over 100 net tons in the Mersey, giving her a worthwhile advantage in her regular trade, taking china clay to Runcorn.

**CORNISH LASS** ON 14032, built 1841 at Padstow by John Tredwen. Tons 81(O) 66(N) 60 net. 55.0 16.5 9.6. This schooner was initially owned in Padstow by J. Hawken with E. Parnall as master, but in 1846 M. T. Hitchens of St Ives bought her and his family owned her for the remaining fifty years of her long life.

On 6th January 1896 the CORNISH LASS was entering St Agnes with coal from Lydney when she was set on to Trevellas Rocks and became a total loss.

**CORNISH OAK** built 1782 at Padstow by John Bone. No surviving register has been found for this brig. *Lloyd's List* of 10th March 1801 confirms that she was a Padstow ship, master's name Boyd. *Lloyd's List* 8th December 1801 informs us of her loss near Padstow on 22nd November 1801.

The Bone family built ships at Polperro, but nothing further has been found of any activity in Padstow.

**CORNUBIA** ON 19274, built 1856 at Padstow by John Tredwen. Tons 78 reg. 70.0 19.9 8.8. Built as a sloop but her Padstow register records an alteration to a two masted dandy rig without giving the date. Her builder was also her owner, but he later sold 32 of his 64 shares to Joseph Tyacke, mariner.

Lost 29th October 1863 (note on register).

**CORNUVIA** ON 63520, built 1869 at South Shields by Readhead Softley & Co. Tons 799 net 832 gross, later 790 net 843 gross. 191.3 32.1 20.0. An iron full-rigged ship with one deck, CORNUVIA was virtually in a class by herself as a Padstow ship. She was built for Henry Wilson of Padstow who registered her in London and captained her in trade to India and elsewhere for over 10 years. She must have been by far the most valuable ship built for a Padstow owner. CORNUVIA was sold to Liverpool owners in the early eighties, and in 1898 she was sold to S. Mazella of Naples and renamed ROSARIO. On the face of it, it is unlikely that this ship ever visited Padstow in the course of her long career.

She was scrapped in Genoa in 1907.

**CORNWALL** date and place of build unknown, *ex* LE GUSTAVE. Prize taken by HMS TELEGRAPH (Timothy Scriven) on 29th December 1813. Tons 79(O). 57.2 18.4 8.9. These details are from her 1814 Padstow register when she was owned by Avery and the Rickard family of Boscastle. James Rickard was her master and she was schooner rigged.

She was registered again at Padstow by E. Billing, owner and master, in 1821, and again in 1833 when Nicholas Marshall, master mariner of St Columb Minor, took over.

Her history fits together well; the French navy had a small GUSTAVE listed 1812-13; HMS TELEGRAPH was an American privateer captured in 1813, previously named VENGEANCE. According to *Lloyd's Register* CORNWALL had been built at Bordeaux in 1811.

In 1837 she was sold to Barnstaple (her tonnage then being measured 55(N) and on the 29th September 1839 she foundered in the Bristol Channel (note on register).

**CORNWALL** ON 5753, built 1855 at Padstow. Tons 120 reg. 80.6 18.7 11.4. It is probable that she was the schooner launched by Tredwen on 20th March and given the name AURORA *pro tem.* (c.f. ARCTIC). A schooner built for the South Devon Shipping Company and registered at Plymouth. This is one of the earliest examples of a Padstow built vessel being owned by a company. Even in the 18th century *Lloyd's Register* lists ships as being owned by Smith and Co. (or Capt. and Co.) but that simply meant Smith the nominated or managing owner and others unnamed.

CORNWALL was owned by a named company. By 1870, however, she was in the ownership of James Lobb of Plymouth (a family name also familiar in Padstow), and she was dropped from the lists by 1874.

**CORSAIR.** The Bude canal records include a 46 ton sloop of Padstow, Hart master, in 1850. No register has been found but it is possible that she was owned in Padstow briefly but registered elsewhere.

**CORSAIR** ON 69458, built 1874 at Padstow by John Cowl. Tons 121 net, 130 gross. 90.9 23.1 11.5. This schooner had an elliptical stern (Cowl's hallmark) and a black figurehead of a man. She was built for William Allport's fleet with Battershill and H. Camps as masters.

CORSAIR has been missing since 29th January 1884 when she left Newcastle for Totnes with coal and a crew of five (note on register).

**COTTAGER** ON 19209, built 1843 at Padstow by John Tredwen. Tons 85(O) 72(N). 56.6 16.7 9.9 (1843). Registered at Padstow by Hockin of Primrose Cottage, Newquay and others with Nicholas Hockin and W. Read as masters.

COTTAGER was essentially a coasting schooner. She was lost in November 1868 (note on register).

**COUNTESS OF DEVON** ON 68327, built 1873 at Plymouth by Shilston. 'Part second-hand material'. Tons 213 net 233 gross. 117.5 23.7 12.7. with raised quarterdeck 28 ft. long. Although the *Mercantile Navy List* describes her as a brigantine, and *Lloyd's Register* in 1874-5 has her as a schooner, she was a barkentine by 1880, and almost certainly she was completed with that rig in 1873.

She was registered at Plymouth (Shilston, owner) and Teignmouth (Finch, owner) but by 1905 G. Randell of Newquay was master, and according to Verran he was also owner when she was lost with all hands on 13th November on the Great Burbo Bank, bringing potter's clay from Poole for Runcorn.

**COURIER** ON 60293, built 1869 at Montrose. Tons 100 net 128 gross (1898). 88.2 21.4 10.9. This schooner was registered at Montrose, and remained so even when in 1875 Benjamin M. Harvey accountant of Padstow, became nominated owner. However, in 1899 she was re-registered at Padstow with Harvey retaining 32 shares and William Allport having the other 32. Padstow masters were J. Mutton, A. Brenton, and W. Durepaire.

On 13th March 1904 she was run down by SS DEUCALION of the Blue Funnel Line in the Crosby Channel whilst on passage Padstow for Runcorn with china clay.

Her net tonnage was, in fact, 99.78 and it seems probable that like CONSTANCE arrangements were made to avoid the compulsory pilotage required for vessels of over 100 tons.

**CRITERION** ON 11635, built 1834 at Southtown, Yarmouth by Frederick Preston. Tons 86(O) 71(N). 66 net. 58.3 16.0 9.9. This schooner was registered at Padstow in 1836 and owned by Tremain until she was sold to Wexford in 1854. Her Padstow masters included G. Bellamy, S. Osborne, Mortly and J. Horsewell.

She lasted until the mid-1880s on the Wexford register.

**DAEDALUS** ON 33084, built 1835 at Portland, New Brunswick. Tons 396(O). 112.4 28.2 18.7. A three masted barque with a sham gallery and a male bust figurehead. *Lloyd's Register* records that her rig became that of a full rigged ship after damage repairs in 1853, and remained so until her loss.

She traded from Liverpool, mainly to Africa, until registered at Padstow in 1844, with Thomas Littlefair Seaton as the principal shareholder, with numerous others having a small number of shares each. In 1845 she was one of Padstow's emigrant ships, being described as an East Indiaman of 700 tons burthen with H. Nichols in command. T. Bullman commanded her later and she traded from Falmouth, Plymouth, Portsmouth and Swansea to America, the Mediterranean, but most often, to Quebec. In 1866 Elford and Co. of Swansea are posted as her owners.

DAEDALUS was abandoned on 16th February 1871 (note on register).

**DALUSIA** built 1826 in Quebec. Tons 187 75/94(O). 85.5 22.2 4.9. A brig with one deck and a half-deck, a square stern, no galleries and a bust head, (details from Bristol register. In this case the 4.9 ft measurement is not the depth of hold but the height of the main deck above the half-deck).

After registry in Quebec and Bristol, she came to Padstow in 1831, Andrew Parnall, master mariner, having command of her with 32 shares. Robert Moon was her master two years later.

In *Lloyd's Shipowners' Register* her rig is given as a snow. 'Total loss per annual list 1834' (note on register).

**DARIA LOUISA** built 1831 at Padstow by Thomas Carter (the register also gives Brewer as a builder). Tons 68(O). 49.8 18.2 8.3. A sloop with running bowsprit and square stern; carvel built (those are all usual characteristics of Padstow built sloops and smacks).

Ownership on register:                                      Shares

| | |
|---|---:|
| Thomas Carter of Padstow | 22 |
| Burnard Carter of Padstow | 5 |
| William Carter of Padstow | 8 |
| Pascoe Billings of Padstow | 4 |
| Thomas Brand of St Columb | 16 |
| James Whitfield of St Columb | 6 |
| William Langdon of St Endellion | 3 |
| | Total: 64 |

But *Lloyd's Register* gave R. Avery as owner. William and Thomas Carter were masters of the ship.

She was lost with all hands in January 1832 (note on register).

**DARING** ON 27299, built 1859 at Salcombe by Vivian. Tons 149 net and gross. 100.0 22.1 12.2. A handsome fruit schooner built for R. Balkwill of Kingsbridge and registered at Dartmouth, with Salcombe as her home port. Balkwill kept her for over twenty years before selling her to W. S. Allport of Padstow, and he kept her registered at Dartmouth. He had F. Moore and J. Daniel in charge of her, and sold her to John Stephens of Fowey in December 1889.

Topgallant schooner DARING
*David Clement Collection*

She sailed from Glasgow for Saint John, New Brunswick on 12th September 1891 and went missing.

**DASHER** built 1815 at Cork. Tons 23(O). 38.5  12.4  7.5. Sold under Commission of Sale, High Court of Admiralty 22nd May 1830. A sloop registered at Padstow 1830, owners Hawken, Davies and John Tredwen, all of Padstow. Benjamin Davies Master. Lost 1833 (note on register).

**DE LANK** ON 53008, built 1866 at Padstow. Tons 50 net. 62.3  18.3  8.0. A cutter registered at Padstow owned by Charles Jorden of Wadebridge and eleven others. Lost about 1st January 1867.

**DEFIANCE** built 1807 at Padstow. Tons 26(O)  38.3  13.4  6.1. A smack registered at Bristol in 1810, owned by W. Kington in 1825 and lost 1837 (note on register).

**DELABOLE** built 1826 at Padstow by John Tredwen. Tons 71(O). 52.8  17.9  9.3. A Padstow schooner owned by Robert Blake of St Teath and Elizabeth Thomas, with Wedlock and William Thomas as masters. She was sold to Truro in 1828. In February 1833 she was ashore on Saunton Sands and almost abandoned, but later that year she was repaired and in the hands of Barnstaple owners.

Finally posted 'SUNK' in *Lloyd's Register*, 1836.

**DELABOLE** ON 26728, built 1848 at Padstow by R & J Tredwen. Tons 49(N). 46 (net 1876). 51.0  15.2  8.4. She was registered in 1848 at Padstow as a schooner but that seems to have been a mistake as she was also endowed with a sliding bowsprit, which the schooners seldom had, and she was later described as a smack. Her builders owned her until 1854 with W. Chalk of Port Isaac in command. Then she was sold to Falmouth and in 1871 to Fowey.

This DELABOLE was lost off Clovelly on 16th September 1880 bringing granite blocks from Par for Swansea. Her crew of three were rescued by the Clovelly lifeboat.

**DESPATCH** (Padstow Port Register) or DISPATCH (*Lloyd's* 1838-1843) ON 13019 built 1831 at Padstow by George Sloggett. Tons 38(O) 26(N). 41.7  15.5  6.8 (1931). A Padstow sloop owned by John Darke Martyn, and from 1842 by Alex Parker, with John Guy and Thomas Chalk as masters early on. She was sold to Newport in 1847 and by 1858 was registered at Bristol where she stayed until her loss in 1874.

**DEVERON** ON 62449, built 1871 at Banff by J & W Geddie. Tons 133 gross, 94 net later. 89.1  20.8  11.4. Although Lloyd's describes her as a schooner, when she came south to Padstow in 1889 she was registered as a brigantine with square stern and billet head, owned by J. Hutchings, accountant of Neath, with F. Couch in command. In 1892 Theophilus Couch became owner and in 1897 G. Couch was master.

On 19th June 1905 DEVERON was anchored in Portland Harbour laden with china clay, when HMS CONFLICT ran her down and sank her. Her crew of six were all picked up, and incidentally such a large crew suggests that she was indeed a brigantine.

**DEVONIA** ON 14054, built 1836 at Salcombe by James Vivian. Tons 84 (1837) 71 (1855). 62.0  16.9  9.4.

A schooner which came to Padstow from Salcombe in 1852, and was owned by Nicholas Hockin of Newquay until she was lost on 19th February 1868. G. Courtis was her master for a time. Lost 19th February 1868 (note on register).

**DEVONIA** ON 47883, built 1865 at Ipswich by Read. Tons 161 gross 146 net. 98.1  24.0  12.3. This brigantine, yellow metalled soon after completion, was built for Dartmouth owners but spent her first year trading from the Northeast Coast to South America and India. In 1890 she was sold to Poole and in 1895 registered at Fowey, but owned by Thomas Trethewey of Newquay, and in 1898 by Fred Harris of Crantock. He moved his home to Par about 1909 and sold her to Grimsby at the end of the Great War.

*Lloyd's* records contain the information that the schooner DEVONIA was broken up in 1932. It is not known when her rig changed.

**DEW DROP, DEWDROP** ON 25208, built 1820 at Hull with major repairs in 1838 and 1845. Tons 204(O) 232(N). 85.3  24.0  5.8. *Lloyd's* has her completed as a snow in the supplement to the 1820 register, but she is described as a brig thereafter. She traded from London mainly to Quebec until coming into the Padstow ownership of M. Wade about 1833. Trade with and emigration to Quebec continued with Wade, R. Brown and E. Key as masters. About 1844 T. Avery of Boscastle bought controlling ownership, but she continued in the same trades, sometimes from Swansea as well as Padstow, with T. Rickard and J. Burke in command. In 1853 she went to Sunderland owners.

She was posted missing in *Lloyd's Register* 1864.

**DICK & HARRY** built 1786 at Salcombe. Tons 27(O). 37.4 13.7 6.7. This tiny sloop was registered at Dartmouth, Fowey, Padstow and Fowey again. During her time at Padstow, 1815-1817, she was owned by Joseph Odgers of Padstow and David Norton, mariner. Her masters were Geach and Thomas Martyn of Padstow. (Odgers was a spirit merchant.)

She last appears in *Lloyd's Register* about 1824.

**DILIGENCE** built 1796 at Bideford and lengthened in 1828. Tons 45(O) as built, 58(O) after lengthening. 49.5 15.5 8.9 as built. Registered at St Ives on completion, the next year she was re-registered at Padstow, owned by Thomas and others, with J. May as master, and later other members of the Thomas family. In 1824 her owner became Bake, gent. of Delabole. She was sloop rigged whilst at Padstow but in 1825 her registry shifted to St Ives, and she was schooner rigged when lengthened.

Lost in collision off Hartland Point 11th May 1842 (note on register).

**DILIGENCE** ON 25287, built 1835 at Aberayron. Tons 37(N). This smack was registered at Cardigan throughout her long life, but she was owned in the sixties and seventies by John Reynolds and Captained by Pappin, both of Newquay. She lasted until about 1890.

**DISPATCH** ON 13803, built 1810 at Bursledon. Tons 70(O) 76 (1858). 60.3 19.4 10.3. (1860 reg.). Built as a smack, she was registered at Southampton, but in 1860 she was registered at Padstow as a ketch owned by J. M. Fishlay of Port Isaac. Subsequent owners were John Willmett, John Stribley and John Courtenay, sailmaker. In 1868 her registry moved to Dundalk and was closed the following year.

**DISPATCH** see DESPATCH, ON 13019.

**DONNA MARIA** ON 45392, built 1862 at Milford by Roberts. Tons 132 reg. 85.5 20.7 11.9. This vessel was registered at Swansea throughout her life, being completed as a brigantine but converted to schooner rig before she was lost. By 1880 she had been bought by J. Male of St Miniver who commanded her thereafter.

DONNA MARIA was lost in collision with a fishing smack on 23rd January 1884. She was sailing from Barry for West Hartlepool with limestone. All four of her crew were saved.

**DORIS** ON 84985, built 1904 at Appledore by R. Cock & Sons. Tons 137 gross 99 net. 98.8 22.5 9.4. A fine steel three masted schooner with an elliptical stern. She was registered on completion at Padstow with ownership William S. Allport 21 shares, Edward Thomas 13 shares, Charles Warden (of Wadebridge) 8 shares, and six other small holdings. T. Magor was captain.

DORIS was wrecked on Rassen Sand, West Kapelle on 14th February 1907, sailing from Plymouth with china clay for Ghent. The wind was south-west force 10 and one man was lost.

**DRIVING MIST** ON 47031, built 1863 at Newquay, Gannel Yard by J. Clemens. Tons 79 gross 68 net. 79.0 19.8 9.2. A schooner with a female figurehead, she was registered at Padstow and managed by Edwin A. Bennett of Newquay, with A. Bennett as master, although there were numerous other shareholders. In 1886 she was sold to Bideford. She foundered off Kinsale 17th November 1902.

**DUCK** Foreign built, date unknown. Tons 110. This brig, probably a prize, appears in *Lloyd's Register* 1810 owned by T. Lockyer with P. Billing as master. On 10th November 1810 she was driven ashore and went to pieces, Billings master (*Lloyd's List* 16th November 1810).

**DUNDARG** ON 63422, built 1875 at Fraserburgh by J. Webster & Co. Tons 145 gross 133 net, later 118. 96.3 23.7 10.7. This schooner (described as a brigantine in some lists) initially traded to Newfoundland, the Mediterranean and the West Indies. She was bought from Fraserburgh in 1889 by William Phillips of St Austell but registered at Padstow whence he had moved. Whilst she remained registered at Padstow, she had Looe owners through the Great War and was sold to Cornish Traders Ltd., Falmouth in 1919.

She was hulked and her register closed 30th September 1924.

**E.C.T.** ON 65139, built 1870 at Falmouth by W. H. Lean. Tons 100 net 114 gross. 86.0 22.4 10.6 (1898). This schooner was registered at Plymouth on completion and traded to Spain. In 1898 John Hawken of Padstow bought her and Padstow became her port of Registry and A. Mitchell her master. In 1901 John Crocker of Portmadoc became master and managing owner.

E.C.T. was wrecked on the North Hooper, Llanelly Bar on 6th January 1908. She was bringing steel scrap from Belfast for Briton Ferry. The wind was SW force 8. All five crew survived.

**E.L.C.** John Cowl & Sons of Padstow were reported to have built a small cutter E.L.C. about 1890.

**EAGLE.** A Padstow ship of this name was abandoned derelict off Stepper Point 30th November 1801.

**EAGLE** ON 16005, built 1839 at Tatmagouche, Nova Scotia. Tons 297(O) 328(N). 93.9 23.8 17.0. She was built with a snow rig, that is a brig but with a small trysail mast immediately abaft the main-mast to take the hoops of the trysail or spanker. She was registered at Liverpool and in 1846 at Plymouth (Parnell owner and master). Then in 1851 Abbott and Mably brought her to Padstow and with W. Mably in command she made 19 voyages to Quebec, often with emigrants until being lost in the Gulf of St Lawrence 16th June 1863.

**EAGLEBUSH.** This Padstow ship was taken by the French off Dungeness in January 1809, but returned to Padstow in August 1911. No register has been found, but see Chapter 9 for more details.

**EARL ST VINCENT** built 1803 at Plymouth. Tons 41(O). 46.0 15.4 7.5. *Lloyd's Register* in 1809 describes this smack as a Cork coaster with W. Cook as owner and master. In 1814 she was

The steel Schooner DORIS                    *Private Collection*

The schooner DRIVING MIST, laid up with sails unbent and with her long lower yard cockbilled. She was sold to Bideford in 1868, which is about the time of this photograph of Newquay. The ketch KITTIE on the right has an unusually long topmast and wide spreaders to enable it to be stayed adequately. *National Maritime Museum*

registered at Padstow with Rawlings owner and John Sheppard master. In 1821 the owner became Margarethe Kunze with Stephen Osborn and then Christian Kunze as masters. Mary Hawker, Sanders, Thomas Chapman and Peter D. Wilson were other Padstow owners. In 1825 her master is given as Charles Kinze (Kenzie in *Lloyd's*).

**EASTERN MAID** ON 69468, built 1876 at Barnstaple by W. Westacott & Sons. Tons 116 net 127 gross. 90.0 22.2 10.6. A schooner with round stern and full woman figurehead. She was a Padstow registered coaster, her 64 shares owned as follows:

| | |
|---|---|
| Mark Kellow of Bickington | 20 |
| Marian Kellow of Bickington | 12 |
| Jane Hoskins, widow of Pt Isaac | 12 |
| Richard Hoskin, Master Mariner | 11 |
| John Kellow of Pentewan | 9 |

She has been missing since 11th October 1885 when she sailed from Morrison's Haven with coal for Plymouth. Richard Hoskin was her master and there were four others in the crew.

**EBENEZER** built 1804 at Plymouth. Tons 54(O). 45.3 17.8 8.3. This sloop rigged smack was owned in Padstow soon after building but her registers make clear that she was built at Plymouth, not Padstow as some editions of the *Lloyd's Register* indicate. Her Padstow owners and masters included Benjamin Harvey, John Billing, Giles Zinney (also Tinney), Sleeman, Martyn, Nicholls of St Colomb and John Tredwen. She was sold to Bristol in 1828.

**EBENEZER** built 1843 at Padstow by Thomas Carter. Tons 17(N). 37.1 10.6 6.2. A lugger with running bowsprit and round stern. This is the first of a series of fishing vessels built by Carter for St Ives owners. She was owned by Thomas Carter and Henry Care who took charge of her. The Carters of Padstow were a branch of the famous Prussia Cove clan, and this business may have resulted from the family connection.

Her St Ives register closed 19th February 1848, 'broken up'.

**EBENEZER** ON 60260, built 1869 at Cardiff by W. H. Tucker and lengthened in 1874. Tons 69 as built. 67.5 16.6 9.6. 88 net, 81.4 18.6 9.4 after lengthening. A schooner with a semi-elliptical stern and a scroll bow, she spent most of her life registered at Shoreham, but Charles Matthews brought her to Padstow in 1892.

On 8th October 1897 she foundered in the Sloyne after collision with the Wigtown schooner RENOWN. She was bringing china clay from Fowey for Runcorn. S. Daniel and his crew of three were all saved.

**ECHO** ON 5729, built 1847 at Port Isaac by John Lakeman. Tons 34(N). 45.7 14.3 7.2 as built. Lengthened 1869 and thereafter 45.4 tons (37 net reg. in 1900) 59.8 17.1 7.6. She remained Padstow registered throughout, being owned by James Stevens and then Mrs Mary Guy of Port Isaac, but in 1900 by Henry Norman of Watchet.

By 1903 she was owned by James Bailey and wrecked near East Quantoxhead on 11th September that year (note on register).

**ECLIPSE** ON 15552, built 1819 at Topsham as a sloop. Tons 76(O). 53.1 16.2 9.4. When her registry came from Truro to Padstow in 1848, her rig is recorded to be schooner, and her tonnage 59(N). At that time she was owned by Arthur Carpenter of Stratton, and later John Jermyn of Bude who was lost at sea in 1860 and left her to his widow. Finally, in 1866 Edward Hockin owned her with Thomas Brinton as master, but she was lost that year with all hands bringing limestone from Plymouth for Bude.

**EDITH** ON 17381, built 1856 at Padstow by John Tredwen. Tons 100(N). 82.6 20.9 10.3. This schooner was one of several owned in joint venture by John Tredwen and John Cory, her first master, who was followed by E. Buse.

Unfortunately she was lost on the Oporto Bar, 14th January 1862.

**EDITH** ON 19759, built 1858 at Padstow by John Tredwen. Tons 81 reg. 70.6 19.5 9.9. This schooner was owned on completion by eighteen local tradesmen, but managed by T. Strout of Port Isaac and subsequently by J. Reynolds of Newquay. W. Maynard was master for many years.

On 23rd January 1884 EDITH was lost with all five hands off Haisborough, Norfolk, wind NW force 10, on passage Sunderland for Emsworth with coal.

**EDITH** ON 53002, built 1865 at Gannel Yard, Newquay, by J. Clemens. Tons 84 net 97 gross. 80.6 20.1 10.0. EDITH was a two masted schooner owned by her builder and master R. Chegwidden until sunk at Falmouth. Sold to local men, she was raised, lengthened and rigged as a three masted schooner in 1884. Tons 94 net, 114 gross. 95.8 21.0 9.7.

In 1913, still Padstow registered, her owners were in Gloucester. On 18th June that year she burnt at Glasgow.

**EDITH MORGAN** ON 56521, built 1866 at Padstow by Willmett. Tons 139 gross 130 net. 96.8 22.9 12.0. This schooner was Willmett's first at the Dennis Cove yard. She went straight to Newport registry, trading to South America. She only survived into the early eighties.

**EDWARD** a French prize made free 1801. Tons 60.3(O). 48.0 16.0 9.4. The only surviving Padstow register is dated 1814, when this brigantine was owned by Thomas Phillips of Padstow. The register is noted 'Re-registered as prev. cert. taken by American privateer.' She was subsequently registered at Plymouth.

**EDWARD** ON 13022. A Spanish prize taken by HMS POMONA and condemned in the High Court of Admiralty 22nd April 1807. Tons 35. 50.2 13.6 7.3. A smack which came to Padstow ownership from Newport in 1847, owned and commanded by Alex. Parker, and then Thomas Burt. By 1865 her registry was at Truro where she lasted until the mid-eighties.

**EDWARD** previous name HOFFNUNG. A ketch of 90 tons (O), prize to HM Cr. ALBION (Lt. Key) 1813. Registered at Padstow 1818, owners Rawlings and Avery, master John Parnall, having previously been registered at Dover. Registration transferred to Dublin in 1819.

**EDWIN**. The Padstow sloop EDWIN was lost off Boscastle sailing for Bideford 2nd July 1815.

**EDWIN** ON 27273, built 1859 at Padstow by Edwin Carter. Tons 26. 55.4 17.0 5.5. A round sterned smack owned by her builder, then in 1862 by Silas Tremain, quarryman and others.

Lost 17th February 1863 (note on Padstow register).

**EIRENE** ON 4007, built 1851 at Padstow by R & J Tredwen. Tons 25. A Bristol Channel pilot cutter, sister to HENRY, she was registered at Bristol and owned initially by Edward Samuel Calloway of Pill.

**ELEANOR** built 1816 at Berkeley. Tons 35(O). 44.5 14.3 6.5. A square sterned sloop owned in Bude 1828-1853 by Davey, Drew and William Tucker. She was a constant trader to Bude until shifting registry from Padstow to Bideford in 1853.

The vessel was wrecked at high water in Combe Martin Harbour on 17th February 1854.

**ELEANOR & JANE** ON 85267, built 1884 at Padstow, begun by Stribley and completed by C. Rawle. Tons 110 net 119 gross. 86.2 22.2 11.1. This schooner was built for Aberystwyth owners. She only lasted ten years.

**ELECTRIC** ON 29363, built 1863 at Port Gavern by Warwick R. Guy (*Lloyd's* gives McOwen as builder). Tons 48. 58.2 18.7 8.8. lengthened 1874. Tons 73 gross 52 net. 79.3 20.4 8.9.

ELECTRIC was built as a cutter rigged smack but converted to fore and aft schooner rig on lengthening in 1874.

Like most Port Isaac and Port Gavern vessels she was owned by Warwick R. Guy who passed all 64 shares to James Stephens Guy (with a Cardiff address) in 1899, who in turn passed them to Mrs Mary Bate of Port Isaac in 1900. J. Walters was her master when she was wrecked on The Stones off Godrevy on 25th January 1909, on passage Newport for St Mary's with coal. All four crew were saved.

**ELFORD**. A Bude vessel named ELFORD was reported lost with four men in January 1823.

**ELIZA** ON 26776, built 1816 at Mevagissey by Peter Smith. Tons 57(O) 45(N). 48.3 17.2 8.2. This square sterned sloop was registered at Fowey throughout her long life, but is included here because in the 1820s and 1830s Edward Fox of Wadebridge and William Rawlins of Padstow, both merchants, had substantial ownership and doubtless provided cargo for her on her typical voyages from Truro to Gloucester with visits to the Camel estuary.

In 1875 ELIZA sailed on, owned by Philip Quenault of Penryn.

**ELIZA** ON 13097, built 1826 at Topsham by Daniel Bishop Davy. Lengthened and repaired by Davy in 1838. Tons 82(O) as built. 107(O) 85(N). 65.9 17.4 9.9. after lengthening. John Martyn of Topsham bought 48 shares in this Exeter schooner in 1839, moved to St Minver as her master in 1850 and had all 64 shares by 1853. He registered her at Padstow in 1859. Up to that time she had been trading from London and Exeter to European ports including Seville, Antwerp and Rotterdam, but he soon sold her to Richard Rowse Chapman of Padstow.

By 1870 she was Cardiff owned, in 1880 Dungarvan, but she was still registered at Padstow when lost on the Taylor Bank, Liverpool on 25th-26th March 1885. There was no loss of life.

**ELIZA**. A 19 ton Padstow sloop, master Baynon, appears in the Bude port book about 1850, but that may be a deadweight tonnage, and the vessel too small to be registered.

**ELIZA** ON 29652, built 1861 at Perth by Smeaton. Tons 99 reg. 79.8 19.4 10.0. This schooner was only briefly owned in Perth, all 64 shares being bought by R. Philp of Padstow in 1862, and he commanded her in the Newfoundland trade apparently for over 10 years, continuing to own her when her port of registry was altered from Padstow to Plymouth in 1867. He renounced ownership in 1884 when Penzance became her home port, but she did not last much longer, being lost on the Doom Bar on 10th October that same year.

ELIZA ANN ON 27389, built 1859 at Padstow by J. Tredwen. Tons 108 reg. 83.4 20.5 10.3. A schooner built for numerous St Agnes owners, she was registered at St Ives. Although described as a coaster, she was wrecked at Gallipoli 8th February 1862 (note on register).

ELIZA ANNIE ON 74625, built 1876 at Padstow by C. Rawle. Tons 96 net 103 gross. 80 net in 1892. 81.1 22.2 10.4. This rather beamy coasting schooner was built for J. Hambly of Calstock, and registered at Plymouth. Sold on to Henry Clarke of Braunton late in the 1890s, she left the registers soon after the turn of the century.

ELIZA JANE ON 13407, built 1837 at Dungarvan, Co. Waterford. Tons 37 (reg. 1864) 51.2 14.4 7.9. This small schooner spent her life on the Penzance and St Ives registers but her ownership moved around Cornwall and Devon, and in 1865-1871 she was owned by Samuel Tucker of Tintagel, a tiny outport of Padstow. She was broken up and her Penzance register closed 21st May 1886.

ELIZABETH built 1783 at Padstow. Tons 50(O). A sloop of which S. Stodder is given as owner in Lloyd's Register 1786. One ELIZABETH of Padstow was a regular trader to Padstow and Boscastle with Bond as master 1793-'4 and Vincent 1801. One ELIZABETH was wrecked at Padstow 21st November 1808 (Lloyd's List). A 60 ton sloop named ELIZABETH was for sale, 'apply Martin Withell' in April 1811.

ELIZABETH ON 19245, built 1805 at Scarborough. Tons 162(O) 166(N). 77.4 23.3 13.8. This Scarborough brig armed with six guns was, for instance, sailing from London to Gibraltar in 1815, the year of the battle of Waterloo, became a collier brig in due course and in 1855 was registered at Padstow, in the ownership of John Tredwen. Barrett was her master then and when, on 17th April 1857, she was abandoned sinking off Clovelly on passage from Newport for Padstow with coals.

ELIZABETH built 1819 at Mevagissey by Peter Smith. Tons 43(O). 43.7 16.8 8.0. A sloop registered at Padstow in 1819 with John Dungey as owner and master. She was registered at Wexford in 1822 and must surely be the ELIZABETH of Wexford stranded and lost at Zennor on 31st October 1823.

ELIZABETH ON 19201, built 1839 at Plymouth. Tons 74(O) 60(N). 52.2 16.0 9.5 as built. Lengthened 1850. Tons 98. 72.0 16.8 10.2. A schooner registered at Padstow on completion as owned by Robert Robinson Langford of Boscastle with B. Carter and J. Bellamy as masters, the latter with 1/64th share!

She was re-registered at Plymouth in 1853 and gone by the end of that decade.

ELIZABETH ON 11458, built 1845 at Fowey. Tons 49(N). Although Lloyd's first described this vessel as a smack, she appears to have been schooner rigged until the last year or so of her life when she was converted into a ketch. ELIZABETH was registered at Fowey on completion and remained so. She only joins this list because T. H. Harvey of Padstow bought her about 1880. On the 19th December 1890 she was wrecked in Portquin Bay bringing coal from Newport to Padstow. J. Spinks, master, and his crew of two were all lost. The wind was NW by N force 10.

ELIZABETH ON 10134, built 1845 at Padstow by Thomas Carter. Tons 17.2485/3500(N). 35.1 11.0 6.9. One of a series of round-sterned luggers built for St Ives where she remained registered despite being in the hands of Waterford owners from 1865 or earlier,

until in 1887 her register was closed with the comment 'existence doubtful'.

ELIZABETH ON 10886, built 1854 at Bridgwater. Tons 36 net 47 gross. A schooner which was re-rigged as a ketch about 1880, but which did not have connections with Padstow until on her last legs after the Great War, when her managing owner became David W. Davis of Wadebridge, and she was used as a barge. She dropped out of the registers about 1930.

ELIZABETH & MARIA (also given as ELIZABETHS & MARIA) built 1821 at Cardiff. Tons 41(O). 42.8 15.1 7.4. This sloop was built for James Harris of Padstow and Richard Tredwen of Cardiff, described as 'builder' although it seems unlikely that he was the Cardiff builder of small ships who operated, so far as is known, from 1830 to 1850. James Harris was her master. In 1887 the Padstow port register records that ownership had passed to House, Jenkin and William Harris of St Columb with Teague of Padstow as master.

She sprang a leak and sank off Lynmouth as reported in Lloyd's List 26th October 1827.

ELIZABETH DAVEY ON 9487, built 1856 at Appledore. Tons 68 net 89 gross. 77.5 20.1 10.5. This Fowey registered schooner with Looe owners was bought by John Ennor of Newquay about 1883 and he owned her for about ten years with E. Lane in command. Then M. T. Clemens of St Blazey took her, and she was lost with all hands near Polperro, having sailed from Plymouth on 23rd September 1896 with grain for Hayle.

ELIZABETH DREW ON 65145, built 1871 at Padstow by J. Stribley. Tons 100 net 110 gross (varied later). 82.5 22.7 10.8. She was registered in Plymouth as a schooner for all sixty-two years of her life. In 1919 she had two Widdop oil engines (total 50 b.h.p.) fitted, but later a single Woodward paraffin motor of 10 n.h.p. sufficed. About 1923 her square topsails were unshipped. On 9th July 1933 when she was on passage Blyth for Padstow with coal, she was rammed and sunk by the German SS MIMI HORN in the Downs. No lives were lost.

The schooner ELIZABETH DREW, painted by C Southey.
*National Maritime Museum*

ELIZABETH HAMPTON ON 45699 built 1863 at Shoreham by Bally. Tons 99 net 108 gross, later 78 net. 87.0 20.0 9.5. A Plymouth registered schooner which traded initially to Spain and the Mediterranean, and came to be owned by William Philp of Padstow about 1878. He captained her himself but later handed command to W. Forward. In 1905 Sydney Bate of Falmouth bought her.

She was sunk by U-boat bomb 25 miles South by West of St Catherine's Point on 14th May 1917, sailing from Cardiff with coal for Carentan.

ELIZABETH HILL ON 14497, built 1856 at Plymouth. Tons 80 gross, 65 net. 81.7 18.0 8.9. This schooner was first registered at Plymouth, then in 1875 at Fowey and finally in 1898 at Padstow, when John Worden became owner of 38 shares. Although she stayed on the Padstow register, ownership went to Watchet by 1900 and Bristol in 1905.

Broken up: register closed 23rd October 1923.

ELIZABETH JANE ON 19271, built 1856 at Newquay, Quay Yard, by J & M Clemens. Tons 73 reg. 66.5 19.1 9.8. A schooner owned by R. Carter and others, and commanded by R. and then W. Carter.

On 14th January 1865 she broke her moorings and was wrecked on Towan Beach.

ELIZABETH MARY ON 24010, built 1840 at Padstow. Tons 74(O) 59(N), 50 net. 53.0 15.7 9.0. She was completed as a schooner registered at Padstow briefly, at Plymouth in 1841 and Truro later. W. Stribley of Padstow owned her in 1878, having converted her to ketch rig, but on 11th March 1878 she was lost in collision with the French brig SANTA ANNA five miles W. by S. of the Scarweather lightship whilst on passage from Newport with coal for Tuckenhay in Devon. Her crew of three were saved.

The other vessel was probably the brigantine SAINTE ANNE of Vannes.

ELLEN FRANCES ON 19206, built at Padstow by Thomas Carter. Tons 50 net 59 gross. 56.7 15.6 8.4 (reg.) This small schooner was owned briefly by her builder with W. Pope as master, but in 1855 her register shifted from Padstow to Fowey.

ELLEN FRANCIS (sic) was reported wrecked on the Hayle Bar on 14th September 1880 bringing coal from Wales.

ELLEN JANE built 1847 at Padstow by R & J Tredwen. Tons 62(N). 64.2 15.2 9.6. This schooner was owned by Tredwen with Horswell and H. Knight in command. She traded from Padstow to Spain. She was lost and her register closed 20th February 1852.

ELLEN VAIR ON 27391, built 1858 at Boscastle by George. Tons 116 gross. 80.2 21.5 11.3. A schooner with standing bowsprit, square stern and female figurehead, and like some of the other few ships built at Boscastle, surprisingly large. She was registered at St Ives with Bain of London as managing owner but several shareholders of St Agnes and Portreath.

Foundered at sea 17th November 1864 (note on register).

EMANUEL prize of 1809. see THOMAS & HARRIOTT.

EMBLEM ON 14046, built 1850 at Padstow by R & J Tredwen. Tons 95(O) 75(N), later 59 net 71 gross. 63.8 18.2 9.8. This schooner may have been launched with the name ACTIVE pro tem. as a newspaper report of such a launch cannot otherwise be explained. EMBLEM was registered at Fowey in 1851, at St Ives in 1876 and at Bideford in 1892. She was converted to ketch rig by 1911.

EMBLEM sank off Lundy on 6th January 1916, having been abandoned.

EMILIE ON 67958, built 1866 at Mandal, Norway. Tons 99 net. 79.0 21.4 9.7. A schooner with a square stern and billet head. Most Padstow ships of overseas origin were either prizes or had come to grief on the Cornish coast, but EMILIE was registered at Wick in 1873 and was bought in 1884 by Mrs Catherine Hocking of St Columb Minor, widow, who registered her at Padstow in 1890. In 1892 she was sold to Joseph Thuillier of Worlds End, Kinsale, and she is out of the registers by 1903.

EMILY ON 18307, built 1854 at Padstow by John Tredwen. Tons 79(O) 57(N). 59.5 15.3 8.4. A schooner registered at Padstow and owned and commanded by Simon Stribley and others. John Stribley of Limerick bought 16 shares in 1855.

Lost at sea and register closed 22nd January 1859.

EMILY ON 29590, built 1861 at Rye by Hoad Bros. Tons 145 net 161 gross. 96.6 22.6 12.6. This brigantine was one of three built by Hoad Bros. for Edward Hain and Co. of St Ives and in 1866 the three of them formed the entire Hain fleet. EMILY, with Edward Hain Jr in command, in 1862 set out on a fifteen month voyage visiting Spain, Canada, Brazil, France, Holland and Ireland. Her cargoes included coal, salt, fish, sugar, oil cake, bran and oats. Hains went on to become one of the largest steamship companies in the world, and an important part of the P & O group.

EMILY was sold to William C. Phillips of Port Isaac in 1882 and registered at Padstow. Phillips moved to St Austell but EMILY remained registered at Padstow. W. Remick was her master for her last years.

EMILY sank in the Scheldt after collision with SS MANITOBA of London (2127 tons, built 1887) on 9th June 1888 whilst on passage from Teignmouth with china clay for Antwerp.

EMILY ON 68329, built 1873 at Plymouth by Marshall. Tons 90 net 94 gross, later 79 net. 77.2 22.1 9.7. Following registry at Plymouth and Bideford, this schooner came onto the Padstow books in 1892, owned by Henry Tabb and William H. Bate. Padstow remained her port of registry when she was bought by Albert Robinson of Cardiff in 1911. EMILY collided with the Danish brigantine TRE-SOSTRE, which sank, off Bull Point, Devon on 3rd October 1896. The Dane was from Cardiff with coal for Lisbon; her large crew of seven were all picked up. EMILY herself foundered off Trevose Head on 12th June 1919 (note on register).

EMILY ELLEN ON 62690, built 1872 at Padstow by J. Stribley. Tons 97 reg. 83.6 23.0 10.8. Registered briefly at Padstow in her builder's name, this schooner went to the well-known Tadd family at Fowey the same year. She was lost with all hands in March 1878 on passage for Liverpool.

EMMA built 1814 at Fowey. Tons 109.5(O). 65.8 20.1 11.2. The Padstow schooner EMMA was owned by the prominent Rawlings clan of merchants, and with Matthew Courtenay in command she traded from Padstow, Falmouth and Bristol to places as far apart as St Petersburg and Leghorn. Sold to Poole in 1825, she entered the Newfoundland trade; indeed by 1841 her home port in Lloyd's Register is given as Newfoundland, and no more is heard of her.

EMMA. The Bude port books show the 49 ton sloop EMMA of Padstow, Drew master, as a frequent visitor in 1850, but no other particulars have been found.

EMMA ON 77401, built 1877 at Padstow by Cowl. Tons 138 net 148 gross, later 128 net. 97.0 23.0 12.0. Registered at Padstow as a schooner, changing to three masted schooner by 1890, she was owned by members of the Jenkin family of Newquay and commanded by W. Jenkin, R. Clemo, R. Brenton, and W. J. Brown who continued as master when Albert Williams of Newquay became managing owner about 1910.

W. H. Bate of Wadebridge took over her management in 1919 but on the 10th December that year she was wrecked on the Devil's

Bank in the River Mersey bringing china clay from Fowey for Runcorn.

**EMMA & AGNES** ON 62795, built 1869 at Milford by Lloyd. Tons 109 net 117 gross. 85.7 21.4 11.0. A schooner owned by John Lloyd, Milford, until acquired in 1872 by William Cock Williams and William Chalk both of Port Isaac, and registered at Padstow.

She has been missing since sailing from Liverpool in January 1883. She was last seen leaving St Tudwals Roads on 3rd January with coal for Looe. She carried a crew of five, including her master J. Tinman.

**EMMA JANE** ON 20359, built 1857 at Plymouth. Tons 66 reg. 66.7 18.4 9.3. This schooner was registered at Plymouth, then at Padstow in 1860.

She was owned by John Tredwen, Merchant of Padstow, and, when he died on 9th June 1870, by his widow.

She was lost near Cardiff 8th December 1872 (note on register).

**EMMA JANE** ON 29352, built 1861 at Gannel Yard, Newquay by John & Richard Clemens. Tons 56 net 65 gross. 71.1 19.1 8.6. This schooner was registered at Padstow on completion, owned by Barry Williams and eleven others, and in 1881 J. Cowl & Sons became the owners with H. Stribley as master, whilst by 1884 John T. Richards of Port Isaac owned her.

She was sunk in collision six miles North of Mort Point on 30th August 1891. There is no mention of a change of rig on her register, but she has been described as a ketch at the time of her loss.

**EMPRESS OF CHINA** ON 68526, built 1874 at Padstow by J. Stribley. Tons 256 net 267 gross. 120.7 26.1 12.8. This barkentine, built for London owners and trading to distant seas, is one of the pinnacles of Padstow shipbuilding activity. She was felted, yellow metalled, copper fastened and salted. Her anchors and chain were approved by testing on a public machine. She was built under Lloyd's 'Special Survey' and classified A1 when surveyed in May 1874. She is described as a brigantine at that time, and as a schooner in *Lloyd's Register* 1881, but three masts are noted in 1885 and finally in the 1890 register she is described as a three masted brigantine.

Her London owners were J. W. Jepps, Lyth and others, but by 1879 she was registered in Hobart, owned by William Fisher, and in 1880 P. Facy, J. Hay and W. Fisher are joint owners.

She was wrecked on 31st December 1888 on Black Pyramid Rock 17 miles W. of Hunter's Island, on passage from Geelong for Hobart. There were no casualties.

**ENCHANTRESS** built 1823 at Padstow by John Tredwen. Tons 17(O). 38.7 10.6 5.0. A decked lugger with a cockpit aft. She was owned by William Carter, mariner, John Carter, fish curer, and William Hockin, blacksmith, all of Newquay, with William Carter in charge of her. 'Unfit for use 1826' (note on register).

**ENDEAVOUR** (ENDEAVOR on St Ives register), built 1788 at Mevagissey. Tons 28.6(O). 39.5 14.4 6.7. (Padstow register). This sloop was registered at Fowey, St Ives and in 1815 at Padstow where she was owned by James Harris of St Columb, then jointly by Richard Tredwen of Cardiff and John Tredwen and others of Padstow. William Sleeman was their master and he had become managing owner by 1824. Finally, in 1825 she moved to Cardiff with Richard Tredwen managing her. Broken up at Cardiff 1829 (Select Committee on shipwrecks 1836).

**ENERGY** ON 14050, built 1853 at Pownal, Prince Edward Island by George Bollum using juniper, birch and spruce. Tons 61.6 reg. 70.3 20.4 7.1. These figures from this schooner's registration at Padstow on 15th September 1858, but the Swansea port register (1854) and *Lloyd's* have widely differing tonnages and dimensions. John Hawken, Padstow merchant, owned all 64 shares and J. Skinner was master.

The register carries this note 'Lost at Sea October 1859'.

**ENGINEER** ON 11457, built 1841 at Charlestown by Anthony Luke. Tons 53(N). 49 reg., later 39 net. This sloop was registered at Fowey throughout her life but about 1890 she was purchased by the Stephens family, Porth's principal merchant for coal and other goods and Alex Stephens was her manager.

On 4th March 1897 she was bringing manure from Cork for Porth when she was lost with all hands near Park Head. One enormous sea overwhelmed her and she was smashed on the rocks. Only one body, that of her mate T. Hocking, was ever found. One report of her loss described her as a ketch.

**ENGLAND'S GLORY** ON 60919, built 1869 at Sunderland by W. Pile & Co. Tons 751 net, 787 gross. 183.3 31.2 19.7. Built of iron by a famous shipbuilder, she was completed as a full rigged ship, but reduced to barque rig about 1880. She was registered in London, owned by Smith & Co. and chartered by the New Zealand Shipping Co. when new and also in 1876 and possibly in 1881. Her first master, E.R.H. Moon was a Plymouth man and when he graduated to being managing owner, W. Knight of Padstow became master. In 1880 she became a Padstow ship, but on 7th November 1881 she was wrecked on the New Zealand coast at Bluff, South Island, to which harbour she was bringing railway iron.

**ENGLISH GIRL** ON 49953, built in France, year and place unknown, as BIENVENU. Tons 76 reg. 66.2 20.1 9.4, after lengthening in 1866. This interesting schooner was registered in Penzance in 1864, then in Hayle and Truro. Notes in the Hicks collection (Royal Institution of Cornwall) indicate that she was at one time owned by Hutchings of Padstow.

In *Lloyd's Register* 1885 she is posted 'Now a hulk'.

**ENTERPRISE.** In 1791 a sloop owned by Capt. Robert Moyse of Stratton: a regular trader from Bristol to Bude. He also owned the MAYFLOWER at that time.

**ENTERPRIZE** ON 14213, built 1846 at Padstow. Tons 110(O) 87(N). This schooner was built for T. Cleary and registered at Waterford. She lasted just over twenty years.

**ENTERPRIZE,** ENTERPRISE ON 14412, built 1846 at Fowey by Brokenshaw. Tons 118(O) 88(N). 83 gross 76 net. 64.9 18.5 10.4. This schooner had been registered at Fowey for 45 years before changing to the Padstow register in 1891 when she was bought by James Parish of St Merryn and managed by Charles Matthews of Padstow.

She has been 'Missing since 21st December 1894, Penzance for Runcorn', (note on register).

**ENTERPRIZE** ON 19667, built 1828 at Bude by Thomas Round. Tons 53(O) 46(N). 42 gross 38 net. 48.0 16.4 8.6. After being launched broadside on into the Bude canal, this sloop was registered at Padstow in 1828, owned and commanded by Thomas Round of Bude. In 1830 she was sold to Portsmouth owners and by 1865 she was registered at Poole as a cutter. She lasted until 1879.

**ETHEL** ON 65164, built 1872 at Plymouth by Gent. Tons 119 net 127 gross. 91.6 20.5 11.5. A schooner registered and largely owned in Plymouth, but commanded by Gill of Newquay in the eighties. Gone by 1899.

**ETHEL** ON 73412, built 1876 at Kingsbridge by Date. Tons 195 net 211 gross. 103.0 24.4 12.9. A handsome brigantine registered at Salcombe but owned by John Ennor of Newquay from 1886, for whom J. Hockin was master. Wrecked 10th February 1891, 2 miles East of Lynmouth (exact date and position varies in different accounts).

**EUGIENE** prize of 1810 renamed HOPE q.v.

**EXCEL** built 1841 at Padstow by Withel for John Hawken. There were press reports of such a vessel but no other record. It appears likely that EXCEL was a *pro tem.* name and that she was registered as CORNISH LASS.

**EXCEL** ON 28508, built 1860 at Newquay by Richard Tredwen. Tons 23 reg. A pilot sloop built for William Dickens of Bristol where she stayed registered when ownership was transferred to Cardiff about 1880. Broken up in 1902.

**EZEL** ON 68146, built 1873 at Cardiff by Tonkin. Tons 155 net 162 gross, later 138 net. 100.0 22.4 12.6. A schooner registered at Cardiff but with a series of Padstow owners: in the early eighties she was owned by John Cory (late of Padstow); in 1885 she was acquired by the Deacon family of Padstow, by which time she was described as a three masted schooner; by 1895 William Hutchings, also of Padstow, was her owner and kept her until about 1906, when she went to Cardigan owners.

EZEL was sunk by U-boat gunfire on 8th September 1917, 20 miles North of St Valery, taking china clay for Treport from Teignmouth. Her crew escaped.

**FAIRY BELLE** ON 62689, built 1872 at Gannel Yard, Newquay, by T & J Clemens. Tons 90 net 101 gross. 87.9 21.8 10.5. One of five fine schooners built between 1868 and 1879 for the Williams family, Newquay, as managing owners, although there were also numerous other share owners. As well as members of the family, R. Burt and S. Lewis were her masters, the latter at the time of her loss.

FAIRY BELLE has been missing since being seen just before the great blizzard on 10th March 1891. She was then between Hartland and Trevose, taking coal from Cardiff for Par with a crew of five.

**FAIRY FLOWER** ON 77406, built 1878 at Padstow by Charles Rawle. Tons 100 net 113 gross. 86.3 22.0 10.7. A schooner with an elliptical stern. Another Williams ship, with W. Allen and N. Wilce as masters, and W. Rich at her loss.

FAIRY FLOWER has not been seen since passing Flamborough Head on 21st December 1894, with china clay and china stone from Par for Kirkaldy.

**FAIRY GLEN** ON 80404, built 1879 at Padstow by John Cowl and subsequently yellow metalled at the Quay Yard, Newquay, by T. Clemens. Tons 100 net, 115 gross. 88.0 23.0 10.8. A schooner with a round stern. W. B. Williams at first owned all 64 shares of this vessel, but he soon distributed many to other owners. J. Penrose was her master when she was lost.

FAIRY GLEN was lost on the Goodwins on 23rd March 1887 when bound from Goole for Plymouth with coal. The wind was SSE force 7, but her crew of five were all saved.

**FAIRY KING** ON 80402, built 1878 at Padstow by Charles Rawle. Tons 100 net, 114 gross, 90 net later. 86.0 22.0 10.9. Although this schooner, like the other FAIRIES, was registered at Padstow, she was owned initially by her builder, and then her managing owner became William R. Allen of Watchet. Amongst her masters were R. Cooper, A. Allen and J. J. Corlett.

She was lost by stranding on Hayling Island 10th September 1903.

**FAIRY MAID** ON 69465, built 1876 at Gannel Yard, Newquay, by T & J Clemens. Tons 100 net 115 gross, later 89 net. 97.0 22.9 11.0. W. B. Williams, then Wm. H. Williams of Newquay were the managing owners of this schooner. Her masters were J. Williams, J. Reeler and E. Cleness.

In an easterly gale she ran aground on North Rock, Cullercoats, on August 7th 1899. Her crew were taken off by the Cullercoats lifeboat and she was later driven inshore and badly damaged but salvage and repair followed.

She stranded on Aberffraw Point on 20th December 1919 near Holyhead, sailing from Runcorn for Newquay with coal (note on register), becoming a total wreck on the rocks. Yet the Rhoscolyn RNLI lifeboat records show that her crew of three were rescued 8th January 1920. Perhaps the three were attempting salvage.

**FAIRY QUEEN** ON 62671, built 1868 at Newquay by T & J Clemens. Tons 85 net 98 gross, 76 net later. 87.0 21.8 10.0. The first of the five Williams family FAIRIES to be built, this schooner was detained at Donaghadee in July 1898 with allegations that her hull was defective. She was released a month later, presumably after repairs. Both this ship and the last had numerous small shareholders apart from the Williams family.

She was wrecked on 22nd January 1900 at Boulmer Stile, Northumberland, bringing granite from Annalong for Newcastle-upon-Tyne. All five of her crew were saved.

**FALMOUTH PACKET** built 1830 at Barnstaple. Tons 50(O) on completion. This smack was lengthened ten feet and converted into a schooner by Tredwen in 1839; otherwise she was a Falmouth vessel.

**FAME** built 1810 at Cork. Tons 52(O). 48.8 16.3 8.5. Although described as a sloop in 1815, she was later registered as a schooner and a 'schooner brig'. She was registered at Padstow in 1816 owned by the Richards family, with J. Richards and then V. Richards in command.

On 30th October 1823, the schooner FAME of Padstow was wrecked at St Ives (*Lloyd's List* 4th November 1823) and her crew saved (note on register), but presumably she was salved and repaired, as she appears on the St Ives port register in 1824.

**FAME** ON 1510, built 1816 at Ringmore, Devon and lengthened in 1853. Tons 75(O) as built, 69 net and 79 gross after lengthening when her dimensions became 69.0 17.5 10.0. First reported as a smack, she became a schooner by 1824, and after many years registered at Penzance, and subsequently at Fowey, she was bought by Joseph Inch of Port Isaac in the 1890s and completed ninety years hard service.

**FANNY** built 1789 at Emsworth. Tons 59(O). 53.0 16.7 9.7. A St Ives schooner owned 1821-1825 by W. Cundall of Padstow and John Vivian, and thus qualifying for this list.

Lost with all hands February 1836 (note on St Ives register).

**FANNY** ON 21129, built 1827 at Ipswich. Tons 60(O) 45(N) in 1851. 48.2 14.0 7.0. This sloop rigged smack was first registered at Padstow in 1847, then owned by W. Oatly (or Oatey) with H. Burd as master. In 1854 Thomas Carter became owner and Henry Carter her master. But the next year she was sold to Abraham Skentlebury of West Looe, and went to the Fowey register. FANNY sprang a leak off the Runnelstone and was abandoned 22nd August 1868. Her crew of three survived miraculously in a small boat with a heavy sea running.

**FARMER.** A ship called FARMER of Padstow was reported wrecked at Castle Cove Tintagel on 28th August 1824. Crew and cargo safe.

**FAVORITE, FAVOURITE** built 1835 at Padstow by Thomas Carter. Tons 60(O) 45(N). Dimensions: 48.8 17.4 8.4 (in 1835), 47.2 15.4 8.4 (in 1836). These dimensions are of interest as the same surveyor was measuring the same vessel, but in 1836 was using the new rules introduced that year. The most significant change is in the breadth, when the old definition of extreme breadth evidently penalised the use of heavy rubbing strakes which were so desirable for the protection of hull and rigging.

FAVORITE was registered at Padstow as a sloop, and although *Lloyd's Register* lists her as a snow in several editions, they revert to smack in 1845, and it seems certain that she was a sloop rigged smack throughout her life. W. Dark was her master until 1841, with

Avery as an important share owner. Then Samuel and Henry Hoskin took her over.

FAVORITE (FAVOURITE later) was lost off Ramsgate 1st November 1848 (note on register).

FAVOURITE ON 24934, built Padstow 1851 (some registers say 1850). Tons 162(O) 149(N). Lengthened 1864 with registered tonnage then 194. 104.0 21.7 12.8.

It is perhaps typical of Padstow that this vessel, when she was launched the largest ever built at Padstow except for the LADY MONA of 1845, has no record of her builders' name on the registers.

She was registered at London as a schooner and traded to the Mediterranean. In 1860 she was described as a brigantine and thereafter she traded to Spain and the West Indies. It is difficult to trace the fate of a ship with such a popular name, but she disappears about 1874.

FAWN ON 21377, built 1858 at Padstow by John Tredwen and briefly registered there in his name. Tons 39 reg. 58.7 16.5 7.8. That same year she was re-registered in Guernsey. In 1860 she was lengthened and in 1870 converted from smack to two masted dandy. Tons 48 net (later reduced to 36). 69.3 17.0 7.6.

Keeping her Guernsey registry until 1894, she was then owned in Jersey and Gloucester, surviving into the twentieth century.

FAWN see MARIA LOUISA, ON 27276.

FAYAWAY ON 16053, built 1853 at Padstow by John Tredwen Jr. Tons 94(N) 85 net. 75.6 19.0 9.7. A schooner with a female bust figurehead, she traded initially to St Michaels under Tredwen ownership and Padstow registry. She was bought by Hoskins of Calstock and registered at Plymouth in 1858. Her Padstow skippers in the early days included Jonas England, J. Skinner and S. Couch.

In the late 1870s Henry Tabbs brought her back into Padstow ownership, but on 28th March 1884, the FAYAWAY, Germyne master, was ashore in Donegal and wrecked.

FEAR NOT. *Lloyd's Register* for a period around 1880 mistakenly put the particulars of FAWN ON 21377 opposite the name FEAR NOT. There never was a Padstow ship of the name.

FERRET built 1827 at Mevagissey by Nicholas Lelean and lengthened the very next year. Tons 18(O) on completion, 23 after lengthening. 30.9 12.1 6.2. This small sloop was registered at Padstow on completion and owned by William Strout of Port Isaac and Boscastle, where she was wrecked 11th June 1833 (*Lloyd's List* 14th June 1833).

FLORA ON 5785, built 1843 at Cardiff by Richard Tredwen and registered there in his name (but not on a list of vessels built by him. Tons 50(N) 44 net. 49.7 15.3 8.5. This schooner went to the Padstow register in 1847 in the ownership of Jenkin, and later William Bennett of St. Merryn (master mariner). Her Padstow masters included Fred and Tom Jenkin and Thomas Teague.

FLORA was lost on Stepper Point on 15th February 1858.

FLORENCE ON 58297, built 1869 at Looe by Shapscott. Tons 181 net 197 gross, later 169 net. 108.1 24.4 12.9. Described as a barque or barquette in the seventies, but as a three masted schooner in the eighties and nineties, FLORENCE was registered first in Fowey and then Plymouth. About 1887 she was bought by T. May of Port Isaac, and with T. May Jr in command she worked extensively in the home trades. On 14th November 1896 she was wrecked on Cross Sands off Great Yarmouth, taking silver sand from Antwerp for Newcastle.

FLORENCE NIGHTINGALE ON 17385, built 1857 at Padstow by John Tredwen. Tons 94 net 105 gross. 81.8 20.8 10.1. This Padstow schooner traded to the Mediterranean for Hoopers of Newquay, with E. Bennett, H. Roach, and H. C. Carter as masters.

In 1882 she went to Renfrew owners and was registered at Greenoch. Apparently she was lost in the Clyde the following year.

FLORENCE VIVIAN ON 47154, built 1864 at Truro. Tons 78 net 99 gross. This Truro registered schooner was owned from 1902 until the end of the Great War by John A. Phillips of Port Isaac. She was altered to be ketch rigged about 1916. She then went to a Grangemouth owner but was lost off Calshot 18th February 1923.

FLORIST ON 25931, built 1851 at Padstow by R & J Tredwen. Tons 192(N) 175 gross. 87.5 19.4 13.8. A Padstow registered brig. owned initially by her builders, but soon the exclusive property of John Tredwen who put her into the River Plate trade. E Key and James Yeo were her commanders.

Wrecked at Giota in Calabria 27th August 1858 (note on register).

FLOWER built 1812 at Salcombe. Tons 39(O). 38.0 15.5 8.0. The sloop FLOWER came from Bristol to the Padstow register in 1853, bought by John Hutchings and others. He, William Henwood and John Sweet were her masters in the following two years.

Run down by the Padstow smack BESS whilst waiting for the tide off Padstow, 6th or 7th March 1855.

FLOWER OF THE FAL ON 62048, built 1870 at Padstow by John Tredwen. Tons 139 net 149 gross, later 98 net. 98.0 23.3 12.0. One of the most celebrated schooners built at Padstow, she was registered and owned at Falmouth throughout her life, starting off mainly in the Mediterranean trades.

On 9th November 1912 she was run down and cut in two by the steamship TURRET HILL off the Owers, bringing coal from Newcastle-on-Tyne for Devonport. Her five crew were saved.

FLY place and date of build unknown. Tons 37. 47.9 ft long. A small schooner, a prize taken by HMS MONTAGU and other vessels 19th December 1800, and made free. The next news of her is her capture as a smuggler (Exchequer), Easter Term 1804, as a result of which she was sold 10th July 1804.

She was then registered at St Ives, and one of her owners was Thomas Smith of Egloskerry in the hinterland of Padstow. She moved to the Newport (Monmouth) register in 1825.

FLY ON 14097, built 1815 at Fowey. Tons 70(O) 48(N), 60 net 66 gross (1866). 50.7 17.0 8.4. (1836 and 1854) 68.7 19.9 8.5 (1859). After Fowey and St Ives owners, the schooner FLY was registered at Padstow in 1854, owned by William Martyn, John Clemens and Richard Ellery, all of Newquay. The last named and S. Ellery both

'FLORENCE' OF 1869 HAD THE BARGUETTE RIG FOR A TIME

took charge of her. It is evident from her dimensions that she was lengthened soon after coming to Padstow.

FLY was sold to Preston owners in 1862, and was still registered there when Irish owners took her over. On 14th October 1891 she burnt at Cultra in Belfast Lough.

**FLY** built 1817 at St Ives. Tons 17(O). 38.0  10.3  6.3. A schooner with a topping or lifting bowsprit and a round stern; carvel built. That is how she was described on joining the Padstow register in 1848. In 1824 she had been termed a lugger with running bowsprit. Her Padstow connection was brief, owned by Bennett and others and with Henry Ivey as master. She was sold to Gloucester in 1849.

**FLYING SCUD** ON 29481, built 1861 at Appledore by Cock. Tons 130 gross (as built). 88.4  20.5  12.0. Lengthened in 1868. Tons 179 gross (after lengthening). 113.4  20.5  12.0. Built as a brigantine, but rigged as a barkentine after lengthening, this Bideford ship's first association with Padstow was in 1872 when she was dismasted and towed in by the Padstow paddle tug AMAZON. About 1882 John Ennor of Newquay added her to his fleet, and according to Verran she was lost in Gourock Bay in 1883. If so, she was salved and registered at Ayr in 1884, and subsequently at Ramsey, Isle of Man.

The next move is intriguing because the 1892 *Mercantile Navy List* has her registered at Sydney, New South Wales, but still owned by T. Corlet of Ramsey. She drops out the next year. Was that perhaps a quiet escape to the South Seas or the start of some infamous blackbirding career?

**FOREST DEER** ON 53009, built 1867 at Newquay (Quay Yard) by M. Clemens. Tons 68 net 79 gross, later 61 net. 77.2  20.9  9.6. This Padstow registered schooner gave twenty years of service to W. Hicks (and other share owners) of Padstow, with Solomon as master. She was  then sold to Stephen Allen of Watchet. On 12th November

1901 she was sailing from Cork with pitwood for Newport when she stranded one mile south of Five Mile Point, Co. Wicklow. The wind was East force 10, but her crew of four were saved.

She was sold as a wreck, but restored and registered at Dublin in 1902. Her Irish owners kept her trading without an engine until November 1932, when she foundered in the Bristol Channel taking coal from Cardiff for Wexford. There was no loss of life.

**FORTUNATE** ON 69845, built 1874 at Padstow by Stribley. Tons 109 net 116 gross. 86.0  22.5  10.9. This schooner was built for R. F. Williams and registered at Fowey, but the masters' names Couch and Harvey show how close were the Cornish family connections. In 1890 Charles Deacon became her master. He went on to command the famous barkentine WATERWITCH, for many years the only British vessel which could qualify officers for the prized square rig certificate.

FORTUNATE joined the fleet of Inkerman Tregaskes about 1895 but she was lost on the Morte Stone, Morte Point, on 26th April 1896.

**FRANCES** ON 95902, built 1889 at Falmouth by C. Burt & Sons. Tons 79 net 89 gross, later 72 net. 83.7  20.4  9.2. FRANCES was a ketch registered at Falmouth but with William Hutchings of Padstow as master. In 1899 he became managing owner and transferred her registry to Padstow, E. P. Hutchings taking charge of her. On 5th September 1917 she was returning from St Malo to Fowey in ballast when she was captured by a U-boat, and had bombs placed on board which duly destroyed her. Her crew escaped in their boat.

**FRANCES ANN** built 1822 at Bideford by William Taylor. Tons 100(O). 61.6  19.8  10.9. A schooner built for Abbott and Parnall of Padstow, where she was registered. Her masters are a notable list of

The ketch FRANCES at Padstow early in the twentieth century.          *Royal Institution of Cornwall*

Padstow families: J. Hicks, V. Richards, J. Dark, Trebilcock and A. Parnall.

*Lloyd's List* 30th January 1836 reports wreckage from FRANCES ANN washed ashore in the Mersey.

**FRANCES ANN** see JANIE.

**FRANK** built 1849 at Padstow by Thomas Carter. Tons 20(N). 39.5 11.4 6.4. This lugger with running bowsprit and round stern must have been a repeat order by the St Ives owners of PAUL PRY.

FRANK was broken up and the register closed 31st August 1855.

**FREDERIC WILLIAM**, FREDERICK WILLIAM ON 11862, built 1837 at Aldborough, Suffolk (Aldeburgh) and lengthened in 1848 and again in 1852. Tons 44(N), 63 (in 1854), 60 (in 1859). 72.2 16.9 7.8 (in 1859). Built as a sloop but rigged as a schooner after 1852. Her original port of registry was Ipswich, then Padstow (1859-1863) and finally Fowey. Her Padstow owner was F. Hocking-Thomas, but later (around 1880) Thomas Trebilcock of Newquay owned her.

She was lost near Cardiff just before the turn of the century.

**FRIENDS** built 1787 at Bridgwater. Tons 60(O). 51.0 17.7 9.2. The first surviving Padstow registration of this sloop is dated 1819 when William Davey and John Tredwen owned her, and Curtis was master. William Hocken owned her in 1822 with H. Nichols and Nicholas Hocken as masters. Her last identifiable appearance in *Lloyd's Register* is in 1834.

**FRIENDS** ON 21552, built 1818 at Appledore, and lengthened in 1853. Tons 36(O) 46(1858). A sloop which was converted to a schooner when lengthened. In her early days she was a regular trader to Bude, with Davey and Whitfield having an interest in her. In 1853 she went to Bridgwater and in 1875 was owned by John Thorne of Watchet. It is difficult to follow her career: in 1875 there were five FRIENDS registered at Bridgwater!

**FRIENDS** built 1826 at Bude by Thomas Round. Tons 29(O) 22(N). 37.0 14.1 7.0. Whereas the last FRIENDS was built in the port of Bideford and traded to Bude in the port of Padstow, but never registered in Padstow, this sloop was built within the port of Padstow and registered there, although built for William Lee of Clovelly in the port of Bideford! Later she was owned by Henry James of Stratton (and others) and William Whitfield was her master, and her frequent visits to Bude make for confusion with the earlier FRIENDS. In 1838 John Sumers James, a limeburner of Bude, was her managing owner but in 1839 she moved to Bideford registry and in 1849 to Barnstaple where a note on the register informs us that she was 'Lost at sea 1851'.

**FRIENDS GOODWILL** built 1784 at Fowey. Tons 45(O). A sloop which is the most likely candidate as a constant trader to Padstow and Boscastle of that name 1799-1806.

One FRIENDS GOODWILL was wrecked at Boscastle (*Lloyd's List* 2nd April 1815).

One FRIENDS GOODWILL was wrecked at Padstow (*Lloyd's List* 19th August 1831).

There was yet another FRIENDS GOODWILL registered at Fowey in 1791. The large number of ships named FRIENDS, FRIENDS ENDEAVOUR and FRIENDS GOODWILL is doubtless a reflection of the intense Quaker activity in Cornwall in the eighteenth and early nineteenth centuries.

**FRIENDS GOODWILL** built 1810 at Fowey by William Geach. Tons 52(O) 41(N). 47.2 16.5 6.8. The Fowey port register confirms her building date and describes her as a sloop-rigged square-sterned lighter. In 1817 she was sold to Robert William Avery of Padstow where she was registered in 1818. Avery had Philp, Phillips, Carter, R. Blythe, Dark, Lovering, H. Carter, Couch and Hicks as masters until she was broken up in 1854 (note on register).

**FRIENDSHIP** built 1781 at Carmarthen. Tons 45(O). 45.5 15.3 6.0. Although the early port registers of Padstow no longer exist, the Cardiff register informs us that this sloop had been registered in Padstow in 1786, was registered in Cardiff in 1814 and went on to be registered in Bristol in 1820. She appears in *Lloyd's Register*, 1829 trading from Bristol to Ireland.

**FRIENDSHIP.** One was rebuilt at Hayle at 1784 and registered at Penzance in 1786, owned by John Tyth of Launceston. Another was a regular Bristol-Padstow trader, with Richards as master 1793-1809. The vessel rebuilt at Hayle was a brigantine of 43 tons.

One FRIENDSHIP was wrecked at Padstow 8th December 1817 (*Lloyd's List*).

**FROLIC** built 1813 at Cardiff. Tons 14(O). 32.0 10.4 5.5. A small sloop transferred to Padstow registry in 1817, when owned by J. Tredwen, William Sleeman and William Hocken.

Her registry was again transferred to Truro that same year.

**FRUIT GIRL** ON 54624, built 1866 at Ipswich by Read. Tons 125 reg. later 96 net. 93.2 22.1 11.2. Built for the Madeira and fruit trades, this schooner later served Newfoundland, taking salt cod to the Mediterranean for Bowrings, and being registered until the 1890s in St John's, Newfoundland. Then she returned to the UK and Falmouth registry, and is included here because in her final years T. Prout of Newquay was her master (Verran) and she was Newquay owned, (Greenhill).

Wrecked near Rye on 5th November 1906.

**GALATEA** ON 56297, built 1868 at Truro by Dyer. Tons 133 net 143 gross, 99 net later. 100.0 22.9 11.1. GALATEA was described as a schooner on the port register but as a brigantine by *Lloyd's*. As she started in the Mediterranean trade from Falmouth, there is probably a painting somewhere which would resolve the doubt about her rig. In 1882 she exchanged Truro for Padstow as port of registry, joining W. S. Allport's fleet with J. Cock as master. W. H. Bull and J. Warden followed him.

The last was in command when on 17th October 1896 she was lost by stranding in the Mersey, sailing from Garston with coal for Padstow. Her crew of five were unharmed.

**GANNEL** (original register)

**GANNELL** (Falmouth register and *Lloyd's*) built 1826 at Plymouth. Tons 51(O). 47.6 16.2 8.3. She was subsequently lengthened in 1839, her tonnage becoming 72(O) 57(N).

On completion this smack was registered at Padstow, owned by Martyn and Symons and in 1837 by Hoskins. Her Padstow masters included G. Hicks, John Martyn and R. Trebilcock. In 1837 she was sold to Falmouth and converted into a schooner on lengthening. She was last reported in *Lloyd's Register* in 1845.

**GAVENWOOD** ON 73896, built 1875 at Limekilns, Fife by Whitehead. Tons 127 net 138 gross, later 100 net. 91.8 22.3 11.5. A schooner with elliptical stern and scroll bow. Her registry was changed from Banff to Padstow in 1891 when she joined the other ships managed by Wm. H. Williams, succeeded by J. T. Williams (who was her master for a time).

GAVENWOOD was wrecked on the Manacles on 7th November 1917, sailing from Runcorn for Dieppe.

**GAZELLE** built 1835 at Leith. Registered at Padstow 1846. Tons 16.5 35.0 11.7 6.6. A cutter with running bowsprit and square stern, carvel built. It is noted on her register that she was 'ex HM Revenue Service, Sold by P.I.A. at Padstow 16th December 1846'. Her Padstow owners were R & J Tredwen with John Reynard as master. In 1847 she was sold to John Paynter of St Ives and registered there in 1849, but that register carries the note 'Lost at Padstow Harbour 25th September 1853'.

The FRUIT GIRL in the Avon Gorge.     *Royal Institution of Cornwall*

GAZELLE has long been a traditional name in the Revenue Service, the latest being a fast motor launch built in 1978.

**GAZELLE** ON 18245, built 1857 at Padstow by Carter. Tons 91 net 99 gross. 81.0  20.9  10.2. This schooner with square stern, and a gazelle as a figurehead, was about 180 tons burthen and built for the Mediterranean trade.

She was registered at Penzance throughout her long and active life.

Abandoned, sinking near the Wolf Rock 25th March 1898.

**GEM** ON 4038, built 1845 at Padstow by Tredwen. Tons 23. Since the early owners of this small cutter were based at Pill, and she was registered at Bristol throughout, it seems safe to assume that she was an example of the famous Bristol Channel Pilot Cutters. She lasted until about 1907.

**GEM** ON 19202, built 1852 at the Quay Yard, Newquay by J & M Clemens. Tons 40(N). 46.4  15.2  7.7. Lengthened 1870. 60 tons net. 69.2  18.1  7.7 after lengthening. Built as a smack for Richard Harvey of Padstow, who was her master, she went to William Oatey of Wadebridge and then in the late 1860s to T. W. Field of Marazion, who had her lengthened very considerably and schooner rigged. Then in the 1870s ownership reverted to Richard Harvey.

On or about 6th April 1874 GEM was lost with all hands, supposedly southwest of Cape Wrath on passage from Runcorn for Wick with salt (note on register).

**GENERAL BURGOYNE** built 1798 in France. Tons 60. An early schooner captured from the French, her owner in 1809 was J. Taylor and her master Underhay. In 1812 her master's name was Williams.

On 21st October 1813 she foundered off the Saltees in a SE gale taking coals from Barry to Padstow. Her crew were saved and landed at Milford 25th October. (*Lloyd's List* 29th October 1813).

**GENESTA** ON 91327, built 1886 at Harwich by J. H. Vaux. Tons 113 net 124 gross, later 97 net. 96.7  22.8  8.5. GENESTA was a fine example of the boomie ketch barge. She was a Harwich barge all her life, trading until hulked about 1934.

She has a place in this list as she was moored between the tidemarks at Rock in the late 1940s as a houseboat. Later she was left to rot with other hulks at Gentle Jane, a little higher up the Camel estuary.

**GEORGE CANNING** ON 1413, built 1827 at Mevagissey by Nicholas Lelean. Tons 64(O). 51.0  17.4  9.0.

Lengthened in 1830, her tonnage became 76(O) 58(N). 57.2  17.8  9.1 (though there were two other measurements later which varied considerably). This smack was built for Rosevear and registered at Padstow, with W. Wivell and then J. Bellamy as masters. On lengthening in 1830 she was re-rigged as a schooner. She had a spell off the Padstow register from 1838 to 1865 but returned to be owned by M. Pascoe, John Couch and George Bennett Jr.

In 1875 she was sold to Watchet and on the 4th July 1899 she foundered one mile ESE of the Scarweather lightship, sailing from Neath Abbey for Watchet with coal. No lives were lost (note on register).

**GEORGES** ON 77404, built 1845 at Bordeaux. Tons 86(N). 65.2  20.7  9.6. A French schooner, foundered off Stepper Point in December 1876, but she was evidently salvaged because she was registered at Padstow the following year, owned by Henry A. Hawkey of Newquay. J. Carrivick and J. Chappell commanded her.

On 12th February 1882 she was wrecked at Weaver's Point, Co. Cork having loaded a cargo of stone at Cork for Newport, Mon.

Note: her date of build is sometimes given as 1847, but 1845 is taken from the French *Registre Maritime*.

**GEORGIANA** ON 5650, built 1823 or 1824 at Bridport. Tons 42(O), lengthened 1844, tons 38(N). 51.2 14.3 7.8 after lengthening. GEORGIANA remained smack rigged after lengthening and came to Padstow from the Guernsey register in 1951. T. Hoskin and then William Couch of Port Isaac had her, and Tabb in 1869. She remained registered at Padstow when sold to Porthcawl in 1873 and Ilfracombe in 1875.

She was detained by the Board of Trade at Barnstaple, 2nd December 1876, with allegations of defective hull and equipment, and she was broken up in 1877 (note on register).

**GIBRALTAR** built 1780 at Padstow. Tons 100(O). A brig owned by J. Luke and others in 1786 and Bynes and others in 1789. She is recorded in *Lloyd's Register* but no port register has been found.

**GILES LANG** ON 48964, built 1864 at Padstow by John Tredwen. Tons 86 net 124 gross. 88.7 21.8 11.5. Although this schooner was registered in Plymouth, her early voyages were from Padstow to Spain, with J. Hoskin of Calstock as owner and Rawlings in command. In 1876 her port of registry became Hayle and in 1892, St Ives.

She was wrecked at Maer Lake on 8th November 1896, bound for St Ives with coal.

**GIPSY MAID** ON 62683, built 1870 at Padstow by Tredwen. Tons 89 net 98 gross, later 75 net. 83.5 22.5 10.2. This Padstow registered schooner had numerous small shareholders throughout her life. Her managing owner and master almost exclusively was J. Matthews, then after 1903, Charles Matthews.

She went ashore on 1st January 1911 on North Copeland Island, Donaghadee, on passage Glasgow for Padstow with coal. All four of her crew survived. Her figurehead survives in the Ulster Folk and Transport Museum, Holywood County Down.

**GIPSY QUEEN** on 62674, built 1869 at Padstow by John Tredwen. Tons 95 net 106 gross. 82.6 22.0 10.6. This schooner, like the GIPSY MAID, was built to be managed by the Matthews family interests. Her masters were successively G. Matthews W. Willcock, and F. Couch. On 13th March 1887 she stranded near the Lizard lights, carrying a cargo of cement from Rochester towards Liverpool.

**GLEANER** ON 74422, built 1875 at Truro by John Stephens. Tons 42 net and gross. 55.3 18.1 7.4. This small smack was only registered at Truro for a short period before joining the Fowey register for the rest of her life.

In 1888 she was bought by Frank Bray of Padstow and sailed with W. Ivey as master. On 14th March 1888 she sailed from Newquay with a part cargo of barley. She was heading for Padstow to complete her cargo, which was destined for Swansea. In working out of the bay in a fresh NNE breeze, she missed stays and went ashore on Towan Head. Her crew of three and her only passenger were all saved, but she became a total wreck.

**GLENDORGAL** ON 17384, built 1857 at Porth by Martyn & Lewarne. Tons 62.09(N). 70.2 19.4 8.1. A Padstow registered schooner with a female figurehead and numerous Westcountry shareholders. Her managing owners included Martin, Richard Devonshire, Nick Lewarne of Porth and J. Bennett of Marazion. Amongst her masters were G. Pappin, J. Bennett, and W. Simmons who was in command when on 10th December 1881 she was wrecked at Ilfracombe whilst on passage from Cardiff with coal for St Michael's Mount. Her crew of four survived.

**GLENDOVEER** ON 43542, built 1861 at Falmouth by Trethowan.

Tons 149 net 161 gross, 128 net later. 100.0 22.2 12.0. As a Falmouth and later a Plymouth schooner, she traded to Spain and the Azores. She is included because of Newquay ownership, first by T. Jenkin of Newquay, then by 1895 by William L. Jenkin of 2 Glendoveer Villas, Newquay. One is tempted to conclude that the GLENDOVEER had contributed substantially to the family fortunes. Her masters included T. Brown, S. Chegwidden, P. Morcon, J. Brown and J. H. Pappin. Jenkin sold her to Albert Williams of Newquay by 1910; she was still registered at Plymouth.

On 30th January 1912, GLENDOVEER was lost in collision off St Catherine's Point on passage from Charlestown with china clay for Terneuzen.

**GRACE** ON 13445, built 1820 at Padstow by Martin Withell. Tons 74(O) 63(N). 57.8 18.0 9.0. She was registered at St Ives in 1820 as a schooner, but was often referred to as a brig. If she was built as a schooner it is quite possible at that date that she would have square topsails on both masts. Her owners throughout her long life were the Rowe family of St Ives, (also spelt Roe and Rowe,) who also provided her masters and much of her crew. Despite her modest size she was no coaster, trading, for instance, to Haiti in the Caribbean. Wrecked at Swansea 20th December 1871 (note on register).

**GRACE** ON 13465, built 1846 at Padstow by Thomas Carter. Tons 15(N). 36.5 10.9 5.7. A lugger with a running bowsprit and a square stern (unlike the other luggers built by Carter for St Ives). She was owned half by the Richards family and half by the Thomases, all St Ives fishermen.

Worn out. Register closed 21st March 1862.

**GUIDING STAR** ON 73582, built 1875 at Kilpinpike, Yorkshire, by Banks Jr. Tons 97 net 106 gross, later 90 net. 81.4 22.4 11.0. A schooner with an elliptical stern and female bust first registered in London. In 1890 J. Mackley of Wadebridge was her master and engaged in the Newfoundland trade. This led to her being registered at Padstow in 1898, with M. Thomas of Wadebridge as managing owner. J. Pinch was her master in the Great War; in the early 1920s she went to George Turner of Plymouth.

Abandoned at sea and drifted ashore to be wrecked on Christmas Eve, 1926.

**GUIDING STAR** ON 80406, built 1879 at Gannel Yard, Newquay by T & J Clemens. Tons 100 net 115 gross. 88.5 23.0 10.9. A schooner with a square stern and a three-quarter female figurehead, registered at Padstow and owned initially by Nicholas Lewarne of Porth, who later sold shares to numerous others. With T. Tretheway as master she traded to the Mediterranean. Some of her logs have survived: one particular entry reads: 'Loaded 600 cases of Benedictine liqueur at Fécamp'. It is perhaps not surprising that there were no further entries in the log for that voyage.

J. B. Baird was her master when on the 23rd April 1888 she was wrecked in Moore Bay, Co. Clare, sailing from Liverpool with salt for Iceland. All five of her crew were saved.

**GURINE** ON 28686, builders unknown. Tons 39.97 net. 52.2 16.5 8.5. This tiny schooner appears in the 1865 *Mercantile Navy List* owned by Thomas Dyer of Southsea. Then in 1867 she is registered at Padstow, owned by John Stribley, the merchant. In 1868 William Taylor of Looe took her over, but returned her to Stribley: perhaps she was security for a loan. Broken up July 1870 (note on register).

**HABBACOT** built (or rebuilt) 1797 at Padstow. Tons 74(O). This sloop first appears in *Lloyd's Register* 1798 edition, owned by Bray with J. Trick as master. HABBACOTT is given in some registers: on today's ordnance survey maps Hobbacot Down is to be found in the area once served by the Bude Canal. No Padstow registration has survived. Later owners and masters included R. Gibbs, R. Lewis, R.

Hodge, J. Ley and W. Gorman. By 1808 *Lloyd's Register* describes her as a brig. Her final entry in Lloyd's (red shipowners) register is in 1814, but it is merely a copy of much earlier editions, and her fate is unknown.

**HANNAH** built 1817 at Padstow by J. Tredwen. Tons 53(O) 39 (N). 48.0 16.4 8.6 (1821 register). A Padstow registered sloop rigged smack. Her first owner was Abbott of Egloshayle (Parnell master) followed by J. Patten and Pettigrew, then J. Tredwen (1829) with William Thomas as master, and finally James Metherill of Bude.

Lost at sea January 1850 (note on register).

**HANNAH** ON 29411, built 1865 at Padstow by Tredwen. Tons 145 net 158 gross, later 129 net. 98.0 23.1 12.2. This vessel registered at Llanelly was consistently described as a schooner by *Lloyd's* but as a brigantine by the port register. Starting work in the Mediterranean trades, her old age was spent as a coaster. She was owned by such familiar figures as W. Rosevear of Pentewan and I. Tregaskis of Par, the latter employing A. Brenton of Newquay as master.

On 17th March 1911 she was lost with all hands on passage from Aberdeen for Leith with granite chippings.

**HAPPY RETURN** ON 19254, built 1801 at Neath. Tons 35 or 37(N). 45.2 13.7 8.2 (1850 register). This sloop came to Padstow registry from Barnstaple in 1850, to be owned and commanded by Samuel Phillips of Port Isaac. In 1854 John Tredwen took her over and George Teague became master.

Wrecked off Boscastle 25th October 1859 (note on register).

**HAPPY RETURN** ON 23477, built 1814 at Topsham, lengthened 1836 and 1868. Tons 62 (O.1815), 32 (O.1832), 42 (N.1854), 46 (1870). 53.4 15.5 8.6 (1867), 66.9 18.3 8.3 (1868). Variously described as sloop (1815), smack (1842), schooner (1854), smack (1867), and ketch (1875).

Registered at Topsham and Falmouth, she came under Padstow ownership in 1856 when the Newquay branch of the Carter clan bought her. In 1864 they re-registered her at Padstow and she remained a Padstow ship when they moved to Connah's Quay about 1878.

She became a total wreck at Portrush on 22nd-23rd August 1882, on passage Teignmouth for Ballyshannon with clay (note on register).

**HARMONY.** The sloop HARMONY was stranded at Port Gaverne in 1806 but was successfully refloated (*Lloyd's List*).

**HARMONY** built 1814 at Shaldon. Tons 75(N). 58.2 17.0 10.4. A schooner which came to Padstow registry from Dartmouth in 1846. She was owned by Samuel Trethewan of St Minver with Fred Cock as master. In 1847 she was sold to Penzance.

**HARMONY** built 1815 at Bristol. Tons 10.36/94 (O). 26.8 9.8 4.8. This counter sterned sloop came to Padstow registry from Bristol in 1825. Her owners/masters included Peter Wilson, Chilcut, H. Langdon of St Teath, J. Marshall of Padstow, and Edgar J. Jeffray of Bude.

Lost 24th April 1836 (note on register).

**HARMONY** ON 58237, built 1868 at Newburgh, Fife, by Scrimgeour. Tons 166 net 173 gross. 101.4 23.2 11.1. *Lloyd's* describes HARMONY as a schooner but the *Mercantile Navy List* as a brigantine, despite the Padstow port register having her as a schooner, with round stern and scroll bow. She was registered at Dundee, then in 1881 at Weymouth and finally at Padstow in 1882, when purchased by Mark Guy of Port Gavern. J. Haynes of Port Isaac took over in 1885, followed in 1900 by W. C. Phillips who by then was based in St Austell and put her in the china clay run to

Runcorn and home with coal. She was feeling her age in 1905 when on 15th March the Holyhead lifeboat rescued her crew of five. She survived that adventure but on 23rd February 1907 she foundered about 21 miles NE of Spurn Point, sailing from Par with china clay for Sunderland.

**HARRIET** built 1834 at Padstow by J. Tredwen. Tons 81(O) 57(N). A schooner built for Cardiff owners which, apparently only lasted until about 1843.

**HARRIET SCOTT** built 1836 at Quebec. Tons 353(N). 104.6 23.4 17.4. A full rigged ship which was registered at Belfast soon after completion and transferred to Padstow in 1851, to be owned by F. Thomas and then Easthope and others. Her Belfast owners had taken her to Africa, India and the United States, but from Padstow her trade was exclusively to N. America.

Lost 16th May 1854 (note on register).

**HEATHERBELL** ON 63370, built 1873 at Cardigan by Williams. Tons 50 reg. later 45 net. 68.4 17.9 7.6. A dandy or ketch with elliptical stern, registered at Cardigan, then at Padstow from 1888 until 1905. During that period she was owned by Francis Ede Bunt of Tintagel and Jos. Knight of Lydney, who changed her port registry to Bideford in 1905. Lost off the Irish coast *c.* 1915.

**HEBE** ON 26325, built 1847 at Berwick-on-Tweed. Tons 94(O) 74(N) 69 net. 59.4 19.2 9.7. This beamy little schooner came to the Padstow register in 1860 from Grangemouth and London. William Mabley of Padstow owned her until he died in 1875, then Sarah his widow. William Hutchings bought her in 1877. Penalegan and G. Harvey were her Padstow masters.

HEBE was wrecked on the Liverpool Bar on 11th March 1878, taking a cargo of brighters from Clonakilty for Liverpool. The wind was WNW force 6. Her crew of four survived.

**HENRIETTA** ON 68281, built 1872 at Point by John Stephens. Tons 99 net 111 gross, 92 net later. 88.0 18.1 11.3. Although this schooner was registered at Truro, she was owned by the Jenkin family of Newquay within two years of completion. Her masters included T. Jenkin, J. Jenkin, T. Gill, J. Brown. W. Pascoe, R. Brenton and S. Hornersham.

On 21st November 1909 whilst at anchor off the Formby lightship she was run down by SS CLAN MACDONALD.

**HENRY** ON 4027 built 1851 at Padstow by R & J Tredwen. Tons 26(N) 44.4 12.9 7.3. This Bristol pilot cutter, a sister to EIRENE, was owned for many years by A. Ray of Pill. Foundered 4 miles NW of Stepper Point whilst out seeking, 15th October 1886.

**HENRY EDMONDS** ON 60763, built 1871 at Aarhus in Denmark by Ulstrup. Tons 162 net 176 gross. 101.9 24.8 10.9. This vessel, described both as a brigantine and as a schooner, was registered at Llanelly in 1874, and at Padstow in 1879. There she was owned by E. R. Tabb, then by Mrs Mary Tabb; in 1890 all 64 shares were in the hands of J. Reney; Mrs E. Merivale was next and then W. S. Allport for the last three or four years of the century. In 1900 K. Pedersen bought her and changed her name to HOWE, registering her at Gloucester.

On March 24th 1917 she was sunk by U-boat, four miles NE by N. of the Arklow light vessel, whilst on passage Garston for Cork with coal.

**HENRY HOLMAN** ON 23955, built 1852 at Plymouth. Tons 158(O) 176(N), 146 net in 1887. 90.6 18.0 12.3.

This small brigantine is unusual in having her 'new' tonnage greater than her 'old'. This phenomenon must be due to her unusually large depth of hold. She was converted to schooner rig at some stage, and although registered at Plymouth she is included here because Charles Matthews of Padstow owned her for her last seven years with J. Hardey and R. Chapman as masters. She was wrecked off Ince in the Mersey on 3rd September 1887, sailing from Runcorn with coal for Plymouth. Her crew of five were all safe.

**HERO** ON 62949, built 1872 on the island of Jersey by J. F. Picot. Tons 80 net 86 gross, later 71 net. 77.8  19.9  9.9. Registered at Jersey throughout her life, she was bought by John T. Keat of Port Isaac in 1911.

This ketch was converted into a houseboat about 1930 and beached at St Mawes. She was finally destroyed by fire in 1940.

**HESPERUS** ON 69463, built 1875 at Padstow by John Cowl. Tons 77 net 85 gross. 75.2  21.9  9.6. A ketch with elliptical stern and gammon knee. Apart from VOLUTINA this Padstow registered ketch was the only one to be built as a ketch in Padstow proper; there were a few others built at Newquay and Bude. She was owned by J. Hawke Jr of Port Isaac.

On 11th January 1880 she was wrecked on St Ives Head whilst sailing from Liverpool with coal for Plymouth. Her crew of four all survived. The wind was SE force 6.

**HETTY** ON 74428, built 1877 at the Carnon Yard, Feock by John Stephens. Tons 100 net 109 gross. 87.2  20.7  11.2. HETTY traded to Newfoundland as a schooner for Truro owners, then in 1890 was registered at Falmouth and owned by William Jenkin of Newquay with S. Chegwidden, W. J. Brown and E. Curry as masters. Albert Williams of Newquay was managing owner from about 1910, and he and W. Olsen, master, saw her through the Great War. In 1919 she was given a two-cylinder paraffin engine of 70 b.h.p.: the engine room allowance reduced her net tonnage to 67. Perhaps it was at that stage that she was converted from schooner to ketch rig. She lifted the last cargo of china clay to be loaded at Newquay in 1921 and in 1924 she was sold to Stanley Harper of Saul, Gloucestershire.

HETTY was abandoned off the Welsh coast in August 1935, but towed into Penzance to be unloaded and condemned.

**HIND** ON 45222, built 1862 at Cardiff by Hill. Tons 123 net 160 gross, later 100 net. 92.0  20.0  11.8. A schooner with a square stern and the figurehead of a young deer (which survived until she was registered at Padstow in 1889).

She was registered at Falmouth on completion but traded mainly from Cardiff to the Mediterranean. In 1873 Liverpool became her port of registry and Aberystwith in 1879. It was Nicholas House of Newquay who bought her in 1889 and appointed R. Hockin, A. Andrews and W. Cock as masters. The last was in command on 12th March 1905 when she was wrecked near Ballymore, Ventry Harbour, Co. Kerry, sailing from Dingle for Cardiff in ballast. The wind was WNW force 10 but her crew of four were saved.

**HOBBACOT.** An area near Bude bears this name, but a ship's name appears in *Lloyd's* and elsewhere spelt HABBACOT q.v.

**HOFFNUNG** see EDWARD.

**HONOR** ON 13509, built 1847 at Padstow by Thomas Carter. Tons 16(N). 36.5  11.2  6.2. A lugger with running bowsprit and round stern built for Job. Stevens of St Ives where she was registered.

'Under 15 tons. Register closed 20th March 1867' (she had been re-measured and being under 15 tons, there was no need to have her registered).

**HOPE** built 1806 at Boscastle. Tons 65(O). 54.0  17.7  9.3. A brig which was registered at Padstow, owned by Rosevear of Boscastle and which appears in *Lloyd's Register* in 1815 with J. Briant as master.

Her port of registry changed to Youghal in 1815. One HOPE, sailing from Yougal, was abandoned and sank on 18th October 1822.

**HOPE** *ex* EUGIENE, prize taken by HMS DEFIANCE in 1810 and made free at London that year. Tons 35(O). 46.5  13.4  6.3. A sloop registered at Plymouth until 1815 when Padstow became her port of registry with John Davey of Bude as master and owner. In 1818 he sold her to Richard Nance of Padstow when her master's name was Power. Lost 1819 (note on register).

**HOPE** ON 13447, built 1846 at Padstow by R & J Tredwen. Tons 94(O) 74(N) 68 net. 62.5  17.6  9.8. A typical coasting schooner with square stern and standing bowsprit, built for John Quick of St Ives, her master and principal owner for almost forty years. She was converted to ketch rig about 1880; her St Ives' registration closes with a note that she was stranded on Puffin Island, North Wales on 13th October 1885.

**HOPE** ON 19247, built 1826 at Mevagissey by Nicholas Lelean. Tons 16(O) 15(N). 35.6  10.4  5.8. A sloop built for Thomas Phillips of Port Isaac and registered at Padstow. Her masters were Thomas Mitchell, Thomas May and Edwin May, the latter being principal owner from 1847 on.

This is probably the HOPE featured in Bude records *c.* 1850, with Richards as master. Lost on Saunton Sands 2nd September 1865 (note on register).

**HOPE** built 1827 at Plymouth. Tons 62(O) 50(N). 46.3  16.0  8.2. Lengthened in 1841 probably at Padstow. A sloop of which the Lloyd's' surveyor commented in 1838, 'she appears to have been raised from her original build'. She was registered at Swansea until transferring to Padstow in 1837. One HOPE was wrecked at Boscastle 16th May 1837, and it is possible that this is the vessel which, when salvaged, was owned by J. Hawken with Brokenshaw as master. Ownership passed to W. Withell then William Darke with Henry Ryley and Frank Prideaux as masters before she was sold to Fowey in 1845.

**HOPEFUL** ON 69466, built 1876 at Dennis Cove Yard at Padstow by Stribley. Tons 216 net 231 gross. 111.4  26.3  12.8. On completion the register describes her rig as a brigantine with three masts; Lloyd's terms her a barkentine (but a barque in 1885).

On completion she was registered at Padstow in the ownership of William Stribley and his bank manager, at times, with William Berry as master. By 1880 she had been sold to Williams & Co., Truro and the next we know she was in Queensland! She dragged her anchors in Liverpool Creek, Cardwell, Queensland, and drove ashore on 12th January 1880. As it was reported, her remains were bought by R. Philp (or Philip) of Townsville for £250, but in fact she survived, and her Padstow registry closes with the note that she had stranded near South Burnard Island, New South Wales on 12th April 1880. But she survived yet again and was registered at Sydney NSW in 1881 and re-rigged as a barque; she was sold to Chinese owners about 1886.

**HOWE** ON 60763, see HENRY EDMONDS

**IDA** ON 66368, built 1873 at Souris, Prince Edward Island by McLaughlin. Tons 199 net and gross, 155 net later. 105.4 24.1 12.9. A brigantine registered at Llanelly in 1874, at Swansea in 1875 and at Padstow in 1886. Her Padstow owners were the Guy family of Port Isaac with Isaac Remick also of Port Isaac as master for the whole period up to her loss.

IDA was wrecked near Dinas in Carnarvon Bay on 20th February 1907, on passage from Teignmouth for Runcorn with pipe clay. The wind at the time was West force 10, but her crew of seven were all saved.

**IDA ELIZABETH** ON 62673, built 1869 at Padstow by John Tredwen. Tons 74 net 82 gross. 77.7  20.7  9.8. A schooner with a female figurehead, she was a Padstow registered coaster all her life. Her owners included H. Buse, J. Tredwen, his widow, J. Casey and eventually Charles Allport. R. Rawlins was her master in the earlier years, then W. Burt. She lost a man overboard about seven miles West of the Tuskar Rock on 17th November 1894 after her bulwarks had been damaged by heavy seas whilst bringing china clay from Fowey for Runcorn.

On 19th February 1902 she was wrecked on the East Mouse, Anglesey (note on register).

**IDEA** probably built in Spain bearing the name SAN JOSEPH. Was taken by the British privateer VIOLET, Henry Dare commanding, and made free in London 23rd February 1811. Tons 30(O). 46.3 12.3 4.7. She was registered at Fowey on 26th February 1811 and at Padstow on 2nd April 1811 (but that register has not survived). Despite her small size and unusually small depth of hold, she was schooner rigged.

On 1st October 1820 after sailing from Plymouth with limestone she struck Carn Du and floated clear, but foundered off Helford. Three men were drowned and only her master, R. Sleeman, survived.

**INDUSTRY** built 1778 at Carmarthen, rebuilt 1801 at Padstow. Tons 43. 44.5 15.8 8.8. This sloop was registered at Padstow, owned by Richard Avery of Boscastle with James Cock of Tintagel as master. Foundered off Land's End 27th September 1816

**INDUSTRY** ON 13109, built 1809 at Carmarthen. Tons 67(O) when she was sloop rigged in early years. She was registered at Penzance in 1826 and St Ives in 1848 when her dimensions were 54.7 16.5 10.1. There is no record of her lengthening but in 1860 her dimensions were 65.5 18.5 10.0. Three successive St Ives registers describe her as a schooner, a schooner-brig and a brigantine. By 1862 she was 79 tons net 85 gross.

In 1848 she was sold to Thomas Richard Avery of Boscastle for £802 and he had her registered at Padstow in 1852. Her local owners and masters included James Richards, William Moyse, Thomas L. Seaton, Jacob Venning, John Mably, Thomas Couch, Richard Blake Hellyer, and Thomas Webb Ward.

Lost by stranding at Ballycroneer on 19th October 1862 (note on register). Her crew were saved by the gallant action of the local population.

**INDUSTRY** ON 4034, built 1818 at Padstow. Tons 31(0). 41.0 13.7 7.4. This pilot cutter, built for J. Calloway and registered at Bristol, was lengthened in 1890 and remeasured as Tons 36(O) 44.6 14.0 7.1. She lasted until about 1860.

**INFANTA** ON 14077, built 1852 at Padstow by R & J Tredwen. Tons 56 net, 63 gross. 59.8 15.3 8.5. Although this schooner was sheathed with zinc sheets in the same year that she was built, she is believed to have spent her life as a Padstow registered coaster owned by E. Knight, T. Prout, Hicks, J. Bellingham, with Richard Blight and M. Osborn among her masters. She went to Arthur Cook of Appledore in 1883 and was converted into a ketch about then. On 19th May 1897 she was wrecked on the north end of Lundy Island, having sailed in ballast from Appledore with the intention of salvaging cargo from a wreck on Lundy. Wind E force 7. All three crew survived.

**INGRID** ON 69453, built 1873 at Padstow by John Stribley. Tons 99 net 109 gross. 83.8 22.7 10.8. The Padstow schooner INGRID carried a good deadweight tonnage; she was owned initially by her builder, then by various members of the Jenkin family (and numerous local tradesmen). G. Bennett and W. Sleeman served as masters.

On 9th December 1889 she was dismasted and lost a man off the Newarp light, Norfolk on passage from Leith with coal for Calstock. On 1st April 1892 she was lost in collision with the Cardiff

steamship LABARROUERE 9 miles NNW of Godrevy (note on register).

**INTREPID** built 1834 at Padstow. Tons 35(O). 38.6 15.2 7.0. This beamy Padstow sloop owned by T. R. Avery with B. Carter as master must have been built to serve the isolated communities north of Port Isaac, but was transferred to the Swansea register in 1835.

**INTREPID** ON 13040, built 1851 at Nappan, Nova Scotia by James Fullerton. Tons 637(O) 702(N), 634 net (1866). 135.7 28.3 20.6. (*Lloyd's Register* gives length 125.3). She was completed as a full rigged ship with two decks, but soon converted to barque rig. She was registered at Limerick, trading from Cork to New York until Padstow became her port of registry in 1854. She was owned by Stribley and later by Samuel Pollard of Wadebridge. Her masters were R. Philp and E. Parnell; under the latter she was one of the vessels which sailed from Padstow with emigrants for North America.

On 28th March 1870 she sprang a leak in a gale and foundered. Her position was 37°N, 126°W. (If the transcription of this note on the register is correct, she sank off the California coast. 12°W in the Atlantic is more probable.)

**IONA** ON 53142, built 1865 at Garmouth by Geddie. Tons 108 net 116 gross, 96 net later. 84.0 21.9 10.4. A schooner with a square stern and a female figurehead, she was registered at Wick and Sligo before Padstow in 1890; but T and J Inch of Port Isaac owned her for a number of years before that, and continued to own her until she was hulked and her register closed 21st April 1904.

**IRIS** built 1836 at Padstow by J. Tredwen. Tons 83(O). 64.3 17.1 10.3. This schooner was initially registered at Padstow with her builder as owner and Benjamin Harvey as master, but she was transferred to Truro almost immediately, owned by Baynard and others.

IRIS was lost 23rd November 1852 (note on register).

**ISABEL** ON 49667, built 1865 at New Quay, Cardigan by Davies. Tons 177 net, 186 gross, 166 net later. 103.4 23.7 12.9. A brig which was registered at Aberystwith but which came to be owned by the Fishley family of Plymouth and Port Isaac in 1883. They converted her to schooner rig in 1885 when James M. Fishley of Port Isaac was managing owner. She lasted until about 1894.

**ISABELLA** ON 14381, built 1856 at Flint. Tons 65 net 81 gross. 75.2 19.0 10.1. Charles Matthews of Padstow bought this schooner in 1898 after she had already served Douglas and Chester owners for over forty years; he registered her at Padstow.

On 8th March 1902 she was wrecked on the Manacles taking oats from Waterford for Penryn; her crew of four including A. Hoskin, the master, survived.

**ISABELLA** ON 62772, built 1872 at Freckleton by P. Rawstone. Tons 83 net 90 gross, later 72 net. 81.0 21.0 9.2. ISABELLA was built as a schooner, converted to ketch rig soon after the turn of the century, and given a 26 b.h.p. auxiliary in 1925.

She was registered at Preston until 1905 and at Gloucester thereafter. She is included here because after dropping out of the register in 1936 she was hulked at Rock opposite Padstow, breaking up in the early 1960s.

**J.C.A.** ON 58242, built 1867 at Padstow by J. Stribley. Tons 89 gross. 74.3 22.0 10.0. A Padstow coasting schooner built for James Strout of Port Isaac, with James Strout Jr in command.

Went missing on 22nd January 1875, leaving Milford with culm for Hayle. Crew five strong (note on register).

**J.K.A.** ON 58249, built 1868 at Padstow by Stribley. Tons 60 net 70 gross. 70.1 19.4 9.4. This schooner was registered at Padstow owned by her builders, with A. Watts as master and later as managing owner. Yet it seems highly probable that her name is a compliment to J. K. Allport, one of Padstow's principal shipowners. By 1887 she was sold to W. Escott of Watchet, and on 11th November 1891 she was lost by stranding on Shag Rock, Scilly, bound from Ballincurra for Poole with oats (note on register).

**J.K. ALLPORT** ON 74623, built 1876 at Padstow by Cowl. Tons 100 net 110 gross, 95 net later. 85.6 22.7 10.8. This schooner was registered at Plymouth, owned first by Charles Allport, then Henry Allport. Her masters included J. Cundy, J. Chapman and E. Wills.

11th December 1901 missing at sea (note on register).

**J.T.A.** ON 51115, built 1866 at Padstow by John Tredwen. Tons 103 gross. 82.6 21.4 10.5. A schooner built for Owen and others of Neath and registered at Swansea. On 5th December 1868 a wreck was seen on Langness, Isle of Man. A part of her stern was sufficiently visible to read her name. No bodies were recovered, the implication being that there were no survivors.

**JAMES** ON 12753, built 1847 at Three Rivers, Prince Edward Island. Tons 208(N) 186 (gross). 88.3 20.0 14.0 A brig coming on to the Padstow register in 1848 with owner P. Wilson, and breaking new ground by trading to the Danube. She was sold to Leith in 1854 and by 1866 was registered in London.

JAMES disappears from the registers in the early seventies.

**JAMES AND ANN** ON 19220, built 1794 at Plymouth, rebuilt at Padstow 1824. Tons 35(O) 26(N). 42.3 14.4 6.8. These dimensions come from the oldest surviving register of this sloop rigged smack at Padstow, 1823. She was then owned by Power and the following year by Nichols and Cock, followed by Martin, and in 1845 by John Brewer of St Minver. Her numerous masters included Webster, Guy, Hawken, J. Cock, Couch, French, Burd, Martyn England and Richard Brewer Rawlins. Lost at sea 5th May 1856 (note on register).

**JAMES AND SAMUEL** built 1783 at Pill, Bristol. Tons 15(O). 36.4 10.0 5.0. Registered at Padstow in 1819 as a sloop with a cockpit owned by A. Teague of St Columb, and in 1820 by George Bowden of St Columb. Broken up at Falmouth in 1821 (note on register).

**JAMES AND SARAH** built 1821 at Cardiff. Tons 30(O) 21(N). 37.9 13.7 5.8. A sloop which came to the Padstow register from Bristol in 1825 with James Cock as owner and Fred Cock as master. Later masters included Richard Wedlake, John and Abel French and George Thomas. Thomas Martyn bought her in 1836 and sold her to Cardiff in 1838. She went on the Swansea register in 1845.

**JANE** ON 11414, built 1802 at Bideford. Tons 64(O) 54(N), 57 gross. 53.2 17.3 8.8. Rebuilt at Padstow 1829. This JANE came to Padstow from Ilfracombe in 1824 to be owned by William Sleeman and E. Parnall. Simon Stribley was her master in the 1830s. T. May of Port Isaac took her over in the '40s and '50s; John Tredwen and John Cory in the '60s. Until 1838 she is described as a brig, but the 1829 register expands on that, noting that the rig is square forward, schooner aft, so she was a brigantine. In 1838 she became a schooner and probably in the 1860s a ketch.

Wrecked on the Doom Bar 22nd January 1868.

**JANE** built 1806 at Plymouth. Tons 65(O). 52.3 17.3 8.2. A Dartmouth sloop which was registered at Padstow in 1825 in the ownership of Robert Pepperell of Portsmouth, with William Symons of Padstow as master. She returned to the Dartmouth register in 1832.

**JANE** Place and date of build unknown. Prize of HM Gunbrig CONSTANT (Lt. John Stokes), 15th June 1811. Tons 63(O). 50.6 17.6 9.8 when registered at Padstow in 1814. This schooner was owned by her master Peter Brabyn of Padstow but he moved to Plymouth where JANE was lengthened, rebuilt and registered in 1820, her tonnage being increased to 103(O). Until about 1830 he

traded her to the Mediterranean and Iberia. A JANE of Padstow was reported to have been blown up in Penzance Harbour on 20th February 1830. A former master was arrested!

**JANE** There was probably another *ex* prize taken by L'EUGENE or EUGENIE and registered at Padstow 1813 and 1814, but the details are lost.

**JANE** built 1816 at Padstow. Tons 53(O). 48.8 16.7 8.4. A Padstow sloop owned initially by William Richards of St Endellion, then in 1832 by Rosevear of Boscastle and Sloggett, with N. Couch as master.

JANE was wrecked trying to beach herself at Trebarwith to load a cargo of slates, 4th June 1844. Press reports described how her mate who was unable to stay awake, steered her onto the rocks.

**JANE** built 1818 at Penzance by John Matthews. Tons 44(O) 34(N). 46.8 15.2 8.4. A sloop with the usual running bowsprit and square stern which was registered briefly at Penzance but in the year of her completion was bought by William Sloggett and had William Withell as master; at Padstow in 1825 they were succeeded by William Knight, and in 1828 he sold to William Philp. He commanded her himself for a while and then handed over to William Heatherington. By then all the Williams of Padstow seem to have had a go and in 1833 she was sold to Ed Paynter of the well-known St Ives family.

Lost near Helwick Rocks 21st February 1850 (note on register, but there is some doubt about the year).

**JANE AND MARGRET** (the name originally registered) or JANE AND MARGARET (as spelt subsequently) built 1830 at Padstow by John Brewer. Tons 55(O) 40(N). 46.8 16.9 8.1. This Padstow registered sloop was commanded by her builder on completion, with John Hawken as managing owner. In 1832 John Brewer handed her over to W. Carsell and went ashore to build the larger sloop MARY. William Burd, Joseph and Thomas Morecombe and Alex Parker were subsequently involved as owners and captains. Lost 16th March 1842 (note on register).

**JANE AND SARAH** built 1829 (probably completed 1830) at Appledore. Tons 66(O) 57(N). 55.7 16.8 9.6. Her rig is variously defined as schooner, brig and "square forward, schooner aft", probably what we would call a brigantine. She was registered at Padstow in 1830 owned and captained by J. Hicks until in 1837 N. Phillips took her to Penzance where she was last registered in 1845.

**JANE AND SARAH** ON 16048, built 1855 at Padstow by Samuel J. Bennett. Tons 50(N) 44 gross, 33 net later. 58.6 15.4 7.7. This long-lived vessel was built as a smack and registered at Padstow with Brenton of St Wenn and others as owners and Richard Brewer Rawlings as master. This linking of surnames was quite usual in the area in the 19th century. The smack was sold to Holyhead owners in 1860 and re-registered at Beaumaris in 1865. In 1889 she was registered at Barnstaple and converted to ketch rig. Although she was reported lost in the Bristol Channel in 1900 she was evidently recovered and traded under sail until her Barnstaple register closed on 2nd September 1928 with the note 'broken up at Braunton Pill'.

**JANE FRANCIS** ON 65155, built 1872 at Padstow by Tredwen. Tons 174 net 184 gross. 107.1 24.2 12.3. Completed as a brig for C. J. Sims and registered at Plymouth, the JANE FRANCIS was salted and yellow metalled and placed in the Iberian and Mediterranean trades. By about 1879, however, she was owned by the May family of Port Isaac and largely employed within home trade limits. Thomas May managed her and R. May and A. May appear as masters in the *Lloyd's Register*.

Lost by collision in the English Channel 22nd July 1893 on

JANE SLADE. A primitive impression of her early days as a fruit schooner, and a photograph of her final three-masted rig.

*David Clement Collection*

passage to Hamburg, by which time she was brigantine rigged.

**JANE LOWDEN** ON 21135, built 1841 at Miramichi, New Brunswick. Tons 500(O) 581(N). 120.8 22.7 19.1. This barque was sold to Liverpool owners soon after completion, then bought by 'Seaton & Co.' and registered at Padstow in 1848. She acquired an Ottoman Pass to trade to the Black Sea in 1851, but her main trades were emigrants to North America and timber from Quebec to Britain.

Lost at sea 31st December 1865 (note on register).

**JANE SLADE** ON 63961, built 1870 at Polruan by Slade. Tons 149 net 158 gross. 97.7 22.9 12.3. A fast fruit schooner built for the Azores and Mediterranean trades. Registered at Fowey, she was owned by the Slades and others, but her managing owner for many years was W. Geake of St Columb. Basil Lubbock wrote of 'the famous JANE SLADE, Captain Peter Avery, which held the record for the fastest passage from St Michaels to Bristol'. Later A. Veale of Newquay was owner and master. In 1905 she was converted to a three masted rig. Her hulk was abandoned in Pont Pill in 1928.

**JANET WORTHINGTON** ON 68623, built 1873 at Ardrossan. Tons 100 net 118 gross, later 79 net. 87.1 21.4 10.6. A schooner registered at Fleetwood and Runcorn and only listed here because John Sherlock of Newquay owned her from 1899 to her loss. J Pappin was her master when she foundered off Prawle Point on 9th August 1902, after a collision with SS RODDAM of London. Only three months earlier the RODDAM had been in the roadstead at Fort de France, Martinique when the volcano Mont Pelee exploded. The 30,000 inhabitatants of St Pierre were annihilated with the single exception of one criminal in a dungeon, and 16 ships were sunk in the harbour. The RODDAM was the only vessel to escape, steaming through a rain of burning lava which killed several members of her crew.

**JANIE** ON 62682, built 1870 at Padstow by Stribley. Tons 87 net 94 gross, 80 net later. 78.7 22.3 10.2. This schooner was registered at Padstow and all 64 shares were owned by Stribley, with H. Pope as captain. Two years later William West of St Blazey bought her, leaving Pope in command (a situation which amused Methodists at the time). After 1890 there were numerous other local shareholders, and by 1904 owners in Looe and later Polruan. In 1915 John M. Cox of Appledore took her to the Bideford register but she was unlisted in 1919.

**JANIE** ON 77409, built 1878 at Padstow by John Cowl. Tons 100 net, 112 gross with minor variations later. 86.2 22.9 10.8. By the time the schooner JANIE was completed, Padstow was no longer such an isolated port fending for itself, and she joined the great pool of schooners trading within home trade limits without reference to the special needs of Padstow (where nevertheless she remained based throughout). Thus, when she was in trouble off Whitby in October 1885, losing one of her crew and suffering storm damage, she was bound from Par with clay and ochre for Burntisland. Her first owners were the Jenkin family, then Kernick (her master) and finally the Allports. Other masters were Chegwidden, S. Veale, G. Vaggers, F.W.J. Myer, and S. Edmonds.

JANIE was wrecked at Holyhead on 19th September 1916. The local RNLI lifeboat saved four. The desperate shortage of shipping led to JANIE being salvaged and she was towed into the Mersey and converted into a steam lighter, a compound engine of 9 nominal horsepower by Bates & Co, Leftwich being installed in 1918. In 1919 she was registered at Liverpool as the FRANCES ANN owned by Kymo Shipping Co. Ltd (Sir H. M. Grayson Bart. KCB, manager). In 1930 she was sold to John Gibney of Wallasey and according to the *Mercantile Navy List* she lasted into the 1950s in his ownership as a salvage vessel.

**JANIE BANFIELD** ON 49989, built 1866 at Padstow by Stribley and yellow metalled for the Mediterranean and Azores trade. Tons 190 gross. 108.8  25.1  12.6. This schooner was registered at Hayle with John Harvey Trevithick as owner (another case of linked surnames) and Jago as master. In 1874 she was bought by Edward Hain of St Ives (founder of the Hain Line) who appointed W. Bickerling to command, but on 17th March 1875 she was wrecked on the island of Nicero (Nicaria, Greece ?).

**JANIE LOUISE** ON 58247, built in France, year and place unknown. Tons 53 gross. 58.9  18.0  8.1. *ex* French COMMERCE, a schooner registered at Padstow in 1868, owned by Samuel Blake of St Minver with Phillips as master.

Broken up and register closed 1875.

**JANIE MORCOM** ON 53161, built 1865 at Padstow by Tredwen. Tons 98 net 119 gross. 87.2  22.1  11.2. A coasting schooner always intended for the china clay and coal trades, owned throughout her life by the Tregaskes family and registered at Fowey.

Lost by collision May 1895 (posted in *Lloyd's Register*).

**JANIE VIVIAN** ON 62675, built 1869 at Padstow by John Tredwen. Tons 92 net 103 gross. 83.6  22.2  10.6. A Padstow registered coasting schooner owned successively by the Brewer family, P. Willcock of Pentewan, Martin Thomas of Wadebridge and J. T. Keat.

On 5th February 1901 leaving for Cardiff with wheat, she went ashore at the entrance to Padstow harbour and became a total loss.

**JASPER** ON 85825, built 1884 at Falmouth by C. Burt. Tons 129 net 139 gross, 99 net later. 96.0  23.0  11.3. This three-masted schooner was registered at Fowey and owned by A. Jenkyns of Charlestown, but in 1899 she was sold to R. J. Hockin of Newquay with H. J. Hockin as captain. She was lost on Haisboro Sands in 1904.

**JEANNE** see ROSALIE.

**JEANNIE SOPHIA** or **JEANNE SOPHIE** see JOHN.

**JEHU** built 1835 at Plymouth. Tons 62(O) 41(N). 47.0  15.7  7.4. This Plymouth smack was bought by James Stephens of Port Isaac in 1842 and registered at Padstow. William Mitchell was her master. She was lost in 1849 (note on register).

**JENNIFER** (JENIFER in *Lloyd's*). ON 11473, built 1845 at Padstow by Thomas Carter. Tons 76(O) 61(N). 54.2  16.6  9.1. A sloop rigged smack registered at Padstow and owned by T. Avery. Thomas Seaton, S. Hoskin and John Steer were her masters.

Lost at sea 16th November 1859; the crew of the French lugger LOUIS of Caen were rewarded for rescuing her crew of three.

**JENOPHER** built 1789 at Barnstaple and registered at Padstow Tons 48 (O). A sloop owned by W. Sluman, trading to Ireland with W. Pascoe and later J. Hawkins as Master. Foundered south of Mousehole, November 1810.

**JEREMIAH** built 1796 at Padstow. Tons 20(O). 38.5  11.8  5.8. This pink sterned cutter was for sale in 1805 as a 'Mackerell boat'. In 1825 she was owned by Hawkins, Stephens and James Hicks of St Columb. William Hockin and Richard Carter were masters in 1825 and 1826.

Broken up in 1834 (note on register).

**JESSIE** ON 21375, built 1858 at Padstow. Tons 164 gross. 92.0  22.0  12.7. A Padstow registered brig with an elliptical stern, she was yellow metalled and entered the deep water trades. Stribley and Allport were managing owners and J. Tippet was her master for many years until R. Rawlings took over not long before her loss.

JESSIE was described as a coaster in *Lloyd's Register* 1873, but she was 'supposed foundered on passage Mazagan [in Morocco] for

The JASPER drying her sails.    *Royal Institution of Cornwall*

Falmouth with maize, mid-January 1874'. Crew of seven all missing (note on register).

**JESSIE** ON 69459, built 1875 at Padstow by Stribley. Tons 92 net 100 gross. 80.5  21.6  10.5. This schooner was registered at Fleetwood and remained so when owned in Lancaster and later in Dublin. She dropped out of the registers in 1912.

**JESSIE** ON 78968, built 1876 at Wadebridge by Billing. Tons 22. Built as a smack rigged barge for Robert Dixon and Samuel Ingram of Truro (her port of registry). (See also the chapter on barges)

**JESSIE** ON 78087 built 1878 at Plymouth by R. Hill & Sons. Tons 41. Net 54.4  17.8  7.6. A beamy square sterned cutter-rigged smack which was built for a Calstock syndicate and registered at Plymouth. In 1892 she was bought by Alexander Stephens, the Porth merchant.

The *Royal Cornwall Gazette* recorded her loss in its issue of 6th April 1893. On Thursday afternoon the JESSIE had struck a rock off Park Head, then slid off and slowly foundered. Seeing her in distress, six young men raced several miles to windward from Newquay, beating the lifeboat WILLIE ROGERS. Captain John Billings and his two-man crew had abandoned the JESSIE in their small punt, and were safely towed back to harbour.

The six men in question were Joseph Pearce fisherman, Edwin Trebilcock labourer, Edward Curry sailor, James Trethewey mason, William James mason, and Richard Clemens shipwright. The JESSIE had been bringing 64 tons of coal from Newport for Porth.

**JOHANN CARL** ON 105153, built 1893 at Seedorf, Germany by G. Kruger. Tons 45 net 58 gross. 65.0  18.4  7.9. A German

The German-built ketch JOHANN CARL at Porth just before the First World War.                                    *Royal Institution of Cornwall*

schooner which came to be registered in Guernsey in 1897 and in Padstow in 1899, where she was owned by Alex. Stephens of Porth and soon altered to ketch rig.

J. Billing senior was her master and he was drowned when, on 1st September 1917, she stranded and was lost at Cliveden in the Bristol Channel. She was taking china clay from Newquay for Bristol. His crew of two were saved (note on register).

JOHN built 1788 at Cleave Houses, Bideford. Tons 67(0) 55.8 17.8 9.3. A pink sterned brig, later brigantine, her first surviving registration at Padstow is in 1817, but *Lloyd's Register* records her owner as Thomas Rawlins and her master J. Hocken before that. She was re-registered at Padstow in 1821 with Hockin, Sleeman and Parnall as owners and William Giles as master.

Missing since leaving Swansea 3rd July 1821, bound for Portreath. Her boat was found near Lundy Island (*Lloyd's List* 31st July 1821).

JOHN date and place of build unknown. Prize to HMS SCEPTRE condemned in the High Court of Admiralty 1811, made free at London 1812. Previous name JEANNIE SOPHIA (note that there was a small French naval vessel named JEANNE SOPHIE built

1793). Tons 29(O). 41.7 13.4 6.7. A sloop previously registered at Plymouth which came to Padstow in 1815, owned by Samuel Billing and others; captain, Abel French. In 1817 she was sold to Abraham Matcott of Boscastle; captain, Thomas Rawson.

On 21st January 1820, sailing from Llanelly for Swansea, JOHN foundered in Roselly Bay, her crew being drowned (*Lloyd's List* 1st February 1820).

JOHN built 1833 at Padstow by Tredwen. This smack, launched sideways on the same tide as the AID was evidently not registered.

JOHN built 1835 at Plymouth. Tons 41. 47.0 15.6 7.3. A sloop apparently registered at Padstow in 1842 as owned by John Stephens of Port Isaac. Lost 1849.

JOHN ON 53034, built 1865 at Penmaen Pool, Merioneth. Tons 40 net later 32 net. 57.2 17.7 6.6. Her rig is variously described as smack, dandy and ketch. She was registered at Aberystwyth, Carnarvon and then in 1893 at Padstow, then owned by Alexander Stephens of Porth, with J. Billing Jr as master.

Supposed foundered, having left Mumbles on 4th November 1900 for Newquay (note on register).

JOHN AND HANNAH built 1818 at Padstow by George Sloggett. Tons 35(O) 23(N). 'Nearly rebuilt 1842' then 28(N). 44.9 14.2 6.8 (1818). This sloop rigged smack was registered successively at Padstow (1818), St Ives (1822), Falmouth (1823) Padstow (1825) and Bristol (1855). The Padstow families involved included Sloggett, Brown, Evans, Nance, Hawken, Parnall, Brokenshaw, Watts, (Port Isaac), Whitford, Corsell, Mitchell Brewer, Bunt and Sinnett. Lost at sea 8th October 1856.

JOHN & JENEFER (early spelling) JOHN & JENIFER ON 11431, built 1840 at Fowey by Marks and Rendle. Tons 91(O) 58(N). Lengthened 1858 thereafter 65 net 71 gross. 71.6 19.3 8.2. Built as

The ketch JOHN at Newquay *c.* 1895. The gig DOVE, already about seventy years old, lies just this side of her.                                    *Private Collection*

a sloop but converted to schooner rig on lengthening. Her port of registry changed from Fowey to Padstow in 1874 when Charles Matthews became managing owner.

On 9th May 1887 she was on passage from Newport with coal for Plymouth when she was in collision with SS R. F. MATTHEWS of London. She sank off the Longships with the loss of one member of crew and one passenger. R. Mably was master at the time.

**JOHN & MARY** built 1779 (port registers) 1783 (*Lloyd's Register*) at Bristol. Tons 50(O). 47.3 16.8 9.0. The oldest surviving Padstow register for this sloop is 1814 when John Tredwen, shipwright, was one of her owners. Avery managed her and J. Gould was master when she went ashore at Fishguard 14th March 1820, but got off much damaged. Nicholas Horsewell of Padstow owned and captained her soon after that. She was sold to Bridgwater and registered there in 1828.

**JOHN & MARY.** A sloop of 59 tons was for sale at Padstow in 1811: Apply Rawlins & Sons'; for sale again in 1813. *Lloyd's Register* 1815 lists one built in 1769 at Bristol, 48 tons; H. Knight owner, J. Vivian master. One was wrecked at Padstow 10th November 1810; another on 31st October 1823.

**JOHN & MARY** built 1827 at Sunderland. Tons 260(O) 287(N). 450 burthen. 86.4 23.7 17.0. The snow JOHN & MARY was registered at Sunderland until purchased by John Tredwen and others and registered at Padstow in 1839. With A. Harvey and later J. Oliver in command, she took Cornish emigrants to Quebec and brought back timber. Late in 1844 her port of registry became Quebec and she was trading to Dublin.

**JOHN & MARY** built 1839 at Newquay by Thomas Clemens. The launch of a 70 ton sloop was reported in the *West Briton* on 19th April 1839. It seems certain that this vessel was subsequently registered as the CAROLINE, and that JOHN & MARY was the name *pro tem.* for this sloop rigged smack which Clemens built as a speculation after completing his apprenticeship.

**JOHN AND MATILDA** built 1802 at Salcombe. Tons 46(O). 43.8 16.3 8.0. This small sloop was registered at Padstow in 1814 (and possibly earlier). Her owner was Edward Martyn, maltster of Lower St Columb, and her master E. Billing. In 1825 her owner was John Tredwen, and her master M. Knight of Padstow who had taken over in 1821. In 1826 she was sold to St Ives and lost in 1829.

**JOHN & SARAH** built 1814 at Padstow by Martin Withell. Tons 66(O). 53.4 17.6 9.3. This Padstow smack had J. Parnell as captain and owner until 1818 when J. Wherry became managing owner and Martyn Parnell, of Padstow and later Swansea, was captain.

Wrecked at Boscastle 5th December 1822 (*Lloyd's List*).

**JOHN & SUSANNA** built 1820 at Plymouth. Tons 24(N). 45.7 12.6 6.6. A sloop which came to Padstow from Plymouth in 1845 to be owned by James Stephens of Port Isaac, with James Skinner as master. She was broken up in 1847 (note on register).

**JOHN BARWISE** built 1828 at Maryport. Tons 50(O). 44.8 16.4 6.1. A sloop with a lifting bowsprit and a round stern (both unusual features at Padstow). When she came to be registered at Padstow, John Barwise of Cumberland retained four shares despite selling the other sixty to J. D. Martyn. Later, F. Cock, Murton and Ryley had shares before she moved to Bridgwater in 1836.

**JOHN HEDLEY** ON 53068, built 1866 at Netstakes, Cornwall, by Emmanuel Crocker & Sons. Tons 60 gross. 65.0 18.3 8.2. A Plymouth registered Tamar barge built as a smack but converted to ketch rig in 1874. Owned by Richard Roose (1875) and Mary Roose (1896) of Port Isaac, then by William Philp, Padstow merchant (1897) and finally John Westcott of Plymouth, who hulked her and cancelled her registry 28th March 1898. (see also chapter on barges)

**JOHN HENRY** ON 577, built 1850 at Newport by Blyth & Co. and yellow metalled in 1852. Tons 514 net 556 gross. 119.0 27.7 20.4. At first this barque was registered at London, and traded to Mauritius. About 1861 her managing owner became John Cory of Padstow, and he registered her at Cardiff, which was to become his home port later. For Cory she traded from South Wales ports to the Mediterranean, doubtless exporting 'black diamonds' and bringing home slightly more romantic cargoes. Her masters included G. Crocker and G. Hore.

*Lloyd's Register* 1881 carries the note 'Now a hulk'.

**JOHN WESLEY** ON 29203 (29303 in later *Mercantile Lists*; an error,) built 1860 at Aberdovey. Tons 98 gross. 76.3 20.5 10.6. A Welsh schooner registered at Aberdovey and then Aberystwyth but owned by John Stribley of Padstow from 1873. Verran gives W. Hockin and A. Burt of Newquay as masters and states 1874 as the date of her loss. *Lloyd's* has a Stribley as master and she is to be found in the *Mercantile Navy List* until 1880, owned by John Reynolds of Newquay.

**JOHNSON & ELIZABETH** ON 14143, built 1837 at Bideford. Tons 95(O) 81(N). 76 gross 64 net. 61.1 16.8 10.4. A Padstow schooner owned for 48 years by the Hicks family of Lower St Columb. She was hulked and her register closed in 1886.

**JOSEPH R.PIM** built 1836 at Passage West, Cork. Tons 109(N). 65.0 19.2 11.5. This Cork registered schooner was bought by James Rowell Rickard of Wadebridge in 1847. V. G. Densten, her master, of Padstow also had shares. In 1847 her port of registry became Padstow. In 1849 John Stribley and Edwin Kelly bought her. Her register closes with the note 'Abandoned at sea 4th June 1849'.

**JOSEPHINE** ON 56364, built 1853 at Bayonne, France, repaired and re-rigged at Newquay 1860. Tons 38 net 48 gross. 55.8 17.4 8.0. Built as the three masted lugger L'UNION, she went ashore in the Gannel 26th October 1859, to be salvaged and re-rigged and registered at Bridgwater as a two masted dandy. In 1868 William Hockin of Newquay registered her at Padstow, and himself commanded her, evidently having given her cutter rig.

The official report of her loss records that on 28th August 1874 she foundered 1½ miles NE of Trevose Head, on passage from Cardiff with coal for Newquay. The wind was E. force 1, so her sails would not have given her steerage way. All four of the crew were members of the Hockin family, and all were lost.

**JUBILEE** built 1809 at Bideford. Tons 51(O). 47.0 16.7 8.5. On completion this sloop was registered at Fowey but two years later moved to Padstow where Giles, Pollard, Harvey, B. Carter, Gurney and Hawken (of Wadebridge) had shares or captained her at different times. In 1834 she was re-registered at Fowey, and the following year seized for smuggling and broken up at Padstow.

**JULIA** ON 44934, built 1862 at Padstow by J. Tredwen. Tons 92 gross. 77.3 20.3 9.8. Little is known about this two masted schooner which went to Swansea owners on completion, then moved to London in 1866. She disappears from the registers about 1879.

**JULIA** ON 80405, built 1879 at Padstow by William Stribley. Tons 169 net 184 gross, later 149 net. 106.5 25.6 12.4. JULIA was built as a three masted schooner and registered at Padstow with J. P. Dunstan owning 64/64ths. She is reputed to have been a regular Newfoundland trader in her early years. J. Hockin, J. Burt and W. George were her masters. About 1906 she was sold to Arklow owners but remained Padstow registered to the end.

On 19th February 1931 she was lost on the N. Arklow bank in a gale with all five hands, including George Kearon who had been her owner and captain for many years. She was on passage from

Glasgow for Newhaven with pig iron.

**KATE** built 1837 at Padstow by John Tredwen. Tons 55(O) 37(N). 49.0 14.2 7.7. A Padstow sloop owned by her builder and by her master John Carveth. John Richards took her over in 1842. Lost December 1845.

**KATE** ON 761, built 1854 at Quay Yard, Newquay, by J & M Clemens. Tons 44 net 58 gross. 53.3 15.7 8.4. The schooner KATE, registered at Padstow, was built for Thomas Jenkins of Newquay who captained her himself in the home trades. One of the Trebilcock family followed him, then S. Ellery in 1874.

On 23rd January 1875 KATE was wrecked on the tiny Channel island of Burhou, off Alderney. She was bound for Le Havre with tin and arsenic from Truro. Her crew of four were saved. The wind was WSW force 8.

**KATE** ON 37793, built 1856 at Pugwash, Nova Scotia. Tons 55 gross. 62.4 18.6 9.0. This schooner was registered at Pictou on completion and brought the first cargo of timber from Nova Scotia to Padstow, where she was bought by W. Martyn. With Padstow as her port of registry, she traded from Liverpool to Spain and from South Wales to many other European destinations, with J. Rowe in command. In 1865 she was sold to Newlyn owners and Penzance became her port of registry.

Lost 15th March 1873 (note on register).

**KATHLEEN** ON 77407, built 1878 at Padstow by William Stribley. Tons 99 net 113 gross. 84.1 22.3 11.0. This schooner, built for Henry House and J. P. Dunstan, with the former as master, was lost in the year of her completion. She sailed from Irvine on 27th September 1878 with two hundred tons of coal for Penzance and a crew of five and went missing.

**KATIE** ON 80401, built 1878 at Padstow by John Cowl. Tons 99 net 113 gross. 86.8 23.0 10.8. A schooner with Cowl's round stern and a female figurehead. The newspapers hailed her launch in October 1878 as 'the second for Tom Jenkin of Newquay in seven weeks'. JANIE had been the first, but KATIE was not such a lucky ship. Foundered off Land's End 17th April 1881 (note on register).

**KATIE** ON 80410, built 1881 at Padstow by John Cowl & Sons. Tons 100 net 116 gross (76 net with engine). 88.6 23.0 10.9. This schooner was built as a replacement for the last, and apart from a marginal increase in registered length, might be described as a replica. This is the famous KATIE, but with so many sailing vessels named KATE and KATIE, there is often confusion. KATIE sailed mostly in the home trades, but she did have a spell in Newfoundland around 1890. The Jenkin family handed her over to Albert Williams, also of Newquay, around 1910. In 1919 he fitted her with a 50 h.p. twin cylindered Robey paraffin engine, and sold shares to a number of people to pay for it. Her topsail yards were removed, making her a fore-and-aft schooner.

In 1931 she was bought by Clunes & Co. a Par syndicate, but remained registered at Padstow. The engine was removed at the end of 1934 and by 1938 she was our last two masted schooner trading under sail alone. Captain Will Cort kept her going into the Second World War.

In 1918-1919 the owners of sailing coasters were encouraged to fit engines so that they should be less at the mercy of German U-boats. In 1940 KATIE was attacked and damaged by enemy aircraft, then forbidden to put to sea as without an engine she was unable to obey routing instructions or to join convoys, so she was laid up in Par Harbour. In 1947 she was sold to Danish owners and renamed BERGFALK. Later she became a houseboat in the Baltic named WIIQUUA. Efforts were made to preserve her, but in 1972 she sank whilst under tow and had to be abandoned.

Her longevity was a tribute to Padstow workmanship and the quality of pitchpine planking on oak frames.

**KILDARE** see THE KILDARE.

**KING'S FISHER** built 1816 at Penzance. Tons 19(O). 37.5 11.6 6.7. A sloop with a hagboat stern. She came to the Padstow registry from Penzance in 1831 when William Brown of Padstow owned 43 shares and Joseph Bullock of Penzance 21 shares.

*Lloyd's List* reported her wrecked at Newquay on 18th January 1834 but she was evidently recovered because her registry closes with the note 'Lost 25th February 1836'.

**KINNAIRD** ON 63421, built 1874 at Fraserburgh by Webster. Tons 138 net 148 gross, later 130 and 120 net. In her early years she was brigantine rigged and traded to Newfoundland and the Baltic. In 1890 her port of registry changed from Fraserburgh to Liverpool, and remained there when in 1900 she joined the fleet of W. S. Allport of Padstow. Captains T. Magor and W. J. Rickard were appointed by him.

On 5th and 6th November 1911 the Holyhead lifeboat DUKE OF NORTHUMBERLAND was credited with saving her crew of four and assisting to save the vessel. However, on 20th December that same year, sailing from Runcorn with coals for Charlestown, KINNAIRD was lost in collision off Holyhead.

**KITTIE** ON 53003, built 1865 at Quay Yard, Newquay, by M. Clemens. Tons 60 reg. 66.0 19.6 8.6. Described in the Padstow register as a schooner with a sharp stern, but photographs show that she appears to have the traditional square stern of the local yards. Her owners were R. M. Clemens (1865), William Varcoe of St Dennis (1870), Samuel Tummon of Newquay (1875), and Nicolas Hockin (1880) also of Newquay. Other members of these families were her masters. KITTIE was cut down to ketch rig in the 1870s and sold to Thomas Kelly of Castletown in the Isle of Man in 1888.

**KITTY** built 1830 at Plymouth. Tons 27(O) 19(N). 37.0 11.6 6.4. In 1837 Robert Knott Ash of Stratton bought this Plymouth sloop and re-registered her at Padstow, and employed William Pickard (Rickard ?) as master. In 1840 Joseph Prust bought her and Edward Mill became master. In 1847 she was sold away to Truro and in 1849 to Bridgwater.

**LA MARIE FRANCOISE** prize to the squadron of HM Ships under Sir John Borlase, condemned in the High Court of Admiralty 13th July 1800, renamed MARY q.v.

**LADY ACLAND** ON 13418, built 1835 at Bude. Tons 53(O) 36(N), 44 net 47 gross, later 32 net. 45.3 16.8 8.2 when registered at Padstow 1835. Owned by the Davey family until 1897 when Edward Rudland of Holsworthy bought her and SIR T.D. ACLAND from Oliver Davey's executors. Rudland continued her in the Bude trade until 1900 when she was leaking badly, so she was hauled out at Bude, much old timber was removed, and her register (which had been at Bideford since 1851) closed. Rudland died in May 1901 and his son (also Edward) was advised to have the bare hull rebuilt for selling unrigged. In 1904 the hull was launched into the Bude canal and given the name MARGARET FRANCES *pro tem*. She was then sold and registered at Bideford as AGNES (q.v.).

The LADY ACLAND started life as a sloop but was converted to ketch rig about 1875.

**LADY AGNES** ON 68865, built 1877 at St Agnes by Hitchins. Tons 84 net 91 gross, later 68 net. 79.1 21.5 10.1. This Hayle registered schooner was bought by R. J. Hockin of Newquay in 1894.

Unfortunately she was wrecked at Great Ormes Head on 8th October 1896, bringing codfish from Newfoundland. However, she was salved and registered anew at Beaumaris in 1897, and went on to have a long second life registered later at Aberystwyth and then Carnarvon, and being re-rigged as a ketch. She was laid up at Portmadoc through the Second World War and broken up there in 1946.

The arrangements at St Agnes were incredibly primitive but the LADY AGNES was only one of hundreds of schooners and ketches which were loaded there before the sea demolished the harbour.
*Royal Institution of Cornwall*

LADY AGNES, now ketch rigged, entering Newlyn.
*David Clement Collection*

**LADY JANE** ON 80409, built 1880 at Porth by J. Osborne. Tons 96 net 107 gross, 82 net later. 84.6   23.3   10.7. This Padstow schooner was the last vessel built at the Porth yard. E. A. Martyn was her first owner but after ten years he sold his 64 shares to various friends and R. E. Bennett became managing owner. J. P. Toms had been master from the start and in 1895 he took over as manager.

On 29th October 1898 she was wrecked on Burrow Head, Calf of Man, sailing from Par with china clay for Irvine. Her crew of four including Captain T. Toms all survived.

**LADY MARY** ON 13191, built 1836 at Clovelly by Thomas Waters. Tons 47(O) 33(N), 29 net. 41.3   14.8   7.6. This sloop transferred registry from Bideford to Padstow in 1841, owned then by John Summers James of Bude and William Whitfield, her master. In 1855 she reverted to Bideford with William Whitfield keeping his shares, but Oliver Davey becoming part owner. In 1861 she went to Barnstaple and about 1867 to Newport, Monmouthshire, where she survived into the twentieth century.

Until 1861 she had traded constantly to Bude.

**LADY MONA** ON 3008, built 1845 at Padstow by R & J Tredwen. Tons 202(O) 196(N). 85.9   20.7   14.2. When this brig was launched she was the largest vessel ever built at Padstow, and she was given the name TEST *pro tem*. She was registered at Liverpool as LADY MONA soon after, owned by E. Thomas and in 1852 at Scilly owned by Weymouth and others. She was essentially a blue water vessel trading to Aden before the Suez canal had been built and continuing in the African trades into the 1860s.

**LADY OF THE LAKE** ON 22386, built 1841 at Gannel yard, Newquay, by T. Clemens. Tons 85(O) 64(N). 56.6   17.1   9.4. A small Padstow registered coasting schooner managed and captained by R. Billing until about 1852 when Francis Webster became master. Lost in the infamous November storm of 1859.

**LADY SALE** ON 25865, built 1843 at Saint John, New Brunswick by F & J Ruddock. Tons 673(O) 737(N), 695 gross. 137.5 32.8 21.2. A full rigged ship built for William Parks and James Hegan who sold her to Greenock in 1844 whence she traded to New Orleans. In 1851 she was owned in Liverpool and in 1862 Robert Easthope bought her and registered her at Padstow. Thereafter, like other large Padstow vessels she tended to trade to Quebec.

It was on a voyage to Quebec that she was lost on 22nd May 1867 (note on register).

**LAETITIA** see LETITIA

**LAFROWDA** ON 56707, built 1867 at Plymouth by Ridley. Tons 122 net 140 gross, 114 net later. 93.5   22.1   11.3. This schooner was registered at Penzance throughout her life and is only included here because she was owned 1903-'5 by Charles Matthews of Duke Street, Padstow. From 1890 onwards *Lloyd's Register* gives her rig as 'smack', but that is believed to be an error as several photographs of that period show her to be a schooner with a rather unusual single topsail.

Broken up 1907 (note on register).

**LANCASHIRE LASS** ON 45343, built 1863 at Newport (Mon.) by Willmott. Tons 94 net 108 gross, evidently lengthened about 1882 whereafter 135 net 146 gross. 91.0   21.3   10.6 (1865). 110.3   23.2   10.6 (1884). Built as a two masted schooner, but becoming a three masted schooner by 1884. Registered at Fleetwood but taken over by A. Sloggett of Padstow in 1884. He was in command when she was sunk in collision with the Dutch pilot schooner SCH No.9, four miles S. of Dungeness on 28th September 1889: Par for Rotterdam with china clay; all saved.

**LANSON CASTLE** see LAWSON CASTLE

**LARCH** ON 19215, built 1841 at Paspebiac, Quebec. Tons 63(N). 56.2   16.6   9.9. The schooner LARCH came from Jersey owners to Padstow registry in 1854, when J. Hawken and Jos. Tippett and others bought her. Ownership passed to John Stribley in 1855 and John Brenton was managing her later that year with Richard Blight as master.

Lost on Lizard rocks, 27th June 1856, in thick fog on passage from Port Talbot with coal for Plymouth.

**LARK** built 1791 at Salcombe. Tons 36(O). 42.0   14.5   7.0. A counter-sterned sloop which came to the Padstow register in 1820 from Llanelly's sub-port Pembrey.

At Padstow she was owned and captained for five years by James Cock; then until 1833 Martyn was her owner and Tumman captain; thereafter Thomas Jollin of Forrabury was owner and captain.

Lost about 1834 with all hands (note on register).

**LAURA EMMA** ON 80407, built 1880 at Padstow by Cowl & Sons. Tons 99 net 116 gross. 88.2   23.1   10.9. A Padstow schooner with elliptical stern and woman figurehead, she was built for W. Philp, who commanded her, and other Padstow investors. By this date Padstow builders knew how to meet the owners' demands for ships of 99 net tons to avoid various expenses which were required for ships of 100 tons or more.

No mere coaster, LAURA EMMA was abandoned in mid-Atlantic on 7th January 1892 on passage from Cardiff to St John's, Newfoundland. Her position was 48° 50'N. 34° 00'W., and the weather was thick with a fresh NW gale, but her five man crew was rescued by SS ASTRAEA of West Hartlepool.

**LAURINA** ON 10919, built 1845 at Bideford by George Williams. Tons 20(N) 17 gross. 44.6  11.2  5.4. A sloop, briefly registered at Bideford and just as briefly at Padstow in 1846 when owned by John Hawken of Padstow, with William Carsell as master, before moving on to Bridgwater in 1847, her home port for many years.

**LAWSON CASTLE, LAUSON CASTLE, LANSON CASTLE,** built 1820 at Padstow by J. Tredwen. Tons 40(O) 43.8  15.1  6.8. This sloop brought the groceries and household goods from Bristol to Bude. Owned first by Southward, then by Nicholas Tucker of Kilkhampton, W. and O. Davey of Bude and Gertrude Mole.

Lost on Bude breakwater 22nd October 1834 (Lloyd's List).

**LE GUSTAVE** see CORNWALL

**LE HEREAUX** built 1813 at Jersey. Tons 15(O). 34.3  10.9  5.7. This Jersey sloop was seized and condemned (presumably for smuggling) in the Easter term, 1826 and sold by public auction to Lowry, agent for William Kent (Knight ?), mariner of Padstow. William Knight, John Knight, Thomas Hoskin, John Mabley, Mayne and Pascoe Billing were all associated with her in the following years. She often traded to Bude and even smaller outports. Lost off St Ives 8th November 1835.

**LEANDER** ON 6141, built 1850 at Hylton, Sunderland. Tons 450 gross. 117.8  28.3  19.6. This barque traded to the Mediterranean and India for Newcastle and Liverpool owners before being registered at Padstow in 1868. Her new owners were J. B. Sergeant (25 shares), Richard Brewer (25 shares) and Francis Brewer (14 shares) all of Padstow. She left the register in 1874 after all 64 shares had passed to John Petters, a Swansea shipbroker, and he sold her foreign.

**LEILA** ON 77405, built 1877 at Gannel Yard, Newquay, by T & J Clemens. Tons 70 net 78 gross. 77.3  20.3  9.9. The managing owner of this Padstow registered schooner was George Hugoe, a Falmouth accountant. Her first master was W. J. Clemens, but W. Kneebow was master when on 28th December 1886 she was sunk in collision with SS ALACRITY of Cardiff, with the loss of three of her crew, off Trevose Head. LEILA was waiting to enter Newquay with coal from Newport.

**LENORA** ON 19225, built 1854 at Padstow by E. Trevethan Bennett. Tons 40 gross, 29 net later. 52.8  15.3  7.3. Initially A. Hutchings owned and commanded this Padstow smack and he was followed by William Bate, S. Hocking and W. Bennett of St Merryn. In 1885 she was sold to Braunton owners, altered to ketch rig and registered at Barnstaple.

On 19th November 1913 she was in collision with the tug ATLAS and had to be beached in Langland Bay to prevent her sinking. Bad weather prevented salvage and she became a total loss.

**LES AMIS** see MARGAM

**LETITIA, LAETITIA,** ON 22774, built 1835 at Plymouth. Tons 76(O) 62(N). 56.5  17.8  9.8. Evidently lengthened as her dimensions in 1859 were 78.0  18.6  9.4 and 90 tons gross. She was built as a schooner for Rosevear of Boscastle and registered at Padstow. Her masters included Ballamy, William Strout and C. Couch. In 1861 she was sold to William Brown of Turnchapel and registered at Plymouth. By that time she was rigged as a ketch.

**LIBERTY** ON 19337, built 1795 at Haverfordwest. Tons 74(O) 69(N) 55 net. 50.5  18.0  9.5 (1825), 59.6  16.0  9.0 (1851). Her rig is described as brig (1815), schooner (1825) schooner-brig (1827, 1837), schooner (1851), and finally ketch (1891). She was registered at Penzance (1815) then St Ives (1826) and finally Barnstaple (1892) and lasted almost until the end of the century and certainly beyond her 100th birthday. In 1875 she was bought by William and Edward Oldham of Padstow, hence her inclusion here. They sailed her until 1892 when she went to James Watts of Braunton.

**LIBERTY** ON 13843, built 1838 at Ilfracombe. Tons 47(N). 47.9  15.8  8.4 rebuilt at Newquay 1851 then tons 66(N) 52 gross. 59.8  16.7  8.9. LIBERTY was registered at Padstow throughout her long life; she was built as a smack, rebuilt as a schooner, and rigged down to a ketch in 1890. William Johns of Crantock was owner and master for her first quarter century and Henry Howe of Newquay managed her for her second. Albert J. Carter of Pentewan owned her briefly in 1883, then William Bate of Padstow until her register closed on 16th March 1905. According to one account, she was lost on the Irish coast, but the note on her register is 'Sold as a hulk at Swansea 1905'.

**LILE** ON 26529, built 1844 at Stonehouse, Plymouth, by Hocking. Tons 163(N) as built. Lengthened in 1860, after which 237 reg. 245 gross, 228 net in 1888. 179 net in 1896. 121.8  22.8  13.9 after lengthening. LILE was built as a schooner and registered at Plymouth, trading mainly to the Mediterranean. She was built by the Hocking family for the Hocking family, and largely captained by the Hocking family.

When she was lengthened she was converted to barque rig and in the early '70s passed to London owners who traded to South Africa.

It was in the '80s that she became Padstow owned, the owner in question being Robert Hoskins of Trewarrow, St Minver. By that time, despite major restoration work at London in 1874 and conversion to barkentine rig in 1880, she must have been showing her age. But she was still good enough for the timber trade and she went successively to Arthur Willyams of Truro, then W. C. Phillips of St Austell, and in 1901 to W. H. Shilston, who ran her for a final year. LILE remained on the Plymouth register throughout.

**LILY** ON 62687, built 1871 at Padstow by John Stribley Tons 70 gross. 73.0  21.3  9.5. Lengthened 1877 then tons 99 net 106 gross, 77 net later. 90.0  21.7  9.4. Built as a schooner, she was given a third mast on lengthening. LILY was built for the Harvey family of Padstow where she was registered, and they retained shares throughout, although William S. Allport bought 32 in 1901. Her masters included Hawke and R. Mitchell, and finally A. Moore.

On 18th October 1907 she was wrecked on the West Mouse, Anglesey, bound from Runcorn with coal for Pentewan. The wind was SSW force 6; her crew of four were all safe.

**LILY OF THE VALLEY.** A small vessel of this name was built by T. R. Avery of Boscastle in 1858. (R.C.G.) It was probably a temporary name for the ELLEN VAIR.

**LISBON PACKET** built 1807 at Padstow. Tons 82(O). No register survives for this brig but she appears in Lloyd's Register 1818-1825 owned by Morgan with R. Kellar as master and is known to have traded between Cork and Lisbon.

**LITTLE JANE** ON 19761, built 1858 at Porth near Newquay by Nicholas Lewarne and Albert E. Martyn. Tons 47 net. 60.2  18.2  7.5. This smack was registered at Padstow, owned initially by her builders with W. Alford and G. Pappin in command. In 1868 Plymouth became her port of registry and by 1892 she was ketch rigged for Lynmouth owners.

She was lost at Clovelly, 30th October 1910, owned by then in Watchet. The lifeboat ELINOR ROGET rescued her crew of three.

**LITTLE MINNIE** see MINNIE, ON 53004.
**LITTLE NELL** ON 48632 built 1864 at Brixham for Dewdney. Tons 132 net. 89.5 20.5 12.0. A Brixham registered schooner for the Newfoundland and Mediterranean trades. She was bought by Henry Buse of Padstow in 1878 but lost in 1880.
**LITTLE RACER** ON 29361, built 1862 at Padstow by Willmet. Tons 54 gross. 62.0 18.6 9.0. Lengthened 1865 then tons 73 gross. 75.7 19.2 9.0. Completed as a cutter rigged smack, but re-rigged as a schooner when lengthened, this Padstow registered vessel, like many others termed coaster, traded extensively to the Continent between Brest and the Baltic. She was owned by J. M. Fishley of Port Isaac who also captained her until his son W. Fishley took over.

LITTLE RACER foundered on 10th February 1884, 25 miles WNW of Lundy island bound from Plymouth with manure for Cork. The wind was SW force 9 and three of her crew of four were lost. It is not recorded how the fourth managed to survive.
**LITTLE REAPER** ON 45225, built 1863 at Falmouth by Lean. Tons 80 reg. 77.0 18.5 10.4. Lengthened 1868 then tons 100 net 108 gross. 95.6 19.8 9.7. Registered at Falmouth as a schooner, but a third mast was added after her lengthening. Her port of registry became Runcorn by 1880: from 1883 J. Sherlock of Newquay was master and a holder of shares, which leads to her inclusion in this list. She was a deep sea trader, especially in her early years, sailing regularly to Newfoundland and Portugal.

LITTLE REAPER was lost by collision off the Smalls on 1st March 1891 carrying pitwood from Bantry towards Newport, Monmouthshire.
**LIZZIE** ON 47038, see LIZZY
**LIZZIE** ON 53010, built 1867 at Padstow by Stribley & Co. Tons 55 gross. 60.4 19.1 8.5. Stribley retained shares in this cutter rigged Padstow smack; other locals involved over the years were E. Tabb, Nicholas Phillips of Bodieve, John Bate of Wadebridge and numerous others. She had a close call on 28th December 1900 in a WNW gale in Swansea Bay when her anchor kept dragging and her crew were rescued by Mumbles lifeboat, but she survived to be converted to a lighter in 1913 (note on register). Finally dismantled at Wadebridge about 1930, having long deteriorated. (Oliver Hill, who described her as a ketch).
**LIZZIE** ON 42560, built 1868 at Padstow by John Tredwen. Tons 153 gross. 97.9 22.9 12.1. A large schooner which was built for George Ward of Teignmouth and registered there. She traded to South America and was lost off Puerto Rico on 3rd November, 1876 (note on register).
**LIZZIE GRACE** ON 19758, built 1857 at Padstow by F. H. Thomas and restored that same year. Tons 69 gross. 75.8 18.4 7.6. A typical Padstow coasting schooner involving the Thomas, Riley, Bennett and Stribley families in ownership and navigation of the ship. May have been ketch rigged before the end of her life.

Supposed foundered about 9th December 1874 on passage Newport for Padstow with coal. Four crew lost (note on register).
**LIZZIE MALE** ON 62679, built 1870 at Padstow by Stribley. Tons 107 net 119 gross. 87.1 22.9 11.0. Another typical Padstow registered schooner built as may be assumed for the Male family (and others). J. Battershill commanded her in 1875. William Stribley bought 24 shares in 1876.

On 29th January 1877 she was flying distress signals, riding out a strong NW gale at anchor off Towan Head with a cargo from Newport for Fécamp. The Newquay lifeboat (Edwin Clemens coxswain) with difficulty rescued her crew of six.

LIZZIE MALE foundered that night.

LITTLE MINNIE riding out a storm.            *Private Collection*

**LIZZIE MARY** ON 69457, built 1874 at Cosheston, Milford Haven by Morgan & Howell. Tons 97 net 109 gross. 84.0 21.2 10.8. A schooner with an elliptical stern and a full lady figurehead built for W. C. Phillips of Padstow, her port of registry. Her masters were successively J. Burton, W. J. Bates and W. E. Haynes.

Not heard of since sailing on 8th March 1891 from Charlestown for Rouen with china clay and a crew of five.
**LIZZIE MAY** ON 17383, built 1857 at Padstow by F. H. Thomas. Tons 86 gross later 71 net. 74.5 19.8 10.1. Built for T. May of Port Isaac, this schooner was registered at Padstow. J. Casey became managing owner about 1880 and Francis Brewer in 1883. Finally in 1895 she joined the fleet of Charles Matthews.

In March 1864 she lost both masts off the South Stack and drove into Towyn Capel Bay. With two anchors out she dragged towards the shore and her crew escaped by ship's boat. But LIZZIE MAY survived against the odds.

Matthews appointed N. England to command her and he was aboard when on 21st March 1898 she was wrecked on the Yew Rock near The Dodman. She had left Par that day with china stone for Runcorn, and had evidently been set on the rocks by tidal streams, since the wind was recorded as East force 1. Her crew of four were all safe.
**LIZZY** ON 47038, built 1864 at Padstow by Willmett. Tons 97 net 106 gross. 86.9 21.5 10.3. A schooner registered at Padstow on completion and briefly owned by 'Willyams of St Columb', banker. In 1866 the port of registry became Hayle and she was owned by Thomas Henwood of St Agnes who was also her captain until R. Carter took over in 1889. In 1892 she was sold to William Hannan of Fowey but remained registered at Hayle.

Lost in Bristol Channel 11th February 1892, (note on register).
**LOFTUS** ON 11435, built 1852 at Mount Batten, Plymouth by William Routleff. Tons 48 net 52 gross. 56.3 19.1 7.7. This Plymouth registered smack was nevertheless owned by R. Avery, and T. Hicks was master. On 9th November 1862 she parted her moorings and drove ashore near Padstow, her crew being rescued by the Padstow lifeboat in heavy surf. Evidently she was salved because in 1863 Padstow became her port of registry and James Rowe of St Minver her principal owner. The following year her master Henry Daggua bought him out and owned all 64 shares.

Lost at sea March 1866 (note on register).

**LONDON** ON 15586, built 1825 at Gosport. Tons 136(O) (106(N). Lengthened 1856 then 97 net 114 gross. 79.1 22.1 11.4. This vessel was built as a smack and converted to schooner rig in the 1830s long before she was lengthened: she remained a schooner after lengthening.

She did not come to the Padstow registry until 1872 after John Stribley had bought her from Penzance owners in 1871. In 1878 J. Osborne senior bought her and that same year on the night 29th-30th March she foundered off St Ives bound from Falmouth for Runcorn with china clay. The wind was NE force 10, but her crew of five all survived.

**LONDON** ON 21697, built 1858 at Bideford by G. Cox. Tons 134 net 148 gross. 96.6 21.3 11.7. This schooner was registered at Plymouth but owned from about 1880 by the Steer family, and from 1885 by John Steer of Port Isaac.

*Lloyd's Register* for 1891-'2 is posted 'Missing since March 1991'.

**LOOK-OUT** ON 21330, built 1858 at Workington. Tons 197 Net 216 gross, 180 net later. 112.7 22.4 14.2. This vessel was built as a barque and registered at Workington, Liverpool and Bristol successively. In 1884 she came into the hands of W. B. Williams of Newquay, and her rig changed to brigantine. That was a very unusual change of rig which might be expected to accompany a major rebuilding, but none is recorded in the registers. M. T. Clemens was her master about then, followed by J. Williams.

Foundered near Boulmer, 29th November 1897, bound from Fowey with china clay for Dundee (*Lloyd's* records).

**LORD DEVON** ON 86467, built 1885 at Salcombe by T. Sanders. Tons 98 net 114 gross. 84.0 21.1 10.7. This Salcombe schooner joined W. S. Allport's fleet in 1906 and remained his until 1918 when she was sold to Frank B. Harvey also of Padstow. Her Padstow masters included J. Keat, G. Crocker, O. Jewel and Edwards.

She lasted until 1927 and was said to be Padstow's last schooner (although still registered at Salcombe).

**LORD PORCHESTER** ON 13140, built 1837 at Padstow by J. Tredwen. Tons 42(O) 28(N). 43.0 13.0 7.0. This sloop was built for O. Davey but he returned her to J. Tredwen who offered her for sale in January 1841 describing her as of 45 tons burthen. E. W. Jago bought her, and for a time based her at Dartmouth, but she was registered at Padstow throughout and subsequently owned by Richard Nicholls of Porth, Thomasin Pascoe (widow of Cuthbert) and Hugh Maunder. William Clemens and William Williams both captained her for the widow. Foundered in the Bristol Channel in 1858, two of her crew being picked up by Clovelly fishermen. (Register closed 1866).

**LOTA** ON 44173, built 1861 at Liverpool by Cato of wood but with partly iron beams. Tons 472 net and gross 447 under deck tonnage. 139.1 28.0 17.9 with poop 38.0 long.

A Liverpool barque which traded to India and South America, she was bought by John Stribley of Padstow and others about 1872, and T. J. Brown was appointed master. (The local Brown family often appear as masters but seldom as owners.)

By 1880 Dudfield of London owned her and she drops out of the lists by 1887.

**LOTTIE** ON 77410, built 1878 at Gannel Yard, Newquay, by T & J Clemens. Tons 98 net 113 gross, later 88 net. 87.8 22.9 10.9.

There were numerous local shareholders in this Padstow registered schooner. Managing owners successively were G. Hugoe, and then W.L. and T. Jenkin. In 1910 Edward Thomas became leading owner with W. S. Allport as manager. Her masters were successively W. H. Tonkin, R. Chapman and C. Thomas.

On 10th January 1917 LOTTIE had to be abandoned off Godrevy and was later driven on to the rocks near Portreath.

**LOTUS** ON 4544, built 1842 at Brixham. Tons 128(O) 112(N), 101 net 112 gross. 72.4 20.1 12.0. A deep narrow hulled schooner compared with most, she came to the Padstow register from Brixham in 1871 when Joseph Passingham Dunstan of St Columb and William Chegwidden of Newquay bought her and appointed W. Darke as captain.

Wrecked on Harry Furlong Rock 26th November 1873.

**LOUISA** built 1824 at Cardiff. Tons 46(O) 35(N). 44.4 14.2 11.8. A sloop rigged smack of Penzance registry before she came to Padstow in 1840 to be owned by Richards, then Avery, Hocking, J. Jenkin, Withell and others. William Couch as well as various members of the aforementioned families acted as master. She returned to the Penzance register in 1847 and was lost on Lundy 18th February 1850.

**LOUISA** ON 481, built 1853 on Prince Edward Island. Tons 156 net 171 gross. 83.1 23.6 13.0. A brig which traded from Liverpool to the West Indies until registered at Padstow in 1860 by Thomas Whetford of St Columb Major, who traded her from Plymouth to the Mediterranean with Popperwell in command. F. Moyse owned her after Whetford and in 1867 sold her to Cork owners. She disappeared from the lists soon afterwards.

**LOUISA** ON 21780, built 1860 at Topsham by William Row & Sons. Tons 54 net. 64.7 17.2 7.4. This sloop was owned for seven years by the family of her builders then sold in instalments to the Hutchings family and Thomas Deacon of Padstow. William and Thomas Hutchings and Robert Chapman were her masters. In 1885 she was sold to Captain John Haynes and he let in Mark Guy to be managing owner. Sold to Bideford in 1892. Wrecked at Bunmahon, Co. Waterford, 23.7.1895. Registered at Exeter throughout.

**LOUISA** ON 61354, built 1868 at Shippegan, New Brunswick by James May. Tons 129 net 138 gross. 88.5 20.8 12.1. A brigantine, registered at Miramichi then at Padstow in 1875 as owned by her master William M. Darke of Newquay. Later W. G. Clemens was her master.

On 11th July 1879 she was lost in the Waterway, Maassluis, bound for Rotterdam with coal from Methil. Her crew of six and a pilot were on board; one member of the crew was lost.

**LOUISA & RACHAEL** (or RACHEL) built 1828 at Bideford by Thomas Evans. Tons 33(O) 24(N). 42.4 14.1 7.3. This sloop was registered at Padstow, owned by Thomas Phillips who was her first master but who later appointed Billings (1835) and William Couch (1837). Wrecked entering Padstow 20th March 1841; crew saved. Loss confirmed by note on register.

**LOUISE** ON 9293, built 1848 at Padstow by Samuel J. Bennett & Bros (their first ship). Tons 99(N) 88 gross. 67.0 17.9 10.7. Registered at Padstow with B. Bennett as manager and J. Bennett as master, this small schooner entered the Black Sea trade soon after completion, sailing from Liverpool to Galatz. In 1852 she was owned by Thomas Whitfield the St Columb banker and re-registered in St Ives, in 1853 at Truro and finally in 1871 at Falmouth.

Lost off Margate Sands 22nd June 1883 (note on register).

**LOUISE** ON 22200, built 1859 at Padstow by J. Tredwen. Tons 52 net 58 gross. 56.5 17.5 8.9. Lengthened 1878, then 67 net 77 gross. 76.8 18.3 8.6. Built as a sloop rigged smack, but rigged as a ketch when lengthened. As a smack she was owned by John Tredwen, John Warne of Perranzabuloe, R. Stephens, then R. Davies. It was Daniel Lloyd of Devoran who had her lengthened; then in 1892 she went to William Hannan of Fowey. She had been registered at Padstow throughout and in 1897 returned there with H. A. Hawkey of Newquay as owner and Joseph Crocker in command.

On 29th November that year she was wrecked off Lowestoft carrying coal and one passenger from Swansea for Burnham Overy (Norfolk). The wind was NNW force 10, but all were saved.

**LOUISE** ON 69469, built 1877 at Gannel Yard, Newquay, by T & J Clemens. Tons 100 net 114 gross, 93 net later. 87.4 22.9 11.0. This Padstow registered schooner had a semi-elliptical stern and a three-quarter woman figurehead.

R. Chegwidden and R. J. Hockin of Newquay owned and captained her into the twentieth century with J. Sharrocks' help. Thomas Chidgey of Watchet took her through the Great War. In the late twenties James St Leger of Falmouth traded her without an engine. In the thirties Gueret and others of Cardiff owned her and she became a storage hulk at Penryn.

Her hull was used to form a breakwater at Falmouth in 1937.

**LOVE & UNITY**, tons 43. A Padstow brigantine of that name was for sale in November 1813. (Note in Hicks Colln, RIC). No register has survived. There was a LOVE & UNITY built at Brixham in 1790 and of 42 tons after lengthening in 1794.

**LUCRETIA** ON 21376, built 1858 at Padstow. Tons 45 gross. 56.2 17.7 7.9. A Padstow registered smack built for J. R. Rickard of Wadebridge who sold her to James Osborne of Little Petherick, who passed her to John Stribley of Padstow in 1869.

In October 1872 she went missing, presumed lost, in the Portland Race on passage from Newhaven to Runcorn in ballast. No traces of Capt. Holder and his crew of two were found.

**L'UNION** (French *chasse-marée*) see JOSEPHINE.

**LUTHA** ON 62281, built 1869 at Leith by Adamson. Tons 124 net 131 gross. 96.7 22.7 11.1. Although this brigantine was registered at Leith, the Tredwens of Padstow (in the name of Mrs C. L. Tredwen) owned her in the '80s, with N. Wilce and W. H. Pendray as masters.

LUTHA stranded half a mile south of Saltfleet on 6th March 1886 on passage from Dublin with artificial manure and one passenger for Scarborough, becoming a total wreck. No lives were lost.

**LYDIA** built 1791 at Bideford. Tons 38(O). 45.6 14.8 7.3. A sloop which was a constant trader from Boscastle to Bristol for many years, including 1797-1809 and 1815-1818. During those periods her masters included Oaks, Gould, Brown Boyd, Wivell (Withell ?) and later R. Hockin and Thomas Teague.

A surviving Padstow register for 1814 gives her owners as Rosevear (of Boscastle), William Sloggett, and John Mitchell (of Camelford). In 1828 her owners were Jenkin and Teague. She was lost on 1st May 1829 (note on register).

**LYDIA CARDELL** ON 69842, built 1873 at Appledore by Cook. Tons 225 net 235 gross. She was built as a three-masted barkentine, a yellow-metalled deepwaterman capable of taking 370 tons of cargo anywhere in the world. She was built for William Geake of St Columb but registered at Fowey with one of the Tadd family in command. Geake soon sold all but a few of his shares to numerous Cornish investors, but he remained for many years managing owner of a fine vessel which traded profitably to North America, the West Indies, the Baltic and the Mediterranean. The Tadds took her over and in 1903 she was bought by the Tyrrells of Arklow and converted into a three masted schooner. In 1919 Edward Stephens brought her back to her port of registry and refettled her as a barkentine, also fitting her with a 6 cylinder Thornycroft paraffin engine of 80 b.h.p. and for nine years she traded in European waters under Captain George Beynon.

On 13th March 1929 she was run down off Flamborough Head by the Sunderland tramp steamer BROADGARTH. The LYDIA CARDELL was bound for Sunderland with silver sand from Rouen. There were no casualties.

**M. D. SARAH** ON 28671, built 1860 at Padstow by John Tredwen. Tons 58 gross. 68.7 17.5 8.4. Registered at Fowey but described in *Lloyd's* as a Padstow coaster, this small schooner was first run by the Sarah family, then the Clarkes, but in 1865 she was bought by Thomas Northcott of St Columb. Lost on passage from Par towards St Valery, 12th March 1876.

**MAGGIE** ON 78213, built 1878 at Fraserburgh by Webster. Tons

LYDIA CARDELL, in her final phase as a barkentine.
*David Clement Collection*

The JUBILEE QUEEN and TRI STAR, the two stalwarts of the Padstow excursion business for many years. *Author's photos*

Plate 13

This lively painting of HELENA ANNA is by Tommy Morrissey of Padstow.

*Malcolm McCarthy Collection*

The MARY BARROW was apparently defensively armed when she was painted by Reuben Chappell.

*Private collection*

Plate 14

The barkentine MALPAS BELLE shows off her clipper bow and handsome sheer, but she was lucky to survive this stranding at Littlestone in 1909.                    *Edward Carpenter Collection*

99 net, 114 gross. 91.9 21.5 10.3. This schooner was registered at Fraserburgh even after John Ennor of Newquay bought her in 1884. She sailed for him, often with J. Pennaligan in command until she was lost on the Kentish Knock in 1900. (Verran).

**MAGNET** or **MAGNET PACKET** built 1825 at Bristol. Tons 79(O) 66(N). 60.3 17.8 10.1. A sloop rigged smack with a woman's bust, coming onto the Padstow register from Bristol in 1827 to be owned and run for fifteen years by Andrew and Benjamin Harvey. With her rig converted to schooner in 1832 (but without lengthening) she started trading to the Mediterranean. The Pax Britannica made all things possible.

Left Plymouth for Santander 12th September 1842 with Couch as master, and went missing (Select Committee on Shipwrecks 1843).

**MAGNET** ON 15611, built 1826 at Ipswich. Tons 73(O) 64(N) 58 gross. MAGNET was built as a smack and converted to schooner rig about 1850. In 1859 she was registered at Padstow, owner William Hancock of St Minver.

Lost at Porthcawl 29th October 1865.

**MAID OF MONA** ON 45475, built 1866 at Ayr by Fullerton. Tons 134 net 147 gross, 120 net later. 96.0 22.4 11.5. Mona's Isle being an old term for the Isle of Man, this schooner was built for Douglas owners and registered there. In the early '80s W. E. R. Hoskin of Calstock bought her and in due course shifted her register to Plymouth. There in 1897, Thomas Jacka of Newquay bought her and T. J. Clemens took command.

Unfortunately she was sunk in collision with a cross-Channel steamer in 1901.

**MALDON** built 1810 at Maldon. Tons 80(O). A large sloop which is assumed to have Padstow ownership, as in *Lloyd's Register* 1820 she is owned by Rawlins with H. Crocker as master, both almost exclusively Padstow names in shipping at that time. But no Padstow register has survived for this vessel.

She went to other owners about 1824 and ceased to be listed four years later.

**MALPAS BELLE** ON 63505, built 1872 at Malpas near Truro by Nicholas Scoble. Tons 180 net, 189 gross, 149 net later. 109.2 22.7 12.1. This Truro registered three masted barkentine made some

Her second stranding in 1922 on Seaton beach proved fatal.
*Private Collection*

famous voyages to South America for her first owner, S. E. Orchard of Truro. In the early '80s W. P. Phillips of Port Isaac became managing owner and she spent more time in home waters commanded by J. Coombes and then F. Nichols.

On 7th January 1909, the MALPAS BELLE was in collision with another vessel in the English Channel and had to be beached at Littlestone The crew got ashore at low water, but the master stood by the ship. Next morning at high water the ship was being raked by heavy seas and the master had to take refuge at the bowsprit end, from which precarious refuge he was rescued by the New Romney lifeboat. After the repair of extensive damage the ship became the property of John Mutton of Truro. She survived the First World War and lasted until 1922, by which time her registry had changed from Truro to Manchester and she was owned by the Anglo-French Coasting Co. Ltd. On 8th February 1922 she ran ashore on Seaton Beach in heavy weather, and became a total loss.

**MARAZION** built 1784 at Bursledon. Tons 70(O) later 65(O). 53.0 17.4 depth unknown. MARAZION was built for Cornish owners. In 1800 she was registered at St Ives, owned by Peter Giles of Egloskerry (which lies in Padstow's hinterland): in 1811 Peter May was her master. The St Ives port register described her as a brigantine: *Lloyd's Register* shows her as a brig — but did not recognise brigantine as a separate rig until 1835.

In 1815 *Lloyd's Register* gave A. Stevens as owner and S. May as master. The port register noted 'broken up' but gave no date. It cannot have been much after 1815.

**MARCHIONESS OF ABERCORN** built 1837 at Quebec. Tons 798(O) 875(N). 140.4 32.4 20.7. This three masted barque was registered at Glasgow soon after completion and at Londonderry in 1845. In February 1848 she was wrecked at Crantock beach, but salved by Richard Tredwen who bought and repaired her and registered her at Padstow. In August 1848 she sailed for Quebec with emigrants with E. Key as captain. The port register notes 'Lost Register Closed, Skibbereen 4th December 1849'.

**MARCO POLO** ON 76706, built 1877 at Grimsby by John Hadfield. Tons 78 net and gross. 71.6 20.4 10.8, later 60 net. This Grimsby ketch was bought and registered at Padstow in 1889 by John Worden of Padstow. In 1896 he sold her to William Bird of Guernsey, but she remained registered at Padstow.

On 9th November 1899 she was bringing a cargo of nuts from Riva de Cella in Spain for London when she was run down and sunk in Sea Reach by SS EIDER of Newcastle. Her crew of three survived.

**MARGAM** captured by His Majesty's Ships LA PENLETTE (Dunbar) and LIBERTY (Coad), this French brigantine, LES AMIS, was condemned in the High Court of Admiralty 10th April 1804 and made free 3rd July 1804. Tons 60(O). 53.8 16.6 8.7. She was renamed MARGAM and her earliest surviving register is Padstow 1811, owner John Tredwen. In 1825 her owners became George Balks of Padstow, John Taylor of London and Martin Hitchens of St Agnes. She was wrecked at St Minver February 1828.

**MARGARET** (*Lloyd's*), MARGARETT (port registers), MARGARETTA (Bude Canal records) built 1829 in Turnchapel Dockyard. Tons 23. 35.3 12.6 5.2. This small sloop was built for R. Pawley of Plymouth and came to Padstow in 1833, bought by J. Fairman of Launceston, with Valentine Richards and James Greenaway as masters. In 1837 she changed to Bideford registry, half owned by Michael Fish of Bude and half by Thomas Warmington of Welcome. She was a constant trader to Bude for many years, and when finally lost off Bude on 9th October 1853, Captain Michael Fish and his mate were rescued by the Bude lifeboat.

**MARGARET** ON 29837, built 1861 at Appledore by Cook. Tons 78 gross. 70.2 19.0 10.1. This Bideford polacre brigantine only joins the Padstow list because she was bought in 1873 or 1874 by T. Jenkin and others of Newquay. She traded mainly to Spain. MARGARET has been missing since 1878.

**MARGARET FRANCES** see LADY ACLAND.

**MARGARET HOBLEY** ON 55374, built 1868 at Pembroke Dock by J. D. Warlow. Tons 124 gross, later 119 gross and 82 net. 86.6 22.2 11.3. A schooner built for Thomas Hobley and registered at Carnarvon, then London in 1868. She was in the South American hide trade, sailing principally to Rio Grande do Sul. The Padstow connection came in 1913 when she was bought by Capt. James Andrew Clemens of Newquay. He sold her to W. A. Jenkins, Cardiff in 1920. In 1921 she was given her first engine, a 2 cylinder Widdop paraffin motor. Next year she was bought by William Quance of Appledore who remained her owner to the end. About 1930 she was re-engined with Svenska diesels and reduced to a three masted fore-and-aft rig. In 1940 she was chartered by the Navy to serve as a BBV (a balloon barrage vessel). After the war she was returned in a condition which did not justify repairs being carried out and she was left to rot near Appledore.

**MARGARET MURRAY** ON 89696, built 1885 by Grangemouth Dockyard Co. Tons 176 net 184 gross (as built), 155 net 195 gross (in 1924). 107.2 23.7 11.7. A steel three masted schooner registered at London, then in 1907 at Liverpool and finally in 1918 at Blyth. She was in the fleet of W. S. Allport of Padstow from 1911 to 1918

when she was sold to the Brito-France Shipping Co., was given a 2 cylinder paraffin motor, and was armed as a Q-ship as described elsewhere in the book.

In 1924 she was on passage from Blyth with coal for Dartmouth; she ran aground at Maasvlakte and was later refloated and towed to Maassluis and then sold to shipbreakers.

**MARGARITA** ON 23083, built 1835 at Blyth, lengthened 1853. Tons 184(O) 187(N). 81.0 23.0 15.2 as built. Tons 281 gross. 105.2 23.0 15.3 after lengthening. Her rig was changed from snow to barque on lengthening. She was built for London owners who traded to Spain, but in 1852 J & R Tredwen bought her and she was registered at Padstow. That same year she changed hands to William Williams and to John Tredwen, but perhaps the changes were connected with payment for her lengthening and re-rigging completed in 1853. Her Padstow masters were J. Richards, R. Easthope, T. Key and Thomas. Her managing owner was also named Thomas from 1854 onwards. Lost in the Gulf of Mexico 27th April 1860 (note on register).

**MARGARITTA & ESTHER** (port registers), MARGARITA & ESTHER, MARGARET & ESTHER (also found), built 1827 at Padstow by George Sloggett and registered there in 1828. Tons

MARGARET HOBLEY reduced to fore and aft rig in the 1930s, but still to play her part in the Second World War.

*David Clement Collection*

35(O) 26(N). 40.0 14.8 7.3. A sloop owned by P. A. Wilson and T. England, who were also her captains as were Christopher Kunze, Moskin and Cobbledick. In 1838 she was sold to Jersey owners, and registered there as a cutter.

**MARIA** built 1801 at Padstow and 'almost rebuilt' in 1815. Tons 71(O). A brig for which no Padstow register survives and which was owned in Plymouth, certainly from 1815 onwards.

Lost on Hoyle Bank in the Mersey on 30th November 1823 with a cargo of clay. Crew saved (*Lloyd's List*).

**MARIA** ON 19204, built 1824 at Salcombe by John Evans. Tons 59(O) 41(N). 59.2 reg. 50.1 17.1 8.7. A Padstow registered sloop with which the following families were associated: Abbott, Egloshayle, Parnell, Knight, Pettigrew, Guy, Avery, Hicks, Berry, Hoskin, Skinner and Fishley; many of them were Port Isaac men. In 1866 she was sold to Bideford and her last owner was William Blackmore of Fremlington.

Wrecked 20th October 1874 (*Mercantile Navy List* supplement).

**MARIA** ON 15509, built 1841 at Bideford by Thomas Evans Tons 32(N). 44.5 14.2 7.6. This smack was bought from Bideford in 1853 by William Hoskin and registered at Padstow.

MARIA was lost near Land's End on 19th May 1863 (note on register).

**MARIA.** A vessel of the name was noted in a report on the Bude breakwater in 1838, with James Metherall as master. In 1840 a MARIA was owned by John Sumers Hames of Bude. These references might be to MARIA ON 19204, or to a smaller unregistered vessel.

**MARIA** ON 18477, built 1857 at Padstow by J. Tredwen. Tons 81 gross 66 net later. 70.7 19.6 10.0. A schooner built for Isle of Man owners and registered at Douglas until 1890 when E. R. Tabb brought her back to Padstow to join Charles Allport's considerable fleet.

Tabb was her master when, on the 14th July 1897 she was sunk in collision with the Bideford ketch ANT between Lundy and Padstow; MARIA was bound from Runcorn for Wadebridge with coal and three passengers.

**MARIA** ON 49985, built 1865 at Hayle by Harvey. Tons 165 net 176 gross, 138 net later. 105.6 24.3 12.2. MARIA was built of wood but with some iron deck beams. She was rigged as a brigantine when newly built, but described as a schooner in *Lloyd's* at the turn of the century and certainly converted into a three masted barkentine by 1910. Although registered at Hayle she was built for Hoopers of Newquay and traded to the Mediterranean, captained by S. Harris and A. Veale. In 1894 she was sold to the May family of Port Isaac and registered at Fowey, perhaps so that William Kellow of Pentewan could manage her. Thomas May Jr was master for a time.

On 13th April 1917 MARIA was sunk by U-boat 25 miles S. by W. of Portland Bill on passage Glasgow and Fowey for Cherbourg with coal.

**MARIA LOUISA** ON 27276, built 1859 at Padstow by John Tredwen. Tons 42 registered. 54.8 16.4 8.1. This sloop rigged smack was given the temporary name FAWN for her launching (as noted on her *Lloyd's* survey report). She was then bought by public subscription for Captain John Casey, master mariner, who had been crippled in a wreck in 1859.

By 1866 she was owned by H. Buse of Padstow with John Massey in command.

On 22nd January 1868 she was lost with all hands on Treguin Rocks, Mullion Island, bound from Plymouth for Penzance with slates.

**MARIAN** ON 43572, built 1861 at Kingsbridge by William Date.

Tons 133 gross. 96.0 21.6 11.9. A yellow metalled clipper of a topsail schooner, with a square stern and female figurehead, she was owned by P. O. Hingston of Kingsbridge and others and registered at Dartmouth, trading to the Mediterranean.

Her Padstow registry was brief. She was bought by W. S. Allport on 28th August 1882. On 21st October 1882 she sailed from Shields with coal for Plymouth under Captain S. Worden with four others, and went missing.

**MARIAN** ON 77403, built 1877 at Barnstaple by Westacott. Tons 97 net 112 gross, 84 net later. 90.2 21.8 10.1. This schooner was registered at Padstow throughout her life despite being built and owned elsewhere! She was owned successively in Bickington (Devon), Watchet, then South Shields in the Great War, Hull immediately after, and finally in Kilkeel. She foundered on 13th April 1925 (note on register).

**MARIE** built 1879 at Elsfleth by G. Wempe. Tons 309 in 1890. This German brig was sold to Danish owners about 1893 and renamed MARIE SOPHIE. ON 108011. Her Danish owners registered her at Ribe but in 1898 she was bought by R. J. Hockin of Newquay and registered at Falmouth, with J. Tyrrell as master. By 1900 she had been re-rigged as a barkentine and was trading to Canada. The Tyrrells of Arklow had shares, but according to *Lloyd's*, R. J. Hocking remained manager. Tons 197 net, 234 gross. 126.7 26.2 12.8 (measurements in 1901)

On 16th October 1902 when she was bound from Dublin for Garston with timber, she ran aground in the Crosby Channel and became a total loss.

**MARINA** ON 5708, built 1838 at Padstow by Thomas Carter. Tons 51(O) 38(N) 37 gross. On completion this small schooner was registered at Padstow as owned and commanded by her builder; but C.Found soon took his place followed by R. Cleave in 1843, then T. Seacombe of Stratton that same year. In 1856 her port of registry became Plymouth, but she was back in 1858 owned by John Brewer of Rock (who died in 1860) followed by Joshua Profitt of St Minver.

Lost 17th April 1869 (note on register).

**MARSHALL** ON 19212, built 1837 at Padstow by John Tredwen, and rebuilt at Newquay 1852. Tons 93(O) 78(N), 67 net. 59.8 17.0 10.0. A typical Padstow coasting schooner, owned by the Marshall and Hicks families for 48 years, carrying endless cargoes of coal,

MARIA entering Bay of Naples 1871. A fine copper-sheathed brigantine 105' x 24' x 12' Reg. ton 175. Built by Harvey & Co. Hayle, 1865 for J. & J. Hooper, Newquay. Christened at launching by Maria Hooper.
*Newquay Old Cornwall Society*

china clay and other local materials. Broken up at Newquay and register closed 21st October 1886.

**MARY.** The earliest Padstow ship known by name was MARY (in 1377) and the name remained so popular that it is often difficult or impossible to tell one MARY from another.

**MARY** ex LA MARIE FRANCOISE (q.v.) French prize built in France and condemned 13th July 1800. Tons 53(O) 44(N). 49.5 16.3 9.2. Her oldest surviving Padstow register is dated 1814 giving Rosevear and Sloggett of Boscastle as owners and Richard Gould as master. This register has her rigged as a brigantine, but she is later variously described as schooner, brig and brigantine. Sleeman (of Newquay), Gould, Edward Buse and Francis Couch all appear as owners or masters, with John Tredwen periodically taking shares, possibly as payment for repairs. Broken up 1851.

**MARY.** A constant trader of this name serving Padstow, and Boscastle from Bristol is recorded in years between 1797 and 1809 with masters named Knight, Brokenshaw, Barratt and Pollard — all suggesting a Padstow register which has not survived.

A 40 ton sloop named MARY owned by R. Baker of Padstow, with A. Baker as master, a French prize, drove ashore at Newquay, Cardiganshire on 21st April 1815 in a severe gale and was lost (*Lloyd's List* 25th April 1815).

**MARY** built 1813 at Bude by William Barrow (*Lloyd's Register* has varying building details). Tons 76(O) later 86(O), 83(N). 59.5 17.9 9.8. This brig was registered at Padstow in 1817 (perhaps an earlier register is missing) owned by Richard Burdon Bray of Bude with William Curtis his master.

In 1825 registration was taken to St Ives, and at some stage she became schooner rigged. The St Ives register ends with the note 'Lost off French coast 1834'. *Lloyd's List* reported 'The MARY, Harvey mr. St Ives for Ancona, foundered off the Raz. Crew picked up by the RENARD of Bordeaux and landed at Brest'. The report was dated 19th February 1834.

**MARY** built 1815 at Grand Rustico, Prince Edward Island. Tons 68(O). 53.8 17.8 9.3. This small schooner had a varied career, both coasting and trading to Canada. She was registered at Exeter in 1832 and Fowey in 1834 and in 1835 Thomas Broad, merchant of St Columb Major owned thirty-two shares, and Thomas Carter and Thomas Richards were her masters. Broken up 16th March 1838 (note on Fowey register).

**MARY** built 1819 at Chepstow by Purchass & Tredwen. Tons 112(O). 65.9 19.9 11.1. A Padstow brig owned by Norway and others, with E. and A. Parnall as masters and by 1829, owners. She traded from Liverpool to Gibraltar, and from Bristol to the Mediterranean. In 1830 she was sold to London owners and although she appears in *Lloyd's Register* until 1838, little more is known.

**MARY** ON 15312 built 1829 at Padstow by J. Tredwen. Tons 37(O) 24(N) 26 gross. 42.8 14.5 7.3 A Padstow registered sloop owned by her captain, Southwood, which traded to Bude under him and after 1833 under Richard Veal who shared ownership with Davy.

In 1838 William Broad owned her, and in 1842 Lawrence Harwood of Stratton. Her port of registry became Barnstaple in 1846, and she was totally wrecked at Minehead on 25th October 1858.

**MARY** ON 13836, built 1833 at Padstow by John Brewer. Tons 86(O) 64(N) 64 gross. 57.2 18.9 9.8. John Brewer himself owned and commanded this Padstow registered sloop in the Bristol Channel trades and owned her until he died about 1860. Then Cecilia Brewer, whom it is presumed was his widow, took over. Masters included W. Mably, Horswell, Richards and E. Jermyn. Wrecked at Barry 10th October 1873 (note on register), by which time she was schooner rigged.

**MARY** built 1834 at Padstow by John Tredwen. The *Royal Cornwall Gazette* reported that 'A 100-ton burthen schooner named MARY was launched on Saturday 3rd November 1834 from Mr Tredwen's yard'. It is probable that MARY was a temporary name as no later reference has been found, in which case she might have been completed as the MARY ANN ON 22374 in 1835.

**MARY** built 1840 at Barnstaple by John Westacott. Tons 51(O) 38(N). 45.1 14.5 8.0. A smack registered at Padstow on completion as owned by Langford and captained by Phillips. She was transferred to Plymouth registry in 1853.

**MARY** ON 9481, built 1854 at Padstow by John Tredwen. Tons 113 net 137 gross, later 86 net. 77.0 17.7 depth uncertain. This schooner was registered at Fowey, and owned by the Trestrail family of Looe for about 30 years. Lost near Land's End, 26th October 1881 (note on register).

**MARY** ON 69883, built 1873 at Garmouth by Geddie. Tons 100 net 108 gross. 85.8 21.5 10.4. This schooner was bought by William C. Phillips of Port Isaac and her registry was changed from Fraserburgh to Padstow in 1882. Her Padstow masters were J. Rosevear, J. Remick and J. A. Phillips.

On the 10th July 1888 she was carrying china clay from Charlestown for Rouen, but she was wrecked near Havre in a NW gale. Her crew of five were landed at Honfleur by the Havre lifeboat (note on register).

**MARY** ON 76745, built 1877 at Ardrossan by Barclay. Tons 100 net 122 gross. 89.1 21.4 10.6. Although Glasgow remained this schooner's port of registry throughout her life of 40 odd years, she was owned by Samuel Yeo of Tywardreath by 1890 and by Henry Lander of Wadebridge by 1910. He managed her through the Great War and sold her to James Crebbin of Milford Haven. She was no longer listed in 1923.

**MARY & ELIZABETH** ON 19221, built 1834 at Penzance by John Matthews. Tons 42(O) 32(N). 41.0 13.7 7.9. This sloop rigged smack came to the Padstow register in 1855, owned by W. C. Martyn with Richard Trebilcock as master. In 1862 Brown of Bude became owner and master. On 14th November that year, bringing coal from Newport, she was dismasted in Bude Bay, and wrecked near Millook. Her crew were saved by lifeboat.

**MARY & HELENA** see MARYS & HELENA.

**MARY ANN** built 1803 at Plymouth. Tons 56(O). 51.5 16.8 8.3. This vessel was described variously as brig and brigantine rigged. She was owned by Rawlings of Padstow by 1809 who sold her to William Knight in 1821. Her Padstow masters included Harding, Horswell, Knight and Hetherington. Padstow ceased to be her port of registry in 1826 when she was sold to Richard Banfield of St Ives. She was lost in 1829.

**MARY ANN** ex LA JEANNE, built in France. Tons 108(O) 68.7. 19.3 9.7. This brigantine was taken by HMS HAZARD and made free at London 15th November 1803. In 1803 she was briefly registered at Plymouth and subsequently at Fowey, her owners including Thomas Shepheard of Stratton, gent. That entitles her to be included in this list.

Retaken by the French (register note; no date).

**MARY ANN** built 1810 at Fowey. 63(O) lengthened and repaired 1827, whereupon tons 76(O). 60.5 17.3 9.4. Originally she worked out of Fowey as a smack, but in 1827, owned by the Daniell family and registered at St Ives, she was lengthened and rigged as a schooner. In 1831 she was bought by Richard Avery of Boscastle.

One MARY ANN was lost in Perran Bay 29th November 1833. The St Ives register of Avery's ship ends 'Lost per B.O.68 3rd May 1834'.

MARY ANN A sloop of the name was wrecked at Boscastle on 24th February 1823. (*Lloyd's List* 4th March 1823)

MARY ANN ON 19229, built 1827 at Cardiff. Tons 58(O) 44(N). 48.8  16.9  8.7. The transfer of this sloop from Cardiff to Padstow registry occurred dramatically on 20th October 1834 when she ran onto the Gannel rocks and was subsequently salved by Richard Tredwen and taken to Padstow for repairs. Richard Carter became her master and John Tredwen managing owner. Then in 1836 Hitchens of St Agnes registered her at St Ives, and in 1846 Richard Peters brought her back to Padstow. In 1848 Varcoe and Kellow took her to Fowey, and in 1852 Joe Coad and W. Chalk of Port Isaac owned her. Finally by 1858 John Harvey of Plymouth was owner. She foundered in calm weather off Dungeness on 31st August 1861.

MARY ANN or ANNE ON 22374, built 1835 at Padstow by J. Tredwen. Tons 100(O) 81(N). 62.5  19.4  10.8. This schooner was built for J. Paddon of Truro, and her first voyages were from Padstow to New York. *Lloyd's Register* 1836 had her posted 'LOST', but she was registered 'de novo' at Truro and resumed work as a coaster. In 1840 she was lengthened, her tonnage becoming 89(N). 67.6  17.7  10.3. In 1853 her port of registry became Llanelly, and she drops out of the lists in 1860.

MARY ANN ON 79954, built 1879 at Kingston, Moray by A. Spence. Tons 164 gross and net. 138 under deck. 99.0 23.7 12.2. This brigantine's port of registry changed from Banff to Fowey in 1886, and she is included in this list because T. J. Hicks of Newquay was her master from 1910 onwards, with Fred Harris of Crantock and Par as managing owner.

On 19th June 1917 she was attacked by a German submarine 20 miles NW by W of the Hanois lighthouse whilst on passage St Brieuc for Swansea with pitwood. Her timber cargo kept her afloat and she was towed into St Peter Port Harbour, Guernsey. There she was bought by F. J. Hubert and registered in Guernsey, but she did not outlast the war.

MARY ANNIE ON 92211, built 1893 at Portmadoc by D. Jones who continued to build beautiful three masted schooners like MARY ANNIE until 1910. Tons 130 net 154 gross. 96.4 23.4 11.9. She was registered at Carnarvon but bought by H. P. Thomas of Newquay in late 1916, and he put J. Pappin in command. His ownership was brief for she was sunk by U-boat bombs on 25th March 1917 SSW of Beachy Head carrying coal from Glasgow for Treport.

MARY BARROW ON 93424, built 1891 at Falmouth by W. H. Lean. Tons 135 net 163 gross, net tonnages were reduced by engine space later. 103.0 24.0. 10.8. This famous three masted schooner was 'launched for the Rio Grande trade', presumably in hides and suchlike. A barkentine rig would have been more suitable, but in British ships that rig required the master to have a full square rig certificate which many otherwise competent master mariners did not possess. That was one reason why the barkentine rig was so much less popular in Britain than in continental Europe.

So much has been written about the MARY BARROW that only the basic outline is given here. She was built for J. Barrow and registered at Barrow, but W. H. Lean is given as her owner in the *Mercantile Navy List* for all her early years: perhaps he had a lien on her!

On 7th January 1908 she stranded on Porthminster beach, but got off and was given a slightly reduced rig at Lean's yard.

In 1912 H. P. Thomas of Newquay became owner and J. Henwood master. They guided her through the Great War and in 1919 T. J. Clemens took over as master.

The Brigantine MARY ANN (ON 79954) with everything set except the fore staysail. The main staysail is on a boom which reduces the pully-hauly work, and the boom is handy for working cargo.
*Newquay Old Cornwall Society*

In 1932 Thomas sold her to Charles P. Couch of Pentewan and she was given her first engine, 60 b.h.p., and registered at Truro. A second engine was added in 1936 so her correct designation became an auxiliary twin screw three masted schooner, with one paraffin and one oil engine, total 104 b.h.p.

On 28th September 1938 she was wrecked on the Calf of Man, on passage from Ayr with coal for Truro.

MARY COAD ON 69456, built 1874 at Padstow by Cowl. Tons 99 net 110 gross. 85.9  22.9  10.9. A schooner with Cowl's usual elliptical stern, registered at Padstow owned by Joseph G. Coad of Port Isaac.

MARY COAD sank following a collision in Haisbro Roads. Register closed 4th March 1885.

MARY ELIZA ON 47033, built 1863 at Padstow by J. Tredwen. Tons 95 net 104 gross. 82.7 21.2 10.5. This schooner was registered at Padstow first in John Tredwen's name, but soon jointly with John Cory and from 1970 on, exclusively in the name of John Cory & Sons Ltd, Cardiff. J. Tyacke was master early on.

Lost in collision with the barque SALISBURY of New Brunswick off Brixey (?), 5th June 1880 (note on register).

MARY ELIZABETH see MARY & ELIZABETH

MARY JAMES ON 29736, built 1862 at Padstow by J. Tredwen. Tons 154 net 163 gross, 144 under deck and 132 net later. 99.2 23.0 12.0. A schooner with square stern and female figurehead, she was known as the Sabbath Breaker because she stuck on the ways, then launched herself the following Sunday. Her early trade was from Padstow to South America (where Cornish miners and mining interests were well established) but later her routine voyage was from Levant mine to Swansea with copper ore and back to Cornwall with coal.

She was registered at Penzance throughout. In March 1898 she had a close call off Penzance when her moorings broke and she was driven across Mounts Bay in a strong SW wind and just brought up before going ashore. She was finally lost on 18th November 1901 off Sennen, when a SSW gale drove her onto the Brissons, taking copper ore and road stone from Newlyn to Swansea.

**MARY JANE** ON 19263, built 1840 at Padstow. Tons 70(O) 53(N) 53 gross. 52.1 15.7 9.0. A Padstow schooner owned by the Knight family for 15 years and then by R. Brewer, and finally Thomas Hambly Harvey. Lost 22nd November 1868 near Clay Castle, Youghal (note on register).

**MARY JANE** ON 17382, built 1856 at Padstow by S. T Bennett. Tons 64 gross. 69.7 18.4 8.4. This small schooner was built for J. Male and others of Padstow. Her Padstow register was closed on 16th May 1859 with the note 'Wrecked at Leith', but the *Mercantile Navy List* continues to quote Padstow as her port of registry and Male as her owner. Meanwhile *Lloyd's* reinstates her as a Leith schooner owned by Innes and others, and in 1875 by R. Smith. The *Mercantile Navy List* then appears to catch up, and carries an identical entry of Leith and R. Smith until 1905!

**MARY JOSEPHINE** ON 19227, built 1842 at Wadebridge. Tons 50(O) 40(N). 46.3 14.2 6.1 lengthened 1850 and then tons 61(N), later 52 net. 61.4 16.7 7.0. A Padstow registered schooner with a woman's bust added in 1842, and the same at the stern in 1850! She was owned by the Wadebridge merchant E. Norway with John Dark, Edward Parnall and W. Hicks as masters until 1864, when ownership passed to William Jennings and about 1880 to John Martin. Willcocks was master in 1869 and Pollard in the 1880s. In 1883 she was nearly wrecked in classic fashion on the Doom Bar; on 1st February she lost her wind and anchored in the surf; as the tide ebbed her situation became more and more desperate, and the crew were taken off; but the anchors held and she survived, with some damage.

She was sunk in collision with SS ACKWORTH of West Hartlepool on 21st September 1894 (note on register).

**MARY KELLOW** ON 28675, built 1862 at Padstow by Willmett. Tons 75 gross. 77.0 19.8 10.1. This schooner was built for John Kellow of Pentewan and registered at Fowey. R. Mably was her captain for many years: and he left a widow and two children when she sailed from the Tyne in December 1891 for Teignmouth and went missing.

**MARY KITTY** built 1819 at Plymouth and believed lengthened 1838 at Padstow. Tons 85(O) 74(N) after lengthening. This schooner is included here because she is mentioned in the Hicks lists of Padstow ships and described in *Lloyd's Register* 1838-1842 as a Padstow coaster, so Padstow was her survey port at that time. Although she was registered at St Ives, H. Richards was her owner and master, and it is probable that he was a Padstow man.

**MARY MARIA** ON 27674, built 1860 at Teignmouth by Mansfield. Tons 58 net 63 gross. 66.9 17.8 9.0. A yawl or dandy registered at Teignmouth until the Lobb family of Port Isaac, who owned her from 1880 onwards, registered her at Padstow in 1889. They sold her to John Curtis of Plymouth in 1905 and she was broken up there in 1907.

Padstow register closed 9th November 1907.

**MARY PEERS** ON 67965, built 1875 at Gannel Yard, Newquay by T & J Clemens. Tons 132 net 144 gross, later 111 net, 97 net with motor. 94.8 23.5 12.0. This three masted schooner was built for John Peers of Connah's Quay, and registered at Chester. Her first master was Henry Charles Carter, and the Carter family of Newquay, which married into the Peers family and already knew the Clemens family, completed the triangle. The Carter family retained an interest in the MARY PEERS through various partnerships in Connah's Quay and in Fowey, and in 1921 she was

fitted with a 22 h.p. motor and registered at Fowey, owned by Toyne, Carter & Co. The engine room reduced her net tonnage to 97, giving her an additional advantage at ports with compulsory pilotage for vessels of over 100 tons.

But on 7th December 1923 she stranded and was lost 1½ miles from Portwrinkle, on passage from Torquay in ballast for Fowey. Her crew was saved by breeches buoy from the shore.

A detailed history of this vessel is given in *Maritime South West* No.6 in an article by Paul Parry.

**MARY PHILLIPS** ON 47036, built 1864 at Padstow by James Willmett at the Dennis Cove yard. Tons 100 net, 116 gross. 86.6 21.6 11.1. Registered at Padstow throughout her life, this schooner had numerous Westcountry share-holders, the managing owners being Seymour of St Agnes, and from 1880, W. Endean of Falmouth. She foundered in the River Seine on 10th October 1884 after colliding with an anchored steamship whilst in tow (note on register).

**MARY SELINA**. A vessel of this name was reported trading in the Gannel and at Porth, 1837. There is also memory of one being wrecked on Goose Rock, East Pentire, Newquay.

**MARY SEYMOUR** ON 47040, built 1865 at Padstow by J. Tredwen. Tons 116 net 149 gross. 97.0 23.2 11.6. This fine schooner, like the MARY PHILLIPS, was registered at Padstow but came under the management of Seymour of St Agnes who had her yellow-metalled and put her into the Spanish trades. Joel Phillips, also of St Agnes, but with strong Padstow connections, managed her 1870-1875, then J. Hawke Jr of Port Isaac, until she was sold away to Portsmouth owners and registry in 1887.

But that was not the last of her Padstow associations for by 1910 she was owned by Benjamin M. Harvey of Padstow, her last owner. On 10th September 1917 she was sunk by gunfire from a German U-boat 7 miles NNE of Pendeen lighthouse, sailing from Ellesmere Port with coal for Cherbourg. Her crew survived.

**MARY SIMMONS** ON 18462, built 1860 at Padstow by J. Tredwen. Tons 110 gross. 82.8 20.5 10.6. A schooner registered at Truro and owned by Michell and others, with J. Donald as master. Lost by collision May 1869 (note on register).

**MARY STEPHENS** ON 5747, built 1839 at Port Isaac by Henry Sandry. Tons 50(O) 35(N) 38 net. 42.6 14.7 8.2. A Padstow sloop throughout, she was built for J. Stephens of Trelights, who in the early 1870s sold her to Warwick Richard Guy of Port Isaac. Over the years her masters included Mitchell, Skinner, James Strout Skinner and R. Mitchell.

Wrecked near North Tail on the Bideford Bar 8th March 1882 on passage Barnstaple for Newport in ballast. Crew and pilot saved.

**MARY WATERS** ON 69464, built 1875 at Padstow by C. Rawle. Tons 100 net 116 gross, later 89 net. 85.0 22.2 11.0. This schooner had an elliptical stern and was registered at Padstow, owned by Joseph Waters of Port Isaac. J. Daniel of St Ives bought her about 1910 and John Renouf of Jersey about 1918, but Padstow remained her port of registry until changed to Jersey in 1920. On 3rd October 1923 Tenby lifeboat rescued her crew of five as she dragged towards rocks, but she was saved the following day.

On 13th April 1925, the vessel stranded at Ardrossan and became a total loss, sailing there from Par with china clay. Crew safe.

**MARY WIGHTON** ON 22684, built 1859 at Dundee by Tay Shipbuilding Co. Tons 100 net 119 gross. 85.4 20.5 10.9. This three masted schooner was registered at Dundee and then Weymouth, but by 1883 was owned by John Bunt of Newquay who registered her at Padstow in 1889. Her register closed 22nd October 1896 with the note that she was to be hulked.

**MARYS & HELENA**, MARY & HELENA ON 22998, built 1826 at Padstow by J. Tredwen. Tons 68(O) 47(N) 47 gross. 51.4 17.8 8.9. This Padstow sloop was built for the Knight family and traded to the Mediterranean, including Smyrna. By 1840 she was owned by E. Martin and was a coaster. R. Moyses, J. Osborne and T. Martin took command.

Lost at Gannel 1st July 1863 (note on register).

**MAYFLOWER.** In 1791 (and doubtless in other years), a sloop of this name with Robert Moyse of Bude as master was a constant trader to Bude. Reported 1805. No register has survived.

**MAYFLOWER** ON 53164, built 1866 at Looe by Pengelly. Tons 99 net 112 gross. 90.7 21.3 10.8. A schooner registered at Fowey but bought in 1881 by N. N. Lewarne of Porth, near Newquay, who had E. May and T. H. Bennett as masters. Lost by stranding in Menai Straits, 3rd December 1885 (note on register).

**MEDORA** ON 18331, built 1847 at Padstow by Thomas Carter. Tons 37(N) 36 gross. 49.3 13.3 7.6. A small schooner registered at Padstow, owned by T. Carter with H. Carter as master. In 1858 she passed to Jennifer Carter, Widow, and was sold to Bridgwater in 1859. Lost in the late 1860s.

**MERMAID** built 1789 at Dartmouth. Tons 112(O). A brig owned by Prideaux, with T. Floud as master, is listed in *Lloyd's Register* in 1790, trading to Newfoundland, and is included here because of the owner's name. No register has been found.

**META** ON 68284, built 1874 at Truro by Dyer. Tons 79 net 85 gross. 79.2 19.7 9.8. META was a schooner registered at Truro, owned by Theophilus Coad. J. Estlick was another share-holder. In 1875, Trebilcock of Newquay had shares and was master. On 14th October, 1875, META was wrecked at Great Yarmouth.

**MILDRED** ON 69462, built 1875 at Plymouth by Banks. Tons 100 net 114 gross. 87.3 22.2 11.0. A schooner with elliptical stern and figurehead. MILDRED was built for W. C. Phillips, then of Port Isaac. Her masters included W. Phillips, J. Vickery, H. Cohring and J. Jenkin.

She was wrecked at Anvil Point on 28th April 1886 following collision with SS EL DORADO of London. One of her crew of five was lost. She was on passage from Liverpool with rock salt for Harlingen.

**MILDRED** ON 84980, built 1889 at Padstow by C. Rawle. Tons 189 net 207 gross. A three masted schooner with square stern and female figurehead, MILDRED was the last schooner and the last sailing vessel of any size to be built at Padstow. Like the previous MILDRED she was built for W. C. Phillips who, by 1889, had moved his headquarters to St Austell; she was registered at Padstow but her masters were not Padstow men.

On 10th May 1907 she lost two of her crew of six when her decks were swept by seas 18 miles SW of the Smalls lighthouse, Pembrokeshire, when she was sailing from Runcorn to Truro with coal. The wind was SSW force 9.

On 7th April 1912 she was wrecked at Gurnards Head on passage Swansea for London with basic slag.

**MILICENT MARY.** A cutter reported built in 1876 (Hicks Colln. RIC). She may have been an unregistered fishing vessel.

**MILLICENT** ON 19231, built 1842 at Padstow by John Tredwen. Tons 52(O) 36(N). 46.2 14.4 7.7. She was built as a sloop, but lengthened about 1867 and rigged as a ketch, then 51 net tons. 64.8 16.9 10.2.

MILLICENT was registered at Padstow. Her managing owners were successively Carveth, James, John Cory, G. Tabb and Henry Tabb, all of whom also acted as her masters, as did Couch, Pinch and T. Hoskin who was captain when she was lost.

On 1st April 1897 she was wrecked on Lundy Island, sailing from Newport, Monmouthshire, with coal for Padstow. Her crew of three survived. Wind ENE force 7.

**MINNIE** ON 53004, built 1866 at Padstow by W. F. Willmett. Tons 87 net 98 gross. 82.0 21.2 10.2. A schooner with square stern and eagle figurehead, she was registered at Padstow, owned by Thomas Jenkin of Newquay and then by Mrs Caroline Jenkin. She was a coaster.

On 11th January 1890 she ran ashore on Kimmeridge Ledges, Dorset, on passage from Portland with scrap iron for Stockton. John Stephens of Fowey bought the wreck and she was rebuilt and renamed LITTLE MINNIE to join his fleet of 'Little' ships. A full female figurehead replaced her eagle and in 1891 she went onto the Fowey register. Joseph Hancock and Charles Jago were her masters trading to Newfoundland.

In January 1897 she was caught in the ice off Labrador and on 23rd January wrecked on Renews Island. Captain Jago was drowned, but the rest of the crew escaped over the ice.

**MIRANDA** ON 62095, built 1870 at Arbroath by Arbroath Shipbuilding Co. Tons 160 gross (1880), 125 net 156 gross (1912). 92.6 22.4 12.1. This Arbroath registered schooner was bought by J. A, Clemens of Newquay in 1902 and sailed with T. J. Clemens and J. Cundy as masters.

On 19th April 1914 she was lost by collision in the Crosby Channel bound from Falmouth for Westonpoint.

**MIRRE** ON 4018, built 1842 at Bude by Robert Stapleton. Tons 26(N) 23 gross. 39.0 13.4 6.2. This sloop was registered at Bideford on completion, owned by Thomas E. Stribling (sic) of Barnstaple. In 1848 Padstow became her port of registry and John Hockin her owner. She was for many years a constant Bude trader. In 1861 John Henry Hooper of Bude owned her and registered her at Bideford (of which Bude had become an outport in 1850). J. B. Cook, Bate, and William Pickard were all masters of her at various times. In 1881 she was sold to Jabez Brown, Boscastle merchant, in 1885 to John E. Stribley of Barnstaple, and in 1897 to Thomas Hayne Fishwick of Appledore. She became a gravel barge at Barnstaple and her register closed 10th July 1903.

**MODEL** ON 11445 built 1840 at Polruan by Nicholas Butson. Tons 60(N) 59 gross 41 net. This sloop was built for the great Cornish industrialist Joseph Treffry of Fowey. She may lack the strict requirements to be included in this list as she was registered at Fowey and not owned substantially by a resident of Padstow or outports. John Hooper of Bude owned her after selling MIRRE, but Bude was by then no longer an outport of Padstow. But the people of Newquay considered her a Newquay ship and indeed she lifted the first 30 ton cargo of lead ore brought from East Wheal Rose Mine to Newquay on Treffry's new railway in 1849, and she went on to trade from Newquay for many years. She was converted into a ketch and owned in Appledore into the twentieth century. Stranded in Barnstaple Bay 13th March 1911, a total loss.

**MOLLY B.** ON 128521, built 1906 at Padstow. A five-ton pilot cutter built for Charles E. Bennett of Barry Island and registered at Cardiff. She is the last vessel built at Padstow (or any of the outports) to be included in this list of sailing ships. Foundered 17th February 1914, seeking from Barry.

**MONARCH** built 1833 at Padstow by Thomas Carter. Tons 81(O). 56.0 18.5 9.8. A sloop registered at Padstow, owned by Avery and John Martyn, the latter being master. Missing since leaving Padstow for Glasgow on 4th November 1834.

**MORFA MAWR** ON 18463, built 1860 at Padstow by Tredwen. Tons 113 gross. 83.7 21.0 10.7. A schooner registered at Truro,

Coal being unloaded from the MODEL.
*Newquay Old Cornwall Society*

owned by Sampson of Devoran and commanded by Capt. Mitchell. Lost by collision off the Scilly Islands, December 1867.

**MORNING STAR** ON 19270, built 1855 at Padstow by John Cowl, foreman shipbuilder to F. H. Thomas, entrepreneur. Tons 480 gross. 114.4 28.4 18.7. A full rigged ship with female figurehead and elliptical stern. She was completed and registered at Padstow in 1856 with Thomas as managing owner, but with 64 shares widely distributed in Padstow, St Issey, Bodmin, St Teath, St Tudy, Camborne, Truro, Rock and Manchester. She was rigged as a barque in 1860 to reduce the number of crew required. She traded from London to India, from Newport to Australia, from Liverpool to the West Indies and so on. Her masters were T. Parnall and R. Key two of Padstow's deep sea captains.

MORNING STAR was abandoned 200 miles west of Scilly on 14th November 1870 (note on register).

**MORNING STAR** ON 70529, built 1878 at Kingston, Elgin by John Duncan. Tons 100 net 117 gross. 88.6 21.7 10.4. In 1890 this schooner was transferred from the Wick to the Padstow register, being owned by Aaron Sloggett who captained her until J. Hellyar took over in 1904, followed by H. J. Purchis in 1911. In 1917 she

was sold to Bertie Corney of Wrafton and registered at Barnstaple. Captain George Welch had owned her for only a few months when, on 11th September 1923, she foundered off Porlock bound from Llanelly for Ballincurra with a cargo of steel bars.

**MOUNTBLAIRY** ON 69891, built 1874 at Kingston, Elgin by Geddie. Tons 138 net 146 gross, later 119 net. 95.1 22.3 11.6. *Lloyd's Register* 1898 describes her as a schooner whereas the 1900 edition describes her as a three masted schooner. Her register was transferred from Banff to Plymouth in 1881 and in 1891 John T. Williams of Newquay became managing owner and ran her until 1906, when she went to Calstock and later Cardiff owners. Lost near Wexford 20th October 1929 (note on Plymouth register).

**MYVANWY** ON 63232, built 1870 at Newport Mon. by Newport Ship Company. Tons 162 net 177 gross, 141 net later. 106.0 23.0 12.6. This schooner was already described as three masted in *Lloyd's Register* of 1880 and was probably built with three masts. She was built for the South American trade and soon registered in Liverpool. However, by 1894 she was registered at Falmouth and in 1897 she was owned and commanded by J. G.Coode of Port Isaac, who transferred her to the Fowey register.

According to *Lloyd's* loss records, she was wrecked on Barrow Sand on 21st May 1904 on passage from Antwerp with slates for Woolwich. That sounds a most unlikely route for that particular cargo in a vessel owned in Port Isaac, but perhaps the cargo consisted of the handsome red roofing tiles of the Netherlands.

**NADIR** ON 5655, built 1827 at Salcombe by John Bull. Tons 68(O) 53(N). 53 gross. 50.2 16.0 8.9. This schooner came to the Padstow register in 1844 with Richards as captain and owner. The Tredwen and Bate families subsequently had large shares and finally Thomas May of Port Isaac in 1866.

Lost about 4th January 1867 on passage from Cardiff for Cork (note on register).

**NANCY.** A Padstow ship named NANCY was reported to have foundered off Hartland in June 1801. (Hicks RIC)

**NANCY.** A ship built at Shoreham in 1784 was owned by one Prideaux (*Lloyd's Register* supplement 1801) but there is no known connection with Padstow except the owner's name.

**NANCY** ON 22385, built 1829 at Padstow. Tons 66(O) 48(N), 48 gross. 52.0 17.5 8.8. A sloop rigged smack with numerous shareholders in Newquay and Bude over the years. The managing owners and captains (usually the same person) were successively H. Nichols, William Darke, J. Clemens and John Ridgman. She worked the whole length of the coast from the Gannel to Hartland Quay and naturally had an adventurous life.

On 21st November 1874, with the wind NW force 10, she was driven ashore at Welcombe Mouth north of Bude, bringing coal from Newport for Bude. All three crew were lost: John Ridgman aged 36, his nephew and his brother-in-law John Hatherly.

**NANSCOW** ON 1461, built 1812 at Padstow by Martin Withell. Tons 53(O) 43(N), 39 gross. 50.3 16.3 8.7. This small Padstow sloop spent her early years under Burt, Harding and Brewer in international trade. Some of her early voyages to Spain must have been in support of the Duke of Wellington's campaigns! Later owners and masters included Bellamy, Tremaine, W. Apps, J. Horsewell (of Boscastle in 1841), A. Hutchings and R. B. Rawlings (1852). In 1854 was sold to Cardiff and later to Strangford owners. She was no longer listed in 1887.

**NAUTILUS** built 1839 at Padstow by J. Tredwen. Tons 100(O) 82(N). 59.4 17.7 10.0. This interesting vessel was described as dandy rigged when registered at Padstow on completion, but *Lloyd's* described her as a sloop. She was sheathed with zinc in 1849 and 'restored' in 1853, after which she was schooner rigged. Her owners were J. Tredwen and then Charles Tredwen in 1849. Her masters were Hawken, Parnall, Knight and in 1854 Robert Brown. In 1855 her port of registry was changed to Melbourne in the colony of Victoria, and the story of her translation to the antipodes is given elsewhere.

On 15th January 1856 she was wrecked near Cape Liptrap, Victoria when she was sailing from Melbourne to pick up a cargo of stone at Westernport.

**NEIROS** see BUSY BEE

**NELLY** built 1825 at Padstow. Tons 58(O). A sloop owned by Sloget with Gould as master. These particulars appear first in the supplement to the 1826 edition of *Lloyd's Shipowners' Register*, the so-called red book, and the 1832 edition has the same entry. It seems probable that George Sloggett built her himself; he launched no other vessel in 1825; but she is not to be found on the Padstow port register, and no registration has been found elsewhere.

**NEW CORNWALL** ON 68196, built 1872 at Barnstaple by W. Westacott. Tons 75 net 84 gross. 74.0  20.0  9.5. This schooner, although registered at Barnstaple was owned by her master Sam Prout of Port Isaac and others. She did not last long, her final appearance in *Lloyd's Register* being in 1876.

**NEW PARLIAMENT** ON 22370, built 1833 at Llanelly. Tons 61(0), 64 gross. 58.0  16.0  8.9. This schooner, registered at Llanelly, is included because she had Newquay shareholders, including two of her captains, B. Williams and A. Lilburn. She was lost in 1880 (Verran).

**NEW QUAY** built 1786 at New Quay, Cardigan. Tons 34(O). 39.2 14.8  7.0. This square sterned sloop was registered at Fowey in 1790 and her owners included Nicholas George, yeoman, and Richard Tinney, yeoman, both of St Columb Minor near Newquay, Cornwall. This register was closed in 1792.

**NEW QUAY** ON 11448, built 1847 at Bideford by Cox. Tons 125(N), 102 net 110 gross. 76.1  20.8  11.6. This schooner (like the MODEL) was built for J. T. Treffry, the industrialist, who acquired Newquay harbour in 1838 and developed it, and became Lord of the Manor there. The schooner was registered at Fowey and according to the *Mercantile Navy List* she stayed in Treffry's name until 1875. She then had a long series of owners in Cornwall and later in Portavogie and Ardglass, ceasing to be listed about 1908.

**NICHOLAS** built 1786 at Brixham, a square sterned sloop, was registered at Fowey in 1793. and one of her owners was Joseph Carne, yeoman, of St Columb. Our only other knowledge of this vessel is that she was seized for smuggling.

**NIMROD** ON 62680, built in France, date unknown. Tons 42 net 48 gross. 59.8  17.9  7.9. *ex* JULES JOSEPHINE. This smack was registered at Padstow in 1870 and that was probably her first appearance in British ownership as no earlier registration is referred to. She was owned by John Bray Edyvane, master mariner, of Padstow. About 1874 he sold her to William Maynard of Bude and in October 1875 she was detained by the Board of Trade at Plymouth as overloading was alleged. Sold to Looe, she was wrecked on the coast of Holland in October 1880 (note on register).

**OCEAN** ON 20971, built 1831 at Padstow by J. Tredwen. Tons 80(O) 65(N). 58.7  18.7  10.1. A brig with fixed bowsprit, square stern and woman's bust. She was described in 1834 as a schooner and *Lloyd's* Survey report calls her a schooner brig. Her rig is described in her second registration in 1838 as 'square forward, schooner aft'. She was quite clearly built as a brigantine, a term not recognised in *Lloyd's Register* as being different from a brig until 1835. Her dimensions in 1838, for 'new' measurement, were 53.6

17.0  9.8. She was lengthened in 1851, and remeasured. Tons 74(N) on dimensions 60.2  17.7  8.7.

In 1858 she was lengthened again and by this time the rules of the 1854 Merchant Shipping Act applied and she measured 92 tons. 80.5 19.5  9.8. These 92 tons would have later been termed gross tons.

Both the lengthening operations were accompanied by major repairs, so the variations in dimensions do not just represent changes in the rules for measurement, but also probably include substantial changes in the shape and size of the structure of the ship.

She was owned until 1847 by Stribley, Tredwen and others. W. Stribley, B. Harvey and Simon Stribley were her masters. In 1847 she was sold to William Holman and registered at Penzance and both lengthening operations took place during his ownership.

The OCEAN foundered off Pentire Point with all hands on 19th March, the notorious March gale of 1869.

**OCEAN BELLE** ON 58241, built 1867 at Gannel Yard, Newquay by T & J Clemens. Tons 67 net 77 gross. 78.1  20.7  9.6. A Padstow registered schooner built for W. H. Tonkin and W. Hicks, both of Newquay and the former as captain. In the mid-eighties she was sold to Welsh owners and on 25th May 1892 she was abandoned and sank 20 miles off Hook Light on passage from London towards Waterford.

**OCEAN QUEEN** ON 19760, built 1858 at Padstow by J. Tredwen. Tons 121 gross. 83.2  20.5  11.0. Described in her 1858 Padstow register as a brigantine with square stern and woman's figurehead, but on registration in 1885 a gammon knee took the place of the figurehead, and in the report of her loss she was said to be schooner rigged.

James Richards of Port Isaac was owner and master until 1884 when A. B. Hutchings of Padstow became owner and W. Day, J. Osborne and J. Chappell were successive masters.

Lost by stranding at Llanddulas 7th November 1890. Wind NW force 10.

**OCEAN QUEEN** ON 58246, built 1868 at Looe by Pengelly. Tons 195 net 207 gross, 164 net later. 124.3  25.2  12.5. This ship, built for John Stribley of Padstow was, on completion, the first three masted schooner in the Padstow fleet. But Stribley sold most of his 64 shares and she was soon re-registered at Plymouth. In the late eighties John Ennor of Newquay became her managing owner and R. J. Hockin her master. His wife would often accompany him and was well known for taking a full trick at the wheel.

One OCEAN QUEEN, a three masted schooner, was abandoned in the North Sea 16th September 1893. (*Lloyd's* casualty returns)

**OCEAN SPRITE** ON 8510, built 1854 at Sunderland. Tons 233 net 319 gross, 167 net later. 114.0  23.6  12.5. This barque was registered at Exeter but her owner and captain until 1872 was Walter Strechley Mear of St Minver near Padstow, and he took her to Rio, to the West Indies and to the Mediterranean. After that she was owned in Hull and Falmouth and dropped out of the registers in 1897.

**OLIVE BRANCH** ON 67649, built 1880 at Aberdovey by Richards. Tons 99 net 118 gross, 92 net later. 85.4  21.7  11.5. This schooner was registered in Aberystwyth and Beaumaris, but when that changed to Truro near the end of the century, B. Phillips of Newquay became her captain and a substantial owner.

W. Thomas of Amlwch and Truro took over command in 1903 and became managing owner after the Great War, and she traded until about 1923.

**ONE & ALL** ON 19328, built 1822 at Padstow. Tons 45(O) 38(N) 33 gross. 42.7  14.3  7.9. This sloop rigged smack was built for the Penzance Shipping Company (founded 1815) and was registered at Penzance until about 1860. In 1849 she was owned by Robert

Glasson Michell, a Marazion draper, (32 shares) and John Johns of Woodland Castle, a Glamorgan butler, (32 shares), and Henry Johns was master (and doubtless benefitted by family arrangements).

Her last quarter of a century was spent on the Plymouth register owned by William Cullis of Turnchapel and she disappears from the lists in the mid-eighties.

**ONTARIO.** The Bunt family of Port Isaac had ownership of a vessel named ONTARIO. (Winstanley)

**ONWARD** ON 13449, built 1853 at Newport, Monmouthshire. Tons 108(O) 85(N), 86 gross. 71.2 17.3 9.1. This schooner was on the St Ives register throughout her life. She traded as far as the Mediterranean but much of her work was between Wales and Cornwall.

In 1882 William Henry Harvey of Padstow bought all 64 shares, and J. Wilcock became master.

Not heard of since sailing on 24th December 1886 from Muckross, County Cork for London with barytes. Crew of four.

**ORB** built 1829 at Padstow by George Sloggett. Tons 55(O) 37(N). 46.8 17.2 8.0. This sloop was registered at Padstow owned by A. Rogers and others, including P. Ellery her captain. John Tredwen became owner about 1840 and in 1841 she was sold to F. Pascoe, a Falmouth grocer, and registered there.

On 26th September 1851 the sailing vessel ORB, Alfred Davey master, sailing from Falmouth with granite for Hull, sank two miles off Bolt Tail.

**ORION** ON 50330, built 1869 at Dysart, Fife, by Watt. Tons 95 net 104 gross, 78 net later. 82.0 21.0 10.4. This schooner came south, transferring registry from Wick to Plymouth about 1882. She is included here because Mrs Elizabeth Lobb of Port Isaac owned her from 1891 onwards, by which time she was ketch rigged. She is dropped from the *Mercantile Navy List* by 1910.

**ORWELL** ON 26720, built 1826 at Ipswich. Tons 108(O) 92 gross. This schooner's register was changed from London to St Ives in 1854. In 1873 she was owned by Fox and John Lobb of Illogan near St Ives. That same year she was bought, all 64 shares, by Richard Chegwidden of Newquay, who appointed Captain Ellery also of Newquay to be master. On 10th September 1873 she was lost near the Mersey (note on register).

**OSPREY** built 1842 at Leith. Tons 91(O) 66(N). 70.3 14.9 9.4. A schooner with a bird at the stemhead. After a period at Kircaldy, her registry came to Padstow in 1850 with Fred Cock of St Minver as owner and master. He had her repaired and yellow metalled and traded to France and the Mediterranean. In 1853 she was sold to Glasgow and disappears from *Lloyd's Register*. For many years (from 1865 to 1891) there is an intriguing entry in the Mercantile Navy List as follows: 'OSPREY ON 49299, of Sydney NSW, schooner built at Leith, date unknown. 64 reg. tons, owner Chas. Miller, Sydney, NSW.' It seems quite probable that these two OSPREYs are one and the same vessel.

**OWNER'S DELIGHT.** On 14th January 1792 the Padstow brigantine OWNER'S DELIGHT, Hetherington master, was wrecked on the Doom Bar. Crew saved.

**P. M. WILLCOCK** ON 58290, built 1868 at Mevagissey by Benjamin H. Roberts. Tons 59 net 74 gross. 75.9 18.8 9.4. She is rather unusual (in England) in being named after her owner. She was registered at Fowey until 1890 when she was bought by Richard Honey, mariner, of Port Isaac, and Padstow became her port of registry. In 1901 Charlotte Ann Harvey, widow, became owner, and in 1905 William Moses of Ramsgate, and it was probably he who altered her to ketch rig and sold her to Aberystwyth owners. She lasted until the start of the Great War.

**PADGY** built 1794 in France. Tons 133(O). This brig first appears in *Lloyd's Register* in 1786, owned by Rawlins, the most prominent Padstow merchant at that time. The entries continue until 1808 with T. Cundy, J. Adam, Williams, and T. Phillips as successive masters, the ship trading from Falmouth, London, Bristol and Padstow to Leghorn, Petersburg, Emden and Cork, and doubtless other destinations. No Padstow registration has survived. There are further entries for this ship in *Lloyd's* until 1814, but with no Padstow connections.

**PADSTOW** built 1789 in Spain. Tons 91(O). This brig first appears in *Lloyd's Register* in 1799, owned by Rawlins like the last, with W. Cundy and P. Billing as masters, before she disappears in 1808. The destinations Bristol, London, Petersburg, Chester and Cork appear in her records.

**PADSTOW.** A vessel named PADSTOW, Richards master, was reported lost near Padstow on 22nd November 1801 (*Lloyd's List* 8th December 1801).

A vessel named PADSTOW, of Padstow, Stevens master, was reported wrecked at Falmouth (*Lloyd's List* 13 January 1804).

**PADSTOW.** The armed brig PADSTOW, 153 tons, was reported in 1811 to be sailing to the Mediterranean, Robert Hansen master. (*Lloyd's List*)

**PADSTOW** built 1816 at Padstow. Tons 29(O). 38.0 13.0 7.3. A pilot cutter built for Bristol pilots and registered there. Lengthened in 1831 and lost in 1836 in the British Channel.

**PASCOE** built 1835 (or 1834) at Swansea. Tons 89(O) 71(N). 58.6 16.4 10.2. A schooner with a griffin at the stemhead. She came to the Padstow register from London in 1849 with E. Knight as owner and master. In 1852 Tredwen was owner and W. Hill master. She last appears in *Lloyd's Register* in 1855.

**PATRA** ON 48629, built 1864 at Brixham by Dewdney. Tons 160 net 183 gross. 101.4 23.5 12.7. This brig was registered at Brixham; *Lloyd's Register* of 1890 posts a change of rig to barkentine. In 1899 she was owned by J. G. Coode of Port Isaac with T. R. Bate as master. She ceases to be listed in 1906.

**PATSEY.** A constant trader Padstow to Bristol 1793 to 1801, with Peters and Brokenshaw in command.

**PAUL PRY** ON 10093, built 1845 at Padstow by Thomas Carter. Tons 17(N). 36.1 11.1 6.1. A lugger with running bowsprit and round stern, registered at St Ives and owned by St Ives fishermen.

She was reduced to an open barge of less than 15 tons and her register closed accordingly in 1859.

**PEACE.** A prize condemned in the High Court of Admiralty 4th September 1810. Tons 29(O). 41.7 13.7 7.0. A sloop registered at Padstow in 1824 with Richard and William Nance as owners, the latter being master. Lost January 1825 sailing from Padstow for Bristol (note on register).

**PEACE** built 1815 at Northam. Tons 18(O) 12(N). 30.0 10.7 6.0. This tiny sloop was registered at Falmouth in 1829, Richard Andrew owner, and at Padstow in 1838 owned by J & R Tredwen. On 13th January 1841 an advertisement appeared: 'Twenty ton cutter PEACE principally used for pleasure, for sale, apply J. Tredwen'. Subsequently R. Stephens of St Columb Minor became owner.

**PEACE** ON 29362, built 1862 at Padstow by Willmett. Tons 66.28 reg. 68.5 19.4 9.1. PEACE was described as a dandy with two masts when registered at Padstow in 1862, but as a cutter in *Lloyd's Register*. Ownership throughout her life was John Hawke (24 shares) R. Neal (16) Isaac Greenwood (24).

'Foundered at Rundlestone 2nd December 1872' (note on register).

**PEACE** ON 69454, built 1873 at Padstow by John Cowl. Tons 89 net 95 gross. 83.1 22.6 10.4. This Padstow registered schooner

The brigantine
PETER & JAMES,
artist unknown.
*National Maritime Museum*

owned by John Hawke Jr. of Port Isaac, with R. Neal as master, sailed from Limerick on 23rd February 1874 with oats for Cardiff and is believed lost with all hands about 24th February.

**PEGGY.** A Padstow brig, was reported lost near Portreath in September 1806 whilst on passage from Cork for Falmouth. However it seems likely that this was the same vessel as a sloop reported lost in December 1805!

**PENALLY** (PENELLY and PENGELLY also found). ON 15546, built 1825 at Padstow by John Tredwen. Tons 49(O) 31(N) 31 reg. 47.6   15.6   7.3. This sloop or smack had strong Boscastle connections. Registered at Padstow, the following families shared ownership or took command over the years: Rosevear, Bellamy, Burt, Gould, Couch, Strout, Honey, Tredwen, and the final owner was Thomas Richards of St Endellion. PENALLY was wrecked at Boscastle on 31st October 1837, parting cables in a heavy NW gale, but she was repaired. She was finally lost at Bude on 22nd August 1868, whilst in ballast on a voyage from Falmouth towards Newport.

**PENDARVES** built 1825 at Padstow by J. Tredwen, and 'rose upon' 1827. Tons 26(O). 36.4   13.3   6.2. The sloop PENDARVES was initially owned by F. Richards and others, including William Phillips master. In 1829 she was owned by her master T. Bate. Lost 27th April 1829 loading slate at Boscastle (note on register).

**PENPOLL** ON 29356, built 1862 at Padstow by J. Tredwen. Tons 55 net 64 gross. 67.9   18.4   8.6. A typical Padstow registered schooner owned by William Martyn of Penpoll who employed J. Crocker and W. Carrivick (or Carrwick) as masters.

Lost on the E side of Holyhead Bay on 27th November 1885, Teignmouth for Ayr with pipeclay. Crew of four all saved. Wind W. by N. force 9.

**PET** ON 19276, built 1856 at Padstow by F. H. Thomas. Tons 64 reg. 71.9   19.1   8.2. William Burd of Wadebridge was the managing owner and master of this schooner, but there were numerous other shareholders. T. Matthews took over as the ship's master in the 1870s.

Foundered about 25th February 1874 on passage Padstow for Campbeltown with barley (note on register).

**PET** ON 41126, built 1856 at Pugwash, Nova Scotia, by Levi W. Eaton. Tons 43 reg. 57.4   16.3   7.5. This schooner was lengthened in 1878 and converted to ketch rig, then tons 59 net. 75.3   18.1   8.1. When first registered at Padstow in 1857 she had a billet head: after lengthening she had a gammon knee.

J. Brown was owner and master in 1857, but Thomas Martyn and Silas E. Martyn of Wadebridge soon had 32 shares each and never sold them. The Bate family of Port Isaac provided masters in the early days. Captain Juliff is recorded as master in the Bude Canal port book in 1911. 'Total loss 19th September 1911 3 miles West of Strumble Head' (note on register).

**PET** ON 17386, built 1857 at Boscastle by T. R. Avery. Tons 35 reg. 48.2   16.6   7.9. Registered at Padstow, this smack was owned by her builder in 1857, by Richard Blake Hellyar of Padstow in 1858, and by Edward Rawle of Boscastle in 1859. Lost at sea 25th October 1859 (note on register).

**PETER & JAMES** ON 9486, built 1856 at Fowey by Christopher Slade. Tons 157 reg. 92.0   22.7   12.5. This Fowey brigantine was owned by the Tadd family and traded initially to the West Indies. She is included here because E. Trebilcock of Newquay was, for a time, her master and part owner. Lost on passage from Salonica 1865.

**PETER & SARAH** ON 19237, built 1809 at Bideford by Richard Chapman. Tons 60(O) 47(N). 49.4   15.2   8.2. She was built as a sloop but soon converted into a Polacca brigantine, that is to say one whose masts were single poles.

She came to the Padstow register from Truro in 1853, to be owned by T & W Martyn of Newquay with W. Clemens as master.

On 1st November 1859 she was lost off Ilfracombe, two of her crew being saved, but Captain Clemens being lost with the ship.

**PHILIPPA** built 1816 at Padstow by John Tredwen. Tons 58(O). 50.5   16.8   8.8. The principal owners of this sloop over the years were the Avery, Tredwen and Billing families. Her masters included

W. Blaney, T. Knight and J. Billing. PHILIPPA was broken up in 1840.

**PHOENIX** ON 18309, built 1854 at Padstow by J. Tredwen. Tons 30 gross 23 net. 50.8 13.2 6.0. A sloop rigged smack registered at Padstow, owned by Seaton and Bryant and James Haynes, her master. She was sold to Evan Evans in 1860 and transferred to the Swansea register in 1865. She lasted until about 1890.

**PHYLLIS.** A small cutter of this name was reported built at Padstow in 1876 (Hicks: RIC).

**PICTOU** built 1832 at Pictou, Nova Scotia. Tons 139(O) 126(N). 67.1 19.6 12.2. PICTOU is described as a barque in *Lloyd's Register* 1836, but as a brig in all subsequent publications. She was registered at St John's, Newfoundland, and then in 1841 at Falmouth, and in 1843 at Padstow with P. Burke as captain and owner. He sold her the same year to John Oxenbury Plint of Penryn. She was lost in 1844.

**PIERRETTE** see ROSALIE

**PILGRIM** ON 15577, built 1855 at Appledore. Tons 61 net 71 gross. 71.3 18.4 9.3. This brigantine, re-rigged as a schooner by 1860, was registered at Bideford, Falmouth and finally Penzance. But she is included here because for many years she was owned by Nicholas Hockin of Lower St Columb. Her last ten years were at Penzance. She was 'supposed lost off Penzance with Captain Hurley and three others' in December 1890, but survived miraculously. (RCG 25.12.90) However, 'The safety of the Penzance schooner PILGRIM is now beyond hope'. (RCG 9.1.96)

**PILOT.** Date and place of building unknown. 16 & 29/94ths tons (O), measured 36 ft long and 11 ft wide by Nathaniel Hickes, survey officer at St Ives 1790. A cutter with pink stern. Her previous registration had been at Padstow in 1787, but has not survived. Ilfracombe became her port of registry in 1791.

**PINK.** A prize made free at Southampton in 1811. Tons 29. 41.7 13.7 6.8. This smack came to Padstow in 1815 from the Jersey register, and was owned by John Gurney and her captain David Manson. S. Osborne was her captain in 1816 but William Nance bought and commanded her in 1817. No fate is indicated on her Padstow register.

**PIONEER** ON 18276, built 1858 at Stirling by Johnstone. Tons 124 gross. 97.5 20.3 11.4. A schooner which remained on the Leith register all her life but which was owned in Falmouth by 1869 and in Padstow by 1870, with H. Buse as captain and owner. She lasted until about 1886.

**PLANET** ON 27809, built 1860 at Pwllheli by Roberts. Tons 134 gross. 81.7 21.7 12.2. PLANET was completed as a brigantine and registered at Carnarvon; by 1879 she was owned by B. M. Harvey of Padstow.

On 7th November 1890, on passage from Runcorn with coal for Calstock, she was wrecked in Llandudno Bay. Wind NW force 11. At the time of her loss she was reported to be a schooner owned by R. Harvey, with T. Tabb as master.

**PLOVER** ON 55350, built 1867 at Sunderland by Pile. Tons 69 gross. 76.9 18.8 9.3. The schooner PLOVER had Fraserburgh registry until Hubert H. Stribley brought her to Padstow about 1890. By then she was ketch rigged but retained her figurehead of a plover. She remained registered at Padstow when he sold her to Plymouth owners and when she went to Samuel Carver of Llandough. Wrecked 29th June 1906 (note on register).

**PLYMOUTH** ON 47901, built 1863 at Plymouth by Jos. Banks. Tons 98 net, 111 gross, later 79 net. 95.3 20.5 10.3. This schooner was owned by South Devon Shipping Co., then Plymouth Mutual Co-op Ltd., in early days for Westcountry ships to be owned by

companies. Then in 1891 John Bunt of Newquay and William Robinson bought her and transferred her from Plymouth to Padstow registry. In 1894 she was sold to John Crocker of Newquay and L. W. Carne was master. On 30th January 1900 she was lost with all five hands off Margate, sailing from London with sleepers for Kilrush. Wind ENE force 6.

**PO** built 1808 at Plymouth. 63(O). 52.4 17.7 8.5. On 14th February 1824 this Plymouth sloop was wrecked at Padstow. However she was repaired and re-registered at Padstow that same year, owned and commanded by W & R Billing. She was transferred to Llanelly in 1829. Wrecked off Ramsgate on 12th May 1832 on passage London for Bristol (*Lloyd's List* 15th May 1832).

**POMARON** ON 47039, built 1865 at Padstow by Willmett. Tons 330 reg. 131.5 29.1 13.9. This barque was built to Henzell's Patent like a large flat-bottomed barge with centreboards in casings on port and starboard sides. She was briefly registered at Padstow by Williams, shipbroker, but Francis T. Barry registered her at London the same year. She spent her life bringing Spanish ores to Liverpool and Newport, trading regularly to Villa Real and Pomaron (now spelt Pomarao).

On 15th December 1874, on passage from Pomaron to Liverpool, she was abandoned 46°N. 8°W. with three feet of water in the hold and with bulwarks and stanchions gone. Her crew were taken off by the London SS TOSKOFF bound from Marianople to Falmouth.

**POMONA** ON 5744, built 1796 (1794 and 1790 also found) at Teignmouth. Tons 32(O). 45.8 14.3 6.8. Lengthened 1815 after which tons 42(O) 30(N) and length 49 ft. Built as a sloop, and rigged as a schooner after lengthening, she was registered at Dartmouth in 1814, Exeter in 1815, and from 1820 until her loss, at Padstow, with Avery (and others) as her owner. Masters included William Dark, Pascoe Billings, J. Cock, William Symons and T. Hicks. Lost April 1856 (note on register).

**PORTH** ON 10876, built 1818 at Porth near Newquay by W. Withell. Tons 35(O) 26(N). 43.5 14.2 7.0. A Padstow sloop in which J. Giles, J. Nicholls, William Carter, Parnall and Charles Fishley had interests until she was sold to Falmouth in 1853. She returned to the North coast to be registered at Bideford by Daniel Walters in 1866. Lost at Neath 4th February 1867 (note on Bideford Register).

**PORTH** ON 69470, built 1877 at Porth near Newquay by Joseph Osborne. Tons 35 net 40 gross. 56.2 18.7 7.65 A smack with semi-elliptical stern registered at Padstow and owned successively by Edward Martyn of Porth, Richard Bennett of Porth and George Bennett of Newquay.

J. Billings Sr was her master when, in the great blizzard of 10th March 1890, bound for Penzance with 60 tons of culm from Swansea, she was wrecked off Annet in the Scilly Isles. Captain Billings and his son were rescued, and Charles Boxer swam ashore but only to die in the snow and ice. Wind NNE force 10.

**PRICE.** The PRICE of Padstow, F. Richards master, was wrecked at Bude on 19th December 1810. She was carrying butter and oats from Waterford for Portsmouth. (*Lloyd's List* 12.1810)

**PRIDE OF THE SOUTH** ON 84976, built 1881 at Padstow by C. Rawle. Tons 133 net 143 gross, later 110 net. 93.5 23.1 11.7. A schooner with an elliptical stern registered at Padstow throughout, although her builder, who was also the first owner (and had therefore probably built her speculatively) sold her soon after her completion to Arthur Jenkyns of Charlestown, like her predecessor PRIDE OF THE WEST. She has been missing since leaving Holyhead on 27th December 1905 with coal for Par.

**PRIDE OF THE WEST** ON 80408, built 1880 at Padstow by C.

Rawle. Tons 109 net 117 gross, 99 net later. 88.6 22.2 11.1. This schooner was registered at Padstow. with her builder owning all 64 shares and J. Battershill as master. Arthur Jenkyns of Padstow became her master but he moved to Charlestown in 1882. In 1898 her port of registry changed from Padstow to Plymouth. She foundered on 5th November 1911.

**PRIMROSE** ON 11416, built 1831 at Padstow by John Tredwen. Tons 80(O) 58(N). 55.1 18.7 9.3. This sloop-rigged Padstow smack was owned for many years by Nicholas Hockin and others (although *Lloyd's Register* varies from Hawkins to Hocking). Then in 1843 the Tredwen family took over and W. James, H. Knight, D. Morton and J. England were employed as masters. About 1846 she was converted to schooner rig, apparently without the usual lengthening operation, and in 1853 she was sold to Oliver Davey of Bude and Bideford became her port of registry.

There are two versions of her fate. She was wrecked on the Doom Bar in December 1860. Alternatively, she was run down and sunk about 1861. These accounts are not necessarily contradictory and perhaps it may be concluded that she had a *contretemps* with another vessel in the approach channel and ended up wrecked on the bar in December 1860, at which time William Maynard was her master.

**PRINCE ALFRED** ON 29353, built 1861 at Padstow by Willmett. Tons 41 net, 47 gross. 58.4 18.5 8.4. This Padstow registered cutter rigged smack was the first built by Willmett, and with thick carvel planking and frames at close centres she survived hundreds of beachings to land coal cargoes and pick up slates and ore from the hamlets of North Cornwall. Her first owner-master was J. Coad of Port Isaac, followed by T. E. Adams, John Neal, (with R. Neal as master) and finally J. Hockaday of Delabole.

On 8th December 1886 she stranded at Port Gavern and broke up. Wind WNW force 9. That sounds like a dramatic wreck, but in fact may just be the culmination of the normal risks of a quarter of a century of arduous service.

**PRINCE EDWARD** built 1786 at Plymouth. Tons 44. A sloop which the St Ives register indicates was registered at Padstow in 1813, although no such register survives. Thereafter she was owned and captained by the Hockins, Hawkins or Hockings (cf. PRIMROSE), and the Row or Rowe family, all of St Ives. Missing since leaving Swansea 22nd January 1821. Loss confirmed by note on register.

**PRINCE EDWARD** built 1802 at Padstow. Tons 42(O). This sloop is listed in *Lloyd's Register* 1805-1809, with William Cowl as owner and master. No Padstow port register has survived.

**PRINCE REGENT** built 1819 at St Mary's, Scilly. Tons 32(O). 39.2 14.7 7.6. A smack with square stern and running bowsprit. She was registered at Ilfracombe in 1829, and at Padstow in 1832, with Abraham Prout of Perranzabuloe as owner and Benjamin Davey as master. Wrecked 1838.

**PRINCESS CHARLOTTE** ON 19253, built 1819 at Dartmouth. Tons 87(O) 71(N). 57.6 16.9 9.8. A schooner which was registered at Dartmouth, at Exeter, and in 1854 at Padstow when Thomas Carter and William Mably owned her. In 1856 the owners became Jennifer Carter, widow, and James Hambly Sr, with James Kerswell as master. In 1858 James Hambly Jr took her and registered her at Plymouth where she was last listed in 1868.

**PRINCESS OF WALES** ON 58244, built 1867 at Padstow by J. Tredwen. Tons 121 net 134 gross. 92.9 22.6 11.3. This schooner was first owned by her builder with W. Garner as master, but in 1870 he sold her to Thomas May of Port Isaac. In 1876 her rig was altered to brigantine; a somewhat unusual change at that date which might have signalled an intention to engage in deep water trades.

She was wrecked near the Grib, Norway, on 16th October 1877, carrying copper ore from Harkedyal for Liverpool. Her crew of six survived.

**PROSPEROUS** ON 58371, built 1868 at Newlyn. Tons 22 gross. 47.3 14.9 6.95. A round sterned lugger altered to a cutter in 1882. In 1874 this Penzance lugger came into the hands of Thomas Allanson, gent. of St Columb (64 shares) as mortgagee for £50 plus 10%. In 1885 she was re-registered at Plymouth by Edgar Bartlett, c/o Naval Bank, Dartmouth, who paid off the mortgage. It seems probable that she was a yacht by then.

**PROVIDENCE** ON 19208, built 1807 at Brixham; almost rebuilt 1854. Tons 74(O) 56(N) 62 reg. 44.0 16.8 9.5. This vessel was built as a sloop and in the course of her career appears to have been converted more than once into schooner and back to sloop. So far as is known, she remained a Brixham ship until Padstow became her port of registry in 1854, when she was owned by Brewer and captained by Edward Jermyn or Jermins. In October 1858 she was in the news when she rescued seven men from the derelict schooner JANE of Carmarthen in the Bristol Channel and landed them at Padstow. Foundered off Cape Cornwall 11th November 1863 (note on register).

**PROVIDENCE** built 1827 at Padstow by George Sloggett. Tons 51(O) 37(N). 47.3 16.3 8.3. A Padstow registered sloop owned by John Sluggett (sic), then by James Marshall and J. Symons. Masters included Heatherington, Richards, Marshall. Lovering and Billing. In 1840 she was sold and registered at Greenock.

**PROVIDENCE** ON 19317, built 1827 at Stonehouse. Tons 25 reg. 42.9 15.4 7.0. A Falmouth sloop which came briefly to Padstow register in 1859 when she was owned by Anscott Hutchings. The following year she was sold to Henry Smith of Minehead and shifted to the Bridgwater register.

**PURSUIT** ON 44244, built 1862 at Nevin, Wales by Robert Thomas. Tons 73 net 89 gross. 70.0 19.5 10.3. A Carnarvon schooner until Padstow became her port of registry in 1890 when John Phillips of Port Isaac bought her and converted her into a ketch. In 1905 Mrs L. J. Gill became owner, succeeded in 1918 by The Jersey Shipping Co. Jersey: but she was still registered at Padstow when broken up in 1929.

**PUZZLE** ON 13063, built 1849 at Salcombe. Tons 73 reg. 63.8 16.2 10.6. This schooner, registered at Dartmouth, St Ives and Fowey, is included because J. Jenkin of Newquay was for a time master and part owner. She lasted until 1879.

**QUEBEC.** On 26th February 1813 the QUEBEC of Padstow. Adams master, was captured by John Paul Jones, but re-captured by HMS DERWENT.

**QUEEN ADELAIDE** ON 14264, built 1830 at Cardiff. Tons 66(O) 56(N) 50 reg. 58.3 15.9 9.0 (1843). Completed as a sloop, this vessel was registered at Padstow in 1843 as a schooner with a running bowsprit, which was a most unusual arrangement at Padstow. She was owned by the Harvey family until her loss.

On 24th June 1865 she went ashore two miles south of Bude whilst sailing from Penzance in ballast towards Cardiff. She was insured for £200. (*Royal Cornwall Gazette* 30th June 1865)

**QUEEN OF THE ISLES** ON 56457, built 1867 at Newburgh, Fife, by Scrimgeour. Tons 149 net, 164 gross. 98,4 23.3 11.2. Described as a schooner in *Lloyd's Register*, but as a brigantine in the *Mercantile Navy List*. She was built for the Mediterranean trades and was based on Perth, Wick and Aberdeen. In 1890, she was bought by Rosevear of Pentewan, and in 1892, still registered at Aberdeen, W. L. Jenkyn became her owner with W. Sleeman as master. The following year she was lost, some say near Salcombe in Devon.

**QUEEN OF THE WEST** ON 19268, built 1855 at Padstow by Samuel T. Bennett. Tons 77 net 87 gross. 76.8  19.8  9.9. A schooner with elliptical stern and female figurehead. This schooner is not to be confused with the famous Salcombe built fruiterer, but nevertheless she had her own high reputation. She was registered at Padstow and owned by Captain Jack Hutchings.

Missing since sailing from Honfleur on 27th March 1872 with barley for Glasgow. Crew of five.

**R.G.D.** ON 42559, built 1866 at Teignmouth by J. B. Mansfield. Tons 68 net 78 gross, 63 net later. 74.2  18.7  9.1. This topgallant schooner is included here because whilst still on the Teignmouth register in the late 1870s she was owned and captained by George Brown of Newquay, and subsequently on the St Ives register her owners included John Penrose of Newquay.

She was nicknamed the 'Roaring Great Devil' at St Ives; whilst registered there she dragged her anchor at Newport and, fouling the bridge, was dismasted. The opportunity was taken to rig her as a ketch, and in the process she retained her topgallant mast on what became the mainmast. In 1914 Scilly became her port of registry. She was given a 35 h.p. motor in 1918, and was sold to Cardiff, then to Portsoy.

'The motor ketch R.G.D. Sunderland for Peterhead with coal, was abandoned four miles off Rattray Head in a gale. Her crew of four were saved by a German trawler, R.G.D. came ashore later at Scotstown Point'. (*Western Echo* 11th November 1919.)

**R.H.G.** ON 83855, built 1881 at Devoran by R. Gilbert. Tons 45 net. 60.5  18.2  7.7. This schooner was named for her builder R. H. Gilbert and registered at Falmouth, but she immediately traded from Newquay, captained by Robert Hooper Hoyle, with James Hoyle aged 18 and William Hoyle aged 13, to complete his crew, all of Newquay. Subsequently she was converted into ketch rig and Captain Galsworthy used to sail her with his son as crew. On one occasion, bringing grain back from Spain, he brought her into Newquay single-handed to let his son get some sleep.

R.H G. went missing in October 1889 sailing from Milford (note on register).

Discharging coal at St Ives *c*. 1896. On the left the schooner RGD (the Roaring Great Devil) before her encounter with Newport Bridge. To the right is the CHYANDOUR, built at Stonehouse, Plymouth in 1824, demonstrating that not all the early schooners were bluff bowed.                    *National Maritime Museum*

Tons 98 net 128 gross. 90.2  21.5  11.7. A Brixham registered schooner until Edmund Tabb brought her to Padstow in 1883. Next year she joined Allport's fleet but members of the Tabb family commanded her throughout.

On 8th October 1896 the Penrhyndu lifeboat had to land all eight from her (including E. R. Tabb's wife and children) when she was on passage from Manchester to Tynemouth; that is the only mention found of a Padstow vessel trading to Manchester.

She was sunk in collision with the London SS HARTLAND about seven miles NE of Pendeen on 17th May 1908, Runcorn for Par with coal. Her crew of five survived.

**RASHLEIGH** built 1802 at Bursledon. Tons 76(O). 56.6  18.8  10.8. Completed as a sloop, she was registered at Southampton in 1802, then that same year at Fowey. In 1823 she was bought by George and Francis Fox, Wadebridge merchants, and Thomas Melhuish was made captain. In 1825 she was rigged as a schooner (without change of tonnage). The Foxes sold their shares in 1829 and she was registered in St Ives. On 10th April 1836, she collided with the schooner EUROPA of Mecklenburg, south of Penzance and foundered.

**REAPER** ON 72551, built 1875 at Pill, Truro by Hitchens. Tons 94 net 102 gross. 81.4  22.1  10.5. Lengthened 1878, tons then 124 net 131 gross. 95.6  22.4  10.5. Originally built as a schooner, she became a three masted schooner, after lengthening. REAPER was registered at Truro throughout her life but in 1895 the Chegwidden family of Newquay bought her and ran her until about 1909 when John T. Williams, also of Newquay. bought her. She foundered 10 miles W. of Horns Reef light vessel in the North Sea, sailing from Bremen with oilcake for Poole on 6th November 1911. (*Lloyd's Wreck Book*)

**REBECCA** built in France. A prize condemned in 1809. Tons 59(O) 51(N). 52.5  16.8  9.6. A schooner with fixed bowsprit (normal) and Hagboat stern (unique at Padstow). Her first surviving registration at Padstow was in 1825 when she was owned by Mary Norway and her captain, William Stribley, but she appears in *Lloyd's Register* with W. Stribley as master for some years before that.

In 1831 J. Tredwen bought her and M. Pope, F. Brewer, Thomas Richards, Richard Morton and John Avery all had charge of her in the following ten years. An advertisement appeared in January 1841 'Schooner REBECCA, 80 tons deadweight, for sale. Apply to J. Tredwen'. The register closes with 'Broken up 1842'.

**REBECCA** built 1814 at Plymouth. Tons 88(O). 58.8  19.3  9.7. This Plymouth brig was registered at Padstow in 1834 with Edward Parnall owner and John Hockin master. In 1835 she was sold on to Thomas Hooper at Bridgwater, appearing in *Lloyd's Register* until 1844.

**REBECCA** ON 56391, built 1866 at Derwenlas, Montgomeryshire by Evans. Tons 202 net, later 209 net and gross, and finally 184 net. 105.0  24.6  13.0. This brig, registered at Aberystwyth, traded to the Mediterranean until Tom May and others of Port Isaac bought her in the early eighties. He converted her to brigantine rig to reduce crew and re-registered her at Plymouth. She dropped out of the lists in 1889.

**REBECCA LANG** ON 14011, built 1852 at Padstow by S. J. Bennett Bros. Tons 60(N). 58.6  16.3  9.5. Lengthened 1854, tons then 76(N) 73 gross. A schooner which was registered at Padstow until 1856, when Plymouth became her port of registry for no apparent reason as her managing owners were the Hoskin (or Hosking) family throughout, with addresses in Padstow and Camelford. One of the first shareholders was Giles Jory Lang, a farmer of St Tudy, which explains the vessel's name. She drops out of the lists in 1869.

WILLIAM HENRY, R H G and CAMELLIA at Newquay.
*Royal Institution of Cornwall*

**RACER** built 1835 at Padstow by John Tredwen. Tons 49(O) 33(N). 47.3  15.8  8.0. This Padstow registered sloop was owned by Rosevear, with P. Burk and J. Strout as masters. *Lloyd's List* for 31st July 1837 records the wreck of the RACE of Padstow at Penzance on 28th July. It seems almost certain that this was one episode in the RACER's life. She was finally lost at sea on 19th June 1853 (note on register).

**RALPH** ON 632, built 1848 at New Glasgow, Prince Edward Island. Tons 90 net 99 gross. 72.4  18.4  10.5. A schooner with male figurehead, she was registered at Bideford, then Bristol and finally in 1866 at Padstow. The Brewer family of Bideford, Padstow and Swansea owned her until 1866 when she was owned by John Stribley, and that same year by William Taylor of Looe. Lost in collision off Ilfracombe 2nd September 1867.

**RANGER** built 1845 at St Peters, Prince Edward Island. Tons 123(N). 77.3  18.6  12.1. This brigantine was registered at Liverpool in 1848 when she was bought by Roger Duggua and William Oatley who registered her at Padstow and traded to the Low Countries. In 1851 the owners became John Martyn and Angelina Oatley of Wadebridge. The final entry in her register, dated 30th July 1852, reads: 'Vessel abandoned off Arklow light vessel'.

**RARE PLANT** ON 51346, built 1866 at Dartmouth by Moore.

**RED JACKET** ON 17887, built 1857 at Brixham. Tons 131 gross. 88.0 20.0 12.0. This schooner was registered at Dartmouth and traded to North America for her Brixham owners. She is included here because Captain J. James of Newquay had shares in her, and command of her for a time. (Verran) She was posted as 'wrecked' in *Lloyd's Register* 1873-4.

**RED ROSE** ON 62040, built 1869 at Bridport by Cox. Tons 145 net 156 gross. 96.0 21.6 12.3 with 24 ft quarterdeck, elliptical stern and demi-woman figurehead. A brigantine built with part iron beams, she was registered at Falmouth and is only included here because Richard James Hockin, master mariner, of Newquay owned and captained her in 1904, and J. Williams of Newquay had been her master earlier. Hockin sold her to Red Sea Transport Co. London, and they passed her on to Rea Transport Co. Liverpool, where she was hulked for use as a lighter in August 1904 and registered in 1905. Her Falmouth register carries the note 'Foundered River Mersey, 22nd February 1917'.

**REGENT** ON 28981, built 1862 at Montrose. Tons 80 net 99 gross. 77.2 21.5 10.4. A schooner of Stornoway and from 1883 of Inverness, she was owned in Scotland until in 1904 she was bought by William Pascoe of Newquay who converted her into a ketch. She dropped out of the lists by 1909.

**REPUBLICAN** ON 24005, built 1841 at Great Yarmouth. Tons 91(O) 81(N), 81 gross, 77 net. This schooner was registered at Yarmouth and then at Plymouth where, by 1882 she was converted to ketch rig and owned by H. Tabb of Padstow with J. Mably as master.

On 11th January 1883 REPUBLICAN was wrecked near Woodabay in Devon whilst sailing from Newport with coal for Padstow.

**RESOLUTION** ON 62672, built 1868 at Island Cove Yard, Newquay by J. Osborne. Tons 42 net 49 gross. 60.7 19.2 7.8. RESOLUTION was built as a smack to enter the trade in coal and slates to remote beaches and havens, which had been carried on for centuries. Her managing owner was Edward A. Martyn of Porth, then Francis E. Bunt of Tintagel, but there were numerous other smaller shareholders.

On 17th February 1888 she was lost at Trebarwith in ballast. The wind was NE force 9. The report of her loss describes her as a ketch. Her crew of four landed safely.

**RETFORD** built 1809 at Ankborough, Lincolnshire. Tons 85(O). 60.3 18.7 9.8. This Hull brig came into the hands of Edward Parnall, sailmaker of Padstow in 1822. He registered her at Padstow and Thomas Parnall became her captain. Lost with all hands off Cape Cornwall, 31st October 1823.

**REVENGE** built 1794, Foreign. Tons 64. An early schooner with no surviving Padstow register, but described in *Lloyd's List* in 1801 and subsequently as being of Padstow.

On 17th February 1804 she was ashore near Milford but was later refloated and repaired. At that time her owner was Kerot and her master, W. May. Subsequently Rowland owned her, and T. Martin, H. Hutchings and W. Pope were masters, all familiar names. Not found listed after 1815.

**REVIRESCO** ON 22440. Perhaps it is not surprising that several other spellings of this name are to be found. Built 1848 at Stockton. Tons 73(N) 64 gross. A schooner registered at Grangemouth and then Wisbech, but owned by John Hooper of Newquay in the 1870s with J. Gustave as captain. She was sold to Robert Hoad of Rye at the start of the '80s and he had her registered there. Register closed in 1887.

**RHODA** ON 27688, built 1859 at Neyland, Pembroke, by Scarlick.

Tons 42 gross, 58 gross after lengthening in 1862. Her dimensions given when registered at Padstow in 1889 were 63.3 17.5 8.1. After years at Milford, Swansea and Fowey, this schooner had Richard Mably, Padstow, as managing owner in 1889, and Mrs Mably in 1892. Charles Rawle took over in 1900 and T. Nugent in 1904.

E. Jenkins was master when, on 17th September 1904, she foundered 13 miles off Pendeen lighthouse. She had sailed from Newport with coal and two passengers for Salcombe; the two passengers were the mate's wife and her three-month old baby. Passengers and crew all saved.

**RHODA MARY** ON 62036. built 1868 at Point, Feock, by John Stephens. Tons 118 net 130 gross, 86 net later. 101.2 21.9 11.0. A fast coaster by a famous builder, she was completed as a two masted schooner, and converted to a three mast rig in 1898. Registered in Falmouth throughout, she came to Padstow ownership in 1908, joining W. S. Allport's fleet, then in 1911 the Harveys of Padstow took her on until she was hulked in the River Camel in 1922. In the 1930s she was moved to the River Medway and became a house-boat at Hoo, finally abandoned there during the Second World War.

**RICHARD** built in France. Prize. Tons 30(O) or 43(O). The involvement of the Couch and Hutchings families in a ship of this name in the period 1815-1825 in *Lloyd's Register*, and in the St Ives port register (1825) lead one to suspect that this was a Padstow ship, but no Padstow register has survived.

**RIPPLING WAVE** ON 62676, built 1869 at the Gannel Yard, Newquay, by T & J Clemens. Tons 73 net 83 gross. 83.0 20.7 9.9. A Padstow coasting schooner not to be confused with the Fowey-Newfoundland trader, she was built for the Carter family (with J. Carter of St Agnes as master). Her next owner was John Christophers also of St Agnes, and finally Francis Henwood of Ivybridge. Missing since 27th October 1880 (note on register).

**RISING SUN** ON 15521, built 1822 at Bideford by William Taylor. Tons 37(O) 24(N). 44.9 14.4 6.9. A sloop which came to Padstow from Bideford in 1825 to be owned by Robert Lewis of Stratton and Robert Wren of Bideford. Robert Lewis, Robert Wren, William Lewis and Jermyn all acted as master before, in 1849, she was re-registered at Bideford with William Tucker of Appledore as owner.

In 1856 she went to Llanelly owners for whom she lasted into the 1870s.

**RITA** ON 51208, built 1865 at Gloucester by Davies as the ketch rigged trow WILLIAM & MARTHA. Tons 67 reg. 69.0 18.5 8.0 and registered at Gloucester, Bridgwater (by 1874) and Cardiff (by 1883) and Gloucester again (by 1895). Lengthened about 1890 after which, tons 76 net (later 66 net with engine), 96 gross. 84.2 21.8 8.5. Renamed RITA by 1904 and thereafter the Beard family of Gloucester were her managing owners until after the Great War. In 1913 she was fitted with a 4 h.p. motor which, according to the *Mercantile Navy List* lasted until the end of her days, which came about in 1927.

She is included in this list because Captain Jenkins of Newquay was for a time her master and part owner. (Verran and Mote).

**RIVAL** ON 44357, built 1862 at Runcorn by Mason. Tons 96 net 106 gross, 78 net later. 85.8 20.6 10.0. The schooner RIVAL was registered at Plymouth soon after completion and in 1867 Thomas Inch of Port Isaac became her master. The owner was Morwellham Ship Co., an early example of a formal company owning a ship in the Westcountry. In 1881 Thomas Inch of Port Isaac became managing owner; at the turn of the century Thomas Inch junior took his place. In 1911 she was sold to J. Mutton of Truro.

The *West Briton* on 18th January 1912 reported that the RIVAL

The Carter family of Newquay had a long term interest in the MARY PEERS.
Reuben Chappell painted her off the Eddystone.

*Paul Parry Collection*

The schooner MORNING STAR was built at Kingston in Elgin in 1878.

*Private collection*

Plate 15

The Chegwidden family of Newquay owned the REAPER when she was painted by John Loos of Antwerp in 1902.      *Private collection*

The TREBISKIN was built as a schooner and converted to ketch rig in 1886.
Painting by Thomas Chidgey.

*Malcolm McCarthy Collection*

Plate 16

had sunk on Monday night after collision with SS SCARSDALE in the outer roads, Holyhead. The RIVAL was bound for Liverpool with china clay from Pentewan. One member of her crew was drowned.

**ROB ROY** built 1832 at St Ives as an open boat. Decked at Padstow in 1835. Tons 9(O). 30.6  9.5  4.7. This small sloop was registered at Padstow in 1836 with James Rowe Williams as owner and master. Sold to Bideford 1845. Register cancelled: 1850, under 15 Tons.

**ROB THE RANTER** ON 62123, built 1874 at Kingston, Elgin by Eddie. Tons 147 net 155 gross, 112 net later. 96.7  22.5  11.8. This vessel was described as a schooner in *Lloyd's Register*, and as a brigantine in the *Mercantile Navy List* throughout her life. She transferred from the Inverness to the Fowey register in 1885 when Joseph G. Coad, or Coode, of Port Isaac was her captain. He was her managing owner a couple of years later, and remained so, with A. Bate taking over as master in 1897.

Wrecked at Hellmouth, 30th October 1899, bound for Cardiff with burnt ore from Belfast. (*Lloyd's Wreck Book*)

**ROBERT COTTLE** ON 24943, built 1853 on Prince Edward Island. Tons 114 net 133 gross. 83.0  19.3  10.7. This brigantine was registered at Padstow from 1858 until 1864, when she was owned by Richard Philip of St Minver, and then by his widow (he died 3rd March 1862). Before that she had been owned in Aberdeen and London. In 1864 she was sold to Ipswich and was unlisted after 1867.

**ROSALIE** ON 81775, built 1879 at Padstow by Charles Rawle. Tons 220 net 230 gross. 116.0  26.1  12.9. This barkentine was built for James H. Cory of Cardiff but in 1881 she was 'sold foreign' to Calais owners and renamed JEANNE. In 1885 Dunkirk became her home port and by 1890 Fécamp, the home of many of the *Morutiers Terrenuevas* which sailed annually with dories nested on their decks over to the Grand Banks off Newfoundland to fish for cod. It seems likely that the JEANNE got involved in that trade: she certainly did in 1900 when she was renamed PIERRETTE and S. M. Legasse Neveu et Cie. of Bayonne became her owners, for they were one of the most famous and successful of the French Grand Banks fishing companies. *Lloyd's* posted her in the 1905 register 'Foundered March 1905'.

**ROSAMOND JANE**, ROSAMOND & JANE ON 21539, built 1834 at Padstow by John Sloggett. Tons 51(O) 38(N), 34 net 52 gross. 46.0  16.6  8.1. One of Padstow's strongly built sloop rigged smacks in which the following families had shares or command over the years: Hawken, Morton, Symons, Tredwen, Peters, Ellery, Teague, Hicks, Williams, Billing, Pascoe and Clemens. Stephen Hare of Appledore bought her in the early 1870s and, in 1877, Bideford became her port of registry. She was the last vessel to trade to Hartland Quay before it was destroyed by the gales of the 1890s. Converted to a barge and register closed 18th July 1907.

**ROSARIO** see CORNUVIA

**ROSE** ON 11471, built 1830 at Padstow by J. Tredwen. Tons 66(O), 47 reg. A smack which was registered first at Swansea, then in 1847 at Fowey where she lasted into the 1880s.

**ROSE** ON 19262, built 1843 at Padstow by Rawle. Tons 92(O) 74(N). 58.3  17.2  9.7. Lengthened 1855 then tons 104 reg. 84.5  19.7  9.4. This Padstow registered schooner was owned first by Brown of Tintagel, then by R. B. Hellyar and Hambly of Padstow, with Key, Burke and Richards as masters. She was zinc sheathed in 1852 and yellow metalled in 1858, and traded to the Mediterranean as well as doing much home trade work. John Richards, her master as early as 1853, went on to become her owner when she was transferred to the St Ives register in 1869. She stranded at St Ives, 29th March 1878,

and broke up (note on register).

**ROSE** ON 19252, built 1847 at Padstow by R & J Tredwen. Tons 70(N) and 70 reg. 57.2  16.6  9.9. This schooner, unlike the last, was essentially a coaster. As owners and masters she had Mitchell, W. Darke and R. Sleeman. She was registered at Padstow throughout.

Lost at Mort Bay on 26th October 1859 during the infamous October gale of that year.

**ROSE OF ST AGNES** ON 47034, built 1863 at Padstow by J. Tredwen. Tons 99 reg. 80.8  20.5  10.2. Although this schooner was registered at Padstow, and had R. Quick as master early on, her owners were Seymour and others of St Agnes, and then the Berehaven Mining Company of Dublin. Wrecked Ballydonegan Bay 20th January 1873 (note on register).

**ROYAL ADELAIDE** ON 32802, built 1831 at Quebec. Tons 410(O) 453(N), 408 reg. 112.0  27.5  19.4. Registered at Falmouth, then at Fowey in 1843 and finally at Padstow in 1869, this barque spent most of her life as a Cornish emigrant ship. It was John Tredwen who bought her in 1869, but he died in 1870 and she passed to William Ruthven of London. Wrecked at Santiago de Cuba 1872 (note on Padstow register).

**ROYALIST** ON 25312, built 1850 at Littlehampton. Tons 141(N). 123 net 135 gross. 88.2  21.4  11.4. Registered first at London, then at Montrose, this schooner, like many others, did not come to the Padstow register until the bloom of youth had passed. In 1879, William Stribley bought all her 64 shares and thereafter J. P. Dunstan, N. House, W. Burt, H. Jones, J. Delbridge all had an interest in her with N. House as manager. In 1890 J. Ennor took over the management. T. Bennett and J. Chapple were masters.

On 7th October 1896 she was lost off Holyhead with three of her four crew, after collision with the Liverpool tug BRITISH KING. ROYALIST was on passage from Runcorn with coal for Fowey.

**RUBY** ON 60834, built 1868 at Rotherhithe, London by Salisbury. Tons 251 net 266 gross, 197 net later. 125.9  26.9  12.9. It is unusual to find a wooden barque built at London as late as 1868, and by a builder who does not appear in *Lloyd's Appendix*, nor in published histories. By that time the listed yards were building iron or composite ships, many of them steamships. After registration in London, Belfast and South Shields, she was registered at Fowey as a barkentine in 1904, owned by J. Williams of Newquay, with W. Cole and T. Hicks as masters.

On 13th November 1915 RUBY was wrecked six miles north of Hartlepool, bound for Tyne with burnt ore from London (*Lloyd's Wreck Book*).

**RUTH** built 1841 at Lower Yard, Padstow by Thomas Carter. Tons 90 burthen. A newspaper report in August 1841 gave news of the completion of this smack. She was not registered at Padstow in that name. It is possible that RUTH was a name *pro tem.* for CATHARINE, completed by Carter that same year. On the other hand, she may have been built for somebody who registered her in say Ireland or Wales.

**S.M.C.** ON 53007, built 1866 at Gannel Yard, Newquay, by T. Clemens, Tons 85 net 93 gross. 86.0  22.1  9.8. G. Pappin was the managing owner and master of the Padstow registered schooner. In January 1868 she was reported wrecked at Mullion but she was repaired and taken over by Nicholas Lewarne of Porth in 1871, when S. Trethewey was captain.

Sunk in collision with the iron paddle tug FLYING SQUALL in the River Clyde, 13th August 1875 (note on register).

**SAINT (THE)** ON 54776, see THE SAINT.

**ST GEORGE** ON 13141, built 1839 at Newport, Monmouthshire. Tons 47 reg. 49.5  14.5  8.1. A smack which came to the Padstow register from Bristol in 1852 to be owned by Thomas Strout, her master, who was highly mobile for the time; coming from Port Isaac, he registered her at Penzance in 1853, giving Penzance as his address, and was back at Padstow again in 1858, giving a Boscastle address. Lost at sea 5th February 1861 (note on register).

**SAINT PETROC** or **ST PETROC** ON 84982, built 1893 at Martenshoek, Holland by G & H Bodewes Gebr. Tons 83 net 98 gross. 87.4  20.5  8.6. A ketch built of iron, described in the port register as clench or clinker built, which in this case can only refer to the lapping of the iron plates. Registered at Padstow in 1893, John Hawken, owner, and F. Conway, master.

On 13th November 1894, on passage from Falmouth to Runcorn with china clay, the wind blew SSW force 10. The main gaff carried away and she lost a man overboard about 8 miles off Trevose Head. Missing since seen off the Skerries, Anglesey, on 18th December 1900 on passage from Runcorn, with coal for Padstow and a crew of four.

**SAINT PETROCK** (SAINT PATRICK in *Mercantile Navy List* 1857) ON 19264, built 1853 at Padstow by John Tredwen Jr, his first ship. Tons 64(N). 60.3  15.4  8.3. A Padstow registered schooner with a male bust figurehead. C. Jordan was her managing owner and Philip James her captain, and there were numerous other small shareholders. Lost at sea January 1857 (note on register).

**ST STEPHEN** or **ST STEPHENS** (SAINT also found) ON 19224, built 1832 at Padstow by John Tredwen. Tons 40(O)  42.8  14.9  7.3. lengthened 1839, then tons 46(O) 32(N). 46.3  13.5  6.9. lengthened again by 1869, then tons 44 reg. 62.0  16.3  7.3. She was sloop rigged until the final lengthening, when she was re-rigged as a ketch.

Padstow registered throughout, the following local families were involved in owning and sailing her: Martyn, Moyse, Tummon, Prideaux, Tredwen, Hutchings and finally John Stribley who owned all 64 shares in 1871, when she was broken up.

**SALAMANDER** ON 21837, built in Sweden, date unknown. Tons 84 net in 1875. This schooner was registered at Woodbridge but owned in the 1870s by T. Davis and her captain William Bate, both of Padstow.

On 3rd August 1879, SALAMANDER was lost in collision with the Sunderland SS LYKUS, ten or twelve miles west of Hartland Point. SALAMANDER was bound from Briton Ferry for Charlestown with culm. Her crew of four were all saved.

**SALLEY** or **SALLY**. One traded regularly to Padstow and Boscastle 1793-4 (Farr). One existed 1800-1830 described as being of Padstow, and was driven ashore at Bude after bringing coal from Neath in 1830, Jenkins of Padstow, master. (John Bray's MS.)

**SALLY ANN** built 1799 in Prussia, and large repairs 1807. Tons 94(O) entered in the supplement to *Lloyd's Register* 1809 as a ketch, but described as a galeas or galiot. She was owned by Rawlins and H. Hutchings was master. There was a similar entry in the 1815 register.

**SALLY ANN** built 1803 at Plymouth. Tons 85(O) 75(N).  60.0  16.3  10.1. This early schooner came from the Plymouth to the Padstow port register in 1838, owned by Robert Stapleton of Bude with James Lee as master. In 1839 Nicholas Tucker became master and owner. Lost in 1845 (note on register).

**SAM SLICK** ON 28162, built 1860 at Galmpton by Gibbs. Tons 146 gross. 88.5  21.0  12.0. A schooner registered at Brixham and then in the '80s at Plymouth, she joined the fleet of W. S. Allport of Padstow in 1885.

On 8th December 1886 she was driven ashore on Pwllheli beach by force 11 winds from the WSW. She was on passage from Fleetwood for Swansea with pitch. Her crew of five were all saved.

**SAMSON** ON 98490, built 1858 in Denmark. Tons 87 net (later 80 net). This schooner first flew the red ensign in 1893, registered at Cowes. Then Thomas Adams of Charlestown bought her, and Fowey became her port of registry in 1900. In 1902 Alex Stephens of Porth bought her and she traded under Captain J. Sluman. She was dropped from the 1905 *Mercantile Navy List*, laid up at Porth, and in due course fell to pieces.

**SAMUEL** ON 28510, built 1860 at Padstow by J. Tredwen. Tons 26 reg. 47.5  14.3  7.7 This cutter was a Bristol Channel pilot vessel owned by Samuel S. Bailey of Pill, and registered at Bristol. She was owned in Porlock from 1887 on, and broken up in 1905.

**SAMUEL & ELIZABETH** ON 18336, built 1834 at Padstow by Thomas Carter. Tons 39(O) 28(N). 43. 2  15.3  7.0. Lengthened 1848, then tons 49 reg. 55.4  14.6  7.8. A sloop converted into a schooner on lengthening. As a sloop she was owned and sailed by T and W Hoskin. When first lengthened, W. Pope was owner and master, then in 1853, Norway was owner, and in 1864 J. S. Pethybridge, a Bodmin accountant, managed her with ten others holding shares. Her captains included W. Hicks and Burt; she was registered at Padstow throughout. Wrecked at Castle (presumably Boscastle) 30th April 1872 (note on register).

**SAMUEL & JANE.** This vessel, said to be of Padstow, was reported detained at Falmouth with contraband on 3rd February 1821.

**SAMUEL & MARY** built 1816 at Polperro. Tons 34(O). 40.8  14.8  6.6. She was registered at Padstow as a cutter in 1822 with William Richards of Boscastle as owner and master. In 1825 the description of the rig was changed to sloop. Lost with all hands 1828.

**SAN JOSEPH** see IDEA

**SAPPHO** ON 58375, built 1869 at Padstow by Stribley. Tons 171 net 187 gross, 145 net later. 111.3  25.3  12.8. A three-masted barentine with elliptical stern and full female figurehead, SAPPHO was built for enterprising Penzance owners who traded to South America and the Black Sea; then she was sold to Inverness in 1881.

In 1890 the May family of Port Isaac brought her to the Padstow register. In 1902 when Edward Stephens of Fowey bought a majority of the shares, Thomas May retained 15. Stephens converted her into a three masted schooner rig as she was by then a coaster. He kept her busy until 1912, when, on 9th January, she sailed from Dysart with coal for Plymouth and went missing. Her crew of six included Captain A. Dixon.

**SARAH** ON 26764, built 1836 at Padstow by J. Tredwen. Tons 36(N) 32 reg. 45.2  14.0  7.0. A Padstow registered smack built for Abbott of Egloshayle (Wadebridge) and others and captained by William Giles and Martyn Parnall. She was sold to Bristol in 1857 and went on to Bridgwater in 1864 and Barnstaple, lasting into the late seventies.

**SARAH** ON 22738, built 1844 at Bristol. Tons 62(O) 54(N), lengthened 1851, then 85(O) 72(N). 64.2  15.4  9.3. A schooner registered at Bristol on completion, at Penzance in 1851, at Plymouth in 1854, finally she had Port Talbot owners in the early sixties. She is listed here because Nicholas Bate, Master Mariner, of Port Isaac was her managing owner with 32 shares for the period of her Plymouth registration.

**SARAH** ON 1830, built 1852 at Northam, Southampton. Tons 84 net 91 gross. 77.1  17.8  9.9. A schooner which spent her early years trading from Southampton to the Mediterranean, and came to Padstow in 1867 after two years on the Penzance register. Her Padstow owners were the Matthews family. Lost on the Bishop Rock, 2nd April 1870 (note on register).

**SARAH** ON 21344, built 1858 at Kingsbridge by W. Date. Tons 149 net 156 reg. 119 net later. 98.0  22.4  12.0. This large schooner, like the last, entered the Mediterranean trades, registered at Salcombe, and then London. John Ennor of Newquay bought her about 1882 and J. Carter started a long and eventful spell as her captain. She was re-registered at Fowey in 1887.

On 26th January 1893 she was driven onto Clippers Rocks, near Holyhead. The Holyhead lifeboat at the time was the famous steam driven DUKE OF NORTHUMBERLAND and she not only rescued the crew of five, but also succeeded in getting the schooner off. By 1906 she was rigged as a three masted schooner.

She ceased trading about 1911, but was not broken up finally until 1932, at Pill.

**SARAH ANN** ON 9484, built 1856 at Padstow by J. Tredwen. Tons 97 net 109 gross, 82 net later. 84.2 20.7 10.5. Although this schooner was registered at Fowey, even early on she was a Padstow coaster and by 1895 was owned by William L. Jenkin of Newquay with R. Sleeman as master. She was sold to P. K. Harris of Appledore about 1909, and was lost 'from natural causes' doing the Great War. In fact she foundered off Morte Point on 25th January 1917 after a collision with the SS NORMANDIET of Copenhagen.

She has been described as a ketch in her later years, but there is no record of the changed rig in the registers.

**SARAH ANNA** built 1815 at Topsham by Robert Davy (the father of Bishop Davy). Tons 62(O). 55.1 16.8 8.5. A sloop with a square stern which was registered at Exeter, then in 1824 at Padstow owned by J. Popham and J. Nichols, her master.

On 30th December 1835 she stranded in Carmarthen Bay and was lost, with all her papers, a few days later. (*Lloyd's List* and note on register.)

**SARAH FOX** ON 58672, built 1868 at Mevagissey by Lelean. Tons 121 net 134 gross. 87.5 22.8 11.8. This Hayle registered schooner is included here because in 1887 Francis, Mary and Thomas Prout of Newquay bought her. Wrecked at Sunderland 14th November 1891.

**SATYR** ON 11917, built 1857 at Gloucester. Tons 92 net 103 gross, 81 net later. 79.0 19.4 11.2. A square sterned schooner which was registered at London, Youghal and then Padstow in 1878 when owned by the Hawkeys of Newquay. Soon after 1900 they sold her to Charles H. Davey of Bude. Lost on the Isle of Wight, 11th July 1905 (note on register).

**SAUGEEN** ON 33241, built 1856 at Quebec. Tons 482 reg. 142.0 28.0 17.6. A barque with an Indian Chief as figurehead. After brief registration in Quebec, SAUGEEN was Liverpool registered in 1857 and after various mortgage transactions was Padstow registered that same year, with E. Knight as managing owner and H. Knight as master. Captain Hambling took over as master and SAUGEEN traded from Liverpool to the West Indies before being sold to a Sunderland owner in 1870, to be lost soon afterwards.

**SAUNDERS HILL** built 1818 at Fowey. Tons 121(O). 63.0 21.3 12.0. A schooner noted on her Padstow register as having a deep waist, she was built for Thomas and William Rawlings with Peter Courtenay as master. Four years later, Courtenay and Paynter became the principal owners. Lost in the Kattegat with all hands (*Lloyd's List* 3rd May 1825).

**SCOUT** ON 909, built 1855 at Dartmouth by William Couch. Tons 163(N) 129 reg. 86.9 20.5 11.6. A London registered schooner which traded to Labrador, Newfoundland, Spain and the Mediterranean. *Lloyd's Register* for 1890 gave M. Guy as manager, but in 1891 Warwick R. Guy of Port Isaac was managing owner and in 1894 SCOUT was registered at Padstow with Edward Murdon of Camelford (Chemist) owning 48 shares and W. R. Guy 16 shares. Sunk in collision off Falmouth 23rd July 1894 (note on register).

**SEA LARK** ON 68169, built 1873 at Brixham by Dewdney. Tons 151 net 159 gross, 124 net later. 94.1 22.7 12.5. SEA LARK was a Brixham schooner but in 1890 she was owned by T. Trethewey of Newquay and is therefore listed here. Lost on Haisboro' Sands in 1897. (Verran)

**SECRET** built 1832 at Padstow by Thomas Carter. Tons 75(O) 54(N), 64(N) later. 54.4 18.3 9.3. Built as a sloop for Josias Sleeman, SECRET was altered to schooner rig during repairs at Padstow in 1838. The Carters retained eight shares throughout, and when Josias came ashore, J. and R. Popham went as masters. Lost about 19th November 1850 (note on Padstow register).

**SELINA ANN** ON 44892, built 1862 at Padstow by J. Tredwen. Tons 116 reg. 83.0 20.0 10.2. She was registered at Fowey, a schooner owned by Richard Staunton of St Clear and by her master S. Walters of Looe.

On 5th January 1867 she was wrecked near Marazion in hurricane force winds, carrying coal for Plymouth. The Penzance lifeboat RICHARD LEWIS was brought to the scene by horses and her crew of five gallantly rescued before she went to pieces.

**SERAPHINA** ON 19239, built 1839 at Appledore by Thomas Green. Tons 38(N). 45.3 14.1 8.0. This smack came from the Barnstaple register to Padstow in 1854, owned by her master James Brown and others. Jane Philips of Plymouth was her next owner in 1863, and she went to Appledore owners and Bideford registration in 1867, lasting until the late seventies.

**SHAMROCK** ON 18382, built 1835 at Baltimore, County Cork. Tons 40(O) 30(N), SHAMROCK was built as a sloop, then lengthened during major repairs in 1840 to measure 50(N) tons, being re-rigged as a schooner. When she came from the Cork to the Padstow register in 1854, her dimensions were 53.7 14.3 8.2. Her narrow beam-to-length ratio is doubtless due to her having been lengthened. Richard Hocken and Richard Chegwidden (master) had her at Padstow, and she moved to Fowey in 1860 and Beaumaris in 1864. Unlisted by 1869.

**SHAMROCK** ON 62049, built 1870 at Falmouth by B. Blamey who was also her managing owner. Tons 37 reg. 51.0 15.0 6.6. This ketch was registered at Falmouth, but R. Hocking of Newquay was her master. Lost 25th March 1873.

**SHEBA** built 1821 at Padstow by George Sloggett. Tons 20(O). 33.7 12.4 6.4. A Padstow sloop built for Thomas Phillips, sold in 1829 to T. Tallow and others and in 1832 to Richard Veal. Lost at Boscastle February 1833 (note on register).

**SHEPHERDESS** ON 51303, built 1865 at Salcombe by Bonker. Tons 215 net and gross, later 179 net. 109.1 23.8 13.9. This vessel was consistently described as a brigantine in the port registers, but as a brig at *Lloyd's*. She remained Salcombe owned until 1888 when ownership passed to Thomas May of Port Isaac, with Thomas May Jr as master. In 1890 she was sold to E. Rillston of Fowey who registered her there early the following year. In 1902 she was dismantled and sold as a hulk.

**SILVER STREAM** ON 58292, built 1868 at Polruan by Slade. Tons 152 net. 163 gross. 100.2 22.7 12.7. A large deep water schooner registered at Fowey but with William Geake of St Columb as managing owner. He put her in the Newfoundland trade under Captain E. Tadd and he was succeeded by P. Tadd. Posted missing in *Lloyd's Register* 1881-'2.

**SIR CHARLES NAPIER** ON 12308, built 1854 at Pugwash, Nova Scotia. Tons 576(N), 543 reg. gross. 132.0 27.5 18.7. This barque like so many from the Maritime provinces, was sold to Liverpool owners but by 1860 Robert Langford of Padstow was the principal owner and E. Broad her captain, trading to Quebec. In 1863 major repairs and alterations were carried out at Padstow and she emerged with revised tonnages, 499 net and 513 gross, with a poop deck 32 ft long and a 16 ft fo'c'sle. About that time the port of registry became Truro, but the Padstow ownership continued with Broad gradually taking over from Langford, and with R. Dixon and R. Mabley taking command. In 1872 she broke new ground for Padstow by trading to Ascension Island in the South Atlantic. W. Bastard was her last Padstow master when she was sold to Norwegians in 1880.

**SIR R.R. VYVYAN**, SIR RICHARD VYVYAN (original registration) Built 1826 at Padstow by George Sloggett. Tons 26(O) 22(N). 35.8  13.8  6.5. Lengthened 1834 becoming Tons 32(O) 42.0 13.1 6.4. A sloop registered at Padstow initially by Edward Haynes of Port Isaac with himself and Edward Brown as masters. Then Edward Parnell of Padstow with William Pearce and H. Hutchings: finally Alex Parker. When Robert Stapleton of Bude bought her in 1836 he shifted her registry to Bideford, but she was back on the Padstow register in 1842, owned by Hockin, also of Bude. John Smith and Richard Found were her masters in these later years. Wrecked at Hartland 9th March 1845 after losing one man overboard on a wild night.

**SIR WILLIAM MOLESWORTH** ON 5726, built 1840 at Padstow by Withell. Tons 60(O) 45(N) 42 gross, 36 net. 49.5  15.0  7.7. This sloop rigged smack was registered at Padstow until 1870 when Cardiff became her home port. Those involved as managing owners and masters at Padstow include Hawken (1840), Tippett (1848), Thomas Whitford (banker: 1851), Richard Peters (1851), Brokenshaw, John Lobb, Thomas Cowling, Joe Harris (1852), Chalk (1854), Thomas Brewer (1866), etc. Her Cardiff registration lasted into the early years of the twentieth century.

**SISTERS** built 1806 at Bideford. Tons 126(O). When registered at Fowey in 1807, the owners of this brigantine included Thomas Shepheard. gent., of Stratton (Bude), hence her inclusion here. He also invested in the prize MARY ANN. In 1816 the SISTERS was sold to Penzance.

**SISTERS** built 1807 at Cork, and rebuilt there in 1822. Tons 27(O). 38.3  13.3  9.0. These were her particulars when this smack transferred from Cork to Padstow registration in 1823, to be owned by J. Tredwen with F. Brewer as master. SISTERS was sold to Bristol in 1824.

**SISTERS** ON 15814, built 1822 at Looe. Tons 50(O). 35 reg. 48.6 16.1  7.2. Registered at Looe as a sloop with counter stern, but subsequently described as a schooner. Registered at Padstow in 1825, she was a constant trader to Bude and district. Her owners and captains included Ed. Shearn, Henry James, John Vowler, Furze, Francis Thorne, James Southwood, Thomas and James Cook, John Sumers James and Barrett. In 1851, Oliver Davey, master mariner, held all 64 shares and Bideford became her port of registry. John Elliott was the last master mentioned on the register. SISTERS was broken up at Bude in 1859 (note on register).

**SLYBOOTS** or SLY BOOTS (in *Lloyd's Register*) ON 60103, built 1868 at Dartmouth by Philip. Tons 178 net 189 gross, later 149 net. 104.0 23.5  13.0. Completed as a brigantine, she was converted into a three masted barkentine when Benjamin M. Harvey of Padstow bought her in about 1882. In 1884 she joined W. S. Allport's considerable fleet, but he sold her to Henry Norman of Watchet in 1891. Her port of registry was Brixham throughout. Wrecked near Aldboro' bound for Poole with coal from Newcastle, 9th November 1897. (*Lloyd's Casualty book*)

**SOPHIA** ON 3916, built 1810 at Pilton (Barnstaple). Tons 66(O) 41(N). 48.0  18.7  7.0. Lengthened 1845, tons 102(O) 74(N). 64.2 16.7 8.2. Her rig varies in different registers, but she was completed as a sloop and it is most probable that she became a schooner on lengthening. She came to the Padstow register from Swansea in 1831 to be owned by R. W. Avery. Captain Cobledick and Josiah Symons sailed her in the Mediterranean trades. *Lloyd's* gives her a ketch rig from 1847. Lost in the port of Plymouth 1856.

**SOUETH** see SUEZ

**SOUTHERNER** ON 22531, built 1859 at Aberdeen by Burns. Tons 62 reg. 67.8  19.0  8.5. Built as a smack with some of her beams of iron, but altered to ketch rig on being registered at Padstow in 1866; owned by Henry Buse of Padstow who traded her Clovelly to Mediterranean with W. Nicol as master. In 1870 J. Casey bought her, and one of the Worden family became master.

Supposedly lost about 15th January 1873 off Grassholm whilst on passage from Runcorn with salt and machinery for Padstow; her crew of four were all lost.

**SOUVENIR** ON 58250, built 1868 at Padstow by Stribley. Tons 97 net 110 gross. 84.9  22.5  10.3. A schooner which started by trading to South America. Stribley kept some shares, but she was built for the Coad family of Port Isaac with Joseph G. Coad as managing owner, and for a time master. Missing since 9th January 1883 when she left Milford with coal for Plymouth and a crew of five.

**SPARK** ON 60825, built 1868 at Rye by Hoad. Tons 197 gross 149 net later. 112.4  24.0  12.6. A schooner converted to a three masted barkentine about 1880 and registered at London, Halifax, St John's, and finally Liverpool, where in 1891 she was bought by J. Ennor of Newquay.

On 13th September 1894 she was wrecked SE of Roselier Point, Côtes du Nord, bound for St Brieuc from Antwerp with phosphate.

**SPRIGHTLY** built 1801 at Dartmouth. Tons 44(O). 45.3  15.6  7.6. This square sterned sloop changed hands frequently. She was registered at Dartmouth (1801), St Ives (1809), Padstow (1811), Truro (1814), Fowey (1819), and Padstow 1824, when she was owned by F. Richards of St Endellion (near Port Isaac), with Edmund Richards as master. Beached at Widemouth near Bude after a collision off-shore: Total loss 10th September 1829.

**SPRIGHTLY** ON 15339, built 1830 at Padstow by John Tredwen. Tons 49(O) 33(N) 38 net 44 gross. 46.2  16.0  8.2. Lengthened 1857 to tons 43(N) 55.3  17  7.5. Registered at Padstow throughout her long life, this Padstow registered sloop must have beached herself on every beach between Perranporth and Watchet to deliver coal to outlying communities. The Richards family had her for about 20 years, then the Guys of Port Isaac until about 1894, then E. E. Bunt of Tintagel. Finally, just before the end of the century, she went to Charles Vickery and later Mrs Catherine Norman, both of Watchet, but remaining on the Padstow register.

Lost on passage Swansea for Watchet with culm. Believed seen off Watchet on 2nd December 1909. Her boat was later picked up near Burnham; crew of two lost.

**SPRING** ON 13118, built 1845 at Padstow by Philip Rawle. Tons 55(O) 43(N). 47.3  15.2  8.3. A sloop rigged smack built for Thomas Rickard Avery with Philip Rawle, William Couch and H. Carter as masters. Thomas Couch took over as managing owner in 1859 with Philip Burke and William Brown as masters. Stranded at St Minver 28th July 1873 and was subsequently broken up (note on register).

**SPRING FLOWER** ON 12517, built 1825 at Sunderland. Tons 226(O) 277(N) 196 reg. 81.8  25.6  14.8. Described on completion as a snow, she was soon ascribed a simple brig rig.

The majority of Padstow larger square rigged ships came to the local owners in middle or old age, but SPRING FLOWER was registered in Padstow only two years after completion and under Captain T. Brown made a series of voyages with emigrants to

Quebec and Miramichi, returning with timber.

*Lloyd's List* of 29th July 1837 reports her being damaged in a gale in Boscastle. Anybody familiar with Boscastle must be amazed at the very idea of taking a two hundred ton square rigger into that tiny twisting hole in the cliffs.

Avery and others became the owners in 1841; *Lloyd's Register* that year commented 'wants repair', but that was crossed out when Avery's ownership was added. She continued in the North American trade, mostly to Quebec until 1859, with J. Symons, May, E. Key, Reynolds, T. Richards, C. H. Boase and William Mabley all taking command in turn, and then she was sold to owners in North Shields and lasted another seven years or so.

**STAG** ON 19203, built 1852 at Topsham by Holman or Rowe. Tons 59(O) 36(N) 35 reg. 50.5  16.9  6.3 Built for Christopher Robinson and registered at Padstow in 1852 with J. Rawlins as master, STAG was one of the first ketches on the Padstow register. Preston Wallis became nominated owner the following year with William Williams as master. In 1865 she went to Bridgwater but continued to trade to Padstow and Bude in the early seventies. A ship called STAG went ashore near Clovelly in 1873.

**STANDARD** ON 11403, built 1837 at Fowey by Brokenshaw. Tons 79(O) 51(N), 39 net in 1916. This sloop, altered to ketch rig in 1889, was registered at Fowey throughout her 80 year's in trade. But she is included here because she was owned 1886-'7 by John Barton and A. Tilbum of Newquay before being sold to the Nicholas family of Watchet.

She was hulked in 1917, and she must have been in desperately poor condition by then because freights were high and Britain needed every vessel which could put to sea that year.

**STAR** ON 14127, built 1818 at Padstow by J. Tredwen. Tons 53(O) 36(N). 48.0  16.5  8.0. A sloop registered at Padstow, owned first by O. and J. Davey, then T. Birch, followed by F. and W. Burt with E. Burt, widow; in 1838 Captain Drew took over and there is a report that STAR was wrecked near Swansea pier, but she and Drew survived to be constant traders to Bude until 1856, when there is a note on the register 'Lost at sea 29th October'. She continued to appear in the *Mercantile Navy List* until 1864 but surely that reflected merely lack of communication between Padstow and London.

**STAR OF GWENT** ON 58245, built 1867 at Padstow. Tons 16 reg. 37.0  13.3  7.1. This small cutter was registered at Padstow on completion, owner Thomas Nichols, gentleman of St Columb. That suggests that she was an early yacht, but the following year Cardiff became her port of registry with first, J. P. Lewis, and then Thomas Morse and David Young, pilots, taking her over. She was a pilot cutter.

The STAR OF GHENT sank off Morte Point on 12th April 1890 as a result of colliding with the Cardiff paddle tug PRINCE OF WALES.

**STAR OF ST AGNES** ON 17564, built 1857 at Padstow. Tons 70 net 76 gross, 61 net later. 65.3  19.0  9.9. This schooner was registered at St Ives and owned by the Hitchins family of St Agnes throughout her life of over forty years, largely engaged in the Bristol Channel and Irish Sea trades. Stranded on Lundy Island on 6th July 1899 in calm conditions but broken up by the ground-swell. The date is sometimes reported as 1900, but as she does not appear in the *Mercantile Navy List* that year it seems certain that 1899 is correct.

**STORM** ON 53006. The Norwegian barque BARBARA was renamed STORM after damage repairs in 1866. Tons 333 reg. 109.8  26.6  16.4. She was registered at Padstow, John Tredwen owner and L. Mably master, and sailed with emigrants to North America, and traded to the Cape Verde Islands.

In 1870 she passed to Tredwen's widow, but in 1871 was sold to W. Taylor of Cardiff.

On 17th November 1871 she went on the rocks near Stolford in the Bristol Channel and the Burnham lifeboat stood by her until she was safely refloated.

On 4th April 1872 she was lost at False Larro de Matto Point (note on register).

**STUCLEY** (STUCKLEY often found) ON 22387, built 1839 at Fowey. Tons 28 reg. 41.7  13.7  6.2. lengthened 1874, then tons 32 net. 58.2  16.2  6.3.

The smack STUCLEY was registered at Bideford in 1839 and came to the Padstow register in 1850. She was a constant trader to Bude with John Goodman, George Barrett (who had her lengthened and ketch rigged), and Nicholas Tregaskes owning and sailing her. Early in the twentieth century William Bryant of Truro owned her, and in the Great War, Miss A. Pickett of Ilfracombe, followed by James Crooks of St Helens, Lancs. Between the wars it was Tom Jones and then William H. Latham, both of Lynton.

In 1939, at the age of 100, she ceased trading and was hulked in Ireland and used as a barge for scrap metal. In the official *Mercantile Navy List* she continued to be listed as a ketch until the final edition in 1976, presumably because nobody informed the registrar of her demise.

**SUCCESS.** In 1790 the Padstow sloop SUCCESS was seized by the Excise Cutter FERRET near Ilfracombe and found to be carrying over 1,000 lbs. of 'manufactured tobacco' and nearly 300 lbs. of snuff. (Graham Smith: *Smuggling in the Bristol Channel*)

**SUEZ** see ALAN (ALLAN)

**SUNBEAM** ON 78962, built 1878 at Portreath by Massey. Tons 123 net, 132 gross. 115 net later. 99.8  23.0  11.0. A three masted schooner owned by Willyams of Truro and registered there throughout. By 1884, J. P. Dunstan of St Columb had become managing owner, and he remained so, with G. Tremberth, N. Tremberth and J. A. Tippet as captains until 1897 when she was sold to J. Reney of Connah's Quay. In 1900 registered in Chester. Sold in 1915 to W. B. Firth of Orkney, but sunk bya German submarine on 4th July 1915 on passage Lieth for Kirkwall.

**SUNSHINE** ON 17387, built 1857 at Padstow by John Tredwen. Tons 112 reg. 85.8  20.7  9.8. According to *Mitchell's Maritime Register*, June 1857, SUNSHINE was ketch rigged, but the Padstow port register of the same year described her as a schooner.

She was owned by her builder and intended for the coastal trade, but she did not last long, being lost on Newcombe Sands near Lowestoft on 10th October 1858.

**SUPERIOR** ON 16028, built 1837 at Scilly. Tons 83(O) 69(N). Lengthened 1849, then tons 88(N) 83 reg. 72.2  16.5 10.6 after lengthening. She was schooner rigged before and after lengthening, and traded to the Azores, the Mediterranean and Newfoundland. She was registered at Scilly, Falmouth and finally in 1861 at Plymouth. Samuel Moss of Boscastle owned her in the 1870s; hence her inclusion here.

A schooner named SUPERIOR was wrecked in Barnstaple Bay on 26th October 1886, and that coincided with the disappearance of ON 16028 from the registers.

**SURPRISE** ON 80403, built 1879 at Port Gaverne by Warwick R. Guy. Tons 42 net 49 gross. 59.1  18.1  8.2. A ketch with an elliptical stern, owned by her builder.

On 28th November 1893 the SURPRISE, S. W. Thomas master, was bound from Plymouth for Watchet with alum cake. Off the Lizard she was run down and sunk by the schooner SILVER SPRAY of Dartmouth. No lives were lost.

SUSAN built 1796 at Padstow. A 17 ton (O) sloop of which no register has survived.

SUSAN built 1813 at Padstow by John Tredwen. Tons 71(O). 55.3 17.8 9.2. This was only the second schooner ever built at Padstow, and she had a square stern and a running bowsprit. She was built for Rawlings and registered at Padstow with B. Harvey as master. In 1825 she was owned by John Williams of St Ives which became her port of registry. In 1836 she was owned by Edward Walmsey Messiden, Attorney-at-law of St Ives. 'Seized, condemned, broken up and sold at Penzance 29th December 1836', (note on St Ives register).

SUSAN built 1820 at Padstow; rose upon 1826 by George Sloggett. Tons 13 13/94(O). 30.5 10.6 5.4. Originally an open boat. In 1826 when registered, a decked sloop. Owner and master in 1826, Alex Parker. In 1831 Abraham Prout became owner and Jonathan Knight, Chalk, Benjamin and Alfred Davey, and James Clemens all served as masters. Condemned as unfit 1st May 1837 (note on register).

SUSAN ON 15345, built 1825 at Plymouth. Tons 93(O) 76(N). 59.0 16.6 10.0. This schooner was built for J. Symonds of Plymouth and St Minver. Initially she was registered at Plymouth and traded from London to the East Mediterranean. In 1834 she was bought by John Courtenay and registered at Padstow. Three years later she was sold to Truro where she lasted until about 1868.

SUSAN VITTERY ON 27753, built 1859 at Dartmouth by Kelly. Tons 140 reg. 99 net later. 100.0 21.0 12.0. A schooner largely rebuilt 1918, rigged as a three masted schooner in 1923. A famous ship of which only the bare outline is given here, she was the last fruiterer built for the Vittery fleet of Brixham, trading to the Azores in the 1860s and active in the Newfoundland trade in the 1870s.

In 1880, still on the Brixham register, she was bought by the Hawkeys of Newquay, and in 1907 by the Daveys of Bude who, towards the end of the Great War, sold her to Grimsby owners. In 1923, bought by the Creenan family of Cork, she started a new career as the three masted schooner BROOKLANDS. She continued trading round Ireland through the Second World War to become the last schooner in the British Isles to cross topsail yards — and they were removed in 1949 when she was fitted with an engine. That year she failed to sail on an expedition to the West Indies. She reverted to her original name SUSAN VITTERY, and she started a prolonged refit, becoming in 1952 a fully powered motor vessel. After various false starts, she had to be abandoned in sinking condition off the Tuskar Rock on 6th April 1953.

SUSIE MAY ON 69467, built 1876 at Padstow by Charles Rawle. Tons 123 net 136 gross, 97 net later. 91.2 22.3 11.6. A schooner with round stern and female figurehead, she was built for Thomas May of Port Isaac and registered at Padstow. On 12th October 1900 she was bound for Kirkaldy with china clay from Par when sunk in collision near the Cross Sands lightship off Norfolk.

SWALLOW built 1837 at Orwell Bay, Prince Edward Island. Tons 157(O) 147(N). 75.3 19.1 13.0. A schooner with a billet head sold to London owners soon after completion, and then in 1841 registered at Padstow with P. Wilson as owner and master, but with H. Hillier and Nance later taking command. She traded Clyde to Archangel, Plymouth to Danube, among other destinations. In 1849 she returned to the London register.

SWIFT ON 22979, built 1836 at Fowey by Nickels. Originally tons 30(N) 41.3 14.5 7.6 but lengthened in 1846 to become tons 40 gross 33 net. 52.3 16.6 7.6. SWIFT was built as a sloop and spent time on the Fowey, Falmouth, Plymouth and Bridgwater registers before coming to Padstow in 1891 as a ketch owned by Mrs F. M. Bray of Padstow. She was converted to a lighter and the register closed 28th January 1910.

SWIFT ON 28501, built 1860 at Padstow by J. Tredwen. Tons 26 reg. 45.6 14.6 7.5. This pilot cutter was registered at Bristol for over 40 years, with owners at Cumberland Basin (Bristol), Pill and Cardiff. She foundered in Barry Roads on 25th November 1903.

SWIFT ON 62193, built 1871 at Portsmouth by Read. Tons 126 gross 97 net in 1906. 88.5 22.3 10.6. Although registered at Fowey this schooner is often referred to as the SWIFT of Padstow, because she was owned by Joseph G. Coad of Port Isaac and captained by himself, W. Martin and W. M. Moyse. Finally, she was owned by Mrs Jessie Lander of Wadebridge; register closed 1910.

SYLPH ON 19223, built 1853 at Port Isaac by James Stephens. Tons 31 net 38 gross. 52.4 15.4 7.6. This cutter rigged smack lifted countless loads of roofing slates from Port Gaverne for Warwick R. Guy of Port Isaac with M. & T. Mitchell as masters, until in 1894 she went to Bideford owners who converted her to ketch rig and carried on as before for another 30 years before selling her to George Binderig of Cardiff.

Her register closed 22nd September 1928 with the note 'Vessel converted to Houseboat'.

SYMMETRY ON 22495, built 1829 at Padstow by J. Tredwen. Tons 118(O) 100(N) 86 reg. 65.6 20.7 11.1 (1829), This schooner was registered at Padstow in 1829, owned by T. Hicks (her master) and others. She was re-registered in Truro in 1832 and lengthened in 1838. Lloyd's survey report that year confirmed that she was 'lengthened 8 ft forward' yet there was no change in tonnage measurement. Her Falmouth register in 1845 gives dimensions 64.9 19.0 10.6, presumably copied from the Truro register before lengthening. She was back in the Truro register in 1852. Foundered 26th October 1876 (note on Truro register).

T.E.J. ON 63060, built 1871 at the Gannel Yard, Newquay, by T & J Clemens. Tons 95 net 108 gross. 89.2 22.0 10.5. This schooner's name is derived from her managing owner's name, Thomas E. Jenkin. Her first master was J. Jenkyn, but T. E. Clemens and J. Hockin also had interests in her. She was registered at St Ives throughout. She was no coaster, as witness her appearances in Lloyd's List. Lost at Genoa on 7th November 1873, but salved, repaired and re-registered. Foundered near Corsica, 23rd April 1878.

T.M.P. ON 68862, built 1874 at Portreath by Thomas Massey. Tons 45 net, 50 gross. 63.2 18.3 7.8. This small vessel was described as a ketch in her port register, but Lloyd's call her a dandy. Her name may derive from Thomas Massey of Portreath. He was her first managing owner as well as building her. She was registered at Hayle but Joseph Cock of Padstow had shares in her, as did R. Brenton of Newquay who was her master at one time.

She moved to the Lynn register in 1881 and to Bideford in 1897, was fitted with a 20 b.h.p. motor in 1915, but was lost on the rocks near Ilfracombe on 12th February 1917, carrying a cargo of gravel from Barnstaple for Newport.

T.P.C. ON 28143, built 1860 at Appledore by Cook. Tons 58 reg. 62.5 18.3 9.0. A schooner with a boy figurehead, the initials are those of her first owner, T. P. Cook of Bideford. In 1863 Padstow became her port of registry when she was bought by Thomas Webb Ward of Boscastle. That same year J. W. Jenkyns of Boscastle became managing owner and master. T.P.C. was lost about 11th September 1869 on passage from St Ives towards Plymouth.

TALBOT ON 840, built 1834 at Plymouth. Tons 62(O) 42(N); lengthened 1848, tons 73(O) 42(N); lengthened again 1863, tons 65 gross. TALBOT was built as a sloop but converted to schooner rig when first lengthened, retaining that rig when re-lengthened. She spent her life registered at Falmouth except that from 1861 to 1864 Padstow was her port of registry. Her dimensions in 1861 were 61.8

16.8 7.9. Her Padstow owner was W. Gray of Wadebridge, with Captain S. Bate as master. On 3rd May 1875 the TALBOT was run down and sunk by an unidentified steamship off Trevose Head. The ketch FLYING CLOUD of Jersey picked up her crew and landed them safely at Padstow.

**TAMAR** (TAMER also found) ON 19214, built 1807 in France. A prize made free in 1809. 40(O) later 46(O) 36 reg. 46.8 15.5 7.7. A sloop registered at Penzance in 1815 but already owned by Sloggett with Bellamy as master; transferred to the Padstow register in 1820, owned by Billing and thereafter run for a time by the Carter family, followed by varying participation from the following: James Charles, Osborne, William Roberts, George Nickels, John England, William Hoskins, Sam Bate and William Corsall. John Tredwen owned her from 1850. Lost off Hartland Point on 4th December 1859 (note on register).

**TARIFF** ON 11415, built 1844 at Fowey by John Marks and William Rendle. Tons 49 reg. 52.9 16.8 8.2 This Fowey smack was owned in the 1860s by Nicholas Hockin of Newquay with T. Hockin as master. Foundered after collision off Wicklow Head 21st March 1868.

**TEAZER** ON 69452, built 1873 at Barnstaple by William Westacott. Tons 50 net 60 gross. 62.0 19.3 8.3, lengthened 1896 at Dennis Cove, then tons 64 net 79 gross. 81.5 20.4 8.3. Built as a smack with elliptical stern, she was converted to ketch rig on lengthening. Despite being built at Barnstaple and having Gould of Barnstaple as a major owner, TEAZER was registered at Padstow. J. Hockaday of Delabole was the other major owner, doubtless reflecting the importance of the Delabole slate quarry as a source of cargo. In 1892 W. S. Allport of Padstow bought 40 of the 64 shares, and in effect she joined his considerable fleet. On 7th January 1901 she was wrecked off Stepper Point bringing coal for Padstow from Runcorn with a crew of three.

**TELEGRAM** ON 19281, built 1857 at Padstow. Tons 52 reg. 64.7 17.4 8.2. A small schooner registered at Fowey, owned by Thomas Varcoe of St Dennis and others. J. Mabley, W. Couch and Sherlock of Newquay were her masters. Lost by collision off Dover 1st September 1878.

**TELEGRAPH** ON 27271, built 1859 at Port Gaverne by Warwick R. Guy. Tons 41 net 52 gross, 36 net later. 55.2 18.0 8.3. A cutter rigged smack registered at Padstow which endured all the usual adventures of her ilk. In 1867 she was wrecked on the Doom Bar, but got off. Guy was her owner until he died on 30th April 1905, when she was sold to Mary Ann Lang, widow, of Braunton, and two years later to J. Cox of Appledore. J. Hutchings was her master on 27th December 1906 when she was wrecked abreast of Monkey Rock in the River Taw bringing coal from Cardiff for Fremlington. It was not winter gales which caused the wreck but swirling tides and a total lack of wind.

**TELEPHONE** ON 77408, built 1878 at Barnstaple by Westacott. Tons 44 net 51 gross, 31 net later. 59.7 19.1 8.5. As with TEAZER, W. Gould of Barnstaple had important ownership of this smack, but she was registered at Padstow with Mark Guy as manager and with W. Thomas, Couch and J. Hill as masters. Also like TEAZER she joined Allport's fleet in the 1890s but was sold to Welsh owners in 1899 and registered at Cardigan in 1902. Lost at Islay on 15th November 1908 (J. G. Jenkins)

**TEMPERANCE** ON 19261, built 1841 at Padstow by Richard Tredwen. Tons 47(O) 34(N) 34 reg. 43.4 14.2 7.6. This Padstow sloop was owned by the Hoskin and Phillips families.

Lost off Morwenstow 1858. (Dudley Stamp). Other sources confirm that she was lost on 24th May 1858 in a N W gale, on passage Newport for Padstow with coal.

**TEST** see LADY MONA

**THE KILDARE** ON 1035, built 1854 at Quebec by Jean Lamelin. Tons 701(N) 812 reg. KILDARE (in *Lloyd's Register*). 150.8 31.3 19.3. This full rigged ship, like so many other Canadian built vessels was sold to UK owners soon after completion. THE KILDARE was registered at Liverpool, but in 1865 John Cory bought all 64 shares and registered her at Padstow. He soon had her rig altered to that of a three masted barque to reduce the size of the crew, and used her in trade to the West Indies and South America with Captains G. Maberly and J. Evans in command. She was sold to South Shields in 1872 and drops out of the registers about 1882.

**THE SAINT** SAINT (THE) ON 54776, built 1870 at Drogheda by Thomas Grendon & Co. Tons 108 net 118 gross, 97 net later. 87.2 21.3 10.7. This schooner was registered at Drogheda and then in 1874 at Runcorn, owned by William Henry Williams of Newquay. For a time she passed to owners in Cheshire and Portmadoc, but in 1895 Williams bought her again and the following year she was registered at Padstow. Her Padstow masters included D. Roberts, G. Randell, J. Lobb, J. Williams and J. Keelon. In 1900 ownership passed to Mrs Towerson of Berwick. On 2nd May 1904 she was lost by stranding near Cowes (note on register).

**THOMAS** built 1797 at Bideford. Tons 214(O) amd 219(O). No Padstow registration of this small full rigged ship has survived, but *Lloyd's Register* 1805 posted the ownership of T. Rawlins and added J. Adams as master. The register then showed her trading from Plymouth to Cork for a number of years. Comparison with the case of the WILLIAM of 1789 makes a convincing case that THOMAS was a Padstow ship bought as a replacement for WILLIAM. THOMAS lasted until about 1819.

**THOMAS** built 1824 at Padstow by George Sloggett. Tons 36(O). 40.9 14.8 7.2. A sloop registered at Padstow, owned by Sloggett and later by Hambley, trading from Bristol to Padstow and round to Falmouth. In 1836 sold to Barnstaple and in 1846 to Swansea.

**THOMAS** ON 27274, built 1859 at Padstow by Edwin Carter. Tons 26 reg. 55.7 17.0 4.4. A round sterned smack registered at Padstow, owned by Edwin Carter, with I. Pappin as master. In 1864 she was sold to Welsh owners and registered at Aberystwith. Foundered following collision off St Govan's Head, Pembrokeshire in December 1892 (note on register).

**THOMAS & ELIZABETH** ON 19219, built 1842 at St Georges Well Yard, Padstow. Tons 60(O) 43(N). 49.9 15.1 7.9. lengthened 1869, then 53 net 60 gross. 68.3 17.7 7.7. She was built as a smack for Richards of Port Isaac; subsequently the Burd, Brewer and Pethybridge families had shares and William Williams was master for a time. William Harvey of Padstow had her lengthened and altered to ketch rig (although she was sometimes described as a schooner). In the 1890s Arthur B. Hutchings also of Padstow bought her and, finally, in 1899 she was sold to Edward Lister of Plymouth. Broken up at Kingsbridge and Padstow register closed 1902.

**THOMAS & HARRIOTT** built in Holland and described in *Lloyd's Register* as 'old'. A prize previously named EMANUEL, made free in 1809, registered at Falmouth in 1811 and at Padstow in 1815. Tons 52(O). 49.0 16.5 5.8. Her owner then was William Rawlins and John Giles was her master. *Lloyd's Register* 1815 gives her intended voyage as Falmouth-Pssage. If that signified Pasajes in Spain, here was another small vessel supporting the Duke of Wellington, like the old CERES. Broken up 1822. (PRO BT 107/153).

**THOMAS & MARY** built 1800 at Newlyn. Tons 19(O). 35.5 12.9 6.0.

She was rigged as a sloop, registered at Penzance and owned by L. Love. The following information is contained in the 1821 Padstow port register: 'This vessel was seized with contraband and condemned in Exchequer in 1804, was sold and registered at Falmouth in 1805'. Her register moved to Padstow in 1821 when Francis Webster was her master and manager, other owners being William Mill James, James and John Phillips, John and Mary Madron, E. Stephens and John Odgers. She was sold on to Ipswich that same year.

**THOMAS & NANCY** built 1821 at Padstow by John Tredwen. Tons 98(O) 79(N). 59.8 19.9 10.7. She was variously described as schooner or brig, but it is well established that she was of polacre rig. Registered at Padstow, her first owner was Avery, with Richards as master. In 1829 J. Yeo took her over and kept her until he sold her to Williams of Bideford where she was registered in 1848. She was run down by the barque BOLTON 5 miles NNE of the Eddystone on 22nd February 1853.

**THOMASINE & MARY** ON 19226, built 1855 at Boscastle by T. R. Avery. Tons 51(N) 49 net 70 gross, 38 net later. 65.0 16.2 8.2. Avery gave this smack the name ANN as she was building, but she was registered at Padstow as THOMASINE & MARY by R. Hellyer. In 1856 she was sold to Swansea and registered there, and in 1858 the Hole family of Watchet bought her and her register moved to Bridgwater. By 1900 she was ketch rigged. The Holes sold her in 1919 but she remained a Bridgwater ship. On 7th September 1926 she was wrecked in Walton Bay, Portishead, carrying barley for Hayle.

**THREE BROTHERS** built 1782 at the Dinas yard, Padstow. Tons 21(O). A sloop of which no register has survived.

**THREE BROTHERS** built 1800 at Brixham; rebuilt 1826 at Padstow, after which tons 36(O) 23(N). 42.7 14.6 6.4. Her registration had been at Bideford before coming to Padstow in 1826. She was a constant trader to Bude and her Padstow owners were R. W. Avery, John Martyn and finally in 1852, John Old, a shoemaker of St Merryn. Her masters included John Dark, P. Billing, William Tremere, George Harvey, John Dark and William Fielding. She was lost at sea with all hands and her register closed 20th February 1854.

**THREE FRIENDS** built 1792 at Padstow. Tons 36(O). A sloop for which no registration survives, not to be confused with the THREE FRIENDS seized by the Revenue Cutter FERRET and sold at Ilfracombe in 1789; she had been built at St Mary's in 1788.

**THREE SISTERS** built 1808 at Bideford by Richard Chapman. Tons 37(O) 32(N). 41.2 13.1 8.1. Unless there is a missing register, which is quite possible, this sloop did not enter the Padstow register until 1846 when J & R Tredwen owned her. William Chalk, Nick Bunt, Ralph Mably and Hicks were her masters until she was lost off Tintagel on 30th August 1849.

**TISDALE** built in France, date and place unknown. *Lloyd's Register* 1809 includes a 45 ton sloop of this name trading from Bristol to Padstow. Her owner was T. Smith and her master W. Cowl.

Between 23rd and 30th December 1809 the Westcountry newspapers reported a TENDALE or TENDELL of Padstow as being wrecked at Tintagel. With the Cowl family established at Padstow, it is possible that TISDALE was a Padstow ship and that it was her loss reported in the papers.

**TITANIA** ON 47275, built 1865 at Dodbrook, Kingsbridge, Devon by Date. Tons 145 net 185 gross. 103.0 22.8 12.8. TITANIA was a fine schooner built for the Sladen fleet of Salcombe. In 1885 John Ennor of Newquay became managing owner with J. Brown as master, but she remained on the Salcombe register. In 1913 she was unrigged and registered at Fowey as a coal lighter. Broken up in 1926 (Librarian, Customs House, Mark Lane).

**TOM HENRY** ON 55383, built 1867 at Fraserburgh by Webster. Tons 124 net 133 gross. 92.0 22.4 11.0. A schooner registered at Kirkwall throughout her life, but bought by John Ennor of Newquay about 1882. Her masters during his ownership included H. Jones, J. Clemens, D. Tinney, J. Solomon and E. J. Reynolds. Lost at Whitehaven 1896.

**TON MAWR** ON 54578, built 1865 at Padstow by Willmett. Tons 100 net 122 gross. 92.0 22.4 10.5. A schooner built as a speculation and launched unnamed and unsold on 18th August 1865. Nevertheless she was registered at London before the end of the year and in 1867 was registered at Ipswich trading thence to the Baltic. In 1875 Fowey became her port of registry and in 1885, at a time when Westcountry owners were buying Scottish schooners, TON MAWR reversed the process by transferring to Ardrossan. 'Missing since October 1889'; *Lloyd's Register* 1890 was posted thus.

**TOWAN** built 1803 at St Mawes. Tons 142(O) 137(N). 70.0 20.6 12.5. A brig with 6 guns (*Lloyd's Register* 1810). In 1816 she was registered at Penzance. In October 1843 she was bound from Llanelly with a cargo of culm for Littlehampton, when a northerly gale forced her to seek shelter in Padstow. On 23rd she grounded under Stepper Point and Richard Tredwen and his boats crew were credited with saving the ship and her crew. Others successfully warped her in to safety. She ended the year in the legal ownership of Thomas Carter of Padstow but under arrest for the non-payment of salvage awards to those who had warped her in. Their claims were soon found to be spurious or excessive. In 1845 Padstow became her port of registry, and Philip Burke of Boscastle was her owner and master. Lost 24th June 1845 (note on register).

**TOWER** ON 19242, built 1851 at Quay Yard, Newquay by J & M Clemens. Tons 95(O) 72 reg. 59 net. 60.2 16.9 9.7. TOWER was built as a schooner but converted to a ketch about 1886. The Clemens family retained shares and others involved were the Carters, the Chalks and William C. Phillips of Port Isaac. She was on the Padstow register throughout.

On 21st August 1896 she was wrecked at the entrance to Queen's Channel, Liverpool Bay, bound from Ellesmere for Polkerris with coal. Captain F. Post and his crew of two were safe, although the wind was WSW force 9.

**TRAVELLER** ON 19267, built 1835 at Padstow by John Sloggett. Tons 53(O) 37(N) and reg. 46.9 16.5 8.3. A typical Padstow sloop rigged smack registered initially with Sloggett as owner, then Stribley in 1836, followed by the May family, with John Tredwen taking a steadying role in the 1850s. But John Bate May was master and managing owner when, on 7th July 1863, she was lost at Gunwalloe (note on register).

**TREBISKIN** ON 22199, built 1859 at Padstow by Edwin Carter. Tons 50 reg. 60.3 17.5 8.7, lengthened 1868, then tons 60 net 69 gross. 77.3 18.7 8.7. TREBISKIN was built as a schooner and registered at Padstow in the ownership of Carter & Co. with E. Tabb as master. In 1866 Thomas Martyn of Wadebridge became owner and in 1886 he had her converted into a ketch. In the mid-1890s the owner became William Chidgey but after 1904 the owners were from Holyhead, Portmadoc and Swansea though the register remained at Padstow. On 13th July 1918 she was damaged by U-boat gunfire 15 miles NW by N. of the Smalls and had to be towed into Milford. She was bound for Swansea with pitwood from Youghal at the time. That November she was lost with all hands on the shoals off the Gower Coast.

**TREFFRY** ON 11021, built 1849 at Quay Yard, Newquay by J & M Clemens. Tons 82(N) 65 net 77 gross. 65.9 17.2 10.4. This schooner was the first vessel built at the Quay Yard, and was named after J. F. Treffry who promoted the new harbour construction and was therefore responsible for the existence of the yard. Reports of her completion say she was built 'for the foreign trade' but she was not yellow metalled, and was described in *Lloyd's Register* as a coaster. F. Jenkin was her first managing owner and master: James Evans of St Agnes had a major share of her in the 1860s; James Trebilcock took over in the 1870s, and finally W. Thomas in the 1880s. She was registered at Padstow throughout. On 14th September 1887 she sank in the River Risle, which runs into the estuary of the Seine. Her master, Captain W. Allen, was taking coal from Swansea for Pont Audemer which is several miles up the river. She was a total loss.

**TREGUNNEL** ON 21378, built 1858. Construction started at the Island Cove Yard but was completed at Gannel by J & M Clemens. Tons 82 net 93 gross 78 net later. 76.3 22.3 10.0. This schooner was built for the Carter family who sold shares to William Thomas also of Newquay. The Carters and T. Gill were her masters for over a quarter of a century. In late 1887 she sank off Penarth, but was raised and sold to Cardiff owners. By 1899 she had been sold again to Dungarvan, County Waterford, but she was still registered at Padstow. Not heard of since leaving Newport on 18th October 1907 with coal for Dungarvan, and a crew of four.

**TREMENHERE** ON 29188, built 1863 at Padstow by John Tredwen. Tons 108 net 120 gross. 85.5 21.4 11.3. This schooner was built for Mitchell and others of Devoran, and was registered at Truro. She ceased to be listed by 1879.

**TREORE** built 1803 at Plymouth. Tons 155(O). A brig armed with two guns. According to *Lloyd's Register*, her first owner was Hambley, with P. Harvey as master. Then, from 1805 to 1810 *Lloyd's Register* gave Mr Norway as owner. All these are names of Padstow (or local) families, and Treore is the name of an estate near Port Gavern and a mine nearby. Furthermore, the Norway family had investments near Treore. It seems very probable, therefore, that TREORE was a Padstow ship of which the port registration has been lost. She last appears in *Lloyd's* 1838 as a Sunderland ship.

**TRETHERRAS** ON 29364, built 1863 at Padstow by Stribley according to her register, but others say Willmett. Tons 67 net 77 gross. 73.3 19.9 9.8. This schooner was registered at Padstow with Stribley as owner, but he soon gave way to Richard Cardell of St Columb Minor and Sarah Jane White. Edward Whitford bought her in 1869. Foundered off St Bees in March 1873 after her cargo had shifted.

**TREVANNANCE** or **TREVAUNANCE** ON 14093 built 1836 by John Tredwen. Tons 88(O) 62(N). 65.1 16.6 9.4. This rather narrow-gutted vessel was built as a sloop with a running bowsprit and square stern, but her mainsail must have been too large for safe handling and she was soon converted to a schooner without being lengthened. She was registered at St Ives in 1836 and again in 1837 when Thomas Avery of Padstow was the surveyor after her re-rigging. Martin Hitchens of St Agnes owned her. In the early hours of 29th March 1857, in a easterly gale, she was driven onto a sandbank off Porthcawl and the tremendous surf sank her within minutes. The crew of four lashed themselves to the topmast and were seen from the shore through the driving mist and spray. They had been there for sixteen hours when, after many gallant attempts, a boat managed to reach them. One was already dead, but the other three were just able to cut their lashings and drop into the boat.

**TREVANNANCE** or **TREVAUNANCE** ON 19892, built 1858 at the Quay Yard, Newquay, by Richard Tredwin. Tons 55 net 65 gross. 65.4 19.0 9.2. This schooner with fixed bowsprit and square stern was built for Martin Hitchens as a replacement for the last vessel and registered at St Ives. J. Henwood of Newquay was her master for many years. Wrecked near Cardiff on 1st November 1887 (note on register).

**TRINITY BUOY YACHT** built 1791 on the Thames, lengthened 1797. Tons 118(O). Sheathed and doubled (*Lloyd's Register* 1800), and rigged as a snow. This vessel, like another of the same name *c.* 1820, was presumably originally owned by Trinity House and used for the provision and maintenance of navigational aids. She was sold for commercial service, appearing in the supplement to *Lloyd's Register* 1798 as owned by Rawlins and trading Bristol-Wales. Since Rawlins was the principal merchant and shipowner of Padstow at the time, she is being included in this list without there being any firm evidence that she was a Padstow ship. She went to other owners in 1805 and was no longer listed in 1812.

**TRIUMPH** ON 84977, built 1881 at the Gannel Yard, Newquay, by T & J Clemens. Tons 84 net 93 gross. 79.9 21.8 9.7. A ketch with elliptical stern rigged to set a squaresail and raffee topsail. The last ship built at Newquay, her history is covered more fully elsewhere in this book. She was registered at Padstow, owned by W. Thomas and J. Hardie, with R. J. Hockin as master. In 1885 she was sunk in collision in the Thames, but raised and repaired and registered at London, then Jersey, and finally London again at the start of the Great War. Missing since leaving Briton Ferry on 3rd November 1915 with coal for Landerneau.

**TRURO** ON 179, built 1853 at Padstow by J. Tredwen Jr. Tons 99(O) 90 reg. 68 net later. 75.0 17.1 9.9. This schooner was registered at Truro on completion, owned by the Truro Shipping Company — a comparatively early example of a genuine shipping company in the Westcountry. In 1882 she was sold to Bridgwater and in 1901 there is a note that she was 'sold foreign', and another that she was owned by the Brazilian Coal Co. of Cardiff in 1902.

**TRY AGAIN** ON 54213, built 1866 at Port Hill, Prince Edward Island by James Yeo Jr. Tons 215 reg. 100.0 24.0 13.9. A brig with an elliptical stern and billet head, she was registered briefly in Prince Edward Island then, still in 1866, at Falmouth with the following ownership:

|                                                          | Shares |
|----------------------------------------------------------|-------:|
| John Ruse Bellamy of Boscastle, Master Mariner            | 36 |
| John Bellamy of Boscastle, Master Mariner                 | 16 |
| William Hicks of Newquay, Draper                          | 8 |
| John Reynolds of Newquay, Jeweller                        | 4 |

John Ruse Bellamy was managing owner and John Bellamy was master. She was felted and yellow metalled and the 1868 register showed her trading from Bideford to the Mediterranean, and in 1871 from Liverpool to South America. Foundered 5th January 1874 (note on Falmouth register).

**TRY AGAIN** ON 58802, built 1868 at Kippford by Cuming (Cumming ?). Tons 139 net 162 gross 128 net later. 95.0 22.1 12.9. This vessel was described as a schooner in *Lloyd's*, but as a brigantine in the *Mercantile Navy List*. She was registered at Dumfries, but the Hawkey family of Newquay bought her about 1882, and moved her to the Padstow register in 1891. That register describes her as a three masted brigantine, a term which was used instead of barkentine. Her barkentine rig is confirmed by a fine pierhead painting in the National Maritime Museum. W. J. M. Hawkey sold her to John Carbines of St Ives in 1904. She was wrecked on the Dodman on 6th October 1908, bound for Dublin with phosphate from Antwerp. Her crew of five survived.

**TRYALL** or **TRIAL** ON 4089, built 1816 at Padstow. Tons 29(O) later 33 reg. This venerable Bristol Channel pilot cutter was owned by Pilot Thomas Vowles of Pill from 1847 until 1878, serving as Pilot Skiff No.17. After that she sailed on into the 1890s, ending up with a Newport owner but still registered at Bristol. Broken up 1892.

**TULLOCHGORUM** ON 55245, built 1867 at Garmouth by Duncan. Tons 157 net 165 gross, 127 net later. 94.0  22.12  12.3. This brigantine was registered at Montrose until 1880, when she shifted to Plymouth and John Haynes of Port Isaac became managing owner, and for much of the time, master, in which capacity G. Brown also served. On 29th December 1894 she was wrecked at Widemouth Bay near Bude, on passage from Cardiff with coal for Plymouth. Her crew were rescued by breeches buoy.

**TULLOCHGORUM** ON 65357, built 1873 at Peterhead by Stephen. Tons 175 net 184 gross, 139 net later. 107.8  23.5  11.7. A three masted schooner registered at Peterhead, but in 1880 she was bought by J. Haynes of Port Isaac and from about 1882 to 1899 she was owned by John Crocker of Newquay who captained her himself for a time and then handed over to a Trebilcock. In 1899 Crocker sold her to W. V. Kellow of Pentewan, and she went onto the Fowey register. On 23rd January 1910 she sank in collision in the Mersey, having sailed from Runcorn with coal for Malpas. Subsequently she was raised and used as an unrigged barge by Kelly's Barges Ltd, then, after the Second World War, by Wadsworth Lighterage & Coaling Co. Ltd, Liverpool. She ceased to be listed in 1950.

**TWO SISTERS.** In March 1812 a sloop named TWO SISTERS of Padstow, Captain Smith, was lost on a voyage from Truro for Bristol. No Padstow register of this vessel survives.

**ULELIA** ON 74429, built 1877 at Truro by Dyer. Tons 69 net 74 gross, 58 net later. 75.4  19.9  9.4. B. Phillips of Newquay was master and part owner of this Truro schooner for 20 years, leading to her inclusion here. By the end of the century she had been sold to William Slade of Appledore, and converted to ketch rig; in due course Bideford became her port of registry. A generation of Appledore men nursed her along until she was lost on the rocks at Ross Carberry, Ireland in April 1930.

**UNION** built 1796 at Pilton. Tons 73(O). 57.0  17.8  10.0. A brigantine which was registered at St Ives, and owned by John Vivian of Padstow mariner.

**UNION** built 1801 at Padstow. Tons 48(O). The register of this sloop has not survived, but *Lloyd's* contains the information that she was owned and captained by T. Richards in 1815; she was advertised for sale in February 1818, and in 1820 owned by Pollard with Boundy as master. A sloop UNION of Padstow, 65 tons, was advertised for sale in July 1812. The vessel above might have been of 65 tons burthen.

**UNION** built 1821 on Prince Edward Island. Tons 66(O). 54.5  17.6  9.5 described both as a schooner and as a schooner-brig and therefore probably a brigantine. In 1826, registered at Plymouth; described as a recovered wreck, lost at Swansea but rebuilt July 1826. In 1827, registered at St Ives with William Philip of Padstow as part owner (warranting her inclusion in this list). Lost and register closed 4th April 1833.

**UNION** see L'UNION later JOSEPHINE

**UNIONEER** According to Ennor, and a poem by Robert Sleeman, a vessel named UNIONEER was wrecked on the Doom Bar in an October gale in 1823.

**UNITY** built 1783 at Bristol. Tons 35(O). 42.5  14.7  7.7. A sloop which was registered at Padstow in 1826, having previously been registered at Truro in 1811. In 1826 she was owned by Joseph Thomas and others and Abel French was her master. Two years later Martin Withell was her owner and William Carter her master. Lost 9th August 1828 (note on register).

**UNITY** ON 19255, built 1812 at Padstow by J. Tredwen, and rebuilt there, after a fire, in 1847 by R & J. Tredwen. Tons 59(O) 47(N) 59 reg. 51.3  17.0  8.8. This sloop was registered at Padstow throughout a long life. Her first owner-master was W. Sargent, and thereafter the following families were successively involved: Carveth, Brewer, Pollard, Richards, Stribley, Philp, and for the last 20 years or so William Chalk of Port Isaac. Lost on 6th March 1872 in Boscastle when the heavy ground swell broke her moorings, allowing her to be battered against quay and cliff.

**UNITY** ON 47255, built 1863 at North Hylton, Sunderland by Wheatley. Tons 126 reg. 83.7  21.8  11.5. This brigantine was fitted with a patent topsail rig which allowed the sail to be reefed from deck. She was registered at Portsmouth but by 1874 owned by Thomas Jenkins of Newquay. Jos. P. Dunstan of St Columb was her managing owner in 1876. Lost with all hands off Whitby in the great October gale of 1880.

**VALENCY** built 1825 at Padstow by J. Tredwen. Tons 60(O). 50.2  16.8  8.8.. Ths sloop VALENCY was named after the stream at Boscastle and registered at Padstow. The Bellamy family owned and navigated her, with the help of W. Pelham, Roseveare and William Sloggett. Lost near Mullion Island 24th November 1834 (note on register).

**VALENCY** ON 21120, built 1838 at Plymouth. Tons 37 (N). 47.3  14.2  7.1. This smack was registered at Padstow, having been built for R. Langford of Boscastle. Her masters included Burnard Carter, Phillips, Philp, Bate and John Nevil of Padstow. In 1865 she was lengthened, becoming 58 tons reg. 75.6  17.0  7.0, and being converted to schooner rig. Willmett had owned her immediately before the conversion, Joseph Tippett in 1865, and John and William Stribley in the seventies. Broke from moorings at Newport, Monmouthshire and was lost 14th October 1877.

**VALENTINE** built 1816 at Padstow. Tons 56(O). This Padstow sloop was built for Richards but only had a short life, being wrecked near Portreath on 20th September 1820. Her crew were saved. (*Lloyd's List* 26.9.1820)

**VEHO** ON 56631, built 1867 at Brixham by Upham. Tons 199 gross. 111.1  23.6  12.9. This fine schooner was yellow metalled and, for Upham, traded initially from Dartmouth to Brazil and later to the Mediterranean. In 1884 Benjamin M. Harvey of Padstow bought her and she briefly entered W. S. Allport's fleet, with J. Worden as master. She remained registered at Brixham. On 16th February 1884 VEHO was wrecked on Skomer Island, sailing with pipeclay from Teignmouth for Runcorn. The wind was SE force 9. She had a crew of six who all survived.

**VELOCITY** ON 13090. built 1842 at Bude by Robert Stapleton. Tons 45(N). 50.1  16.2  7.8. This vessel was registered at Padstow as a sloop owned by John Found of Bude with C. Found as master. In 1844 she was sold to John Salcombe of Tavistock for 224 Pounds, and in 1845 registered at Bideford. In 1853 Milford became her home port and her rig was changed to schooner without lengthening. She lasted into the '90s as a Welsh coaster registered at Aberystwith. Reported foundered off Cape Cornwall.

**VENUS** built 1820 at Padstow by G. Sloggett and William Hambly. Tons 46(O). 45.5  16.0  7.7. A sloop rigged smack built for R. Avery with Thomas Brown as master. She was registered in 1820 and again in 1825 when her ownership was as follows:

Thomas Brown of Tintagel                                          32
George Sloggett of Padstow                                        8
William Hambly of Padstow                                        8
Thomas Rickard Avery of Boscastle                           16

On 16th May 1826 she struck the Manacles and was lost (note on register).

**VESPER** ON 25621, built 1837 at Barnstaple by John Westacott. Tons 87(O) 77(N). 56.1  16.6  10.3. lengthened 1839, then tons 119(O) 99(N). 68.0  17.8  10.4. VESPER was a schooner both before and after lengthening. She was built on spec. and sold to Robert Langford of Boscastle (22 shares), R. W. Avery of Padstow (21 shares), and John Bellamy of Boscastle (21 shares) with John Bellamy as managing owner, even when in 1853 her register was transferred from Padstow to Plymouth. H. Swaffen and J. & W. James were her masters as well as Bellamy himself. Thomas Bate of Port Isaac took over command of her about 1865, and was later her managing owner. She foundered off Ilfracombe after hitting floating wreckage on 30th November 1880.

**VESTA** ON 24516, built 1845 at Padstow by R & J Tredwen. Tons 45(N). 48.5  15.0  9.0. A Padstow sloop owned by William Pollan of Egloshayle. Her masters included Richard Blight, Sam Phillips, R. Philp, Oats, Lobb and W. Gill. On 22nd November 1877 she arrived at Port Gaverne with coal from Cardiff, but the wind went round to the NNW and blew force 10. VESTA was driven ashore and wrecked, but her crew of three survived. (note on register)

**VIA** ON 48634, built 1864 at Brixham by J. Upham. Tons 99 net 126 gross. 91.0  21.3  12.0. The schooner VIA was built for the Newfoundland trade and registered at Brixham throughout her long life. She is included here because Francis Brewer of Padstow bought her in the late '70s and sold her in 1880 to Llanelly owners. After a spell in Scottish ownership she was back in the Bristol Channel in 1891, owned by Frank Nurse of Gloucester. Eventually in 1927 she was sold to Kilkeel owners and lost by stranding off Carlingford on 5th June 1931.

**VICTOR** ON 4037, built 1845 at Padstow by R & J Tredwen. Tons 22(N). A pilot cutter registered at Bristol, and owned by various pilots at Pill until sold to Cardiff about 1881. No longer listed in 1900.

**VICTORIA** built 1837 at Bude by Stapleton. Tons 61(O) 37(N). A sloop registered at Padstow in 1837, owned by John Found of Bude (who was her master), J. Sullivan of Bude and T. Andrew of Kilkhampton. Lost April 1842 (note on register).

**VICTORIA** ON 19228, built 1847 at Padstow. Tons 37(N) and 37 reg. 45.9  15.1  7.6 as built. Lengthened 1872, then tons 49 reg. 65.6  17.6  6. She was converted from sloop to ketch rig on being lengthened. VICTORIA was a typical Padstow registered smack, owned in Newquay until 1867 by J. Cardell and then Johnson Hicks, with J & M Osborne as masters. Richard Lobb of Port Isaac bought her in 1867. C. Beer was master when, on 27th October 1882, she was attempting the Padstow entrance with coal from Newport. The wind was NE force 9, and she was lost with all three crew on the Doom Bar.

**VICTORIA** ON 18391, built 1853 at Port Gaverne by James Stephens. Tons 40 (N and gross). 52.0  15.4  7.4. A sloop rigged smack with Carter and later Joseph Coad of Port Isaac as managing owners, and T. May as master. In 1888 she was sold to Thomas Clarke of Wrafton, converted to ketch rig and registered at Barnstaple. She was broken up at Barnstable in 1907.

**VILLAGE BELLE** ON 72555, built 1875 at Malpas near Truro by N. Scoble. Tons 137 net and gross. 93.0  22.7  11.6. This schooner,

like the MALPAS BELLE, was built by Nicholas Scoble, and also had G. Gregory as a deepwater master for Truro owners before joining the fleet of W. C. Phillips of Port Isaac about 1883, with R. Honey as master. Posted 'lost' in *Lloyd's Register* 1885.

**VILLIERS** ON 1349, built 1820 at Swansea,. Tons 112(O) 108(N). 64.3  20.6  12.2 lengthened 1854, then tons 142 net 159 gross. She was registered at Swansea as a brig and at Padstow in 1847 as a brigantine, with J. Hawken as owner and captain. Thomas Whitford of St Columb owned her in 1851 and John Tredwen in 1853. Other Padstow men involved as masters were J. Tippett, A. Harvey and H. Knight. In 1857 she was sold to London owners and lasted until 1866.

VIOLA

**VIOLA** ON 68256, built 1872 at Appledore by William Pickard. Tons 159 net 168 gross, 140 net later, 87 net with engine. 99.1  22.7  12.5. She was completed as a schooner with semi-elliptical stern and what was described as a semi-female figurehead. She was first registered at Hull, then briefly in 1884 at London. That same year she was bought by J. H. Male and registered at Padstow. He ran her until 1905 with J. Lewis and Worden, as well as himself, as captains. In 1905 she passed to William Hutchings who had her re-rigged as a three masted schooner. His captains were O. Watts and C. Tucker during the Great War. In 1918 she was taken up by the Royal Navy to become a Q-ship as described elsewhere; her 80 h.p. engine was fitted, and the following year Edwin P. Hutchings became owner. Having sailed from Teignmouth with china clay for Glasgow, she refuelled at Brixham and then, in thick fog, ran aground on rocks near Kennack Sands near the Lizard at 4 a.m. on 21st May 1922. Although she broke her back, she apparently survived to be bought by the Willows family of London, but her register was closed on 3rd February 1926.

**VITULA** ON 62930, built 1871 at Jersey by George Deslandes Jr. Tons 157 gross. 109.1  19.5  10.9. In the Jersey records she is described as a brig of 202 tons, but in the *Lloyd's Register* she is a brigantine, and in 1881 a brigantine with three masts, i.e. a barkentine, which she may well have been throughout. After five years in the Deslandes fleet she was registered at London and bought by the Darke family of Newquay. She traded largely from Newquay with W. G. Clemens and J. Roberts in command. Unlisted by 1883.

**VIXEN** ON 62677, built 1870 at the Island Cove Yard Newquay by J. Osborne. Tons 27 net 35 gross. 55.4  19.8  7.0 lengthened in the Gannel 1873, then tons 35 net 44 gross. 67.8  18.2  7.0. VIXEN was registered at Padstow as a smack with elliptical stern owned by E. A. Martyn and J. Osborne. In 1873 she went to Edward L. Johns of Crantock and was lengthened and ketch rigged. In 1883 Henry Rowse of Lerryn bought her and in 1912 George Irwin of Combe Martin and G. Irons of Newquay. Her last owner was Reuben Chichester of Braunton and she was broken up and the register closed 16th November 1923.

**VOLANT** ON 13158, built 1849 at Brixham by Matthews. Tons 115(O) 96(N). 70.0  16.5  11.2 lengthened 1872, then tons 112 net 122 gross. 88.7  19.5  11.2. Her builder put this schooner into the Portuguese, Newfoundland and Mediterranean trades with H. May as master. In 1866 he sold her to James H. Fishley of Port Isaac and her register moved from Brixham to Padstow, but she continued in the Newfoundland trade. After lengthening she was in the home bulk trades. Abandoned in the North Sea, 13th December 1883 (note on register).

**VOLUNA** ON 17125, built 1826 at St Mary's Bay, Nova Scotia. Tons 331(O) 336(N). 96.2  23.7  17.4. Although occasionally described as a brig, this vessel was snow rigged. Like so many vessels built in the Maritime Provinces, she was soon sold to Liverpool owners. By 1835 T. Seaton of Padstow was her managing owner, and in 1838 Padstow became her port of registry, Tom Seaton her owner. She had a whole series of Padstow captains, including Seaton himself, Robson, Smith, Easthope and Thomas Bulman. From Liverpool she had traded to Savannah and New Orleans, but from Padstow her destination was generally Quebec and she became one of Padstow's emigrant ships, coming home with timber (lumber). She stranded at St Agnes in the Isles of Scilly in fog on 31st May 1857 bound for Quebec in ballast. Her people all got ashore and the wreckage was auctioned at St Marys in June.

**VOLUNTEER** ON 27279, built 1860 at Padstow by John Tredwen. Tons 77 net 88 gross. 74.9  19.2  10.2. This schooner is one of several ships which the young John Cory owned in equal partnership with John Tredwen: but not for long because in 1862 they sold her to Plymouth and built a larger VOLUNTEER (ON 29357). The two are sometimes confused in the records.

VOLUNTEER (ON 27279) came back on to the Padstow register in 1892 when she was bought by Thomas Brown of Port Isaac. Hannah Maria Brown had all 64 shares in 1900 and sold 32 to Samuel Couch. On 25th August 1902 she was becalmed off Pentire Point and the tide carried her on to the Newland islet and then off again, damaged, when she foundered (note on register).

**VOLUNTEER** ON 29286, built 1861 at Bowling, Dumbarton by Scott. Tons 83 reg. 68.5  19.3  10.1. A schooner with a 'demi-man' figurehead, she was registered at Glasgow until Warwick R. Guy and James Bate bought her in 1865, and registered her at Padstow. On 7th October 1878 she was bound for Plymouth with coal from Liverpool when she foundered off the breakwater lighthouse, losing three of her crew of four. There is a note on her Padstow register that she was registered at Beaumaris in 1879.

**VOLUNTEER** ON 29357, built 1862 at Padstow by John Tredwen. Tons 134.3 gross. 91.8  22.2  11.6. A schooner built to replace ON 27279, with 32 shares owned by John Tredwen and 32 by John Cory, who was listed as her captain, trading to the Mediterranean.

She was, however, sold to Plymouth owners, George Prout and others, in 1863 and lost on 11th December 1865 when Captain Skinner of Padstow was in command. The SS MINERVA of the London Steam Navigation Co. ran her down off Trevose Head just after midnight; four of her crew were drowned, but Skinner and his helmsman were picked up. The steamship was found solely to blame.

**VOLUNTEER** ON 47032, built 1862 at St Peters, Prince Edward Island by Cox. Tons 199 reg. 107.5  23.2  12.8. The ambitious young captain and owner John Cory, already in command of VOLUNTEER ON 29357, persuaded his partner John Tredwen to trade up yet again by selling ON 29357 and buying this much larger brigantine in 1863, when she was registered at Padstow and started trading to the Mediterranean. The *Mercantile Navy List* and *Lloyd's* had C. J. Jutson as owner in 1875 and her Padstow register notes that she 'was sold to a foreigner in 1879'. The last reference found is in *Lloyd's Register* 1881 where it was noted that her home port was in France.

**VOLUNTEER** ON 65148, built 1864 at Plymouth. Tons 24 gross. A barge which probably spent all her life on the River Tamar, but which is included here because although she was registered at Plymouth, William Symons of Tintagel owned her in her early years. Broken up 1926 (see also chapter on barges).

**VOLUTINA** ON 19273, built 1856 at Padstow by John Carter. Tons 78 net 87 gross. 73.4  19.8  10.1. This vessel was registered on completion at Padstow as a ketch and so described in *Lloyd's Register* until 1862, when her designation was changed to schooner. She was owned by Thomas Seaton, then John Haynes of Port Isaac. Cobaldick was her first master; Haynes looked after her himself. In 1879 Thomas Honey of Devonport was owner. On 29th October 1880 she left Antwerp bound for Middlesbrough with glass sand and went missing (note on register).

**VOLZY** ON 84981, built 1853 at Libourne near Bordeaux, VOLZY traded for many years as a French brig measuring 106 tons with La Nouvelle as her home port. The circumstances of her becoming a British vessel are not known, but in 1892 she was registered at Padstow, tons 77 net 97 gross. 73.0  21.8  10.1, rigged as a ketch and owned wholly by George Sloggett of Cardiff, Engineer. That same year Arthur Bennett Hutchings and William Edward Hutchings each bought 16 of his 64 shares. The loss report described her as a Dartmouth ketch owned by A. B. Hutchings, with J. Andoire as master. She foundered off Ventnor on 9th April 1893, bound from London for Dartmouth with cement. No lives were lost.

**W.J.C.** ON 78969, built 1880 at Sunny Corner, Truro by Charles Dyer. Tons 80 net 86 gross. 79.2  20.8  9.5. This schooner was the last ship he built and W.J.C. stood for William Martin, John Burley and Charles Dyer, each owning about a third when she was registered at Truro. By 1884 A. J. Burt of Newquay was her master and there was a degree of Newquay ownership justifying her inclusion here. She remained registered at Truro, trading through the Great War, after which William R. Cock of Malpas was managing owner. She continued trading under sail in the 1920s before being abandoned in the River Fal. She was listed until 1928 when she was reported broken up.

**WANDERER** ON 18326, built 1848 at New London, Prince Edward Island. Tons 74(O) 55(N) 56 reg. 55.8  15.2  8.1. A small schooner with a billet head which was registered in Prince Edward Island on completion, but sold to Henry Hoskin and registered at Padstow that same year. Henry and then Thomas Hoskin commanded her. In 1860 Henry Hoskin moved to Swansea, taking WANDERER with him to be registered there. The move was doubtless to be closer to the rapidly developing ore and coal trades, and it seems to have been successful, as by 1890 Henry was the owner of three barkentines of over 500 tons apiece, all built like WANDERER on Prince Edward Island. WANDERER was evidently lost in 1860 or 1861.

**WATER LILY** ON 62686, built 1871 at Padstow by Stribley. Tons 71 net 80 gross, 64 net later. 73.0 20.9 9.4. A schooner with a female figurehead, registered at Padstow, and owned by the Hutchings family throughout. Arscott Hutchings Sr owned her to start with, and B. Hutchings commanded her. Then Arthur B. Hutchings became managing owner and W. J. Rickard was master until her loss. WATER LILY was sunk by collision with SS REBECCA of Carnarvon in the Crosby Channel on 13th September 1899. She had sailed from Garston with coal for Wadebridge.

**WATER NYMPH** ON 58248, built 1868 at Padstow by J. Tredwen. Tons 61 net 67 gross. 69.2 19.2 8.8. This Padstow schooner was built for Cardell and others, with R. J. Hocking as master. Other principal shareholders were J. P. Dunstan of St Columb, William Trebilcock of Newquay, W. Thomas, and William Stribley, and there were numerous others with a share or two each. On 3rd August 1884 she was intending to sail in ballast from Clifden Harbour to Benowen. Her cables parted and she ran aground outside the harbour and was lost. Her crew were able to get away safely in their own boat.

**WELCOME** ON 6530, built 1841 at Portmadoc by Henry Jones. Tons 66(N) and 65 gross. 56.4 18.7 9.4. After 25 years of hard work for Portmadoc, Pwllheli and Plymouth owners, this schooner was bought by Francis Burt of Padstow and registered there in 1866. He sold 32 shares to John Thomas that same year. They kept her working mostly in the Bristol Channel. On 1st June 1877 she was wrecked on Sully Island whilst sailing from Padstow for Newport in ballast.

**WELCOME** ON 13474, built 1846 at Padstow by Thomas Carter. Tons 17(N) 15 gross. 37.2 11.2 6.2. One of a series of round sterned luggers built for St Ives fishermen (two Grenfell brothers in this case). They sold her to Dublin in 1863 and she was last reported in 1866.

**WELSH BELLE** ON 70490, built 1875 at Bideford by Cox. Tons 103 net 120 gross, 85 net later. 93.0 20.8 10.7. This schooner was registered at Neath, Swansea and then Falmouth. In the 1890s when she was registered at Falmouth she was owned by W. Kernick with W. Pascoe in command, both of Newquay; hence her inclusion here. Then Frank Nurse of Gloucester was followed as owner by Thomas Hutchings of Appledore, who sailed her through the Great War. She ceased being listed in 1921.

**WESTERN STAR** ON 62894, built 1869 at Appledore by Robert Cock. Tons 75 net 82 gross. 76.9 19.1 10.0. Her builder retained ownership of this schooner for about three years, and put her into the Spanish trades. Bideford was her port of registry but N. Lewarne of Porth owned her from 1875 onwards and other Newquay and Padstow men commanded her, including C. W. Bennett, T. Tretheway and J. Bennett. She went missing in November 1890 sailing from Liverpool (Verran).

**WESTFA** ON 60774, built 1876 at Llanelly by Rees. Tons 142 net 153 gross. 103.0 22.5 11.4. Registered at Llanelly, this brigantine was bought by J. Jenkin of Newquay in 1891, and he took command himself. Missing since sailing from Rouen on 7th November 1891 with oats for London (Lloyd's).

**WHIM** ON 51332, built 1865 at Brixham by Dewdney. Tons 112 net 135 gross, 96 net later. 96.5 21.5 12.3. This top-gallant schooner was tiller steered, which was unusual having regard to her rig, size

and date of construction. She was registered at Brixham and sailed deep water for the Vittery family before being bought in 1881 by Henry A. Hawkey of Newquay. J. J. Matthews immediately became her master and remained with her until her loss. WHIM left Newcastle for Plymouth on 23rd November 1900 and was lost with all hands 26th-27th November off Harwich.

**WHY NOT?** ON 13837, built 1851 at Bideford by Thomas Waters. Tons 37(N) 34 gross. 49.0 15.0 7.0. Built for Fernandez and others of Instow, this Bideford smack was bought by J. Strout and registered at Padstow in 1853. In 1861 she returned to Devon to be registered at Barnstaple. Much of her time was spent lifting cargoes of slate from the beach at Tintagel, which must have been a risky operation; but she lasted until 1911. Her hull was used to close a breach in the river bank at Braunton and her register was closed on 28th December 1911.

**WIIQUUA** see KATIE

**WILD PIGEON** ON 76251, built 1877 at Dundalk by Cennick. Tons 54 net 60 gross, 48 net later. 68.4 19.2 7.9. In 1877 Robert Neal of Port Isaac bought this Dundalk schooner and registered her at Padstow. In 1892 she was converted to ketch rig. George W. Barrett of Bude became her owner and master in 1895. On 7th November 1898 she was ashore on Bude Sands with coal from Lidney but got off.

Her end was dramatic. On 3rd February 1904 the sea broke the lock gates leading to the Bude Canal. WILD PIGEON was washed out to sea with the water escaping through the lock and wrecked under Summerlease Point. Fortunately there was nobody on board.

**WILLIAM** built 1789 in Britain, but location unknown. Tons 114(O). A brig first reported arriving at Padstow (from Petersburg) in 1799 captained by T. Cundy, and almost certainly already owned by Thomas Rawlins of Padstow. No Padstow register survives. Lloyd's List for 24th January 1804 intimated that the WILLIAM, Captain Adams, had been wrecked on the Baltic island of Anholt on 30th November 1803. Her crew had been saved.

**WILLIAM** ON 18978, built 1799 at Padstow by Withell. Tons 45(O) 30(N). 46.8 16.0 7.8. A sloop with square stern and running bowsprit. No Padstow register survives, but on her St Ives registry in 1805 it is noted that she had been registered in Padstow in 1799. In 1817 she went to Exeter, thence to Newport and later Milford owners. When 'official numbers' were allotted in 1856, she was on the Bideford register. Lost in 1868 (note on register).

**WILLIAM** built 1801 at Padstow. Tons 120(O) and 124(O). This brig appears in Lloyd's Registers in the 1820s but without any apparent Padstow connection, apart from her having been built there.

**WILLIAM & CATHERINE** built 1815 (one register gives 1811) at Plymouth: almost rebuilt 1822. Tons 60(O) 46(N). 51.0 17.9 8.4. This sloop's register moved from Plymouth to Padstow in 1829 and thereafter she was owned by T. Martyn who was also her master, as were J. Guy, W. Jones and T. Mabley. She was lost in Mullion Roads on 4th April 1839. Her crew was saved.

**WILLIAM & EMMA** ON 95138, built 1880 at Stonehouse, Plymouth by Francis Hawke. Tons 19 net. 43.0 15.8 5.0. She was built as a smack and converted to a ketch soon after 1900. She was probably lengthened then as her tonnage increased to 27 net. Her register moved from Plymouth to Falmouth in 1900. David W. Davies of Wadebridge bought her soon after the Great War and used her to take stone from the Stepper Point Quarry to Bude and to Wadebridge. She ended up as a barge: no longer listed in the Mercantile Navy List 1928.

**WILLIAM & JANE** built 1802 at Brixham. Tons 32(O) 20(N), 40.8

14.2 7.5. This sloop came from the Plymouth register to Padstow in 1835 when she was bought by William Haynes of Port Isaac. Her ownership passed to John and then Richard Tredwen, but Haynes remained master until succeeded by William Chalk in 1843. The following year she was sold to Bideford.

A smack named WILLIAM & JANE was wrecked at Ilfracombe on 15th February 1850.

WILLIAM & MARTHA 51208. see RITA

WILLIAM GEAKE ON 76711, built 1876 at Bideford by Cox & Son. Tons 277 net 290 gross. 127.5 25.8 13.8, a barkentine with a raised quarterdeck 27 ft long. Built for William Geake of St Columb, like her consort LYDIA CARDELL in many ways she epitomised the peak of development of the small Westcountryman, and therefore also the start of the decline. She was registered at Fowey, salted and yellow-metalled, and traded worldwide, J. Hockin her master having a full square rig certificate. In the early nineties she was sold to Monmouth owners. Lost on Byron Island on 2nd August 1896, on passage from Barbados for Montreal. (*Lloyd's Wreck Returns*)

WILLIAM HENRY ON 18367, built 1854 at Feock, Truro by Thomas Ferris. Tons 103(N) 87 net, 94 gross, 80 net later. 73.0 18.0. 10.6. This schooner is remembered as starting life with topgallant rig, registered at Falmouth. In 1865 Truro became her port of registry, and remained so when James Trebilcock of Newquay became managing owner in the early eighties. In 1897 Thomas Jacka, also of Newquay, took over from him but she was back in Truro hands by 1904 and no longer listed in 1915. In her Newquay days she was altered from 'topgallant' to 'Garibaldi' rig, that is to say, she became a fore-and-aft schooner with one less in the crew.

WILLIAM MARTYN ON 69455, built 1873 at Gannel yard, Newquay, by T & J Clemens. Tons 93 net 104 gross, 82 net later. 87.1 22.2 10.4. J. Crocker, master and owner, registered his new schooner at Padstow and sailed her in the traditional home trades. John Ennor took a hand in her management and F. Harris of Newquay took command of her briefly before she was sold to James Kearns of Arklow and registered at Dublin in 1892. At the start of the Great War, William Corney of Rafton bought her and she became a Barnstaple ship.

She was sunk by U-boat off Ram Head, Youghal on 16th March 1917. According to Oliver Hill's notes (N.M.M.) the U-boat forced them out of their boat onto her casing, removed the water from their boat and then submerged without giving them time to re-board. The WILLIAM MARTYN was on passage from Newport for Cork with a cargo of coal at the time.

WILLIAMS built 1823 at Flushing (Falmouth). Tons 9(O) 27.5 9.2 7.5. The registry of this tiny sloop was transferred from Falmouth to Padstow in 1825 when John Jenkin of Crantock became her owner and Richard Phillips her master. In 1828 T. F. Paynter of St Columb bought her and sailed her himself, altering her to yawl rig in 1829 when she was re-registered. There is no information as to her fate.

WILLIE ON 29354, built 1861 at Padstow by John Henry Willmett. Tons 41.39 reg. 53.7. 17.3 8.0. This cutter rigged smack was registered at Padstow throughout her life. She traded to the dangerous beaches of North Cornwall in the charge of William Stribley and then John Courtney, both of Padstow. In 1879 ownership passed to John J. Prout, blacksmith of St Agnes, but when she was wrecked at Portreath pierhead on 11th December 1883, entering with slates from Padstow, Francis Ede Bunt of Trewethen (or Trevethan) was her owner and C. Honey was her master. The crew of three were all saved.

WILLIE ON 53422, built 1865-1866 at Galmpton by W. A. Gibbs. Tons 93 reg. 80.9 19.9 10.3. This Dartmouth registered schooner was bought by J. P. Dunston of St Columb in 1879. The Trebilcock family of Newquay also owned shares, and Trembeth, W. George and F. Harris captained her. WILLIE sank in collision off Lowestoft on 14th October 1894.

WINDSOR ON 798, built 1850 at Quebec by Thomas C. Lee. Tons 947(O) 1099(N), 1009 reg. 162.3 36.0 22.7. A full rigged ship with a woman's figurehead, she was registered at London then at Liverpool soon after completion, but in 1859 was bought by R. Easthope (or Easthorpe) and others and registered at Padstow, the largest ship ever to be so registered. She had been trading to Panama, Australia and Ceylon but Easthope converted her to barque rig and put her in the Quebec trade which he knew so well, commanding her himself but with S. Harding and J. Evans taking over from him. Abandoned at sea on 13th May 1866 (note on register).

WINDSWORTH ON 3511, built 1843 at East Looe by Henry Shepcott. Tons 126(O) 108(N). 84 net 97 gross 79 net later. 70.0 20.5 11.0. A schooner with gammon knee, WINDSWORTH was registered at Fowey and traded to the Mediterranean. Soon after 1880 Charles Rawle of Padstow became her owner and in 1886 Padstow became her port of registry. Henry Tabb was then her master and in 1887 her owner. H. W. Freethy was master when, on 28th December 1894 she was wrecked in South Bay, Troon, bound from Glasgow to Castletown Beerhaven in Ireland with coal. The wind was NW force 11.

WINLAY. The Bude Canal records refer to a Padstow sloop WINLAY of 27 tons with Gill as master in 1850. The tonnage was probably deadweight and the sloop was not registered.

WINNIE. A small sloop was built in 1890 at Padstow by Cowl; it later became the JIMBET of Ramsgate mentioned in the chapter on fishing vessels.

WONDER ON 56023 built 1866 at Padstow by J. Tredwen. Tons 165 gross, 126 net at loss. 101.2 23.4 12.4. This large topgallant schooner was built for Port Talbot owners, registered at Swansea and traded to the West Indies. In 1887 she was bought by W. C. Phillips of St Austell (previously of Port Isaac) and registered at Fowey.

Wrecked near Honfleur 8th February 1897, sailing from Rouen with glass sand for Sunderland (*Lloyd's Wreck Returns*)

YACHT ON 62124, built 1874 at Garmouth by Spence. Tons 72 net. 74.0 19.6 9.4 This schooner was owned successively in Lossiemouth, Tarbert (Argyll), Wigtown and Sherkin (Co. Cork). She was registered successively at Glasgow, Wigtown and Bideford. Soon after 1900 when she was registered at Bideford, Andrew Bate of Port Isaac became her managing owner and she sailed in the Irish Sea trades. On 23rd November 1916 'vessel took fire and consumed'. Register closed.

YEOMAN'S GLORY ON 19248, built 1826 at Fowey by William Geach & Son. Tons 57(O) 33(N) 34 reg. 47.7 17.1 7.2. A sloop rigged smack with counter stern and running bowsprit. She was registered at Fowey 1826, London 1833, Plymouth 1838, Padstow 1846 and Bideford 1859.

Lawrence Harwood of Bude was her master and owner in the late '30s and '40s, followed by William Moyse of Port Isaac in the '50s. She served her Bideford owners until her loss in the Bristol Channel in 1867.

YOUNG HENRY. The wreck of the YOUNG HENRY of Padstow at Tintagel was recorded in the *Royal Cornwall Gazette* 28 November 1807, and *Lloyd's List* 1st December 1807.

YSTWYTH ON 42580, built 1861 at Aberystwyth by Evans. Tons

The Ketch YSTWITH stranded in Carbis Bay in 1908, her final resting place.
*David Clement Collection*

63 gross, 51 net. 68.5  18.4  8.2. This Aberystwyth schooner was bought by Hubert Henry Stribley in 1891 and registered at Padstow. About 1894 he converted her to ketch rig. She was owned for a time around the turn of the century by John Hitchins of St Agnes, but at the time of her loss in 1908 T. G. Reveley of Padstow was her master and owner.

YSTWYTH was lost by stranding in Carbis Bay near St Ives on 29th January 1908 with a coal cargo. Her crew of three were all saved. The wind was NNW force 7.

**ZARAH** ON 11543, built 1846 at Sunderland. Tons 310(N) 357 net 383 gross. 104.0  26.7  18.1. This barque was registered at Glasgow and traded to Singapore, Bombay, the West Indies, etc. In 1865 Robert Langford of Padstow became managing owner and with T. Morris and later Crowther in command, she traded from Padstow and Falmouth to Quebec, Nova Scotia and the Mediterranean. She lasted until about 1874, still registered at Glasgow.

**ZEPHYR** ON 11484, built 1841 at Padstow by Thomas Carter. Tons 97(O) 86(N), 77 net 85 gross. 62.0  16.9  10.0. The schooner ZEPHYR was built for Avery and registered at Padstow, trading to the Baltic with W. Dark as master. He became managing owner in 1849 and his brother Richard Dark was master for a time. In 1862

Richard Dark, then of Pentewan, bought a controlling interest and Fowey became her port of registry. Lost by collision off Dungeness 29th July 1869.

*Notes*

The use of punctuation, or the lack of it, in conjunction with initials and the spelling of proper names are taken from the various registers. Elsewhere in this book the old spellings of place-names are usually kept but the use of punctuation is somewhat less inconsistent.

The histories of ships are as comprehensive as possible for periods when they were registered at Padstow or owned in North Cornwall. Inevitably the rest of their lives are covered less thoroughly.

# BIBLIOGRAPHY

## Principal Sources

Hicks, The Hicks Collection (of notes on Padstow) held at the Royal Institution of Cornwall, Truro.
*Lloyd's List*, Guildhall Library and National Maritime Museum
*Lloyd's Registers*, 1764-1994                                      annually
*Lloyd's Yacht Registers*, 1889-1980                               "
*Mercantile Navy Lists*, HMSO 1857-1976                            "
*Olsen's Fisherman's Nautical Almanack*, 1880-1992                 "
Port Books, various, incl. Padstow 1565-1719, Public Records Office
Port Registers, Padstow and neighbouring ports; the transcriptions by the late Grahame Farr and others now available in the National Maritime Museum have been particularly helpful.

The early history of Padstow was written with the help of C. S. Gilbert's work, of which the wording of the title page is reproduced as follows:

### AN HISTORICAL SURVEY OF THE COUNTY OF CORNWALL

to which is added a complete Heraldy of the same with
numerous engravings, Plymouth Dock.
Vol I 1817, Vol II 1820

Printed and Published by J. Congdon:
Published in London by Longman, Hurst, Rees,
Orme and Brown, Paternoster Row,
and by R. Ackerman, Strand

To the most Noble Hugh Percy, Duke of Northumberland, Earl Percy,
General in the Army, Vice Admiral of Northumberland
and Newcastle-upon-Tyne. One of the Council of State of the
Prince of Wales.

In Cornwall
Constable of Launceston Castle, and High Steward of Launceston.
Knight of the Garter and Fellow of the Royal Society.'

Also used in compiling the early history were the following two works:

Richard Carew *Survey of Cornwall* published 1602. Carew was born 1555, High Sheriff of Cornwall 1586, by which time he had largely written his survey which lay dormant for sixteen years.
*A Complete Parochial History of the County of Cornwall*, compiled from the Best Authorities etc. Truro, Wm. Lake, Boscawen Street (in four volumes), 1867.

## General Bibliography

**A**
| | |
|---|---|
| Acland, Capt. John E. | *Bude Haven, Some Links with the Past*, 1914 |
| Acton, Viv & Carter, Derek | *Operation Cornwall 1940-1944*, 1994 |
| Anderson, John | *Coastwise Sail*, 1934 & 1948 |
| Archibald, E.H.H. | *Dictionary of Sea Painters*, 1980 & 1989, *The Wooden Fighting Ship*, 1968 |

**B**
| | |
|---|---|
| Bainbridge, George | *The Wooden Ships and the Iron Men of the Cornish China Clay Trade*, 1980 |
| Baker & Wishart | *Tidal Power for Small Estuaries*, Water for Energy Conference, Brighton, 1986 |
| Barton, R.M. | *A History of the Cornish China Clay Industry*, 1966 |
| Benham, Harvey & Finch, Roger | *The Big Barges*, 1983 |
| Bere, Rennie | *The Story of Bude Haven*, 1977 |
| Berry, Claude | *Padstow, 1895-1925*, 1976, *Padstow's Lifeboats 1827-1977*, 1977 |
| Bolton Letters, The | Vol II 1701-1714, printed by John Blandy, 1976 |
| Bouquet, Michael | *No Gallant Ship*, 1959, *Westcountry Sail*, 1971 |

Bray, Donald                                    *Stories of the North Cornish Coast*, 1983
Bray, John                                      *An Account of Wrecks on the North Coast of Cornwall 1759-1830.* 1975
Brett, Henry                                    *White Wings*, New Zealand 1924
Buckley K and Klugman, K.                       *The History of Burns Philp*, 1981
Butcher, David                                  *Follow the Fishing*, 1987
C
Carter, Capt. Harry                             *The Autobiography of a Cornish Smuggler*, 1894
Colledge, J.J.                                  *Ships of the Royal Navy*, Vol I, 1969, Vol 2, 1970
Cliff, James Henry Treloar                      *Down to the Sea in Ships*, Memoirs, 1983
Coombes, Nigel                                  *Passenger Steamers of the Bristol Channel*, 1990
D
Damer Powell, Commander J.W.                    *Bristol Privateers and Ships of War*, 1930
Daniell, Rev. J.J.                              *A Compendium of the History & Geography of Cornwall*, 4th ed. Truro, 1906
David, Pat                                      *The First Fifty Years of the Rock Sailing and Water Ski Club*, 1988
Davies, Alun                                    *The History of the Falmouth Working Boats*, 1989
Dittmar, F.J. and Colledge, J.J.               *British Warships 1914-1919*, 1972
Drew, John Henry                                *Rail & Sail to Pentewan*, 1986
Duxbury, Brenda & Williams, Michael             *The River Camel*, 1987
E
Eglinton, Edmund                                *The Last of the Sailing Coasters*, 1982
Ekwall, Eilert                                  *The Concise Oxford Dictionary of English Place Names*
England, Capt. Richard                          *Schoonerman*, 1981
F
Farr, Grahame E.                                *Ships and Harbours of Exmoor*, 1970, *West Country Passenger Steamers*, 1956, *Shipbuilding in the Port of Bristol*, 1977, *Records of Bristol Ships 1800-1838*, 1950, *Chepstow Ships*, 1954, *Shipbuilding in North Devon*, 1976, *The Ship Registers of the Port of Hayle*, 1975, *Wreck & Rescue in the Bristol Channel I*, 1966, *Wreck & Rescue in the Bristol Channel II*, 1967, *Wreck & Rescue on the Coast of Devon, (South Coast)*, 1986, *Wreck & Rescue on the Dorset Coast*, 1971,
Finch, Roger                                    *The Ship Painters*, 1975, *The Pierhead Painters*, 1983
Fitzhugh, Rod                                   *Bridgwater & the River Parrett in Old Photographs*, 1993
G
Gascoyne, Joel                                  *A Map of the County of Cornwall*, 1699
Gillis, R. H. C.                                *Mariners' Mirror*, Vol.55, pp.117-138
Goodwin, Deborah                                *Padstow Past and Present*, 1984
Gosson, P.R. and Parsons, R.M.                  *The Golden Harvest — The Story of Sand Dredging in the Bristol Channel*, 1989
Grant, Alison                                   *North Devon Pottery, The Seventeenth Century*, 1983
Grant, Alison and Hughes, Barry                 *North Devon Barges*, 1975
Gray, Todd                                      *Early Stuart Mariners and Shipping*, 1990
Greenhill, Basil                                *The Merchant Schooners*, 1951, 1959, 1988, *Sailing for a Living*, 1962
Greenhill, Basil and Giffard, Ann               *The Merchant Sailing Ship, A Photographic History*, 1970
Greenhill, Basil and Manning, Sam               *The Evolution of the Wooden Ship*, 1988
Grimshaw, Geoffrey                              *British Pleasure Steamers 1920-1939*, 1939
H
Hadfield, Charles                               *The Canals of South West England*
Harris, John                                    *The Sea Shall Not Have Them*
Harris, Helen and Ellis, Monica                 *The Bude Canal*, 1972
Harris, K.                                      *Hevva! Cornish Fishing in the Days of Sail*, 1983
Hill, H. O.                                     Various articles in the *Mariners' Mirror*
Hippisley Coxe, Antony, D.                      *A Book about Smuggling in the West Country*, 1984
Husband, S. Teague                              *Old Newquay*, 1923
I
Ingram, Charles *et al*                         *Shipwrecks - New Zealand Disasters 1775-1936*, 1936
J
Jenkins, Alf                                    *The Scillonian and his Boat*, 1982, *Gigs and Cutters of the Isles of Scilly*, 1975
K
Kemp, Dixon                                     *A Manual of Yacht and Boat Sailing*, 1888
Kittridge, Alan                                 *Cornwall's Maritime Heritage*, 1989, *Passenger Steamers of the River Tamar*, 1984
L
Langley M, & Small, E.                          *Estuary & River Ferries of South West England*, 1984, *Lost Ships of the West Country*, 1988
Larn, Richard                                   *Shipwreck Index of the British Isles*, Vol.1, 1995, *Cornish Shipwrecks Vol.3 — The Isles of Scilly*, 1971
Larn, Richard & Carter, Clive                   *Cornish Shipwrecks, Vol.1 — The South Coast*, 1969, *Cornish Shipwrecks, Vol.2 — The North Coast*, 1970

Loney, Jack — *Australian Shipwrecks*, Vol. 3, 1982

**M**

MacGregor, David R. — *Merchant Sailing Ships 1775-1815*, 1985, *Merchant Sailing Ships 1815-1850*, 1984, *Merchant Sailing Ships 1850-1875*, 1984, *Schooners in Four Centuries*, 1982,

Marsh, Edgar J. — *Sailing Drifters*, 1952, *Sailing Trawlers*, 1953, *Inshore Craft of Great Britain*, 1970

Merry, Ian D. — *The Westcotts and their Times*, 1977, *The Shipping and Trade of the River Tamar*, 1980

Mitchell, Percy — *A Boat-builder's Story*, 1968

Morton-Raymont, Christine — *Padstow in the Mid-Nineteenth Century*, 1989

Mote, Gordon — *The Westcountrymen*, 1986

**N**

Neale, W. G. — *At the Port of Bristol*, Vols. I, II, 1968, 1970, *The Tides of War 1914-1918*, 1976

Nix, Michael & Myers, Mark R. — *Hartland Quay, The Story of a Vanished Port*, 1982

Noall, Cyril and Farr, Grahame — *Wreck & Rescue Round the Cornish Coast*, (Three volumes 1964-5)

Norman, W. H. — *Tales of Watchet Harbour*, 1985

Norton, Peter — *The End of the Voyage*. 1959

**O**

Oliver, A. S. — *Boats and Boat-building in West Cornwall*, 1971

Oppenheim, M. — *The Victoria History of the County of Cornwall: Maritime History (in Vol.I)*, 1906

Orme, Nicholas editor — *Nicholas Roscarrock's Lives of the Saints: Cornwall & Devon*, 1992

**P**

Parry, Henry — *Wreck & Rescue on the Coast of Wales*, (two volumes) 1969, 1973

Powell, see Damer Powell

**R**

Rawe, Donald R. and Ingrey, Jack — *Padstow and District*, 1984

Rendell, Joan — *North Cornwall in the Old Days*, 1983

Richards, Mark — *Walking the North Cornwall Coastal Footpath*, 1974

Roddis, Roland — *Cornish Harbours*, 1951

Rogers, Inkerman — *Ships and Shipyards of Bideford*, 1947

**S**

Shaw, Captain Hugh — *Schooner Captain*

Slade, W. J. — *Out of Appledore*, 1959

Slade, W. J. and Greenhill, Basil — *Westcountry Coasting Ketches*, 1974

Smith, Graham — *Smuggling in the Bristol Channel, 1700-1850*, 1989

Starkey, H. F. — *Schooner Port, Two Centuries of Upper Mersey Sail*, 1983

Stuckey, Peter J. — *The Sailing Pilots of the Bristol Channel*, 1977

**T**

Tangyye, Michael — *Portreath, Some Chapters in its History*, 1968

Tregenna, Lyn — *Cornwall and Isles of Scilly Gig Guide*, 1991

**U**

Underhill, Harold H. — *Sailing Ship Rigs and Rigging*, 1938

**V**

Vale, Edmund — *The Harveys of Hayle*, 1966

Verran, W. H. — *Shipbuilding at Newquay and Notes on Local Vessels, Mariner's Mirror*, 1945

**W**

Wall, Robert — *Bristol Channel Pleasure Steamers*, 1973

Wallace, Frederick William — *Record of Canadian Shipping*, 1929

Ward-Jackson, C. H. — *Ships and Shipbuilders of a Westcountry Seaport 1786-1939*, 1986, *Stephens of Fowey*, 1980

Ward, Lock & Co's — *Newquay and North Cornwall, Illustrated Guidebook*, 1922

Williams, Michael — *About Boscastle*, 1990

Winstanley, Monica — *High Tide at Port Isaac*, 1978, *The Story of Port Isaac, Port Quin and Port Gaverne*, 1976

Miscellaneous — *Bristol Channel Pilot*, Admiralty, 1872

*A Century of Family Shipowning — John Cory & Sons Ltd. 1854-1954* by R. C. (presumably Raymond Cory), Cardiff, 1954

*Concise Catalogue of Oil Paintings in the National Maritime Museum*, 1988

*Lloyd's War Losses: The First World War, The Second World War*, Vols. 1 & 2

*Maritime History*, Vols. 1 & 2, David and Charles, 1972, 1973

*Maritime Wales* Gwynned Archives Service, annually since 1976

*West Coast of England Pilot* Admiralty, various dates

Newspapers and Periodicals

*Fishing News*
*The Lifeboat Journal*
*Mariner's Mirror*, Journal of the Society for Nautical Research
*Maritime South West*, Journal of the SW Maritime History Society
*Royal Cornwall Gazette*
*Royal Cruising Club Journals*, 1908-1939
*Sea Breezes* (old and new series)
*Ships & Ship Models*, 1931-1939
*West 'Briton*
*Western Morning News*

# REFERENCES

*Chapter 1*
1  Gilbert, C. S. *An Historical Survey of the County of Cornwall*, 1817-1820
2  Oppenheim, M. 'Maritime History' *The Victoria History of the County of Cornwall*, Vol. 1, 1906
3  Ekwall, Eilert. *The Concise Oxford Dictionary of English Place Names*
4  *A Complete Parochial History of the County of Cornwall*, 1867, Wm Lake, Truro
5  Carew, Richard. *Survey of Cornwall*, 1602
6  Hippisley Coxe, Antony D. *A Book about Smuggling in the West Country* 1700-1850, Tabb House, Padstow, 1984

*Chapter 2*
1  *Tidal Power from Small Estuaries*, Baker & Wishart, Water for Energy Conference, Brighton, 1986

*Chapter 3*
1  Carew, Richard. *Survey of Cornwall*, 1602
2  Harris, Helen & Ellis, Monica. *The Bude Canal*
3  Acland, Capt. John E. *Bude Haven*, 1914
4  Williams, Michael. *About Boscastle*, 1990
5  Verran, W. H. 'Shipbuilding at Newquay', etc. in the *Mariners' Mirror*, Vol 31

*Chapter 4*
1  Much of this information is taken from Archibald E. H. H. *The Wooden Fighting Ship in the Royal Navy*
2  Excerpt from Haws and Hurst. *The Maritime History of the World*
3  *The Bolton Letters*, Vol II, 1701-1714, printed by John Blandy, 1976
4  Powell, D. *Bristol Privateers and Ships of War*
5  *Ibid*. The HAWK in 1744. Capt. Henry Sussex shipped her hands at Padstow.
6  Oil paintings in the National Maritime Museum, Ref. BHC0848

*Chapter 7*
1  Historical MSS Commission Report V. App. I. 176, 178, 214.
2  Oppenheim, M. 'Maritime History' *Victoria Hist. of Cornwall*, Vol. 1, p.506

*Chapter 9*
1  Jeffreys, D.E. *Maritime Memories of Cardiff*, 1978
2  Ward-Jackson, C. H. *Ships and Shipbuilders of a Westcountry Seaport*
3  Verran, W. H. 'Shipbuilding at Newquay and Notes on Local Vessels', *Mariners' Mirror*, Vol. 31

# INDEX OF SHIPS' NAMES

*Abbreviations used in index*

| | |
|---|---|
| Bg | Brig |
| Bn | Brigantine |
| Bg | Barge |
| Cr | Cutter |
| FV | Fishing Vessel |
| K | Ketch |
| MB | Motor Boat |
| MFV | Motor Fishing Vessel |
| ML | Motor Launch |
| MV | Motor Vessel |
| Rev.Cr | Revenue Cutter |
| Sr | Schooner |

# LIST OF SHIPS ILLUSTRATED

# GENERAL INDEX